MACROECONOMICS

National income and related statistics for selected years, 1929–1970

National income statistics are in billions of current dollars. Details may not add to totals because of rounding.

			1929	1933	1939	1940	1942	1944	1946	1948	1950	1952
THE SUM OF	1	Personal consumption expenditures	77.3	45.8	67.0	71.0	88.6	108.2	143.9	174.9	192.1	219.1
	2	Gross private domestic investment	16.7	1.6	9.5	13.4	10.3	7.7	31.5	47.1	55.1	53.5
	3	Government purchases	8.9	8.3	13.6	14.2	59.9	97.1	29.1	32.6	38.8	75.8
	4	Net exports	0.2	−0.1	0.7	1.4	−0.3	−2.0	7.4	5.7	1.0	1.3
EQUALS	5	Gross domestic product	103.1	55.6	90.8	100.0	158.5	211.0	211.9	260.3	287.0	349.7
LESS	6	Consumption of fixed capital	9.9	7.6	9.0	9.4	11.3	12.0	14.2	20.4	23.6	29.2
EQUALS	7	Net domestic product	93.2	48.0	81.8	90.6	147.2	199.0	197.7	239.9	263.4	320.5
LESS	8	Net foreign factor income earned in the U.S.	−0.8	−0.3	−0.4	−0.4	−0.5	−0.5	−0.7	−1.5	−1.5	−2.2
LESS	9	Indirect business taxes	9.3	9.0	11.1	11.5	11.5	16.8	17.5	19.7	24.6	30.9
EQUALS	10	National income	84.7	39.3	71.1	79.5	136.2	182.7	181.0	221.7	240.3	291.9
LESS	11	Social security contributions	0.3	0.3	2.2	2.4	3.5	5.2	7.7	6.0	7.4	9.3
	12	Corporate income taxes	1.4	0.5	1.4	2.8	11.4	12.9	9.1	12.4	17.9	19.4
	13	Undistributed corporate profits	2.4	−4.0	0.3	2.0	4.0	6.7	2.5	10.9	8.2	9.6
PLUS	14	Transfer payments	3.7	3.7	4.8	5.2	5.1	6.7	16.2	17.0	21.8	20.5
EQUALS	15	Personal income	84.3	46.2	72.0	77.5	122.4	164.6	177.9	209.4	228.6	274.1
LESS	16	Personal taxes	2.6	1.4	2.4	2.6	5.9	18.9	18.7	21.0	20.6	34.0
EQUALS	17	Disposable income	81.7	44.8	69.6	74.9	116.4	145.7	159.2	188.3	208.0	240.1
	18	Real gross domestic product (in 1987 dollars)	821.8	587.1	840.7	906.0	1,284.9	1,670.0	1,272.1	1,300.0	1,418.5	1,624.9
	19	Percent change in real GDP	—	−2.1	7.9	7.8	20.0	8.4	−20.6	3.8	8.7	4.3
	20	Real disposable income per capita (in 1987 dollars)	4,807.0	3,477.0	4,505.0	4,747.0	6,115.0	6,516.0	6,083.0	5,953.0	6,214.0	6,433.0

RELATED STATISTICS			1929	1933	1939	1940	1942	1944	1946	1948	1950	1952
	21	Consumer price index (1982–84 = 100)	17.0	13.0	13.9	14.0	16.3	17.6	19.5	24.1	24.1	26.5
	22	Rate of inflation (%)	0.0	−5.1	−1.4	0.7	10.9	1.7	8.3	8.1	1.3	1.9
	23	Index of industrial production (1987 = 100)	—	—	—	—	—	—	—	23.6	25.8	29.1
	24	Supply of money, $M1$ (in billions of dollars)	26.6	19.9	34.2	39.7	55.4	85.3	106.5	112.3	114.1	125.2
	25	Prime interest rate (%)	5.50	1.50	1.50	1.50	1.50	1.50	1.50	1.75	2.07	3.0
	26	Population (in millions)	121.8	125.6	131.0	132.1	134.9	138.4	141.4	146.6	152.3	157.6
	27	Civilian labor force (in millions)	49.2	51.6	55.2	55.6	56.4	54.6	57.5	60.6	62.2	62.1
	28	Unemployment (in millions)	1.6	12.8	9.5	8.1	2.7	0.7	2.3	2.3	3.3	1.9
	29	Unemployment rate as % of civilian labor force	3.2	24.9	17.2	14.6	4.7	1.2	3.9	3.8	5.3	3.0
	30	Index of productivity (1982 = 100)	—	—	—	—	—	—	—	45.7	50.1	53.7
	31	Annual change in productivity (%)	—	—	—	—	—	—	—	—	8.3	3.1
	32	Trade balance on current account (in billions of dollars)	—	—	—	—	—	—	4.9	2.4	−1.8	0.6
	33	Public debt (in billions of dollars)	16.9	22.5	48.2	50.7	79.2	204.1	271.0	252.0	256.9	259.1

1954	1956	1958	1959	1960	1961	1962	1963	1964	1965	1966	1967	1968	1969	1970
239.8	270.6	294.6	318.1	332.4	343.5	364.4	384.2	412.5	444.6	481.6	509.3	559.1	603.7	646.5
54.1	72.7	63.6	78.8	78.7	77.9	87.9	93.4	101.7	118.0	130.4	128.0	139.9	155.2	150.3
76.0	79.7	95.4	99.0	99.8	107.0	116.8	122.3	128.3	136.3	155.9	175.6	191.5	201.8	212.7
1.0	3.3	1.2	−1.7	2.4	3.4	2.4	3.3	5.5	3.9	1.9	1.4	−1.3	−1.2	1.2
370.9	426.2	454.7	494.2	513.4	531.8	571.6	603.1	648.0	702.7	769.8	814.3	889.3	959.5	1,010.7
32.5	38.1	42.8	44.6	46.3	47.7	49.3	51.3	53.9	57.3	62.1	67.4	73.9	81.5	88.8
338.4	388.1	412.0	449.6	467.1	484.1	522.3	551.8	594.1	645.4	707.7	746.9	815.4	878.0	921.9
−2.2	−3.0	−2.9	−2.8	−3.2	−3.6	−4.3	−4.5	−5.0	−5.4	−5.2	−5.5	−6.2	−6.1	−6.4
33.7	33.8	39.0	42.3	44.6	47.2	52.1	54.8	60.0	63.9	69.2	72.5	80.6	85.5	94.8
306.9	357.3	375.8	410.1	425.7	440.5	474.5	501.5	539.1	586.9	643.7	679.9	741.0	798.6	833.5
10.6	13.5	15.9	18.8	21.9	22.9	25.4	28.5	30.1	31.6	40.6	45.5	50.4	57.9	62.2
17.6	22.0	19.0	23.6	22.7	22.8	24.0	26.2	28.0	30.9	33.7	32.7	39.4	39.7	34.4
9.9	12.6	10.0	15.9	14.5	14.3	14.2	22.6	26.1	31.9	34.0	31.2	28.5	24.6	19.3
24.8	29.0	37.0	39.4	42.6	46.0	42.5	52.2	55.8	60.4	66.3	76.0	87.2	97.3	113.4
293.6	338.2	367.9	391.2	409.2	426.5	453.4	476.4	510.7	552.9	601.7	646.5	709.9	773.7	831.0
32.5	39.7	42.2	44.5	48.7	50.3	54.8	58.0	56.0	61.9	71.0	77.9	92.1	109.9	109.0
261.1	298.5	325.7	346.7	360.5	376.2	398.7	418.4	454.7	491.0	530.7	568.6	617.8	663.8	722.0
1,673.8	1,803.6	1,829.1	1,928.8	1,970.8	2,023.8	2,128.1	2,215.6	2,340.6	2,470.5	2,616.2	2,796.9	2,796.9	2,873.0	2,875.9
−0.7	2.0	−0.5	5.5	2.2	2.7	5.2	4.1	5.6	5.5	5.9	2.6	4.2	2.7	0.0
6,598.0	7,046.0	7,098.0	7,256.0	7,264.0	7,382.0	7,583.0	7,718.0	8,140.0	8,508.0	8,822.0	9,114.0	9,399.0	9,606.0	9,875.0

1954	1956	1958	1959	1960	1961	1962	1963	1964	1965	1966	1967	1968	1969	1970
26.9	27.2	28.9	29.1	29.6	29.9	30.2	30.6	31.0	31.5	32.4	33.4	34.8	36.7	38.8
0.7	1.5	2.8	0.7	1.7	1.0	1.0	1.3	1.3	1.6	2.9	3.1	4.2	5.5	5.7
29.9	35.1	33.3	37.3	38.1	38.4	41.6	44.0	47.0	51.7	56.3	57.5	60.7	63.5	61.4
130.3	136.0	138.4	140.0	140.7	145.2	147.9	153.4	160.4	167.9	172.1	183.3	197.5	204.0	214.5
3.05	3.77	3.83	4.48	4.82	4.50	4.50	4.50	4.50	4.54	5.63	5.61	6.30	7.96	7.91
163.0	168.9	174.9	177.9	180.7	183.7	186.5	189.2	191.9	194.3	196.6	198.7	200.7	202.7	205.1
62.3	66.6	67.6	68.4	69.6	70.5	70.6	71.8	73.1	74.5	75.8	77.3	78.7	80.7	82.8
3.5	2.8	4.6	3.7	3.9	4.7	3.9	4.1	3.8	3.4	2.9	3.0	2.8	2.8	4.1
5.5	4.1	6.8	5.5	5.5	6.7	5.5	5.7	5.2	4.5	3.8	3.8	3.6	3.5	4.9
56.7	59.2	62.5	64.6	65.6	68.1	70.4	73.3	76.5	78.6	81.0	83.0	85.4	85.9	87.0
1.6	1.3	3.0	3.3	1.6	3.7	3.5	4.1	4.3	2.7	3.0	2.5	3.0	0.5	1.3
0.2	2.7	0.8	−1.3	2.8	3.8	3.4	4.4	6.8	5.4	3.0	2.6	0.6	0.4	2.3
270.8	272.7	279.7	287.5	290.5	292.6	302.9	310.3	316.1	322.3	328.5	340.4	368.7	365.8	380.9

(Continued)

MACROECONOMICS
PRINCIPLES, PROBLEMS, AND POLICIES
THIRTEENTH EDITION

CAMPBELL R. McCONNELL

Professor of Economics, Emeritus
University of Nebraska

STANLEY L. BRUE

Professor of Economics
Pacific Lutheran University

McGRAW-HILL, INC.

New York • St. Louis • San Francisco • Auckland
Bogotá • Caracas • Lisbon • London • Madrid
Mexico City • Milan • Montreal • New Delhi
San Juan • Singapore • Sydney • Tokyo • Toronto

To Mem
and to Terri and Craig

MACROECONOMICS
Principles, Problems, and Policies

Copyright © 1996, 1993, 1990 by McGraw-Hill, Inc. All rights reserved. Portions of this text have been taken from *Economics,* Thirteenth Edition. Copyright © 1996 by McGraw-Hill, Inc. All rights reserved. Printed in the United States of America. Except as permitted under the United States Copyright Act of 1976, no part of this publication may be reproduced or distributed in any form or by any means, or stored in a data base or retrieval system, without the prior written permission of the publisher.

This book is printed on acid-free paper.

4 5 6 7 8 9 0 VNH VNH 9 0 9 8 7

ISBN 0-07-046819-2

This book was set in Century Oldstyle by York Graphic Services, Inc.
The editors were Michael R. Elia, Lucille H. Sutton, and Edwin Hanson;
the designer was Joseph A. Piliero;
the production supervisor was Annette Mayeski.
Illustrations were drawn by Cathy Hull and Roy Wiemann.
Drawings were done by Vantage Art.
Von Hoffmann Press, Inc., was printer and binder.

ABOUT THE AUTHORS

Campbell R. McConnell earned his Ph.D. from the University of Iowa after receiving degrees from Cornell College and the University of Illinois. He taught at the University of Nebraska—Lincoln from 1953 until his retirement in 1990. He is also coauthor of *Contemporary Labor Economics,* 4th ed. (McGraw-Hill) and has edited readers for the principles and labor economics courses. He is a recipient of both the University of Nebraska Distinguished Teaching Award and the James A. Lake Academic Freedom Award, and is past-president of the Midwest Economics Association. Professor McConnell was awarded an honorary Doctor of Laws degree from Cornell College in 1973 and received its Distinguished Achievement Award in 1994. His primary areas of interest are labor economics and economic education. He has an extensive collection of jazz recordings and enjoys reading jazz history.

Stanley L. Brue did his undergraduate work at Augustana College (S.D.) and received his Ph.D. from the University of Nebraska—Lincoln. He teaches at Pacific Lutheran University, where he has been honored as a recipient of the Burlington Northern Faculty Achievement Award. He has also received the na-tional Leavey Award for excellence in economic education. Professor Brue is national President and member of the International Executive Board of Omicron Delta Epsilon International Economics Honorary. He is coauthor of *Economic Scenes,* 5th ed. (Prentice-Hall) and *Contemporary Labor Economics,* 4th ed. (McGraw-Hill) and author of *The Evolution of Economic Thought,* 5th ed. (HB/Dryden). For relaxation, he enjoys boating on Puget Sound and skiing trips with his family.

CONTENTS IN BRIEF

CONTENTS

PART 2

National Income, Employment, and Fiscal Policy

LIST OF KEY GRAPHS

PREFACE

We are pleased to present the thirteenth edition of *Economics* (and its companion editions *Macroeconomics* and *Microeconomics*). *Economics* continues to be the top-selling economics text in the United States —with an expanded market share in the twelfth edition. Moreover, the Russian-language version of *Economics* is the leading economics text in Russia. More than 1 million Russians have learned about market economics from it since the fall of communism. The Canadian and Australian adaptations of this book, and its translations into French, Spanish, and other languages, have further extended its reach.

Capitalism in Russia, interest-rate hikes, GATT and NAFTA, renewed productivity growth, the balanced budget amendment—what a remarkable time for teaching and learning macroeconomics! More than ever before it is clear that people who comprehend economic principles will be better able to make sense of the emerging world and have an advantage functioning in it. We thank each of you using *Macroeconomics,* wherever you are in this rapidly changing world, for granting us a modest role in your efforts to teach or learn this vital subject.

WHAT'S NEW?

This edition has been thoroughly revised, polished, and updated. Many of the changes have been motivated by the comments of 43 reviewers, 9 participants in focus groups and 124 respondents to a questionnaire. We sincerely thank each of these contributors and have acknowledged them at the end of this preface.

Here, we strive only for an overview of the changes in the thirteenth edition; chapter-by-chapter details are provided in the *Instructor's Resource Manual.*

New Chapter

We have written a new chapter for this edition.

- *The United States in the Global Economy*. The material throughout Part 1 has been condensed and rearranged to allow for an early and comprehensive new chapter (Chapter 6) on the global economy. This chapter contains not only descriptive material (volume and pattern of world trade), but also essential theory (comparative advantage, exchange rates) and institutional features (trade barriers, GATT, EU, NAFTA). By providing the basics of international trade and finance, the chapter is a springboard for the instructor who wishes to fully integrate macro materials into a global framework.

New Features

The thirteenth edition contains two new features— one adding another global dimension to *Macroeconomics,* the other making the book more interactive.
- *Global Perspectives*. We have added twenty-five Global Perspective sections—most containing charts—throughout the book to compare the United States economy with other nations. To merely state, for example, United States' rates of inflation, unemployment, or taxes, the size of the public debt and the underground economy, or the amount of exports without international comparisons denies students the global context needed for meaningful comparisons.
- *Key Questions (with Answers)*. In each chapter we have designated two to five end-of-chapter questions as "Key Questions," providing answers in the back of the text. Many of these questions are quantitative and are designed to help the student work through and understand basic concepts. The student is alerted within the chapters as to when a particular Key Question is relevant. Students wanting to immediately test their understanding can turn to the specially marked Key Question, checking their answer against the end-of-book answer. Others may want to wait until they have read the full chapter before an-

swering the Key Questions. Either way, the Key Questions make this edition of *Macroeconomics* more interactive.

Reconstituted Macro Theory

The macro analysis has been carefully rethought and restructured for logical development of the ideas and to provide greater flexibility for instructors. Because these changes are extensive, we describe them more fully.

- *Chapters 7 and 8* on national income accounting and macroeconomic instability have undergone only minor revision.
- *Chapter 9* addresses the components of the private, closed aggregate expenditures (AE) model and examines equilibrium GDP. We have abridged the discussion of classical economics, quickly getting the student into the AE model. We present the AE theory as part of integrated modern macro rather than emphasizing disputes between "camps." Comparison of schools of macroeconomic thought is deferred to Chapter 16 on alternative perspectives.
- *Chapter 10* examines changes in equilibrium GDP and the multiplier in the private, closed economy. It then brings in the net export and government components of the aggregate expenditures model, the latter from the previous edition's chapter on fiscal policy. Then, recessionary and inflationary gaps are considered, along with historical applications of these concepts (the Great Depression and Vietnam inflation).
- *Chapter 11* develops the aggregate demand–aggregate supply (AD-AS) model, with two optional sections which (1) derive the AD curve from the AE model, and (2) show how shifts in the AD curve and AE curve are related. We anticipate that most instructors will assign the AE chapters, but instructors wishing to use only AD-AS can delete the AE chapters along with these optional sections in Chapter 11. With in-class supplementation, Chapter 11's section on the multiplier with inflation could serve as a springboard for instructors to develop the concepts of the MPC, MPS, and multiplier (the latter in an AD-AS framework).
- *Chapter 12* on fiscal policy has been recast entirely in terms of AD-AS.

We believe the new organization of the macroeconomic theory accomplishes three goals.

- Most importantly, by eliminating all "jumping" between models, the AE and AD-AS models are bet-

ter integrated for the majority of professors who teach both. The new progression is: National income accounting, macroeconomic instability, the AE model, derivation of AD from the AE model, addition of AS, and application of the AD-AS model to fiscal policy (and later to monetary policy).

- Second, the new organization provides an exclusive AD-AS option (Chapters 11 and 12 and beyond) for those desiring it.
- Finally, the two AE chapters are now unencumbered with AD-AS sections for instructors wishing to emphasize the AE model.

Consolidated Introductory Chapters

We have consolidated the introductory chapters for clearer focus and to make room for the new Chapter 6 on the global economy. The two twelfth-edition chapters on the private and public sectors are combined into new Chapter 5 (The Mixed Economy) in this edition. Also, new Chapter 4 (previously Chapter 5) now meshes the former Chapter 3 discussion of pure capitalism with analysis of the market system. This is facilitated by relocating supply and demand analysis as Chapter 3 in this edition.

The Economic Perspective

We have placed greater emphasis on the economic way of thinking. In Chapter 1 we have greatly expanded the section on the economic perspective, discussing scarcity and choice, rational behavior, and marginal analysis. In Chapter 2 we use the ideas of marginal benefits and marginal costs (Figure 2-2) to determine the optimal position on the production possibilities curve. We then take opportunities to reinforce the economic perspective in the remainder of the book.

Culling and Tightening

Our considerable culling and tightening in the twelfth edition has been well received by instructors and, of course, students. Buoyed by that response, we have again looked to delete the archaic, remove redundancy, tighten sentences, and reduce formality. In further economizing on words, we were careful *not* to reduce the thoroughness of our explanations. Where needed, the "extra sentence of explanation" remains a distinguishing characteristic of *Macroeconomics*.

Other New Topics and Revised Discussions

Along with the changes just discussed, there are many other revisions.

• *Part 1. Chapter 1:* Reorganization of the "policy" section; new discussion of the correlation-causation fallacy. *Chapter 2:* Clarification of productive versus allocative efficiency; new application on lumber versus owls. *Chapter 3:* New examples: increased demand for broccoli, carrots, guns; reduced supply of haddock. *Chapter 4:* Expanded discussion of property rights. *Chapter 5:* New discussions on growth of transfer payments and lottery revenues.

• *Part 2. Chapter 8:* Revised Figure 8-7 to allow for output beyond the full-employment output; new Figure 8-8 on nominal versus real interest rate. *Chapter 10:* Major new aggregate expenditure applications: the Great Depression and Vietnam inflation. *Chapter 11:* Removal of "Keynesian" and "classical" labels from the horizontal and vertical ranges of AS; new distinction between full-employment GDP and full-capacity GDP. *Chapter 12:* New presentation of fiscal policy in the AD-AS framework (Figures 12-1 and 12-2); revised discussion of the full-employment budget (new Figure 12-4).

• *Part 3. Chapter 13:* New discussions on the relative decline of bank and thrift assets and globalization of financial activity. *Chapter 15:* New AD-AS presentation of monetary policy (Figure 15-2); new discussions of recent successes of monetary policy; the "loss of control" issue; the effect of interest-rate changes on interest income; and the recent policy focus on the Federal funds rate. New Figure 15-3 provides an extended AD-AS "overview" of macro theory and policy.

• *Part 4. Chapter 16:* New title: "Alternative Views of Macro Theory and Policy"; AD-AS comparison of classical and Keynesian analysis (from twelfth-edition Chapter 10). *Chapter 17:* New discussion of employment and training policy. *Chapter 18:* New topics: entitlements; ownership of the public debt (Figure 18-1); debt as a curb on fiscal policy; Deficit Reduction Act of 1993. *Chapter 19:* Clarification of demand and efficiency factors in growth (Figure 19-1); new Figure 19-4 on the educational attainment of the population; discussions of slow growth of median family income (new Figure 19-5) and the new resurrection of Doomsday models (Figure 19-6).

• *Part 5. Chapter 20:* New topics: supply and demand analysis of exports and imports (Figures 20-3, 20-4, and 20-5); government export promotion policies; renewal of China's most-favored-nation status; and negotiations with Japan. *Chapter 21:* Revised discussion of the managed float; updated discussion of recent American trade deficits. *Chapter 22:* New table on the distribution of world income (Table 22-1); a reworked and extended discussion of population problems; new discussion of the difficulties associated with foreign aid; reworked discussion of the debt crisis; new section on the "New Global Compact." *Chapter 23:* Progress report on the Russian transition to capitalism.

New Last Words

Reviewers have indicated they appreciate the "Last Word" minireadings and their placement toward the conclusion of each chapter. These selections serve several purposes: Some provide current or historical real-world applications of economic concepts; others reveal human interest aspects of economic problems; some present contrasting or nonmainstream points of view; and still others present economic concepts or issues in a global context. Eight of the Last Words are new and others have been revised and updated.

The new topics are: Cuba's declining production possibilities (Chapter 2); ticket scalping (Chapter 3); alternative views on why Europe's unemployment rate is so high (Chapter 11); the use of the dollar around the world (Chapter 13); the problem of entitlements (Chapter 18); pros and cons of economic growth (Chapter 19); speculation in currency markets (Chapter 21); and China as an emerging economic power (Chapter 23).

New Software and Multimedia Materials

The extensive ancillaries available with the thirteenth edition for either students or instructors are described later in the Preface. Three new items are described here.

PowerPoint Presentation/Tutorial Software for Windows

C. Norman Hollingsworth of Dekalb College, North Campus, Dunwoody, Georgia, has prepared a multi-slide presentation for every chapter in the thirteenth edition (2000 slides in all). This Windows software includes a full run-time version of PowerPoint, allowing instructors to use these presentations "right out of the box" without having to purchase the PowerPoint software program. Owners of PowerPoint software can edit any slide in the set or add additional slides to the set to more closely match their classroom needs. This software is interactive, flexible, and in full color. While designed to enhance the instructor's classroom lecture/discussion, it can also be used in a computer lab for tutorial/review purposes.

Interactive Key Graphs Presentation/Tutorial Software for Windows

The twelve Key Graphs in the thirteenth edition are critical for student understanding of the concepts in introductory economics. With this Key Graphs Tutorial Software students will be able to study and review critical concepts in the IBM-PC/Windows environment in a computer lab or on their own PC. Instructors may also use this software in class, manipulating the full-color graphs to dynamically illustrate concepts in ways that a book or overhead transparencies never can.

MULTIMEDIA: Principles of Economics on CD-ROM

Charles Link, Jeffrey Miller, and Fred Hofstetter of the University of Delaware have prepared a stand-alone multimedia CD-ROM for principles of economics that contains both an instructor and a tutorial component. The CD-ROM, with sound, video, and animation, includes substantial interactive tutorial material for creative learning. There are eight content modules covering the topics in macroeconomics and eight modules covering microeconomics.

In addition we continue to provide *Concept Master,* a DOS-based student tutorial by William and Irene Gunther, updated to reflect the changes in the thirteenth edition, *Macroeconomics: A Lab Course* by Norris Peterson, for use with IBM-PCs, and *DiscoverEcon* by Gerald Nelson and Wesley Seitz, for use with the Macintosh computer.

FUNDAMENTAL GOALS

Although the thirteenth edition bears only a modest resemblance to the first, the basic purpose remains the same—to introduce the beginning economics student to principles essential in understanding the basic economizing problem, specific economic issues, and the policy alternatives available for dealing with them. We hope that an ability to reason accurately and objectively about economic matters and a lasting interest in economics will be two byproducts of this basic objective. Our intention remains to present the principles and problems of economics in a straightforward, logical fashion. Therefore, we continue to stress clarity of presentation and organization.

PRODUCT DIFFERENTIATION

This text embraces a number of distinguishing features.

* *Comprehensive explanations at an appropriate level.* We have attempted to craft a comprehensive, analytical text which is challenging to better students, yet accessible—with appropriate diligence—to average students. We think the thoroughness and accessibility of *Macroeconomics* enables the instructor to select topics for special classroom emphasis with confidence that students can independently read and comprehend other assigned material in the book.

* *Comprehensive definition of economics.* The principles course sometimes fails to provide students with a comprehensive and meaningful definition of economics. To avoid this shortcoming, all of Chapter 2 is devoted to a careful statement and development of the economizing problem and an exploration of its implications. This foundation should be helpful in putting the many particular subject areas of economics in proper perspective.

* *Fundamentals of the market system.* Economies the world over are making the difficult transition from planning to markets. Our detailed description of the institutions and operation of the market *system* in Chapter 4 is even more relevant than before. Property rights, freedom of enterprise and choice, competition, the role of profits—these and related concepts are poorly understood by the typical student. We think we have accorded them the elaboration they require.

* *Early integration of international economics.* The principles and institutions of the global economy are given early treatment. Chapter 6 examines the growth of world trade, the major participants in world trade, specialization and comparative advantage, the foreign exchange market, tariffs and subsidies, and various trade agreements. This strong, accessible, introduction to international economics permits "globalization" of later discussions of macroeconomics.

- *Early and extensive treatment of government.* Government is an integral component of modern capitalism. Its economic role, therefore, should not be treated piecemeal nor as an afterthought. This text introduces the economic functions of government early and accords them systematic treatment in Chapter 5. The controversy about the proper role of government in stabilizing the economy is central to the macroeconomic policy chapters.

- *Emphasis on economic growth.* This volume continues to emphasize economic growth. Chapter 2 employs the production possibilities curve to show the basic ingredients of growth. Chapter 19 discusses the rate and causes of American growth, in addition to some of the controversies surrounding it. Chapter 22 focuses on the less-developed countries and the growth obstacles they confront. A segment of Chapter 23 concerns the stalling of growth in the former Soviet Union.

ORGANIZATION AND CONTENT

The prerequisite of an understandable economics text is the logical arrangement and clear exposition of subject matter. This book has been organized so the exposition of each particular topic and concept is directly related to the level of difficulty which the average student is likely to encounter. For this reason we have given the aggregate expenditures model, aggregate demand and aggregate supply, money and banking, and international economics comprehensive and careful treatments. Simplicity here is correlated with comprehensiveness, not brevity.

Furthermore, our experience suggests that in treating each basic topic it is desirable to couple analysis with policy. Generally, a three-step development of analytical tools is employed: (1) verbal descriptions and illustrations, (2) numerical examples, and (3) graphical presentation based on these numerical illustrations.

The material in this book is organized into five parts: Part 1: An Introduction to Economics and the Economy; Part 2: National Income, Employment, and Fiscal Policy; Part 3: Money, Banking, and Monetary Policy; Part 4: Problems and Controversies in Macroeconomics; and Part 5: International Economics and the World Economy. The Table of Contents lists the specific chapters in each part and the topics within each chapter.

PEDAGOGICAL AIDS

As in previous editions, *Macroeconomics* is highly student-oriented. The new "To the Student" statement at the beginning of Part 1 details the many pedagogical aids.

SUPPLEMENTS

The thirteenth edition is accompanied by a variety of high-quality supplements.

Study Guide

Professor William Walstad—one of the nation's foremost experts on economic education—has prepared the thirteenth edition of the *Study Guide,* which many students find to be indispensable. It contains for each chapter an introductory statement, a checklist of behavioral objectives, an outline, a list of important terms, hints and tips, fill-in questions, problems and projects, objective questions, and discussion questions. The glossary found at the end of *Macroeconomics* also appears in the *Study Guide.*

The *Guide* is a superb "portable tutor" for the principles student. Separate *Study Guides* have been prepared to correspond with the individual macro and micro paperback editions of the text.

Instructors' Resource Manual

Professor Joyce Gleason of Nebraska Wesleyan University has revised and updated the *Instructor's Resource Manual.* It comprises chapter summaries, listings of "what's new" in each chapter, teaching tips and suggestions, learning objectives, chapter outlines, data and visual aid sources with suggestions for classroom use, and questions and problems. Answers to the text's end-of-chapter questions are also found in the manual (with the exception of the answers to the Key Questions, which are found at the end of *Macroeconomics*).

Available again in this edition is a computerized version of the *Manual,* suitable for use with IBM-PC compatibles and Macintosh computers. Users of *Economics* can print out portions of the *Manual's* contents, complete with their own additions and alterations, for use as student handouts or in whatever ways they might wish. This capability includes printing out answers to the end-of-chapter questions not answered in the textbook.

Three Test Banks

This edition of *Macroeconomics* is supplemented by two test banks of objective, predominately multiple-choice questions and a third test bank of short-answer essay questions and problems.

- *Test Bank I* now comprises about 5200 questions, all written by the text authors.
- *Test Bank II,* by Professor Walstad, contains over 4700 questions.
- *Test Bank III,* also prepared by Professor Walstad, contains "constructive response" testing to evaluate student understanding in a manner different from conventional multiple-choice and true-false questions. Suggested answers to the essay and problem questions are included.

For all test items in Test Banks I and II, the nature of each question is identified (for example, G = graphical; C = conceptual, etc.) as are the page numbers in the text containing the material which is the basis for each question. Also, each chapter in Test Banks I and II begins with a list which groups questions by topics. Text adopters can use this sizable number of questions, organized into three test banks of equal quality, with maximum flexibility. The fact that the text authors and *Study Guide* authors have prepared all the test items assures the fullest possible correlation with the text content.

Additional Supplements

- *Computerized testing.* Test Banks I, II, and III are available in computerized versions, both for IBM-PC and compatibles and for Macintosh computers. These systems include test generation, capable of producing high-quality graphs from the test banks. They also can generate multiple tests, with versions "scrambled" to be distinctive, and other useful features. This software will meet the various needs of the widest spectrum of computer users. Separate versions of the Computerized Test Banks have been prepared to correspond with the individual macro and micro editions of the text.
- *Color transparencies (figures and tables).* Over 250 new full-color transparencies for overhead projectors have been prepared especially for the thirteenth edition. They encompass all the figures appearing in *Economics* and are available on request to adopters. New to this edition are overhead transparencies for the tables in the book. As with the Computerized Test Banks, the transparencies are also available in versions corresponding to *Macroeconomics* and *Microeconomics.*
- *Student software. Concept Master III,* a student software package, has been prepared for users of IBM-PCs and compatibles by William Gunther of the University of Alabama and Irene Gunther. The previous version of this software was widely praised by its users. It provides extensive and varied computer-assisted study material.

More than twelve graphic-based tutorial programs provide an opportunity for students to study key topics in the book in an interactive way. The tutorial programs are linked to the text. Selected end-of-chapter questions relating to the content of one of the tutorial programs are highlighted by a floppy disk symbol 💾. The questions themselves are not necessarily contained within the tutorial program, but the tutorial does contain material relating directly to the concepts underlying the highlighted questions.

In addition to the tutorial programs, students can quiz themselves with a self-testing program accompanying each text chapter. The package also features three macroeconomic simulation games. Some of the simulations are elementary, others are more complex. Wherever possible, they include a global perspective. Also included in the package are a list of key terms, a pop-up calculator for computations, and a section using the Key Graphs in the text to direct students to the appropriate tutorial lesson.

- *Macroeconomics: A Lab Course.* Professor Norris Peterson of Pacific Lutheran University, working with the talented staff of Intellipro, Inc., has created the software package *Macroeconomics: A Lab Course,* to be used in macroeconomics courses. It builds the basic macroeconomic framework in sequential, "building block" laboratory simulations that allow students to grasp the fundamental concepts of macroeconomics in a dynamic and creative manner.
- *DiscoverEcon.* For users of MacIntosh computers, there is an exciting tutorial program, *DiscoverEcon.* Developed by Professors Gerald Nelson and Wesley Seitz of the University of Illinois, this innovative package uses Apple's HYPERCARD programming environment to produce an extremely interactive learning experience. Dynamic shifts of curves, screen animation, sound effects, and simple-to-use command keys are features of this program.
- *Videos.* New videotape materials have been assembled for this edition to illustrate fundamental concepts and economic issues in a manner that will be

equally effective in classroom settings or media resource centers. Among these materials are numerous videos selected from "Adam Smith's Money World" that may be used when covering such topics as production possibilities, the role of government, the labor market, monopolistic competition, and international economics. Your local McGraw-Hill representative can provide details on all video ancillaries for the text.

DEBTS

The publication of this thirteenth edition will extend the life of *Economics* well into its fourth decade. This gracious acceptance has no doubt been fostered by the many teachers and students kind enough to provide their suggestions and criticisms.

Our colleagues at the University of Nebraska—Lincoln and Pacific Lutheran University have generously shared knowledge of their specialties with us and have provided encouragement. We are especially indebted to Jerry Petr and Norris Peterson, who have been most helpful in offsetting our comparative ignorance in their areas of specialty.

As indicated, the thirteenth edition has benefited from a number of perceptive reviews. In both quantity and quality, they provided us the richest possible source of suggestions for this revision. These contributors are listed at the end of this Preface.

Professor Thomas Barbiero of Ryerson Polytechnical Institute in his role as coauthor of the Canadian edition of *Macroeconomics* has provided helpful ideas. Also, we are most appreciative of several good suggestions for improvement provided by Professor Walstad, the author of the *Study Guide*. Thanks also go to Professor Mark Lovewell, who coded the new Test Bank items by type of question and identified the corresponding text page numbers for all the items.

We are greatly indebted to the many professionals at McGraw-Hill—and in particular Lucille Sutton, Mike Elia, Edwin Hanson, Joseph Murphy, Joe Piliero, Victoria Richardson, Annette Mayeski, and Jonathan Hulbert, for their expertise in the production and distribution of the book. Cathy Hull and Roy Weimann provided the creative illustrations for the Last Word readings. The positive contributions of these highly skilled professionals are gratefully acknowledged.

With this much assistance, we see no compelling reason why the authors should assume full responsibility for errors of omission or commission. But we bow to tradition.

Campbell R. McConnell
Stanley L. Brue

CONTRIBUTORS

REVIEWERS

Mamhoud Arya, Edison Community College
Noel Bennett, Metro Community College
Trent Bogges, Plymouth State College
Frank Bonello, University of Notre Dame
Mark Chopin, Louisiana Tech University
Chris Colburn, Old Dominion University
Gordon Crocker, Community College of Allegheny
    County
John Dorsey, University of Maryland
Paul Farnham, Georgia State University
Rashi Fein, Harvard Medical School
Paul Feldstein, University of California—Irvine
Arthur Friedberg, Mohawk Valley Community
    College
Nicholas Grunt, Tarrant County College
Will Harris, University of Delaware
Yu Hsing, Southeast Louisiana University
Mark Huston, San Diego Mesa College
Leo Kahane, California State University
Charles Link, University of Delaware
Patrick Litzinger, Robert Morris College
Ray Mack, Community College of Allegheny County
Drew Mattson, Anoka-Ramsey Community College
Frank Musgrave, Ithaca College
Asghan Nazemzadeh, University of Houston
Kathy Parkison, Indiana University—Kokomo
Martin Perliene, Wichita State University
Mary Pitts, Onondaga Community College
Jeff Pliskin, Hamilton College
Joseph Prizginger, Lynchburg College
Chris Rhoden, Solano College
Philip Rothman, East Carolina University
John Saussy, Harrisburg Area Community College
Carol Scott, West Georgia College
David Shorow, Richland College
Jerry Schwartz, Broward Community College
Phil Smith, Dekalb College
Jeff Summers, Lynnfield College
Donna Thompson, Brookdale Community College
Ted Tsukahara, St. Mary's College

Percy Vera, Sinclair Community College
Harold Warren, East Tennessee State University
Art Welsh, Pennsylvania State University
Janet West, University of Nebraska—Omaha
Dieter Zschock, SUNY—Stony Brook

FOCUS GROUP PARTICIPANTS

Joseph Barr, Framingham State College
Marc C. Chopin, Louisiana Tech University
Sharon Ehrenburg, Eastern Michigan University
Paul Farnham, Georgia State University
David E. R. Gay, University of Arkansas
Paul W. Grimes, Mississippi State University
Michael N. Hayes, Radford University
Delores Linton, Tarrant County College
Kathy Parkison, Indiana University—Kokomo
Ted Tsukahara, St. Mary's College

QUESTIONNAIRE RESPONDENTS

Steve Ahn, Mercer Community College
A.K. Barakeh, University of Southern Alabama
Doris Beuttenmuller, Webster University
Jerry Bodily, School of Business
Bernard Bogar, Indiana University—Indianapolis
George Bohler, Florida Community College
R. Bohm, University of Tennessee—Knoxville
Barry Bombay, J. Sargent Reynolds Community
    College
Joseph Brandt, Incarnate Word College
Robert Brooker, Gannon University
Louis Buda, Nassau Community College
Norman Caldwell, Iowa Central Community College
Jack Chambless, Valencia Community College
Arshad Chawdhry, California University
    of Pennsylvania
Jane Clary, College of Charleston
Don Coffin, Indiana University Northwest

Tom Cole, Amarillo College

George Collier, Southeastern Oklahoma State University

John Connelly, Corning Community College

Jerry Crawford, Arkansas State University

Norman Cure, Macomb Community College

Maria DaCosta, University of Wisconsin—Eau Claire

Cynthia Dempster, Pellissippi State Technical Community College

Bruce Donelson, Bellevue College

Michael Doyle, Dana College

Robert Eggleston, Shippensburg University

Bernice Evans, Morgan State University

John Ewing-Smith, Burlington County College

Loretta Fairchild, Nebraska Wesleyan University

William Foeller, State University of New York— Fredonia

Kaya Ford, North Virginia Community College

Thomas Fox, Pennsylvania State University

Julie Granthen, Oakland Community College- Auburn Hills

Ron Gunderson, Northern Arizona University

Ron Hansen, Muscatine Community College

Paul Harris, Camden County College

Will Harris, University of Delaware

Mark Healy, William Rainey Harper College

Alfred Herschede, Indiana University South Bend

Charles Hiatt, Delta College

Cal Hoerneman, Delta College

Brad Hoppes, Southwest Missouri State University

Pat Hunston, Bee County College

Bruce Hutchinson, University of Tennessee— Chattanooga

Eric Jacobsen, University of Delaware

Wayne Jesswein, University of Minnesota—Duluth

Chuck Jewell, Charles County Community College

Kay Johnson, Pennsylvania State University at Erie- Behrend

Mary Ann Keating, Valparaiso University

John Kinworthy, Concordia College

Andrew Kliman, New York Institute of Technology

Peter Kressler, Rowan College of New Jersey

Jim Kyle, Indiana State University

William Laughlin, Fairmont State University

Nancy Lawler, Oakton Community College

Molly Lee, New York Institute of Technology

Secunderabad Leela, Millersville University of Pennsylvania

Delores Linton, Tarrant County College

Louis McClain, Texas Wesleyan University

Michael McGuire, Incarnate Word College

Eugene McKibbins, Fullerton College

John Manzer, Indiana/Purdue at Fort Wayne

David Martin, State University of New York at Geneseo

Saul Mekies, Kirkwood Community College

Ed Mills, Clackamas College

John Muth, Regis University

Ron Noreen, Camden County College

Gerard O'Boyle, St. Johns University

Dennis O'Connor, Loras College

Alex Obiya, San Diego City College

Duane Oyen, University of Wisconsin—Eau Claire

Deborah Paige, McHenry County College

Young Park, California University of Pennsylvania

Kathy Parkison, Indiana University—Kokomo

John Peck, Indiana University South Bend

Hilda Pope, Jones County Junior College

Gary Rourke, Lakewood Community College

Noel Rozells, San Diego Miramar College

Paul Schmitt, St. Clair County Community College

Ken Seidenstricker, Regis University

Jack Sheeks, Broward Community College— Central Campus

Dorothy Siden, Salem State College

Donald Sparks, The Citadel

Theresa Spencer, Meredith College

Gerald Stollman, Oakland Community College— Auburn Hills

Roger Traver, Johnson County Community College

John Walgreen, Wheaton College

Irvin Weintraub, Towson State University

Janet West, University of Nebraska at Omaha

Howard Yergan, Southwest Texas State University

Other respondents wished to remain anonymous.

PART ONE

An Introduction to Economics and the Economy

TO THE STUDENT

Economics is concerned with efficiency—accomplishing goals using the best methods. Therefore, we offer some brief introductory comments on how to improve your efficiency—and your understanding and grade—in studying economics. Several features of this book will aid your learning.

- *Appendix on graphs* Being comfortable with graphical analysis and a few related quantitative concepts will be a big advantage to you in understanding principles of economics. The appendix to Chapter 1 reviews graphing, line slopes, and linear equations. Be sure not to skip it!

- *Introductions* The introductory paragraphs of each chapter are designed to stimulate interest, state the main objectives, and present an organizational overview of the chapter.

- *Terminology* A significant portion of any introductory course is terminology. To designate key terms, we have put them in **boldface type,** listed them at the end of each chapter, and provided a glossary at the end of the book.

- *Reviews* Important things should be said more than once. You will find a chapter summary at the conclusion of every chapter plus two or three "Quick Reviews" within each chapter. These review statements will help you focus on the essential ideas of each chapter and also to study for exams. If any of these statements are unclear, you should reread the appropriate section of the text.

- *Key Graphs* We have labeled graphs having special relevance as "Key Graphs." Your instructor may or may not emphasize each of these figures, but pay special attention to those your instructor discusses in class. You can bet there will be exam questions on them!

- *Figure legends* Economics is known for its many graphs. The legends accompanying the diagrams in this book are self-contained analyses of the concepts shown. Study these legends carefully—they are quick synopses of important ideas.

- *Globalization* Each nation functions increasingly in a global economy. To gain appreciation of this wider economic environment, be sure to take a look at the "Global Perspectives" which compare the United States to other selected nations.

- *Last Words* Each chapter concludes with a "Last Word" minireading. While it is tempting to ignore these sections, doing so is a mistake. Some of them are revealing applications of economic concepts; others are short case studies; still others present views which contrast with mainstream thinking; some are easy and delightful to read. All will deepen and broaden your grasp of economics.

- *Questions* A comprehensive list of questions is located at the end of each chapter. The old cliché that you "learn by doing" is very relevant to economics. Use of these questions will enhance your understanding. We designate several of them as "Key Questions" and answer them at the end of the book. You can immediately turn to these particular questions when they are cited in each chapter, or later, after you have read the full chapter.

- *Software* Many of the end-of-chapter questions deal with subject matter reinforced by the computerized tutorial, *Concept Master III,* which complements this text. A floppy disk symbol 🖥 identifies questions whose content correlates to a lesson in the tutorial program.

- *Study Guide* We enthusiastically recommend the *Study Guide* accompanying this text. This "portable tutor" contains not only a broad sampling of various kinds of questions, but a host of useful learning aids.

You will find in Chapter 1 that economics involves a special way of thinking—a unique approach to analyzing problems. The overriding goal of this book is to help you acquire that skill. If our cooperative efforts—yours, ours, and your instructor's—are successful, you will be able to comprehend a whole range of economic, social, and political problems which otherwise would have remained murky and elusive.

So much for the pep talk! Let's get on with the show.

THE NATURE AND METHOD OF ECONOMICS

Human beings, unfortunate creatures, are plagued with wants. We want, among other things, love, social recognition, and the material necessities and comforts of life. Our striving to improve our material well-being, to "make a living," is the concern of economics. Economics is the study of our behavior in producing, distributing, and consuming material goods and services in a world of scarce resources.

Humans are characterized by both biologically and socially determined wants. We seek food, clothing, shelter, and the many goods and services associated with a comfortable or affluent standard of living. We are also blessed with aptitudes and surrounded by quantities of property resources—both natural and manufactured. We use available human and property resources—labor and managerial talents, tools and machinery, land and mineral deposits—to produce goods and services which satisfy material wants. This is done through the organizational mechanism we call the *economic system.*

Quantitative considerations, however, rule out an ideal solution. The blunt fact is that the total of all our material wants is beyond the productive capacity of available resources. Thus, absolute material abundance is not possible. This unyielding fact is the basis for our definition of economics: *Economics is concerned with the efficient use or management of limited productive resources to achieve maximum satisfaction of human material wants.* Though it may not be self-evident, all the headline-grabbing issues of the day—inflation, unemployment, health care problems, government and international trade deficits, free-trade agreements among nations, poverty and inequality, pollution, and government regulation of business—are rooted in the one issue of using limited resources efficiently.

In this first chapter, however, we will not plunge into problems and issues. Our immediate concern is with some basic preliminary questions: (1) Of what importance or consequence is the study of economics? (2) How should we study economics—what are the proper procedures? What is the methodology of this subject? (3) What specific problems, limitations, and pitfalls might we encounter in studying economics? (4) How do economists think about problems? What is the "economic perspective"?

THE AGE OF THE ECONOMIST

Is studying economics worth your time and effort? Half a century ago John Maynard Keynes (1883–1946) —the most influential economist of this century —said this:

> The ideas of economists and political philosophers, both when they are right and when they are wrong, are more powerful than is commonly understood. Indeed the world is ruled by little else. Practical men, who believe themselves to be quite exempt from any intellectual influences, are usually the slaves of some defunct economist.

Most of the ideologies of the modern world have been shaped by the great economists of the past— Adam Smith, David Ricardo, John Stuart Mill, Karl Marx, and John Maynard Keynes. And it is currently common for world leaders to receive and invoke the advice and policy prescriptions of economists.

For example: The President of the United States benefits from the ongoing counsel of his Council of Economic Advisers. The broad spectrum of economic issues facing political leaders is suggested by the contents of the annual *Economic Report of the President.* Areas covered include unemployment and inflation, economic growth and productivity, taxation and public expenditures, poverty and income maintenance, the balance of payments and the international monetary system, labor-management relations, health care, pollution, discrimination, immigration, and competition and industrial regulation, among others.

Economics for Citizenship

A basic understanding of economics is essential if we are to be well-informed citizens. Most of today's problems have important economic aspects, and as voters we can influence the decisions of our political leaders in coping with these problems. What are the causes and consequences of the "twin deficits"—the Federal budget deficit and the international trade deficit—that are constantly reported by the news media? What of the depressing stories of homeless street people? Why is inflation undesirable? What can be done to reduce unemployment? Are existing welfare programs effective and justifiable? Should we continue to subsidize farmers? Do we need further reform of our tax system? Does America need to "reindustrialize" to reassert its dominant position in world trade and finance?

Since responses to such questions are determined largely by our elected officials, intelligence at the polls depends on a basic working knowledge of economics. Needless to say, a sound grasp of economics is more than helpful to politicians themselves!

A recent survey by the National Center for Research in Economic Education suggests economic illiteracy is widespread. The American public, high school seniors, and college seniors show widespread ignorance of basic economics that is needed to understand economic events and changes in the national economy. When asked questions about fundamental economics, only 35 percent of high school seniors, 39 percent of the general public, and 51 percent of college seniors gave correct answers.

Personal Applications

Economics is also vital in business. An understanding of the overall operation of the economic system enables the business executive to better formulate policies. The executive who understands the causes and consequences of inflation can make more intelligent business decisions during inflationary periods. That's why economists are on the payrolls of most large corporations. Their job is to gather and interpret economic information on which rational business decisions can be made.

Economics also gives the individual as a consumer and worker insights on how to make wiser buying and employment decisions. How can you "hedge" against the reduction in the dollar's purchasing power which accompanies inflation? Which occupations pay well; which are most immune to unemployment? Should you buy or lease a car? Should you use a credit card or pay cash? Similarly, someone who understands the relationship between budget and trade deficits, on the one hand, and security (stock and bond) values, on the other, can make more enlightened personal investment decisions.

In spite of its practical benefits, you must be forewarned that economics is mainly an academic, not a vocational, subject. Unlike accounting, advertising, corporation finance, and marketing, economics is not primarily a how-to-make-money area of study. A knowledge of economics will help you run a business or manage personal finances, but this is not its primary objective. In economics, problems are usually examined from the *social,* rather than the *personal,* point of view. The production, exchange, and consumption of goods and services are discussed from the viewpoint of society as a whole, rather than from the standpoint of one's own bankbook.

METHODOLOGY

What do economists do? What are their goals? What procedures do they employ? The subtitle of this textbook—*Principles, Problems, and Policies*—contains a thumbnail answer to the first two questions. Economists formulate economic *principles* useful in the establishment of *policies* designed to solve economic *problems.*

The procedures employed by the economist are summarized in Figure 1-1. The economist ascertains and gathers facts relevant to a specific economic problem. This task is sometimes called **descriptive** or **empirical economics** (box 1). The economist also states economic principles, that is, generalizes about the way individuals and institutions actually behave. Deriving principles is called **economic theory** or "economic analysis" (box 2).

As we see in Figure 1-1, economists are as likely to move from theory to facts in studying economic behavior as they are to move from facts to theory. Stated more formally, economists use both deductive and inductive methods. **Induction** distills or creates principles from facts. Here an accumulation of facts is arranged systematically and analyzed to permit the derivation of a generalization or principle. Induction moves from facts to theory, from the particular to the general. The inductive method is suggested by the left upward arrow from box 1 to box 2 in the figure.

Generalizations may also be created through *deduction* or the hypothetical method. Here economists draw upon casual observation, insight, logic, or intuition to frame a tentative, untested principle called an **hypothesis.** For example, they may conjecture, on the basis of "armchair logic," that it is rational for consumers to buy more of a product when its price falls.

To test the validity of the hypothesis they have deduced, economists must subject it to systematic and repeated examination of relevant facts. Do "real-world" data in fact reveal a negative or inverse relationship between price and the amount purchased? This testing process is suggested by the right downward arrow from box 2 to box 1 in Figure 1-1.

Deduction and induction are complementary, rather than opposing, techniques of investigation. Hypotheses formulated by deduction provide guidelines for the economist in gathering and systematizing em-

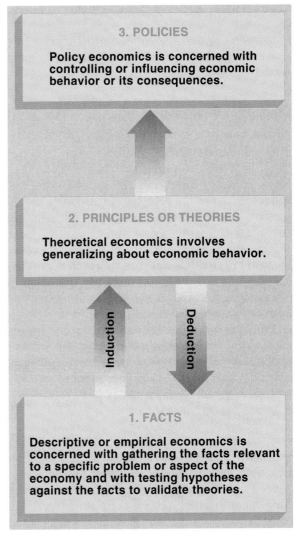

FIGURE 1-1 The relationship between facts, principles, and policies in economics
In analyzing problems or aspects of the economy, economists may use the inductive method whereby they gather, systematically arrange, and generalize on facts. Alternatively, the deductive method entails the development of hypotheses which are then tested against facts. Generalizations derived from either method of inquiry are useful not only in explaining economic behavior, but also as a basis for formulating economic policies.

pirical data. Conversely, some understanding of factual evidence—of the "real world"—is prerequisite to formulation of meaningful hypotheses.

Finally, the general knowledge of economic behavior which economic principles provides can then be used in formulating policies, that is, remedies or solutions, for correcting or avoiding the problem under scrutiny. This final aspect of economics is sometimes called "applied economics" or **policy econom-ics** (box 3).

Continuing to use Figure 1-1 as a reference, we now examine the economist's methodology in more detail.

Descriptive Economics

All sciences are empirical; they are based on facts, that is, on observable and verifiable behavior of certain data or subject matter. In the physical sciences the factual data are inorganic. As a social science, economics examines the behavior of individuals and institutions engaged in the production, exchange, and consumption of goods and services.

Fact-gathering can be a complex task. Because the world of reality is cluttered with innumerable interrelated facts, economists must use discretion in gathering them. They must distinguish economic from noneconomic facts and then determine which economic facts are relevant and which irrelevant for the problem under consideration. But even when this sorting process is complete, the relevant economic facts may appear diverse and unrelated.

Economic Theory

The task of economic theory or analysis is to systematically arrange, interpret, and generalize upon facts. Principles and theories—the end result of economic analysis—bring order and meaning to facts by tying them together, putting them in correct relationship to one another, and generalizing upon them. "Theories without facts may be barren, but facts without theories are meaningless."[1]

Principles and theories are meaningful statements drawn from facts, but facts, in turn, serve as a check on the validity of principles already established. Facts—how individuals and institutions actually behave in producing, exchanging, and consuming goods and services—may change with time. This is why economists must continually check principles and theories against the changing economic environment.

Terminology Economists talk about "laws," "principles," "theories," and "models." These terms all mean essentially the same thing: generalizations, or statements of regularity, concerning the economic behav-

ior of individuals and institutions. The term "economic law" is a bit misleading because it implies a high degree of exactness, universal application, and even moral rightness. So, to a lesser degree, does the term **principle.** And some people incorrectly believe "theory" has nothing to do with the facts and realities of the world. The term "model" has much to commend it. A model is a simplified picture of reality, an abstract generalization of how relevant data actually behave.

In this book these four terms will be used synonymously. The choice of terms in labeling any particular generalization will be governed by custom or convenience. Thus, the relationship between the price of a product and the quantity consumers purchase will be called the "law" of demand, rather than the theory or principle of demand, simply because this is the customary designation.

Several other points regarding the character and derivation of economic principles are in order.

Generalizations Economic principles are **generalizations** and, as the term implies, characterized by somewhat imprecise quantitative statement. Economic facts are usually diverse; some individuals and institutions act one way and some another way. Economic principles are therefore frequently stated as averages or statistical probabilities. For example, when economists say that the average family earned an income of about $37,000 in 1993, they are generalizing. It is recognized that some families earned much more and a good many others much less. Yet this generalization, properly handled and interpreted, can be very meaningful and useful.

Similarly, economic generalizations are often stated in terms of probabilities. A researcher may tell us there is a 95 percent probability that every $1.00 reduction in personal income taxes will result in a $.92 increase in consumer spending.

"Other Things Equal" Assumption Like other scientists, economists use the *ceteris paribus* or **other things equal assumption** to construct their generalizations. They assume all other variables except those under immediate consideration are held constant. This simplifies the reasoning process by isolating the relationship under consideration. For example, in considering the relationship between the price of Pepsi and the amount purchased, it helps to assume that, of all the factors which might influence the amount of Pepsi purchased (for example, the price of Pepsi, the prices of other goods such as Coke, con-

[1]Kenneth E. Boulding, *Economic Analysis: Microeconomics,* 4th ed. (New York: Harper & Row, Publishers, Incorporated, 1966), p. 5.

sumer incomes and preferences), only the price of Pepsi varies. The economist can then focus on the "price of Pepsi–purchases of Pepsi" relationship without reasoning being blurred or confused by intrusion of other variables.

In the natural sciences controlled experiments usually can be performed where "all other things" are in fact held constant or virtually so. Thus, scientists can test the assumed relationship between two variables with great precision. But economics is not a laboratory science. The economist's process of empirical verification is based on "real-world" data generated by the actual operation of the economy. In this rather bewildering environment "other things" *do* change. Despite the development of complex statistical techniques designed to hold other things equal, such controls are less than perfect. As a result, economic principles are less certain and less precise in application than those of laboratory sciences.

Abstractions Economic principles, or theories, are necessarily abstractions. They do not mirror the full complexity of reality. The very process of sorting out noneconomic and irrelevant facts in the fact-gathering process involves abstracting from reality. Unfortunately, the abstractness of economic theory prompts the uninformed to identify theory as impractical and unrealistic. This is nonsense! Economic theories are practical simply because they are abstractions. The level of reality is too complex and bewildering to be very meaningful. Economists theorize to give meaning to a maze of facts which would otherwise be confusing and useless, and to put facts into a more usable, practical form. Thus, to generalize is to abstract or purposely simplify; generalization for this purpose is practical, and therefore so is abstraction.

An economic theory is a model—a simplified picture or map—of some segment of the economy. This model helps us understand reality better *because* it avoids the confusing details of reality. Theories—*good* theories—are grounded on facts and therefore are realistic. Theories which do not fit the facts are simply not good theories.

Macro and Micro There are two levels of analysis at which the economist may derive laws concerning economic behavior. **Macroeconomics** deals either with the economy as a whole or with the basic subdivisions or aggregates—such as the government, household, and business sectors—making up the

economy. An aggregate is a collection of specific economic units treated *as if* they were one unit. Thus, we might find it convenient to lump together the over twenty million businesses in our economy and treat them as if they were one huge unit.

In dealing with aggregates, macroeconomics is concerned with obtaining an overview, or general outline, of the structure of the economy and the relationships among the major aggregates constituting the economy. No attention is given to specific units making up the various aggregates. Macroeconomics speaks of such magnitudes as *total* output, *total* level of employment, *total* income, *aggregate* expenditures, the *general* level of prices, and so forth, in analyzing various economic problems. Macroeconomics examines the forest, not the trees. It gives us a bird's-eye view of the economy.

Microeconomics deals with *specific* economic units and a *detailed* consideration of these individual units. At this level of analysis, the economist figuratively puts an economic unit, or very small segment of the economy, under the microscope to observe details of its operation. Here we talk of an individual industry, firm, or household, and concentrate on such magnitudes as the output or price of a specific product, the number of workers employed by a single firm, the revenue or income of a particular firm or household, or the expenditures of a given firm or family. In microeconomics we examine the trees, not the forest. Microeconomics is useful in achieving a worm's-eye view of some specific component of our economic system.

The macro–micro distinction does not mean that the subject matter of economics is so highly compartmentalized that each topic can be readily labeled as "macro" or "micro"; many topics and subdivisions of economics are rooted in both. There has been a convergence of macro- and microeconomics in important areas in recent years. While the problem of unemployment was treated as a macroeconomic topic some twenty or twenty-five years ago ("unemployment depends on *aggregate* spending"), economists now recognize that decisions made by *individual* workers in searching for jobs and the way specific product and labor markets function are also critical in determining the unemployment rate. *(Key Question 5)*

Graphical Expression Many of the economic models or principles in this book will be expressed graphically. The most important of these models are labeled "Key Graphs." You should read the appendix to this chapter to review graphing and other relevant quantitative relationships.

QUICK REVIEW 1-1

■ Economics is concerned with the efficient management of scarce resources.

■ Induction is observing regularities in factual data and drawing generalizations from them; deduction uses logic to create hypotheses which are then tested with factual data.

■ Economic theories ("laws," "principles," or "models") are generalizations, based on facts, concerning the economic behavior of individuals and institutions.

■ Macroeconomics deals with the economy as a whole; microeconomics focuses on specific units which comprise the economy.

Policy Economics

Economic theories are the basis for **economic policy.** Our understanding of economic principles can be applied in resolving or alleviating specific problems and in furthering the realization of society's overall goals (box 3 of Figure 1-1). Economic principles are valuable as predictive devices. And accurate prediction is required if we want to alter some event or outcome. If some undesirable event such as unemployment or inflation can be predicted or understood through economic theory, we may then be able to influence or control that event.

Formulating Economic Policy   The creation of policies designed to achieve specific goals is no simple matter. Here's a brief examination of the basic steps in policy formulation.

1 Stating Goals   The first step is to make a clear statement of a goal. If we say that we want "full employment," do we mean that everyone between, say, 16 and 65 years of age should have a job? Or do we mean that everyone who wants to work should have a job? Should we allow for some "normal" unemployment caused by inevitable changes in the structure of industry and workers' voluntarily changing jobs?

2 Policy Options   Next, we must state and recognize the possible effects of alternative policies designed to achieve the goal. This requires a clear un-

derstanding of the economic impact, benefits, costs, and political feasibility of alternative programs. For example, economists debate the relative merits and demerits of fiscal policy (which involves changing government spending and taxes) and monetary policy (which entails altering the supply of money) as alternative means of achieving and maintaining full employment.

3 Evaluation   We are obligated to ourselves and future generations to review our experiences with chosen policies and evaluate their effectiveness; it is only through this evaluation that we can hope to improve policy applications. Did a specific change in taxes or the supply of money alter the level of employment to the extent originally predicted? Did deregulation of a particular industry (for example, the airlines) yield the predicted beneficial results? If not, why not? *(Key Question 1)*

Economic Goals   If economic policies are designed to achieve certain **economic goals,** then we need to recognize a number of goals which are widely accepted in our own and many other societies. They include:

1 Economic Growth   The production of more and better goods and services, or, more simply, a higher standard of living, is desired.

2 Full Employment   Suitable jobs should be available for all willing and able to work.

3 Economic Efficiency   We want maximum benefits at minimum cost from the limited productive resources available.

4 Price Level Stability   Sizable upswings or downswings in the general price level, that is, inflation and deflation, should be avoided.

5 Economic Freedom   Business executives, workers, and consumers should enjoy a high degree of freedom in their economic activities.

6 An Equitable Distribution of Income   No group of citizens should face stark poverty while others enjoy extreme luxury.

7 Economic Security   Provision should be made for those who are chronically ill, disabled, handicapped, laid off, aged, or otherwise unable to earn minimal levels of income.

8 Balance of Trade We seek a reasonable balance in our international trade and financial transactions.

This list of goals is the basis for several significant points.

1 Interpretation This or any other statement of basic economic goals inevitably involves problems of interpretation. What are "sizable" changes in the price level? What is a "high degree" of economic freedom? What is an "equitable" distribution of income? Although most of us might accept these goals as generally stated, we might also disagree substantially on their specific meanings and hence the types of policies needed to attain them. Although goals 1 to 4 and 8 are subject to reasonably accurate measurements, the inability to quantify goals 5 to 7 contributes to controversy over their precise meaning.

2 Complementary Certain of these goals are complementary in that when one goal is achieved, some other goal or goals will also be realized. For example, achieving full employment (goal 2) means eliminating unemployment, a basic cause of low incomes (goal 6) and economic insecurity (goal 7). Comparing goals 1 and 6, a particular degree of income inequality is more acceptable if economic growth is raising all incomes absolutely.

3 Conflicting Some goals may be conflicting or mutually exclusive. They entail **tradeoffs,** meaning that to achieve one goal we must sacrifice some other goal. For example, goals 1 and 6 may be in conflict. Efforts to achieve greater equality in the distribution of income may weaken incentives to work, invest, innovate, and take business risks, all of which promote rapid economic growth. If government tries to equalize the distribution of income by taxing high-income people heavily and transferring those tax revenues to low-income people, the incentives of a high-income individual may diminish because taxation reduces income rewards. Similarly, a low-income person may be less motivated to work and engage in other productive activities when government stands ready to subsidize that individual.

International example: In the former Soviet Union, central planning virtually eliminated unemployment so that this source of worker insecurity disappeared. With little fear of losing their jobs, Soviet workers were quite cavalier regarding work effort and therefore productivity and efficiency in the Soviet Union were quite low. Here we have a conflict between goal 7, economic security, and goal 1, the growth of worker productivity.

4 Priorities When goals conflict, society must develop a system of priorities for the objectives it seeks. If full employment and price stability are to some extent mutually exclusive, that is, if full employment is accompanied by some inflation *and* price stability entails some unemployment, society must decide on the relative importance of these two goals. There is clearly ample room for disagreement here. But society must assess the tradeoffs and make decisions.

Positive and Normative As we move from the fact and principles levels (boxes 1 and 2) of Figure 1-1 to the policy level (box 3) we make a critical leap from positive to normative economics.

Positive economics deals with facts (once removed at the level of theory) and avoids value judgments. Positive economics attempts to set forth scientific statements about economic behavior.

Normative economics, in contrast, involves someone's value judgments about what the economy should be like or what particular policy action should be recommended based on a given economic generalization or relationship.

Positive economics concerns *what is,* while normative economics embodies subjective feelings about *what ought to be.* Positive economics deals with what the economy is actually like; normative economics examines whether certain conditions or aspects of the economy are desirable or not.

Examples: Positive statement: "Unemployment is 7 percent of the labor force." Normative statement: "Unemployment ought to be reduced." Second positive statement: "Other things being the same, if tuition is increased, enrollment at Gigantic State University will fall." Normative statement: "Tuition should be lowered at GSU so that more students can obtain an education." Whenever words such as "ought" or "should" appear in a sentence, there is a strong chance you are dealing with a normative statement.

Most of the apparent disagreement among economists involves normative, value-based policy questions. To be sure, various economists present and support different theories or models of the economy and its component parts. But by far most economic controversy reflects differing opinions or value judgments as to what our society should be like. For example, there is greater agreement about the actual distribution of income in our society than how income should be distributed. The point we reemphasize is that value judgments or normative statements come into play at the level of policy economics. *(Key Question 6)*

QUICK REVIEW 1-2

■ Policy economics entails the clear statement of goals, the assessing of policy options, and the evaluation of policy results.

■ Some of society's economic goals are complementary while others are conflicting.

■ Positive economics deals with factual statements ("what is"), while normative economics concerns value judgments ("what ought to be").

PITFALLS TO OBJECTIVE THINKING

Our discussion of the economist's procedure has skirted some specific problems and pitfalls which frequently hinder our thinking objectively about economic problems. Consider the following impediments to valid economic reasoning.

Bias

In contrast to a neophyte physicist or chemist, the budding economist ordinarily brings into economics a bundle of biases and preconceptions about the field. For example, you might be suspicious of business profits or feel that deficit spending is evil. Biases may cloud your thinking and interfere with objective analysis. The beginning economics student must be willing to shed biases and preconceptions not warranted by facts.

Loaded Terminology

The economic terminology in newspapers and popular magazines is sometimes emotionally loaded. The writer—or the interest group he or she represents—may have a cause to further or an ax to grind, and terms will be slanted to solicit the support of the reader. A governmental flood-control project in the Great Plains region may be called "creeping social-

ism" by its opponents and "intelligent democratic planning" by its proponents. We must be prepared to discount such terminology to objectively understand economic issues.

Definitions

No scientist is obligated to use popularized or immediately understandable definitions of his or her terms. The economist may find it convenient and essential to define terms in such a way that they are at odds with the definitions held by most people in everyday speech. No problem, so long as the economist is explicit and consistent in these definitions. For example, the term "investment" to the average citizen is associated with the buying of bonds and stocks in the securities market. How often have we heard someone talk of "investing" in General Motors stock or government bonds? But to the economist, "investment" means the purchase of real capital assets such as machinery and equipment, or the construction of a new factory building, not the purely financial transaction of swapping cash or part of a bank balance for a neatly engraved piece of paper.

Fallacy of Composition

Another pitfall in economic thinking is assuming "what is true for the individual or part of a group is necessarily true for the group or whole." This is a logical **fallacy of composition;** it is *not* correct. The validity of a particular generalization for an individual or part does *not* necessarily ensure its accuracy for the group or whole.

A noneconomic example: You are watching a football game and the home team executes an outstanding play. In the excitement, you leap to your feet to get a better view. Generalization: "If you, *an individual,* stand, then your view of the game is improved." But does this also hold true for the group—for everyone watching the game? Not necessarily! If everyone stands to watch the play, everyone—including you—will probably have the same or worse view than when seated.

Consider two examples from economics: A wage increase for Smith is desirable because, with constant product prices, it increases Smith's purchasing power and standard of living. But if everyone gets a wage increase, product prices may rise, that is, inflation might occur. Therefore, Smith's standard of living may be unchanged as higher prices offset her larger salary.

Second illustration: An *individual* farmer fortunate enough to reap a bumper (particularly large) crop is likely to realize a sharp gain in income. But this generalization does not apply to farmers as a *group*. For the individual farmer, crop prices will not be influenced (reduced) by this bumper crop, because each farmer produces a negligible fraction of the total farm output. But to farmers as a group, prices vary inversely with total output. Thus, as *all* farmers realize bumper crops, the total output of farm products rises, thereby depressing crop prices. If price declines are relatively greater than the increased output, farm incomes will *fall*.

Recalling our earlier discussion between macroeconomics and microeconomics, the fallacy of composition reminds us that *generalizations valid at one of these levels of analysis may or may not be valid at the other.*

Causation Fallacies

Causation is sometimes difficult to discern in economics. Consider these two fallacies.

Post Hoc Fallacy You must be very careful before concluding that because event A precedes event B, A is the cause of B. This kind of faulty reasoning is known as the **post hoc, ergo propter hoc,** or **after this, therefore because of this, fallacy.**

Example: Suppose early each spring the medicine man of a tribe performs his ritual by cavorting around the village in a green costume. A week or so later the trees and grass turn green. Can we safely conclude that event A, the medicine man's gyrations, has caused event B, the landscape's turning green? Obviously not. The rooster crows before dawn, but this doesn't mean the rooster is responsible for the sunrise!

Gigantic State University hires a new basketball coach and the team's record improves. Is the new coach the cause? Maybe. But perhaps the presence of more experienced players, an easier schedule, or the violation of NCAA recruiting rules is the true cause.

Correlation versus Causation We must not confuse **correlation** with **causation.** *Correlation* is a technical term indicating that two sets of data are associated in some systematic and dependable way. For example, we may find that when X increases, Y also increases. But this does not necessarily mean that X

is the cause of Y. The relationship could be purely coincidental or determined by some other factor, Z, not included in the analysis.

Example: Economists have found a positive correlation between education and income. In general, people with more education earn higher incomes than people with less education. Common sense suggests education is the cause and higher incomes are the effect; more education suggests a more productive worker and such workers receive larger monetary rewards.

But might not causation run the other way? Do people with higher incomes buy more education, just as they buy more automobiles and steaks? Or is the relationship explainable in terms of still other factors? Are education and income positively correlated because the bundle of characteristics—ability, motivation, personal habits—required to succeed in education are the same characteristics required to be a productive and highly paid worker? *(Key Question 9)*

THE ECONOMIC PERSPECTIVE

The methodology used by economists is common to all the natural and social sciences. And all scholars try to avoid the reasoning errors just discussed. Thus, economists do *not* think in a special way, but they *do* view things from a special perspective.

The **economic perspective** entails several critical and closely interrelated features, including scarcity, rational behavior, and benefit-cost comparisons.

Scarcity and Choice

From our definition of economics, it is easy to see why economists view the world from the vantage point of scarcity. Human and property resources are scarce. It follows that outputs of goods and services must be scarce or limited, and scarcity limits our options and necessitates choices. We "can't have it all." If not, what should we choose to have?

At the core of economics is the idea that "there is no free lunch." Someone may treat you to lunch, making it "free" to you, but there is a cost to someone—ultimately to society. Scarce inputs of farm products and the labor of cooks and waiters are required. These resources could have been used in alternative productive activities, and those activities—those other goods and services—are sacrificed in providing your lunch.

LAST WORD

FAST-FOOD LINES: AN ECONOMIC PERSPECTIVE

How might the economic perspective help us understand the behavior of fast-food consumers?

You enter a fast-food restaurant. Which line will move fastest? What do you do when you are in the middle of a long line and a new station opens? Have you ever gone to a fast-food restaurant, only to see long lines, and then leave? Have you ever had someone in front of you in a fast-food line place an order which takes a long time to fill?

The economic perspective is useful in analyzing the behavior of fast-food customers. These customers are at the restaurant because they expect the marginal benefit or satisfaction from the food they buy to match or exceed its marginal cost. When customers enter the restaurant they scurry to the *shortest* line, believing that the shortest line will reduce their time cost of obtaining their food. They are acting purposefully; time is limited and most people would prefer using it in some way other than standing in line.

All fast-food lines normally are of roughly equal lengths. If one line is temporarily shorter than other

lines, some people will move toward that line. These movers apparently view the time saving associated with the shorter line to exceed the cost of moving from their present line. Line changing normally results in an equilibrium line length. No further movement of customers between lines will occur once all lines are of equal length.

Fast-food customers face another cost-benefit decision when a clerk opens a new station at the counter.

Rational Behavior

Economics is grounded on the assumption of "rational self-interest." Individuals make rational decisions to achieve the greatest satisfaction or maximum fulfillment of their goals. Thus, consumers seek to spend their incomes rationally to get the greatest benefit or satisfaction from the goods and services their incomes allow them to buy.

Rational behavior means people will make different choices, because their circumstances (constraints) and available information differ. You may have decided that it is in your self-interest to attend college before entering the labor force, but a high school classmate has decided to forgo additional schooling and take a job. Why the different choices? Your academic abilities, along with your family's income, may be greater than those of your classmate. You may also be better informed, realizing that college-educated workers make much higher incomes and are less likely to be unemployed than workers

with a high school education. Thus, you opt for college while your high school classmate with fewer human and financial resources and less information chooses a job. Both are rational choices, but based on differing constraints and information.

Of course, rational decisions may change as circumstances change. Suppose the Federal government decides it is in the national interest to increase the supply of college-educated workers. As a result, government policy changes to provide greater financial assistance to college students. Under these new conditions, your high school classmate may opt for college rather than a job after graduating from high school.

Rational self-interest is not the same as being selfish. People make personal sacrifices to help family members or friends and contribute to charities because they derive pleasure from doing so. Parents contribute financially to their childrens' educations because they derive satisfaction from that choice.

Should you move to the new station or stay put? Those who do shift to the new line decide that the benefit of the time savings from the move exceeds the extra cost of physically moving. In so deciding, customers must also consider just how quickly they can get to the new station compared to others who may be contemplating the same move. (Those who hesitate in this situation are lost!)

Customers at the fast-food establishment select lines without having perfect information. For example, they do not first survey those in the lines to determine what they are ordering before deciding on which line to enter. There are two reasons for this. First, most customers would tell them "It is none of your business," and therefore no information would be forthcoming. Second, even if they could obtain the information, the amount of time necessary to get it (cost) would most likely exceed any time saving associated with finding the best line (benefit). Because information is costly to obtain, fast-food patrons select lines on the basis of imperfect information. Thus, not all decisions turn out to be as expected. For example, some people may enter a line in which the person in front of them is ordering hamburgers and fries for the forty people in the Greyhound bus parked out back! Nevertheless, at the time the customer made the decision, he or she thought that it was optimal.

Imperfect information also explains why some people who arrive at a fast-food restaurant and observe long lines decide to leave. These people conclude that the marginal cost (monetary plus time costs) of obtaining the fast food is too large relative to the marginal benefit. They would not have come to the restaurant in the first place had they known the lines were so long. But, getting that information by, say, employing an advance scout with a cellular phone would cost more than the perceived benefit.

Finally, customers must decide what to order when they arrive at the counter. In making these choices they again compare marginal costs and marginal benefits in attempting to obtain the greatest personal satisfaction or well-being.

Economists believe that what is true for the behavior of customers at fast-food restaurants is true for economic behavior in general. Faced with an array of choices, consumers, workers, and businesses rationally compare marginal costs and marginal benefits in making decisions.

Marginalism: Benefits and Costs

The economic perspective focuses largely on **marginal analysis**—decisions which compare marginal benefits and marginal costs. *Marginal* means "extra," "additional," or "a change in." Most economic choices or decisions entail changes in the status quo. When you graduated from high school you faced the question of whether you should get *additional* education. Similarly, businesses are continuously deciding whether to employ more or fewer workers or to produce more or less output.

In making such choices rationally, we must compare marginal benefits and marginal costs. Because of scarcity, any option or choice will entail both extra benefits and additional costs. Example: Your time is scarce. What will you do with, say, two "free" hours on a Saturday afternoon? Option: Watch Gigantic State University's Fighting Aardvarks play basketball on television. Marginal benefit: The pleasure of seeing the game. Marginal cost: Any of the other things you sacrifice by spending an extra two hours in front of the tube, including studying (economics, hopefully), jogging, or taking a nap. If the marginal benefit exceeds the marginal cost, then it is rational to watch the game. But if you perceive the marginal cost of watching the game to exceed its marginal benefits, then one of the other options should be chosen.

On the national level government is continuously making decisions involving marginal benefits and costs. More spending on health care may mean less spending on homeless shelters, aid for the poor, or military security. Lesson: In a world of scarcity the decision to obtain the marginal benefit with some specific choice includes the marginal cost of forgoing something else. Again, there's no free lunch.

One implication of decisions based on marginal analysis is that there *can* be too much of a "good thing." Although certain goods and services seem inherently desirable—education, health care, a clean environment—we can in fact have too much of them. "Too much" occurs when we push their production to some point where their marginal cost (the value of the forgone options) exceeds their marginal benefit. If we choose to produce health care to the extent that its marginal cost exceeds its marginal benefit, we are providing "too much" health care even though health care is a good thing. If the marginal cost of health care is greater than its marginal benefit, then we are sacrificing alternative products (for example, education and pollution reduction) which are more valuable than health care at the margin. *(Key Question 13)*

The accompanying Last Word provides an everyday application of the economic perspective.

> ### QUICK REVIEW 1-3
>
> ■ Beware of logical errors such as the fallacy of composition, the post hoc fallacy, and confusing correlation with causation when engaging in economic reasoning.
>
> ■ The economic perspective stresses *a* resource scarcity and the necessity of making choices; *b* the assumption of rational behavior; and *c* marginal analysis.

CHAPTER SUMMARY

1   Economics deals with the efficient use of scarce resources in the production of goods and services to satisfy material wants.

2   A knowledge of economics contributes to effective citizenship and provides useful insights for consumers and businesspersons.

3   The tasks of descriptive or empirical economics are a gathering those economic facts relevant to a particular problem or specific segment of the economy, and b testing hypotheses against facts to validate theories.

4   Generalizations stated by economists are called "principles," "theories," "laws," or "models." The derivation of these principles is the task of economic theory.

5   Induction distills theories from facts; deduction uses logic to derive hypotheses which are then tested against facts.

6   Some economic principles deal with macroeconomics (the economy as a whole or major aggregates); others pertain to microeconomics (specific economic units or institutions).

7   Economic principles are valuable as predictive devices; they are the bases for the formulation of economic policy designed to solve problems and control undesirable events.

8   Economic growth, full employment, economic efficiency, price level stability, economic freedom, equity in the distribution of income, economic security, and reasonable balance in our international trade and finance are all widely accepted economic goals in our society. Some of these goals are complementary; others are mutually exclusive.

9   Positive statements deal with facts ("what is"), while normative statements express value judgments ("what ought to be").

10   In studying economics the beginner may encounter pitfalls, such as a biases and preconceptions, b terminological difficulties, c the fallacy of composition, and d the difficulty of establishing clear cause-effect relationships.

11   The economic perspective envisions individuals and institutions making rational decisions based on marginal costs and marginal benefits.

TERMS AND CONCEPTS

economics
descriptive or
   empirical economics
economic theory
induction and
   deduction
principles or
   generalizations

hypothesis
ceteris paribus or
   "other things equal"
   assumption
policy economics
macroeconomics and
   microeconomics

economic goals
tradeoffs
positive and normative
   economics
correlation and
   causation
fallacy of composition

post hoc, ergo propter
   hoc or "after this,
   therefore because of
   this" fallacy
economic perspective
marginal analysis

QUESTIONS AND STUDY SUGGESTIONS

1   *Key Question   Explain in detail the interrelationships between economic facts, theory, and policy. Critically evaluate: "The trouble with economics is that it is not practical. It* *has too much to say about theory and not enough to say about facts."*

2 Analyze and explain the following quotation.[2]

Facts are seldom simple and usually complicated; theoretical analysis is needed to unravel the complications and interpret the facts before we can understand them . . . the opposition of facts and theory is a false one; the true relationship is complementary. We cannot in practice consider a fact without relating it to other facts, and the relation is a theory. Facts by themselves are dumb; before they will tell us anything we have to arrange them, and the arrangement is a theory. Theory is simply the unavoidable arrangement and interpretation of facts, which gives us generalizations on which we can argue and act, in the place of a mass of disjointed particulars.

3 Of what significance is the fact that economics is not a laboratory science? What problems may be involved in deriving and applying economic principles?

4 Explain each of the following statements:
    a "Like all scientific laws, economic laws are established in order to make successful prediction of the outcome of human actions."[3]
    b "Abstraction . . . is the inevitable price of generality . . . indeed abstraction and generality are virtually synonyms."[4]
    c "Numbers serve to discipline rhetoric."[5]

5 *Key Question* *Indicate whether each of the following statements pertains to microeconomics or macroeconomics:*
    a *The unemployment rate in the United States was 5.9 percent in September of 1994.*
    b *The Alpo dogfood plant in Bowser, Iowa, laid off 15 workers last month.*
    c *An unexpected freeze in central Florida reduced the citrus crop and caused the price of oranges to rise.*
    d *Our national output, adjusted for inflation, grew by about 3.1 percent in 1993.*
    e *Last week Manhattan Chemical Bank lowered its interest rate on business loans by one-half of 1 percentage point.*
    f *The consumer price index rose by 2.7 percent in 1993.*

6 *Key Question* *Identify each of the following as either a positive or a normative statement:*
    a *The high temperature today was 89 degrees.*
    b *It was too hot today.*
    c *The general price level rose by 4.4 percent last year.*
    d *Inflation eroded living standards last year and should be reduced by government policies.*

7 To what extent would you accept the eight economic goals stated and described in this chapter? What priorities would you assign to them? It has been said that we seek only four goals: progress, stability, justice, and freedom. Is this list of goals compatible with that given in the chapter?

8 Analyze each of the following specific goals in terms of the eight general goals stated on pages 6 and 7, and note points of conflict and compatibility: a the lessening of environmental pollution; b increasing leisure; and c protection of American producers from foreign competition. Indicate which of these specific goals you favor and justify your position.

9 *Key Question* *Explain and give an illustration of* a *the fallacy of composition, and* b *the "after this, therefore because of this" fallacy. Why are cause-and-effect relationships difficult to isolate in the social sciences?*

10 Suppose empirical studies show that students who study more hours receive higher grades, as suggested by the graph accompanying question 4 in this chapter's appendix. Does this relationship guarantee that any particular student who studies longer will get higher grades?

11 A recent psychiatric study found that there is a positive correlation between the amount of time children and youth spend watching television and mental depression. Speculate on possible cause-effect relationships.

12 "Economists should never be popular; men who afflict the comfortable serve equally with those who comfort the afflicted and one cannot suppose that American capitalism would long prosper without the critics its leaders find such a profound source of annoyance."[6] Interpret and evaluate.

13 *Key Question* *Use the economic perspective to explain why someone who normally is a light eater at a standard restaurant may become somewhat of a glutton at a buffet-style restaurant which charges a single price for all you can eat.*

14 (Last Word) Explain how the economic perspective can be used to explain the behavior of customers in fast-food restaurants.

[2]Henry Clay, *Economics for the General Reader* (New York: The Macmillan Company, 1925), pp. 10–11.

[3]Oskar Lange, "The Scope and Method of Economics," *Review of Economic Studies,* vol. 13, 1945–1946, p. 20.

[4]George J. Stigler, *The Theory of Price* (New York: The Macmillan Company, 1947), p. 10.

[5]Victor R. Fuchs, *How We Live* (Cambridge, Mass.: Harvard University Press, 1983), p. 5.

[6]John Kenneth Galbraith, *American Capitalism,* rev. ed. (Boston: Houghton Mifflin Company, 1956), p. 49.

APPENDIX TO CHAPTER 1

GRAPHS AND THEIR MEANING

If you glance quickly through this text, you will find graphs. Some seem simple, while others seem more formidable. Contrary to student folklore, graphs are *not* designed by economists to confuse students! Graphs are employed to help you visualize and understand important economic relationships. The physicist and chemist sometimes illustrate their theories by building TinkerToy arrangements of multicolored wooden balls representing protons, neutrons, and so forth, held in proper relation to one another by wires or sticks. Economists often use graphs to illustrate their models. By understanding these "pictures" you can more readily comprehend what economists are saying.

Most of our principles or models will explain the relationship between just two sets of economic facts, which can be conveniently represented with two-dimensional graphs.

Constructing a Graph

A graph is a visual representation of the relationship between two variables. Table 1 is a hypothetical illustration showing the relationship between income and consumption. Without ever having studied economics, you would expect intuitively that high-income people would consume more than low-income people. Thus we are not surprised to find in Table 1 that consumption increases as income increases.

How can the information in Table 1 be expressed graphically? Glance at the graph shown in Figure 1.

Now look back at the information in Table 1 and we will explain how to represent it in a meaningful way by constructing the graph you just examined.

What we want to show visually, or graphically, is how consumption changes as income changes. Since income is the determining factor, we represent it on the horizontal axis of the graph, as is customary. And, because consumption depends on income, we represent it on the vertical axis of the graph, as is also customary. Actually, what we are doing is representing the independent variable on the horizontal axis and the dependent variable on the vertical axis.

Now we must arrange the vertical and horizontal scales of the graph to reflect the range of values of consumption and income, as well as mark the steps in convenient graphic increments. As you can see, the ranges in the graph cover the ranges of values in Table 1. The increments on both scales are $100 for approximately each half-inch.

Next, we must locate for each consumption value, and the income value that it depends on, a single point which reflects the same information graphically. Our five income–consumption combinations are plotted by drawing perpendiculars from the appropriate points on the **vertical** and **horizontal axes.** For example, in plotting point *c*—the $200 income–$150 consumption point—perpendiculars must be drawn up from the horizontal (income) axis at $200 and across from the vertical (consumption) axis at $150. These perpendiculars intersect at point *c,* which locates this particular income–consumption combination. You should

TABLE 1 The relationship between income and consumption

Income (per week)	Consumption (per week)	Point
$ 0	$ 50	a
100	100	b
200	150	c
300	200	d
400	250	e

TABLE 2 The relationship between ticket prices and attendance

Ticket price	Attendance (thousands)	Point
$25	0	a
20	4	b
15	8	c
10	12	d
5	16	e
0	20	f

verify that the other income–consumption combinations shown in Table 1 are properly located in Figure 1. By assuming that the same general relationship between income and consumption prevails at all other points between the five points graphed, a line or curve can be drawn to connect these points.

Using Figure 1 as a benchmark, we can make several additional comments.

Direct and Inverse Relationships

Our upsloping line depicts a direct relationship between income and consumption. By a positive or **direct relationship** we mean that the two variables—in this case consumption and income—change in the *same* direction. An increase in consumption is associated with an increase in income; a decrease in consumption accompanies a decrease in income. When

two sets of data are positively or directly related, they will always graph as an *upsloping* line as in Figure 1.

In contrast, two sets of data may be inversely related. Consider Table 2, which shows the relationship between the price of basketball tickets and game attendance at Gigantic State University. We observe a negative or **inverse relationship** between ticket prices and attendance; these two variables change in *opposite* directions. When ticket prices decrease, attendance increases. When ticket prices increase, attendance decreases. In Figure 2 the six data points of Table 2 are plotted following the same procedure outlined before. Observe that an inverse relationship will always graph as a *downsloping* line.

FIGURE 1 Graphing the direct relationship between consumption and income
Two sets of data which are positively or directly related, such as consumption and income, graph as an upsloping line. In this case the vertical intercept is 50 and the slope of the line is $+\frac{1}{2}$.

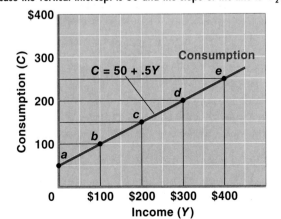

FIGURE 2 Graphing the inverse relationship between ticket prices and game attendance
Two sets of data which are negatively or inversely related, such as ticket price and the attendance at basketball games, graph as a downsloping line. The slope of this line is $-1\frac{1}{4}$.

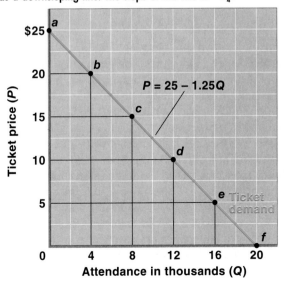

Dependent and Independent Variables

Although it is not always easy, economists seek to determine which variable is "cause" and which "effect." Or, more formally, we want to ascertain the independent and the dependent variable. By definition, the **dependent variable** is the "effect" or outcome; it is the variable which changes because of a change in another (independent) variable.

The **independent variable** is the "cause"; it is the variable which causes the change in the dependent variable. As noted in our income–consumption example, generally, income is the independent variable and consumption the dependent variable. Income causes consumption to be what it is rather than the other way around. Similarly, ticket prices determine attendance at GSU basketball games; attendance does not determine ticket prices. Ticket price is the independent variable and the quantity purchased is the dependent variable.

You may recall from your high school courses that mathematicians always put the independent variable (cause) on the horizontal axis and the dependent variable (effect) on the vertical axis. Economists are less tidy; their graphing of independent and dependent variables is more arbitrary. Thus, their conventional graphing of the income–consumption relationship is consistent with mathematical presentation. But economists put price and cost data on the vertical axis. Hence, economists' graphing of GSU's ticket price–attendance data conflicts with normal mathematical procedure.

Other Variables Held Constant

Our simple two-variable graphs ignore many other factors which might affect the amount of consumption occurring at each income level or the number of people who attend GSU basketball games at each possible ticket price. When economists plot the relationship between any two variables, they invoke the *ceteris paribus* or "other things equal" assumption. Thus, in Figure 1 all other factors (that is, all factors other than income) which might affect the amount of consumption are presumed to be constant or unchanged. Similarly, in Figure 2 all factors other than ticket price which might influence attendance at GSU basketball games are assumed constant. In reality, we know "other things" often change, and when they do, the specific relationships presented in our two tables and graphs will change. Specifically, we

would expect the lines we have plotted to shift to new locations.

For example, what might happen to the income–consumption relationship if a stock market "crash" such as that of October 1987 occurred? The expected impact of this dramatic fall in the value of stocks would be to make people feel less wealthy and therefore less willing to consume at each income level. We would anticipate a downward shift of the consumption line in Figure 1. You should plot a new consumption line, assuming that consumption is, say, $20 less at each income level. Note that the relationship remains direct, but the line has merely shifted to reflect less consumer spending at each level of income.

Similarly, factors other than ticket prices might affect GSU game attendance. If the government abandoned its program of student loans, GSU enrollment and hence attendance at games might be less at each ticket price. You should redraw Figure 2, assuming that 2000 fewer students attend GSU games at each ticket price. *(Key Appendix Questions 1 and 2)*

Slope of a Line

Lines can be described in terms of their slopes. The **slope of a straight line** between any two points is defined as the ratio of the vertical change (the rise or fall) to the horizontal change (the run) involved in moving between those points.

Positive Slope   In moving from point b to point c in Figure 1 the rise or vertical change (the change in consumption) is +$50 and the run or horizontal change (the change in income) is +$100. Therefore:

$$\text{Slope} = \frac{\text{vertical change}}{\text{horizontal change}} = \frac{+50}{+100} = +\frac{1}{2}$$

Note that our slope of $\frac{1}{2}$ is positive because consumption and income change in the same direction, that is, consumption and income are directly or positively related.

This slope of $+\frac{1}{2}$ tells us that there will be a $1 increase in consumption for every $2 increase in income. Similarly, it indicates that for every $2 decrease in income there will be a $1 decrease in consumption.

Negative Slope   For our ticket price–attendance data the relationship is negative or inverse with the result that the slope of Figure 2's line is negative. In particular, the vertical change or fall is 5 and the horizontal change or run is 4. Therefore:

$$\text{Slope} = \frac{\text{vertical change}}{\text{horizontal change}} = \frac{-5}{+4} = -1\frac{1}{4}$$

This slope of $-5/+4$ or $-1\frac{1}{4}$ means that lowering the price of a ticket by $5 will increase attendance by 4000 people—which is the same as saying that a $1 price reduction will increase attendance by 800 persons.

Three Addenda Our discussion of line slopes needs three additional comments.

1 Measurement Units The slope of a line will be affected by the choice of units for either variable. If, in our ticket price illustration we had chosen to measure prices in dimes rather than dollars, our vertical change for a price cut would be -50 (dimes) instead of -5 (dollars) and the slope would be $-12\frac{1}{2}$ $(= -50 \div 4)$ rather than $-1\frac{1}{4}$. The measurement of slope depends on the way the relevant variables are denominated.

2 Marginal Analysis Economics is largely concerned with *marginal* or incremental changes—changes from the status quo. Should you work an hour more or an hour less each day on your part-time job? Should you buy one more or one less GSU basketball ticket? Should a fast-food restaurant, now employing eight workers, hire an extra or marginal worker?

This is relevant because the slopes of lines measure marginal changes. For example, in Figure 1, the slope shows that $50 of extra or marginal consumption is associated with each $100 increase in income. Consumers will spend half of any increase in their income and reduce their consumption by half of any decline in income. The concept of slope is important in economics because it reflects marginal changes.

3 Infinite and Zero Slopes Many variables are unrelated or independent of one another. We would not expect the price of bananas to be related to the quantity of wristwatches purchased. If we put the price of bananas on the vertical axis and the quantity demanded of watches on the horizontal axis, the absence of a relationship between them would be described by a line parallel to the vertical axis, indicating that changes in the price of bananas have no impact on watch purchases. The slope of such a line is *infinite*. Similarly, if aggregate consumption was completely unrelated to, say, the quantity of rainfall and we put consumption on the vertical axis and rainfall on the horizontal axis, this unrelatedness would be represented by a line parallel to the horizontal axis. This line has a slope of *zero*.

Intercept

In addition to its slope, the only other information needed in locating a line on a graph is the vertical intercept. The **vertical intercept** is the point where the line meets the vertical axis. For Figure 1 the intercept is $50. This means that, if current income were zero, consumers would still spend $50. How might they manage to consume when they have no current income? Answer: By borrowing or by selling off some of their assets. Similarly, the vertical intercept in Figure 2 shows us that at a $25 ticket price GSU's basketball team would be playing in an empty auditorium.

Equation Form

With a specific intercept and slope, our consumption line can be succinctly described in equation form. In general, a linear equation is written as $y = a + bx$, where y is the dependent variable, a is the vertical intercept, b is the slope of the line, and x is the independent variable. For our income–consumption example, if C represents consumption (the dependent variable) and Y represents income (the independent variable), we can write $C = a + bY$. By substituting the values of the intercept and the slope for our specific data, we have $C = 50 + .5Y$. This equation allows us to determine consumption at *any* level of income. At the $300 income level (point d in Figure 1), our equation predicts that consumption will be $200 $[= \$50 + (.5 \times \$300)]$. You should confirm that at the $250 income level consumption will be $175.

When economists reverse mathematical convention by putting the independent variable on the vertical axis and the dependent variable on the horizontal axis, the standard linear equation solves for the independent, rather than the dependent, variable. We noted earlier that this case is relevant for our GSU ticket price–attendance data. If P represents the ticket price and Q represents attendance, our relevant equation is $P = 25 - 1.25Q$, where the vertical intercept is 25 and the negative slope is $-1\frac{1}{4}$ or -1.25. But knowing the value for P lets us solve for Q, which is actually our dependent variable. For example, if $P = 15$, then the values in our equation become: $15 = 25 - 1.25(Q)$, or $1.25Q = 10$, or $Q = 8$. You should check this answer against Figure 2 and also use this equation to predict GSU ticket sales when price is $7.50. *(Key Appendix Question 3)*

Slope of a Nonlinear Curve

We now move from the simple world of linear relationships (straight lines) to the more complex world of nonlinear relationships (curves). By definition, the slope of a straight line is constant at every point on it. The slope of a curve changes as we move from one point to another on the curve.

For example, consider the downsloping curve in Figure 3. Although its slope is negative throughout, it diminishes or flattens as we move southeast along the curve. Because the slope is constantly changing, we can only measure the slope at some particular point on the curve.

We begin by drawing a straight line which is tangent to the curve at that point where we want to measure its slope. A line is **tangent** at that point where it touches, but does not intersect, the curve. Thus, line *aa* is tangent to the curve at point *A* in Figure 3. Having done this, we can measure the slope of the curve at point *A* by measuring the slope of the straight tangent line *aa*. Specifically, in Figure 3 the vertical change (fall) in *aa* is −20 and the horizontal change (run) is +5. Thus the slope of the tangent *aa* line is −20/+5 or −4 and therefore the slope of the curve at *A* is also −4.

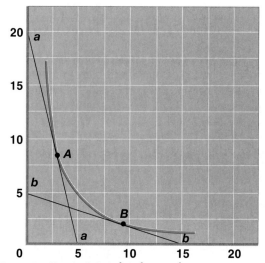

FIGURE 3   Determining the slopes of curves
The slope of a nonlinear curve changes as one moves from point to point on the curve. The slope at any point can be determined by drawing a straight line tangent to that point and calculating the slope of that straight line.

We can now draw line *bb* tangent to a flatter part of the curve at point *B*. Following the same procedure, we find the negative slope to be smaller, specifically −5/+15 or −$\frac{1}{3}$. Similar analysis applies to upsloping curves. *(Key Appendix Question 6)*

APPENDIX SUMMARY

1   Graphs are a convenient and revealing means of presenting economic relationships or principles.

2   Two variables are positively or directly related when their values change in the same direction. Two directly related variables will plot as an upsloping line on a graph.

3   Two variables are negatively or inversely related when their values change in opposite directions. Two variables which are inversely related will graph as a downsloping line.

4   The value of the dependent variable ("effect") is determined by the value of the independent variable ("cause").

5   When "other factors" which might affect a two-variable relationship are allowed to change, the plotted relationship will likely shift to a new location.

6   The slope of a straight line is the ratio of the vertical

change to the horizontal change in moving between any two points. The slope of an upsloping line is positive; the slope of a downsloping line is negative.

7   The slope of a line   a depends on the choice of units in denominating the variables and   b are especially relevant for economics because they measure marginal changes.

8   The slope of a horizontal line is zero; the slope of a vertical line is infinite.

9   The vertical intercept and the slope of a line establish its location and are used in expressing the relationship between two variables as an equation.

10   The slope of a curve at any point is determined by calculating the slope of a straight line drawn tangent to that point.

APPENDIX TERMS AND CONCEPTS

vertical and horizontal
   axes
slope of a straight line

direct and inverse
   relationships

dependent and
   independent variables

vertical intercept
tangent

APPENDIX QUESTIONS AND STUDY SUGGESTIONS

*1 Briefly explain the use of graphs as a means of presenting economic principles. What is an inverse relationship? How does it graph? What is a direct relationship? How does it graph? Graph and explain the relationships one would expect to find between **a** the number of inches of rainfall per month and the sale of umbrellas, **b** the amount of tuition and the level of enrollment at a university, and **c** the size of a university's athletic scholarships and the number of games won by its football team.

In each case cite and explain how considerations other than those specifically mentioned might upset the expected relationship. Is your second generalization consistent with the fact that, historically, enrollments and tuition have both increased? If not, explain any difference.

2 *Key Appendix Question Indicate how each of the following might affect the data shown in Table 2 and Figure 2 of this appendix.*

    a *GSU's athletic director schedules higher-quality opponents.*

    b *GSU's Fighting Aardvarks experience three losing seasons.*

    c *GSU contracts to have all its home games televised.*

3 *Key Appendix Question The following table contains data on the relationship between saving and income. Rearrange these data as required and graph the data on the accompanying grid. What is the slope of the line? The vertical intercept? Interpret the meaning of both the slope and the intercept. Write the equation which represents this line. What would you predict saving to be at the $12,500 level of income?*

Income (per year)	Saving (per year)
$15,000	$1,000
0	−500
10,000	500
5,000	0
20,000	1,500

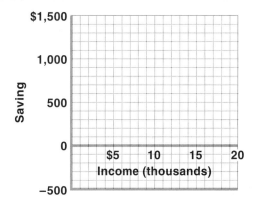

4 Construct a table from the data shown on the graph below. Which is the dependent and which the independent variable? Summarize the data in equation form.

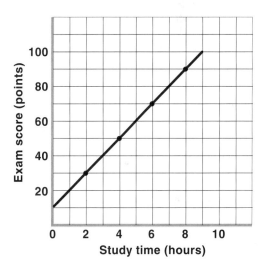

5 Suppose that when the interest rate which must be paid to borrow funds is 16 percent, businesses find it unprofitable to invest in machinery and equipment. However, when the interest rate is 14 percent, $5 billion worth of investment is profitable. At 12 percent, a total of $10 billion of investment is profitable. Similarly, total investment increases by $5 billion for each successive 2 percentage point decline in the interest rate. Indicate the relevant relationship between the interest rate and investment verbally, tabularly, graphically, and as an equation. Put the interest rate on the vertical axis and investment on the horizontal axis. In your equation use the form $i = a - bI$, where i is the interest rate, a is the vertical intercept, b is the slope of the line, and I is the level of investment. Comment on advantages and disadvantages of verbal, tabular, graphical, and equation forms of presentation.

---

*Note to the reader: A floppy disk symbol ⌷ precedes each of the questions in this appendix. This icon is used throughout the text to indicate that a particular question relates to the content of one of the tutorial programs in the student software which accompanies this book. Please refer to the Preface for more detail about this software.

6 *Key Appendix Question* *The accompanying diagram shows curve XX and three tangents at points A, B, and C. Calculate the slope of the curve at these three points.*

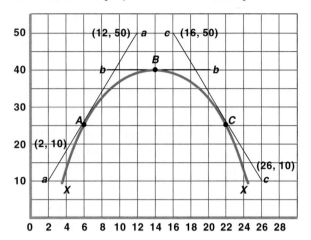

7 In the accompanying diagram, is the slope of curve *AA'* positive or negative? Does the slope increase or decrease as we move from *A* to *A'*? Answer the same two questions for curve *BB'*.

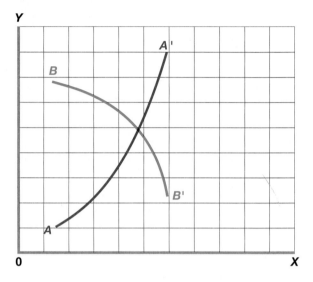

THE ECONOMIZING PROBLEM

You make decisions every day which capture the essence of economics. Suppose you have $30 and are deciding how to spend it. Should you buy a new pair of jeans? A couple of compact discs? A ticket for a rock concert? Similarly, what to do with your time between three and six o'clock on, say, a Thursday afternoon? Should you work extra hours on your part-time job? Do research on a term project? Prepare for an economics quiz? Watch TV? Take a nap? Money and time are both scarce and making decisions in the context of scarcity implies costs. If you choose the jeans, the cost is the forgone CDs or concert. If you nap or watch TV, the cost might be a low grade on your quiz. Scarcity, choices, and costs—these are the building blocks of this chapter.

Here we introduce and explore the fundamentals of economic science. We expand on the definition of economics introduced in Chapter 1 and explore the essence of the economizing problem. We will illustrate, extend, and modify our definition by using production possibilities tables and curves. Next, we will briefly survey different ways by which institutionally and ideologically diverse economies respond to the economizing problem. Finally, we present an overview of the market system in the form of the circular flow model.

THE FOUNDATION OF ECONOMICS

Two fundamental facts which constitute the **economizing problem** provide a foundation for the field of economics. We must carefully state and fully understand these two facts, because everything that follows depends directly or indirectly on them.

1 *Society's material wants, that is, the material wants of its citizens and institutions, are virtually unlimited or insatiable.*

2 *Economic resources—the means of producing goods and services—are limited or scarce.*

Unlimited Wants

In the first statement, what do we mean by "material wants"? We mean, first, the desires of consumers to obtain and use various *goods* and *services* which provide **utility,** the economist's term for pleasure or satisfaction.[1] An amazingly wide range of products fills the bill in this respect: houses, automobiles, toothpaste, compact-disc players, pizzas, sweaters, and the like. Innumerable products sometimes classified as

---

[1]This definition leaves a variety of wants—recognition, status, love, and so forth—for the other social sciences to worry about.

necessities (food, shelter, clothing) and *luxuries* (perfumes, yachts, mink coats) all can satisfy human wants. Of course, what is a luxury to Smith may be a necessity to Jones, and what is a common necessity today may have been a luxury a few years ago.

Services satisfy our wants as much as products. Repair work on our car, the removal of our appendix, a haircut, and legal advice also satisfy human wants. On reflection, we realize that we buy many goods, for example, automobiles and washing machines, for the services they render. The differences between goods and services are often less than they first appear.

Businesses and units of government also seek to satisfy material wants. Businesses want factory buildings, machinery, trucks, warehouses, communications systems, and other things that help them realize their production goals. Government, reflecting the collective wants of its citizenry or goals of its own, seeks highways, schools, hospitals, and military hardware.

As a group, these material wants are *insatiable,* or *unlimited,* meaning material wants for goods and services cannot be completely satisfied. Our wants for a *particular* good or service can be satisfied; over a short period of time we can get enough toothpaste or beer. Certainly one appendicitis operation is par for the course.

But goods *in general* are another story. We do not, and presumably cannot, get enough. A simple experiment will help verify this. Suppose all members of society are asked to list those goods and services they want but do not now possess. Chances are this list will be impressive!

Furthermore, over time, wants multiply. As we fill some of the wants on the list, we add new ones. Material wants, like rabbits, have a high reproduction rate. The rapid introduction of new products whets our appetites, and extensive advertising persuades us that we need items we might not otherwise buy. Not long ago, we didn't want personal computers, light beer, video recorders, fax machines, and compact discs because they didn't exist. Furthermore, we often cannot stop with simple satisfaction: The acquisition of an Escort or Geo has been known to whet the appetite for a Porsche or Mercedes.

At any specific time the individuals and institutions constituting society have innumerable unfulfilled material wants. Some—food, clothing, shelter—have biological roots. But some are also influenced by the conventions and customs of society: The specific kinds of food, clothing, and shelter we seek are frequently determined by the general social and cultural environment in which we live. Over time, wants change and multiply, fueled by development of new products and extensive advertising and sales promotion.

The overall objective of all economic activity is the attempt to satisfy all these diverse material wants.

Scarce Resources

In considering the second fundamental fact—*economic resources are limited or scarce*—what do we mean by **economic resources?** In general, we mean all natural, human, and manufactured resources that go into the production of goods and services. This covers a lot of ground: factory and farm buildings and all equipment, tools, and machinery used to produce manufactured goods and agricultural products; transportation and communication facilities; innumerable types of labor; and land and mineral resources of all kinds. Economists broadly classify these as either (1) *property* resources—land or raw materials and capital; or (2) *human* resources—labor and entrepreneurial ability.

Resource Categories   Let's examine these various resource categories.

Land   **Land** means much more to the economist than to most people. Land is all natural resources—all "gifts of nature"—usable in the productive process. Such resources as arable land, forests, mineral and oil deposits, and water resources come under this classification.

Capital   **Capital,** or investment goods, is all manufactured aids to production, that is, all tools, machinery, equipment, and factory, storage, transportation, and distribution facilities used in producing goods and services and getting them to the ultimate consumer. The process of producing and purchasing capital goods is known as **investment.**

Two other points are pertinent. First, *capital goods* ("tools") differ from *consumer goods* in that the latter satisfy wants directly, whereas the former do so indirectly by facilitating production of consumable goods. Second, the term "capital" as here defined does *not* refer to money. True, business executives and economists often talk of "money capital," meaning money available to purchase machinery, equipment, and other productive facilities. But money, as such, produces nothing; hence, it is not considered an economic resource. *Real capital*—tools, machinery, and other productive equipment—is an economic resource; *money* or *financial capital* is not.

Labor   **Labor** is a broad term the economist uses for all the physical and mental talents of men and women available and usable in producing goods and services. (This excludes a special set of talents—entrepreneurial ability—which, because of their special significance in a capitalistic economy, we consider separately.) The services of a logger, retail clerk, machinist, teacher, professional football player, and nuclear physicist all fall under the general heading of labor.

Entrepreneurial Ability   Finally, there is the special human resource we label **entrepreneurial ability,** or, simply, *enterprise.* We can assign four related functions to the entrepreneur.

1   The entrepreneur takes the *initiative* in combining the resources of land, capital, and labor to produce a good or service. Both a sparkplug and a catalyst, the entrepreneur is the driving force behind production and the agent who combines the other resources in what is hoped will be a profitable venture.

2   The entrepreneur makes basic *business-policy decisions,* that is, those nonroutine decisions which set the course of a business enterprise.

3   The entrepreneur is an *innovator*—the one who attempts to introduce on a commercial basis new products, new productive techniques, or even new forms of business organization.

4   The entrepreneur is a *risk bearer.* This is apparent from a close examination of the other three entrepreneurial functions. The entrepreneur in a capitalistic system has no guarantee of profit. The reward for his or her time, efforts, and abilities may be profits *or* losses and eventual bankruptcy. The entrepreneur risks not only time, effort, and business reputation, but his or her invested funds and those of associates or stockholders.

Resource Payments   The income received from supplying property resources—raw materials and capital equipment—is called *rental* and *interest income,* respectively. The income accruing to those who supply labor is called *wages* which includes salaries and various wage and salary supplements in the form of bonuses, commissions, royalties, and so forth. Entrepreneurial income is called *profits,* which may be a negative figure—that is, losses.

These four broad categories of economic resources, or *factors of production* or *inputs* as they are often called, leave room for debate when it comes to classifying specific resources. For example, suppose you receive a dividend on some newly issued Exxon stock which you own. Is this an interest return for the capital equipment the company bought with the money you provided in buying Exxon stock? Or is this return a profit which compensates you for the risks involved in purchasing corporate stock? What about the earnings of a one-person consulting firm where the owner is both entrepreneur and labor force? Are the owner's earnings considered wages or profit income? The answer in both examples is "some of each." The point is that while we might quibble about classifying a particular flow of income as wages, rent, interest, or profits, all income can be fitted under one of these general headings.

Relative Scarcity   Economic resources, or factors of production, have one fundamental characteristic in common: *They are scarce or limited in supply.* Our "spaceship earth" contains only limited amounts of resources to use in producing goods and services. Quantities of arable land, mineral deposits, capital equipment, and labor (time) are all limited; they are available only in finite amounts. Because of the scarcity of productive resources and the constraint this scarcity puts on productive activity, output will necessarily be limited. Society will *not* be able to produce and consume all the goods and services it might want. Thus, in the United States—one of the most affluent nations—output per person was limited to $25,847 in 1994. In the poorest nations, annual output per person is as low as $200 or $300!

ECONOMICS: EMPLOYMENT AND EFFICIENCY

Restating the basic definition of economics: *Economics is the social science concerned with the problem of using or administering scarce resources (the means of producing) to attain the greatest or maximum fulfillment of society's unlimited wants (the goal of producing).* Economics is concerned with "doing the best with what we have." If our resources are scarce, we cannot satisfy all of our unlimited material wants. The next best thing is to achieve the greatest possible satisfaction of these wants.

Economics is a science of efficiency—efficiency in the use of scarce resources. Society wants to use its limited resources efficiently; it wants to get the maximum amount of useful goods and services produced with its available resources. To achieve this desirable outcome it must realize both full employment and full production.

Full Employment: Using Available Resources

By **full employment** we mean all available resources should be employed. No workers should be involuntarily out of work; the economy should provide employment for all who are willing and able to work. Nor should capital equipment or arable land sit idle. Note we say all *available* resources should be employed. Each society has certain customs and practices which determine what particular resources are available for employment. For example, legislation and custom provide that children and the very aged should not be employed. Similarly, it is desirable for productivity to allow farmland to lie fallow periodically. And it is desirable to "conserve" some resources for use by future generations.

Full Production: Using Resources Efficiently

But the employment of all available resources is insufficient to achieve efficiency. Full production must also be realized. By **full production** we mean that all employed resources should be used so that they provide the maximum possible satisfaction of our material wants. If we fail to realize full production, economists say our resources are *underemployed.*

Full production implies two kinds of efficiency—allocative and productive efficiency.

Allocative Efficiency **Allocative efficiency** means that resources are being devoted to that combination of goods and services most wanted by society. It is obtained when we produce the best or optimal output-mix. For example, society wants resources allocated to compact discs and cassettes, rather than 45 rpm or long-playing records. We prefer word processors and personal computers, not manual typewriters. Xerox copiers are desired, not mimeograph machines.

Productive Efficiency **Productive efficiency** is realized when desired goods and services are produced in the least costly ways. When we produce, say, compact discs at the lowest achievable unit cost, this means we are expending the smallest amount of resources to produce CDs and therefore making available the largest amount of resources for the production of other wanted products. Suppose society has only $100 worth of resources available. If we can produce a CD with only $5 of resources, then $95 of resources would be available to produce other goods. This is clearly better than producing the CD for $10 and only having $90 of resources for alternative uses.

In real-world terms, productive efficiency requires that Tauruses and Grand Ams be produced with computerized and roboticized assembly techniques rather than with the primitive assembly lines of the 1920s. Nor do we want our farmers harvesting wheat with scythes or picking corn by hand when elaborate harvesting equipment will do the job at a much lower cost per bushel.

In summary, allocative efficiency means resources are apportioned among firms and industries to obtain the particular mix of products society wants the most. Productive efficiency means each good or service in this optimal product-mix is produced in the least costly fashion. Full production means producing the "right" goods (allocative efficiency) in the "right" way (productive efficiency). *(Key Question 5)*

QUICK REVIEW 2-1

■ Human material wants are virtually unlimited.

■ Economic resources—land, capital, labor, and entrepreneurial ability—are scarce or limited.

■ Economics is concerned with the efficient management of scarce resources to achieve the maximum fulfillment of our material wants.

■ Economics entails the pursuit of full employment and full production, the latter involving both allocative and productive efficiency.

Production Possibilities Table

We can clarify the economizing problem through the use of a production possibilities table. This device reveals the core of the economizing problem: *Because resources are scarce, a full-employment, full-production economy cannot have an unlimited output of goods and services. As a result, people must choose which goods and services to produce and which to forgo.*

Assumptions Several assumptions will set the stage for our illustration.

1 *Efficiency* The economy is operating at full employment and achieving productive efficiency. (We will consider allocative efficiency later.)

2 *Fixed Resources* The available supplies of the factors of production are fixed in both quantity and quality. But they can be shifted or reallocated, within limits, among different uses; for example, a relatively unskilled laborer can work on a farm, at a fast-food restaurant, or as a gas station attendant.

3 *Fixed Technology* The state of the technological arts is constant; that is, technology does not change during our analysis. Assumptions 2 and 3 are another way of saying that we are looking at our economy at a specific point in time, or over a very short period of time. Over a relatively long period it would be unrealistic to rule out technological advances and the possibility that resource supplies might vary.

4 *Two Products* To further simplify, suppose our economy is producing just two products—industrial robots and pizza—instead of the innumerable goods and services actually produced. Pizza is symbolic of **consumer goods,** those goods which directly satisfy our wants; industrial robots are symbolic of **capital goods,** those goods which satisfy our wants *indirectly* by permitting more efficient production of consumer goods.

Necessity of Choice From our assumptions we see that a choice must be made among alternatives. Available resources are limited. Consequently, the total amounts of robots and pizza that our economy can produce are limited. *Limited resources mean a limited output.* Since resources are limited in supply and fully employed, any increase in the production of robots will mean shifting resources away from the production of pizza. And the reverse holds true: If we step up the production of pizza, needed resources must come at the expense of robot production. *Society cannot have its cake and eat it, too.* Facetiously put, there's no such thing as a "free lunch." This is the essence of the economizing problem.

Let's generalize by noting in Table 2-1 alternative combinations of robots and pizza which our economy might choose. Though the data in this and the following **production possibilities tables** are hypothetical, the points illustrated have tremendous practical significance. At alternative A, our economy would be devoting all its resources to the production of ro-

TABLE 2-1 Production possibilities of pizza and robots with full employment and productive efficiency, 1996

Type of product	Production alternatives				
	A	B	C	D	E
Pizza (in hundred thousands)	0	1	2	3	4
Robots (in thousands)	10	9	7	4	0

bots (capital goods). At alternative E, all available resources would go to pizza production (consumer goods). Both these alternatives are unrealistic extremes; any economy typically strikes a balance in dividing its total output between capital and consumer goods. As we move from alternative A to E, we step up the production of consumer goods (pizza), by shifting resources away from capital goods (robot) production.

Remembering that consumer goods directly satisfy our wants, any movement toward E—producing more pizza—looks tempting. In making this move, society increases the current satisfaction of its wants. But there is a cost—fewer robots. This shift of resources catches up with society over time as its stock of capital goods dwindles—or at least ceases to expand at the current rate—with the result that the potential for greater future production is impaired. In moving from alternative A toward E, society chooses "more now" at the expense of "much more later."

In moving from E toward A, society chooses to forgo current consumption. This sacrifice of current consumption frees resources which can be used to increase production of capital goods. By building up its stock of capital in this way, society can anticipate greater production and, therefore, greater consumption in the future. In moving from E toward A, society is choosing "more later" at the cost of "less now."

At any point in time, an economy which is achieving full employment and productive efficiency must sacrifice some of product X to obtain more of product Y. The basic fact that economic resources are scarce prohibits such an economy from having more of both X and Y.

Production Possibilities Curve

To ensure our understanding of the production possibilities table, let's view these data graphically. We employ a simple two-dimensional graph, arbitrarily

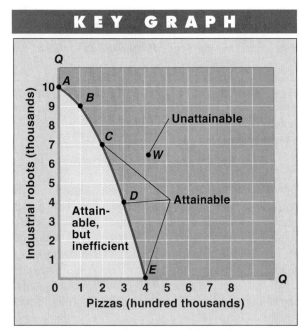

FIGURE 2-1   The production possibilities curve
Each point on the curve represents some maximum combination of any two products which can be achieved if full employment and full production are realized. When operating on the curve, more robots mean less pizza, and vice versa. Limited resources and a fixed technology make any combination of robots and pizza lying outside the curve, such as *W,* unattainable. Points inside the curve are attainable, but indicate that full employment and productive efficiency are not being realized.

putting the output of robots (capital goods) on the vertical axis and the output of pizza (consumer goods) on the horizontal axis, as in Figure 2-1 (Key Graph). Following the plotting procedure in the appendix to Chapter 1, we can locate the "production possibilities" curve, as shown in Figure 2-1.

Each point on the production possibilities curve represents some maximum output of the two products. Thus the curve is a *frontier.* To realize the various combinations of pizza and robots which fall *on* the production possibilities curve, society must achieve both full employment and productive efficiency. Points lying *inside* the curve are also attainable, but are not as desirable as points on the curve. These interior points imply a failure to achieve full employment and productive efficiency. Points lying *outside* the production possibilities curve, like point *W,* would represent greater output than at any point on the curve; but such points are unattainable with the current supplies of resources and technology. The production barrier of limited resources and existing technological knowl-

edge prohibits production of any combination of capital and consumer goods lying outside the production possibilities curve.

Law of Increasing Opportunity Costs

Because resources are scarce relative to the virtually unlimited wants which these resources can be used to satisfy, people must choose among alternatives. More of X (pizza) means less of Y (robots). *The amount of other products which must be forgone or sacrificed to obtain some amount of a specific product is called the* **opportunity cost** *of that good.* In our case the amount of Y (robots) which must be forgone or given up to get another unit of X (pizza) is the *opportunity cost,* or simply the *cost,* of that unit of X.

In moving from possibility A to B in Table 2-1, we find that the cost of 1 additional unit of pizza is 1 less unit of robots. But, as we now pursue the concept of cost through the additional production possibilities— B to C, C to D, and D to E—an important economic principle is revealed. In shifting from alternative A to alternative E, the sacrifice or extra cost of robots involved in getting each additional unit of pizza *increases.* In moving from A to B, just 1 unit of robots is sacrificed for 1 more unit of pizza; but going from B to C sacrifices 2 additional units of robots for 1 more unit of pizza; then 3 more of robots for 1 more of pizza; and finally 4 for 1. Conversely, you should confirm that in moving from E to A the cost of an additional robot is $\frac{1}{4}, \frac{1}{3}, \frac{1}{2}$, and 1 unit of pizza, respectively, for each of the four shifts.

Note two points about opportunity costs:
1   The analysis is in *real* or physical terms. We will shift to monetary comparisons in a moment.
2   Our explanation also is in terms of *marginal* (meaning "added" or "extra") cost, rather than cumulative or *total* opportunity cost. For example, the marginal opportunity cost of the third unit of pizza in Table 2-1 is 3 units of robots ($= 7 - 4$). But the total opportunity cost of 3 units of pizza is 6 units of robots ($= 10 - 4$ or $1 + 2 + 3$).

Concavity   Graphically, the **law of increasing opportunity costs** is reflected in the shape of the production possibilities curve. The curve is *concave* or bowed out from the origin. As verified in Figure 2-1, when the economy moves from *A* toward *E,* it must give up successively larger amounts of robots (1, 2, 3, 4) as shown on the vertical axis to acquire equal increments of pizza (1, 1, 1, 1) as shown on the horizontal axis. The slope of the production possibilities curve becomes steeper as we move from *A* to *E* and such a curve, by definition, is concave as viewed from the origin.

Rationale   What is the economic rationale for the law of increasing opportunity costs? *Why* does the sacrifice of robots increase as we get more pizza? The answer is that *economic resources are not completely adaptable to alternative uses.* As we step up pizza production, resources which are less and less adaptable to making pizza must be induced, or "pushed," into pizza production. If we start at *A* and move to *B,* we can first pick resources whose productivity of pizza is greatest in relation to their productivity of robots. But as we move from *B* to *C, C* to *D,* and so on, resources highly productive of pizza become increasingly scarce. To get more pizza, resources whose productivity in robots is great in relation to their productivity in pizza will be needed. It will take more and more of such resources—and hence a greater sacrifice of robots—to achieve each increase of 1 unit in the production of pizza. This lack of perfect flexibility, or interchangeability, on the part of resources and the resulting increase in the sacrifice of one good that must be made in acquiring more and more units of another good is the rationale for the law of increasing opportunity costs. In this case, these costs are stated as sacrifices of goods and not in terms of dollars and cents. *(Key Question 6)*

Allocative Efficiency Revisited

Our analysis has purposely stressed full employment and productive efficiency, the realization of which allows society to achieve *any point* on its production possibilities curve. We now focus again on allocative efficiency, the question of determining the most-valued or *optimal point* on the production possibilities curve. Of all the attainable combinations of pizza and robots on Figure 2-1's curve, which is optimal or "best"? That is, what quantities of resources should be allocated to pizza and what quantities to robots?

Our discussion of the "economic perspective" in Chapter 1 puts us on the right track. Recall that economic decisions center on comparisons of marginal benefits and marginal costs. Any economic activity— for example, production or consumption—should be expanded so long as marginal benefits exceed marginal costs and should be reduced if marginal costs are greater than marginal benefits.

Consider pizza. We already know from the law of increasing opportunity costs that the marginal cost

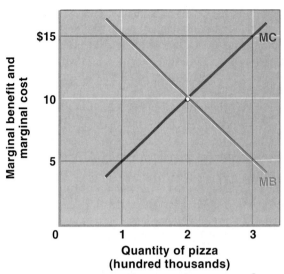

FIGURE 2-2   Allocative efficiency: MB = MC
Resources are efficiently allocated to any product when its output is such that marginal benefits equal marginal costs.

(MC) of additional units of pizza will rise as more units are produced. This is shown by the upsloping MC curve in Figure 2-2. We are also aware that we obtain extra or marginal benefits (MB) from additional units of pizza. However, although material wants *in the aggregate* are insatiable, the consumption of each *particular* product yields less and less extra satisfaction or, in other words, less MB. A consumer can become relatively saturated with a specific product. A second pizza provides less additional utility or benefit to you than the first. And a third will provide even less MB than the second. So it is for society as a whole. Hence, we can portray the marginal benefits from pizza by the downsloping MB line in Figure 2-2.

The optimal amount of pizza to produce is 200,000 units as indicated by the intersection of the MB and MC curves. Why is this optimal? If only 100,000 pizzas were produced, the MB of pizzas would be greater than their MC. In money terms the MB of a pizza here might be $15 while its MC is only $5. This suggests that society is *underallocating* resources to pizza production.

Why? Because society values an additional pizza as being worth $15, while the alternative products or services the required resources could have produced are only worth $5 as indicated by MC. Society will benefit—it will be better off in the sense of having a larger total output to enjoy—whenever it can gain something worth $15 by giving up or forgoing something (alternative goods and services) worth only $5. A reallocating of resources from other products to pizza means society is using its resources more efficiently. Each additional pizza up to 200,000 provides such gains, indicating that allocative efficiency is improved by this production. But when MB = MC the value of producing pizza or alternative products with available resources is the same. Allocative efficiency is achieved where MB = MC.

The production of 300,000 pizzas would represent an *overallocation* of resources to their production. Here the MC of pizza is $15 and MB is only $5. This means a unit of pizza is worth only $5 to society while the alternative products the resources required for its production could have otherwise produced are valued at $15. By producing one less unit society loses a pizza worth $5, but by reallocating the freed resources it gains other products worth $15. When society can gain something worth $15 by forgoing something (a pizza) worth only $5, it has realized a net gain. The net gain in this instance is $10 worth of total output. In Figure 2-2 net gains can be realized so long as pizza production is reduced from 300,000 back to 200,000. A more valued output from the same aggregate amount of inputs means greater allocative efficiency.

Generalization: Resources are being efficiently allocated to any product when its output is such that its marginal benefit equals its marginal cost (MB = MC). Suppose that by applying the same analysis to robots we find that 7000 is their optimal or MB = MC output. This would mean that alternative C on our production possibilities curve—200,000 pizzas and 7000 robots—would result in allocative efficiency for our hypothetical economy. *(Key Question 9)*

QUICK REVIEW 2-2

■ The production possibilities curve illustrates four concepts: *a* the *scarcity* of resources is implicit in that all combinations of output lying outside the production possibilities curve are unattainable; *b* *choice* is reflected in the need for society to select among the various attainable combinations of goods lying on the curve; *c* the downward slope of the curve implies the notion of *opportunity cost;* *d* the concavity of the curve reveals *increasing opportunity costs.*

■ Full employment and productive efficiency must be realized for the economy to operate on its production possibilities curve.

■ A comparison of marginal benefits and marginal costs is needed to determine allocative efficiency— the best or optimal output-mix on the curve.

UNEMPLOYMENT, GROWTH, AND THE FUTURE

Let's now release the first three assumptions underlying the production possibilities curve to see what happens.

Unemployment and Productive Inefficiency

The first assumption was that our economy is characterized by full employment and productive efficiency. How would our analysis and conclusions be altered if idle resources were available (unemployment) or if least-cost production was not realized? With full employment and productive efficiency, our five alternatives in Table 2-1 represent a series of maximum outputs; they illustrate combinations of robots and pizzas which might be produced when the economy is operating at full capacity. With unemployment or inefficient production, the economy would produce less than each alternative shown in the table.

Graphically, a situation of unemployment or productive inefficiency can be illustrated by a point *inside* the original production possibilities curve, reproduced in Figure 2-3. Point *U* is such a point. Here the economy is falling short of the various maximum combinations of pizza and robots reflected by all the points

FIGURE 2-3   Unemployment and the production possibilities curve
Any point inside the production possibilities curve, such as *U,* indicates unemployment or a failure to achieve productive efficiency. By realizing full employment and productive efficiency, the economy can produce more of either or both of the two products, as the arrows indicate.

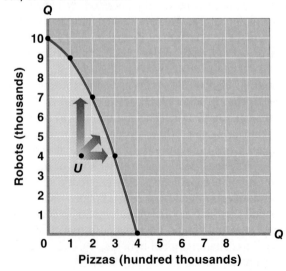

on the production possibilities curve. The arrows in Figure 2-3 indicate three of the possible paths back to full employment and least-cost production. A move toward full employment and productive efficiency will entail a greater output of one or both products.

A Growing Economy

When we drop the remaining assumptions that the quantity and quality of resources and technology are fixed, the production possibilities curve will shift position; that is, the potential total output of the economy will change.

Expanding Resource Supplies Let's abandon the assumption that total supplies of land, labor, capital, and entrepreneurial ability are fixed in both quantity and quality. Common sense tells us that over time a nation's growing population will bring about increases in supplies of labor and enterpreneurial ability.[2] Also, labor quality usually improves over time. Historically, our stock of capital has increased at a significant, though unsteady, rate. And although we are depleting some of our energy and mineral resources, new sources are being discovered. The drainage of swamps and the development of irrigation programs add to our supply of arable land.

The net result of these increased supplies of the factors of production will be the ability to produce more of both robots and pizza. Thus, in the year 2016, the production possibilities of Table 2-1 for 1996 may be obsolete, having given way to those shown in Table 2-2. The greater abundance of resources results in a greater potential output of one or both products at each alternative. Economic growth, in the sense of an expanded potential output, has occurred.

But such a favorable shift in the production possibilities curve does not guarantee the economy will actually operate at a point on that new curve. The economy might fail to realize fully its new potentialities. Some 125 million jobs will give us full employment now, but ten or twenty years from now our labor force, because of a growing population, will be larger, and 125 million jobs will not be sufficient for full employment. The production possibilities curve

[2]This does not mean that population growth as such is always desirable. Overpopulation can be a constant drag on the living standards of many less developed countries. In advanced countries overpopulation can have adverse effects on the environment and the quality of life.

TABLE 2-2 Production possibilities of pizza and robots with full employment and productive efficiency, 2016

Type of product	Production alternatives				
	A'	B'	C'	D'	E'
Pizza (in hundred thousands)	0	2	4	6	8
Robots (in thousands)	14	12	9	5	0

may shift, but the economy may fail to produce at a point on that new curve.

Technological Advance Our other assumption is a constant or unchanging technology. We know that technology has progressed remarkably over a long period. An advancing technology involves new and better goods *and* improved ways of producing them. For now, let's think of technological advance as comprising merely improvements in capital facilities— more efficient machinery and equipment. Such technological advance alters our earlier discussion of the economizing problem by improving productive efficiency, allowing society to produce more goods with fixed resources. As with increases in resource supplies, technological advance permits the production or more robots *and* more pizza.

When the supplies of resources increase or an improvement in technology occurs, the production possibilities curve of Figure 2-3 shifts outward and to the right, as illustrated by the A'B'C'D'E' curve in Figure 2-4. **Economic growth**—*the ability to produce a larger total output*—*is reflected in a rightward shift of the production possibilities curve; it is the result of increases in resource supplies, improvements in resource quality, and technological progress.* The consequence of growth is that our full-employment economy can enjoy a greater output of *both* robots and pizza. While a static, no-growth economy must sacrifice some of X to get more Y, a dynamic, growing economy can have larger quantities of both X and Y.

Economic growth does *not* typically mean proportionate increases in a nation's capacity to produce various products. Note in Figure 2-4 that, while the economy can produce twice as much pizza, the increase in robot production is only 40 percent. You should pencil in two new production possibilities curves: one to show the situation where a better technique for producing robots has been developed, the

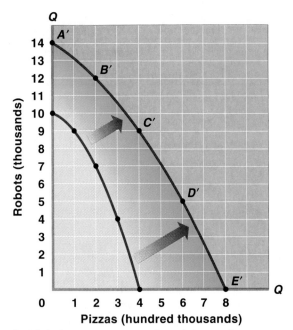

FIGURE 2-4 Economic growth and the production possibilities curve

The expanding resource supplies, improved resource quality, and technological advances which characterize a growing economy move the production possibilities curve outward and to the right. This permits the economy to enjoy larger quantities of both types of goods.

technology for producing pizza being unchanged, and the other to illustrate an improved technology for pizza, the technology for producing robots being constant.

Present Choices and Future Possibilities *An economy's current choice of position on its production possibilities curve is a basic determinant of the future location of that curve.* Let's designate the two axes of the production possibilities curve as "goods for the future" and "goods for the present," as in Figures 2-5a and b. "Goods for the future" are such things as capital goods, research and education, and preventive medicine, which increase the quantity and quality of property resources, enlarge the stock of technological information, and improve the quality of human resources. As we have already seen, "goods for the future" are the ingredients of economic growth. "Goods for the present" are pure consumer goods such as foods, clothing, "boom boxes," and automobiles.

Now suppose there are two economies, Alphania and Betania, which are initially identical in every respect except that Alphania's current (1996) choice of position on its production possibilities curve strongly favors "present goods" as opposed to "future goods." The dot in Figure 2-5a indicates this choice. Betania,

FIGURE 2-5 An economy's present choice of position on its production possibilities curve helps determine the curve's future location

A current choice favoring "present goods," as made by Alphania in (a), will cause a modest rightward shift of the curve. A current choice favoring "future goods," as made by Betania in (b), will result in a greater rightward (outward) shift of the curve.

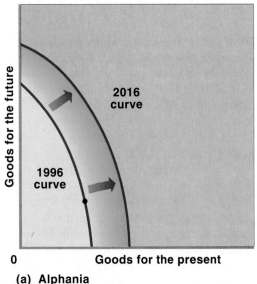

(a) Alphania

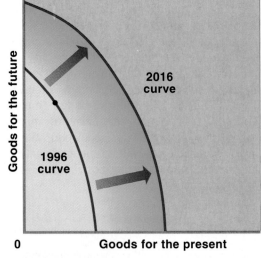

(b) Betania

on the other hand, makes a current (1996) choice which stresses large amounts of "future goods" and lesser amounts of "present goods" as shown by the dot in Figure 2-5b.

Now, all other things the same, we can expect the future (2016) production possibilities curve of Betania to be farther to the right than Alphania's curve. By currently choosing an output more conducive to technological advance and to increases in the quantity and quality of property and human resources, Betania will tend to achieve greater economic growth than Alphania, whose current choice of output places less emphasis on those goods and services which cause the production possibilities curve to shift rightward. In terms of capital goods, Betania is choosing to make larger current additions to its "national factory"—to invest more of its current output—than Alphania. The payoff from this choice is more rapid growth—greater future productive capacity—for Betania. The opportunity cost is fewer consumer goods in the present. *(Key Questions 10 and 11)*

QUICK REVIEW 2-3

■ Unemployment and the failure to realize productive efficiency cause the economy to operate at a point inside its production possibilities curve.

■ Expanding resource supplies, improvements in resource quality, and technological progress cause economic growth, depicted as an outward shift of the production possibilities curve.

■ An economy's present choice of output—particularly of capital and consumer goods—helps determine the future location of its production possibilities curve.

Applications

There are many possible applications of the production possibilities curve.

1   Microeconomic Budgeting   While our discussion is in macroeconomic terms—in terms of the output of the entire economy—the concepts of scarcity, choice, and opportunity cost also apply at the microeconomic level. You should reread the first paragraph of this chapter.

2   Going to War   In beginning to produce war goods for World War II (1939–1945), the United States

GLOBAL PERSPECTIVE 2-1

Investment and economic growth, selected countries

Nations which invest large proportions of their national outputs enjoy high growth rates, measured here by output per person. Additional capital goods make workers more productive and this means greater output per person.

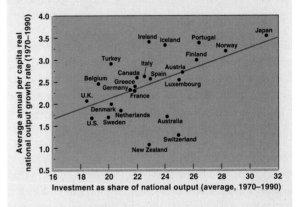

Source: International Monetary Fund data, as reported in *Economic Report of the President, 1994*, p. 37.

found itself with considerable unemployment. Our economy was able to produce an almost unbelievably large quantity of war goods and at the same time increase the output of consumer goods (Figure 2-3). The Soviet Union, on the other hand, entered World War II at almost capacity production; it was operating close to full employment. Its military preparations required considerable shifting of resources from production of civilian goods with a drop in the standard of living.

The United States' position during the Vietnam War was similar to that of the Soviet Union during World War II. Our economy was at full employment in the mid-1960s and the government accelerated military spending for Vietnam while simultaneously increasing expenditures on domestic "war on poverty" programs. This attempt to achieve simultaneously more pizza and more robots—or, more guns and more butter—in a full-employment economy was doomed to failure. The attempt to spend beyond our capacity to produce—to realize a point like *W* in Figure 2-1—contributed to the double-digit inflation of the 1970s.

3 Discrimination Discrimination based on race, gender, age, or ethnic background impedes the efficient employment of human resources, keeping the economy operating at some point inside its production possibilities curve. Discrimination prevents blacks, women, and others from obtaining jobs in which society can use efficiently their skills and talents. Elimination of discrimination would help move the economy from some point inside the production possibilities curve toward a point on the curve.

4 Lumber versus Owls The tradeoffs portrayed in the production possibilities curve occur regularly in environmental issues. An example is the much-publicized conflict between the logging industry of the Pacific Northwest and environmentalists. Envision a production possibilities curve with "lumber production" on one axis and "environmental quality" or "biodiversity" on the other. It so happens that the spotted owl depends on the mature or old-growth trees of that region for survival. Increasing the output of lumber limits the owl's habitat, destroys the species, and thus reduces environmental quality. Maintaining the old-growth forests preserves the owl, but destroys thousands of jobs in the logging and lumber industries. The production possibilities curve is an informative context within which to grasp the many difficult environmental decisions confronting society.

5 Productivity Slowdown Since the mid-1960s the United States has experienced an alarming decline in the rate of growth of labor productivity, defined as output per worker-hour. One cause of this decline is that the rate of increase in the mechanization of labor has slowed because of reduced investment relative to total output. One remedy is to increase investment as compared to consumption—a D to C type of shift in Figure 2-1. Special tax incentives to make business investment more profitable might be an appropriate policy to facilitate this shift. The expectation is that the restoration of a more rapid rate of productivity growth will accelerate the growth of the economy (the rightward shifting of the production possibilities curve) through time.

6 Growth: Japan versus United States The growth impact of a nation's decision on how much of its domestic output will be devoted to investment and how much to consumption is illustrated vividly in comparing Japan and the United States. Japan has been investing over 25 percent of its domestic output in productive machinery and equipment compared to only about 10 percent for the United States. The consequences are in accord with our earlier discussion. Over the 1960–1990 period Japan's domestic output expanded at about 6.4 percent per year compared to only 3.2 percent for the United States. Japan's production possibilities curve shifted outward more rapidly than the United States' curve. This is reflected in living standards. In 1980 the per capita output of Japan was $16,711 as compared to $17,643 for the United States. By 1992 these figures had changed to $28,190 and $23,240, respectively.

7 International Trade Aspects The message of the production possibilities curve is that a nation cannot live beyond its means or production potential. When the possibility of international trade is taken into account, this statement must be modified in two ways.

Trade and Growth We will discover in later chapters that a nation can circumvent the output constraint imposed by its domestic production possibilities curve through international specialization and trade. International specialization and trade have the same impact as having more and better resources or discovering improved production techniques. Both increase the quantities of capital and consumer goods available to society. The output gains from international specialization and trade are the equivalent of economic growth.

Trade Deficits Within the context of international trade, a nation can achieve a combination of goods outside its domestic production possibilities curve (such as point W in Figure 2-1) by incurring a *trade deficit*. A nation may buy and receive an amount of imported goods from other nations which exceeds the amount of goods it exports. The United States has been doing just that recently. In 1993 the United States had a trade deficit of approximately $133 billion. We imported $133 billion more worth of goods than we exported. The net result was that in 1993 we enjoyed some $133 billion of output over what we produced domestically.

This looks like a favorable state of affairs. Unfortunately, there is a catch. To finance its deficit—to pay for its excess of imports over exports—the United

States must go into debt to its international trading partners *or* it must give up ownership of some of its assets to those other nations. Analogy: How can you live beyond your current income? Answer: Borrow from your parents, the sellers of goods, or a financial institution. Or sell some of the real assets (your car or stereo) or financial assets (stocks or bonds) you own. This is what the United States has been doing.

A major consequence of our large and persistent trade deficits is that foreign nationals hold larger portions of American private and public debt and own larger amounts of our business corporations, agricultural land, and real estate. To pay our debts and repurchase those assets we must in the future live well *within* our means. We must settle for some combination of goods within our production possibilities curve so that we can export more than we import—incur a *trade surplus*—to pay off our world debts and reacquire ownership of those assets. On the other hand, to the extent that some of our imports are capital goods, our future production possibilities curve will be farther rightward than it might otherwise be.

8   Famine in Africa   Modern industrial societies take economic growth—more-or-less continuous rightward shifts of the production possibilities curve—for granted. But, as the recent catastrophic famines in Somalia and other sub-Saharan nations of Africa indicate, in some circumstances the production possibilities curve may shift leftward. In addition to drought, a cause of African famines is ecological degradation—poor land-use practices. Land has been deforested, overfarmed, and overgrazed, causing the production possibilities of these highly agriculturally oriented countries to diminish. In fact the per capita national outputs of most of these nations declined in the last decade or so.

9   Castro's Cuba   This chapter's Last Word chronicles how the inefficiencies inherent in central planning, along with an American trade embargo and the loss of foreign aid, have diminished Cuba's production possibilities.

THE "ISMS"

A society can use many different institutional arrangements and coordinating mechanisms to respond to the economizing problem. Historically, the industrially advanced economies of the world have differed essentially in two ways: (1) the ownership of the means of production, and (2) the method of coordinating and directing economic activity. Let's examine the main characteristics of two "polar" types of economic systems.

Pure Capitalism

Pure, or **laissez faire, capitalism** is characterized by the private ownership of resources and the use of a system of markets and prices to coordinate and direct economic activity. In such a system each participant is motivated by his or her own self-interests; each economic unit seeks to maximize its income through individual decision making. The market system communicates and coordinates individual decisions and preferences. Because goods and services are produced and resources are supplied under competitive conditions, there are many independently acting buyers and sellers of each product and resource. As a result, economic power is widely dispersed. Advocates of pure capitalism argue that such an economy is conducive to efficiency in the use of resources, output and employment stability, and rapid economic growth. Hence, there is little or no need for government planning, control, or intervention. The term *laissez faire* means "let it be," that is, keep government from interfering with the economy, because such interference will disturb the efficient working of the market system. Government's role is therefore limited to protecting private property and establishing an appropriate legal framework for free markets.

The Command Economy

The polar alternative to pure capitalism has been the **command economy** or **communism,** characterized by public ownership of virtually all property resources and the rendering of economic decisions through central economic planning. All major decisions concerning the level of resource use, the composition and distribution of output, and the organization of production are determined by a central planning board. Business firms are governmentally owned and produce according to state directives. Production targets are determined by the planning board for each enterprise and the plan specifies the amounts of resources to be allocated to each enterprise so that it might realize its production goals. The division of output between capital and consumer goods is centrally decided and capital goods are allocated among industries in terms of the central planning board's long-term priorities.

Mixed Systems

Real-world economies fall between the extremes of pure capitalism and the command economy. The United States economy leans toward pure capitalism, but with important differences. Government plays an active role in our economy in promoting economic stability and growth, in providing certain goods and services which would be underproduced or not produced at all by the market system, and in modifying the distribution of income. In contrast to the wide dispersion of economic power among many small units which characterizes pure capitalism, American capitalism has spawned powerful economic organizations in the form of large corporations and labor unions. The ability of these power blocs to manipulate and distort the functioning of the market system to their advantage is a further reason for governmental involvement in the economy.

While the former Soviet Union historically approximated the command economy, it relied to some extent on market-determined prices and had some vestiges of private ownership. Recent reforms in the former Soviet Union, China, and most of the eastern European nations are designed to move these command economies toward more capitalistic, market-oriented systems. North Korea and Cuba are the best remaining examples of centrally planned economies.

But private ownership and reliance on the market system do not always go together, nor do public ownership and central planning. For example, the *fascism* of Hitler's Nazi Germany has been dubbed **authoritarian capitalism** because the economy had a high degree of governmental control and direction, but property was privately owned. In contrast, the former Yugoslavian economy of the 1980s was **market socialism,** characterized by public ownership of resources coupled with considerable reliance on free markets to organize and coordinate economic activity. The Swedish economy is also a hybrid system. Although over 90 percent of business activity is in private hands, government is deeply involved in achieving economic stability and in redistributing income. Similarly, the capitalistic Japanese economy entails a great deal of planning and "coordination" between government and the business sector.

The Traditional Economy

Many less developed countries have **traditional** or **customary economies.** Production methods, ex-

change, and distribution of income are all sanctioned by custom. Heredity and caste circumscribe economic roles of individuals and socioeconomic immobility is pronounced. Technological change and innovation may be closely constrained because they clash with tradition and threaten the social fabric. Economic activity is often secondary to religious and cultural values and society's desire to perpetuate the status quo.

The point is that there is no unique or universally accepted way to respond to the economizing problem. Various societies, having different cultural and historical backgrounds, different mores and customs, and contrasting ideological frameworks—not to mention resources which differ both quantitatively and qualitatively—use different institutions in dealing with the reality of relative scarcity. China, the United States, and Great Britain, for example, are all—in terms of their accepted goals, ideology, technologies, resources, and culture—attempting to achieve efficiency in the use of their respective resources. The best method for responding to the unlimited wants–scarce resources dilemma in one economy may be inappropriate for another economic system.

THE CIRCULAR FLOW MODEL

Market-oriented systems now dominate the world scene. Thus, our focus in the remainder of this chapter and in the following two chapters is on how nations use markets to respond to the economizing problem. Our goal in this last section is modest; we want to identify the major groups of decision makers and the major markets in the market system. Our point of reference is the circular flow diagram.

Resource and Product Markets

Figure 2-6 (Key Graph) shows two groups of *decision makers*—households and businesses. (Government will be added as a third decision maker in Chapter 5.) The *coordinating mechanism* which brings the decisions of households and businesses into alignment with one another is the market system, in particular resource and product markets.

The upper half of the diagram portrays the **resource market.** Here, households, which directly or indirectly (through their ownership of business corporations) own all economic resources, *supply* these

KEY GRAPH

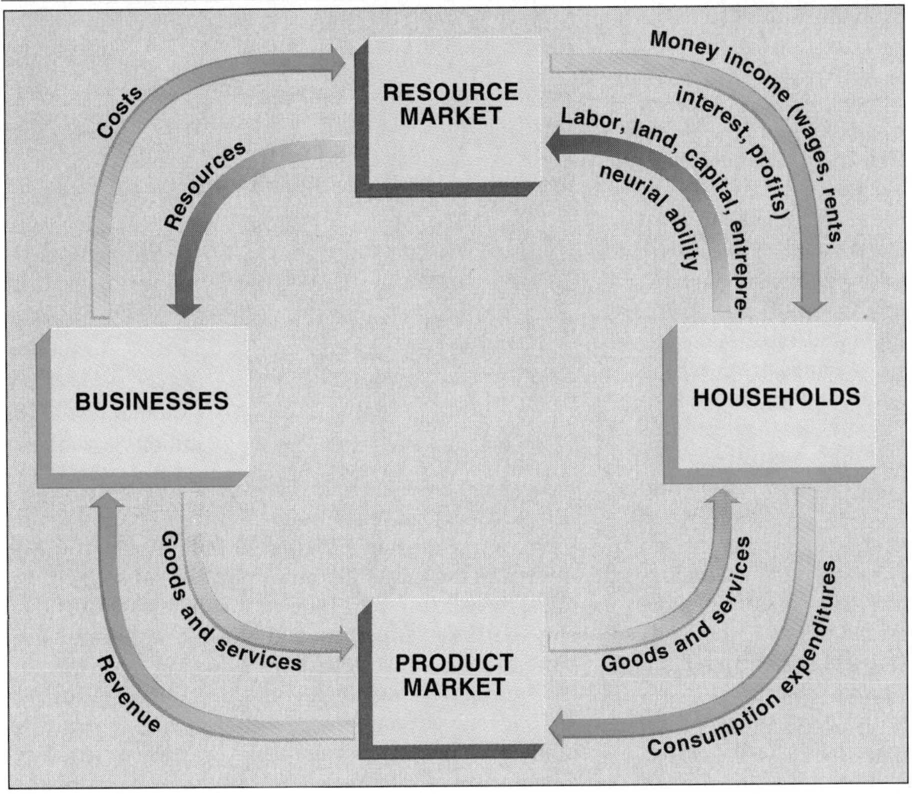

FIGURE 2-6 The circular flow of output and income
The prices paid for the use of land, labor, capital, and entrepreneurial ability are determined in the resource market shown in the upper loop. Businesses are on the demand side and households on the supply side of this market. The prices of finished goods and services are determined in the product market located in the lower loop. Households are on the demand side and businesses on the supply side of this market.

resources to businesses.[3] Businesses will *demand* resources because they are the means by which firms produce goods and services. The interaction of demand and supply for the immense variety of human and property resources establishes the price of each. The payments which businesses make in obtaining resources are costs to businesses, but simultaneously constitute flows of wage, rent, interest, and profit income to the households supplying these resources.

Now consider the **product market** shown in the bottom half of the diagram. The money income received by households from the sale of resources does not, as such, have real value. Consumers cannot eat or wear coins and paper money. Thus, through the expenditure of money income, households express

their *demand* for a vast array of goods and services. Simultaneously, businesses combine the resources they have obtained to produce and *supply* goods and services in these same markets. The interaction of these demand and supply decisions determines product prices (Chapter 3). Note, too, that the flow of consumer expenditures for goods and services constitutes sales revenues or receipts from the viewpoint of businesses.

The **circular flow model** implies a complex, interrelated web of decision making and economic activity. Note that households and businesses participate in both basic markets, but on different sides of each. Businesses are on the buying or demand side of resource markets, and households, as resource owners and suppliers, are on the selling or supply side. In the product market, these positions are reversed; households, as consumers, are on the buying or demand side, and businesses are on the selling or supply side. Each group of economic units both buys and sells.

[3]For present purposes think of businesses simply as organizational charts, that is, institutions on paper apart from the capital, raw materials, labor, and entrepreneurial ability which breathe life into them and make them "going concerns."

LAST WORD

THE DIMINISHING PRODUCTION POSSIBILITIES OF CASTRO'S CUBA

Inefficiencies associated with its command economy, a thirty-year United States trade embargo, and the recent loss of Soviet aid are causing the Cuban economy to collapse.

The fortieth anniversary of Cuba's communist revolution in 1993 was overshadowed by a collapsing economy. Shortages of essential goods began to appear on the island by mid-1989 and have since become widespread and severe. Long lines are common as consumers attempt to buy rationed goods such as eggs, fish, meat, and soap. Some 50,000 Cubans have been diagnosed as having optic neuritis, a disease causing gradual blindness from malnutrition and vitamin deficiencies. Energy shortages have closed factories and disrupted construction projects. Shortages of gasoline and spare parts have idled automobiles, buses, and farm tractors. Ox carts are being substituted for tractors in agriculture and hundreds of thousands of bicycles are being imported from China as substitutes for autos and buses.

There are three reasons behind the collapse of Fidel Castro's Cuban economy. First, the Cuban economy has suffered increasingly from the kinds of central planning problems which brought about the fall of the command economies of eastern Europe and the former Soviet Union. Central planning has simply failed to (a) accurately assess consumer wants, (b) provide the market signals needed to minimize production costs, and (c) furnish adequate economic incentives for workers and business managers.

The second factor in Cuba's economic decline is an American trade embargo. Although Cuba is only 90 miles from the vast American market, that market has been denied to Cuba for some thirty years, causing a substantial decline in and distortion of Cuba's world trade.

Third, Soviet patronage has ended. For decades the Soviet Union heavily subsidized its communist partner in the Western Hemisphere. The Soviets bought Cuban exports (primarily sugar) at inflated prices and sold oil and other goods to Cuba at low prices. Best estimates suggest Soviet economic and military aid averaged about $5 billion per year. The decline of the Soviet economy and the subsequent political breakup of the Soviet Union has brought an end to these subsidies and dealt a very damaging blow to the Cuban economy.

Estimates of the decline in Cuba's production possibilities vary. Some suggest that in recent years the domestic output has fallen by one-half; others indicate a three-quarters decline. In either case this decline in output is not simply a temporary move to a point inside Cuba's production possibilities curve, but rather a significant inward shift of the curve itself.

Castro has attempted to rejuvenate the Cuban economy in several ways. First, an attempt is being made to revitalize the tourist industry through joint ventures—for example, hotel and resort construction —with foreign firms. Second, Cuba has invited foreign companies to explore the island for oil. Third, Cuba is making a concerted effort to cultivate trade relations with new trading partners such as China and Japan. Whether such efforts will be successful is doubtful and most experts predict the economic crisis in Cuba to spark either widespread reforms toward a market economy or the overthrow of the Castro regime.

Furthermore, the specter of scarcity haunts these transactions. Because households have only limited amounts of resources to supply to businesses, the money incomes of consumers will be limited. This means that each consumer's income will go only so far. A limited number of dollars clearly will not permit the purchase of all the goods and services the consumer might like to buy. Similarly, because resources are scarce, the output of finished goods and services is also necessarily limited. Scarcity and choice permeate our entire discussion.

To summarize: In a monetary economy, households, as resource owners, sell their resources to businesses and, as consumers, spend the money income received buying goods and services. Businesses must buy resources to produce goods and services; their finished products are then sold to households in exchange for consumption expenditures or, as businesses view it, revenues. The net result is a counterclockwise *real* flow of economic resources and finished goods and services, and a clockwise *money* flow of income and consumption expenditures. These flows are simultaneous and repetitive.

Limitations

Our model simplifies in many ways. Intrahousehold and intrabusiness transactions are concealed. Government and the "rest of the world" are ignored as decision makers. The model subtly implies constant flows of output and income, while in fact these flows are unstable over time. Nor is the circular flow a perpetual motion machine; production exhausts human energies and absorbs physical resources, the latter giving rise to problems of environmental pollution. Finally, our model does not explain how product and resource prices are actually determined, which is examined in Chapter 3.

CHAPTER SUMMARY

1   Economics centers on two basic facts: first, human material wants are virtually unlimited; second, economic resources are scarce.

2   Economic resources may be classified as property resources—raw materials and capital—or as human resources—labor and entrepreneurial ability.

3   Economics is concerned with the problem of administering scarce resources in the production of goods and services to fulfill the material wants of society. Both full employment and full production of available resources are essential if this administration is to be efficient.

4   Full production consists of productive efficiency—producing any output in the least costly way—and allocative efficiency—producing the specific output-mix most desired by society.

5   An economy which is achieving full employment and productive efficiency—that is, operating *on* its production possibilities curve—must sacrifice the output of some types of goods and services to achieve increased production of others. Because resources are not equally productive in all possible uses, shifting resources from one use to another yields the law of increasing opportunity costs; that is, the production of additional units of product X entails the sacrifice of increasing amounts of product Y.

6   Allocative efficiency means achieving the optimal or most desired point on the production possibilities curve. It is determined by comparing marginal benefits and marginal costs.

7   Over time, technological advance and increases in the quantity and quality of human and property resources permit the economy to produce more of all goods and services. Society's choice as to the composition of current output is a determinant of the future location of the production possibilities curve.

8   The various economic systems of the world differ in their ideologies and also in their responses to the economizing problem. Critical differences have centered on **a** private versus public ownership of resources, and **b** the use of the market system versus central planning as a coordinating mechanism.

9   An overview of the operation of the capitalistic system can be gained through the circular flow of income. This simplified model locates the product and resource markets and presents the major income-expenditure flows and resources-output flows which constitute the lifeblood of the capitalistic economy.

TERMS AND CONCEPTS

economizing problem	full production	law of increasing	authoritarian
utility	allocative efficiency	opportunity costs	capitalism
economic resources	productive efficiency	economic growth	traditional or
land, capital, labor,	consumer goods	pure or laissez faire	customary
and entrepreneurial	capital goods	capitalism	economies
ability	production possibilities	command economy or	resource market
investment	table (curve)	communism	product market
full employment	opportunity cost	market socialism	circular flow model

QUESTIONS AND STUDY SUGGESTIONS

1 "Economics is the study of the principles governing the allocation of scarce means among competing ends when the objective of the allocation is to maximize the attainment of the ends."[4] Explain.

2 Comment on the following statement from a newspaper article: "Our junior high school serves a splendid hot meal for $1 without costing the taxpayers anything, thanks in part to a government subsidy."

3 Critically analyze: "Wants aren't insatiable. I can prove it. I get all the coffee I want to drink every morning at breakfast." Explain: "Goods and services are scarce because resources are scarce." Analyze: "It is the nature of all economic problems that absolute solutions are denied us."

4 What are economic resources? What are the major functions of the entrepreneur?

5 *Key Question* *Why is the problem of unemployment a part of the subject matter of economics? Distinguish between allocative efficiency and productive efficiency. Give an illustration of achieving productive, but not allocative, efficiency.*

6 *Key Question* *The following is a production possibilities table for war goods and civilian goods:*

Type of production	Production alternatives				
	A	B	C	D	E
Automobiles	0	2	4	6	8
Rockets	30	27	21	12	0

a Show these data graphically. Upon what specific assumptions is this production possibilities curve based?

b If the economy is at point C, what is the cost of one more automobile? One more rocket? Explain how this curve reflects the law of increasing opportunity costs.

c What must the economy do to operate at some point on the production possibilities curve?

7 What is the opportunity cost of attending college?

8 Suppose you arrive at a store expecting to pay $100 for an item, but learn that a store two miles away is charging $50 for it. Would you drive there and buy it? How does your decision benefit you? What is the opportunity cost of your decision? Now suppose that you arrive at a store expecting to pay $6000 for an item, but learn that it costs $5950 at the other store. Do you make the same decision as before? Perhaps surprisingly, you should! Explain why.

9 *Key Question* *Specify and explain the shapes of the marginal-benefit and marginal-cost curves and use these curves to determine the optimal allocation of resources to a particular product. If current output is such that marginal cost exceeds marginal benefit, should more or less resources be allocated to this product? Explain.*

10 *Key Question* *Label point G inside the production possibilities curve you have drawn in question 6. What does it indicate? Label point H outside the curve. What does this point indicate? What must occur before the economy can attain the level of production indicated by point H?*

11 *Key Question* *Referring again to question 6, suppose improvement occurs in the technology of producing rockets but not in the production of automobiles. Draw the new production possibilities curve. Now assume that a technological advance occurs in producing automobiles but not in producing rockets. Draw the new production possibilities curve. Finally, draw a production possibilities curve which reflects technological improvement in the production of both products.*

12 Explain how, if at all, each of the following affects the location of the production possibilities curve.

a Standardized examination scores of high school and college students decline

b The unemployment rate falls from 9 to 6 percent of the labor force

c Defense spending is reduced to allow government to spend more on health care

d Society decides it wants compact discs rather than long-playing records

e A new technique improves the efficiency of extracting copper from ore

f A new "baby boom" increases the size of the nation's work force

13 Explain: "Affluence tomorrow requires sacrifice today."

14 Explain how an international trade deficit may permit an economy to acquire a combination of goods in excess of its domestic production potential. Explain why nations try to avoid trade deficits.

15 Contrast how pure capitalism, market socialism, and a command economy try to cope with economic scarcity.

16 Describe the operation of pure capitalism as portrayed by the circular flow model. Locate resource and product markets and emphasize the fact of scarcity throughout your discussion. Specify the limitations of the circular flow model.

17 (Last Word) What are the major causes of Cuba's diminishing production possibilities?

---

[4]George J. Stigler, *The Theory of Price* (New York: The Macmillan Company, 1947), p. 12.

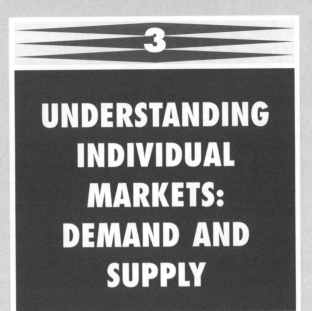

3

UNDERSTANDING INDIVIDUAL MARKETS: DEMAND AND SUPPLY

Teach a parrot to say, "Demand and supply," and you have an economist! There is a strong element of truth in this quip. The tools of demand and supply can take us far in understanding not only specific economic issues, but also how the entire economy works.

In this chapter we examine the nature of markets and how prices and outputs are determined. Our circular flow model in Chapter 2 identified the participants in both product and resource markets. But we assumed there that product and resource prices were "given"; we will now explain how prices are determined by discussing the concept of a market more fully.

MARKETS DEFINED

A **market** is *an institution or mechanism which brings together buyers ("demanders") and sellers ("suppliers") of particular goods and services.* Markets exist in many forms. The corner gas station, the fast-food outlet, the local music store, a farmer's roadside stand—all are familiar markets. The New York Stock Exchange and the Chicago Board of Trade are highly organized markets where buyers and sellers of stocks and bonds and farm commodities, respectively, from all over the world may communicate with one another. Auctioneers bring together potential buyers and sellers of art, livestock, used farm equipment, and sometimes real estate. The all-American quarterback and his agent bargain with the owner of an NFL team. A graduating finance major interviews with Citicorp or Chase Manhattan at the university placement office.

All these situations which link potential buyers with potential sellers constitute markets. As our ex- amples imply, some markets are local while others are national or international in scope. Some are highly personal, involving face-to-face contact between demander and supplier; others are impersonal in that buyer and seller never see or know one another.

This chapter concerns *purely competitive markets.* Such markets presume large numbers of independently acting buyers and sellers exchanging a standardized product. These markets are not the music store or corner gas station where products have price tags, but competitive markets such as a central grain exchange, a stock market, or a market for foreign currencies where the equilibrium price is "discovered" by the interacting decisions of buyers and sellers.

DEMAND

Demand is *a schedule which shows the various amounts of a product consumers are willing and able* to purchase at each price in a series of possible prices during a specified period of time.[1] Demand portrays a series of alternative possibilities which can be set down in tabular form. It shows the quantities of a product which will be demanded at various possible prices, *all other things equal.*

We usually view demand by looking at price; that is, we read demand as showing the amounts consumers will buy at various possible prices. It is equally correct and sometimes more useful to view demand by looking at quantity. Instead of asking what quantities can be sold at various prices, we ask what prices can be gotten from consumers for various quantities of a good. Table 3-1 is a hypothetical **demand schedule** for a single consumer purchasing bushels of corn.

This tabular portrayal of demand reflects the relationship between the price of corn and the quantity the consumer would be willing and able to purchase at each of these prices. We say willing and *able,* because willingness alone is not effective in the market. I may be willing to buy a Porsche, but if this willingness is not backed by the necessary dollars, it will not be effective and, therefore, not reflected in the market. In Table 3-1, if the price of corn were $5 per bushel, our consumer would be willing and able to buy 10 bushels per week; if it were $4, the consumer would be willing and able to buy 20 bushels per week; and so forth.

The demand schedule does not tell us which of the five possible prices will actually exist in the corn market. This depends on demand *and supply.* Demand is simply a tabular statement of a buyer's plans, or intentions, with respect to the purchase of a product.

To be meaningful the quantities demanded at each price must relate to a specific period—a day, a week, a month. To say "a consumer will buy 10 bushels of corn at $5 per bushel" is meaningless. To say "a consumer will buy 10 bushels of corn *per week* at $5 per bushel" is clear and meaningful. Without a specific time period we would not know whether demand for a product was large or small.

Law of Demand

A fundamental characteristic of demand is this: *All else being constant, as price falls, the quantity demanded rises. Or, other things being equal, as price increases, the corresponding quantity demanded falls.* In short,

TABLE 3-1 An individual buyer's demand for corn

Price per bushel	Quantity demanded per week
$5	10
4	20
3	35
2	55
1	80

there is a negative or *inverse* relationship between price and quantity demanded. Economists call this inverse relationship the **law of demand.**

The "other things being constant" assumption is critical here. Many factors other than the price of the product under consideration affect the amount purchased. The quantity of Nikes purchased will depend not only on the price of Nikes, but also on the prices of such substitutes as Reeboks, Adidas, and L.A. Gear. The law of demand in this case says that fewer Nikes will be purchased if the price of Nikes rises *and the prices of Reeboks, Adidas, and L.A. Gear all remain constant.* In short, if the *relative price* of Nikes increases, fewer Nikes will be bought. However, if the price of Nikes and all other competing shoes increase by some amount—say $5—consumers might buy more, less, or the same amount of Nikes.

What is the foundation for the law of demand? There are several levels of analysis on which to argue the case.

1 Common sense and simple observation are consistent with the law of demand. People ordinarily *do* buy more of a product at a low price than they do at a high price. Price is an obstacle which deters consumers from buying. The higher this obstacle, the less of a product they will buy; the lower the price obstacle, the more they will buy. A high price discourages consumers from buying; a low price encourages them to buy. The fact that businesses have "sales" is evidence of their belief in the law of demand. "Bargain days" are based on the law of demand. Businesses reduce their inventories by lowering prices, not by raising them.

2 In any given time period each buyer of a product will derive less satisfaction or benefit or utility from each successive unit consumed. The second "Big Mac" will yield less satisfaction to the consumer than the first; and the third still less added benefit or utility than the second. Because consumption is subject to **diminishing marginal utility**—consuming successive units of a particular product yields less and

---

[1]In adjusting this definition to the resource market, substitute the word "resource" for "product" and "businesses" for "consumers."

less extra satisfaction—consumers will only buy additional units if price is reduced.

3 The law of demand also can be explained in terms of income and substitution effects. The **income effect** indicates that, at a lower price, you can afford more of the good without giving up other goods. A decline in the price of a product will increase the purchasing power of your money income, enabling you to buy more of the product than before. A higher price will have the opposite effect.

The **substitution effect** suggests that, at a lower price, you have the incentive to substitute the cheaper good for similar goods which are now relatively more expensive. Consumers tend to substitute cheap products for dear products.

For example, a decline in the price of beef will increase the purchasing power of consumer incomes, enabling them to buy more beef (the income effect). At a lower price, beef is relatively more attractive and is substituted for pork, mutton, chicken, and fish (the substitution effect). The income and substitution effects combine to make consumers able and willing to buy more of a product at a low price than at a high price.

The Demand Curve

This inverse relationship between product price and quantity demanded can be represented on a simple graph where, by convention, we measure quantity demanded on the horizontal axis and price on the vertical axis. To graph those five price–quantity possibilities in Table 3-1 we draw perpendiculars from the appropriate points on the two axes. In plotting the "$5-price–10-quantity-demanded" possibility, we draw a perpendicular from the horizontal (quantity) axis at 10 to meet a perpendicular drawn from the vertical (price) axis at $5. If this is done for all five possibilities, the result is a series of points as shown in Figure 3-1. Each point represents a specific price and the corresponding quantity the consumer will purchase at that price.

Now, assuming the same inverse relationship between price and quantity demanded at all points between the ones graphed, we can generalize on the inverse relationship between price and quantity demanded by drawing a curve to represent *all* price–quantity-demanded possibilities within the limits shown on the graph. The resulting curve is called a **demand curve,** labeled *DD* in Figure 3-1. It slopes downward and to the right because the relationship it portrays between price and quantity demanded is negative or inverse. The law of demand—people buy more at a low price than at a high price—is reflected in the downward slope of the demand curve.

What is the advantage of graphing our demand schedule? After all, Table 3-1 and Figure 3-1 contain exactly the same data and reflect the same relationship between price and quantity demanded. The advantage of graphing is that we can represent clearly a given relationship—in this case the law of demand—more simply than if we relied on verbal and tabu-

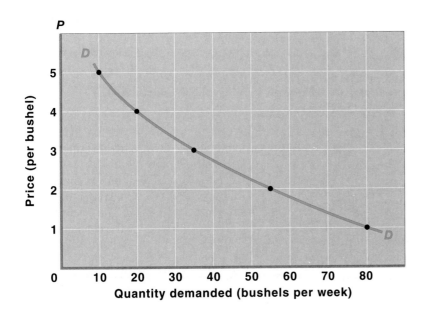

FIGURE 3-1 An individual buyer's demand curve for corn
An individual's demand schedule graphs as a downsloping curve such as *DD*, because price and quantity demanded are inversely related. Specifically, the law of demand generalizes that consumers will buy more of a product as its price declines.

TABLE 3-2   Market demand for corn, three buyers

Price per bushel	Quantity demanded			Total quantity demanded per week
	First buyer	Second buyer	Third buyer	
$5	10 +	12 +	8 =	30
4	20 +	23 +	17 =	60
3	35 +	39 +	26 =	100
2	55 +	60 +	39 =	154
1	80 +	87 +	54 =	221

lar presentation. A single curve on a graph, if understood, is simpler to state *and manipulate* than tables and lengthy verbal descriptions. Graphs are invaluable tools in economic analysis. They permit clear expression and handling of sometimes complex relationships.

Individual and Market Demand

Until now we have assumed just one consumer. Competition assumes many buyers are in the market. We can get from an *individual* to a *market* demand schedule by summing the quantities demanded by each consumer at the various possible prices. If there were just three buyers in the market, as is shown in Table 3-2, it would be easy to determine the total quantities demanded at each price. Figure 3-2 shows the same summing procedure graphically, using only the $3 price to illustrate the adding-up process. Note that we are simply summing the three individual demand curves *horizontally* to derive the total demand curve.

Competition, of course, entails many more than three buyers of a product. So—to avoid a lengthy addition process—suppose there are 200 buyers of corn in the market, each choosing to buy the same amount at each of the various prices as our original consumer. Thus, we can determine total or market demand by multiplying the quantity-demanded data of Table 3-1 by 200, as in Table 3-3. Curve D_1 in Figure 3-3 indicates this market demand curve for the 200 buyers.

Determinants of Demand

An economist constructing a demand curve such as D_1 in Figure 3-3 assumes that price is the most important influence on the amount of any product purchased. But the economist knows that other factors can and do affect purchases. In locating a specific demand curve such as D_1, it must be assumed that "other things are equal"; that is, certain *determinants* of the amount demanded are assumed to be constant. When any of these determinants change, the location of the demand curve will shift to the right or left of D_1. For this reason determinants of demand are referred to as *demand shifters*.

The basic determinants of market demand are: (1) the tastes or preferences of consumers, (2) the number of consumers in the market, (3) the money incomes of consumers, (4) prices of related goods, and (5) consumer expectations about future prices and incomes.

Changes in Demand

A change in one or more of the determinants of de-

FIGURE 3-2   The market demand curve is the sum of the individual demand curves
Graphically the market demand curve (*D* total) is found by summing horizontally the individual demand curves (*D₁, D₂,* and *D₃*) of all consumers in the market.

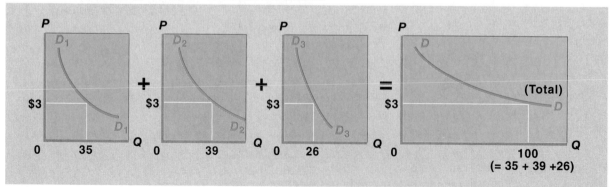

TABLE 3-3 Market demand for corn, 200 buyers

(1) Price per bushel	(2) Quantity demanded per week, single buyer		(3) Number of buyers in the market		(4) Total quantity demanded per week
$5	10	×	200	=	2,000
4	20	×	200	=	4,000
3	35	×	200	=	7,000
2	55	×	200	=	11,000
1	80	×	200	=	16,000

mand will change the demand schedule data in Table 3-3 and therefore the location of the demand curve in Figure 3-3. A change in the demand schedule data, or, graphically, a shift in the location of the demand curve, is called a *change in demand.*

If consumers become willing and able to buy more corn at each possible price than is reflected in column 4 of Table 3-3, the result will be an *increase in demand.* In Figure 3-3, this increase in demand is reflected in a shift of the demand curve to the *right,* as from D_1 to D_2. Conversely, a *decrease in demand* occurs when, because of a change in one or more of

the determinants, consumers buy less corn at each possible price than indicated in column 4 of Table 3-3. Graphically, a decrease in demand is shown as a shift of the demand curve to the *left,* for example, from D_1 to D_3 in Figure 3-3.

Let's now examine how changes in each determinant affect demand.

1 Tastes A change in consumer tastes or preferences favorable to a product—possibly prompted by advertising or fashion changes—will mean that more will be demanded at each price; that is, demand will increase. An unfavorable change in consumer preferences will decrease demand, shifting the curve to the left. Technological change in the form of a new product may affect consumer tastes. For example, the introduction of compact discs has greatly decreased the demand for long-playing records. Consumer concerns over the health hazards posed by cholesterol and obesity have increased the demands for broccoli, low-calorie sweeteners, and fresh fruits, while decreasing the demands for beef, veal, eggs, and whole milk. Medical studies linking beta carotene to the prevention of heart attacks, strokes, and some types of cancer have greatly boosted the demand for carrots.

FIGURE 3-3 Changes in the demand for corn
A change in one or more of the determinants of demand—consumer tastes, the number of buyers in the market, money incomes, the prices of other goods, or consumer expectations—will cause a change in demand. An increase in demand shifts the demand curve to the right, as from D_1 to D_2. A decrease in demand shifts the demand curve to the left, as from D_1 to D_3. A change in the quantity demanded is caused by a change in the price of the product, and is shown by a movement from one point to another—as from a to b—on a fixed demand curve.

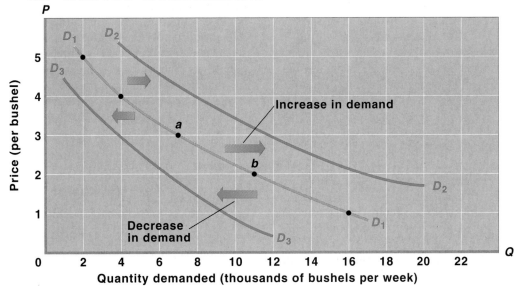

2 Number of Buyers An increase in the number of consumers in a market will increase demand. Fewer consumers will decrease demand. For example, improvements in communications have given financial markets international range, increasing demand for stocks and bonds. And the "baby boom" after World War II increased demand for diapers, baby lotion, and services of obstetricians. When the "baby boomers" reached their twenties in the 1970s, the demand for housing increased. Conversely, the aging of the baby boomers in the 1980s and 1990s has been a factor in the recent "slump" in housing demand. Also, increasing life expectancy has increased demands for medical care, retirement communities, and nursing homes. And recent international trade agreements such as the North American Free Trade Agreement (NAFTA) and the General Agreement on Tariffs and Trade (GATT) have reduced foreign trade barriers to American farm products, increasing demands for those products.

3 Income How changes in money income affect demand is more complex. For most commodities, a rise in income will cause an increase in demand. Consumers typically buy more steaks, sunscreen, and stereos as their incomes increase. Conversely, the demand for such products will decline as incomes fall. Commodities whose demand varies *directly* with money income are called **superior,** or **normal, goods.**

Although most products are normal goods, there are a few exceptions. As incomes increase beyond some point, the amounts of bread or lard or cabbages purchased at each price may diminish because higher incomes allow consumers to buy more high-protein foods, such as dairy products and meat. Rising incomes may also decrease demands for used clothing and third-hand automobiles. Similarly, rising incomes may cause demands for hamburger and margarine to decline as wealthier consumers switch to T-bones and butter. Goods whose demand varies *inversely* with a change in money income are called **inferior goods.**

4 Prices of Related Goods Whether a particular change in the price of a related good will increase or decrease the demand for a product will depend on whether the related good is a substitute for it or a complement to it. A substitute is a good which can be used in place of another good. A complement is a good used in conjunction with another good.

Substitutes Butter and margarine are examples of **substitute goods.** When the price of butter rises, consumers buy less butter, increasing the demand for margarine.[2] Conversely, as the price of butter falls, consumers will buy more butter, decreasing the demand for margarine. *When two products are substitutes, the price of one good and the demand for the other are directly related.* So it is with Nikes and Reeboks, sugar and Nutrasweet, Toyotas and Hondas, and Coke and Pepsi.

Complements Other products are related and are **complementary goods;** they "go together" in that they are used in tandem and jointly demanded. If the price of gasoline falls and, as a result, you drive your car more, this extra driving will increase your demand for motor oil. Conversely, an increase in the price of gasoline will diminish the demand for motor oil.[3] Thus gas and oil are jointly demanded; they are complements. So it is with ham and eggs, tuition and textbooks, movies and popcorn, VCRs and video cassettes, golf clubs and golf balls, cameras and film. *When two commodities are complements, the price of one good and the demand for the other are inversely related.*

Many goods are not related to one another—they are *independent* goods. For example, with such pairs as butter and golf balls, potatoes and automobiles, bananas and wristwatches, a change in the price of one would have little or no impact on the demand for the other.

5 Expectations Consumer expectations about future product prices, product availability, and future income can shift demand. Consumer expectations of higher future prices may prompt them to buy now to "beat" anticipated price rises; similarly, the expectation of rising incomes may induce consumers to be freer in current spending. Conversely, expectations of falling prices and income will decrease current demand for products.

---

[2]Note that the consumer is moving up a stable demand curve for butter. But the demand curve for margarine shifts to the right (increases). Given the supply of margarine, this rightward shift in demand means more margarine will be purchased and that its price will also rise.

[3]While the buyer is moving up a stable demand curve for gasoline, the demand for motor oil shifts to the left (decreases). Given the supply of motor oil, this decline in the demand for motor oil will reduce both the amount purchased and its price.

First example: If freezing weather destroys much of Florida's citrus crop, consumers may reason that forthcoming shortages of frozen orange juice will escalate its price. They may stock up on orange juice by purchasing large quantities now.

Second example: In late 1993 there was a substantial increase in the demand for guns. Reason? The expectation of Congress passing more stringent gun control laws.

Third example: A first-round NFL draft choice might splurge for a new Mercedes in anticipation of a lucrative professional football contract.

Final example: Additional Federal excise taxes imposed on beer, wine, and distilled liquor on January 1, 1991, sharply increased demand in December of 1990 as consumers "bought early" to beat anticipated price increases.

In summary, an *increase* in demand—the decision by consumers to buy larger quantities of a product at each possible price—can be caused by:

1   A favorable change in consumer tastes
2   An increase in the number of buyers
3   Rising incomes if the product is a normal good
4   Falling incomes if the product is an inferior good
5   An increase in the price of a substitute good
6   A decrease in the price of a complementary good
7   Consumer expectations of higher future prices and incomes

Be sure you can "reverse" these generalizations to explain a *decrease* in demand. Table 3-4 provides additional illustrations to reinforce your understanding of the determinants of demand. *(Key Question 2)*

Changes in Quantity Demanded

A "change in demand" must not be confused with a "change in quantity demanded." A **change in demand** is a shift in the entire demand curve either to the right (an increase in demand) or to the left (a decrease in demand). The consumer's state of mind concerning purchases of this product has been altered. The cause: a change in one or more of the determinants of demand. The term "demand" refers to a schedule or curve; therefore, a "change in demand" means that the entire schedule has changed and that graphically the curve has shifted its position.

In contrast, a **change in the quantity demanded** designates the movement from one point to another point—from one price-quantity combination to another—on a fixed demand curve. The cause of a change in quantity demanded is a change in the

TABLE 3-4   Determinants of demand: factors that shift the demand curve

1   **Change in buyer tastes**   Example: Physical fitness increases in popularity, increasing the demand for jogging shoes and bicycles

2   **Change in number of buyers**   Examples: Japanese reduce import quotas on American telecommunications equipment, increasing the demand for it; a birthrate decline reduces the demand for education

3   **Change in income**   Examples: An increase in incomes increases the demand for such normal goods as butter, lobster, and filet mignon, while reducing the demand for such inferior goods as cabbage, turnips, retreaded tires, and used clothing

4   **Change in the prices of related goods**   Examples: A reduction in airfares reduces the demand for bus transportation (substitute goods); a decline in the price of compact disc players increases the demand for compact discs (complementary goods)

5   **Change in expectations**   Example: Inclement weather in South America causes the expectation of higher future coffee prices, thereby increasing the current demand for coffee

price of the product under consideration. In Table 3-3 a decline in the price from $5 to $4 will increase the quantity of corn demanded from 2000 to 4000 bushels.

In Figure 3-3 the shift of the demand curve D_1 to either D_2 or D_3 is a "change in demand." But the movement from point a to point b on curve D_1 is a "change in the quantity demanded."

Is a change in demand or a change in quantity demanded illustrated in each of the following?

1   Consumer incomes rise, with the result that more jewelry is purchased.
2   A barber raises the price of haircuts and experiences a decline in volume of business.
3   The price of Toyotas goes up, and, as a consequence, the sales of Chevrolets increase.

QUICK REVIEW 3-1

■ A market is any arrangement which facilitates purchase and sale of goods, services, or resources.

■ The law of demand indicates that, other things being constant, the quantity of a good purchased will vary inversely with its price.

■ The demand curve will shift because of changes in *a* consumer tastes, *b* the number of buyers in the market, *c* incomes, *d* the prices of substitute or complementary goods, and *e* expectations.

■ A "change in quantity demanded" refers to a movement from one point to another on a stable demand curve; a "change in demand" designates a shift in the entire demand curve.

SUPPLY

Supply is *a schedule which shows the amounts of a product a producer is willing and able to produce and make available for sale at each price in a series of possible prices during a specified period.*[4] This **supply schedule** portrays a series of alternative possibilities, such as shown in Table 3-5, for a single producer of corn. Supply tells us the quantities of a product which will be supplied at various prices, all other factors held constant.

Our definition of supply indicates that supply is usually viewed from the vantage point of price. That is, we read supply as showing the amounts producers will offer at various prices. It is equally correct and more useful in some instances to view supply from the reference point of quantity. Instead of asking what quantities will be offered at various prices, we can ask what prices will induce producers to offer various quantities of a good.

Law of Supply

Table 3-5 shows a positive or *direct* relationship between price and quantity supplied. As price rises, the corresponding quantity supplied rises; as price falls, the quantity supplied also falls. This particular relationship is called the **law of supply.** Producers will produce and offer for sale more of their product at a high price than at a low price. This again is basically a commonsense matter.

Price is a deterrent from the consumer's standpoint. A high price means that the consumer, being on the paying end of this price, will buy a relatively small amount of the product; the lower the price obstacle, the more the consumer will buy. The supplier is on the receiving end of the product's price. To a supplier, price is revenue per unit and therefore an inducement or incentive to produce and sell a product. Given production costs, a higher product price means

TABLE 3-5 An individual producer's supply of corn

Price per bushel	Quantity supplied per week
$5	60
4	50
3	35
2	20
1	5

greater profits and thus an incentive to increase the quantity supplied.

Consider a farmer who can shift resources among alternative products. As price moves up in Table 3-5, the farmer will find it profitable to take land out of wheat, oats, and soybean production and put it into corn. Furthermore, higher corn prices will make it possible for the farmer to cover the costs associated with more intensive cultivation and the use of larger quantities of fertilizers and pesticides. The result is more corn.

Now consider a manufacturer. Beyond some point manufacturers usually encounter increasing production costs per added unit of output. Therefore, a higher product price is necessary to cover these rising costs. Costs rise because certain productive resources — in particular, the firm's plant and machinery — cannot be expanded quickly. As the firm increases the amounts of more readily variable resources such a labor, materials, and component parts, the fixed plant will at some point become crowded or congested. Productive efficiency will decline and the cost of successive units of output will increase. Producers must receive a higher price to produce these more costly units. Price and quantity supplied are directly related.

The Supply Curve

As with demand, it is convenient to represent graphically the concept of supply. Our axes in Figure 3-4 are the same as those in Figure 3-3, except for the change of "quantity demanded" to "quantity supplied" on the horizontal axis. The graphing procedure is the same, but the quantity data and relationship involved are different. The market supply data graphed in Figure 3-4 as S_1 are shown in Table 3-6, which assumes there are 200 suppliers in the market having the same supply schedules as the producer previously portrayed in Table 3-5.

---

[4]In talking of the resource market, our definition of supply reads: a schedule which shows the various amounts of a resource which its owners are willing to supply in the market at each possible price in a series of prices during a specified time.

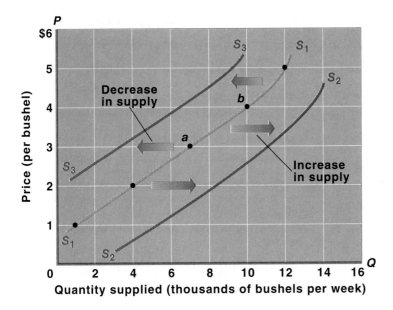

FIGURE 3-4 Changes in the supply of corn
A change in one or more of the determinants of supply—resource prices, productive techniques, the prices of other goods, taxes and subsidies, price expectations, or the number of sellers in the market—will cause a change in supply. An increase in supply shifts the supply curve to the right, as from S_1 to S_2. A decrease in supply is shown graphically as a shift of the curve to the left, as from S_1 to S_3. A change in the quantity supplied is caused by a change in the price of the product and is shown by a movement from one point to another—as from a to b—on a fixed supply curve.

Determinants of Supply

In constructing a supply curve, the economist assumes that price is the most significant influence on the quantity supplied of any product. But, as with the demand curve, the supply curve is anchored on the "other things are equal" assumption. The supply curve is drawn assuming that certain determinants of the amount supplied are given and do not change. If any of these determinants of supply do change, the supply curve will shift.

The basic determinants of supply are (1) resource prices, (2) the technique of production, (3) taxes and subsidies, (4) prices of other goods, (5) price expectations, and (6) the number of sellers in the market. A change in any one or more of these determinants or *supply shifters* will cause the supply curve for a product to shift either to the right or the left. A shift to the

right, from S_1 to S_2 in Figure 3-4, designates an *increase in supply:* Producers will supply larger quantities of the product at each possible price. A shift to the *left,* S_1 to S_3 in Figure 3-4, indicates a *decrease in supply:* Suppliers offer less at each price.

Changes in Supply

Let's consider how changes in each of these determinants affect supply.

1   Resource Prices   The relationship between production costs and supply is an intimate one. A firm's supply curve is based on production costs; a firm must receive higher prices for additional units of output because those extra units cost more to produce. It follows that a decrease in resource prices will lower production costs and increase supply, shifting the supply curve to the right. If prices of seed and fertilizer decrease, we can expect the supply of corn to increase. Conversely, an increase in resource prices will raise production costs and reduce supply, shifting the supply curve to the left. Increases in the prices of iron ore and coke will increase the cost of producing steel and reduce its supply.

2   Technology   A technological improvement means new knowledge permits us to produce a unit of output with fewer resources. Given the prices of these resources, this will lower production costs and increase supply. Recent breakthroughs in supercon-

TABLE 3-6 Market supply of corn, 200 producers

(1) Price per bushel	(2) Quantity supplied per week, single producer		(3) Number of sellers in the market		(4) Total quantity supplied per week
$5	60	×	200	=	12,000
4	50	×	200	=	10,000
3	35	×	200	=	7,000
2	20	×	200	=	4,000
1	5	×	200	=	1,000

ductivity portend the possibility of transporting electric power with little or no loss. Currently, about 30 percent of electric power transmitted by copper cable is lost. Consequence? Significant cost reductions and supply increases might occur in a wide range of products where electricity is an important input.

3 **Taxes and Subsidies** Businesses treat most taxes as costs. An increase in sales or property taxes will increase costs and reduce supply. Conversely, subsidies are "taxes in reverse." If government subsidizes the production of a good, it in effect lowers costs and increases supply.

4 **Prices of Other Goods** Changes in the prices of other goods can also shift the supply curve for a product. A decline in the price of wheat may cause a farmer to produce and offer more oats at each possible price. Conversely, a rise in the price of wheat may make farmers less willing to produce and offer oats in the market. A firm making athletic equipment might reduce its supply of basketballs in response to a rise in the price of soccer balls.

5 **Expectations** Expectations concerning the future price of a product can affect a producer's current willingness to supply that product. It is difficult, however, to generalize how the expectation of higher prices will affect the present supply of a product. Farmers might withhold some of their current corn harvest from the market, anticipating a higher corn price in the future. This will cause a decrease in the current supply of corn. Similarly, if the price of IBM stock is expected to rise significantly in the near future, the supply offered today for sale might decrease. On the other hand, in many types of manufacturing, expected price increases may induce firms to add another shift of workers or expand their production facilities, causing supply to increase.

6 **Number of Sellers** Given the scale of operations of each firm, the larger the number of suppliers, the greater the market supply. As more firms enter an industry, the supply curve will shift to the right. The smaller the number of firms in an industry, the less the market supply will be. This means that as firms leave an industry, the supply curve will shift to the left. Example: The United States and Canada recently imposed restrictions on haddock fishing to replenish dwindling stocks. The requirement that every haddock fishing boat remain in dock 80 days a year

TABLE 3-7 **Determinants of supply: factors that shift the supply curve**

1 **Change in resource prices** Examples: A decline in the price of fertilizer increases the supply of wheat; an increase in the price of irrigation equipment reduces the supply of corn

2 **Change in technology** Example: The development of a more effective insecticide for corn rootworm increases the supply of corn

3 **Changes in taxes and subsidies** Examples: An increase in the excise tax on cigarettes reduces the supply of cigarettes; a decline in subsidies to state universities reduces the supply of higher education

4 **Change in prices of other goods** Example: A decline in the prices of mutton and pork increases the supply of beef

5 **Change in expectations** Example: Expectations of substantial declines in future oil prices cause oil companies to increase current supply

6 **Change in number of suppliers** Examples: An increase in the number of firms producing personal computers increases the supply of personal computers; formation of a new professional football league increases the supply of professional football games

put a number of fishermen out of business and reduced the supply of haddock.

Table 3-7 provides a checklist of the determinants of supply; the accompanying illustrations deserve careful study. *(Key Question 5)*

Changes in Quantity Supplied

The distinction between a "change in supply" and a "change in quantity supplied" parallels that between a change in demand and a change in quantity demanded. A **change in supply** means the entire supply curve shifts. An increase in supply shifts the curve to the right; a decrease in supply shifts it to the left. The cause of a change in supply is a change in one or more of the determinants of supply. The term "supply" refers to a schedule or curve. A "change in supply" therefore must mean that the entire schedule has changed and that the curve has shifted.

A **change in the quantity supplied** refers to the movement from one point to another on a stable supply curve. The cause of such a movement is a change in the price of the specific product under consideration. In Table 3-6 a decline in the price of corn from $5 to $4 decreases the quantity of corn supplied from 12,000 to 10,000 bushels.

Shifting the supply curve from S_1 to S_2 or S_3 in Figure 3-4 entails "changes in supply." The movement from point a to point b on S_1, however, is a "change in quantity supplied."

You should determine which of the following involves a change in supply and which a change in quantity supplied:

1   Because production costs decline, producers sell more automobiles.

2   The price of wheat declines, causing the number of bushels of corn sold per month to increase.

3   Fewer oranges are offered for sale because their price has decreased in retail markets.

4   The Federal government doubles its excise tax on liquor.

QUICK REVIEW 3-2

■ The law of supply states that, other things being unchanged, the quantity of a good supplied varies directly with its price.

■ The supply curve will shift because of changes in **a** resource prices, **b** technology, **c** taxes or subsidies, **d** prices of other goods, **e** expectations regarding future product prices, and **f** the number of suppliers.

■ A "change in supply" means a shift in the supply curve; a "change in quantity supplied" designates the movement from one point to another on a given supply curve.

SUPPLY AND DEMAND: MARKET EQUILIBRIUM

We may now bring supply and demand together to see how interaction of the buying decisions of households and the selling decisions of producers determines the price of a product and the quantity actually bought and sold. In Table 3-8, columns 1 and 2 reproduce the market supply schedule for corn (from Table 3-6), and columns 2 and 3, the market demand schedule for corn (from Table 3-3). Note that in column 2 we are using a common set of prices. We assume competition—a large number of buyers and sellers.

Surpluses

Of the five[5] possible prices at which corn might sell in this market, which will actually prevail as the market price? Let's derive our answer through the process of trial and error. For no particular reason, we start with $5. Could this be the prevailing market price for corn? The answer is "No," because producers are willing to produce and offer in the market some 12,000 bushels of corn at this price while buyers are willing to buy only 2000 bushels at this price. The $5 price encourages farmers to produce a great deal of corn, but discourages most consumers from buying it. Other products appear as "better buys" when corn is high-priced. The result here is a 10,000-bushel **surplus** or *excess supply* of corn. This surplus, shown in column 4, is the excess of quantity supplied over quantity demanded at $5. Corn farmers find themselves with unwanted inventories of output.

A price of $5—even if it existed temporarily in the corn market—could not persist over a period of time. The very large surplus of corn would prompt competing sellers to bid down the price to encourage buyers to take this surplus off their hands.

Suppose price goes down to $4. The lower price has encouraged buyers to take more of this product off the market and, at the same time, has induced farmers to use a smaller amount of resources in producing corn. The surplus has diminished to 6000 bushels. However, a surplus or excess supply still exists and competition among sellers will once again bid down the price of corn. We can conclude, then, that prices of $5 and $4 will be unstable because they are "too high." The market price for corn must be less than $4.

Shortages

Let's jump to $1 as the possible market price for corn. Observe in column 4 that at this price, quantity de-

TABLE 3-8   Market supply and demand for corn

(1) Total quantity supplied per week	(2) Price per bushel	(3) Total quantity demanded per week	(4) Surplus (+) or shortage (−) (arrows indicate effect on price)
12,000	$5	2,000	+10,000 ↓
10,000	4	4,000	+ 6,000 ↓
7,000	3	7,000	0
4,000	2	11,000	− 7,000 ↑
1,000	1	16,000	−15,000 ↑

[5]There are many possible prices; our example shows only five.

manded exceeds quantity supplied by 15,000 units. This price discourages farmers from devoting resources to corn production and encourages consumers to attempt to buy more than is available. The result is a 15,000-bushel **shortage** of, or *excess demand* for, corn. The $1 price cannot persist as the market price. Competition among buyers will bid up the price to something greater than $1. At $1, many consumers who are willing and able to buy at this price will be left out in the cold. Many potential consumers will express a willingness to pay a price above $1 to ensure getting some of the available corn.

Suppose competitive bidding by buyers boosts the price of corn to $2. This higher price has reduced, but not eliminated, the shortage of corn. For $2, farmers will devote more resources to corn production, and some buyers who were willing to pay $1 for a bushel of corn will choose not to buy at $2. But a shortage of 7000 bushels still exists at $2. We can conclude that competitive bidding among buyers will push the market price above $2.

Equilibrium

By trial and error we have eliminated every price but $3. At $3, *and only at this price,* the quantity farmers are willing to produce and supply in the market is identical with the amount consumers are willing and able to buy. As a result, there is neither a shortage nor a surplus. A surplus causes price to decline and a shortage causes price to rise.

With neither a shortage nor a surplus at $3, there is no reason for the price of corn to change. The economist calls this price the *market-clearing* or **equilibrium price,** equilibrium meaning "in balance" or "at rest." At $3, quantity supplied and quantity demanded are in balance; that is, **equilibrium quantity** is 7000 bushels. Hence $3 is the only stable price of corn under the supply and demand conditions shown in Table 3-8. The price of corn will be established where the supply decisions of producers and the demand decisions of buyers are mutually consistent. Such decisions are consistent with one another only at a price of $3. At any higher price, suppliers want to sell more than consumers want to buy and a surplus will result; at any lower price, consumers want to buy more than producers are willing to offer for sale, as shown by the consequent shortage. Discrepancies between supply and demand intentions of sellers and buyers will prompt price changes which will bring these two sets of plans into accord with one another.

A graphical analysis of supply and demand should yield the same conclusions. Figure 3-5 (Key Graph) puts the market supply and market demand curves for corn on the same graph, the horizontal axis now measuring both quantity demanded and quantity supplied.

At any price above the equilibrium price of $3, quantity supplied will exceed quantity demanded. This surplus will cause a competitive bidding down of price by sellers eager to rid themselves of their surplus. The falling price will cause less corn to be offered and will simultaneously encourage consumers to buy more.

Any price below the equilibrium price will entail a shortage; quantity demanded will exceed quantity supplied. Competitive bidding by buyers will push the price up toward the equilibrium level. This rising price will simultaneously cause producers to increase the quantity supplied and ration buyers out of the market, eliminating the shortage. *Graphically, the intersection of the supply curve and the demand curve for the product will indicate the equilibrium point.* In this case equilibrium price and quantity are $3 per bushel and 7000 bushels.

Rationing Function of Prices

The ability of the competitive forces of supply and demand to establish a price where selling and buying decisions are synchronized or coordinated is called the **rationing function of prices.** In this case, the equilibrium price of $3 "clears the market," leaving no burdensome surplus for sellers and no inconvenient shortage for potential buyers. The composite of freely made individual buying and selling decisions sets this price which clears the market. In effect, the market mechanism of supply and demand says that any buyer willing and able to pay $3 for a bushel of corn will be able to acquire one; those who are not, will not. Similarly, any seller willing and able to produce bushels of corn and offer them for sale at $3 will be able to do so; those who are not, will not. *(Key Question 7)*

Changes in Supply and Demand

We know demand might change because of fluctuations in consumer tastes or incomes, changes in consumer expectations, or variations in the prices of related goods. Supply might vary in response to changes in technology, resource prices, or taxes. Now we are ready to consider the effect of changes

KEY GRAPH

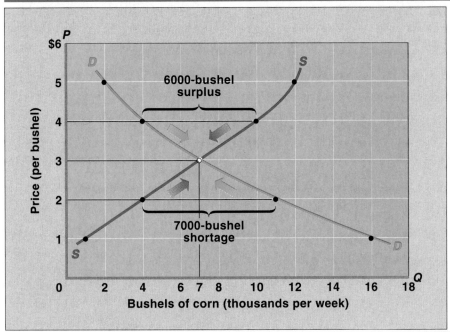

FIGURE 3-5 The equilibrium price and quantity for corn as determined by market demand and supply
The intersection of the downsloping demand curve *D* and the upsloping supply curve *S* indicates the equilibrium price and quantity, $3 and 7000 bushels in this instance. The shortages of corn which would exist at below-equilibrium prices, for example, 7000 bushels at $2, drive price up, and in so doing, increase the quantity supplied and reduce the quantity demanded until equilibrium is achieved. The surpluses which above-equilibrium prices would entail, for example, 6000 bushels at $4, push price down and thereby increase the quantity demanded and reduce the quantity supplied until equilibrium is achieved.

in supply and demand on equilibrium price and quantity.

Changing Demand First, we analyze the effects of a change in demand, assuming supply is constant. Suppose demand *increases,* as shown in Figure 3-6a. What is the effect on price? Since the new intersection of the supply and demand curves is at a higher point on both the price and quantity axes, an increase in demand, other things (supply) equal, will have a *price-increasing effect* and a *quantity-increasing effect.* (The value of graphical analysis is now apparent; we need not fumble with columns of figures in determining the effect on price and quantity but only compare the new with the old point of intersection on the graph.)

A *decrease* in demand, shown in Figure 3-6b, reveals both *price-decreasing* and *quantity-decreasing effects.* Price falls and so does quantity. *In brief, we find a direct relationship between a change in demand and resulting changes in both equilibrium price and quantity.*

Changing Supply Let's now see how a change in supply affects price, assuming demand is constant. If

supply increases, as in Figure 3-6c, the new intersection of supply and demand is located at a lower equilibrium price. Equilibrium quantity, however, increases. If supply decreases, product price will rise, but quantity declines. Figure 3-6d illustrates this situation.

An increase in supply has a *price-decreasing* and a *quantity-increasing effect.* A decrease in supply has a *price-increasing* and a *quantity-decreasing effect. There is an inverse relationship between a change in supply and the resulting change in equilibrium price, but the relationship between a change in supply and the resulting change in equilibrium quantity is direct.*

Complex Cases Many complex cases might arise, involving changes in both supply and demand.

1 Supply Increase; Demand Decrease Assume first that supply increases and demand decreases. What effect does this have on equilibrium price? This example couples two price-decreasing effects, and the net result will be a price fall greater than what would result from either change alone.

How about equilibrium quantity? Here the effects of the changes in supply and demand are opposed:

AN INTRODUCTION TO ECONOMICS AND THE ECONOMY

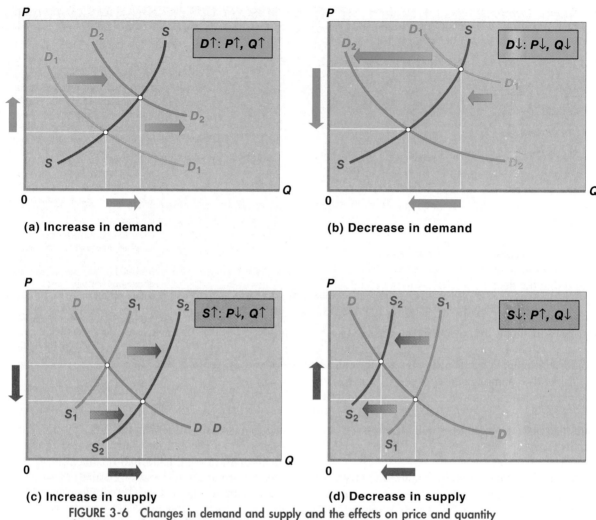

FIGURE 3-6 Changes in demand and supply and the effects on price and quantity
The increase in demand of (a) and the decrease in demand of (b) indicate a direct relationship between a change in demand and the resulting changes in equilibrium price and quantity. The increase in supply of (c) and the decrease in supply of (d) show an inverse relationship between a change in supply and the resulting change in equilibrium price, but a direct relationship between a change in supply and the accompanying change in equilibrium quantity.

The increase in supply increases equilibrium quantity, but the decrease in demand reduces the equilibrium quantity. The direction of the change in quantity depends on the relative sizes of the changes in supply and demand. If the increase in supply is larger than the decrease in demand, the equilibrium quantity will be larger than it was originally. But if the increase in supply is relatively smaller than the decrease in demand, equilibrium quantity will decrease. You should use graphs to verify these results.

2 Supply Decrease; Demand Increase Another possibility is for supply to decrease and demand to

increase. Two price-increasing effects are involved here. We can predict an increase in equilibrium price greater than that caused by either change separately. The effect on equilibrium quantity is again indeterminate, depending on the relative size of the changes in supply and demand. If the decrease in supply is relatively larger than the increase in demand, the equilibrium quantity will be less than initially. But if the decrease in supply is relatively smaller than the increase in demand, the equilibrium quantity will increase. You should trace through these two cases graphically to verify these conclusions.

3 *Supply Increase; Demand Increase* What if supply and demand both increase? What is the effect on equilibrium price? It depends. Here we must compare two conflicting effects on price—the price-decreasing effect of the increase in supply and the price-increasing effect of the increase in demand. If the increase in supply is greater than the increase in demand, the equilibrium price will decrease. If the opposite holds, equilibrium price will increase.

The effect on equilibrium quantity is certain: Increases in supply and in demand both have quantity-increasing effects. This means that equilibrium quantity will increase by an amount greater than either change alone.

4 *Supply Decrease; Demand Decrease* A decrease in both supply and demand can be similarly analyzed. If the decrease in supply is greater than the decrease in demand, equilibrium price will rise. If the reverse holds true, equilibrium price will fall. Because decreases in supply and demand both have quantity-decreasing effects, we can predict with certainty that equilibrium quantity will be less than it was initially.

Table 3-9 summarizes these four cases. You should draw a supply and demand diagram for each case to confirm the effects on equilibrium price and quantity indicated in the table.

Special cases might arise where a decrease in demand and a decrease in supply, on the one hand, and an increase in demand and an increase in supply, on the other, exactly cancel out. In both these cases, the net effect on equilibrium price will be zero; price will not change. *(Key Question 8)*

The Resource Market

As in the product market, resource supply curves are typically upsloping, and resource demand curves are downsloping.

Resource supply curves reflect a *direct* relationship between resource price and quantity supplied, because it is in the interest of resource owners to supply more of a particular resource at a high price than at a low price. High income payments in a particular occupation or industry encourage households to supply more human and property resources. Low income payments discourage resource owners from supplying resources in this occupation or industry and encourage them to supply their resources elsewhere.

On the demand side, businesses buy less of a given resource as its price rises, and they substitute other relatively low-priced resources for it. Entrepreneurs will find it profitable to substitute low- for high-priced resources as they try to minimize costs. More of a particular resource will be demanded at a low price than at a high price. The result? A downsloping demand curve for the various resources.

Just as supply decisions of businesses and the demand decisions of consumers determine prices in the product market, so the supply decisions of households and demand decisions of businesses set prices in the resource market.

"Other Things Equal"

In Chapter 1 we explained that because economists cannot conduct controlled experiments, they assume "other things are equal" in their analyses. We have seen in this chapter that a number of forces bear on both demand and supply. Therefore, in locating specific supply and demand curves, such as D_1 and S in Figure 3-6a, economists isolate the impact of what they judge to be the most important influence on the amounts supplied and demanded—the price of the specific product under consideration. In thus representing the laws of demand and supply by downsloping and upsloping curves, respectively, the economist assumes that the determinants of demand (incomes, tastes, and so forth) and of supply (resource prices, technology, and other factors) are constant or unchanging. That is, price and quantity demanded are inversely related, *other things equal*. And price and quantity supplied are directly related, *other things equal.*

If you forget the "other things equal" assumption, you can encounter situations which *seem* to be in conflict with the laws of demand and supply. For example, suppose Ford sells 200,000 Escorts in 1993 at $10,000; 300,000 at $11,000 in 1994; and 400,000 in 1995 at $12,000. Price and the number purchased vary *directly,* and these real-world data seem to be at odds

TABLE 3-9 **Effects of changes in both supply and demand**

Change in supply	Change in demand	Effect on equilibrium price	Effect on equilibrium quantity
1 increase	decrease	decrease	indeterminate
2 decrease	increase	increase	indeterminate
3 increase	increase	indeterminate	increase
4 decrease	decrease	indeterminate	decrease

LAST WORD

TICKET SCALPING: A BUM RAP?

Some market transactions get a bad name which is unwarranted.

Tickets to athletic and artistic events are sometimes resold at higher-than-original prices—a market transaction known by the unsavory term "scalping." For example, a $40 ticket to a college bowl game may be resold by the original buyer for $200, $250, or more. The media often denounces scalpers for "ripping off" buyers by charging "exorbitant" prices. Scalping and extortion are synonymous in some people's minds.

But is scalping really sinful? We must first recognize that such ticket resales are voluntary, not coerced, transactions. This correctly implies that both buyer and seller gain from the exchange or it would not occur. The seller must value the $200 more than seeing the game and the buyer must value seeing the game more than the $200. There are no losers or victims here; both buyer and seller benefit from the transaction. The "scalping" market simply redistributes assets (game tickets) from those who value them less to those who value them more.

Does scalping impose losses or injury on other parties—in particular, the sponsors of the event? If the sponsors are injured, it is because they initially priced tickets below the equilibrium level. In so doing they suffer an economic loss in the form of less revenue and profit than they might have otherwise received. But the loss is self-inflicted because of their pricing error. That mistake is quite separate and distinct from the fact that some tickets were later resold at a higher price.

What about spectators? Does scalping somehow impose losses by deteriorating the quality of the game's audience? No! People who most want to see the game—generally those with the greatest interest in and understanding of the game—will pay the scalper's high prices. Ticket scalping will benefit athletic teams and performing artists—they will appear before more understanding and appreciative audiences.

So, is ticket scalping undesirable? Not on economic grounds. Both seller and buyer of a "scalped" ticket benefit and a more interested and appreciative audience results. Game sponsors may sacrifice revenue and profits, but that derives from their own misjudgment of equilibrium price.

---

with the law of demand. But there is really not a conflict here; these data do *not* refute the law of demand. The catch is that the law of demand's "other things equal" assumption has been violated over the three years in the example. Specifically, because of, for example, growing incomes, population growth, and relatively high gasoline prices, all increasing the attractiveness of compact cars, the demand curve for Escorts has increased over the years—shifted to the right as from D_1 to D_2 in Figure 3-6a—causing price to rise and, simultaneously, a larger quantity to be purchased.

Conversely, consider Figure 3-6d. Comparing the original S_1D and the new S_2D equilibrium positions, *less* of the product is being sold or supplied at a higher price; that is, price and quantity supplied seem to be *inversely* related, rather than *directly* related as the law of supply indicates. The catch again is that the "other things equal" assumption underlying the upsloping supply curve has been violated. Perhaps production costs have gone up or a specific tax has been levied on this product, shifting the supply curve from S_1 to S_2.

These examples also emphasize the importance of our earlier distinction between a "change in quantity demanded (or supplied)" and a "change in demand (supply)." In Figure 3-6a a "change in demand" has caused a "change in the quantity supplied." In Figure 3-6d a "change in supply" has caused a "change in the quantity demanded."

QUICK REVIEW 3-3

■ In competitive markets price adjusts to the equilibrium level at which quantity demanded equals quantity supplied.

■ A change in demand alters both equilibrium price and equilibrium quantity in the same direction as the change in demand.

■ A change in supply causes equilibrium price to change in the opposite direction, but equilibrium quantity to change in the same direction, as the change in supply.

■ Over time equilibrium price and quantity may change in directions which seem at odds with the laws of demand and supply because the "other things equal" assumption is violated.

CHAPTER SUMMARY

1 A market is any institution or arrangement which brings together buyers and sellers of some product or service.

2 Demand refers to a schedule representing the willingness of buyers to purchase a given product during a specific time period at each of the various prices at which it might be sold. According to the law of demand, consumers will ordinarily buy more of a product at a low price than they will at a high price. Therefore, other things equal, the relationship between price and quantity demanded is negative or inverse and demand graphs as a downsloping curve.

3 Changes in one or more of the basic determinants of demand—consumer tastes, the number of buyers in the market, the money incomes of consumers, the prices of related goods, and consumer expectations—will cause the market demand curve to shift. A shift to the right is an increase in demand; a shift to the left, a decrease in demand. A "change in demand" is distinguished from a "change in the quantity demanded," the latter involving movement from one point to another point on a fixed demand curve because of a change in the price of the product under consideration.

4 Supply is a schedule showing the amounts of a product which producers would be willing to offer in the market during a given period at each possible price. The law of supply says that, other things equal, producers will offer more of a product at a high price than they will at a low price. As a result, the relationship between price and quantity supplied is a direct one, and the supply curve is upsloping.

5 A change in resource prices, production techniques, taxes or subsidies, the prices of other goods, price expectations, or the number of sellers in the market will cause the supply curve of a product to shift. A shift to the right is an increase in supply; a shift to the left, a decrease in supply. In contrast, a change in the price of the product under consideration will result in a change in the quantity supplied, that is, a movement from one point to another on a fixed supply curve.

6 Under competition, the interaction of market demand and market supply will adjust price to that point where quantity demanded and quantity supplied are equal. This is the equilibrium price. The corresponding quantity is the equilibrium quantity.

7 The ability of market forces to synchronize selling and buying decisions to eliminate potential surpluses or shortages is termed the "rationing function" of prices.

8 A change in either demand or supply will cause equilibrium price and quantity to change. There is a positive or direct relationship between a change in demand and the resulting changes in equilibrium price and quantity. Though the relationship between a change in supply and resulting change in equilibrium price is inverse, the relationship between a change in supply and equilibrium quantity is direct.

9 The concepts of supply and demand also apply to the resource market.

TERMS AND CONCEPTS

market	income and	change in demand	law of supply
demand	substitution effects	(supply) versus	surplus
demand schedule	normal (superior)	change in the	shortage
(curve)	good	quantity demanded	equilibrium price and
law of demand	inferior good	(supplied)	quantity
diminishing marginal	substitute goods	supply	rationing function of
utility	complementary goods	supply schedule (curve)	prices

QUESTIONS AND STUDY SUGGESTIONS

1 Explain the law of demand. Why does a demand curve slope downward? What are the determinants of demand? What happens to the demand curve when each of these determinants changes? Distinguish between a change in demand and a change in the quantity demanded, noting the cause(s) of each.

2 *Key Question* *What effect will each of the following have on the demand for product B?*

  a *Product B becomes more fashionable*

  b *The price of substitute product C falls*

  c *A decline in incomes if B is an inferior good*

  d *Consumers anticipate the price of B will be lower in the near future*

  e *The price of complementary product D falls*

  f *Foreign tariff barriers on B are eliminated*

3 Explain the following news dispatch from Hull, England: "The fish market here slumped today to what local commentators called 'a disastrous level'—all because of a shortage of potatoes. The potatoes are one of the main ingredients in a dish that figures on almost every café-menu —fish and chips."

4 Explain the law of supply. Why does the supply curve slope upward? What are the determinants of supply? What happens to the supply curve when each of these determinants changes? Distinguish between a change in supply and a change in the quantity supplied, noting the cause(s) of each.

5 *Key Question* *What effect will each of the following have on the supply of product B?*

  a *A technological advance in the methods of producing B*

  b *A decline in the number of firms in industry B*

  c *An increase in the prices of resources required in the production of B*

  d *The expectation that the equilibrium price of B will be lower in the future than it is currently*

  e *A decline in the price of product A, a good whose production requires substantially the same techniques and resources as does the production of B*

  f *The levying of a specific sales tax on B*

  g *The granting of a 50-cent per unit subsidy for each unit of B produced*

6 "In the corn market, demand often exceeds supply and supply sometimes exceeds demand." "The price of corn rises and falls in response to changes in supply and demand." In which of these two statements are the terms "supply" and "demand" used correctly? Explain.

7 *Key Question* *Suppose the total demand for wheat and the total supply of wheat per month in the Kansas City grain market are as follows:*

Thousands of bushels demanded	Price per bushel	Thousands of bushels supplied	Surplus (+) or shortage (−)
85	$3.40	72	_____
80	3.70	73	_____
75	4.00	75	_____
70	4.30	77	_____
65	4.60	79	_____
60	4.90	81	_____

  a *What will be the market or equilibrium price? What is the equilibrium quantity? Using the surplus-shortage column, explain why your answers are correct.*

  b *Using the above data, graph the demand for wheat and the supply of wheat. Be sure to label the axes of your graph correctly. Label equilibrium price "P" and equilibrium quantity "Q."*

  c *Why will $3.40 not be the equilibrium price in this market? Why not $4.90? "Surpluses drive prices up; shortages drive them down." Do you agree?*

  d *Now suppose that the government establishes a ceiling (maximum legal) price of, say, $3.70 for wheat. Explain carefully the effects of this ceiling price. Demonstrate your answer graphically. What might prompt government to establish a ceiling price?*

8 *Key Question* *How will each of the following changes in demand and/or supply affect equilibrium price and equilibrium quantity in a competitive market; that is, do price and quantity rise, fall, remain unchanged, or are the answers indeterminate, depending on the magnitudes of the shifts in supply and demand? You should rely on a supply and demand diagram to verify answers.*

  a *Supply decreases and demand remains constant*

  b *Demand decreases and supply remains constant*

  c *Supply increases and demand is constant*

  d *Demand increases and supply increases*

  e *Demand increases and supply is constant*

  f *Supply increases and demand decreases*

  g *Demand increases and supply decreases*

  h *Demand decreases and supply decreases*

9 "Prices are the automatic regulator that tends to keep production and consumption in line with each other." Explain.

10 Explain: "Even though parking meters may yield little or no net revenue, they should nevertheless be retained because of the rationing function they perform."

11 Use two market diagrams to explain how an increase in state subsidies to public colleges might affect tuition and enrollments in both public and private colleges.

12 Critically evaluate: "In comparing the two equilibrium positions in Figure 3-6a, I note that a larger amount is actually purchased at a higher price. This refutes the law of demand."

13 Suppose you go to a recycling center and are paid 25 cents per pound for your aluminum cans. However, the recycler charges you 20 cents per bundle to accept your old newspapers. Use demand and supply diagrams to portray both markets. Can you explain how different government policies with respect to the recycling of aluminum and paper might account for these different market outcomes?

14 Advanced analysis: Assume that demand for a commodity is represented by the equation $P = 10 - .2Q_d$ and supply by the equation $P = 2 + .2Q_s$, where Q_d and Q_s are quantity demanded and quantity supplied, respectively, and P is price. Using the equilibrium condition $Q_s = Q_d$, solve the equations to determine equilibrium price. Now determine equilibrium quantity. Graph the two equations to substantiate your answers.

15 (Last Word) Discuss the economic aspects of ticket scalping, specifying gainers and losers.

4

PURE CAPITALISM AND THE MARKET SYSTEM

In Chapter 3 we saw how equilibrium prices and quantities are established in *individual* product and resource markets. We now widen our focus to take in all product and resource markets—the *competitive market system,* also known as the private enterprise system or capitalism. In the past few years, the press and television have regularly reported how Russia and other centrally planned economies are trying to shift toward capitalism. Precisely what are the features and institutions of capitalism which these nations are trying to emulate?

First we will describe the capitalist ideology and explain how pure, or laissez faire, capitalism would function. Although pure capitalism has never existed, describing it provides a useful approximation of how the economies of the United States and many other industrially advanced nations function. We will modify our model of pure capitalism in later chapters to correspond more closely to the reality of modern capitalism.

In explaining pure capitalism, we will discuss: (1) the institutional framework and basic assumptions which make up the capitalist ideology; (2) certain institutions and practices common to all modern economies; and (3) how a market system can coordinate economic activity and contribute to the efficient use of scarce resources. In achieving this third goal we will rely heavily on Chapter 3's explanation of how individual markets work.

CAPITALIST IDEOLOGY

There is no neat, universally accepted definition of capitalism. We therefore must examine in some detail the basic tenets of pure capitalism to understand what it entails. In short, the framework of capitalism embraces the following institutions and assumptions: (1) private property, (2) freedom of enterprise and choice, (3) self-interest as the dominant motive, (4) competition, (5) reliance on the price or market system, and (6) a limited role for government.

Private Property

Under a capitalistic system, property resources are owned by private individuals and private institutions, not by government. **Private property,** coupled with the freedom to negotiate binding legal contracts, permits private persons or businesses to obtain, control, employ, and dispose of property resources as they see fit. The institution of private property is sustained over time by the *right to bequeath*—the right of a property owner to designate who receives his or her property at the time of death.

Property rights—rights to own, use, and dispose of property—are significant because they encourage investment, innovation, exchange, and economic growth. Why would anyone build a house, construct a factory, or clear land for farming if someone or some institution (for example, government) could confiscate that property for their own benefit?

Property rights also apply to "intellectual property" and function similarly. Patents and copyrights exist to encourage individuals to write books, music, and computer programs and to invent new products and production processes without fear that others will expropriate them along with the associated economic rewards.

Another important role of property rights is that they facilitate exchange. A title to an automobile or a deed to a house assures the buyer that the seller is the legitimate owner. Finally, without property rights people would have to devote considerable energy and resources simply to protect and retain the property they have produced or acquired.

There are broad legal limits to this right of private ownership. For example, the use of resources to produce illicit drugs is prohibited. Nor is public ownership nonexistent. Even in pure capitalism, public ownership of certain "natural monopolies" may be essential to realize efficiency in the use of resources.

Freedom of Enterprise and Choice

Closely related to private ownership of property is freedom of enterprise and choice. Capitalism charges its component economic units with the responsibility of making certain choices, which are registered and made effective through the free markets of the economy.

Freedom of enterprise means that private business enterprises are free to obtain economic resources, to organize these resources in the production of a good or service of the firm's own choosing, and to sell it in the markets of their choice. In pure capitalism no artificial obstacles or restrictions imposed by government or other producers block an entrepreneur's choice to enter or leave a particular industry.

Freedom of choice means that owners of property and money can employ or dispose of them as they see fit. It also means that laborers are free to enter any lines of work for which they are qualified. Finally, it means that consumers are at liberty, within the limits of their incomes, to buy that collection of

goods and services most appropriate in satisfying their wants.

Freedom of *consumer* choice is perhaps the most profound of these freedoms. The consumer is in a particularly strategic position in a capitalistic economy; in a sense, the consumer is sovereign. The range of free choices for suppliers of human and property resources depends on the choices of consumers. The consumer ultimately decides what the capitalistic economy should produce, and resource suppliers must make their free choices within these constraints. Resource suppliers and businesses are not really "free" to produce goods and services consumers do not desire because producing them would be unprofitable.

Again, broad legal limitations prevail in the expression of all these free choices.

Role of Self-Interest

The primary driving force of capitalism is **self-interest.** Each economic unit attempts to do what is best for itself. Entrepreneurs aim to maximize their firm's profits or, as the case might be, minimize losses. And, other things equal, property owners attempt to get the highest price for the rent or sale of these resources. Given the amount and irksomeness of the effort involved, those who supply human resources will also try to obtain the highest possible incomes from their employment. Consumers, in purchasing a specific product, will seek to obtain it at the lowest price. Consumers also apportion their expenditures to maximize their utility or satisfaction. In short, capitalism presumes self-interest as the fundamental *modus operandi* for the various economic units as they express their free choices. The motive of self-interest gives direction and consistency to what might otherwise be an extremely chaotic economy.

Pursuit of economic self-interest should not be confused with selfishness. A stockholder may invest to receive the best available corporate dividends and then may contribute a portion to the United Way or leave bequests to grandchildren.

Competition

Freedom of choice exercised in terms of promoting one's own monetary returns is the basis for **competition,** or economic rivalry, as a fundamental feature of capitalism. Competition entails:

1   Large numbers of independently acting buyers

and sellers operating in the market for any particular product or resource.

2   Freedom of buyers and sellers to enter or leave particular markets.

Large Numbers   The essence of competition is the widespread diffusion of economic power within the two major aggregates—businesses and households—which comprise the economy. When many buyers and sellers are in a particular market, no one buyer or seller will be able to demand or offer a quantity of the product sufficiently large to noticeably influence its price. Let's examine this statement in terms of the selling or supply side of the product market.

We know that when a product becomes unusually scarce, its price will rise. An unseasonable frost in Florida may seriously curtail the supply of citrus crops and sharply increase the price of oranges. Similarly, *if* a single producer, or a small group of producers acting together, can somehow control or restrict the total supply of a product, then price can be raised to the seller's advantage. By controlling supply, the producer can "rig the market" on his or her own behalf. The idea of pure competition is that there are so many independently acting sellers that each, *because he or she is contributing an almost negligible fraction of the total supply,* has virtually no influence over the supply or, therefore, over product price.

Suppose there are 10,000 farmers, each supplying 100 bushels of corn in the Kansas City grain market when the price of corn is $4 per bushel. Could a single farmer who feels dissatisfied with that price cause an artificial scarcity of corn and thereby boost the price above $4? The answer clearly is "No." Farmer Jones, by restricting output from 100 to 75 bushels, exerts virtually no effect on the total supply of corn. The total amount supplied is reduced only from 1,000,000 to 999,975 bushels. This is not much of a shortage! Supply is virtually unchanged, and, therefore, the $4 price persists.

Competition means that each seller is providing a drop in the bucket of total supply. Individual sellers can make no noticeable dent in total supply; thus, a seller cannot *as an individual producer* manipulate product price. This is what is meant when it is said that an individual competitive seller is "at the mercy of the market."

The same rationale applies to the demand side of the market. Buyers are plentiful and act independently. Thus single buyers cannot manipulate the market to their advantage.

The widespread diffusion of economic power underlying competition controls the use and limits the potential abuse of that power. Economic rivalry prevents economic units from wreaking havoc on one another as they attempt to further their self-interests. Competition imposes limits on expressions of self-interest by buyers and sellers. It is a basic regulatory force in capitalism.

Entry and Exit   Competition also implies it is simple for producers to enter or leave an industry; there are no artificial legal or institutional obstacles to prohibit expansion or contraction of specific industries. This freedom of an industry to expand or contract provides a competitive economy with the flexibility it needs to remain efficient over time. Freedom of entry and exit is necessary for the economy to adjust appropriately to changes in consumer tastes, technology, or resource supplies.

Markets and Prices

The basic coordinating mechanism of a capitalist economy is the market or price system. *Capitalism is a market economy.* Decisions rendered by buyers and sellers of products and resources are made effective through a system of markets. We know from Chapter 3 that a **market** is a mechanism or arrangement which brings buyers or "demanders" and sellers or "suppliers" of a good or service into contact with one another. A McDonald's, a gas station, a grocery supermarket, a Sotheby's art auction, the New York Stock Exchange, and worldwide foreign exchange markets are illustrations. The preferences of sellers and buyers are registered on the supply and demand sides of various markets, and the outcome of these choices is a system of product and resource prices. These prices are guideposts on which resource owners, entrepreneurs, and consumers make and revise their free choices in furthering their self-interests.

Just as competition is the controlling mechanism, so a system of markets and prices is a basic organizing force. The market system is an elaborate communication system through which innumerable individual free choices are recorded, summarized, and balanced against one another. Those who obey the dictates of the market system are rewarded; those who ignore them are penalized by the system. Through this communication system, society decides what the economy should produce, how production can be efficiently organized, and how the fruits of productive endeavor are distributed among the individual economic units which make up capitalism.

Not only is the market system the mechanism through which society decides how it allocates its resources and distributes the resulting output, but it is through the market system that these decisions are carried out. All of this will be detailed in the final sections of this chapter.

Limited Government

A competitive capitalist economy promotes a high degree of efficiency in the use of its resources. There is allegedly little need for governmental intervention in the operation of such an economy beyond its role of imposing broad legal limits on the exercise of individual choices and the use of private property. The concept of pure capitalism as a self-regulating and self-adjusting economy precludes any extensive economic role for government. However, as we will find in Chapter 5, a number of limitations and potentially undesirable outcomes associated with capitalism and the market system have resulted in an active economic role for government.

QUICK REVIEW 4-1

■ Pure capitalism rests on the private ownership of property and freedom of enterprise and choice.

■ Economic entities—businesses, resource suppliers, and consumers—seek to further their own self-interest.

■ The coordinating mechanism of capitalism is a competitive system of prices or markets.

■ The efficient functioning of the market system under capitalism allegedly precludes significant government intervention.

OTHER CHARACTERISTICS

Private property, freedom of enterprise and choice, self-interest as a motivating force, competition, and reliance on a market system are all institutions and assumptions more or less exclusively associated with pure capitalism.

In addition, there are certain institutions and practices which are characteristic of all modern economies: (1) the use of advanced technology and large amounts of capital goods, (2) specialization, and (3)

the use of money. Specialization and an advanced technology are prerequisites to efficient employment of any economy's resources. The use of money is a mechanism which allows society more easily to practice and reap the benefits of specialization and advanced productive techniques.

Extensive Use of Capital Goods

All modern or "industrially advanced" economies are based on state-of-the-art technology and the extensive use of capital goods. Under pure capitalism it is competition, coupled with freedom of choice and the motivation of self-interest, which create the opportunities for achieving technological advance. The capitalistic framework is highly effective in harnessing incentives to develop new products and improved techniques of production, because monetary rewards accrue directly to the innovator. Pure capitalism therefore presupposes extensive use and rapid development of complex capital goods: tools, machinery, large-scale factories, and facilities for storage, communication, transportation, and marketing.

Why are advanced technology and capital goods important? Because the most direct method of producing a product is usually the least efficient.[1] Even Robinson Crusoe avoided the inefficiencies of direct production in favor of **roundabout production.** It would be ridiculous for a farmer—even a backyard farmer—to go at production with bare hands. It pays huge dividends in terms of more efficient production and, therefore, a more abundant output, to create tools of production—capital equipment—to aid in the productive process. There is a better way of getting water out of a well than to dive in after it!

But there is a catch. Recall our discussion of the production possibilities curve and the basic nature of the economizing problem. For any economy operating on its production possibilities curve, resources must be diverted from the production of consumer goods to be used in the production of capital goods. We must currently tighten our belts as consumers to free resources for the production of capital goods which will give us a greater output of consumer goods in the future. Greater abundance tomorrow requires sacrifice today. *(Key Question 2)*

---

[1]Remember that consumer goods satisfy wants directly, while capital goods do so indirectly through the more efficient future production of consumer goods.

Specialization and Efficiency

The extent to which society relies on **specialization** is astounding. The vast majority of consumers produce virtually none of the goods and services they consume and consume little or nothing of what they produce. The worker who spends a lifetime stamping out parts for jet engines may never "consume" an airplane trip. The worker who devotes 8 hours a day to installing windows in Fords may own a Honda. Few households seriously consider any extensive production of their own food, shelter, and clothing. Many farmers sell their milk to the local dairy and then buy margarine at the local general store. Society learned long ago that self-sufficiency breeds inefficiency. The jack-of-all-trades may be a very colorful individual, but is certainly not efficient.

Division of Labor   In what ways might human specialization—the **division of labor**—enhance a society's output?

1   Ability Differences   Specialization permits individuals to take advantage of existing differences in their abilities and skills. If caveman A is strong, swift, and accurate with a spear, and caveman B is weak and slow, but patient, this distribution of talents can be most efficiently used if A hunts and B fishes.

2   Learning by Doing   Even if the abilities of A and B are identical, specialization may be advantageous. By devoting all your time to a single task, you are more likely to develop the appropriate skills and to discover improved techniques than when apportioning your time among a number of diverse tasks. You learn to be a good hunter by hunting!

3   Saving Time   Specialization—devoting all one's time to, say, a single task—avoids the loss of time involved in shifting from one job to another.

For all these reasons the division of labor results in greater total output from society's limited human resources.

Geographic Specialization   Specialization also works on a regional and international basis. Oranges could be grown in Nebraska, but because of the unsuitability of the land, rainfall, and temperature, the costs would be very high. Florida could achieve some success in the production of wheat, but for similar reasons such production would be costly. That's why Nebraskans produce those products—wheat in particular—for which their resources are best adapted, and Floridians do the same, producing oranges and other citrus fruits. In so doing, both produce surpluses of their specialties. Then, very sensibly, Nebraskans and Floridians swap some of their surpluses. Specialization permits each area to turn out those goods which its resources can most efficiently produce. In this way both Nebraska and Florida can enjoy a larger amount of both wheat and oranges than would otherwise be the case.

Similarly, on an international basis the United States specializes in such items as commercial aircraft and computers which it sells abroad in exchange for video recorders from Japan, bananas from Honduras, shoes from Italy, and woven baskets from Thailand. In short, human and geographical specialization are both essential in achieving efficiency in the use of resources.

Use of Money

Virtually all economies, advanced or primitive, use money. Money performs several functions, but first and foremost it is a **medium of exchange.**

In our example, Nebraskans must trade or exchange wheat for Florida's oranges if both states are to share in the benefits of specialization. If trade was highly inconvenient or prohibited for some reason, gains from specializing would be lost to society. Consumers want a wide variety of products and, without trade, would devote their human and material resources to many diverse types of production. If exchange could not occur or was very inconvenient to transact, Nebraska and Florida would be forced to be more self-sufficient, and the advantages of specialization would not occur. *A convenient means of exchanging goods is a prerequisite of specialization.*

Exchange can, and sometimes does, occur on the basis of **bartering,** that is, swapping goods for goods. But bartering as a means of exchange can pose serious problems for the economy. Exchange by barter requires a *coincidence of wants* between the two transactors. In our example, we assumed that Nebraskans had excess wheat to trade and that they wanted oranges. And we assumed Floridians had excess oranges to swap and that they wanted wheat. So exchange occurred. But if this coincidence of wants did not exist, trade would be stymied.

Suppose Nebraska does not want any of Florida's oranges but is interested in buying potatoes from Idaho. Ironically, Idaho wants Florida's oranges but

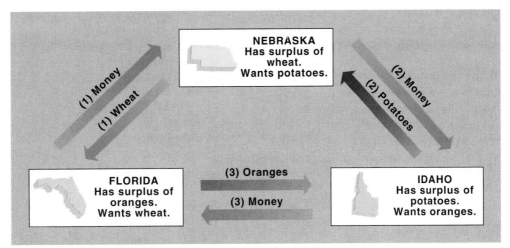

FIGURE 4-1 Money facilitates trade where wants do not coincide
By the use of money as a medium of exchange, trade can be accomplished, as indicated by the arrows, despite a noncoincidence of wants. By facilitating exchange, the use of money permits an economy to realize the efficiencies of specialization.

not Nebraska's wheat. And, to complicate matters, suppose that Florida wants some of Nebraska's wheat but none of Idaho's potatoes. The situation is summarized in Figure 4-1.

In no case do we find a coincidence of wants. Trade by barter clearly would be difficult. To overcome such a stalemate, economies use *money,* which is simply a convenient social invention to facilitate exchange of goods and services. Historically, cattle, cigarettes, shells, stones, pieces of metal, and many other commodities have been used, with varying degrees of success, as a medium for facilitating exchange. But to be money, an item needs to pass only one test: *It must be generally acceptable by buyers and sellers in exchange.* Money is socially defined; whatever society accepts as a medium of exchange *is* money.

Most economies use pieces of paper as money. This is the case with the Nebraska–Florida–Idaho economy; they use pieces of paper called "dollars" as money. Can the use of paper dollars as a medium of exchange overcome our stalemate?

Yes, with trade occurring as shown in Figure 4-1:
1 Floridians can exchange money for some of Nebraska's wheat.
2 Nebraskans use the money from the sale of wheat and exchange it for some of Idaho's potatoes.
3 Idahoans exchange the money received from the sale of potatoes for some of Florida's surplus oranges.

The willingness to accept paper money (or any other kind of money) as a medium of exchange has permitted a three-way trade which allows each state to specialize in one product and obtain the other product(s) its residents desire, despite the absence of a coincidence of wants between any two of the parties. Barter, resting as it does on a coincidence of wants, would have impeded this exchange and in so doing would have induced the three states not to specialize. Of course, the efficiencies of specialization would then have been lost to those states. Strange as it may first seem, two exchanges—surplus product for money and then money for a wanted product—are simpler than the single product-for-product exchange which bartering entails. In this example, product-for-product exchange would likely not occur.

On a global basis the fact that different nations have different currencies complicates international specialization and exchange. However, foreign exchange markets permit Americans, Japanese, Germans, Britons, and Mexicans to exchange dollars, yen, marks, pounds, and pesos for one another to complete international exchanges of goods and services.

A final example: Imagine a Detroit laborer producing crankshafts for Oldsmobiles. At the end of the week, instead of receiving a piece of paper endorsed by the company comptroller, or a few pieces of paper engraved in green and black, the worker receives from the company paymaster four Oldsmobile crankshafts. Inconvenient as this is, and with no desire to hoard crankshafts, the worker ventures into the Detroit business district to spend this income on a bag of groceries, a pair of jeans, and a movie. Obviously, the worker is faced with some inconvenient and time-consuming trading, and may not be able to negotiate any exchanges at all. Finding a clothier with jeans who happens to be in the market for an Oldsmobile crankshaft can be a formidable task. And, if the jeans do not trade evenly for crankshafts, how do the transactors "make change"? It is fair to say that money is one of the great social inventions of civilization.

QUICK REVIEW 4-2

■ Advanced economies achieve greater efficiency in production through the use of large quantities of capital goods.

■ Specialization enhances efficiency by having individuals, regions, and nations produce those goods and services for which their resources are best suited.

■ The use of money facilitates the exchange of goods which specialization entails.

THE COMPETITIVE MARKET SYSTEM

We noted earlier that a fundamental feature of capitalism is its reliance on a market system. We have also stressed that a capitalistic system is characterized by freedom of enterprise and choice. Consumers are free to buy what they choose; businesses, to produce and sell what they choose; and resource suppliers, to make their property and human resources available in whatever occupations they choose. We may wonder why such an economy does not collapse in chaos. If consumers want breakfast cereal, businesses choose to produce aerobic shoes, and resource suppliers want to offer their services in manufacturing computer software, production would seem to be deadlocked because of the apparent inconsistency of these free choices.

In reality, the millions of decisions made by households and businesses are highly consistent with one another. Firms do produce those particular goods and services consumers want. Households provide the kinds of labor businesses want to hire. Here we will see how a competitive market system constitutes a coordinating mechanism which overcomes the potential chaos suggested by freedom of enterprise and choice. The competitive market system is a mechanism both for communicating decisions of consumers, producers, and resource suppliers to one another and for synchronizing those decisions toward consistent production objectives.

THE FIVE FUNDAMENTAL QUESTIONS

To understand the operation of a market economy we must first recognize that there are **Five Fundamental Questions** to which *every* economy must respond:
1 *How much* is to be produced? At what level—to what degree—should available resources be employed or used in the production process?
2 *What* is to be produced? What collection of goods and services will best satisfy society's material wants?
3 *How* is that output to be produced? How should production be organized? What firms should do the producing and what productive techniques should they use?
4 *Who* is to receive the output? How should the output of the economy be shared by consumers?
5 Can the system *adapt* to change? Can it appropriately adjust to changes that occur in consumer wants, resource supplies, and technology?

Two points are relevant. First, we will defer the "how much" question for now. Macroeconomics deals in detail with the complex question of the level of resource employment.

Second, the Five Fundamental Questions are merely an elaboration of the choices underlying Chapter 2's production possibilities curve. These questions would be irrelevant were it not for the economizing problem.

THE MARKET SYSTEM AT WORK

Chapter 2's circular flow diagram (Figure 2-6) provides the setting for our discussion. In examining how the market system answers the Fundamental Questions, we must add demand and supply diagrams as developed in Chapter 3 to represent the various product and resource markets embodied in the circular flow model.

Determining What Is to Be Produced

Given the product and resource prices established by

competing buyers and sellers in both the product and resource markets, how would a purely capitalistic economy decide the types and quantities of goods to be produced? Remembering that businesses seek profits and want to avoid losses, we can generalize that those goods and services which can be produced at a profit will be produced and those whose production entails a loss will not. Two things determine profits or losses.

1   The total revenue a firm receives when it sells a product.

2   The total costs of producing the product.

Both total revenue and total costs are price-times-quantity figures. Total revenue is found by multiplying product price by the quantity of the product sold. Total costs are found by multiplying the price of each resource used by the amount employed and summing the costs of each.

Economic Costs and Profits

To say that those products which can be produced profitably will be produced and those which cannot will not is only an accurate generalization if the meaning of **economic costs** is clearly understood.

Let's again think of businesses as simply organizational charts, that is, businesses "on paper," distinct from the capital, raw materials, labor, and entrepreneurial ability which make them going concerns. To become actual producing firms, these "on paper" businesses must secure all four types of resources. *Economic costs are the payments which must be made to secure and retain the needed amounts of these resources.* The per unit size of these costs—that is, resource prices—will be determined by supply and demand in the resource market. Like land, labor, and capital, entrepreneurial ability is a scarce resource and has a price tag on it. Costs therefore must include not only wage and salary payments to labor and interest and rental payments for capital and land, but also payments to the entrepreneur for the functions he or she performs in organizing and combining the other resources in the production of a commodity. The cost payment for these contributions by the entrepreneur is called a **normal profit.**

A product will be produced only when total revenue is large enough to pay wage, interest, rental, *and* normal profit costs. Now if total revenues from the sale of a product exceed all production costs, including a normal profit, the remainder will go to the entrepreneur as the risk taker and organizing force. This return above all costs is called a **pure, or economic, profit.** It is *not* an economic cost, because it need not be realized for the business to acquire and retain entrepreneurial ability.

Profits and Expanding Industries

A few examples will explain how the market system determines what to produce. Suppose the most favorable relationship between total revenue and total cost in producing product X occurs when the firm's output is 15 units. Assume, too, that the least-cost combination of resources to use in producing 15 units of X is 2 units of labor, 3 units of land, 1 of capital, and 1 of entrepreneurial ability, selling at prices of $2, $1, $3, and $3, respectively. Finally, suppose that the 15 units of X which these resources produce can be sold for $1 per unit. Will firms produce X? Yes, because the firm will be able to pay wage, rent, interest, and normal profit costs of $13 $[= (2 \times \$2) + (3 \times \$1) + (1 \times \$3) + (1 \times \$3)]$. The difference between total revenue of $15 and total costs of $13 will be an economic profit of $2.

This economic profit is evidence that industry X is a prosperous one. It will become an **expanding industry** as new firms, attracted by these above-normal profits, are created or shift from less profitable industries.

But the entry of new firms will be self-limiting. As new firms enter industry X, the market supply of X will increase relative to the market demand. This will lower the market price of X (Figure 3-6c) and economic profits will in time be competed away. The market supply and demand condition prevailing when economic profits become zero will determine the total amount of X produced. At this point the industry will be at its "equilibrium size," at least until a further change in market demand or supply upsets that equilibrium.

Losses and Declining Industries

But what if the initial market situation for product X were less favorable? Suppose conditions in the product market were such that the firm could sell the 15 units of X at a price of just 75 cents per unit. Total revenue would be $11.25 (= 15 × 75 cents). After paying wage, rental, and interest costs of $10, the firm would obtain a below-normal profit of $1.25. In other words, *losses* of $1.75 (= $11.25 − $13) would be incurred.

Certainly, firms would not be attracted to this unprosperous **declining industry.** On the contrary, if these losses persisted, entrepreneurs would seek the normal profits or possibly even the economic profits offered by more prosperous industries. In time existing firms in industry X would go out of business or migrate to other industries where normal or better profits prevail. However, as this happens, the market supply of X will fall relative to the market demand. Product price will rise (Figure 3-6d) and losses will eventually disappear. Industry X will then stabilize itself in size. The supply and demand situation that prevails at that point where economic profits are zero will determine the total output of product X. Again, the industry for the moment will have reached its equilibrium size.

"Dollar Votes"   Consumer demand is crucial in determining the types and quantities of goods produced. Consumers, unrestrained by government and with money incomes from the sale of their resources, spend their dollars on those goods they are most willing and able to buy. These expenditures are **dollar votes** by which consumers register their wants through the demand side of the product market. If these votes for a product are great enough to provide a normal profit, businesses will produce it. An increase in consumer demand, that is, an increase in the dollar votes cast for a product, will mean economic profits for the industry producing it. These profits will signal expansion of that industry and increases in the output of the product.

Conversely, a decrease in consumer demand, that is, fewer votes cast for the product, will result in losses and, in time, contraction of the industry. As firms leave the industry, the output of the product declines. Indeed, the industry may cease to exist. The dollar votes of consumers play a key role in determining what products profit-seeking businesses will produce. The capitalistic system is characterized by **consumer sovereignty** because of the strategic role consumers have in determining the types and quantities of goods produced.

Illustration: In 1991, responding to doctors and nutritionists, McDonald's introduced its low-fat McLean burger. Good idea? Not really. Most consumers have found the new product "too dry" and "not tasty" so sales have been meager. While the McLean burger remains on McDonald's menu, it is there largely for public relations reasons and not as a source of significant profits. Hardee's, Burger King, and other fast-food franchises have also found that consumers have rejected their low-fat products.

Market Restraints on Freedom   From the viewpoint of businesses, we now see that firms are not really "free" to produce what they wish. The demand decisions of consumers, by making production of some products profitable and others not, restrict the choice of businesses in deciding what to produce. Businesses must match their production choices with consumer choices or face losses and eventual bankruptcy.

It's the same for resource suppliers. The demand for resources is a **derived demand**—derived, that is, from the demand for the goods and services which the resources help produce. There is a demand for autoworkers only because there is a demand for automobiles. Resource suppliers will not be "free" to allocate their resources to the production of goods which consumers do not value highly. Firms will not produce such products, because consumer demand is not sufficient to make it profitable.

In brief: Consumers register their preferences on the demand side of the product market; producers and resource suppliers respond appropriately in seeking to further their own self-interests. The market system communicates the wants of consumers to businesses and resource suppliers and elicits appropriate responses.

Organizing Production

How is production to be organized in a market economy? This Fundamental Question is composed of three subquestions:

1   How should resources be allocated among specific industries?
2   What specific firms should do the producing in each industry?
3   What combinations of resources—what technology—should each firm employ?

Production and Profits   The preceding section has answered the first subquestion. The market system steers resources to those industries whose products consumers want badly enough to make their production profitable. It simultaneously deprives unprofitable industries of scarce resources.

The second and third subquestions are closely intertwined. In a competitive market economy, the firms which do the producing are the ones willing and able to employ the economically most efficient technique

TABLE 4-1 Techniques for producing $15 worth of product X

Resource	Price per unit of resource	Units of resource		
		Technique no. 1	Technique no. 2	Technique no. 3
Labor	$2	4	2	1
Land	1	1	3	4
Capital	3	1	1	2
Entrepreneurial ability	3	1	1	1
Total cost of $15 worth of X		$15	$13	$15

of production. And the most efficient technique depends on:

1 Available technology, that is, the alternative combinations of resources of inputs which will produce the desired output.
2 The prices of needed resources.

Least-Cost Production The combination of resources which is most efficient economically depends not only on the physical or engineering data provided by available technology but also on the relative worth of the required resources as measured by their market prices. A technique which requires just a few physical inputs of resources to produce a given output may be highly *in*efficient economically *if* the required resources are valued very highly in the market. *Economic efficiency entails getting a given output of product with the smallest input of scarce resources, when both output and resource inputs are measured in dollars-and-cents.* That combination of resources which will produce, say, $15 worth of product X at the lowest possible money cost is the most efficient.

Suppose there are three possible techniques to produce the desired $15 worth of product X. The quantity of each resource required by each production technology and the prices of the required resources are shown in Table 4-1. By multiplying the quantities of each resource required by its price in each of the three techniques, the total cost of producing $15 worth of X by each technique can be determined.

Technique No. 2 is economically the most efficient because it is the least costly. It permits society to obtain $15 worth of output by using a smaller amount of resources—$13 worth—than the $15 worth required by the two other techniques.

But will firms actually use technique No. 2? The answer is "Yes." Firms will want to use the most efficient technique because it yields the greatest profit.

A change in *either* technology *or* resource prices may cause the firm to shift from the technology it is using. If the price of labor falls to 50 cents, technique No. 1 will now be superior to technique No. 2. Businesses will find they can lower their costs by shifting to a technology which uses more of that resource whose price has fallen. You should verify that a new technique involving 1 unit of labor, 4 of land, 1 of capital, and 1 of entrepreneurial ability will be preferable to all three techniques listed in Table 4-1, assuming the resource prices given there. (*Key Question 8*)

Distributing Total Output

The market system enters the picture in two ways in solving the problem of distributing total output. Generally, any given product will be distributed to consumers on the basis of their ability and willingness to pay the existing market price for it. If the price of X is $1 per unit, those buyers who are able and willing to pay that price will get a unit of this product; those who are not, will not. This is the rationing function of equilibrium prices.

The size of consumers' money incomes determines their abilities to pay the equilibrium price for X and other products. And money income depends on the quantities of the various property and human resources which the income receiver supplies and their prices in the resource market. Thus, resource prices play a key role in determining the size of each household's income claim against the total output of society. Within the limits of a consumer's money income, his or her willingness to pay the equilibrium price for

X determines whether or not some of this product is distributed to that person. And this willingness to buy X will depend on one's preference for X compared to available close substitutes for X and their relative prices. Thus, product prices play a key role in determining spending patterns of consumers.

There is nothing particularly ethical about the market system as a mechanism for distributing output. Households which accumulate large amounts of property resources by inheritance, through hard work and frugality, through business acumen, or by crook will receive large incomes and thus command large shares of the economy's total output. Others, offering unskilled and relatively unproductive labor resources which elicit low wages, will receive meager money incomes and small portions of total output.

Accommodating Change

Industrial societies are dynamic: Consumer preferences, technology, and resource supplies all change. This means that the particular allocation of resources which is *now* the most efficient for a *given* pattern of consumer tastes, for a *given* range of technological alternatives, and for *given* supplies of resources will become obsolete and inefficient as consumer preferences change, new techniques of production are discovered, and resource supplies change over time. Can the market economy adjust to these changes so that resources are still used efficiently?

Guiding Function of Prices   Suppose consumer tastes change. Specifically, assume that, because of greater health consciousness, consumers decide they want more exercise bikes and fewer cigarettes than the economy currently provides. This change in consumers' tastes will be communicated to producers through an increase in demand for bikes and a decline in demand for cigarettes. Bike prices will rise and cigarette prices will fall. Now, assuming firms in both industries were enjoying precisely normal profits before these changes in consumer demand, higher exercise bike prices mean economic profits for the bike industry, and lower cigarette prices mean losses for the cigarette industry. Self-interest induces new competitors to enter the prosperous bike industry. Losses will in time force firms to leave the depressed cigarette industry.

These adjustments in the business sector are appropriate to changes in consumer tastes. Society—

meaning consumers—wants more exercise bikes and fewer cigarettes, and that is precisely what it is getting as the bike industry expands and the cigarette industry contracts. These adjustments portray the concept of consumer sovereignty at work.

This analysis assumes resource suppliers are agreeable to these adjustments. Will the market system prompt resource suppliers to reallocate their human and property resources from the cigarette to the bike industry, permitting the output of bikes to expand at the expense of cigarette production? The answer is "Yes."

The economic profits which initially follow the increase in demand for bikes will not only induce that industry to expand but will also give it the revenue needed to obtain the resources essential to its growth. Higher bike prices will permit firms in that industry to pay higher prices for resources, increasing resource demand and drawing resources from less urgent alternative employments.

The reverse occurs in the adversely affected cigarette industry. The losses following the decline in consumer demand will cause a decline in the demand for resources in that industry. Workers and other resources released from the shrinking cigarette industry can now find employment in the expanding bike industry. Furthermore, the increased demand for resources in the bike industry will mean higher resource prices in that industry than those being paid in the cigarette industry, where declines in resource demand have lowered resource prices. The resulting differential in resource prices will provide the incentive for resource owners to further their self-interests by reallocating their resources from the cigarette to the bike industry. And this is the precise shift needed to permit the bike industry to expand and the cigarette industry to contract.

The ability of the market system to communicate changes in such basic data as consumer tastes and to elicit appropriate responses from businesses and resource suppliers is called the **directing** or **guiding function of prices.** By affecting product prices and profits, changes in consumer tastes direct the expansion of some industries and the contraction of others. These adjustments carry through to the resource market as expanding industries demand more resources and contracting industries demand fewer. The resulting changes in resource prices guide resources from the contracting to the expanding industries. Without a market system, some administrative agency, presumably a governmental planning board, would have to direct businesses and resources into specific lines of production.

Similar analysis would indicate that the market system would adjust to other fundamental changes— for example, to changes in technology and in the relative supplies of various resources.

Initiating Progress Adjusting to changes is one thing; initiating changes, particularly desirable changes, is something else. Is the competitive market system congenial to technological improvements and capital accumulation—the interrelated changes which lead to greater productivity and a higher level of material well-being for society?

Technological Advance The competitive market system contains the incentive for technological advance. A firm developing new cost-cutting techniques has a temporary advantage over its rivals. Lower production costs mean economic profits for the innovating firm. By passing part of its cost reduction to the consumer through a lower product price, the firm can increase sales and obtain economic profits at the expense of rival firms. Furthermore, the competitive market system provides an environment favorable to the rapid spread of a technological advance throughout the industry. Rivals *must* follow the lead of the most progressive firm or suffer immediate losses and eventual bankruptcy.

The lower product price which technological advance permits will cause the innovating industry to expand. This expansion may be the result of existing firms' expanding their rates of output or of new firms entering the industry lured by the economic profits initially created by technological advance. This expansion, that is, the diversion of resources from less progressive to more progressive industries, is as it should be. Sustained efficiency in the use of scarce resources demands that resources be continually reallocated from industries whose productive techniques are relatively less efficient to those whose techniques are relatively more efficient.

Capital Accumulation But technological advance typically requires more capital goods. The entrepreneur as an innovator can command through the market system the resources necessary to produce the machinery and equipment upon which technological advance depends.

If society registers dollar votes for capital goods, the product market and the resource market will adjust to these votes by producing capital goods. The market system acknowledges dollar voting for both consumer and capital goods.

But who will register votes for capital goods? First, the entrepreneur as a receiver of profit income can be expected to apportion part of that income to accumulation of capital goods. By doing so, an even greater profit income can be achieved in the future if innovation is successful. Furthermore, by paying interest, entrepreneurs can borrow portions of the incomes of households and use these borrowed funds in casting dollar votes for the production of more capital goods.

Competition and Control

In pure capitalism the market system is the organizing mechanism and competition is the mechanism of control. Supply and demand communicate the wants of consumers (society) to businesses and through businesses to resource suppliers. It is competition, however, which forces businesses and resource suppliers to make appropriate responses.

To illustrate: We have seen that an increase in consumer demand for some product will raise that good's price and generate economic profits. These profits signal producers that society wants more of the product. It is competition—new firms entering the industry—that simultaneously brings an expansion of output and a lowering of price back to a level just consistent with production costs. However, if the industry was dominated by, say, one huge firm (a monopolist) which was able to prohibit entry of potential competitors, that firm could continue to enjoy economic profits.

But competition does more than guarantee responses appropriate to the wishes of society. It also forces firms to adopt the most efficient productive techniques. In a competitive market, a firm that fails to use the least costly production technique will eventually be eliminated by more efficient firms. And we have seen that competition provides an environment conducive to technological advance.

The "Invisible Hand"

The operation and adjustments of a competitive market system create a curious and important identity—

the identity of private and social interests. Firms and resource suppliers, seeking to further their own self-interest and operating within the framework of a highly competitive market system, will simultaneously, as though guided by an **"invisible hand,"**[2] promote the public or social interest. For example, we have seen that given a competitive environment, business firms use the least costly combination of resources in producing a given output because it is in their private self-interest to do so. To act otherwise would be to forgo profits or even to risk bankruptcy. But, at the same time, it is clearly also in the social interest to use scarce resources in the least costly, that is, most efficient, manner. Not to do so would be to produce a given output at a greater cost or sacrifice of alternative goods than is necessary.

In our more-bikes–fewer-cigarettes illustration, it is self-interest, awakened and guided by the competitive market system, which induces responses appropriate to the change in society's wants. Businesses seeking to make higher profits and to avoid losses, on the one hand, and resource suppliers pursuing greater monetary rewards, on the other, negotiate the changes in the allocation of resources and therefore the composition of output society demands. The force of competition controls or guides the self-interest motive in such a way that it automatically, and quite unintentionally, furthers the best interests of society. The "invisible hand" tells us that when firms maximize their profits, society's domestic output is also maximized.

The Case for the Market System

The virtues of the market system are implicit in our discussion of its operation. Three merit emphasis.

Efficiency The basic economic argument for the market system is that it promotes the efficient use of resources. The competitive market system guides re-sources into production of those goods and services most wanted by society. It forces use of the most efficient techniques in organizing resources for production, and leads to the development and adoption of new and more efficient production techniques.

Incentives The market system effectively harnesses incentives. Greater work effort means higher money incomes which can be translated into a higher standard of living. Similarly, the assuming of risks by entrepreneurs can result in substantial profit incomes. Successful innovations may also generate economic rewards.

Freedom The major noneconomic argument for the market system is its great emphasis on personal freedom. In contrast to central planning, the market system can coordinate economic activity without coercion. The market system permits—indeed, it thrives on—freedom of enterprise and choice. Entrepreneurs and workers are not herded from industry to industry by government directives to meet production targets established by some governmental agency. On the contrary, they are free to further their own self-interests, subject to the rewards and penalties imposed by the market system itself.

QUICK REVIEW 4-3

■ The output mix of the competitive market system is determined by profits. Profits cause industries to expand; losses cause them to contract.

■ Competition forces firms to use the least costly (most efficient) production methods.

■ The distribution of output in a market economy is determined by consumer incomes and product prices.

■ Competitive markets reallocate resources in response to changes in consumer tastes, technological progress, and changes in resource supplies.

CHAPTER SUMMARY

1 The capitalistic system is characterized by private ownership of resources and the freedom of individuals to engage in economic activities of their choice to advance their material well-being. Self-interest is the driving force of such an economy, and competition functions as a regulatory or control mechanism.

2 Capitalistic production is not organized in terms of a government plan, but rather features the market system as a means of organizing and making effective the many millions of individual decisions which determine what is pro-

[2]Adam Smith, *The Wealth of Nations* (New York: Modern Library, Inc., originally published in 1776), p. 423.

LAST WORD

BACK TO BARTER

Despite the advantages of using money, there is evidence that bartering is a "growth industry."

Because money facilitates exchange, it may seem odd that a considerable and growing volume of both domestic and international trade occurs through barter.

Suppose you own a small firm selling equipment to television stations. The economy is in recession; business is slow; your cash flow is down; and your inventories are much higher than desired. What do you do? You approach a local TV station which needs new equipment. But it, too, is feeling the effects of recession. Its advertising revenues are down and it also faces a cash-flow crunch. So a deal is struck. You provide $50,000 worth of equipment in exchange for $50,000 worth of "free" advertising. Advantage to seller: You move unwanted inventory, eliminating warehousing and insurance costs. You also receive valuable advertising time. The TV station gets needed equipment and pays for it with advertising time slots which would otherwise be unfilled. Both parties gain and no money changes hands.

Internationally, a firm might encounter an obstacle in selling its goods to a nation which does not have "hard" (exchangeable) currencies such as dollars, marks, or yen. Barter circumvents this problem. Example: Arcon Manufacturing of North Carolina sold its grain silos to a Nicaraguan firm, knowing that the buyer had no hard currency for making payment. Arcon took payment in sesame seeds, which it delivered to a Middle Eastern food manufacturer which was able to pay Arcon in hard currency. PepsiCo swaps cola syrup for Russian vodka. Coca-Cola has traded its syrup for Egyptian oranges, Turkish tomato paste, Polish beer, and Hungarian soft-drink bottles. Recently, large American oil companies such as Chevron and Amoco have negotiated "joint ventures" with the former Soviet Union based on barter. The Russians get updated capital equipment, new technologies, and increased oil production; American oil companies take their earnings in oil rather than currency.

Estimates differ on the volume of barter transactions within the United States. One estimate is that 175,000 businesses engaged in barter transactions of almost $1 billion in 1990, a fivefold increase in dollar volume since 1980. Other estimates put the dollar value of barter transactions as high as $6 billion per year.

The increasing popularity of barter has partly resulted from the development of "exchange companies" which coordinate barter transactions. The exchange company provides trade credits to members who make goods or services available; these accounts are debited when members make purchases. For its services the exchange company charges a membership fee and receives a percentage of the value of each transaction. At present there are over 400 barter exchanges in America.

Barter does involve time-consuming negotiation and it could undermine and distort the flow of open multilateral trade (Figure 4-1). Yet, as our illustrations make clear, barter is sometimes a means of bringing about mutually advantageous transactions which otherwise would not have occurred.

---

duced, the methods of production, and the sharing of output. The capitalist ideology envisions government playing a minor and relatively passive economic role.

3 Specialization and an advanced technology based on the extensive use of capital goods are common to all modern economies.

4 Functioning as a medium of exchange, money circumvents problems of bartering and thereby permits greater specialization both domestically and internationally.

5 Every economy faces Five Fundamental Questions: a At what level should available resources be employed? b What goods and services are to be produced?　c How is that output to be produced?　d To whom should the out-

put be distributed? **e** Can the system adapt to changes in consumer tastes, resource supplies, and technology?

6 In a market economy those products whose production and sale yield total revenue sufficient to cover all costs, including a normal profit, will be produced. Those whose production will not yield a normal profit will not be produced.

7 Economic profits designate an industry as prosperous and signal its expansion. Losses mean an industry is unprosperous and result in contraction of that industry.

8 Consumer sovereignty means that both businesses and resource suppliers channel their efforts in accordance with the wants of consumers.

9 Competition forces firms to use the least costly, and therefore the most economically efficient, productive techniques.

10 The prices commanded by the quantities and types of resources supplied by each household will determine the number of dollar claims against the economy's output which each household receives. Within the limits of each household's money income, consumer preferences and the relative prices of products determine the distribution of total output.

11 The competitive market system can communicate changes in consumer tastes to resource suppliers and entrepreneurs, thereby prompting appropriate adjustments in the allocation of the economy's resources. The competitive market system also provides an environment conducive to technological advance and capital accumulation.

12 Competition, the primary mechanism of control in the market economy, will foster an identity of private and social interests; as though directed by an "invisible hand," competition harnesses the self-interest motives of businesses and resource suppliers to simultaneously further the social interest in using scarce resources efficiently.

TERMS AND CONCEPTS

private property	specialization and	economic costs	dollar votes
freedom of enterprise	division of labor	normal versus	consumer sovereignty
freedom of choice	medium of exchange	economic profits	derived demand
self-interest	bartering	expanding industry	directing (guiding)
competition	**Five Fundamental**	versus declining	function of prices
market	**Questions**	industry	"invisible hand"
roundabout production			

QUESTIONS AND STUDY SUGGESTIONS

1 "Capitalism may be characterized as an automatic self-regulating system motivated by the self-interest of individuals and regulated by competition."[3] Explain and evaluate.

2 *Key Question* *What advantages result from "roundabout" production? What problem is involved in increasing a full-employment economy's stock of capital goods? Illustrate this problem in terms of the production possibilities curve. Does an economy with unemployed resources face the same problem?*

3 What are the advantages of specialization in the use of human and material resources? Explain: "Exchange is the necessary consequence of specialization."

4 What problems does barter entail? Indicate the economic significance of money as a medium of exchange. "Money is the only commodity that is good for nothing but to be gotten rid of. It will not feed you, clothe you, shelter you, or amuse you unless you spend or invest it. It imparts value only in parting."[4] Explain this statement.

5 Describe in detail how the market system answers the Fundamental Questions. Why must economic choices be made?

6 Evaluate and explain the following statements:
  a "The capitalistic system is a profit and loss economy."
  b "Competition is the indispensable disciplinarian of the market economy."
  c "Production methods which are inferior in the engineering sense may be the most efficient methods in the economic sense."

---

[3]Howard R. Bowen, *Toward Social Economy* (New York: Holt, Rinehart and Winston, Inc., 1948), p. 249.

[4]Federal Reserve Bank of Philadelphia, "Creeping Inflation," *Business Review,* August 1957, p. 3.

7   Explain fully the meaning and implications of the following quotation.

> The beautiful consequence of the market is that it is its own guardian. If output prices or certain kinds of remuneration stray away from their socially ordained levels, forces are set into motion to bring them back to the fold. It is a curious paradox which thus ensues: the market, which is the acme of individual economic freedom, is the strictest taskmaster of all. One may appeal the ruling of a planning board or win the dispensation of a minister; but there is no appeal, no dispensation, from the anonymous pressures of the market mechanism. Economic freedom is thus more illusory than at first appears. One can do as one pleases in the market. But if one pleases to do what the market disapproves, the price of individual freedom is economic ruination.[5]

8   *Key Question   Assume that a business firm finds that its profits will be at maximum when it produces $40 worth of product A. Suppose also that each of the three techniques shown in the following table will produce the desired output.*

Resource	Price per unit of resource	Technique no. 1	Technique no. 2	Technique no. 3
Labor	$3	5	2	3
Land	4	2	4	2
Capital	2	2	4	5
Entrepreneurial ability	2	4	2	4

a   *Given the resource prices shown, which technique will the firm choose? Why? Will production entail profits or losses? Will the industry expand or contract? When is a new equilibrium output achieved?*

b   *Assume now that a new technique, technique No. 4, is developed. It entails the use of 2 units of labor, 2 of land, 6 of capital, and 3 of entrepreneurial ability. Given the resource prices in the table, will the firm adopt the new technique? Explain your answer.*

c   *Suppose now that an increase in labor supply causes the price of labor to fall to $1.50 per unit, all other resource prices being unchanged. Which technique will the producer now choose? Explain.*

d   *"The market system causes the economy to conserve most in the use of those resources which are particularly scarce in supply. Resources which are scarcest relative to the demand for them have the highest prices. As a result, producers use these resources as sparingly as is possible." Evaluate this statement. Does your answer to question 8c bear out this contention? Explain.*

9   (Last Word) What considerations have increased the popularity of barter in recent years?

---

[5]Robert L. Heilbroner, *The Worldly Philosophers,* 3d ed. (New York: Simon & Schuster, Inc., 1967), p. 42.

5

THE MIXED ECONOMY: PRIVATE AND PUBLIC SECTORS

This chapter will put meat on the bear-bones model of capitalism developed thus far. Here we will provide some descriptive detail about the private sector (households and businesses) and introduce and analyze the public sector (government) of the economy. Because government is new to our discussion, it will receive most of our attention. Our goal is to understand households, businesses, and governmental units as the primary *decision makers* of our economy.

HOUSEHOLDS AS INCOME RECEIVERS

The household sector is currently composed of some 96 million households. They are the ultimate suppliers of all economic resources and simultaneously the major spenders in the economy. We will consider households first as income receivers and second as spenders.

There are two related approaches to studying income distribution.

1 The **functional distribution** of income indicates how society's money income is divided among wages, rents, interest, and profits. Here total income is distributed according to the function performed by the income receiver. Wages are paid to labor, rents and interest compensate property resources, and profits flow to the owners of corporations and unincorporated businesses.

2 The **personal distribution** of income shows the way total money income of society is apportioned among individual households.

The Functional Distribution of Income

The functional distribution of the nation's total earned income for 1994 is shown in Figure 5-1. The largest source of income for households is the wages and salaries paid to workers by the businesses and governmental units hiring them. In our capitalist system the bulk of total income goes to labor, not to "capital." Proprietors' income—the incomes of doctors, lawyers, small business owners, farmers, and other unincorporated enterprises—is in fact a combination of wage, profit, rent, and interest incomes. The other three sources of earnings are self-defining. Some households own corporate stock and receive dividend income on their holdings. Many households also own bonds and savings accounts which yield interest income. Rental income results from households pro-

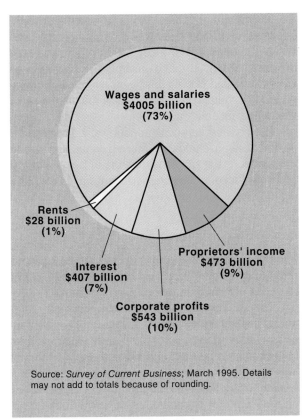

FIGURE 5-1 The functional distribution of income, 1994
Almost three-fourths of national income is received as wages and salaries. Capitalist income—corporate profits, interest, and rents—only account for less than one-fifth of total income.

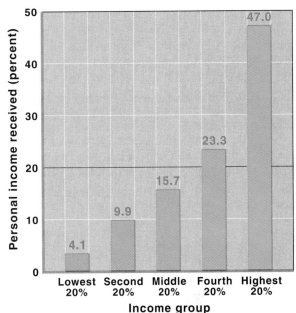

FIGURE 5-2 The distribution of income among families, 1993
Personal income is quite unequally distributed in the United States. An equal distribution would mean that all vertical bars would be equal to the horizontal line drawn at 20 percent; each 20 percent of the families would get 20 percent of total personal income. In fact, the richest fifth of the families gets over eleven times as much income as does the poorest fifth.

Personal Distribution of Income

Figure 5-2 is an overall view of how total income is distributed among households. Here we divide families into five numerically equal groups or *quintiles* and show the percentage of total income received by each group. In 1993 the poorest 20 percent of all families received about 4 percent of total personal income in contrast to the 20 percent they would have received if income were equally distributed. In comparison the richest 20 percent of all families received over 47 percent of personal income. The richest fifth of the population received over eleven times as much income as the poorest fifth. Most economists agree

there is considerable inequality in the distribution of income. *(Key Question 2)*

HOUSEHOLDS AS SPENDERS

How do households dispose of their income? Part flows to government as personal taxes, and the rest is divided between personal consumption expenditures and personal saving. In 1994, households disposed of their total personal income as shown in Figure 5-3.[1]

Personal Taxes

Personal taxes, of which the Federal personal income tax is the major component, have risen in both absolute and relative terms since World War II. In 1941,

viding buildings, land, and other natural resources to businesses.

---

[1]The income concepts used in Figures 5-1 and 5-3 are different, accounting for the quantitative discrepancy between "total income" in the two figures.

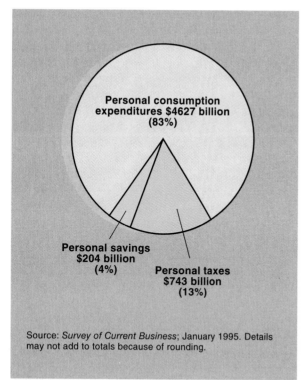

Source: *Survey of Current Business*; January 1995. Details may not add to totals because of rounding.

FIGURE 5-3   The disposition of household income, 1994 Household income is apportioned between taxes, saving, and consumption, with consumption being the dominant use of income.

households paid $3.3 billion, or 3 percent of their $95.3 billion total income, in personal taxes, compared to $743 billion, or 13 percent of $5574 billion total income in 1994.

Personal Saving

Economists define saving as "that part of after-tax income which is *not* consumed"; hence, households have just two choices with their incomes after taxes —to consume or to save. Saving is that portion of current (this year's) income not paid in taxes nor used in the purchase of consumer goods, but which flows into bank accounts, insurance policies, bonds and stocks, and other financial assets.

Reasons for saving center around *security* and *speculation*. Households save to provide a nest egg for unforeseen contingencies—sickness, accident, unemployment—for retirement from the work force, to finance the education of children, or simply for financial security. Also, people save for speculation. You might channel part of your income to purchase securities, speculating they will increase in value.

The desire or willingness to save is not enough. You must be *able* to save, which depends on the size of your income. If your income is very low, you may *dissave;* that is, you may consume in excess of your after-tax income. You do this by borrowing and by digging into savings you may have accumulated in years when your income was higher.

Both saving and consumption vary directly with income; as households get more income, they divide it between saving and consumption. In fact, the top 10 percent of income receivers account for most of the personal saving in our society.

Personal Consumption Expenditures

Figure 5-3 shows that over four-fifths of total income flows from income receivers back into the business sector as personal consumption expenditures.

The size and composition of the economy's total output depend on the size and composition of the flow of consumer spending. So we must examine how households divide their expenditures among the various goods and services competing for their dollars. Consumer spending is classified as (1) expenditures on durables, (2) expenditures on nondurables, and (3) expenditures on services.

If a product generally has an expected life of three years or more, it is called a **durable good;** if its life is less than three years, it is labeled **nondurable.** Automobiles, video recorders, washing machines, personal computers, and most furniture are durables. Most food and clothing items are nondurables. **Services** refer to the work done by lawyers, barbers, doctors, mechanics, and others for consumers. Note in Table 5-1 that *ours is a service-oriented economy in that over one-half of consumer outlays are for services.*

QUICK REVIEW 5-1

■ The functional distribution of income indicates how income is divided among wages, rents, interest, and profits; the personal distribution of income shows how income is apportioned among households.

■ Wages and salaries are the major component of the functional distribution of income. The personal distribution reveals considerable inequality

■ Over 80 percent of household income is consumed; the rest is saved or paid in taxes.

■ Over half of consumer spending is for services.

TABLE 5-1 The composition of personal consumption expenditures, 1994*

Types of consumption	Amount (billions of dollars)		Percent of total
Durable goods		$ 591	13
Motor vehicles and parts	$251		5
Furniture and household equipment	229		5
All others	111		2
Nondurable goods		1394	30
Food	679		15
Clothing and shoes	247		5
Gasoline and oil	107		2
Fuel oil and coal	14		0
All others	347		8
Services		2642	57
Housing	660		14
Household operations	264		6
Medical care	727		16
Transportation	180		4
Personal services recreation, and others	811		18
Personal consumption expenditures		$4627	100

*Excludes interest paid to businesses.
Source: Survey of Current Business, January 1995. Details may not add to totals because of rounding.

THE BUSINESS POPULATION

Businesses constitute the second major aggregate of the private sector. To avoid confusion, we first explain some terms. In particular, we distinguish among a plant, a firm, and an industry.

1 A **plant** is a physical establishment—a factory, farm, mine, retail or wholesale store, or warehouse which performs one or more functions in the fabrication and distribution of goods and services.

2 A business **firm** is the business organization which owns and operates these plants. Most firms operate only one plant, but many own and operate a number of plants. Multiplant firms may be "horizontal," "vertical," or "conglomerate" combinations. For example, every large steel firm—USX Corporation (United States Steel), Bethlehem Steel, Republic Steel, and the others—are **vertical combinations** of plants; that is, each company owns plants at various stages of the production process. Each steelmaker owns ore and coal mines, limestone quarries, coke

ovens, blast furnaces, rolling mills, forge shops, foundries, and, in some cases, fabricating shops.

The large chain stores in the retail field—A&P, Kroger, Safeway, J.C. Penney—are **horizontal combinations** in that each plant is at the same stage of production.

Other firms are **conglomerates;** they comprise plants which operate across many different markets and industries. For example, International Telephone and Telegraph, apart from operations implied by its name, is involved through affiliated plants on a large-scale basis in such diverse fields as hotels, baking products, educational materials, and insurance.

3 An **industry** is a group of firms producing the same, or similar, products. Though an apparently uncomplicated concept, industries are usually difficult to identify in practice. For example, how do we identify the automobile industry? The simplest answer is, "All firms producing automobiles." But automobiles are heterogeneous products. While Cadillacs and Buicks are similar products, and Buicks and Fords are similar, and Fords and Geos are similar, it is clear that Geos and Cadillacs are very dissimilar. At least most buyers think so. And what about trucks? Certainly, small pickup trucks are similar in some respects to vans and station wagons. Is it better to speak of the "motor vehicle industry" rather than of the "automobile industry"?

Delineating an industry becomes even more complex because most enterprises are multiproduct firms. American automobile manufacturers also make such diverse products as diesel locomotives, buses, refrigerators, guided missiles, and air conditioners. For these reasons, industry classifications are usually somewhat arbitrary.

LEGAL FORMS OF BUSINESSES

The business population is extremely diverse, ranging from giant corporations like General Motors with 1993 sales of $134 billion and 711,000 employees to neighborhood speciality shops and "mom and pop" groceries with one or two employees and sales of only $100 or $150 per day. This diversity makes it necessary to classify business firms by some criterion such as legal structure, industry or product, or size. Figure 5-4a shows how the business population is distributed among the three major legal forms: (1) the sole proprietorship, (2) the partnership, and (3) the corporation.

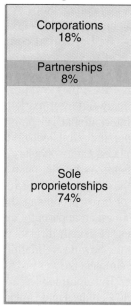

Percentage of firms

Corporations 18%

Partnerships 8%

Sole proprietorships 74%

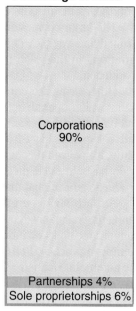

Percentage of sales

Corporations 90%

Partnerships 4%

Sole proprietorships 6%

The business population by form of legal organization

Form	Number of firms
Sole proprietorships*	14,783,000
Partnerships	1,554,000
Corporations	3,717,000
Total	20,054,000

*Excludes farmers.

FIGURE 5-4   The business population and shares of domestic output
Although sole proprietorships dominate the business population numerically, corporations account for 90 percent of total sales.

Sole Proprietorship

A **sole proprietorship** is an individual in business for himself or herself. The proprietor owns or obtains the materials and equipment needed by the business and personally supervises its operation.

Advantages   This simple type of business organization has certain advantages:
1   A sole proprietorship is easy to organize—there is virtually no legal red tape or expense.
2   The proprietor is his or her own boss and has substantial freedom of action. Since the proprietor's profit income depends on the enterprise's success, there is a strong and immediate incentive to manage the business efficiently.

Disadvantages   But the disadvantages of this form of business organization are great.
1   With rare exceptions, the financial resources of a sole proprietorship are insufficient to permit the firm to grow into a large enterprise. Finances are usually limited to what the proprietor has in the bank and to what he or she can borrow. Since proprietorships often fail, commercial banks are not eager to extend them credit.
2   Being in complete control of an enterprise forces the proprietor to carry out all management functions. A proprietor must make decisions concerning buying, selling, and the hiring and training of personnel, not

to mention the technical aspects involved in producing, advertising, and distributing the product. In short, the potential benefits of specialization in business management are usually inaccessible to the typical small-scale proprietorship.
3   Most important, the proprietor is subject to *unlimited liability*. Individuals in business for themselves risk not only the assets of the firm but also their personal assets. If assets of an unsuccessful proprietorship are insufficient to satisfy the claims of creditors, claims can be filed by creditors against the proprietor's personal property.

Partnership

The **partnership** form of business organization is a natural outgrowth of the sole proprietorship. Partnerships were developed to overcome some of the shortcomings of proprietorships. In a partnership, two or more individuals agree to own and operate a business. Usually they pool their financial resources and business skills. Similarly, they share the risks and the profits or losses.

Advantages   What are the advantages of a partnership?
1   Like the sole proprietorship, it is easy to organize. Although a written agreement is almost invariably involved, legal red tape is not great.
2   Greater specialization in management is possible because there are more participants.
3   Because there are several participants, the odds are that the financial resources of a partnership should be greater than those of a sole proprietorship. Partners can pool their money capital and are usually

somewhat better risks in the eyes of lending institutions.

Disadvantages   The partnership may not overcome the shortcomings of the proprietorship as expected, and may raise some potential problems the sole proprietorship does not have.

1   Whenever several people participate in management, this division of authority can lead to inconsistent policies or to inaction when action is required. Worse yet, partners may disagree on basic policy.

2   The finances of partnerships are still limited, although generally superior to those of a sole proprietorship. But the financial resources of three or four partners may still not be enough for the growth of a successful enterprise.

3   The continuity of a partnership is precarious. The withdrawal or death of a partner generally means dissolution and complete reorganization of the firm, disrupting its operations.

4   Unlimited liability plagues a partnership, just as it does a proprietorship. In fact, each partner is liable for all business debts incurred, not only as a result of each partner's own management decisions, but also as a consequence of the actions of any other partner. A wealthy partner risks money on the prudence of less affluent partners.

Corporation

Corporations are legal entities, distinct and separate from the individuals who own them. These governmentally designated "legal persons" can acquire resources, own assets, produce and sell products, incur debts, extend credit, sue and be sued, and carry on all those functions any other type of enterprise performs.

Advantages   The advantages of the corporate form of business enterprise have catapulted it into a dominant position in modern American capitalism. Although corporations are relatively small in number, they are frequently large in size and scale of operations. As Figure 5-4 indicates, less than 20 percent of all businesses are corporations, but they account for roughly 90 percent of all business sales.

1   The corporation is by far the most effective form of business organization for raising money capital. As this chapter's Last Word reveals, the corporation features unique methods of finance—the selling of stocks and bonds—which allow the firm to tap the savings of untold thousands of households. Through the securities market, corporations can pool the financial resources of extremely large numbers of people.

Financing by the sale of securities also has advantages from the viewpoint of the purchasers of these securities. First, households can now participate in enterprise and share the expected monetary reward without assuming an active part in management. In addition, an individual can spread any risks by buying the securities of several corporations. Finally, it is usually easy for the holder of corporate securities to sell those holdings. Organized stock exchanges make it easy to transfer securities among buyers and sellers, which increases the willingness of savers to buy corporate securities.

Corporations have easier access to bank credit than other types of business organizations. Corporations are better risks and are more likely to provide banks with profitable accounts.

2   Corporations have the distinct advantage of **limited liability.** The owners (stockholders) of a corporation risk *only* what they paid for their stock. Their personal assets are not at stake if the corporation suffers bankruptcy. Creditors can sue the corporation as a legal person, but cannot sue the owners of the corporation as individuals. Limited liability clearly eases the corporation's task in acquiring money capital.

3   Because of their advantage in attracting money capital, successful corporations find it easier to expand the size and scope of their operations and to realize the benefits of expansion. They can take advantage of mass-production technologies and greater specialization in the use of human resources. While the manager of a sole proprietorship may be forced to share her time among production, accounting, and marketing functions, a corporation can hire specialized personnel in these areas and achieve greater efficiency.

4   As a legal entity, the corporation has a life independent of its owners and its officers. Proprietorships are subject to sudden and unpredictable demise, but, legally at least, corporations are immortal. The transfer of corporate ownership through the sale of stock will not disrupt the continuity of the corporation. Corporations have a permanence, lacking in other forms of business organization, which is conducive to long-range planning and growth.

Disadvantages   The corporation's advantages are of tremendous significance and typically override any accompanying disadvantages. Yet there are drawbacks of the corporate form.

1   There are some red tape and legal expense in obtaining a corporate charter.

2   From the social point of view, the corporate form of enterprise lends itself to certain abuses. Because the corporation is a legal entity, unscrupulous business owners sometimes can avoid personal responsibility for questionable business activities by adopting the corporate form of enterprise.

3   A further disadvantage of corporations is the **double taxation** of corporate income. That part of corporate income paid out as dividends to stockholders is taxed twice—once as part of corporate profits and again as part of stockholders' personal incomes.

4   In sole proprietorships and partnerships, the owners of the real and financial assets of the firm also directly manage or control those assets. In large corporations where ownership is widely diffused over tens or hundreds of thousands of stockholders, there is **separation of ownership and control.**

The roots of this cleavage lie in the lethargy of the typical stockholder. Most stockholders do not vote, or, if they do, merely delegate their votes to the corporation's present officers. Not voting, or the automatic signing over of proxy votes to current corporate officials, makes those officials self-perpetuating.

The separation of ownership and control is of no consequence so long as the actions of the control (management) group and the wishes of the ownership (stockholder) group are in accord. But the interests of the two groups are not always identical. Management, seeking the power and prestige which accompany control over a *large* enterprise, may favor unprofitable expansion of the firm's operations. Or a conflict of interest can develop over dividend policies. What portion of corporate earnings after taxes should be paid out as dividends, and what amount should be retained by the firm as undistributed profits? And corporation officials may vote themselves large salaries, pensions, bonuses, and so forth, out of corporate earnings which might otherwise be used for increased dividend payments.

Postscript: A number of states have passed legislation authorizing **limited-liability companies** (LLCs) which seeks to make the corporate advantage of limited liability available to a partnership. The LLC is like an ordinary partnership for tax purposes, but resembles a corporation on liability issues. Like a partnership, a LLC distributes income directly to owners and investors which is treated as personal income for tax purposes. But like a corporation, a LLC shields the personal assets of participants from liability claims.

LLCs have a limited life, typically 30 or 40 years. *(Key Question 4)*

Incorporate or Not?

The need for money capital is critical to whether or not a firm incorporates. The money capital required to establish and operate a barbershop, a shoeshine stand, or a small gift shop is modest, making incorporation unnecessary. In contrast, modern technology and a much larger dollar volume of business make incorporation imperative in many lines of production. In most branches of manufacturing—automobiles, steel, fabricated metal products, electrical equipment, and household appliances—substantial amounts of money are needed for investment in fixed assets and working capital. Here, there is no choice but to incorporate.

Big Business

A glance back at Figure 5-4 reminds us that, although relatively small in number, corporations are the major source of production in our economy. Many of our major industries are dominated by corporate giants which enjoy assets and annual sales revenues of billions of dollars, employ hundreds of thousands of workers, have a hundred thousand or more stockholders, and earn annual profits after taxes running into hundreds of millions of dollars. We have already cited the vital statistics of General Motors, America's largest corporation, for 1993: sales, about $134 *billion;* assets, about $188 *billion;* employees, about 711,000. Remarkably, there are only 20 or so nations in the world whose annual domestic outputs are more than GM's annual sales!

In 1993 some 20 industrial corporations had annual sales over $20 billion; 47 industrial firms realized sales over $10 billion. Realizing that corporations constitute less than 20 percent of the business population, yet produce 90 percent of total business output, suggests the dominant role of large corporations in our economy.

But the influence of large corporations varies significantly from industry to industry. Big business dominates manufacturing and is pronounced in the transportation, communications, power utilities, and banking and financial industries. At the other extreme are some 2 million farmers whose total sales in 1993 were less than the economy's two largest industrial corporations! In between are a variety of retail and service industries characterized by relatively small firms.

Nevertheless, large corporations dominate the American business landscape and grounds exist for labeling the United States a "big business" economy.

ECONOMIC FUNCTIONS OF GOVERNMENT

All economies in the real world are "mixed"; government and the market system share the responsibility of responding to the Five Fundamental Questions. Our economy is predominantly a market economy, yet the economic activities of government are of great significance. Here we want to (1) state and illustrate the major economic functions of the public sector; (2) add government to Chapter 2's circular flow model; and (3) examine the major expenditures and sources of tax revenue for Federal, state, and local governments.

Some economic functions of government strengthen and facilitate the operation of the market system; others supplement and modify pure capitalism.

LEGAL AND SOCIAL FRAMEWORK

Government provides the legal framework and the services needed for a market economy to operate effectively. The legal framework provides the legal status of business enterprises, defines the rights of private ownership, and makes it possible to provide for enforcement of contracts. Government also establishes legal "rules of the game" governing the relationships of businesses, resource suppliers, and consumers with one another. Through legislation, government can referee economic relationships, detect foul play, and exercise authority in imposing appropriate penalties.

Services provided by government include police powers to maintain internal order, a system of standards for measuring the weight and quality of products, and a monetary system to facilitate exchange of goods and services.

The Pure Food and Drug Act of 1906 is an example of how government has strengthened the market system. This act sets rules of conduct governing producers in their relationships with consumers. It prohibits the sale of adulterated and misbranded foods and drugs, requires net weights and ingredients of products to be specified on their containers, establishes quality standards which must be stated on labels of canned foods, and prohibits deceptive claims on patent-medicine labels. These measures are designed to prevent fraudulent activities by producers and to increase the public's confidence in the integrity of the market system. Similar legislation pertains to labor-management relations and relations of business firms to one another.

This type of government activity is presumed to improve resource allocation. Supplying a medium of exchange, ensuring product quality, defining ownership rights, and enforcing contracts increase the volume of exchange. This widens markets and permits greater specialization in the use of property and human resources. Such specialization means a more efficient allocation of resources. However, some argue that government overregulates interactions of businesses, consumers, and workers, stifling economic incentives and impairing productive efficiency.

MAINTAINING COMPETITION

Competition is the basic regulatory mechanism in a capitalistic economy. It is the force which subjects producers and resource suppliers to the dictates of consumer sovereignty. With competition, buyers are the boss, the market is their agent, and businesses are their servants.

It's completely different with **monopoly.** *Monopoly exists when the number of sellers becomes small enough for each seller to influence total supply and therefore the price of the commodity being sold.*

In a monopoly sellers can influence, or "rig," the market in their own self-interests, to the detriment of society as a whole. Through their ability to influence total supply, monopolists can restrict the output of products and enjoy higher prices and, frequently, persistent economic profits. These above-competitive prices and profits directly conflict with the interests of consumers. Monopolists are not regulated by the will of society as are competitive sellers. Producer sovereignty supplants consumer sovereignty to the degree that monopoly supplants competition. In a monopoly resources are allocated in terms of the profit-seeking interests of sellers rather than in terms of the wants of society as a whole. Monopoly causes a misallocation of economic resources.

In the United States, government has attempted to control monopoly primarily in two ways.

1 Regulation and Ownership In the case of "natural monopolies"—industries in which technological and economic realities rule out competitive markets—government has created public commissions to regulate prices and service standards. Transportation, communications, and electric and other utilities are industries which are regulated in varying degrees. At local levels of government, public ownership of electric and water utilities is common.

2 Antimonopoly Laws In nearly all markets, efficient production can be attained with a high degree of competition. The Federal government has therefore enacted a series of antimonopoly or antitrust laws, beginning with the Sherman Act of 1890, to maintain and strengthen competition as a regulator of business behavior.

Even if the legal foundation of capitalistic institutions is assured and competition is maintained, there is still a need for certain additional economic functions on the part of government. *The market economy has certain biases and shortcomings which compel government to supplement and modify its operation.*

REDISTRIBUTION OF INCOME

The market system is impersonal. It may distribute income with more inequality than society desires. The market system yields very large incomes to those whose labor, by virtue of inherent ability and acquired education and skills, commands high wages. Similarly, those who possess—through hard work or easy inheritance—valuable capital and land receive large property incomes.

But others in our society have less ability, have received modest amounts of education and training, and have accumulated or inherited no property resources. Thus, their incomes are very low. Furthermore, many of the aged, the physically and mentally handicapped, and female-headed families earn only very small incomes or, like the unemployed, no incomes at all through the market system. In the market system there is considerable inequality in the distribution of money income (recall Figure 5-2) and therefore in the distribution of total output among individual households. Poverty amidst overall plenty in our economy persists as a major economic and political issue.

Government's role in ameliorating income inequality is reflected in a variety of policies and programs.

1 Transfers *Transfer payments* provide relief to the destitute, aid to the dependent and handicapped, and unemployment compensation to the unemployed. Social security and Medicare programs provide financial support for the retired and aged sick. These programs transfer income from government to households which would otherwise have little or none.

2 Market Intervention Government also alters the distribution of income by *market intervention,* that is, by modifying the prices established by market forces. Price supports for farmers and minimum-wage legislation are illustrations of government price fixing designed to raise incomes of specific groups.

3 Taxation The personal income tax has been used historically to take a larger proportion of the incomes of the rich than the poor.

REALLOCATION OF RESOURCES

Economists recognize *market failure* occurs when the competitive market system either (1) produces the "wrong" amounts of certain goods and services, or (2) fails to allocate any resources whatsoever to the production of certain goods and services whose output is economically justified. The first case involves "spillovers" or "externalities," the second "public" or "social" goods.

Spillovers or Externalities

The idea that competitive markets automatically bring about efficient resource use rests on the assumption that *all* the benefits and costs of production and consumption of each product are fully reflected in the market demand and supply curves respectively. It is assumed that there are no *spillovers* or *externalities* associated with the production or consumption of any good or service.

A *spillover* occurs when some of the benefits or costs of production or consumption of a good "spillover" onto parties other than the immediate buyer or seller. Spillovers are also called *externalities* because they are benefits and costs accruing to some third party external to the market transaction.

Spillover Costs When production or consumption of a commodity inflicts costs on a third party without compensation, these costs are **spillover costs.** Examples of spillover costs include environmental pollution. When a chemical manufacturer or meat-packing plant dumps its wastes into a lake or river, swimmers, fishermen, and boaters—not to mention communities' water supplies—suffer spillover costs. Human health hazards may arise and wildlife may be damaged or destroyed. When a petroleum refinery pollutes the air with smoke or a paint factory creates distressing odors, the community bears spillover costs for which it is not compensated. Acid rain and global warming are spillover costs which receive almost daily media attention.

What are the economic effects? Recall that costs underlie the firm's supply curve. When a firm avoids some costs by polluting, its supply curve will lie further to the right than when it bears the full costs of production. This results in a larger output and causes an *overallocation* of resources to the production of this good.

Correcting for Spillover Costs Government can do two things to correct this overallocation of resources. Both are designed to *internalize* the external costs, that is, to make the offending firm pay these costs rather than shift them to society.

1   Legislation In our examples of air and water pollution, the most direct action is *legislation* prohibiting or limiting pollution. Such legislation forces potential polluters to bear costs of properly disposing of industrial wastes. Firms must buy and install smoke-abatement equipment or facilities to purify water contaminated by manufacturing processes. The idea is to force potential offenders, under the threat of legal action, to bear *all* costs associated with their production.

2   Specific Taxes A less direct action is based on the fact that taxes are a cost and therefore a determinant of a firm's supply curve (Chapter 3). Government might levy a *specific tax* which equals or approximates the spillover costs per unit of output. Through this tax, government attempts to shove back onto the offending firm those external or spillover costs—which private industry would otherwise avoid—and thus eliminate the overallocation of resources.

Spillover Benefits But spillovers may also appear as benefits. Production or consumption of certain goods and services may confer spillover or external benefits on third parties or the community at large for which payment of compensation is not required. Measles and polio immunization shots result in direct benefits to the immediate consumer. But immunization against these contagious diseases yields widespread and substantial spillover benefits to the entire community. Discovery of an AIDS vaccine would benefit society far beyond those vaccinated. Unvaccinated individuals would clearly benefit by the slowing of the spread of the disease.

Education is another example of **spillover benefits.** Education benefits individual consumers: "More educated" people generally achieve higher incomes than "less educated" people. But education also provides benefits to society. The economy as a whole benefits from a more versatile and more productive labor force, on the one hand, and smaller outlays on crime prevention, law enforcement, and welfare programs, on the other. There is evidence indicating that any worker with a *given* educational or skill level will be more productive if associated workers have more education. In other words, worker X becomes more productive simply because fellow-workers Y and Z are more educated. Significant, too, is the fact that political participation correlates positively with the level of education in that the percentage of persons who vote increases with educational attainment.

Spillover benefits mean the market demand curve, which reflects only private benefits, understates total benefits. The demand curve for the product lies further to the left than if all benefits were taken into account by the market. This means that a smaller amount is produced or, alternatively stated, there is an *underallocation* of resources to the product.

Correcting for Spillover Benefits How might the underallocation of resources associated with spillover benefits be corrected? The answer is to either subsidize consumers (increase demand), subsidize producers (increase supply), or, in the extreme, have government produce the product.

1   Increase Demand In the case of higher education, government provides low-interest student loans and grants to provide student employment. Second example: Our food stamp program is designed to improve the diets of low-income families. The food stamps which government provides can be spent only on food. Stores accepting food stamps are reimbursed with money by the government. Part of the rationale for this program is that improved nutrition will help disadvantaged children perform better in school and disadvantaged adults to be better employees. In helping disadvantaged people become productive participants in the economy, society as a whole benefits.

2 Increase Supply In some cases government might find it more convenient and administratively simpler to subsidize producers. This is also true with higher education where state governments provide substantial portions of the budgets of public colleges and universities. These subsidies lower costs to students and increase educational supply. Public subsidization of immunization programs, hospitals, and medical research are additional examples.

3 Government Provision A third policy option arises if spillover benefits are extremely large: Government may simply choose to finance or, in the extreme, to own and operate such industries. This option leads us into a discussion of public goods and services.

Public Goods and Services

Private goods, which are produced through the market system, are *divisible* in that they come in units small enough to be afforded by individual buyers. Also, private goods are subject to the **exclusion principle,** the idea that those willing and able to pay the equilibrium price get the product, but those unable or unwilling to pay are excluded from the benefits provided by that product.

Certain goods and services—**public** or **social goods**—would not be produced by the market system because their characteristics are opposite those of private goods. Public goods are *indivisible,* involving such large units that they cannot ordinarily be sold to individual buyers. Individuals can buy hamburgers, computers, and automobiles through the market, but not Patriot missiles, highways, space telescopes, and air-traffic control.

More importantly, the exclusion principle does *not* apply to public goods; there is no effective way of excluding individuals from their benefits once those goods come into existence. Obtaining the benefits of private goods is predicated on *purchase;* benefits from public goods accrue to society from the *production* of such goods.

Illustrations The classic public goods example is a lighthouse on a treacherous coast. The construction of a lighthouse would be economically justified if benefits (fewer shipwrecks) exceed production costs. But the benefit accruing to each individual user would not justify the purchase of such a large and indivisible product. But once in operation, its warning light is a guide to *all* ships. There is no practical way to exclude certain ships from its benefits. Therefore, why should any ship owner voluntarily pay for the benefits received from the light? The light is there for all to see, and a ship captain cannot be excluded from seeing it if the ship owner chooses not to pay. Economists call this the **free-rider problem;** *people can receive benefits from a good without contributing to its costs.*

Because the exclusion principle does not apply, there is no economic incentive for private enterprises to supply lighthouses. If the services of the lighthouse cannot be priced and sold, it will be unprofitable for private firms to devote resources to lighthouses. Here is a service which yields substantial benefits but for which the market would allocate no resources. National defense, flood-control, public health, satellite navigation systems, and insect-abatement programs are other public goods. If society is to enjoy such goods and services, they must be provided by the public sector and financed by compulsory charges in the form of taxes.

Large Spillover Benefits While the inapplicability of the exclusion principle distinguishes public from private goods, many other goods and services are provided by government even though the exclusion principle *could* be applied. Such goods and services as education, streets and highways, police and fire protection, libraries and museums, preventive medicine, and sewage disposal could be subject to the exclusion principle. All could be priced and provided by private producers through the market system. But, as noted earlier, these are all services with substantial spillover benefits and would be underproduced by the market system. Therefore, government provides them to avoid the underallocation of resources which would otherwise occur. Such goods and services are called *quasi-public goods.* One can understand the long-standing controversies surrounding the status of medical care and housing. Are these private goods to be provided through the market system, or are they quasi-public goods to be provided by government?

Allocating Resources to Public Goods

The price system will fail to allocate resources for public goods and will underallocate resources for quasi-public goods. What, then, is the mechanism by which such goods get produced?

Public goods are purchased through the government on the basis of group, or collective, choices, in contrast to private goods, which are purchased from private enterprises on the basis of individual choices. The types and quantities of public goods produced are determined in a democracy by political voting. The quantities of the various public goods consumed are a matter of public policy.[2] These group decisions, made in the political arena, supplement the choices of households and businesses in answering the Five Fundamental Questions.

How are resources reallocated from production of private goods to production of public goods? In a full-employment economy, government must free resources from private employment to make them available for production of public goods. The means of releasing resources from private uses is to reduce private demand for them. This is accomplished by levying taxes on businesses and households, diverting some of their incomes—some of their potential purchasing power—out of the income-expenditure stream. With lower incomes, businesses and households must curtail their investment and consumption spending. *Taxes diminish private demands for goods and services, which in turn prompts a drop in the private demand for resources.* By diverting purchasing power from private spenders to government, taxes free resources from private uses.

Government expenditure of the tax proceeds can then reabsorb these resources in the provision of public goods and services. Corporation and personal income taxes release resources from production of investment goods—printing presses, boxcars, warehouses—and consumer goods—food, clothing, and television sets. Government expenditures can reabsorb

these resources in production of post offices, military aircraft, and new schools and highways. Government purposely reallocates resources to bring about significant changes in the composition of the economy's total output. *(Key Questions 9 and 10)*

Stabilization

Historically, the most recent function of government is that of stabilizing the economy—assisting the private economy to achieve the full employment of resources and a stable price level. Here we will only outline (rather than fully explain) how government tries to do this.

The level of output depends directly on total or aggregate expenditures. A high level of total spending means it will be profitable for industries to produce large outputs. This means that both property and human resources will be employed at high levels. But aggregate spending may either fall short of, or exceed, that particular level which will provide for full employment and price stability. Two possibilities, unemployment or inflation, may then occur.

1 Unemployment The level of total spending in the private sector may be too low for full employment. Thus, the government may choose to augment private spending so that total spending—private *and* public—will be sufficient to generate full employment. Government can do this by using the same techniques—government spending and taxes—as it uses to reallocate resources to production of public goods. Specifically, government might increase its own spending on public goods and services on the one hand, and reduce taxes to stimulate private spending on the other.[3]

2 Inflation The economy may attempt to spend more than its capacity to produce. If aggregate spending exceeds the full-capacity output, the price level will rise. Excessive aggregate spending is inflationary. Government's obligation here is to eliminate the excess spending. It can do this by cutting its own expenditures and by raising taxes to curtail private spending.

---

[2]There are differences between *dollar voting,* which dictates output in the private sector of the economy, and *political voting,* which determines output in the public sector. The rich person has many more votes to cast in the private sector than does the poor person. In the public sector, each—at least in theory—has an equal say. Furthermore, the children who cast their votes for bubble gum and comic books in the private sector are banned by virtue of their age from the registering of social choices.

[3]In macroeconomics we learn that government can also use monetary policy—changes in the nation's money supply and interest rates—to help achieve economic stability.

QUICK REVIEW 5-2

■ Government enhances the operation of the market system by providing an appropriate legal foundation and promoting competition.

■ Transfer payments, direct market intervention, and the tax system are ways government can lessen income inequality.

■ Government can correct the overallocation of resources associated with spillover costs through legislation or specific taxes; the underallocation of resources associated with spillover benefits can be offset by government subsidies.

■ Government must provide public goods because they are indivisible and the exclusion principle does not apply to them.

■ Government spending and tax revenues can be manipulated to stablize the economy.

THE CIRCULAR FLOW REVISITED

Government is thoroughly integrated into the real and monetary flows comprising our economy. Let's reexamine the redistributional, allocative, and stabilization functions of government in terms of Chapter 2's circular flow model. In Figure 5-5 flows (1) through (4) restate Figure 2-6. Flows (1) and (2) show business expenditures for the resources provided by households. These expenditures are costs to businesses, but represent wage, rent, interest, and profit income to households. Flows (3) and (4) portray households making consumer expenditures for the goods and services produced by businesses.

Now consider the modifications resulting from the addition of government. Flows (5) through (8) tell us that government makes purchases in both product and resource markets. Specifically, flows (5) and (6) represent government purchasing such things as paper, computers, and military hardware from private businesses. Flows (7) and (8) reflect government purchases of resources. The Federal government employs and pays salaries to members of Congress, the armed forces, Justice Department lawyers, various bureaucrats, and so on. State and local governments hire teachers, bus drivers, police, and firefighters. The Federal government might lease or purchase land to expand a military base; a city may buy land to build a new elementary school.

Government then provides public goods and services to both households and businesses as shown by flows (9) and (10). Financing public goods and services require tax payments by businesses and households as reflected in flows (11) and (12). We have labeled these flows as *net* taxes to acknowledge that they also include "taxes in reverse" in the form of transfer payments to households and subsidies to businesses. Thus, flow (11) entails not merely corporate income, sales, and excise taxes flowing from businesses to government, but also various subsidies to farmers, shipbuilders, and some airlines. Most business subsidies are "concealed" in the form of low-interest loans, loan guarantees, tax concessions, or public facilities provided at prices less than costs. Similarly, government also collects taxes (personal income taxes, payroll taxes) directly from households and makes available transfer payments, for example, welfare payments and social security benefits as shown by flow (12).

Our circular flow model clearly shows how government can alter the distribution of income, reallocate resources, and change the level of economic activity. The structure of taxes and transfer payments can have a significant impact on income distribution. In flow (12) a tax structure which draws tax revenues primarily from well-to-do households combined with a system of transfer payments to low-income households will result in greater equality in the distribution of income.

Flows (6) and (8) imply an allocation of resources different from that of a purely private economy. Government buys goods and labor services which differ from those purchased by households.

Finally, all governmental flows suggest ways government might try to stabilize the economy. If the economy was experiencing unemployment, an increase in government spending with taxes and transfers held constant would increase aggregate spending, output, and employment. Similarly, given the level of government expenditures, a decline in taxes or an increase in transfer payments would increase spendable incomes and boost private spending. Conversely, with inflation the opposite government policies would be in order: reduced government spending, increased taxes, and reduced transfers.

GOVERNMENT FINANCE

How large is the public sector? What are the main economic programs of Federal, state, and local governments? How are these programs financed?

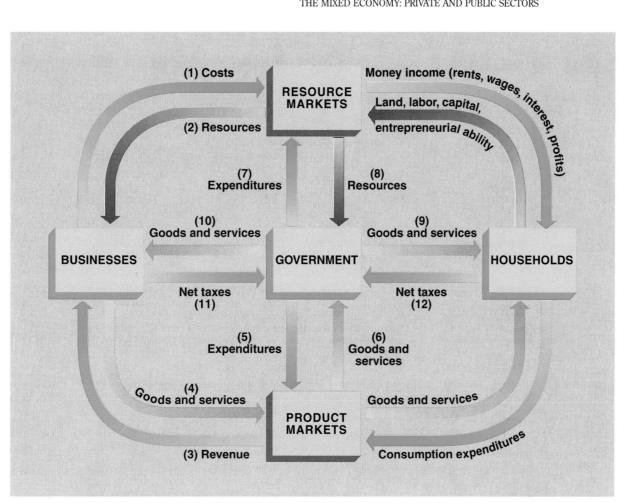

FIGURE 5-5 The circular flow and the public sector
Government expenditures, taxes, and transfer payments affect the distribution of income, the allocation of resources, and the level of economic activity.

Government Growth: Purchases and Transfers

We can get a general impression of the size and growth of government's economic role by examining government purchases of goods and services and government transfer payments. The distinction between these two kinds of outlays is significant.

1 Government purchases are "exhaustive"; they directly absorb or employ resources and the resulting production is part of the domestic output. For example, the purchase of a missile absorbs the labor of physicists and engineers along with steel, explosives, and a host of other inputs.

2 Transfer payments are "nonexhaustive"; they do not directly absorb resources or account for production. Social security benefits, welfare payments,

veterans' benefits, and unemployment compensation are examples of transfer payments. Their key characteristic is that recipients make no current contribution to output in return for these payments.

Figure 5-6 shows that *government purchases* of goods and services have been approximately 20 percent of domestic output over the past 45 years. Of course, domestic output has increased greatly during that time so that the *absolute* volume of government purchases has increased substantially. Government purchases were $75 billion in 1955 as compared to $1,175 billion in 1994.

But if we now look at *transfer payments* we get a different impression of government's role and growth. As Figure 5-6 reveals, transfers have grown significantly since the 1960s, rising from 5 percent of do-

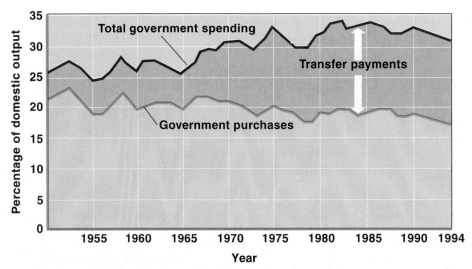

FIGURE 5-6 Government purchases, transfers, and total spending as a percentage of domestic output, 1950–1994
Government purchases have tightly fluctuated around 20 percent of domestic output since 1950. Transfer payments, however, have increased as a percentage of domestic output so that total government spending (purchases plus transfers) have grown and are now about one-third of domestic output.

mestic output in 1960 to over 14 percent in 1994. The net result is that tax revenues required to finance total government spending—purchases plus transfers —are equal to about one-third of domestic output. In 1994 the average taxpayer spent about 2 hours and 45 minutes of each 8-hour workday to pay taxes.

FEDERAL FINANCE

Now let's look separately at the Federal, state, and local units of government to compare their expenditures and taxes. Figure 5-7 tells the story for the Federal government.

FIGURE 5-7 Federal expenditures and tax revenues, 1993
Federal spending is largely on pensions and income security, national defense, health, and interest payments on the public debt. Major revenue sources are the personal income tax, payroll taxes, and the corporate income tax.

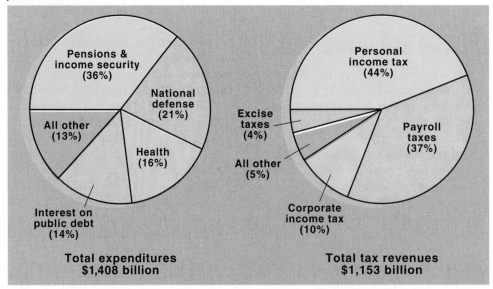

Federal Expenditures

Four important areas of Federal spending stand out: (1) pensions and income security, (2) national defense, (3) health, and (4) interest on the public debt. The *pensions and income security* category reflects the myriad income-maintenance programs for the aged, the disabled, the unemployed, the handicapped, and families with no breadwinner. *National defense* constitutes about one-fifth of the Federal budget and underscores the high costs of military preparedness. *Health* reflects dramatic increases in costs of government health programs for the retired and poor. *Interest on the public debt* has grown dramatically in recent years because the public debt itself has grown.

Federal Tax Revenues

The revenue side of Figure 5-7 clearly shows that the personal income tax, payroll taxes, and the corporate income tax are the basic revenue getters, accounting for 44, 37, and 10 cents of each dollar collected.

Personal Income Tax The **personal income tax** is the kingpin of our national tax system and merits special comment. This tax is levied on *taxable income,* that is, on the incomes of households and unincorporated businesses after certain exemptions ($2,450 for each household member) and deductions (business expenses, charitable contributions, home mortgage interest payments, certain state and local taxes) are taken into account.

The Federal personal income tax is a *progressive tax,* meaning that people with higher incomes pay a larger percentage of their income as taxes than do persons with lower incomes. The progressivity is achieved through a system of higher tax rates which apply to successive layers or brackets of income.

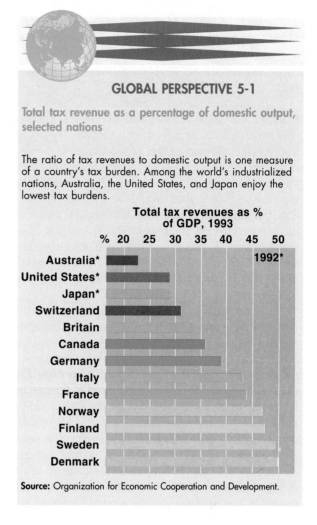

GLOBAL PERSPECTIVE 5-1

Total tax revenue as a percentage of domestic output, selected nations

The ratio of tax revenues to domestic output is one measure of a country's tax burden. Among the world's industrialized nations, Australia, the United States, and Japan enjoy the lowest tax burdens.

Source: Organization for Economic Cooperation and Development.

Columns 1 and 2 of Table 5-2 portray the mechanics of the income tax for a married couple filing a joint return. Note that the 15 percent rate applies to all taxable income up to $36,900, at which point any *additional* income up to $89,150 is taxable at the 28

TABLE 5-2 Federal personal income tax rates, 1995*

(1) Total taxable income	(2) Marginal tax rate (4) ÷ (3)	(3) Change in income Δ(1)	(4) Change in taxes Δ(5)	(5) Total tax	(6) Average tax rate (5) ÷ (1)
$ 0	0%	—	—	—	—
36,900	15	$ 36,900	$ 5,535	$ 5,535	15%
89,150	28	52,250	14,630	20,165	22.6
140,000	31	50,850	15,764	35,929	25.7
250,000	36	110,000	39,600	75,529	30.2
Over 250,000	39.6	—	—	—	—

*Data are for a married couple filing a joint return.

percent rate. Additional income between $89,150 and $140,000 is taxed at 31 percent with a 36 percent rate applying to income in the $140,000–$250,000 range. All taxable income above $250,000 is taxed at 39.6 percent.

The tax rates shown in column 2 of Table 5-2 are marginal tax rates. A **marginal tax rate** is the tax paid on additional or incremental income. By definition, it is the *increase* in taxes paid (column 4) divided by the *increase* in income (column 3). Thus, if our couple's taxable income increased from $0 to $36,900, the increase in taxes paid would be $5,535 (= .15 × $36,900) as shown in column 4. If the couple's taxable income rose by an additional $52,250 (column 3)— that is, from $36,900 to $89,150—a higher marginal tax rate of 28 percent would apply so an additional tax of $14,630 (= .28 × $52,250) would have to be paid (column 4).

The marginal tax rates of column 2 overstate the personal income tax bite because the rising rates apply only to income falling within each successive tax bracket. To get a better picture of the tax burden we must consider average tax rates. The **average tax rate** is the total tax paid divided by total taxable income. In column 6 of Table 5-2 for the $0 to $36,900 tax bracket, the average tax rate is $5,535 (column 4) divided by $36,900 (column 1) or 15 percent, the same as the marginal tax rate. But the couple earning $89,150 does *not* pay 28 percent of its income as taxes as the marginal tax rate would suggest. Rather, its average tax rate is only about 22.6 percent (= $20,165 ÷ $89,150). The reason is that the first $36,900 of income is taxed at 15 percent and only the next $52,250 is subject to the 28 percent rate. You should calculate the average tax rate for a couple earning $350,000. What we observe here is that, if the marginal tax rate is higher than the average tax rate, the average tax rate will rise. The arithmetic is the same as what you may have encountered in school. You must get a score on an additional or "marginal" examination higher than your existing average grade to pull your average up!

A tax whose average tax rate rises as income increases is called a *progressive tax.* Such a tax claims both a larger absolute amount and a larger proportion of income as income rises. Thus we can say that our current personal income tax is modestly progressive. *(Key Question 15)*

Payroll Taxes   Social security contributions, or **payroll taxes,** are the premiums paid on the compulsory insurance plans—old age insurance and Medicare—

provided under social security legislation. These taxes are paid by both employers and employees. Improvements in, and extensions of, our social security programs, plus growth of the labor force, have resulted in very significant increases in payroll taxes in recent years. In 1995 employees and employers each paid a tax of 7.65 percent on the first $61,200 of an employee's annual earnings. Also, employers and employees each pay a 1.45 percent tax on all wages to finance Medicare.

Corporate Income Tax   The Federal government also taxes corporate income. This **corporate income tax** is levied on a corporation's profits—the difference between its total revenue and its total expenses. The basic rate is 35 percent, which applies to annual profits above $10 million. A firm with profits of $15 million would pay corporate income taxes of $1,750,000 (= $5 million × .35). Firms making annual profits less than $10 million are taxed at lower rates.

Excise Taxes   Commodity or consumption taxes may take the form of **sales taxes** or **excise taxes.** The difference between the two is basically one of coverage. Sales taxes fall on a wide range of products, whereas excises are taxes on a small, select list of commodities. As Figure 5-7 suggests, the Federal government collects excise taxes (on such commodities as alcoholic beverages, tobacco, and gasoline). The Federal government does *not* levy a general sales tax; sales taxes are the bread and butter of most state governments.

STATE AND LOCAL FINANCE

Note in Figure 5-8 that the basic sources of tax revenue at the state level are sales and excise taxes, which account for about 49 percent of all sales tax revenues. State personal income taxes, which entail much more modest rates than those of the Federal income taxes are the second most important source of revenue. Taxes on corporate income, property, inheritances, and licenses and permits constitute the remainder of state tax revenue.

The major outlays of state governments are for (1) public welfare, (2) education, (3) health and hospitals, and (4) highway maintenance and construction.

Figure 5-8 contains aggregated data, telling us little about the finances of individual states. States vary

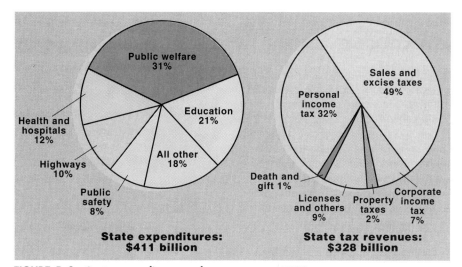

FIGURE 5-8   State expenditures and tax revenues, 1992
State governments spend mainly on public welfare and education. Their primary source of tax revenue comes from sales and excise taxes.

significantly in the types of taxes employed. Thus, although personal income taxes are a major source of revenue for all state governments combined, six states do not use the personal income tax. Furthermore, great variations in the size of tax receipts and disbursements exist among the states.

The receipts and expenditures shown in Figure 5-9 are for all units of local government, including not only cities and towns but also counties, municipalities, townships, and school districts. One source of revenue and one use of revenue stand out: The bulk of the revenue received by local government comes from **property taxes.** And most local revenue is spent for education.

The gaping deficit found by comparing revenue and expenditure in Figure 5-9 is largely removed when nontax resources of income are taken into account: In 1992 the tax revenues of local governments were supplemented by some $216 billion in intergovernmental grants from Federal and state governments. Furthermore, local governments received an additional $56 billion as proprietary income, that is,

FIGURE 5-9   Local expenditures and tax revenues, 1992
The expenditures of local governments are largely for education and are financed mostly by property taxes.

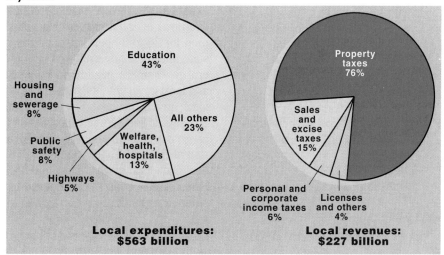

LAST WORD

THE FINANCING OF CORPORATE ACTIVITY

One of the advantages of corporations is their ability to finance their operations through the sale of stocks and bonds. It is informative to examine the nature of corporate finance in more detail.

Generally speaking, corporations finance their activities in three different ways. First, a very large portion of a corporation's activity is financed internally out of undistributed corporate profits. Second, like individuals or unincorporated businesses, corporations may borrow from financial institutions. For example, a small corporation planning to build a new plant may obtain the funds from a commercial bank, a savings and loan association, or an insurance company. Third, unique to corporations, they can issue common stocks and bonds.

Stocks versus Bonds A common stock is an ownership share. The purchaser of a stock certificate has the right to vote for corporate officers and to share in dividends. If you buy 1000 of the 100,000 shares issued by Specific Motors, Inc. (hereafter SM), then you own 1 percent of the company, are entitled to 1 percent of any dividends declared by the board of directors, and control 1 percent of the votes in the annual election of corporate officials.

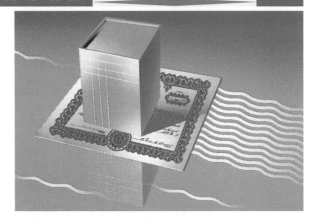

In contrast, a bond is not an ownership share. A bond purchaser is simply lending money to a corporation. A bond is merely an IOU, in acknowledgment of a loan, whereby the corporation promises to pay the holder a fixed amount at some specified future date and other fixed amounts (interest payments) every year up to the bond's maturity date. For example, you might purchase a ten-year SM bond with a face value of $1000 with a 10 percent stated rate of interest. This means that in exchange for your $1000 SM guarantees you a $100 interest payment

---

as revenue from government-owned hospitals and utilities.

QUICK REVIEW 5-3

■ Government purchases are about 20 percent of the domestic output; the addition of transfers increases government spending to almost one-third of domestic output.

■ Income security and national defense are the main Federal expenditures; personal income, payroll, and corporate income taxes are the primary sources of revenue.

■ States rely on sales and excise taxes for revenue; their spending is largely for public welfare, education, health, and highways.

■ Education is the main expenditure for local governments and most of their revenue comes from property taxes.

Fiscal Federalism

Historically, the tax collections of both state and local governments have fallen substantially short of their expenditures. These revenue shortfalls are largely filled by Federal transfers or grants. It is not uncommon for 15 to 20 percent of all revenue received by state and local governments to come from the Federal government. In addition to Federal grants to state and local governments, the states also make grants to local governmental units. This system of intergovernmental transfers is called **fiscal federalism.** Because the Federal budget has suffered large and persistent deficits, Federal grants in recent years have declined. That's why state and local governments have increased tax rates, imposed new taxes, and restrained expenditures.

Lotteries

Both state and local governments have increasingly

for each of the next ten years and then to repay your $1000 principal at the end of that period.

Differences There are clearly important differences between stocks and bonds. First, as noted, the bondholder is not an owner of the company, but is only a lender. Second, bonds are considered to be less risky than stocks for two reasons. On the one hand, bondholders have a "legally prior claim" upon a corporation's earnings. Dividends cannot be paid to stockholders until all interest payments that are due to bondholders have been paid. On the other hand, holders of SM stock do not know how much their dividends will be or how much they might obtain for their stock if they decide to sell. If Specific Motors falls on hard times, stockholders may receive no dividends at all and the value of their stock may plummet. Provided the corporation does not go bankrupt, the holder of an SM bond is guaranteed a $100 interest payment each year and the return of his or her $1000 at the end of ten years.

Bond Risks But this is not to imply that the purchase of corporate bonds is riskless. The market value of your SM bond may vary over time in accordance with the financial health of the corporation. If SM encounters economic misfortunes which raise questions about its financial integrity, the market value of your bond may fall. Should you sell the bond prior to maturity you may receive only $600 or $700 for it (rather than $1000) and thereby incur a capital loss.

Changes in interest rates also affect the market prices of bonds. Specifically, increases in interest rates cause bond prices to fall and vice versa. Assume you purchase a $1000 ten-year SM bond this year (1996) when the interest rate is 10 percent. This obviously means that your bond provides a $100 fixed interest payment each year. But now suppose that by next year the interest rate has jumped to 15 percent and SM must now guarantee a $150 fixed annual payment on its new 1997 $1000 ten-year bonds. Clearly, no sensible person will pay you $1000 for your bond which pays only $100 of interest income per year when new bonds can be purchased for $1000 which pay the holder $150 per year. Hence, if you sell your 1993 bond before maturity, you will suffer a capital loss.

Bondholders face another element of risk due to inflation. If substantial inflation occurs over the ten-year period you hold a SM bond, the $1000 principal repaid to you at the end of that period will represent substantially less purchasing power than the $1000 you loaned to SM ten years earlier. You will have lent "dear" dollars, but will be repaid in "cheap" dollars.

turned to **lotteries** as a means of closing the gaps between their tax receipts and expenditures. In 1993 some 37 states had lotteries which sold $25 billion of tickets.

Lotteries are controversial. Critics argue that (1) it is morally wrong for states to sponsor gambling; (2) lotteries generate compulsive gamblers who impoverish themselves and their families; (3) low-income families spend a larger proportion of their incomes on lotteries than do high-income families; (4) as a cash business, lotteries attract criminals and other undesirables; and, (5) lotteries send the message that luck and fate—rather than education, hard work, and saving and investing—are the route to wealth.

Defenders contend that (1) lotteries are preferable to taxes because they are voluntary rather than compulsory; (2) they are a painless way to finance government services such as education, medical care, and welfare; and (3) lotteries are competitive with illegal gambling and thus socially beneficial in curtailing organized crime.

CHAPTER SUMMARY

1 The functional distribution of income shows how society's total income is divided among wages, rents, interest, and profits; the personal distribution of income shows how total income is divided among individual households.

2 Households divide their total incomes among personal taxes, saving, and consumer goods. Over half of consumption expenditures are for services.

3 Sole proprietorships, partnerships, and corporations are the major legal forms of business enterprises. Corporations dominate the business sector because they **a** have limited liability, and **b** can acquire money capital for expansion more easily than other firms.

4 Government enhances the operation of the market system by **a** providing an appropriate legal and social framework, and **b** acting to maintain competition.

5 Government alters the distribution of income by direct market intervention and through the tax-transfer system.

6 Spillovers or externalities cause the equilibrium output of certain goods to vary from the optimal output. Spillover costs result in an overallocation of resources which can be corrected by legislation or specific taxes. Spillover benefits are accompanied by an underallocation of resources which can be corrected by subsidies to either consumers or producers.

7 Government must provide public goods because such goods are indivisible and entail benefits from which non-paying consumers cannot be excluded.

8 The manipulation of taxes and its expenditures is one way by which government can reduce unemployment and inflation.

9 The circular flow model helps us envision how government performs its redistributional, allocative, and stabilizing functions.

10 Government purchases exhaust or absorb resources; transfer payments do not. Government purchases have been about 20 percent of domestic output since 1950. However, transfers have grown significantly, so total government spending is now about one-third of domestic output.

11 The main categories of Federal spending are for pensions and income security, national defense, health, and interest on the public debt; revenues come primarily from personal income, payroll, and corporate income taxes.

12 The primary sources of revenue for the states are sales and excise taxes; public welfare, education, health and hospitals, and highways are the major state expenditures.

13 At the local level, most revenue comes from the property tax, and education is the most important expenditure.

14 Under our system of fiscal federalism, state and local tax revenues are supplemented by sizable revenue grants from the Federal government.

TERMS AND CONCEPTS

functional and personal distribution of income	conglomerates	limited-liability companies	personal income tax
	industry		marginal and average tax rates
durable and nondurable goods	sole proprietorship	monopoly	payroll taxes
	partnership	spillover costs and spillover benefits	
services	corporation	exclusion principle	corporate income tax
plant	limited liability	public or social goods	sales and excise taxes
firm	separation of ownership and control	free-rider problem	property taxes
horizontal and vertical combinations	double taxation	government purchases transfer payments	fiscal federalism lotteries

QUESTIONS AND STUDY SUGGESTIONS

1 Distinguish between functional and personal distributions of income.

2 *Key Question* *Assume the five residents of Econoville receive incomes of $50, $75, $125, $250, and $500. Present the resulting personal distribution of income as a graph similar to Figure 5-2. Compare the incomes of the lowest and highest fifth of the income receivers.*

3 Distinguish clearly between a plant, a firm, and an industry. Why is an "industry" often difficult to define in practice?

4 *Key Question* *What are the major legal forms of business organization? Briefly state the advantages and disadvantages of each. How do you account for the dominant role of corporations in our economy?*

5 "The legal form which an enterprise assumes is dictated primarily by the financial requirements of its particular line of production." Do you agree?

6 Enumerate and briefly discuss the main economic functions of government.

7 What divergencies arise between equilibrium and an efficient output when **a** spillover costs and **b** spillover benefits are present? How might government correct for these discrepancies? "The presence of spillover costs suggests underallocation of resources to that product and the need for governmental subsidies." Do you agree? Explain how zoning and seat belt laws might be used to deal with a problem of spillover costs.

8 UCLA researchers have concluded that injuries caused

by firearms cost about $429 million a year in hospital expenses alone. Because the majority of those shot are poor and without insurance, almost 86 percent of hospital costs must be borne by taxpayers. Use your understanding of externalities to recommend appropriate policies.

9 *Key Question   What are the basic characteristics of public goods? Explain the significance of the exclusion principle. By what means does government provide public goods?*

10 *Key Question   Draw a production possibilities curve with public goods on the vertical axis and private goods on the horizontal axis. Assuming the economy is initially operating on the curve, indicate the means by which the production of public goods might be increased. How might the output of public goods be increased if the economy is initially functioning at a point inside the curve?*

11   Use your understanding of the characteristics of private and public goods to determine whether the following should be produced through the market system or provided by government: **a** bread;   **b** street lighting;   **c** bridges;   **d** parks;   **e** swimming pools;   **f** medical care;   **g** mail delivery;   **h** housing;   **i** air traffic control;   **j** libraries.

12   Explain how government might manipulate its expenditures and tax revenues to reduce   **a** unemployment and **b** the rate of inflation.

13   "Most governmental actions simultaneously affect the distribution of income, the allocation of resources, and the levels of unemployment and prices." Use the circular flow model to confirm this assertion for each of the following: **a** the construction of a new high school in Blackhawk County;   **b** a 2 percent reduction in the corporate income tax;   **c** an expansion of preschool programs for disadvantaged children;   **d** a $50 million increase in spending for space research;   **e** the levying of a tax on air polluters; and **f** a $1 increase in the minimum wage.

14   What is the most important source of revenue and the major type of expenditure at the Federal level? At the state level? At the local level?

15 *Key Question   Suppose in Fiscalville there is no tax on the first $10,000 of income, but earnings between $10,000 and $20,000 are taxed at 20 percent and income between $20,000 and $30,000 at 30 percent. Any income above $30,000 is taxed at 40 percent. If your income is $50,000, how much in taxes will you pay? Determine your marginal and average tax rates. Is this a progressive tax?*

6

THE UNITED STATES IN THE GLOBAL ECONOMY

Backpackers in the wilderness like to think they are "leaving the world behind," but, like Atlas, they carry the world on their shoulders. Much of their backpacking equipment is imported—knives from Switzerland, rain gear from South Korea, cameras from Japan, aluminum pots made in England, miniature stoves from Sweden, sleeping bags from China, and compasses from Finland. Some backpackers wear hiking boots from Italy, sunglasses made in France, and watches from Japan or Switzerland. Moreover, they may drive to the trailheads in Japanese-made Toyotas or Swedish-made Volvos, sipping coffee from Brazil or snacking on bananas from Honduras.

International trade and the global economy affect all of us daily, whether we are hiking in the wilderness, driving our cars, listening to music, or working at our jobs. We cannot "leave the world behind." We are enmeshed with the rest of the world in a complex web of economic relationships—trade of goods and services, multinational corporations, cooperative ventures among the world's firms, and ties among the world's financial markets. This web is so complex that it is difficult to determine just what is—or isn't—an American product! RCA television sets are made by a company based in France; a Canadian company owns Tropicana Orange Juice; and the parent company of Gerber baby food is Swiss. The Chevrolet Lumina sedan is manufactured in Canada and a British corporation owns Burger King. Many "American" products are made with components from abroad. For example, international firms supply major components of the new "American" Boeing 777 airplane (see Figure 6-1), and, conversely, many "foreign" products contain numerous American-produced parts.

This chapter will introduce the basic principles underlying the global economy (a more advanced discussion of international economics is found in the last Part). We first look at the growth of world trade, the United States' role in it, and factors causing the growth. Next, Chapter 5's circular flow diagram is modified to account for international trade flows. We then explore the basis for world trade, focusing on the concept of comparative advantage. Foreign currencies and exchange rates are discussed. Next, some restrictive trade practices implemented by nations are examined, leading to a discussion of multilateral trade agreements and free-trade regions of the globe. We conclude with some answers to the question: "Can American firms compete?"

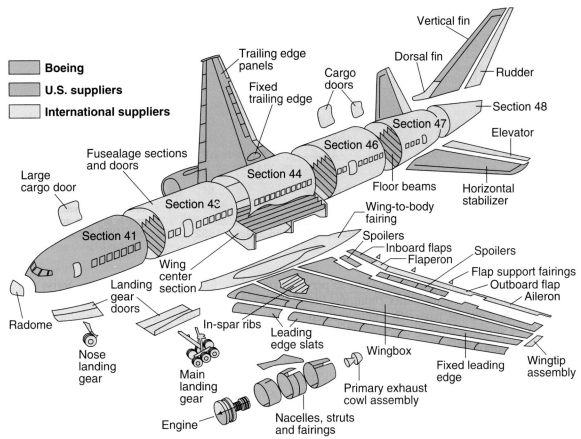

FIGURE 6-1   The Boeing 777: who supplies the parts?
International firms supply major components of the "American" Boeing 777 aircraft. (*Seattle Post Intelligencer.* **Reprinted by permission.**)

GROWTH OF WORLD TRADE

The volume of world trade is so large and its characteristics so unique that it requires special consideration.

Volume and Pattern

Table 6-1 provides a rough index of the importance of world trade for several representative countries. Many nations with restricted resource bases and limited domestic markets cannot produce with reasonable efficiency the variety of goods they want to consume. For such countries, exports—sales abroad—are the route for obtaining imported goods they de-

TABLE 6-1   Exports of goods and services as a percentage of GDP, selected countries, 1993

Country	Exports as percentage of GDP
The Netherlands	52
Germany	37
New Zealand	33
Canada	30
United Kingdom	27
France	23
Italy	22
United States	11
Japan	9

Source: IMF, International Financial Statistics, 1994.

and Standard Oil and Holiday Inns are in British hands.

Facilitating Factors

Several factors have facilitated the rapid growth of international trade since World War II.

Transportation Technology High transportation costs are a barrier to any type of trade, particularly trade between distant places. But improvements in transportation have shrunk the globe, fostering world trade. Airplanes now transport low-weight, high-value items such as diamonds and semiconductors quickly from one nation to another. We now routinely transport oil in massive tankers, greatly reducing the cost of transportation per barrel. Grain is loaded onto ocean-going ships at modern, efficient grain silos at Great Lakes and coastal ports. Container ships transport self-contained railroad boxes directly to foreign ports, where cranes place the containers onto railroad cars for internal shipment. Natural gas flows through large-diameter pipelines from exporting to importing countries—for instance, from Russia to Germany and Canada to the United States. Workers clean fish on large processing ships directly on the fishing grounds. Refrigerated vessels then transport the fish to overseas ports. Commercial airplane manufacturers deliver new aircraft within a matter of hours by simply flying them directly to their foreign customers.

Communications Technology World trade has expanded as well due to dramatic improvements in communications technology. Telephones, fax (facsimile) machines, and computers now directly link traders around the world, allowing exporters to assess the potential for selling products abroad and consummate trade deals. New communications methods enable us to move money around the world in the blink of an eye. Exchange rates, stock prices, and interest rates flash onto computer screens nearly simultaneously in Los Angeles, London, and Lisbon.

In short, exporters and importers today can as easily communicate between Sweden and Australia as between San Francisco and Oakland. A distributor in Florida can get a price quote on 1000 woven baskets in Thailand as quickly as a quotation on 1000 bottles of bourbon in Kentucky.

General Decline in Tariffs Tariffs—excise taxes or duties on imported products—have had their ups and downs, but since 1940 have generally fallen worldwide. A glance ahead to Figure 6-6 shows that United States' tariff duties as a percentage of dutiable imports are now about 5 percent, down from 40 percent in 1940. Many nations still have barriers to free trade, but, on average, tariffs have fallen greatly, increasing international trade.

Peace During World War II powerful industrial countries fought one another, certainly disrupting international trade. Not only has trade since been restored, it has been bolstered by peaceful relations and by trade-conducive institutions linking most industrial nations. In particular, Japan and Germany—two defeated World War II powers—now are major participants in world trade.

Participants

All nations of the world participate to some extent in international trade.

United States, Japan, and western Europe As shown in Global Perspective 6-1, the top participants in world trade are the United States, Germany, and Japan. In 1993 these three nations had combined exports of $1.2 trillion. Along with Germany, other western European nations such as France, Britain, and Italy are major exporters and importers. In fact, three major "players"—the United States, Japan, and the western European nations—now dominate world trade. These three areas also form the heart of the world's financial system and headquarter most of the world's large **multinational corporations**—firms with sizable foreign production and distribution assets. Among the world's top twenty-five multinationals are Royal Dutch Shell and Unilever (Britain/Netherlands); Ford Motor, General Motors, and IBM (United States); British Petroleum (Britain); Nestlé (Switzerland); Fiat (Italy); Siemens and Bayer Chemicals (Germany); Mitsubishi and Mitsui (Japan); and Alcatel Alstrom (France).

New Players New, important participants have arrived on the world trade scene. One such group of nations is the newly industrializing Asian economies of Hong Kong, Singapore, South Korea, and Taiwan. These **"Asian tigers"** have expanded their share of world exports from about 3 percent in 1972 to more than 9 percent today. Together, they export about as much as Japan and much more than either France,

Britain, or Italy. Other countries in southeast Asia, particularly Malaysia and Indonesia, have also expanded their international trade.

China, with its increasing reliance on the market system, is another emerging trading power. Since initiating market reforms in 1979, its annual growth of output has averaged nearly 10 percent (compared to 2 to 3 percent annually in the United States). At this remarkable rate, China's total output nearly doubles every seven years! An upsurge of exports and imports has accompanied this expansion of output. In 1989 Chinese exports and imports each were about $50 billion. In 1994 they each topped $90 billion, with 30 percent of China's exports going to the United States. Also, China has been attracting much foreign investment. In 1993 alone, it contracted for about $100 billion of foreign-produced capital to be delivered during the next several years. Experts predict China will become one of the world's leading trade nations.

The collapse of communism in eastern Europe and the former Soviet Union has also altered world trade patterns. Before this collapse, the eastern European nations of Poland, Hungary, Czechoslovakia, and East Germany mainly traded with the Soviet Union and its political allies such as North Korea and Cuba. Today, East Germany is reunited with West Germany, and Poland, Hungary, and the Czech Republic have established new trade relationships with Europe and America.

Russia itself has initiated far-reaching market reforms, including widespread privatization of industry, and has consummated major trade deals with firms from across the globe. Although its transition to capitalism has not been smooth, no doubt Russia can be a major trading power. Other former Soviet republics —now independent nations—such as Ukraine and Estonia also are opening their economies to international trade and finance.

BACK TO THE CIRCULAR FLOW

Now that we have an idea of the size and growth of world trade, we need to represent it as "the Rest of the World" in Chapter 5's circular flow model. In Figure 6-3 we make two adjustments to Figure 5-5:

1 Our previous "Resource Markets" and "Product Markets" now become "U.S. Resource Markets" and "U.S. Product Markets." Similarly, we add the modifier "U.S." to the "Businesses," "Government," and "Households" sectors.

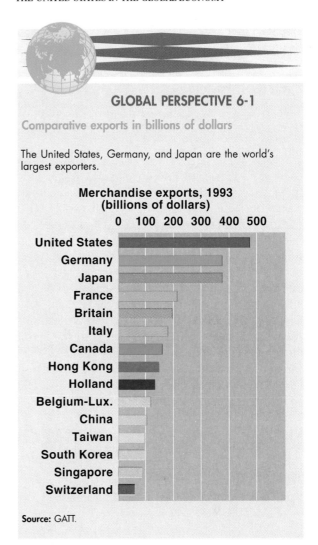

GLOBAL PERSPECTIVE 6-1

Comparative exports in billions of dollars

The United States, Germany, and Japan are the world's largest exporters.

Merchandise exports, 1993 (billions of dollars)

Source: GATT.

2 We place the foreign sector—the "Rest of the World"—at the bottom of the circular flow diagram. This sector designates all foreign nations with which we deal and the individuals, businesses, and governments comprising them.

Flow (13) shows that people, businesses, and governments abroad buy American products—our exports—from our product market. This real flow of American exports to foreign nations is accompanied by a monetary revenue flow (14) from the rest of the world to us. In response to these revenues from abroad, American businesses demand more domestic resources to produce the goods for export; they are on the demand side of the resource market. Thus, the domestic flow (1) of money income (rents, wages, interest, and profits) to American households rises.

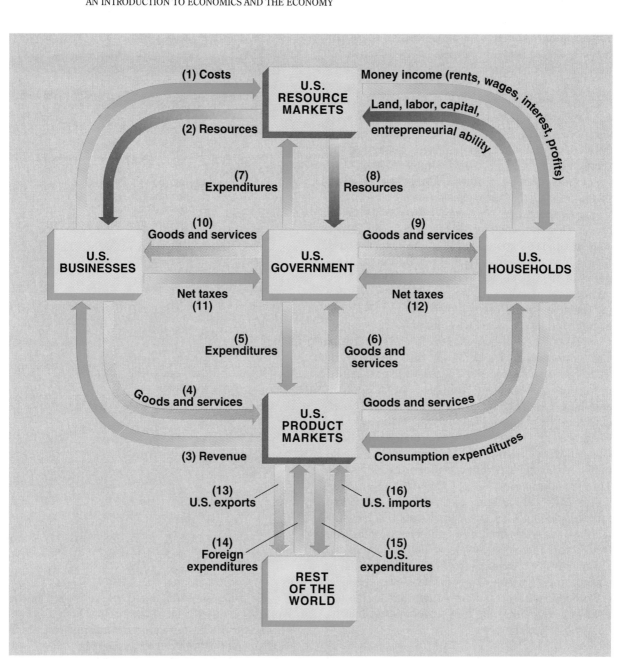

FIGURE 6-3 The circular flow with the foreign sector
Flows 13–16 in the lower portion of the diagram show how the United States economy interacts with the "Rest of the World." People abroad buy American exports, contributing to our business revenues and money incomes. Americans, in turn, spend part of their incomes to buy imports from abroad. Income from a nation's exports helps pay for its imports.

But U.S. exports are only half the picture. Flow (15) shows that American households, businesses, and government spend some of their income on foreign products. These products, of course, are our imports—flow (16)—in the circular flow. Purchases of imports, say, autos and electronics, contribute to foreign output and income, which in turn enable foreign households to buy U.S. exports.

Our circular flow model is a simplification which emphasizes product market effects, but a few other

United States–Rest of the World relationships also merit mention. Specifically, there are linkages between the U.S. resource market and the rest of the world.

America imports and exports not only products but resources as well. For example, we import crude oil and export raw logs. Moreover, some American firms engage in "offshore" production, which diverts spending on capital from our domestic resource market to resource markets in other nations. For instance, General Motors might build an auto assembly plant in Canada or Germany. Or, flowing in the other direction, Sony might construct a plant for manufacturing CD players in the United States.

There are also international flows of labor. About 1 million legal and illegal immigrants enter the United States each year, expanding the availability of labor resources in the United States and raising our total output and income. On the other hand, immigration increases labor supply in specific American labor markets, pulling down wage rates for some types of American labor.

The expanded circular flow model (Figure 6-3) also demonstrates that a nation engaged in world trade risks instability which would not affect a "closed" nation (Figure 5-5). For example, recessions and inflation can be highly contagious among trading nations. Suppose that the nations of western Europe experience a severe recession. As their incomes decline, they would purchase fewer American exports. As a result, flows (13) and (14) in Figure 6-3 would decline and inventories of unsold American goods would rise. American firms would respond by reducing their production and employment, which diminishes the flow of money income to American households [flow (1)]. Recession in Europe might contribute to a recession in the United States.

Figure 6-3 also helps us see that the foreign sector alters resource allocation and incomes in the U.S. economy. With a foreign sector, we produce more of some goods (our exports) and fewer of others (our imports) than we would otherwise. Thus, American labor and other productive resources are shifted toward export industries and away from import industries. We use more of our resources to make commercial aircraft and to grow wheat and less to make autos and clothing. So we ask: "Do these shifts of resources make any economic sense? Do they enhance our total output and thus our standard of living?" We look at some answers next. *(Key Question 3)*

QUICK REVIEW 6-1

■ World trade has increased globally and nationally. The United States is the world's leading international trader—our exports and imports are about 11 to 13 percent of our GDP.

■ Advances in transportation and communications technology, declines in tariffs, and peaceful relations among major industrial countries all have helped to expand world trade.

■ World trade is dominated by the United States, Japan, and the western European nations. Recent new traders are the "Asian tigers" (Hong Kong, Singapore, South Korea, and Taiwan), China, eastern European nations, and the newly independent states formerly comprising the Soviet Union.

■ The circular flow model now incorporates the foreign sector by adding flows of exports from our domestic product market, imports to our domestic product market, and the corresponding flows of spending.

SPECIALIZATION AND COMPARATIVE ADVANTAGE

Specialization and trade increase the productivity of a nation's resources and allow for larger total output than otherwise. This notion is not new! According to Adam Smith in 1776:

It is the maxim of every prudent master of a family, never to attempt to make at home what it will cost him more to make than to buy. The taylor does not attempt to make his own shoes, but buys them from the shoemaker. The shoemaker does not attempt to make his own clothes, but employs a taylor. The farmer attempts to make neither the one or the other, but employs those different artificers. . . .

What is prudence in the conduct of every private family, can scarce be folly in that of a great kingdom. If a foreign country can supply us with a commodity cheaper than we can make it, better buy it of them with some part of the produce of our own industry, employed in a way in which we have some advantage.[1]

Nations specialize and trade for the same reasons as individuals: Specialization and exchange among in-

---

[1]Adam Smith, *The Wealth of Nations* (New York: Modern Library, Inc., 1937), p. 424. (Originally published in 1776.)

dividuals, regions, and nations result in greater over-all output and income.

Basic Principle

In the early 1800s British economist David Ricardo expanded Smith's idea, correctly observing that it pays for a person or a country to specialize and exchange even if that person or nation is more productive than a potential trading partner in *all* economic activities.

Consider the certified public accountant (CPA) who is also a skilled house painter. Suppose the CPA can paint her house in less time than the professional painter she is thinking of hiring. Also suppose the CPA can earn $50 per hour doing her accounting and must pay the painter $15 per hour. Let's say that it will take the accountant 30 hours to paint her house; the painter, 40 hours.

Should the CPA take time from her accounting to paint her own house or should she hire the painter? The CPA's opportunity cost of painting her house is $1500 (= 30 hours × $50 per hour of sacrificed income). The cost of hiring the painter is only $600 (= 40 hours × $15 per hour paid to the painter). Although the CPA is better at both accounting and painting, her relative or comparative advantage lies in accounting. She will *lower the cost of getting her house painted* by specializing in accounting and using some of the earnings from accounting to hire a house painter.

Similarly, the house painter can reduce his cost of obtaining accounting services by specializing in painting and using some of his income to hire the CPA to prepare his income tax forms. Suppose that it would take the painter 10 hours to prepare his tax return, while the CPA could handle this task in 2 hours. The house painter would sacrifice $150 of income (= 10 hours × $15 per hour of sacrificed time) to accomplish a task which he could hire the CPA to do for $100 (= 2 hours × $50 per hour of the CPA's time).

By using the CPA to prepare his tax return, the painter *lowers his cost of getting the tax return completed.*

What is true for our CPA and house painter is also true for nations. Countries can reduce their cost of obtaining desirable goods by specializing in production where they have comparative advantages.

Comparative Costs

Our simple example clearly shows that specialization is economically desirable because it results in more efficient production. To understand the global economy, let's now put specialization in the context of trading nations, employing the familiar concept of the production possibilities table for our analysis. Suppose production possibilities for Mexico and the United States are as shown in Tables 6-4 and 6-5. In these tables we assume constant costs. Each country must give up a constant amount of one product in securing constant increments of the other product. (This assumption will simplify our discussion without impairing the validity of our conclusions.)

Specialization and trade are mutually beneficial or "profitable" to the two nations if the comparative costs of the two products within the two nations differ. What are the domestic comparative costs of avocados and soybeans in Mexico? Comparing production alternatives A and B in Table 6-4, we see that 5 tons of soybeans (= 15 − 10) must be sacrificed to produce 20 tons of avocados (= 20 − 0). Or, more simply, in Mexico it costs 1 ton of soybeans to produce 4 tons of avocados—that is, $1S = 4A$. Because we assumed constant costs, this domestic comparative-cost relationship will not change as Mexico expands the output of either product. This is evident from production possibilities B and C, where we see that 4 more tons of avocados (= 24 − 20) cost 1 unit of soybeans (= 10 − 9).

Similarly, in Table 6-5, comparing production alternatives R and S reveals that at a domestic opportunity cost of 10 tons of soybeans (= 30 − 20),

TABLE 6-4 Mexico's production possibilities table (in tons)

Product	Production alternatives				
	A	B	C	D	E
Avocados	0	20	24	40	60
Soybeans	15	10	9	5	0

TABLE 6-5 United States' production possibilities table (in tons)

Product	Production alternatives				
	R	S	T	U	V
Avocados	0	30	33	60	90
Soybeans	30	20	19	10	0

Americans can obtain 30 tons of avocados (= 30 − 0). That is, the domestic comparative-cost ratio for the two products in the United States is $1S = 3A$. Comparing production alternatives S and T demonstrates this clearly. Note that an extra 3 tons of avocados (= 33 − 30) comes at the direct sacrifice of 1 ton of soybeans (= 20 − 19).

The comparative cost of the two products within the two nations is clearly different. Economists say that the United States has a domestic comparative-cost advantage or, simply, a **comparative advantage,** in soybeans. The United States must forgo fewer avocados—3 tons—to get 1 ton of soybeans than in Mexico where 1 ton of soybeans costs 4 tons of avocados. In terms of domestic opportunity costs, soybeans are relatively cheaper in the United States. *A nation has a comparative advantage in some product when it can produce that product at a lower domestic opportunity cost than can a potential trading partner.* Mexico, on the other hand, has a comparative advantage in avocados. While it costs $\frac{1}{3}$ ton of soybeans to get 1 ton of avocados in the United States, by comparison 1 ton of avocados only costs $\frac{1}{4}$ ton of soybeans in Mexico. Comparatively speaking, avocados are cheaper in Mexico. In summary: Mexico's domestic cost conditions: $1S = 4A$; United States' domestic cost conditions: $1S = 3A$.

Because of these differences in domestic opportunity costs, if both nations specialize, each according to its comparative advantage, each can achieve a larger total output with the same total input of resources. Together, they will be using their scarce resources more efficiently.

Terms of Trade

Since the United States' cost ratio of $1S$ equals $3A$, it makes sense that Americans would specialize in soybeans, if they could obtain *more than* 3 tons of avocados for a ton of soybeans through trade with Mexico. Similarly, recalling Mexico's $1S$ equals $4A$ cost ratio, it will be advantageous to Mexicans to specialize in avocados, provided they can get 1 ton of soybeans for *less than* 4 tons of avocados.

Suppose through negotiation the two nations agree on an exchange rate of 1 ton of soybeans for $3\frac{1}{2}$ tons of avocados. These **terms of trade** will be mutually beneficial to both countries since each can "do better" through trade than by domestic production alone. Americans get $3\frac{1}{2}$ tons of avocados by sending 1 ton of soybeans to Mexico, while they can get only 3 tons of avocados by shifting resources domestically from soybeans to avocados. It would cost Mexicans 4 tons of avocados to obtain 1 ton of soybeans by shifting their domestic resources. Instead, they can obtain 1 ton of soybeans through trade with the United States at the lower cost of $3\frac{1}{2}$ tons of avocados.

Gains from Specialization and Trade

Let's pinpoint the size of the gains in total output from specialization and trade. Suppose that, before specialization and trade, production alternative C in Table 6-4 and alternative T in 6-5 were the optimal product-mixes for each country. These outputs are shown in column 1 of Table 6-6. That is, Mexicans preferred 24 tons of avocados and 9 tons of soybeans (Table 6-4) and Americans preferred 33 tons of avocados and 19 tons of soybeans (Table 6-5) to all other alternatives available within their respective domestic economies.

Now assume both nations specialize according to comparative advantage, Mexico producing 60 tons of avocados and no soybeans (alternative E) and the United States producing no avocados and 30 tons of soybeans (alternative R) as reflected in column 2 of Table 6-6. Using our $1S = 3\frac{1}{2}$ terms of trade, assume Mexico exchanges 35 tons of avocados for 10 tons of American soybeans. Column 3 of Table 6-6 shows quantities exchanged in this trade. As observed in column 4, Mexicans will now have 25 tons of avocados and 10 tons of soybeans, while Americans will obtain

TABLE 6-6 Specialization according to comparative advantage and the gains from trade (in tons)

Country	(1) Outputs before specialization	(2) Outputs after specialization	(3) Amounts traded	(4) Outputs available after trade	(5) = (4) − (1) Gains from specialization and trade
Mexico	24 avocados	60 avocados	−35 avocados	25 avocados	1 avocados
	9 soybeans	0 soybeans	+10 soybeans	10 soybeans	1 soybeans
United States	33 avocados	0 avocados	+35 avocados	35 avocados	2 avocados
	19 soybeans	30 soybeans	−10 soybeans	20 soybeans	1 soybeans

GLOBAL PERSPECTIVE 6-2

Exchange rates: foreign currency per United States dollar

The amount of foreign currency which a dollar will buy varies greatly from nation to nation. These amounts are for February 1995 and fluctuate in response to supply and demand changes in the foreign exchange market.

One dollar will buy:

1.76 German marks
.685 British pounds
1.34 Canadian dollars
3.11 Mexican pesos
1.48 Swiss francs
5.97 French francs
108 Japanese yen
807 South Korean won
21,719 Polish zloty

duction possibilities frontiers of the two countries have not been pushed outward, specialization and trade have circumvented the constraints of the production possibilities curve. The economic effects of specialization and trade between two nations are tantamount to having more or better resources or to having achieved technological progress. The national self-interest of trading partners is the foundation of the world economy. Such trade provides mutual gains in consumable output and thus higher domestic standards of living. *(Key Question 4)*

FOREIGN EXCHANGE MARKET

People, firms, or nations specializing in the production of specific goods or services exchange those products for money and then use the money to buy other products or to pay for the use of resources. Within an economy—for example, Mexico—prices are stated in pesos and buyers use pesos to purchase domestic products. The buyers possess pesos, exactly the currency sellers want.

International markets are different. How many dollars does it take to buy a truckload of Mexican avocados selling for 3000 pesos, a German automobile selling for 90,000 marks, or a Japanese motorcycle priced at 300,000 yen? Producers in Mexico, Germany, and Japan want payment in pesos, marks, and yen, respectively, so they can pay their wages, rent, interest, dividends, and taxes. This need is served by a **foreign exchange market,** *the market where various national currencies are exchanged for one another.* (See Global Perspective 6-2.) Two points about this market require emphasis.

1 A Competitive Market Real-world foreign exchange markets conform closely to the kinds of markets studied in Chapter 3. These are competitive markets characterized by large numbers of buyers and sellers dealing in a standardized "product" such as the American dollar, the German mark, the British pound, Swedish krona, or the Japanese yen.

2 Linkage to All Domestic and Foreign Prices The price or exchange value of a nation's currency is an unusual price; it links all domestic (say, United States) prices with all foreign (say, Japanese or German) prices. Exchange rates enable consumers in one country to translate prices of foreign goods into units of their own currency—just multiply the foreign prod-

35 tons of avocados and 20 tons of soybeans. Compared with their optimum product-mixes before specialization and trade (column 1), *both* nations now enjoy more avocados and more soybeans! Specifically, Mexico will gain 1 ton of avocados and 1 ton of soybeans. The United States will gain 2 tons of avocados and 1 ton of soybeans. These gains are shown in column 5 where we have subtracted the *before*-specialization outputs of column 1 from the outputs realized *after*-specialization in column 4.

Specialization according to comparative advantage improves global resource allocation. The same total inputs of world resources and technology have resulted in a larger global output. If Mexico and the United States allocate all their resources to avocados and soybeans respectively, the same total inputs of resources have produced more output between them, indicating that resources are being more efficiently used or allocated.

We saw in Chapter 2 that through specialization and international trade a nation can overcome the production constraints imposed by its domestic production possibilities curve. Although the domestic prouct price by the exchange rate. If the dollar–yen exchange rate is $.01 (1 cent) per yen, a Sony cassette player priced at ¥20,000 will cost an American $200 (= 20,000 × $.01). If the exchange rate is $.02 per yen, it would cost an American $400 (= 20,000 × $.02). Similarly, all other Japanese products will double in price to American buyers. As we will see, a change in exchange rates has important implications for a nation's levels of domestic production and employment.

Dollar–Yen Market

How does the foreign exchange market for dollars and yen work? (We defer technical details until later.) When nations trade, they must exchange their currencies. American exporters want to be paid in dollars, not yen; but Japanese importers of American goods possess yen, not dollars. This problem is resolved by Japanese importers who offer to supply their yen in exchange for dollars. Conversely, there are American importers who need to pay Japanese exporters with yen, not dollars. So these Americans go to the foreign exchange market as demanders of yen.

Figure 6-4 shows Japanese importers as suppliers of yen and American importers as demanders of yen. The intersection of the demand for yen curve D_y and the supply of yen curve S_y establishes the equilibrium dollar price of yen. Note that the equilibrium dollar price of 1 yen—the dollar–yen exchange rate —is $.01 = ¥1, or $1 = ¥100. At this price, the yen market clears; there is neither a shortage nor a surplus of yen. The equilibrium $.01 price of 1 yen means that $1 will buy 100 yen and therefore 100 yen worth of Japanese goods. Conversely, 100 yen will buy $1 worth of American goods.

Changing Rates: Depreciation and Appreciation

What might cause the exchange rate to change? The determinants of the demand for and the supply of yen are similar to the determinants of supply and demand discussed in Chapter 3. In the United States, several things might increase the demand for—and therefore the dollar price of—yen. Incomes might rise in the United States, enabling Americans to buy not only more domestic goods, but also more Sony televisions, Nikon cameras, and Nissan automobiles from Japan. So Americans need more yen and the demand for yen increases. Or, a change in American tastes may enhance our preferences for Japanese goods. When gas prices soared in the 1970s, many American auto buyers shifted their demands from gas-guzzling domestic cars to gas-efficient Japanese compact cars. The result? An increased demand for yen.

An increase in the American demand for Japanese goods will increase the demand for yen and raise the dollar price of yen. Suppose the dollar price of yen rises from $.01 = ¥1 (or $1 = ¥100) to $.02 = ¥1 (or $2 = ¥100). When the dollar price of yen increases, a **depreciation** of the dollar relative to the yen has occurred: It takes more dollars (pennies in this case) to

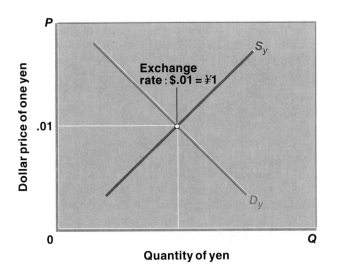

FIGURE 6-4 The market for foreign exchange
American imports from Japan create a demand for yen, while American exports to Japan create a supply of yen. The dollar price of one yen—the exchange rate—is determined at the intersection of the supply and demand curves. In this case the equilibrium price is $.01, meaning that 1 cent will buy 1 yen (or $1 will buy 100 yen).

buy a single unit of a foreign currency (the yen). A dollar is worth less because it will buy fewer yen and therefore fewer Japanese goods; the yen and therefore all Japanese goods become more expensive to Americans. Result: American consumers shift their expenditures from Japanese to American goods. The Ford Taurus becomes relatively more attractive than the Honda Accord to American consumers. Conversely, because each yen will buy more dollars, American goods become cheaper to people in Japan and our exports to them rise.

If opposite events occurred—if incomes rose in Japan and Japanese preferred more American goods—then the supply of yen in the foreign exchange market would increase. This increase in the supply of yen relative to demand would decrease the equilibrium dollar price of yen. For example, yen supply might increase, causing the dollar price of yen to decline from $.01 = ¥1 (or $1 = ¥100) to $.005 = ¥1 (or $1 = ¥200). This decrease in the dollar price of yen means there has been an **appreciation** of the dollar relative to the

yen. It now takes fewer dollars (or pennies) to buy a single yen; the dollar is worth more because it can purchase more yen and therefore more Japanese goods. Each Sony Walkman becomes less expensive in terms of dollars, so Americans purchase more of them. In general, American imports rise. Meanwhile, because it takes more yen to get a dollar, American exports to Japan fall.

We summarize these currency relationships in Figure 6-5, which you should examine closely. *(Key Question 6)*

QUICK REVIEW 6-2

■ A country has a comparative advantage in some product when it can produce it at a lower domestic opportunity cost than can a potential trading partner.

■ Specialization based on comparative advantage increases the total output available for nations which trade with one another.

■ The foreign exchange market is the market where the currency of one nation is exchanged for that of another nation.

■ Appreciation of the dollar is an increase in the international value of the dollar relative to the currency of some other nation; a dollar now buys more units of another currency. Depreciation of the dollar is a decrease in the international value of the dollar relative to other currencies; a dollar now buys fewer units of another currency.

FIGURE 6-5 Currency appreciation and depreciation
An increase in the dollar price of foreign currency is equivalent to a decline in the international value of the dollar (dollar depreciation). An increase in the dollar price of foreign currency also implies a decline in the foreign currency price of dollars. That is, the international value of foreign currency rises relative to the dollar (foreign currency appreciates).

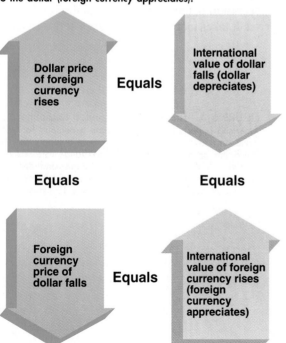

GOVERNMENT AND TRADE

If people and nations benefit from specialization and international exchange, why do governments sometimes try to restrict the free flow of imports or to subsidize exports? What kinds of world trade barriers exist? And what is the rationale for them?

Trade Impediments and Subsidies

The major government interferences with free trade are fourfold:

1 **Protective tariffs** are excise taxes or duties placed on imported goods. Most are designed to shield domestic producers from foreign competition. They impede free trade by increasing the prices of imported goods, shifting demand toward domestic products.

2   Import quotas are maximum limits on the quantity or total value of specific imported items. Once quotas are "filled," they choke off imports which domestic consumers might prefer to domestic goods. Import quotas can be more effective in retarding international commerce than tariffs. A particular product might be imported in large quantities despite high tariffs; low import quotas completely prohibit imports once quotas are filled.

3   Nontariff barriers include licensing requirements, unreasonable standards pertaining to product quality, or simply unnecessary bureaucratic red tape in customs procedures. Some nations require their domestic importers of foreign goods to obtain licenses. By restricting the issuance of licenses, imports can be effectively impeded. Great Britain bars coal importation in this way. Also, some nations impede imports of fruit by insisting that each crate be inspected for worms and insects.

4   Export subsidies consist of governmental payments to domestic producers to reduce their production costs. With lower production costs, domestic producers can charge lower prices and thus sell more exports in world markets. Two examples: Participating European governments have heavily subsidized Airbus Industries, which produces commercial aircraft. These subsidies have helped Airbus compete against two American firms, Boeing and McDonnell Douglas. The United States and other nations have subsidized domestic farmers, boosting domestic food supply. This has reduced the market price of food, artificially decreasing export prices on agricultural produce.

Why Government Trade Interventions?

Why would a nation want to send more of its output for consumption abroad than it gains as imported output in return? Why the impulse to impede imports or boost exports through government policy when free trade is beneficial to a nation? There are several reasons—some legitimate, most not. We will look at two here, and examine others in a later chapter.

1   Misunderstanding of the Gains from Trade   It is a commonly accepted myth that the fundamental benefit of international trade is larger domestic employment in the export sector. This suggests that exports are "good" because they increase domestic employment, whereas imports are "bad" since they deprive people of jobs at home. In reality, the true ben-

efit from international trade is the *overall* increase in output obtained through specialization and exchange. A nation can fully employ its resources, including labor, with or without international trade. International trade, however, enables society to use its resources in ways that increase its total output and therefore its overall well-being.

A nation does not need international trade to locate *on* its production possibilities curve. A closed (nontrading) national economy can have full employment without international trade. But through world trade an economy can reach a point *beyond* its domestic production possibilities curve. The gain from trade is the extra output obtained from abroad—the imports gotten for less cost than if they were produced using domestic resources. The only valid reason for exporting part of our domestic output is to obtain imports of greater value to us. Specialization and international exchange make this possible.

2   Political Considerations   While a nation as a whole gains from trade, trade may harm particular domestic industries and groups of resource suppliers. In our example of comparative advantage, specialization and trade adversely affected the American avocado industry and the Mexican soybean industry. These industries may seek to preserve or improve their economic positions by persuading their respective governments to impose tariffs or quotas to protect them from harm.

> The direct beneficiaries of import relief or export subsidy are usually few in number, but each has a large individual stake in the outcome. Thus, their incentive for vigorous political activity is strong.
>
> But the costs of such policies may far exceed the benefits. It may cost the public [$60,000–$80,000] a year to protect a domestic job that might otherwise pay an employee only half that amount in wages and benefits. Furthermore, the costs of protection are widely diffused—in the United States, among 50 states and [263] million citizens. Since the cost borne by any one citizen is likely to be quite small, and may even go unnoticed, resistance at the grass-roots level to protectionist measures often is considerably less than pressures for their adoption.[2]

Also, the costs of protectionism are hidden because tariffs and quotas are embedded in the prices of goods. Thus policy makers face fewer political restraints in responding positively to demands for pro-

---

[2]*Economic Report of the President, 1982,* p. 177. Updated.

tectionism. Indeed, the public may be won over, not only by the vigor of the arguments for trade barriers, but also by the apparent plausibility ("Cut imports and prevent domestic unemployment") and patriotic ring ("Buy American!") of the protectionists. Alleged tariff benefits are immediate and clear-cut to the public. The adverse effects cited by economists are obscure and dispersed over the economy. Then, too, the public is likely to stumble on the fallacy of composition: "If a quota on Japanese automobiles will preserve profits and employment in the American automobile industry, how can it be detrimental to the economy as a whole?" When political considerations are added in— "You back tariffs for the apparel industry in my state and I'll back tariffs for the auto industry in your state" —the sum can be protective tariffs, import quotas, and export subsidies.

Costs to Society

Tariffs and quotas benefit domestic firms in the protected industries, but hurt American consumers who must pay higher than world prices. The cost of trade protection to American consumers exceeds the gain to American producers, resulting in a *net* cost to Americans. In the early 1990s this net cost exceeded $21 billion annually. Removing trade barriers, on average, would reduce product prices in protected industries by 3 percent. Prices of apparel products would fall by 11.4 percent, luggage prices by 9.1 percent, and sugar prices by 8.3 percent. Prices would also decline for footwear, watches, roller bearings, pressed and blown glass, costume jewelry, machine tools, frozen fruit and vegetables, ceramic tiles, and leather goods.[3]

Tariffs and quotas on textiles and apparel cost our economy about $16 billion annually. Other net costs of trade protection, by industry, include $3 billion in maritime transport, $850 million in dairy products, $657 million in sugar, $353 million in peanuts, $177 million in meat, $170 million in nonrubber footwear, and $101 million in watches and clocks.

MULTILATERAL AGREEMENTS AND FREE-TRADE ZONES

When one nation enacts barriers against imports, the nations whose exports suffer may retaliate with trade barriers of their own. In a "trade war" tariffs escalate,

choking off world trade and reducing everyone's economic well-being. The **Smoot-Hawley Tariff Act of 1930** is a classic example. Rather than reducing imports and stimulating domestic production, its high tariffs prompted affected nations to retaliate with equally high tariffs. International trade across the globe fell, lowering the output, income, and employment levels of all nations. Economic historians generally agree that the Smoot-Hawley tariff was a contributing cause of the Great Depression. In view of this fact, the world's nations have worked to lower tariffs worldwide. This pursuit of free trade has been aided by the expansion of powerful domestic interest groups. Specifically, exporters of goods and services, importers of foreign components used in "domestic" products, and domestic sellers of imported products all strongly support lower tariffs worldwide.

Figure 6-6 makes clear that the United States has been a high tariff nation over much of its history. But it also demonstrates that, in general, American tariffs have declined during the past half-century.[4]

Reciprocal Trade Agreements Act and GATT

The **Reciprocal Trade Agreements Act of 1934** started the downward trend of tariffs. Specifically aimed at reducing tariffs, this act had two main features:

1 *Negotiating Authority* It authorized the President to negotiate with foreign nations agreements reducing American tariffs up to 50 percent of the existing rates. Tariff reductions hinged on other nations reciprocating by lowering tariffs on American exports.
2 *Generalized Reductions* By incorporating **most-favored-nation clauses** in these agreements, the reduced tariffs would not only apply to the specific nation negotiating with the United States, but to all nations previously granted most-favored-nation status.

But the Reciprocal Trade Act gave rise to only bilateral (between-two-nations) negotiations. This approach was broadened in 1947 when twenty-three nations, including the United States, signed a **General Agreement on Tariffs and Trade (GATT).** GATT is based on three cardinal principles: (1) equal, nondiscriminatory treatment for all member nations;

---

[3]United States International Trade Commission.

[4]Average tariff-rate figures understate the importance of tariffs, however, by not accounting for the fact that some goods are excluded from American markets because of existing tariffs. Also, average figures conceal the high tariffs on particular items.

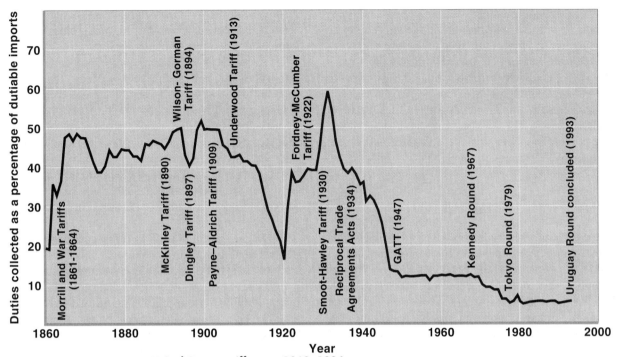

FIGURE 6-6   United States tariff rates, 1860–1994
American tariff rates have fluctuated historically. But beginning with the Reciprocal Trade Agreements Act of 1934, the trend has been downward. (U.S. Department of Commerce data.)

(2) the reduction of tariffs by multilateral negotiations; and (3) the elimination of import quotas.

Basically, GATT is a forum to negotiate reductions in trade barriers on a multilateral basis among nations. More than 120 nations now belong to GATT, and there is little doubt that it has been a positive force in the trend toward liberalized trade. Under its sponsorship, member nations have completed eight "rounds" of negotiations to reduce trade barriers in the post-World War II period.

Uruguay Round   The eighth "round" of GATT negotiations began in Uruguay in 1986. After seven years of wrangling, in 1993 the 124 participant nations reached a new agreement. This new agreement took effect on January 1, 1995 and its provisions will be phased in through 2005.

The major provisions of the new GATT agreement are:

1   *Tariff Reduction*   Tariffs will be eliminated or reduced on thousands of products, including construction equipment, medical equipment, paper, steel, chemicals, wood, memory chips, and aluminum. Overall, tariffs will drop by about 33 percent.

2   *Inclusion of Services*   Services are now a $900 billion segment of world trade and GATT will apply to them for the first time. The GATT accord will liberalize governmental rules which in the past have impeded the global market for advertising, insurance, consulting, accounting, legal, tourist, financial, and other services.

3   *Agriculture*   All member nations together agree to cut agricultural subsidies they pay to farmers, reducing the collective total subsidy by about 21 percent, or $300 billion annually. The agreement lifts Japanese and South Korean bans on rice importation and phases out American quotas on sugar, dairy products, and peanuts. These quotas will be replaced with tariffs.

4   *Intellectual Property*   International protection against piracy is provided for intellectual property such as patents, trademarks, and copyrights. This protection will greatly benefit American book publishers, music producers, and software firms.

5   *Phased Reduction of Quotas on Textiles and Apparel*   Quotas on imported textiles and apparel will be phased out over a ten-year period, to be replaced with tariffs. These quotas have choked off apparel and clothing imports to the industrial nations. Eliminating them will benefit developing countries having comparative advantages in these areas.

6 *World Trade Organization* GATT creates the World Trade Organization with judicial powers to mediate among members disputing the new rules.

When fully implemented, the GATT agreement will boost the world's GDP by an estimated $6 trillion, or 8 percent! Consumers in the United States will gain about $30 billion annually.

European Union

Countries have also sought to reduce tariffs by creating regional free-trade zones or trade blocs. The most dramatic example is the **European Union (EU),** formerly called the European Economic Community. Initiated as the Common Market in 1958, the EU now comprises fifteen western European nations—France, Germany, Italy, Belgium, the Netherlands, Luxembourg, Denmark, Ireland, United Kingdom, Greece, Spain, Portugal, Austria, Finland, and Sweden.

Goals The original Common Market called for (1) gradual abolition of tariffs and import quotas on all products traded among the participating nations; (2) establishment of a common system of tariffs applicable to all goods received from nations outside the EU; (3) free movement of capital and labor within the Common Market; and (4) creation of common policies in other economic matters of joint concern, such as agriculture, transportation, and restrictive business practices. The EU has achieved most of these goals and is now a strong **trade bloc.**

Results Motives for creating the European Union were both political and economic. The main economic motive was freer trade for members. While it is difficult to determine how much of EU prosperity and growth has resulted from economic integration, integration clearly has created the mass markets essential to EU industries. The economies of large-scale production have enabled European industries to achieve the lower costs historically denied them by small, localized markets.

Effects on nonmember nations, such as the United States, are less certain. On the one hand, a peaceful and increasingly prosperous EU makes its member nations better customers for American exports. On the other, American and other nonmember firms encounter tariffs which make it difficult to compete against firms within the EU trade bloc. For example, before the establishment of the EU, American German, and French automobile manufacturers all faced the same tariff selling their products in, say, Belgium. However, with the establishment of internal trading among EU members, Belgian tariffs on German Volkswagens and French Renaults fell to zero, but an external tariff still applies to American Chevrolets and Fords. This puts American firms at a serious disadvantage. Similarly, EU trade restrictions hamper eastern European exports of metals, textiles, and farm products, goods which the eastern Europeans produce in abundance.

By giving preferences to other countries within their free-trade zone, trade blocs such as the EU may reduce their trade with nonbloc members. Thus, the world loses some of the benefits of a completely open global trading system. Eliminating this disadvantage has been one of the motivations for promoting freer global trade through GATT.

North American Free Trade Agreement

In 1993 Canada, Mexico, and the United States formed a trade bloc. The **North American Free Trade Agreement (NAFTA)** established a free-trade zone having about the same combined output as the EU, but a much larger geographical area. A 1989 free-trade agreement between the United States and Canada preceded NAFTA. Through this United States–Canada accord, Canadian producers have gained increased access to a market ten times the size of Canada; United States' consumers have gained advantage of lower-price Canadian goods. Eliminating the high Canadian tariffs has helped American producers and Canadian consumers. Because Canada is the United States' largest trade partner, there have been large gains to each country from the United States–Canadian accord. When fully implemented in 1999, the agreement is expected to generate $1 billion to $3 billion of annual gains for each nation.

Free trade with Mexico is more controversial in the United States than is free trade with Canada. NAFTA will eliminate tariffs and other trade barriers between Mexico and the United States and Canada over a fifteen-year period. Critics of the agreement fear a loss of American jobs as firms move to Mexico to take advantage of lower wages and less stringent regulations on pollution and workplace safety. Also, there is concern that Japan and South Korea will build plants in Mexico to transport goods duty-free to the United States, further hurting American firms and workers.

Defenders of NAFTA reject these concerns and cite several strong arguments in its favor:

1 Specialization according to comparative advantage will enable the United States to obtain more total output from its scarce resources.

2 The reduction of high Mexican tariffs will greatly increase American exports to Mexico.

3 This free-trade zone will encourage worldwide investment in Mexico, enhancing Mexican productivity and national income. Mexican consumers will use some of that increased income to buy United States exports.

4 A higher standard of living in Mexico eventually will help stem the flow of illegal immigrants to the United States.

5 The higher standard of living in Mexico will enable Mexico to afford more pollution control equipment and to provide safer workplaces.

6 The loss of specific American jobs to Mexico may have occurred anyway to low-wage countries such as South Korea, Taiwan, and Hong Kong. NAFTA will enable and encourage American firms to be more efficient, enhancing their long-term competitiveness with firms in Japan and the European Union.

7 By binding Mexico to an international agreement, NAFTA will lock in the politically fragile free-market reforms already implemented by Mexico.

It may appear that the world's nations are combining into potentially hostile trade blocs. But NAFTA constitutes a vehicle to negotiate reductions in trade barriers with the EU, Japan, and other trading countries. Access to the vast North American market is as important to the EU and Japan as is access to their markets by the United States, Canada, and Mexico. NAFTA gives the United States a lever in future trade negotiations with the EU and Japan. Conceivably, direct negotiations between NAFTA and the EU could eventually link the two free-trade zones. Japan and other major trading nations, not wishing to be left out of the world's wealthiest trade markets, would be forced to eliminate their high trade barriers—to open their domestic markets to additional imports. Nor do other nations and trade blocs want to be excluded from free-trade zones. Examples:

1 *APEC* In late 1994 the United States and seventeen other members of the Asia-Pacific Economic Cooperation (APEC) nations agreed to establish freer trade and more open investment over the next few decades. APEC nations are Australia, Brunei, Canada, Chile, Hong Kong, Indonesia, Japan, Malaysia, Mexico, New Zealand, the Philippines, Papua New Guinea, Singapore, South Korea, Taiwan, Thailand, and the United States.

2 *Admission of Chile into NAFTA* At the invitation of Canada, Mexico, and the United States, Chile has agreed to become the fourth partner in NAFTA.

3 *Mercosur* The free-trade area encompassing Brazil, Argentina, Uruguay, and Paraguay—called *Mercosur*—is interested in linking up with NAFTA. So are other South American countries. In late 1994 President Clinton and thirty-three other presidents and prime ministers of Western hemisphere nations agreed to begin negotiations on a free-trade area from "Alaska to Argentina."

Economists agree that the *ideal* free-trade area would be the world. *(Key Question 10)*

QUICK REVIEW 6-3

■ Governments promote exports and reduce imports through tariffs, quotas, nontariff barriers, and export subsidies.

■ The various "rounds" of the General Agreement on Tariffs and Trade (GATT) have established multinational reductions in tariffs and import quotas among the more than 120 member nations.

■ The Uruguay Round of GATT which went into effect in 1995: *a* reduced tariffs worldwide; *b* liberalized rules impeding barriers to trade in services; *c* reduced agricultural subsidies; *d* created new protections for intellectual property; *e* phased out quotas on textiles and apparel; and *f* set up the World Trade Organization, the successor to GATT.

■ The European Union (EU) and the North American Free Trade Agreement (NAFTA) have reduced internal trade barriers by establishing large free-trade zones.

CAN AMERICAN FIRMS COMPETE?

Freer international trade has brought with it intense competition in a number of product markets in the United States and the world. Not long ago three large domestic producers dominated our automobile industry. Imported autos were an oddity, accounting for a minuscule portion of auto sales. But General Motors, Ford, and Chrysler now face intense competition as they struggle for sales against Nissan, Honda, Toyota, Hyundai, BMW, and others. Similarly, imports

LAST WORD

BUY AMERICAN: THE GLOBAL REFRIGERATOR

Humorist Art Buchwald looks at the logic of the "Buy American" campaign.

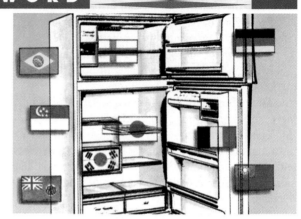

"There is only one way the country is going to get on its feet," said Baleful.

"How's that?" I asked, as we drank coffee in his office at the Baleful Refrigerator Company.

"The consumer has to start buying American," he said, slamming his fist down on the desk. "Every time an American buys a foreign refrigerator it costs one of my people his job. And every time one of my people is out of work it means he or she can't buy refrigerators."

"It's a vicious circle," I said.

Baleful's secretary came in. "Mr. Thompson, the steel broker is on the phone."

My friend grabbed the receiver. "Thompson, where is that steel shipment from Japan that was supposed to be in last weekend? . . . I don't care about weather. We're almost out of steel, and I'll have to close down the refrigerator assembly line next week. If you can't deliver when you promise, I'll find myself another broker."

"You get your steel from Japan?" I asked Baleful.

"Even with shipping costs, their price is still lower than steel made in Europe. We used to get all our sheets from Belgium, but the Japanese are now giving them a run for their money."

The buzzer on the phone alerted Baleful. He listened for a few moments and then said, "Excuse me, I have a call from Taiwan. Mark Four? Look, R&D designed a new push-button door handle and we're going to send the specs to you. Tell Mr. Chow if his people send us a sample of one and can make it for us at the same price as the old handle, we'll give his company the order."

---

have gained major market shares in automobile tires, clothing, sporting goods, electronics, motorcycles, outboard motors, and toys.

Nevertheless, thousands of American firms—large and small—have thrived and prospered in the global marketplace. Boeing, McDonald's, Dow Chemicals, Intel, Coca-Cola, 3M, Microsoft, AT&T, Monsanto, Procter & Gamble, and Hewlett-Packard are just a few cases. These and many other firms have continued to retain high market shares at home and have dramatically expanded their sales abroad. Of course, not all firms have been so successful. Some corporations simply have not been able to compete; their international competitors make better-quality products, have lower production costs, or both. Not surprisingly, the American firms which have been most vulnerable to foreign competition are precisely those which have enjoyed long periods of trade protection via tariffs and quotas. These barriers to imports have artificially limited competition, dampening incentives to innovate, reduce costs, and improve

products. Also, trade barriers have shielded some domestic firms from the usual consequences of national shifts in comparative advantages over time. As trade protection declines under GATT and NAFTA, some American firms will surely discover that they are producing goods for which America clearly has a comparative *dis*advantage (apparel, for example).

Is the greater competition accompanying the global economy a good thing? Although some domestic producers and their workers do not like it, foreign competition clearly benefits consumers. Imports reduce product prices and provide consumers with a greater variety of goods. Foreign competition also forces domestic producers to become more efficient and to improve product quality—precisely the outcome in several American industries, including autos and steel. Evidence shows that most—clearly not all —American firms *can* and *do* compete successfully in the global economy.

What about American firms which cannot successfully compete in open markets? The harsh reality

A man came in with a plastic container and said, "Mr. Baleful, you said you wanted to see one of these before we ordered them. They are the containers for the ice maker in the refrigerator."

Baleful inspected it carefully and banged it on the floor a couple of times. "What's the price on it?"

"Hong Kong can deliver it at $2 a tray, and Dong-Fu Plastics in South Korea said they can make it for $1.70."

"It's just a plastic tray. Take the South Korea bid. We'll let Hong Kong supply us with the shelves for the freezer. Any word on the motors?"

"There's a German company in Brazil that just came out with a new motor, and it's passed all our tests, so Johnson has ordered 50,000."

"Call Cleveland Motors and tell them we're sorry, but the price they quoted us was just too high."

"Yes, sir," the man said and departed.

The secretary came in again and said, "Harry telephoned and wanted to let you know the defroster just arrived from Finland. They're unloading the box cars now."

"Good. Any word on the wooden crates from Singapore?"

"They're at the dock in Hoboken."

"Thank heaven. Cancel the order from Boise Cascade."

"What excuse should I give them?"

"Tell them we made a mistake in our inventory, or we're switching to plastic. I don't care what you tell them."

Baleful turned to me. "Where were we?"

"You were saying that if the consumer doesn't start buying American, this country is going to be in a lot of trouble."

"Right. It's not only his patriotic duty, but his livelihood that's at stake. I'm going to Washington next week to tell the Senate Commerce Committee that if they don't get on the stick, there isn't going to be a domestic refrigerator left in this country. We're not going to stay in business for our health."

"Pour it to them," I urged him.

Baleful said, "Come out with me into the showroom."

I followed him. He went to his latest model, and opened the door. "This is an American refrigerator made by the American worker, for the American consumer. What do you have to say to that?"

"It's beautiful," I said. "It puts foreign imports to shame.

Source: Art Buchwald, "Being Bullish on Buying American." Reprinted by permission. We discovered this article in *Master Curriculum Guide in Economics: Teaching Strategies for International Trade* (New York: Joint Council on Economic Education, 1988).

---

is that they should go out of business, much like an unsuccessful corner boutique. Persistent economic losses mean valuable scarce resources are not being used efficiently. Shifting these resources to alternative, profitable uses will increase the total value of American output.

CHAPTER SUMMARY

1 International trade is growing in importance globally and for the United States. World trade is vital to the United States in two respects. **a** The absolute volumes of American imports and exports exceed those of any other single nation. **b** The United States is completely dependent on trade for certain commodities and materials which cannot be obtained domestically.

2 Our principal exports include chemicals, computers, consumer durables, aircraft, and grain; our major imports are petroleum, automobiles, clothing, computers, and household appliances. Quantitatively, Canada is our most important trading partner.

3 Global trade has been greatly facilitated by **a** improvements in transportation technology; **b** improvements in communications technology;   **c** general declines in tariffs; and   **d** peaceful relations among major industrial nations. The United States, Japan, and the western European nations dominate the global economy. But the total volume of trade has been increased by several new trade participants, including the "Asian tigers" (Hong Kong, Singapore, South Korea, and Taiwan), China, the eastern European countries, and the new independent countries of the former Soviet Union.

4 The open-economy circular flow model connects the domestic U.S. economy to the rest of the world. Customers from abroad enter our product market to buy some of our output. These American exports create business revenues and generate income in the United States. American households spend some of their money income on products made abroad and imported to the United States.

5   Specialization according to comparative advantage permits nations to achieve higher standards of living through exchange with other countries. A trading partner should specialize in products and services where its domestic opportunity costs are lowest. The terms of trade must be such that both nations can get more of a particular output via trade than they can at home.

6   The foreign exchange market sets exchange rates between nations' currencies. Foreign importers are suppliers of their currencies and American importers are demanders of foreign currencies. The resulting equilibrium exchange rates link the price levels of all nations. Depreciation of the dollar reduces our imports and increases our exports; dollar appreciation increases our imports and reduces our exports.

7   Governments shape trade flows through a protective tariffs; b quotas; c nontariff barriers; and d export subsidies. These are impediments to free trade; they result from misunderstanding about the gains from trade and from political considerations. By driving up product prices, trade barriers cost American consumers billions of dollars annually.

8   The Reciprocal Trade Agreements Act of 1934 marked the beginning of a trend toward lower American tariffs. In 1947 the General Agreement on Tariffs and Trade (GATT) was formed to a encourage nondiscriminatory treatment for all trading nations; b reduce tariffs; and c eliminate import quotas.

9   The Uruguay Round of GATT negotiations, completed in 1993: a reduced tariffs; b liberalized trade in services; c reduced agricultural subsidies; d reduced pirating of intellectual property; e phased out import quotas on textiles and apparel; and f established the World Trade Organization, which replaces GATT.

10   Free-trade zones (trade blocs) may liberalize trade within regions but may also impede trade with nonbloc members. Two examples of free-trade arrangements are a the European Union (EU), formerly the European Community or "Common Market"; and b the North American Free Trade Agreement (NAFTA), comprising Canada, Mexico, the United States, and later, Chile.

11   The global economy has created intense foreign competition in many American product markets.

TERMS AND CONCEPTS

multinational corporations	appreciation	Reciprocal Trade Agreements Act of 1934	European Union (EU)
"Asian tigers"	protective tariffs		trade bloc
comparative advantage	import quotas	most-favored-nation clauses	North American Free Trade Agreement (NAFTA)
terms of trade	nontariff barriers		
foreign exchange market	export subsidies	General Agreement on Tariffs and Trade (GATT)	
depreciation	Smoot-Hawley Tariff Act of 1930		

QUESTIONS AND STUDY SUGGESTIONS

1   What is the quantitative importance of world trade to the United States? Who is the United States' most important trade partner, quantitatively? How have persistent United States trade deficits been financed? "Trade deficits mean we get more merchandise from the rest of the world than we provide them in return. Therefore, trade deficits are economically desirable." Do you agree?

2   Account for the rapid growth of world trade since World War II. Who are the major players in international trade? Who are the "Asian tigers" and how important are they in world trade?

3   *Key Question   Use the circular flow model (Figure 6-3) to explain how an increase in exports would affect revenues of domestic firms, money income of domestic households, and imports from abroad. Use Table 6-3 to find the exact*

amounts (1993) of United States exports (flow 13) and imports (flow 16) in the circular flow model. What do these amounts imply for flows 14 and 15?

4   *Key Question   The following are production possibilities tables for South Korea and the United States. Assume that before specialization and trade the optimal product-mix for South Korea is alternative B and for the United States alternative U.*

Product	South Korea's production possibilities					
	A	B	C	D	E	F
Radios (in thousands)	30	24	18	12	6	0
Chemicals (in tons)	0	6	12	18	24	30

Product	U.S. production possibilities					
	R	S	T	U	V	W
Radios (in thousands)	10	8	6	4	2	0
Chemicals (in tons)	0	4	8	12	16	20

a *Are comparative-cost conditions such that the two areas should specialize? If so, what product should each produce?*

b *What is the total gain in radio and chemical output which results from this specialization?*

c *What are the limits of the terms of trade? Suppose actual terms of trade are 1 unit of radios for $1\frac{1}{2}$ units of chemicals and that 4 units of radios are exchanged for 6 units of chemicals. What are the gains from specialization and trade for each area?*

d *Can you conclude from this illustration that specialization according to comparative advantage results in more efficient use of world resources? Explain.*

5 Suppose that the comparative-cost ratios of two products—baby formula and tuna fish—are as follows in the hypothetical nations of Canswicki and Tunata.

Canswicki: 1 can baby formula = 2 cans tuna fish

Tunata: 1 can baby formula = 4 cans tuna fish

In what product should each nation specialize? Explain why terms of trade of 1 can baby formula = $2\frac{1}{2}$ cans tuna fish would be acceptable to both nations.

6 *Key Question* "*Our exports create a demand for foreign currencies; foreign imports of our goods generate supplies of foreign currencies.*" *Do you agree? Would a decline in American incomes or a weakening of American preferences for foreign products cause the dollar to depreciate or appreciate? What would be the effects of that depreciation or appreciation on our exports and imports?*

7 If the French franc declines in value (depreciates) in the foreign exchange market, will it be easier or harder for the French to sell their wine in the United States? Suppose you were planning a trip to Paris. How would the depreciation of the franc change the dollar price of this trip?

8 True or False? "An increase in the American dollar price of the German mark implies that the German mark has depreciated in value." Explain.

9 What tools do governments use to promote exports and restrict imports? What are the benefits and the costs of protectionist policies? What is the net outcome for society?

10 *Key Question What is GATT? How does it affect nearly every person in the world? What were the major outcomes of the Uruguay Round of GATT? How is GATT related to the European Union (EU) and the North American Free Trade Agreement (NAFTA)?*

11 Explain: "Free-trade zones such as the EU and NAFTA lead a double life: They can promote free trade among members, but pose serious trade obstacles for nonmembers." Do you think the net effects of these trade blocs are good or bad for world trade?

12 Do you think American firms will be able to compete with foreign firms in world trade during the next twenty years? What do you see as the competitive strengths of American firms? Competitive weaknesses? Explain: "Even if Japan captured the entire worldwide auto market, that simply would mean that Japan would have to buy a whole lot of other products from abroad. Thus, the United States and other industrial nations would necessarily experience an increase in exports to Japan."

13 (Last Word) What point is Art Buchwald making in his humorous essay on the Baleful Refrigerator Company? Why might Mr. Baleful *oppose* tariffs on imported goods, even though he wants consumers to buy "American" refrigerators?

PART TWO

National Income, Employment and Fiscal Policy

MEASURING DOMESTIC OUTPUT, NATIONAL INCOME, AND THE PRICE LEVEL

"**D**isposable Income Flat"; "Personal Consumption Surges"; "Domestic Investment Stagnates"; "Japan Suffers GDP Decline"; "GDP Deflator Rises Less Rapidly Than CPI"

Typical headlines in the business and economics news. Gibberish—unless you know the language of macroeconomics and national income accounting. This chapter will help you learn this language and understand the ideas it communicates.

There are two substantial payoffs from carefully studying this chapter. One is an understanding of the basics of how government statisticians and accountants measure and record the levels of domestic output, national income, and prices for the economy. Second, knowledge of the terms and ideas examined in this chapter—for example, consumption, investment, government purchases, net exports, real GDP, national income, and the price level—will help you comprehend material in subsequent chapters.

In the present chapter we will first explain why it is important to measure the performance of the economy. Second, we define the key measure of total output—gross domestic product (GDP)—and show how it is measured. We then derive and explain several other important measures of output and income. Next, measurement of the overall level of prices —the price level—is examined. We then demonstrate how GDP is adjusted for inflation or deflation so that changes in the physical amount of a nation's production are more accurately reflected. Finally, some limitations of the measures of domestic output and national income are listed and explained.

MACROECONOMIC MEASUREMENT

Our first goal is to explain the ways the overall production performance of the economy is measured. This comes under the heading of national income accounting, which does for the economy as a whole what private accounting does for the individual business enterprise or, for that matter, for the household. The

business executive must know how well his or her firm is doing, but that is not always immediately discernible.

A firm measures its flows of income and expenditures to assess its operations, usually for a three-month period or for the current year. With this information in hand the firm can gauge its economic health. If things are going well, the accounting data can be used to explain this success. Costs might be down or output or prices up, resulting in large profits. If things are going badly, accounting measures can help discover why. And by examining the accounts over a specific period, the firm can detect growth or decline of profits and what caused the change. All this information helps the firm's managers make intelligent business decisions.

National income accounting operates in much the same way for the economy.

1 It allows us to keep a finger on the economic pulse of the nation. Our national income accounting system permits us to measure the level of production in the economy at some point in time and explain why it's at that level.

2 By comparing national income accounts over a number of years, we can track the long-run course of the economy and see whether it has grown, been steady, or stagnated.

3 Information supplied by national income accounts provides a basis for formulating and applying public policies to improve the performance of the economy. Without national income accounts, economic policy would be based on guesswork. *National income accounting allows us to keep tabs on the health of the economy and formulate polices which will maintain and improve that health.*

GROSS DOMESTIC PRODUCT

There are many measures of the economic well-being of society. But the best available measure is its annual total output of goods and services or, as it is sometimes called, the economy's aggregate output. There are two ways of measuring an economy's total output of goods and services: gross national product and gross domestic product. Both measure *the total market value of all final goods and services produced in the economy in one year.* They are closely related, differing only in how the "economy" is defined.

Gross national product (GNP) consists of the total output produced by land, labor, capital, and entrepreneurial talent supplied by Americans, *whether these resources are located in the United States or abroad.* For example, the share of output (income) produced by an American working in France or Saudi Arabia is included in our GNP. Conversely, the share of output (income) produced in the United States by foreign-owned resources is excluded from our GNP.

Gross domestic product (GDP) is slightly different. It comprises the value of the total goods and services *produced within the boundaries of the United States,* whether by American or foreign-supplied resources. For instance, the value of the autos produced at a Japanese-owned Nissan factory in the United States, including profits, is a part of American GDP. Conversely, profits earned by an American-owned IBM plant in France are excluded from our GDP.

Specifically, the difference between GDP and GNP consists of *net foreign factor income earned (output produced) in the United States.* This amount is found by subtracting receipts of factor (resource) income *from* the rest of the world from payments of factor income *to* the rest of the world. Net foreign factor income earned in the United States can be positive or negative. In 1994 it was a *positive* $12 billion, meaning that foreign-owned resources produced and earned more in the United States than American-supplied resources produced and earned abroad.

	Billions
Factor payments to the rest of the world	$178
Less: Factor receipts from the rest of the world	166
Net foreign factor income earned in the U.S.	$12

Since net foreign factor income earned in the United States is positive, GDP in the United States exceeds GNP. The total value of output produced within the borders of the United States (GDP) is greater than the total value of output produced by Americans, wherever located (GNP):

	Billions
Gross national product	$6725
Plus: Net foreign factor income earned in the U.S.	12
Gross domestic product	$6737

Because most nations, including the United States, use GDP as the measure of their output, our focus will be on GDP. *(Key Question 2)*

A Monetary Measure

If the economy produces three oranges and two apples in year 1 and two oranges and three apples in year 2, in which year is output greater? We cannot answer this question until price tags are attached to the various products as indicators of society's evaluation of their relative worth.

That's what GDP does. It measures the market value of annual output; it is a monetary measure. In-

...rogeneous outputs by using money prices

...uts	Market values
...nd 2 apples	3 at 20 cents + 2 at 30 cents = $1.20
...nd 3 apples	2 at 20 cents + 3 at 30 cents = $1.30

...he heteroge-
...produced in
...of their rel-

...is 20 cents
...'s output is
...es year 2's
...$.10 more
...2 than for

Avoiding Double Counting

To measure total output accurately, all goods and services produced in any specific year must be counted once, but not more than once. Most products go through a series of production stages before reaching a market. As a result, parts or components of most products are bought and sold many times. To avoid counting several times the parts of products that are sold and resold, GDP includes only the market value of final goods and ignores transactions involving intermediate goods.

By **final goods** we mean goods and services being purchased for final use and not for resale or further processing or manufacturing. *They are "purchases not resold."* Transactions involving **intermediate goods** refer to purchases of goods and services for further processing and manufacturing or for resale.

The sale of *final goods is included* and the sale of *intermediate goods is excluded* from GDP. Why? Because the value of final goods already includes all intermediate transactions involved in producing those final goods. To count intermediate transactions separately would be **double counting** and exaggerating the value of GDP.

To clarify this, suppose there are five stages of production in getting a wool suit manufactured and to the consumer—the ultimate or final user. As Table 7-2 indicates, firm A, a sheep ranch, provides $120 worth of wool to firm B, a wool processor. Firm A pays out the $120 it receives in wages, rents, interest, and profits. Firm B processes the wool and sells it to firm C, a suit manufacturer, for $180. What does firm B do with this $180? As noted, $120 goes to firm A, and the remaining $60 is used by B to pay wages, rents, interest, and profits for the resources needed in processing the wool. The manufacturer sells the suit to firm D, a clothing wholesaler, who sells it to firm E, a retailer, and then, at last, it is bought for $350 by a consumer, the final user.

At each stage, the difference between what a firm has paid for the product and what it receives for its sale is paid out as wages, rent, interest, and profits for

TABLE 7-2 Value added in a five-stage production process

(1) Stage of production	(2) Sales value of materials or product	(3) Value added
	0	
Firm A, sheep ranch	$ 120	$120 (= $120 − $ 0)
Firm B, wool processor	180	60 (= 180 − 120)
Firm C, suit manufacturer	220	40 (= 220 − 180)
Firm D, clothing wholesaler	270	50 (= 270 − 220)
Firm E, retail clothier	350	80 (= 350 − 270)
Total sales values	$1140	
Value added (total income)		$350

NATIONAL INCOME, EMPLOYMENT, AND FISCAL POLICY

the resources used by that firm in helping to produce and distribute the suit.

How much should we include in GDP in accounting for the production of this suit? Just $350, the value of the final product. This figure includes all the intermediate transactions leading up to the product's final sale. It would be a gross distortion to sum all the intermediate sales figures and the final sales value of the product in column 2 and include the entire amount, $1140, in GDP. This would be double counting: counting the final product *and* the sale and resale of its various parts in the multistage productive process. The production and sale of the suit has generated $350, *not* $1140, worth of output and income.

To avoid double counting, national income accountants are careful to calculate only the *value added* by each firm. **Value added** is the market value of a firm's output *less* the value of the inputs which it has purchased from others. In column 3 of Table 7-2 the value added of firm B is $60, the difference between the $180 value of its output and the $120 it paid for the inputs provided by firm A. By adding together the values added by the five firms in Table 7-2, the total value of the suit can be accurately determined. Similarly, by calculating and summing the values added by all firms in the economy, we can determine the GDP—the market value of total output.

GDP Excludes Nonproduction Transactions

GDP measures the annual production of the economy. The many nonproduction transactions which occur each year must be excluded. *Nonproduction transactions* are of two major types: (1) purely financial transactions, and (2) secondhand sales.

Financial Transactions Purely financial transactions are of three general kinds.

1 Public Transfer Payments These are the social security payments, welfare payments, and veterans' payments which government makes to particular households. The basic characteristic of public transfer payments is that recipients make no contribution to *current* production in return for them. To include them in GDP would be to overstate this year's production.

2 Private Transfer Payments These payments, for example, a university student's monthly subsidy from home or an occasional gift from a wealthy relative, do not entail production but simply the transfer of funds from one private individual to another.

3 Security Transactions Buying and selling of stocks and bonds are also excluded from GDP. Stock market transactions involve swapping paper assets. The amount spent on these assets does not directly create current production. Only the services provided by the security broker are included in GDP. However, sales of *new* issues of stocks and bonds transfer money from savers to businesses which often spend the proceeds on capital goods. Thus, these transactions may indirectly contribute to spending, which does account for output and hence add to GDP.

Secondhand Sales Secondhand sales are excluded from GDP because they either reflect no *current* production, or involve double counting. If you sell your 1965 Ford Mustang to a friend, this transaction would be excluded in determining GDP because no current production is involved. Including the sales of goods produced some years ago in this year's GDP would be an exaggeration of this year's output. Similarly, if you purchased a brand new Mustang and resold it a week later to your neighbor, we would still exclude the resale transaction from the current GDP. When you originally bought the new car, that's when its value was included in GDP. To include its resale value at a later time would be to count it twice.

Two Sides to GDP: Spending and Income

We now must consider how the market value of total output—or for that matter, any single unit of output—is measured. Returning to Table 7-2, how can we measure the market value of a suit?

We can determine how much a consumer, the final user, pays for it. Or we can add up all the wage, rental, interest, and profit incomes created in its production. This second approach is the value-added technique discussed in Table 7-2.

The final-product and value-added approaches are two ways of looking at the same thing. *What is spent on a product is received as income by those who contributed to its production.* Chapter 2's circular flow model demonstrated this. If $350 is spent on the suit, then $350 is the total amount of income derived from its production. You can verify this by looking at the incomes generated by firms A, B, C, D, and E in Table 7-2—$120, $60, $40, $50, and $80—which total $350.

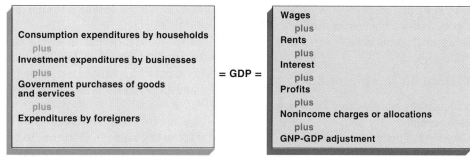

FIGURE 7-1   The output and income approaches to GDP
There are two general approaches to measuring gross domestic product. We can determine the value of output by summing the expenditures on that output. Alternatively, with some modifications, we can determine GDP by adding up the components of income arising from producing that output.

This equality of the expenditure for a product and the income derived from its production is guaranteed, because profit income is a balancing item. Profit—or loss—is the income remaining after wage, rent, and interest incomes have been paid by the producer. If the wage, rent, and interest incomes the firm must pay in getting the suit produced are less than the $350 expenditure for the suit, the difference will be the firm's profits.[1] Conversely, if wage, rent, and interest incomes exceed $350, profits will be negative. That is, losses will be realized, to balance the expenditure on the product and the income derived from its production.

It is the same for the output of the economy as a whole. There are two ways of looking at GDP: One is to see GDP as the sum of all the expenditures in buying that total output. This is the *output,* or **expenditures, approach.** The other views GDP in terms of the income derived or created from producing it. This is the *earnings,* or *allocations,* or **income, approach.**

GDP can be determined either by adding up all that is spent to buy this year's total output or by summing up all the incomes derived from the production of this year's output. Putting this as an equation, we can say

$$\left.\begin{array}{l}\text{Amount spent to}\\ \text{purchase this year's}\\ \text{total output}\end{array}\right\} = \left\{\begin{array}{l}\text{money income}\\ \text{derived from}\\ \text{production of}\\ \text{this year's output}\end{array}\right.$$

This is more than an equation: It is an identity. Buying (spending money) and selling (receiving money

income) are two aspects of the same transaction. *What is spent on a product is income to those who have contributed their human and property resources in getting that product produced and to market.*

For the economy as a whole, we can expand our identity to read as in Figure 7-1. Considered as output, all final goods produced in the American economy are purchased by the three domestic sectors—households, businesses, and government—and by foreign buyers. On the income side of GDP, this figure shows that (aside from a few complicating factors, discussed later) the total receipts businesses acquire from the sale of total output are allocated among resource suppliers as wage, rent, interest, and profit income. Using this diagram as a point of reference, we next examine the types of expenditures and the incomes derived from them.

EXPENDITURES APPROACH

To determine GDP through expenditures, we add up all types of spending on finished or final goods and services. But national income accountants have more precise terms for the different types of spending than those in Figure 7-1.

Personal Consumption Expenditures (C)

What we have called "consumption expenditures by households" is **personal consumption expenditures** to national income accountants. It includes expenditures by households on *durable consumer goods* (automobiles, refrigerators, video recorders), *non-*

---

[1]The term "profits" is used here in the accounting sense to include both normal profits and economic profits as defined in Chapter 4.

durable consumer goods (bread, milk, vitamins, pencils, shirts, toothpaste), and *consumer expenditures for services* (of lawyers, doctors, mechanics, barbers). We will use C to designate the total of these expenditures.

Gross Private Domestic Investment (I_g)

This refers to all investment spending by American business firms. It includes:
1 All final purchases of machinery, equipment, and tools by business enterprises
2 All construction
3 Changes in inventories

This is more than we have meant by "investment" thus far. We therefore must explain why each of these three items is included under the general heading of gross private domestic investment.

The first group simply restates our definition of investment spending as the purchase of tools, machinery, and equipment.

The second—all construction—such as building a new factory, warehouse, or grain elevator is also a form of investment. But why include residential construction as investment rather than consumption? Because apartment buildings are investment goods which, like factories and grain elevators, are income-earning assets. Other residential units which are rented are for the same reason investment goods. Owner-occupied houses are investment goods because they could be rented out to yield a money income return, even though the owner may not do so. For these reasons all residential construction is considered as investment.

Finally, changes in inventories are counted as investment because an increase in inventories is, in effect, "unconsumed output." And that precisely is what investment is!

Inventory Changes as Investment   Because GDP measures total current output, we must include in GDP any products produced this year even though *not sold* this year. To be an accurate measure of total production, GDP must include the market value of any additions to inventories accruing during the year. A tube of lipstick produced in 1995 must be counted as GDP in 1995, even though it remains unsold as of February of 1996. If we excluded an increase in inventories, GDP would understate the current year's total production. If businesses have more goods on their shelves and in warehouses at year's end than they had at the start, the economy has produced more

than it has purchased during this year. This increase in inventories must be added to GDP as a measure of *current* production.

What about a decline in inventories? This must be subtracted in figuring GDP. The economy can sell a total output which exceeds its production by dipping into, and thus reducing its inventories. Some of the GDP purchased this year reflects not current production but, rather, a drawing down of inventories on hand at the beginning of this year. And inventories on hand at the start of any year's production represent the production of previous years. The tube of lipstick produced in 1995, but sold in 1996, cannot be counted as 1996 GDP. Consequently, a decline in inventories in any specific year means the economy has purchased more than it has produced during that year. This means society has purchased all of that year's output plus some of the inventories inherited from the previous year's production. Because GDP is a measure of the *current* year's output, we must omit any purchases of past production, that is, any drawing down of inventories, in determining GDP.[2]

Noninvestment Transactions   We have discussed what investment is. Now we need to emphasize what it isn't. Investment does *not* refer to the transfer of paper assets or secondhand tangible assets. Economists exclude the buying of stocks and bonds from their definition of investment, because such purchases merely transfer the ownership of existing assets. It's the same for the resale of existing assets.

Investment is the construction or manufacture of *new* capital assets. The production of these assets creates jobs and income; the exchange of claims to existing capital goods does not.

Gross versus Net Investment   Our concepts of investment and investment goods include purchases of machinery and equipment, all construction, and changes in inventories. Let's now focus on the modifiers, "gross," "private," and "domestic," which describe investment. "Private" and "domestic" tell us we are talking about spending by private business enterprises as opposed to governmental (public) agencies, and that the investment is in America—rather than abroad.

---

[2]Both *planned* and *unplanned* changes in inventories are included as part of investment. In the former, firms may intentionally increase their inventories because aggregate sales are growing. In the latter, an unexpected drop in sales may leave firms with more unsold goods (larger inventories) than intended.

"Gross" is not as simple. **Gross private domestic investment** includes production of *all* investment goods—those which replace machinery, equipment, and buildings used up to produce the current year's output *plus* any net additions to the economy's stock of capital. Gross investment includes both replacement and added investment. **Net private domestic investment** refers only to the added investment in the current year.

To make the distinction clear: In 1994 our economy produced about $1038 billion of capital goods. However, in producing the GDP in 1994, the economy used up $716 billion of machinery and equipment. Thus, our economy added $322 (or $1038 minus $716) billion to its stock of capital in 1994. Gross investment was $1038 billion in 1994; net investment was only $322 billion. The difference is the value of the capital used up or depreciated in the production of 1994's GDP.

Net Investment and Economic Growth   The relationship between gross investment and *depreciation* —the amount of the nation's capital worn out or used up in a particular year—indicates whether our economy is expanding, static, or declining. Figure 7-2 illustrates these cases.

1   Expanding Economy   When gross investment exceeds depreciation (Figure 7-2a), the economy is expanding since its production capacity—measured by its stock of capital goods—is growing. Net investment is a positive figure in an expanding economy. For example, in 1994 gross investment was $1038 billion, and $716 billion of capital goods was consumed in producing that year's GDP. Our economy ended 1994 with $322 billion more capital goods than it had on hand at the start of the year. Bluntly stated, we added $322 billion to our "national factory" in 1994.

Increasing the supply of capital goods is a basic means of expanding the productive capacity of the economy (Chapter 2).

2   Static Economy   In a stationary or static economy gross investment and depreciation are equal (Figure 7-2b). The economy is standing pat; it produces just enough capital to replace what is consumed in producing the year's output—no more, no less. Example: During World War II, the Federal government purposely restricted private investment to free resources to produce war goods. In 1942 gross private investment and depreciation (replacement investment) were each about $10 billion. Thus net invest-

ment was about zero. At the end of 1942 our stock of capital was roughly the same as at the start of that year. Our economy was stationary; its production facilities failed to expand.

3   Declining Economy   An economy declines when gross investment is less than depreciation, that is, when the economy uses up more capital in a year than it produces (Figure 7-2c). When this happens net investment will be negative—the economy will be *disinvesting*. Depressions foster such circumstances. During bad times, when production and employment are low, the nation has a greater productive capacity than it is currently using. There is no incentive to replace depreciated capital equipment, much less add to the existing stock. Depreciation is likely to exceed gross investment, with the result that the nation's stock of capital is less at the end of the year than it was at the start.

This was the case during the Great Depression. In 1933 gross investment was only $1.6 billion, while the capital consumed during that year was $7.6 billion. Net disinvestment was therefore $6 billion. That is, net investment was a minus $6 billion, indicating that the size of our "national factory" shrunk during that year.

We will use I for domestic investment spending and attach the subscript g when referring to gross and n when referring to net investment. *(Key Question 5)*

Government Purchases (G)

Government purchases *include* all governmental spending (Federal, state, and local) on the finished products of businesses and all direct purchases of resources—labor, in particular. It *excludes* all government transfer payments, because such outlays do not reflect any current production but merely transfer governmental receipts to certain specific households. We'll use G to indicate **government purchases.**

Net Exports (X_n)

Do American international trade transactions enter into national income accounting? They do, and in this way: On the one hand, we include all spending in American markets accounting for or inducing the production of goods and services in the American economy. Spending by people abroad on American goods will account for American output just as will spending by Americans. Thus, we must add in what the rest of

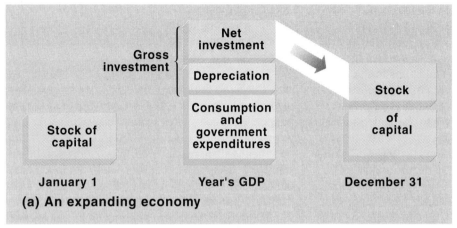

(a) An expanding economy

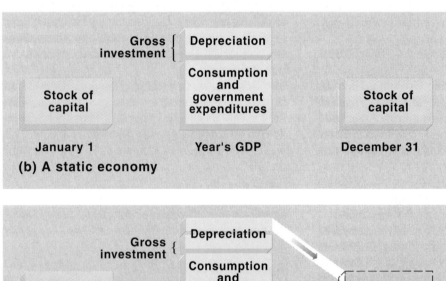

(b) A static economy

(c) A declining economy

FIGURE 7-2 Expanding, static, and declining economies

In an expanding economy (a), gross investment exceeds depreciation, which means that the economy is making a net addition to its stock of capital facilities. In a static economy (b), gross investment precisely replaces the capital facilities depreciated in producing the year's output, leaving the stock of capital goods unchanged. In a declining economy (c), gross investment is insufficient to replace the capital goods depreciated by the year's production. As a result, the economy's stock of capital declines.

the world spends on American goods and services—we must add in the value of American exports—in determining GDP by the expenditures approach.

On the other hand, we know that part of consumption, investment, and government purchases is for imports, meaning goods and services produced abroad. This spending does *not* reflect production activity in the United States. The value of imports is subtracted to avoid overstating total production in the United States.

Rather than treat American exports and imports separately, our national income accountants take the difference between them. Thus, net exports of goods and services, or **net exports,** is *the amount by which foreign spending on American goods and services exceeds American spending on foreign goods and services.*

If people abroad buy $45 billion worth of American exports and Americans buy $35 billion worth of foreign imports in a year, net exports would be *plus*

TABLE 7-3 The income statement for the economy, 1994 *(in billions of dollars)*

Receipts: expenditures approach		Allocations: income approach	
Personal consumption expenditures (C)	$4627	Compensation of employees	$4005
Gross private domestic investment (I_g)	1038	Rents	28
Government purchases (G)	1174	Interest	407
Net exports (X_n)	−102	Proprietors' income	473
		Corporate income taxes	203
		Dividends	205
		Undistributed corporate profits	135
		National income	5456
		Indirect business taxes	553
		Consumption of fixed capital	716
		Gross national product	6725
		Plus: Net foreign factor income earned in the U.S.	12
Gross domestic product	$6737	Gross domestic product	$6737

Source: U.S. Department of Commerce data. Because of rounding, details may not add up to totals.

$10 billion. Our definition of net exports might result in a negative figure. If the rest of the world spends $30 billion on American exports and Americans spend $40 billion on foreign imports, our "excess" of foreign spending over American spending is *minus* $10 billion.

Note in Table 7-3 that in 1994 Americans spent $102 billion more on foreign goods and services than the rest of the world spent on American goods and services, a matter which will receive our attention in later chapters.

The letter X_n will designate net exports.

$C + I_g + G + X_n =$ GDP

These four categories of expenditures—personal consumption expenditures *(C)*, gross private domestic investment *(I_g)*, government purchases *(G)*, and net exports *(X_n)*—are comprehensive. They include all possible types of spending. Added together, they measure the market value of the year's output or, in other words, the GDP. That is,

$$C + I_g + G + X_n = \text{GDP}$$

For 1994 (Table 7-3):

$$\$4627 + \$1038 + \$1174 - \$102 = \$6737$$

Global Perspective 7-1 compares GDPs for selected nations.

GLOBAL PERSPECTIVE 7-1

Comparative GDPs in trillions of dollars, 1993

The United States, Japan, and Germany have the world's highest GDPs. The GDP data are converted to dollars via international exchange rates.

GDP in Trillions of Dollars

0 1 2 3 4 5 6 7

- U.S.
- Japan
- Germany
- Britain
- France
- Italy
- Canada
- China
- Brazil
- Spain
- Mexico
- India
- Sweden

Source: International Monetary Fund data.

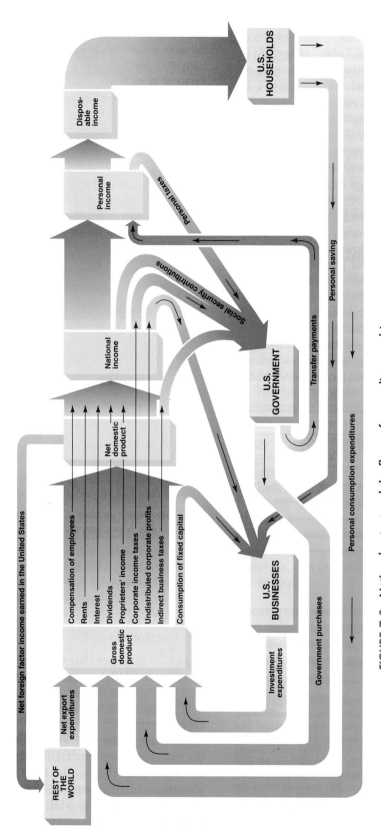

FIGURE 7-3 National output and the flows of expenditure and income

This figure is an elaborate circular flow diagram which fits the expenditures and allocations sides of GDP to one another. The income or allocations flows are shown in red; the expenditure flows, in green. You should trace through the income and expenditures flows, relating them to the five basic national income accounting measures.

TABLE 7-4   The relationships between GDP, NDP, NI, PI, and DI in 1994

	Billions
Gross domestic product (GDP)	$6737
Consumption of fixed capital	−716
Net domestic product (NDP)	$6021
Net foreign factor income earned in the U.S.	−12
Indirect business taxes	−553
National income (NI)	$5456
Social security contributions	−626
Corporate income taxes	−203
Undistributed corporate profits	−135
Transfer payments	+1210
Personal income (PI)	$5702
Personal taxes	−743
Disposable income (DI)	$4959

Note the flow of personal taxes out of PI and the division of DI between consumption and personal saving in the household sector. In the government sector the flows of revenue in the form of four basic types of taxes are denoted on the right; on the left, government disbursements take the form of purchases of goods and services and transfers. The position of the business sector emphasizes, on the left, investment expenditures and, on the right, the three major sources of funds for business investment.

Finally, observe the role of the rest of the world in the flow diagram. Spending by people abroad on our exports adds to our GDP, but our consumption, government, and investment expenditures buy imported products as well as domestically produced goods. The flow emanating from "Rest of the World" shows that we handle this complication by calculating *net* exports (exports minus imports). This may be a positive or a negative amount. Also, note that *net* foreign factor income earned in the United States is subtracted from NDP in deriving NI.

Figure 7-3 simultaneously portrays the expenditure and income aspects of GDP, fitting the two approaches to one another. These flows of expenditure and income are part of a continuous, repetitive process. Cause and effect are intermingled: Expenditures create income, and out of this income arise expenditures, which again flow to resource owners as income.

The table inside the covers of this book contains a useful historical summary of the national income accounts and related statistics.

MEASURING THE PRICE LEVEL

Thus far we have focused primarily on domestic output and national income. We now consider how the price level is measured.

Measurement of the price level is significant for two reasons.

1   Measuring Inflation and Deflation   It is useful to know how much the price level has changed, if at all, from one period to another. That is, we must be aware of whether and to what extent inflation (a rising price level) or deflation (a falling price level) has occurred.

2   Comparing GDPs   Because GDP is the market value, or total money value, of all final goods and services produced in a year, money values are used as the common measure to sum a heterogeneous output into a meaningful total. The value of different years' output (GDPs) can be meaningfully compared only if we account for changes in the value of money.

Price Indexes

The price level is stated as an index number. A **price index** measures the combined price of a particular collection of goods and services, called a "market basket," in a *specific* period relative to the combined price of an identical or similar group of goods and services in a *reference* period. This point of reference, or benchmark, is called the "base year." More formally,

$$\text{Price Index in a given year} = \frac{\text{price of market basket in a specific year}}{\text{price of the same market basket in the base year}} \times 100$$

By convention the price ratio between the specific year and the base year is multiplied by 100. For example, a price ratio of 2/1 (= 2) is expressed as an index number of 200. Similarly, a price ratio of 1/3 (= .33), is expressed as 33.

The Federal government computes indexes of the prices of several different collections or market baskets of goods and services. The best known of these indexes is the **consumer price index** (CPI), which measures the prices of a fixed market basket of some 300 consumer goods and services purchased by a "typical" urban consumer. In the CPI the items in the market basket are determined in a base year and their relative importance—their so-called "weights"—remain fixed in subsequent years. Neither the items nor their composition change from year to year. Because the CPI is an important measure of inflation, we will consider it in detail in this chapter's Last Word.

Another price index—the **GDP deflator**—is more relevant than the CPI for measuring the price level for all the goods comprising the GDP. The GDP deflator is broader than the CPI. The GDP deflator includes not only the prices of consumer goods and services, but also the prices of investment goods, goods and services purchased by government, and goods and services entering into world trade. For this reason, the GDP deflator is the price index used to account for inflation or deflation when comparing GDP from year to year.

The GDP deflator differs from the CPI in another respect. While the CPI employs a historic, fixed-composition market basket to calculate the CPI, the GDP deflator uses the *current* composition of output to determine the relative importance of the items in the market basket for the base year. This fact will become evident in the discussion which follows.

Computing a GDP Price Index

Table 7-5 gives an example of how a GDP price index or deflator can be computed in a particular year for a hypothetical economy. Observe from column 1 that in 1996 this economy produces only four goods: pizzas (a consumption good); industrial robots (a capital good); paper clips (a good purchased by government); and computer disks (an export good). Suppose that in 1996 the outputs of the four goods are 2, 1, 1, and 1 units, respectively, as shown in column 2. Also, assume that the per unit prices of these four products in 1996 are those shown in column 3. The total price (cost) of the 1996 output therefore is $64, an amount found by summing the expenditures on each of the four goods (column 4).

Now, let's arbitrarily select 1987 as our reference or base year to establish a price index for 1996. The 1987 prices of the components of the 1996 output are listed in column 5 of Table 7-5. From columns 5 and 3, we observe that the prices of pizza and paper clips were lower in 1987 than in 1996, the price of robots was higher, and the price of computer disks did not change. Most importantly, the total price (cost) of the 1996 output—shown at the bottom of column 6—was $50 in 1987 rather than $64 as in 1996. This tells us that the 1996 output would have cost $50 if 1987 prices had persisted. To determine the 1996 price index, we divide the 1996 price of the market basket ($64) by the 1987 price of that same collection of goods ($50). The quotient is then multiplied by 100 to express the price index in its conventional form.

$$\text{GDP price index}_{1996} = \frac{\text{price of market basket}_{1996}}{\text{price of 1996 market basket in the base year}_{1987}} \times 100$$

TABLE 7-5 Computing a GDP price index for 1996

(1) Product	(2) Quantities in market basket in 1996	(3) Prices of 1996 market basket in 1996	(4) Expenditures on 1996 market basket in 1996 (3) × (2)	(5) Prices of 1996 market basket in 1987 prices (base year)	(6) Expenditures on 1996 market basket in 1987 prices (5) × (2)
Pizzas	2	$12	$24	$ 5	$10
Robots	1	18	18	20	20
Paper clips	1	8	8	6	6
Computer disks	1	14	14	14	14
Total price (cost)			$64		$50
GDP price index 1996			$128 \left(= \frac{\$64}{\$50} \times 100 \right)$		

$$\text{GDP price index}_{1993} = \frac{\$64}{\$50} \times 100 = 128$$

The price index for 1996 is 128. This index value may be thought of as the price level for 1996.

These steps can be used to calculate the price level for all years in a series of years. For example, the price index in the 1987 base year is found by discovering the price of the particular collection of goods and services produced in 1987 and comparing this price to the price of that same market basket in the base year. However, in this special case, the "specific year" and the "reference year" are the same. That is,

$$\text{GDP price index}_{1987} = \frac{\text{price of market basket}_{1987}}{\text{price of market basket}_{1987}} \times 100$$

The GDP price index for the 1987 base year therefore is 100. In effect, we automatically set the price index at 100 in the base year.

Likewise, if we wanted to know the GDP price index for 1950, we would determine 1950 output and then estimate what that same or a similar collection of goods and services would have cost in the 1987 base year. If prices on the 1950 output had quadrupled between 1950 and 1987, the price ratio of the market basket would be $\frac{1}{4}$ (= .25) and the 1950 GDP price index would be 25 (= .25 × 100).

Once a GDP price index has been constructed for each year in a series of years, comparisons of price levels between years is possible. Examples:

1 If the price indexes for 1996 and 1987 are 128 and 100, respectively, we can calculate that the price level increased by 28 percent [= (128 − 100)/100] between the two years.

2 If, as suggested by our previous illustration, the price index for 1950 is 25, we can say that the price level rose by 412 percent [(128 − 25)/25] between 1950 and 1993.

3 If the price index fell from 100 in 1987 to 98 in 1988, we would know that the price level declined by 2 percent [= (98 − 100)/100].

Conclusions: The GDP price index or deflator compares the price of each year's output to the price of that same output in the base year or reference year. A series of price indexes for various years enables us to compare price levels among years. An increase in the GDP price index from one year to the next constitutes *inflation*; a decrease in the price index constitutes *deflation*. *(Key Question 10)*

NOMINAL AND REAL GDP

Inflation or deflation complicates GDP because GDP is a price-times-quantity figure. The data from which the national income accountants estimate GDP are the total sales revenues of business firms; however, these revenue figures include changes in *both* the quantity of output *and* the level of prices. This means that a change in either the quantity of total physical output or the price level will affect the size of GDP. However, it is the quantity of goods produced and distributed to households which affects their standard of living, not the size of the price tags on these goods. The hamburger of 1970 which sold for 65 cents yielded the same satisfaction as will an identical hamburger selling for $2.00 in 1996.

The situation facing government accountants is this: In gathering statistics from financial reports of businesses and deriving GDP in various years, they get nominal GDP figures. They do *not* know directly to what extent changes in price and changes in quantity of output have accounted for the changes in nominal GDP. For example, they would not know directly if a 4 percent increase in nominal GDP resulted from a 4 percent rise in output and zero inflation, from a zero percent change in output and 4 percent inflation, or some other combination of changes in output and the price level, say, a 2 percent increase in output and 2 percent inflation. The problem is adjusting a price-times-quantity figure so it will accurately reflect changes in physical output or quantity, not changes in prices.

As we will soon see, this problem is resolved by *deflating* GDP for rising prices and *inflating* it when prices are falling. These adjustments give us a picture of GDP for various years *as if* prices and the value of the dollar were constant. A GDP figure which reflects current prices, that is, *not* adjusted for changes in the price level, is called *unadjusted, current dollar, money,* or nominal GDP. Similarly, GDP figures which are inflated or deflated for price level changes measure *adjusted, constant dollar,* or **real GDP**.

The Adjustment Process

The process for adjusting current dollar or nominal GDP for inflation or deflation is straightforward. The GDP deflator for a specific year tells us the ratio of that year's prices to the prices of the same goods in the base year. The GDP deflator or GDP price index therefore can be used to inflate or deflate nominal GDP figures for each year to express them in real terms—in other words, *as if* base year prices prevailed. *The simplest and most direct method of deflating or inflating a year's nominal GDP is to express that year's index number in decimal form, and divide it into the nominal GDP.* This yields the same result as the more complex procedure of dividing nominal GDP by the corresponding index number and multiplying the quotient by 100. In equation form:

$$\frac{\text{Nominal GDP}}{\text{Price index (in hundredths)}} = \text{real GDP}$$

To illustrate in Table 7-5, in 1996 nominal GDP is $64 and the price index for that year is 128 (= 1.28 in hundredths). Real GDP in 1996, therefore, is:

$$\frac{\$64}{1.28} = \$50$$

In summary, the real GDP figures measure the value of total output *as if* the prices of the products had been constant from the reference or base year throughout all the years being considered. Real GDP thus shows the market value of each year's output measured in dollars of the same value, or purchasing power, as the base year.

Real GDP is clearly superior to nominal GDP as an indicator of the economy's production performance.

Inflating and Deflating

Table 7-6 illustrates the **inflating** and **deflating** process. Here we are taking actual nominal GDP figures for selected years and adjusting them with the GDP deflator for these years to obtain real GDP. Note the base year is 1987.

Because the long-run trend has been for the price level to rise, we need to increase, or *inflate,* the pre-1987 figures. This upward revision of nominal GDP acknowledges that prices were lower in years before 1987 and, as a result, nominal GDP figures understated the real output of those years. Column 4 reveals what GDP would have been had the 1987 price level prevailed.

The rising price level has caused the nominal GDP figures for the post-1987 years to overstate real output. These figures must be reduced, or *deflated,* as in column 4, to gauge what GDP would have been in 1988, 1991, and so on, if 1987 prices had prevailed.

In short, while the *nominal* GDP figures reflect both output and price changes, the *real* GDP figures

TABLE 7-6 Adjusting GDP for changes in the price level *(selected years, in billions of dollars)*

(1) Year	(2) Nominal, or unadjusted, GDP	÷	(3) Price level index,* percent (1987 = 100)	=	(4) Real, or adjusted, GDP, 1987 dollars
1960	$ 513.4		26.0		$1974.6 (= 513.4 ÷ 0.260)
1965	702.7		28.4		_____
1970	1010.7		35.1		$2879.5 (= 1010.7 ÷ 0.351)
1975	1585.9		49.2		_____
1980	2708.0		71.7		$3776.8 (= 2708.0 ÷ 0.717)
1983	3405.0		87.2		$3904.8 (= 3405.0 ÷ 0.872)
1985	4038.7		94.4		_____
1986	4268.6		96.9		$4405.2 (= 4268.6 ÷ 0.969)
1987	4539.9		100.0		$4539.9 (= 4539.9 ÷ 1.000)
1988	4900.4		103.9		_____
1989	5250.8		108.5		$4839.4 (= 5250.8 ÷ 1.085)
1991	5724.8		117.6		$4893.0 (= 5724.8 ÷ 1.170)
1994	6736.9		126.1		$5342.5 (= 6736.9 ÷ 1.261)

*U.S. Department of Commerce implicit price deflators.
Source: U.S. Department of Commerce data.

allow us to estimate changes in real output, because the real GDP figures, in effect, hold the price level constant.

Example: For 1994 nominal GDP was $6736.9 billion and the price index was 126.1 or 26.1 percent higher than 1987. To compare 1994's GDP with 1987's we express the 1994 index in hundredths (1.261) and divide it into the nominal GDP of $6736.9 as shown in column 4. The resulting real GDP of $5342.5 is directly comparable to the 1987 base year's GDP because both reflect only changes in output and *not* price level changes. You should trace through the computations involved in deriving the real GDP figures given in Table 7-6 and also determine real GDP for years 1965, 1975, 1985, and 1988, for which the figures have been purposely omitted. *(Key Question 11)*

QUICK REVIEW 7-3

■ A price index compares the combined price of a specific market basket of goods and services in a particular year to the combined price of the same basket in a base year.

■ Nominal GDP is output valued at current prices; real GDP is output valued at constant prices (base year prices).

■ A year's nominal GDP can be adjusted to real GDP by dividing nominal GDP by the GDP price index (expressed in hundredths).

GDP AND SOCIAL WELFARE

GDP is a reasonably accurate and extremely useful measure of domestic economic performance. It is not, and was never intended to be, an index of social welfare. GDP is merely a measure of the annual volume of market-oriented activity.

> . . . any number of things could make the Nation better off without raising its real [GDP] as measured today: we might start the list with peace, equality of opportunity, the elimination of injustice and violence, greater brotherhood among Americans of different racial and ethnic backgrounds, better understanding between parents and children and between husbands and wives, and we could go on endlessly.[5]

---

[5]Arthur M. Okun, "Social Welfare Has No Price Tag," *The Economic Accounts of the United States: Retrospect and Prospect* (U.S. Department of Commerce, July 1971), p. 129.

Nevertheless, it is widely held that there should be a strong positive correlation between real GDP and social welfare, that is, greater production should move society toward "the good life." Thus, we must understand some of the shortcomings of GDP—why it might understate or overstate real output and why more output will not necessarily make society better off.

Nonmarket Transactions

Certain production transactions do not appear in the market. Thus, GDP as a measure of the market value of output fails to include them. Examples include the production services of a homemaker, the work of the carpenter who repairs his or her own home, or the work of the professor who writes a scholarly article. Such transactions are *not* reflected in the profit and loss statements of business firms and therefore escape the national income accountants, causing GDP to be understated. However, some large nonmarket transactions, such as that part of farmers' output which farmers consume themselves, are estimated by national income accountants.

Leisure

Over many years, leisure has increased significantly. The workweek declined from about 53 hours at the turn of the century to approximately 40 hours by the end of World War II. Since then the average workweek has declined more slowly and is currently about 35 hours. Also, the expanded availability of paid vacations, holidays, and leave time has reduced the work year. This increased leisure has had a positive effect on our well-being. Our system of social accounting understates our well-being by not directly recognizing this. Nor do the accounts reflect the satisfaction—the "psychic income"—which people derive from their work.

Improved Product Quality

GDP is a quantitative, not a qualitative, measure. It does not accurately reflect improvements in product quality. For example, there is a fundamental qualitative difference between a $3000 personal computer purchased today and a computer for that same amount bought just a few years ago. Today's $3000 computer has far more speed and storage capacity, as

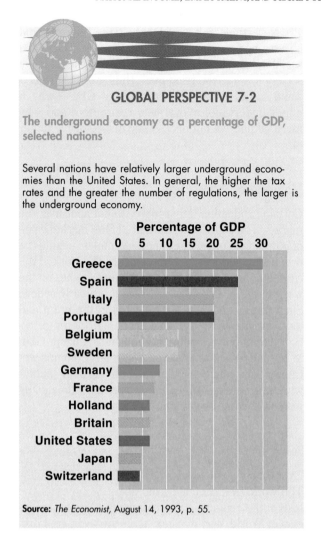

GLOBAL PERSPECTIVE 7-2

The underground economy as a percentage of GDP, selected nations

Several nations have relatively larger underground economies than the United States. In general, the higher the tax rates and the greater the number of regulations, the larger is the underground economy.

Percentage of GDP

	0 5 10 15 20 25 30
Greece	
Spain	
Italy	
Portugal	
Belgium	
Sweden	
Germany	
France	
Holland	
Britain	
United States	
Japan	
Switzerland	

Source: *The Economist,* August 14, 1993, p. 55.

well as a clearer monitor and improved multimedia capabilities.

Failure to account for quality improvement is a shortcoming of GDP accounting: Quality improvements clearly affects economic well-being as much as does the quantity of goods. Because product quality has improved over time, GDP understates improvement in our material well-being.

Composition and Distribution of Output

Changes in the composition and the allocation of total output among specific households may influence economic welfare. GDP, however, reflects only the size of output and tells us nothing about whether this collection of goods is "right" for society. A hand gun and a set of encyclopedias, both selling for $350, are weighted equally in the GDP. And some economists feel that a more equal distribution of total output would increase national economic well-being. If they are correct, a future trend toward a less unequal distribution of GDP would enhance the economic welfare of society. A more unequal distribution—which appears to be occurring—would have the reverse effect.

Conclusion: GDP measures the size of the total output but does not reflect changes in the composition and distribution of output which might also affect the economic well-being of society.

Per Capita Output

For many purposes the most meaningful measure of economic well-being is per capita output. Because GDP measures the size of total output, it may conceal or misrepresent changes in the standard of living of individual households. GDP may rise, but if population is also growing rapidly, the per capita standard of living may be constant or even declining.

This is the plight of many of the less developed countries. Ethiopia's domestic output grew at 1.2 percent per year in 1980–1992. But annual population growth exceeded 3 percent, resulting in a yearly decrease in per capita output of 1.9 percent.

GDP and the Environment

There are undesirable and much publicized "gross domestic by-products" accompanying the production and growth of the GDP such as dirty air and water, automobile junkyards, congestion, noise, and other forms of environmental pollution. The costs of pollution reduce our economic well-being. These spillover costs associated with the production of the GDP are not now deducted from total output and, thus, GDP overstates our national economic welfare.

Ironically, the final physical product of economic production and consumption is garbage. A rising GDP means more garbage, and may mean more pollution and a greater divergence between GDP and economic well-being. In fact, under existing accounting procedures, when a manufacturer pollutes a river and government spends to clean it up, the cleanup expense is added to the GDP while the pollution is not subtracted!

The Underground Economy

Economists agree there is a large underground or subterranean sector in our economy. Some participants in this sector engage in illegal activities such as gambling, loansharking, prostitution, and the narcotics trade. These may well be "growth industries." Obviously, persons receiving income from illegal businesses choose to conceal their incomes.

Most participants in the underground economy are in legal activities, but do not fully report their incomes to the Internal Revenue Service (IRS). A waiter or waitress may underreport tips from customers. A businessperson may record only a portion of sales receipts for the tax collector. A worker who wants to retain unemployment compensation or welfare benefits may obtain an "off the books" or "cash only" job so there is no record of his or her work activities. A nanny who is an illegal immigrant may wish to be paid in cash, so as not to be detected by the immigration service, and her employer may acquiesce, as a way to avoid paying social security taxes.

Although there is no consensus on the size of the underground economy, estimates suggest it is between 7 to 12 percent of the recorded GDP. In 1994, that meant GDP was understated by between $472 and $808 billion. If this additional income had been taxed at a 20 percent average tax rate, the Federal budget deficit for 1994 would have declined from $203 billion to between a $109 billion and a $41 billion deficit.

Global Perspective 7-2 indicates the relative sizes of underground economies of selected nations.

CHAPTER SUMMARY

1 Gross domestic product (GDP), a basic measure of society's economic performance, is the market value of all final goods and services produced within the borders of the United States in a year. It is more than GNP—output produced by Americans, regardless of where located—by the amount of net foreign factor income earned (output produced) in the United States.

2 Intermediate goods, nonproduction transactions, and secondhand sales are purposely excluded in calculating GDP.

3 GDP may be calculated by summing total expenditures on all final output or by summing the income derived from the production of that output.

4 By the expenditures approach GDP is determined by adding consumer purchases of goods and services, gross investment spending by businesses, government purchases, and net exports; GDP $= C + I_g + G + X_n$.

5 Gross investment can be divided into **a** replacement investment (required to maintain the nation's stock of capital at its existing level), and **b** net investment (the net increase in the stock of capital). Positive net investment is associated with a growing economy; negative net investment with a declining economy.

6 By the income or allocations approach GDP is calculated as the sum of compensation to employees, rents, interest, proprietors' income, corporate income taxes, dividends, undistributed corporate profits, *plus* the two nonincome charges (indirect business taxes and capital consumption allowance) and *plus* net foreign factor income earned in the United States.

7 Other national income accounting measures are derived from GDP. Net domestic product (NDP) is GDP less the consumption of fixed capital. National income (NI) is total income earned by American resource suppliers; it is found by subtracting both net foreign factor income earned in the United States and indirect business taxes from NDP. Personal income (PI) is the total income paid to households prior to any allowance for personal taxes. Disposable income (DI) is personal income after personal taxes have been paid. DI measures the amount of income households have available to consume or save.

8 Price indexes are computed by comparing the price of a specific collection or "market basket" of output in a particular period to the price (cost) of the same market basket in a base period and multiplying the outcome (quotient) by 100. The GDP deflator is the price index associated with adjusting nominal GDP to account for inflation or deflation and thereby obtaining real GDP.

9 Nominal (current dollar) GDP measures each year's output valued in terms of the prices prevailing in that year. Real (constant dollar) GDP measures each year's output in terms of the prices which prevailed in a selected base year. Because it is adjusted for price level changes, real GDP measures the level of production activity.

10 National income accounting measures exclude nonmarket and illegal transactions, changes in leisure and product quality, the composition and distribution of output, and the environmental effects of production. Nevertheless, these measures are reasonably accurate and very useful indicators of the nation's economic performance.

years, for example, 25, 50, or 100 years. The long-run secular trend for American capitalism has been remarkable expansion (Chapter 19). For present purposes, the importance of this long-run expansion is that the business cycle fluctuates around a long-run growth trend. Note that in Figure 8-1 cyclical fluctuations are measured as deviations from the secular growth trend and that the stylized cycle of Figure 8-2 is drawn against a trend of growth.

Cyclical Impact: Durables and Nondurables

The business cycle is felt in every nook and cranny of the economy. The elements of the economy are related in such a way that few, if any, escape the negative effects of depression or surging inflation. However, the business cycle affects various individuals and segments of the economy in different ways and degrees.

Insofar as production and employment are concerned, service industries and industries producing nondurable consumer goods are somewhat insulated from the most severe effects of recession. And, of course, recession actually helps some firms such as pawnbrokers and law firms specializing in bankruptcies! Who is hit hardest by recession? Those firms and industries producing capital goods and consumer durables. The construction industry is particularly vulnerable. Industries and workers producing housing and commercial buildings, heavy capital goods, farm implements, automobiles, refrigerators, gas ranges, and similar products bear the brunt of bad times. Conversely, these "hard goods" industries are stimulated most by expansion.

Two facts help explain the vulnerability of these industries to the business cycle.

1 Postponability Within limits, purchase of hard goods is postponable. As the economy slips into bad times, producers frequently defer the acquisition of more modern production facilities and construction of new plants. The business outlook simply does not warrant increases in the stock of capital goods. The firm's present capital facilities and buildings will likely still be usable and in excess supply. In good times, capital goods are usually replaced before they completely depreciate. When recession strikes, however, business firms patch up their outmoded equipment and make it do. As a result, investment in capital goods will decline sharply. Some firms, having excess plant capacity, may not even bother to replace all the capi-

tal they are currently consuming. Net investment for them may be negative.

It's the same for consumer durables. When recession occurs and the family must trim its budget, plans for the purchases of durables such as major appliances and automobiles first feel the ax. People repair their old appliances and cars rather than buy new models. Food and clothing—consumer nondurables—are a different story. A family must eat and clothe itself. These purchases are much less postponable. To some extent the quantity and quality of these purchases will decline, but not so much as with durables.

2 Monopoly Power Most industries producing capital goods and consumer durables are industries of high concentration, where a small number of large firms dominate the market. These firms have sufficient monopoly power to temporarily resist lowering prices by restricting output in the face of a declining demand. Therefore, the impact of a fall in demand centers primarily on production and employment. The reverse is true in nondurable, or soft, goods industries, which are highly competitive and have low concentration. Firms are unable to resist price declines in such industries, and the declining demand reduces prices more than the levels of production.

Figure 8-3 provides historical evidence from the Great Depression on this point. It shows the percentage declines in price and quantity in ten selected industries as the economy fell from peak prosperity in 1929 to the depth of depression in 1933. Generally, high-concentration industries make up the top half of the table and low-concentration industries the bottom half. Note the drastic production declines and relatively modest price declines of the high-concentration industries. Contrast those outcomes to the large price declines and relatively small output declines which occurred in the low-concentration industries. *(Key Question 1)*

QUICK REVIEW 8-1

■ The long-term secular trend of real domestic output has been upward in the United States.

■ The typical business cycle has four phases: peak, recession, trough, and recovery.

■ Industries producing capital goods and consumer durables normally suffer greater output and employment declines during recession than do service and nondurable consumer goods industries.

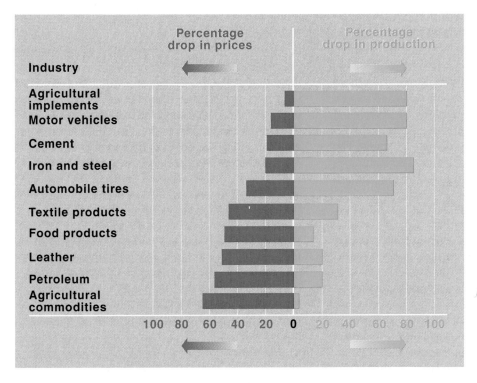

FIGURE 8-3 Relative price and production declines in ten industries, 1929–1933 The high-concentration industries shown in the top half had relatively small price declines and large declines in output during the early years of the Great Depression. In the low-concentration industries of the bottom half, price declines were relatively large, and production fell by relatively small amounts. [Gardiner C. Means, *Industrial Prices and Their Relative Flexibility* (Washington, 1953), p. 8.]

UNEMPLOYMENT

"Full employment" is hard to define. A person might think it means that everyone in the labor market—100 percent of the labor force—is employed. But that's not so; some unemployment is normal or warranted.

Types of Unemployment

Before defining full employment, we first need to know about three types of unemployment: frictional, structural, and cyclical.

Frictional Unemployment   With freedom to choose occupations and jobs, at any time some workers will be "between jobs." Some will be voluntarily switching jobs. Others will have been fired and are seeking reemployment. Still others will be temporarily laid off from their jobs because of seasonality, for example, bad weather in the construction industry. And there will be some particularly young workers searching for their first jobs.

As these unemployed people find jobs or are called back from temporary layoffs, other job seekers and temporarily laid-off workers will replace them in the "unemployment pool." Therefore, even though

the specific individuals who are unemployed for these reasons change from month to month, this type of unemployment persists.

Economists use the term **frictional unemployment**—consisting of *search unemployment* and *wait unemployment*—for workers who are either searching for jobs or waiting to take jobs in the near future. "Frictional" correctly implies that the labor market does not operate perfectly nor instantaneously—without friction—in matching workers and jobs.

Frictional unemployment is inevitable and, at least in part, desirable. Many workers who are voluntarily "between jobs" are moving from low-paying, low-productivity jobs to higher-paying, higher-productivity positions. This means more income for workers and a better allocation of labor resources—and therefore a larger real output—for the economy as a whole.

Structural Unemployment   Frictional unemployment blurs into a category called **structural unemployment.** Here, economists mean "structural" in the sense of "compositional." Changes occur over time in the "structure" of consumer demand and in technology, which alter the "structure" of the total demand for labor. Because of such changes, some skills will be in less demand or may even become obsolete. Demand for other skills will expand, including skills which did not exist. Unemployment results because the composition of the labor force does not respond quickly or completely to the new structure of job opportunities. Some workers therefore find they have no readily marketable talents; their skills and experience become obsolete and unwanted by changes in technology and consumer demand. Similarly, the geographic distribution of jobs constantly changes. The migration of industry and employment opportunities from the Snow Belt to the Sun Belt over the past few decades is an example.

We can cite many illustrations of structural unemployment.

1 Many years ago, highly skilled glass blowers were thrown out of work by the invention of bottle-making machines.

2 Historically, mechanization of agriculture in the South dislodged thousands of low-skilled, poorly educated blacks from their jobs. Many migrated to northern cities and suffered prolonged unemployment because of racial bias and insufficient skills.

3 Many oil-field workers in the American "oil-patch" states found themselves structurally unemployed when the world price of oil nosedived in the 1980s. Less drilling and oil-related activity took place, resulting in widespread layoffs.

4 In the 1980s many pilots, mechanics, flight attendants, and other airline employees became structurally unemployed as a result of mergers following deregulation of the airline industry.

5 Recently, "corporate downsizing" has occurred in several major American manufacturing industries. Many people losing their jobs have been corporate managers, who have found it difficult to find new work.

6 Recent closures of military bases and other defense cutbacks have displaced many workers, adding them to the roles of the structurally unemployed.

The distinction between frictional and structural unemployment is hazy, however. The key difference is that frictionally unemployed workers have salable skills, while structurally unemployed workers are not readily reemployable without retraining, additional education, and possibly geographic relocation. Frictional unemployment is short-term; structural unemployment is more long-term, and therefore regarded as more serious.

Cyclical Unemployment Cyclical unemployment is caused by the recession phase of the business cycle, that is, by a deficiency of total spending. As the overall demand for goods and services decreases, employment falls and unemployment rises. For this reason, cyclical unemployment is sometimes called *deficient-demand unemployment*. During the recession year 1982, for example, the unemployment rate rose to 9.7 percent. This compares to a 6.7 percent unemployment rate in the recession year 1991. Cyclical unemployment at the depth of the Great Depression in 1933 was about 25 percent of the labor force.

Defining "Full Employment"

Full employment does *not* mean zero unemployment. Economists regard frictional and structural unemployment as essentially unavoidable. Thus, "full employment" is defined as something less than 100 percent employment of the labor force. Specifically, the **full-employment unemployment rate** is equal to the total of frictional and structural unemployment. Stated differently, the full-employment unemployment rate is achieved when cyclical unemployment is zero. The full-employment rate of unemployment is also referred to as the **natural rate of unemployment.** The real level of domestic output associated with the natural rate of unemployment is called the economy's **potential output.** The economy's potential output is the real output forthcoming when the economy is "fully employed."

From a slightly different vantage point the full or natural rate of unemployment results when labor markets are in balance in the sense that the number of job seekers equals the number of job vacancies. The natural rate of unemployment is some positive amount because it takes time for frictionally unemployed job seekers to find open jobs they can fill. Also, regarding the structurally unemployed, it takes time to achieve the skills and geographic relocation needed for reemployment. If the number of job seekers exceeds available vacancies, labor markets are not in balance; there is a deficiency of aggregate demand and cyclical unemployment is present. But if aggregate demand is excessive a "shortage" of labor will arise; the number of job vacancies will exceed the number of workers seeking employment. In this situation the actual rate of unemployment is below the natural rate. Unusually "tight" labor markets such as this are associated with inflation.

The concept of the natural rate of unemployment merits elaboration in two respects.

1 Not Automatic "Natural" does *not* mean the economy will always operate at the natural rate and realize its potential output. Our brief discussion of the business cycle demonstrated that the economy frequently operates at an unemployment rate higher than the natural rate. On the other hand, the economy may on some occasions achieve an unemployment rate lower than the natural rate. For example, during World War II, when the natural rate was about 4 percent, the pressure of wartime production resulted in an almost unlimited demand for labor. Overtime work was common as was "moonlighting" (working at more than one job). The government also froze some people working in "essential" industries in their jobs, reducing frictional unemployment. The actual rate of unemployment was below 2 percent in 1943–1945 and dropped to 1.2 percent in 1944. The economy was producing beyond its potential output, but incurred considerable inflationary pressure in the process.

2 Not Immutable The natural rate of unemployment itself is *not* immutable. It is subject to periodic revision because of the shifting demographics of the labor force or institutional changes (changes in society's laws and customs). In the 1960s this unavoidable minimum of frictional and structural unemployment was about 4 percent of the labor force. That is, full employment meant 96 percent of the labor force was employed. But today, economists generally agree that the natural rate of unemployment is about 5.5 to 6 percent.

Why is the natural rate of unemployment higher today than in the 1960s? First, the demographic makeup of the labor force has changed. Young workers—who traditionally have high unemployment rates—have become relatively more important in the labor force. Second, laws and customs have changed. For example, our unemployment compensation program has been expanded both in terms of numbers of workers covered and size of benefits. By cushioning the economic impact of unemployment, unemployment compensation permits unemployed workers to engage in a more deliberate, lengthy job search, increasing frictional unemployment and the overall unemployment rate.

Measuring Unemployment

Defining the full employment rate of unemployment is complicated by problems in measuring unemployment. Figure 8-4 is a helpful starting point. The total

Total population	260,991,000
Less: Under 16 and institutionalized	−64,177,000
Not in labor force.................................	−65,758,000
Equals: Labor force..................................	131,056,000
Employed..	123,060,000
Unemployed	7,996,000

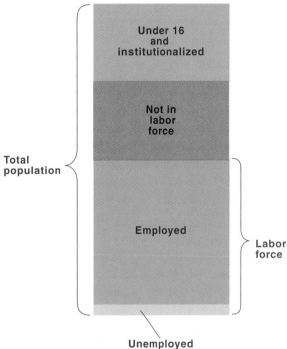

FIGURE 8-4   The labor force, employment, and unemployment, 1994
The labor force consists of persons sixteen years of age or older who are not in institutions and who are employed or unemployed.

population is divided into three groups. One comprises people under 16 years of age and people who are institutionalized, for example, in mental hospitals or correctional institutions. These people are not considered potential members of the labor force.

A second group, labeled "not in labor force," are adults who are potential workers, but for some reason—they are homemakers, in school, or retired—are not employed and are not seeking work.

The third group is the **labor force,** which constituted about 50 percent of the total population in 1994. The labor force is all people who are able and willing to work. Both those who are employed and those who are unemployed but actively seeking work are counted as being in the labor force. The *unemployment rate* is the percentage of the labor force which is unemployed:

$$\text{Unemployment rate} = \frac{\text{unemployed}}{\text{labor force}} \times 100$$

In 1994 the unemployment rate was

$$6.1\% = \frac{7,996,000}{131,056,000} \times 100$$

Unemployment rates for selected years between 1929 and 1994 are provided on the inside covers of this book.

The Bureau of Labor Statistics (BLS) determines who is employed and who is not by a nationwide random survey of some 60,000 households each month. A series of questions is asked as to which members of the household are working, unemployed and looking for work, not looking for work, and so on. Despite the careful sampling and interview techniques used, the data collected from this survey are subject to a number of criticisms.

1 Part-time Employment The official data include all part-time workers as fully employed. In 1994 about 17.5 million people worked part time because of personal choice. Another 6.5 million part-timer workers either wanted to work full time, but could not find suitable full-time work, or worked fewer hours because of a temporary slack in consumer demand. These last two groups were, in effect, partially employed and partially unemployed. By counting them as fully employed the official BLS data *understate* the unemployment rate.

2 Discouraged Workers You must be actively seeking work to be counted as unemployed. An unemployed individual who is not actively seeking employment is classified as "not in the labor force." The problem is there are numerous workers who, after unsuccessfully seeking employment for a time, become discouraged and drop out of the labor force. The number of **discouraged workers** is larger during recession than prosperity; an estimated 1.25 million people fell into this category in recession-year 1991. By not counting discouraged workers as unemployed, official data *understate* the unemployment rate.

3 False Information Alternatively, the unemployment rate may be *overstated*. Some respondents who are not working may claim they are looking for work, even though they are not. These individuals will be classified as "unemployed," rather than "not in the labor force." A person's motivation for giving this false information is that unemployment compensation or welfare benefits may depend on professed job pursuit. The underground economy (Chapter 7) may also cause the official unemployment rate to be overstated. Someone fully employed in the South Florida drug traffic or "running numbers" for the Chicago Mafia may identify himself as "unemployed."

The point is that, although the unemployment rate is a basic consideration in policy making, it has certain shortcomings. And, while the unemployment rate is one of the best measures of the economic condition of the nation, it is not an infallible barometer. *(Key Question 5)*

Economic Cost of Unemployment

Problems in measuring the unemployment rate and defining the full-employment unemployment rate do not negate the fact that above-normal unemployment involves great economic and social costs.

GDP Gap and Okun's Law The basic economic cost of unemployment is forgone output. *When the economy fails to generate enough jobs for all who are able and willing to work, potential production of goods and services is irretrievably lost.* In Chapter 2's analysis, unemployment keeps society from moving to its production possibilities curve. Economists measure this sacrificed output in terms of the **GDP gap**—the amount by which *actual GDP* falls short of *potential GDP.*

Potential GDP is determined by assuming the natural rate of unemployment exists and projecting the economy's "normal" growth rate. Figure 8-5 shows the GDP gap for recent years and the close correlation between the actual unemployment rate (Figure 8-5b) and the GDP gap (Figure 8-5a). The higher the unemployment rate, the larger the GDP gap.

Macroeconomist Arthur Okun quantified the relationship between the unemployment rate and the GDP gap. **Okun's law** indicates that *for every 1 percent that the actual unemployment rate exceeds the natural rate, a $2\frac{1}{2}$ percent GDP gap occurs.* With this $1:2\frac{1}{2}$, or $1:2.5$, unemployment rate–GDP gap link, we can calculate the absolute loss of output associated with any unemployment rate. For example, in 1992 the unemployment rate was 7.4 percent, or 1.6 per-

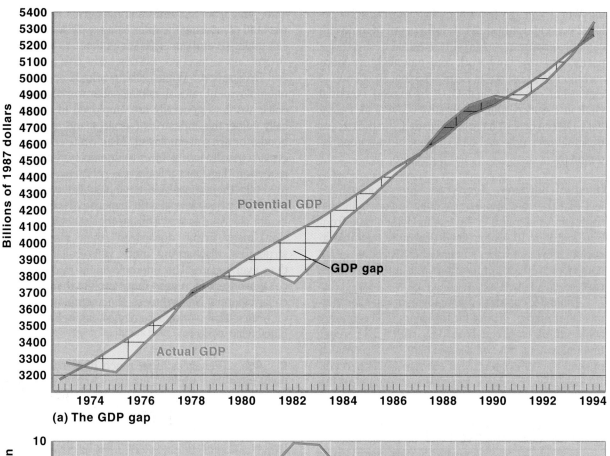

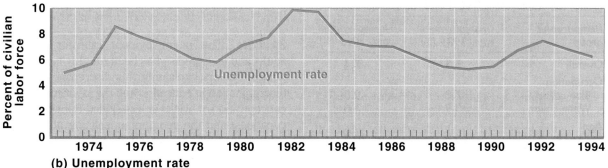

FIGURE 8-5 **Potential and actual GDP (a) and the unemployment rate (b)**
The difference between potential GDP and actual GDP is the GDP gap. The GDP gap measures the output the economy sacrifices because it fails to use fully its productive potential. A high unemployment rate means a large GDP gap. [*Economic Report of the President* and Robert J. Gordon, *Macroeconomics,* 6th ed. (New York: HarperCollins, 1993). Updated.]

centage points above an assumed 6 percent natural rate. Multiplying this 1.6 percent by Okun's 2.5 figure indicates that 1992's GDP gap was 4 percent. Stated differently, 1992's GDP would have been 4 percent larger than it actually was had the economy realized its full employment rate of unemployment. Applying this 4 percent loss to 1992's $6020 billion

nominal GDP, we find that the economy sacrificed almost $241 billion (= $6020 × 4 percent) of output because the natural rate of unemployment was not achieved. *(Key Question 3)*

As you see in Figure 8-5, sometimes the economy's actual output can exceed its potential output. We have already mentioned that this happened dur-

INFLATION: DEFINED AND MEASURED

We now turn to inflation as an aspect of macroeconomic instability. The problems posed by inflation are more subtle than those of unemployment.

The Meaning of Inflation

Inflation is a rising general level of prices. This does not mean that *all* prices are rising. Even during periods of rapid inflation, some prices may be relatively constant and others falling. For example, although the United States experienced high rates of inflation in the 1970s and early 1980s, the prices of video recorders, digital watches, and personal computers declined. As we will see, one of the troublesome aspects of inflation is that prices rise unevenly. Some streak upward; others ascend leisurely; others do not rise.

Measuring Inflation

Inflation is measured by price index numbers such as those introduced in Chapter 7. Recall that a price index measures the general level of prices in reference to a base period.

To illustrate, the consumer price index uses 1982–1984 as the base period, meaning that period's price level is set equal to 100. In 1994 the price index was approximately 148. This means that prices were 48 percent higher in 1994 than in 1982–1984, or that a set of goods which cost $100 in 1982–1984 cost $148 in 1994.

The *rate* of inflation can be calculated for any specific year by subtracting last year's (1993) price index from this year's (1994) index, dividing that difference by the prior year's (1993) index, and multiplying by 100 to express it as a percentage. For example, the consumer price index was 144.5 in 1993 and 148.2 in 1994. The rate of inflation for 1994 is calculated as follows:

$$\frac{\text{Rate of}}{\text{inflation}} = \frac{148.2 - 144.5}{144.5} \times 100 = 2.6\%$$

The so-called **rule of 70** provides a quantitative appreciation of inflation. It permits quick calculation of the number of years it takes the price level to double. We divide the number 70 by the annual rate of inflation:

$$\frac{\text{Approximate number of years required to double}} = \frac{70}{\text{percentage annual rate of increase}}$$

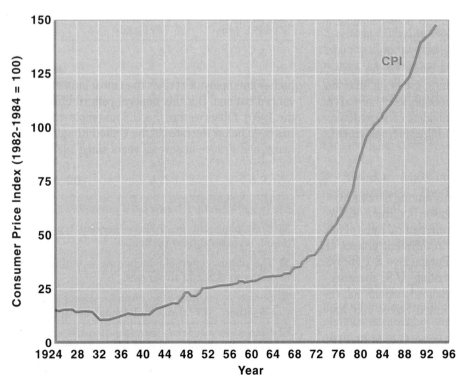

FIGURE 8-6   Price level behavior in the United States since 1924
The price stability of the 1920s and the deflation of the 1930s gave way to sharp inflation in the immediate post-World War II period. The 1951–1965 period had a reasonably stable price level, but the period since 1965 has clearly been an "age of inflation." (Bureau of Labor Statistics.)

For instance, a 3 percent annual rate of inflation will double the price level in about $23 (= 70 \div 3)$ years. Inflation of 8 percent per year will double the price level in about $9 (= 70 \div 8)$ years. Inflation at 12 percent will double the price level in only about 6 years. The rule of 70 is generally applicable. This rule will allow you, for example, to estimate how long it will take for real GDP *or* your savings account to double. *(Key Question 7)*

The Facts of Inflation

Figure 8-6 surveys inflation in the United States since 1924. The CPI curve represents annual increases in the consumer price index, which is constructed using a base period of 1982–1984. That is, the CPI for the 1982–1984 period is arbitrarily set at 100.

Although most of you have grown up in an "age of inflation," our economy has not always been inflation-prone. The price level was stable in the prosperous 1920s and declined—*deflation* occurred—during the early years of the Great Depression of the 1930s. Prices then rose sharply in the immediate post–World War II period (1945–1948). However, overall price stability characterized the 1951–1965 period in which the average annual increase in the price level was less than $1\frac{1}{2}$ percent. But the inflation starting in the late 1960s and then surging in the 1970s introduced Americans to double-digit inflation. In 1979 and 1980 the price level rose at 12 to 13 percent annual rates. By the 1990s, the inflation rate had settled into a 2–4 percent annual range. Historical annual rates of inflation can be found on the inside covers of this textbook.

Inflation is not distinctly American. All industrial nations have experienced this problem. Global Perspective 8-2 traces the post-1983 annual inflation rates of the United States, the United Kingdom, Japan, France, and Germany. Observe that inflation in the United States has been neither unusually high nor low relative to inflation in these other industrial countries.

Some nations have had double-digit, triple-digit, or still higher annual rates of inflation in recent years. In 1993, for example, the annual inflation rate in Hungary was 23 percent; in Turkey, 66 percent; and in Romania, 256 percent. A few nations experienced astronomical rates of inflation in 1993: Zaire, 1,987 percent; and Brazil, 2,148 percent!

Causes: Theories of Inflation

Economists distinguish between two types of inflation.

GLOBAL PERSPECTIVE 8-2

Inflation rates in five industrial nations, 1984–1994

Inflation rates in the United States over the past ten years have neither been extraordinarily high nor low relative to rates in other industrial nations.

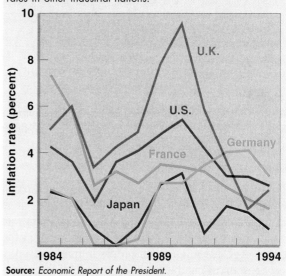

Source: *Economic Report of the President.*

1   Demand-Pull Inflation   Traditionally, changes in the price level have been attributed to an excess of total demand. The economy may attempt to spend beyond its capacity to produce; it may seek some point beyond its production possibilities curve. The business sector cannot respond to this excess demand by expanding real output because all available resources are already fully employed. This excess demand will bid up the prices of the fixed real output, causing **demand-pull inflation.** The essence of demand-pull inflation is "too much money chasing too few goods."

But the relationship between the total demand, on the one hand, and output, employment, and the price level, on the other, is not so simple. Figure 8-7 will help unravel the complications.

Range 1   In *range 1* total spending—the sum of consumption, investment, government, and net export spending—is so low that domestic output is far short of its maximum full-employment level. That means there's a substantial GDP gap. Unemployment rates

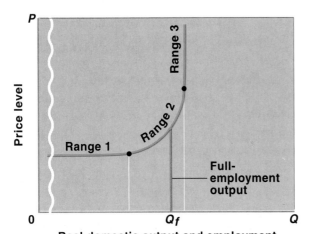

FIGURE 8-7 The price level and the level of employment

As aggregate expenditures increase, the price level generally begins to rise before full employment is reached. At some point, additional spending is purely inflationary.

are high and businesses have much idle production capacity. Now assume total demand increases. Real domestic output will rise and the unemployment rate will fall. But there will be little or no increase in the price level. Large amounts of idle human and property resources can be put back to work at their *existing* prices. An unemployed worker does not ask for a wage increase when called back to a job!

Range 2 As demand continues to rise, the economy enters *range 2* where it approaches—and then surpasses—full employment. Before full employment is achieved, the price level may begin to rise. As production expands, supplies of idle resources do not vanish simultaneously in all sectors and industries of the economy. Bottlenecks develop in some industries even though most have excess production capacity. Some industries are using fully their production capacity before others and cannot respond to further increases in demand for their products by increasing output. So their prices rise. As still more labor is hired, workplaces become increasingly congested and each added worker contributes less to output. Labor costs thus rise, forcing up product prices. As full employment is approached many firms hire less qualified workers and this, too, contributes to rising costs and prices. The inflation which occurs in this portion of range 2 is sometimes called *premature inflation* because it occurs before the economy reaches full employment.

Once the economy achieves full employment, additional spending and still higher prices in range 2 may induce some businesses to demand—and some households to supply—resources beyond the full-employment level of output. Firms may employ additional work shifts and use overtime to achieve greater output. Households may supply secondary workers such as teenagers and spouses, who normally would not choose to enter the labor force. In this part of range 2, the rate of unemployment falls below the natural rate of unemployment and actual GDP exceeds potential GDP. Here, the pace of inflation usually quickens.

Range 3 As total spending increases into *range 3,* the economy simply cannot supply more resources. Firms cannot respond to increases in demand by increasing output. Real domestic output is at an absolute maximum so that further increases in demand do only one thing—raise the price level. The rate of inflation may be high and growing because total demand greatly exceeds society's absolute capacity to produce. The demand-pull inflation of range 2 becomes the *pure* demand-pull inflation of range 3. There is no increase in real output to absorb some of the increased spending.

Reprise: Chapter 7's distinction between nominal and real GDP is helpful at this point. So long as the price level is constant (range 1), increases in nominal and real GDP are identical. But with inflation in range 2, nominal GDP is rising faster than real GDP, so nominal GDP must be "deflated" to measure changes in physical output. In range 3, nominal GDP is rising—perhaps rapidly due to high inflation—but real GDP is constant. In brief, the demand-pull inflation of ranges 2 and 3 breaks the link between nominal and real GDP.

2 Cost-Push or Supply-Side Inflation Inflation may also arise on the supply or cost side of the market. During several periods in our recent economic history the price level has risen even though aggregate demand was not excessive. These were periods when output and employment were both *declining* (evidence of a deficiency of total demand), while at the same time the general price level was *increasing*.

The theory of **cost-push inflation** explains rising prices in terms of factors which raise **per unit production cost.** Per unit production cost is the average cost of a particular level of output. This average cost is found by dividing the total cost of resource inputs by the amount of output produced. That is,

$$\text{Per unit production cost} = \frac{\text{total input cost}}{\text{units of output}}$$

Rising per unit production costs squeeze profits and reduce the amount of output firms are willing to supply at the existing price level. As a result, the economywide supply of goods and services declines. This decline in supply drives up the price level. Under this scenario, costs are *pushing* the price level upward, rather than demand *pulling* it upward, as with demand-pull inflation.

Two sources of cost-push inflation are increases in nominal wages and increases in the prices of nonwage inputs such as raw materials and energy.

Wage-Push Variant   This theory of cost-push inflation suggests that, under some circumstances, unions may be a source of inflation. That is, unions exert some control over nominal wage rates through collective bargaining. Suppose large unions demand and receive large increases in wages. Let's also assume that these wage gains set the standard for wage increases paid to nonunion workers. If the economywide wage gains are excessive relative to any offsetting factors such as rises in output per hour, then producers' per unit production costs will rise. Firms will respond by reducing the amount of goods and services offered for sale. Assuming no change in demand, this decline in supply will increase the price level. Because the culprit is an excessive increase in nominal wages, this type of inflation is called the *wage-push variant* of cost-push inflation.

Supply-Shock Variant   The *supply-shock* theory of cost-push inflation traces rising production costs—and therefore product prices—to abrupt, unanticipated increases in the costs of raw materials or energy inputs. The rocketing prices of imported oil in 1973–1974 and again in 1979–1980 are good illustrations. As energy prices rose during these periods, the costs of producing and transporting virtually every product in the economy increased. Rapid cost-push inflation ensued.

Complexities

The real world is more complex than our distinction between demand-pull and cost-push inflation suggests. Usually, it is difficult to distinguish between the two types of inflation. For example, suppose a boost in health care spending occurs which increases total spending, causing demand-pull inflation. As the demand-pull stimulus works its way through product and resource markets, individual firms find their wage costs, material costs, and fuel prices rising. From their perspective they must raise their prices because production costs have risen. Although this inflation is clearly demand-pull, it appears to be cost-push to business firms. It is not easy to label inflation as demand-side or supply-side without knowing the original cause of price and wage increases.

Cost-push and demand-pull inflation differ in another respect. Demand-pull inflation will continue so long as there is excess total spending. Cost-push inflation automatically is self-limiting; it will die out or cure itself. Reduced supply will decrease real domestic output and employment and these declines will constrain further cost increases. Cost-push inflation generates a recession and the recession inhibits additional cost increases. We'll see this in more detail in Chapter 17.

QUICK REVIEW 8-3

■ Inflation is a rising general level of prices, measured as a percentage change in a price index.

■ The United States' inflation rate has been within the middle range of rates of other advanced industrial nations, and far below the rates experienced by some nations.

■ Demand-pull inflation occurs when total spending exceeds the economy's ability to provide goods and services at the existing price level; total spending *pulls* the price level upward.

■ Cost-push inflation occurs when factors such as excessive wage increases and rapid increases in raw material prices drive up per unit production costs; higher costs *push* the price level upward.

REDISTRIBUTIVE EFFECTS OF INFLATION

Shifting from what causes inflation, we now look at its effects. We first consider how inflation redistributes income; then we examine possible effects on domestic output.

The relationship between the price level and the domestic output is ambiguous. Historically, real output and the price level have risen and fallen together.

In the past two decades, however, there have been times when real output has fallen while prices have continued to rise. We will dodge this matter for a moment by assuming that real output is constant and at the full-employment level. By holding real output and income constant we can isolate the effects of inflation on the distribution of that income. With a fixed national income pie, how does inflation affect the size of the slices going to different incomes receivers?

Nominal and Real Income   To answer this question we must understand the difference between money income or nominal income and real income.[2] *Money* income or **nominal income** is the number of dollars received as wages, rent, interest, or profits. **Real income** measures the amount of goods and services nominal income can buy.

If your nominal income increases faster than the price level, your real income will rise. If the price level increases faster than your nominal income, your real income will decline. We can approximate a change in real income through this formula:

$$
\begin{array}{lll}
\text{Percentage} & \text{percentage} & \text{percentage} \\
\text{change in} = & \text{change in} & - \text{change in} \\
\text{real income} & \text{nominal income} & \text{price level}
\end{array}
$$

If your nominal income rises by 10 percent and the price level rises by 5 percent in the same period, your real income will *increase* by about 5 percent. Conversely, a 5 percent increase in nominal income accompanied by 10 percent inflation will *decrease* your real income by approximately 5 percent.[3]

The point is this: While inflation reduces the purchasing power of the dollar—the amount of goods and services each dollar will buy—it does not neces-

sarily follow that a person's real income will fall. The purchasing power of the dollar declines whenever inflation occurs; a decline in your real income or standard of living occurs only when your nominal income fails to keep pace with inflation.

Anticipations   The redistribution effects of inflation depend on whether or not it is expected. With **anticipated inflation,** an income receiver *may* be able to take steps to avoid or lessen the adverse effects inflation would otherwise have on real income. The generalizations which immediately follow assume **unanticipated inflation.** We will then modify our generalizations to reflect the anticipation of inflation.

Fixed-Nominal-Income Receivers

Our distinction between nominal and real incomes shows that *inflation penalizes people who receive fixed nominal incomes.* Inflation redistributes income away from fixed income receivers toward others in the economy. The classic case is the elderly couple living on a private pension or annuity providing a fixed amount of nominal income each month. The pensioner who retired in 1980 on what appeared to be an adequate pension finds by 1995 that the purchasing power of that pension had been cut by one-half.

Similarly, landlords who receive lease payments of fixed dollar amounts will be hurt by inflation as they receive dollars of declining value over time. To a lesser extent some white-collar workers, some public sector employees whose incomes are dictated by fixed pay scales, and families living on fixed levels of welfare will be victims of inflation. Note, however, that Congress has *indexed* social security benefits; social security payments are tied to the consumer price index to prevent erosion from inflation.

Some people living on flexible incomes *may* benefit from inflation. The nominal incomes of such households may spurt ahead of the price level, or cost of living, with the result that their real incomes are enhanced. Workers in expanding industries and represented by aggressive unions may keep their nominal wages apace with, or ahead of, the rate of inflation.

Some wage earners are hurt by inflation. Those in declining industries or without strong unions may find that the price level skips ahead of their money incomes.

Business executives and other profit receivers might benefit from inflation. If product prices rise

---

[2]Chapter 7's distinction between nominal and real GDP is pertinent and you may want to review the "inflating" and "deflating" process involved in converting nominal GDP to real GDP (Table 7-6).

[3]A more precise calculation follows Chapter 7's process for changing nominal GDP to real GDP. Thus,

$$
\text{Real income} = \frac{\text{nominal income}}{\text{price index (in hundredths)}}
$$

In our first illustration, if nominal income rises by 10 percent from $100 to $110 and the price level (index) increases by 5 percent from 100 to 105, then real income has increased as follows:

$$
\frac{\$110}{1.05} = \$104.76
$$

The 5 percent increase in real income shown by the simple formula in the text is a good approximation of the 4.76 percent yielded by our more complex formula.

faster than resource prices, business receipts will grow at a faster rate than costs. Thus some—but not necessarily all—profit incomes will outdistance the rising tide of inflation.

Savers

Inflation hurts savers. *As prices rise, the real value, or purchasing power, of a nest egg of savings will deteriorate.* Savings accounts, insurance policies, annuities, and other fixed-value paper assets once adequate to meet rainy-day contingencies or provide for a comfortable retirement decline in real value during inflation. The simplest case is the individual who hoards money as a cash balance. A $1000 cash balance would have lost one-half its real value between 1980 and 1995. Of course, most forms of savings earn interest. But the value of savings will still decline if the rate of inflation exceeds the rate of interest.

Example: A household may save $1000 in a certificate of deposit (CD) in a commercial bank or savings and loan association at 6 percent annual interest. But if inflation is 13 percent (as in 1980), the real value or purchasing power of that $1000 will be cut to about $938 at the end of the year. That is, the saver will receive $1060 (equal to $1000 plus $60 of interest), but deflating that $1060 for 13 percent inflation means that the real value of $1060 is only about $938 (equal to $1060 divided by 1.13).

Debtors and Creditors

Inflation redistributes income by altering the relationship between debtors and creditors. *Unanticipated inflation benefits debtors (borrowers) at the expense of creditors (lenders).* Suppose you borrow $1000 from a bank, to be repaid in two years. If in that time the general level of prices were to double, the $1000 which you repay will have only half the purchasing power of the $1000 originally borrowed. True, if we ignore interest charges, the same number of dollars is repaid as was borrowed. But because of inflation, each of these dollars will now buy only half as much as it did when the loan was negotiated. As prices go up, the value of the dollar comes down. Thus, because of inflation, the borrower is given "dear" dollars but pays back "cheap" dollars.

The inflation of the past several decades has been a windfall to those who purchased homes in, say, the mid-1960s with fixed-interest-rate mortgages. Inflation has greatly reduced the real burden of their mortgage indebtedness. Also, until very recently the nominal value of housing has increased more rapidly than the overall price level.

The Federal government, which has amassed $4600 billion of public debt over the decades, has also been a beneficiary of inflation. Historically, the Federal government has regularly paid off its loans by taking out new ones. Inflation has permitted the Treasury to pay off its loans with dollars which have less purchasing power than the dollars it originally borrowed. Nominal national income and therefore tax collections rise with inflation; the amount of public debt owed does not. Thus, inflation reduces the real burden of the public debt to the Federal government. Because inflation benefits the Federal government in this way, some economists have questioned whether society can really expect government to be zealous in its efforts to halt inflation.

In fact, some nations such as Brazil once used inflation so extensively to reduce the real value of their debts that lenders forced them to borrow money in U.S. dollars or in some other relatively stable currency instead of their own currency. This prevents them from using domestic inflation as a means of subtly "defaulting" on their debt. Any inflation which they generate will reduce the value of their own currencies, but not the value of the dollar-denominated debt they must pay back.

Anticipated Inflation

The redistributive effects of inflation will be less severe or eliminated if people (1) anticipate inflation and (2) can adjust their nominal incomes to reflect expected price level changes. The prolonged inflation which began in the late 1960s prompted many unions in the 1970s to insist on labor contracts with **cost-of-living adjustment (COLA)** clauses to automatically adjust workers incomes for inflation.

Similarly, the redistribution of income from lender to borrower might be altered if inflation is anticipated. Suppose a lender (perhaps a commercial bank or savings and loan) and a borrower (a household) both agree that 5 percent is a fair rate of interest on a one-year loan, *provided* the price level is stable. But assume inflation has been occurring and is expected to be 6 percent over the next year. If the bank lends the household $100 at 5 percent, the bank will be paid back $105 at the end of the year. But if 6 percent inflation does occur during the year, the purchasing power of that $105 will have been reduced to triggers another round of price increases. The net effect is a cumulative *wage-price inflationary spiral*. Nominal-wage and price rises feed on each other, and this creeping inflation bursts into galloping inflation.

Potential Economic Collapse Aside from disruptive redistributive effects, hyperinflation can cause economic collapse. Severe inflation encourages speculative activity. Businesses may find it increasingly profitable to hoard both materials and finished products, anticipating further price increases. But restricting the availability of materials and products relative to the demand for them will intensify inflationary pressures. Rather than invest in capital equipment, businesses and individual savers may purchase nonproductive wealth—jewels, gold and other precious metals, real estate, and so forth—as hedges against inflation.

In the extreme, as prices shoot up sharply and unevenly, normal economic relationships are disrupted. Business owners do not know what to charge for their products. Consumers do not know what to pay. Resource suppliers will want to be paid with actual output, rather than with rapidly depreciating money. Creditors will avoid debtors to escape the repayment of debts with cheap money. Money becomes virtually worthless and ceases to do its job as a measure of value and medium of exchange. The economy may be thrown into a state of barter. Production and exchange grind toward a halt, and the net result is economic, social, and possibly political chaos. Hyperinflation has precipitated monetary collapse, depression, and sociopolitical disorder.

Examples History reveals a number of examples which fits this scenario. Consider the effects of World War II on price levels in Hungary and Japan:

The inflation in Hungary exceeded all known records of the past. In August, 1946, 828 octillion (1 followed by 27 zeros) depreciated pengös equaled the value of 1 prewar pengö. The price of the American dollar reached a value of 3×10^{22} (3 followed by 22 zeros) pengös. Fishermen and farmers in 1947 Japan used scales to weigh currency and change, rather than bothering to count it. Prices rose some 116 times in Japan, 1938 to 1948.[4]

The German inflation of the 1920s was also catastrophic:

The German Weimar Republic is an extreme example of a weak government which survived for some time through inflationary finance. On April 27, 1921, the German government was presented with a staggering bill for reparations payments to the Allies of 132 billion gold marks. This sum was far greater than what the Weimar Republic could reasonably expect to raise in taxes. Faced with huge budget deficits, the Weimar government simply ran the printing press to meet its bills.

During 1922, the German price level went up 5,470 percent. In 1923, the situation worsened; the German price level rose 1,300,000,000,000 times. By October of 1923, the postage on the lightest letter sent from Germany to the United States was 200,000 marks. Butter cost 1.5 million marks per pound, meat 2 million marks, a loaf of bread 200,000 marks, and an egg 60,000 marks. Prices increased so rapidly that waiters changed the prices on the menu several times during the course of a lunch. Sometimes customers had to pay double the price listed on the menu when they ordered.[5]

A closing word of caution: Dramatic hyperinflations like these are almost invariably the consequence of imprudent expansion of the money supply by government. With appropriate public policies, mild inflation need not become hyperinflation.

CHAPTER SUMMARY

1 Our economy has been characterized by fluctuations in domestic output, employment, and the price level. Although having common phases—peak, recession, trough, recovery—business cycles vary greatly in duration and intensity.

2 Although economists explain the business cycle in terms of such ultimate causal factors as innovations, political events, and money creation, they generally agree that the level of total spending is the immediate determinant of real output and employment.

3 The business cycle affects all sectors of the economy,

but in varying ways and degrees. The cycle has greater output and employment ramifications in the capital goods and durable consumer goods industries than it does in services and nondurable goods industries. Over the cycle, price fluctuations are greater in competitive than in monopolistic industries.

---

[4]Theodore Morgan, *Income and Employment,* 2d ed. (Englewood Cliffs, N.J.: Prentice-Hall, Inc., 1952), p. 361.

[5]Raburn M. Williams, *Inflation! Money, Jobs, and Politicians* (Arlington Heights, Ill.: AHM Publishing Corporation, 1980), p. 2.

LAST WORD

THE STOCK MARKET AND MACROECONOMIC INSTABILITY

How, if at all, do changes in stock prices relate to the macroeconomy?

Financial investors daily buy and sell the stock certificates of thousands of corporations. These corporations pay dividends—a portion of their profits—to the owners of their stock shares. The price of a particular company's stock is determined by supply and demand. Individual stock prices generally rise and fall in concert with the collective expectations for each firm's profits. Greater profits normally result in higher dividends to the owners of the stock, and in anticipation of these higher dividends, financial investors are willing to pay more for the stock.

Stock market averages such as the Dow Jones industrial average—the average price of the stocks of a selected list of major United States industrial firms—are closely watched and reported. It is common for these price averages to change over time, or even to rise or fall sharply during a single day. On "Black Monday," October 19, 1987, the Dow Jones industrial average experienced a record one-day fall of 20 percent. About $500 billion in stock market wealth evaporated in a single day!

The volatility of the stock market raises this question: Do changes in stock price averages *cause* macroeconomic instability? There are linkages between the stock market and the economy which might lead us to think the answer is "Yes." Consider a sharp decline in stock prices. Feeling poorer, owners of stock may respond by reducing their spending on goods and services. Because it is less attractive to raise funds by issuing new shares of stock, firms may react by cutting back on their purchases of new capital goods.

Research studies find, however, that the consumption and investment impacts of stock price changes are relatively mild. Therefore, although stock price averages do influence total spending, the stock market is *not* a major cause of recession or inflation.

A related question emerges: Even though changes in stock prices do not *cause* significant changes in domestic output and the price level, might they *predict* such changes? That is, if stock market values are based on expected profits, wouldn't we expect rapid changes in stock price averages to forecast changes in future business conditions? Indeed, stock prices often *do* fall prior to recessions and rise prior to expansions. For this reason stock prices are among a group of eleven variables which constitute an index of leading indicators (Last Word, Chapter 12). This index often provides a useful clue to the future direction of the economy. But taken alone, stock market prices are not a reliable predictor of changes in domestic output. Stock prices have fallen rapidly in some instances with no recession following. Black Monday itself did not produce a recession during the following two years. In other instances, recessions have occurred with no prior decline in stock market prices.

In summary, the relationship between stock market prices and the macroeconomy is quite loose. Changes in stock prices are not a major source of macroeconomic instability nor are they reliable in forecasting business recessions or expansions.

---

4   Economists distinguish between frictional, structural, and cyclical unemployment. The full-employment or natural rate of unemployment is currently between 5.5 and 6 percent. Part-time and discouraged workers complicate the accurate measurement of unemployment.

5   The economic cost of unemployment, as measured by the GDP gap, consists of the goods and services which so-

ciety forgoes when its resources are involuntarily idle. Okun's law suggests that every 1 percent increase in unemployment above the natural rate causes a $2\frac{1}{2}$ percent GDP gap.

6   Unemployment rates and inflation rates vary greatly among nations. Unemployment rates differ because nations have different natural rates of unemployment and often are

TABLE 9-1   Consumption and saving schedules *(columns 1 through 3 in billions)*

(1) Level of output and income (GDP = DI)	(2) Consump- tion, C	(3) Saving, S (1) − (2)	(4) Average propensity to consume (APC) (2)/(1)	(5) Average propensity to save (APS) (3)/(1)	(6) Marginal propensity to consume (MPC) Δ(2)/Δ(1)*	(7) Marginal propensity to save (MPS) Δ(3)/Δ(1)*
(1) $370	$375	$−5	1.01	−.01		
(2) 390	390	0	1.00	.00	.75	.25
(3) 410	405	5	.99	.01	.75	.25
(4) 430	420	10	.98	.02	.75	.25
(5) 450	435	15	.97	.03	.75	.25
(6) 470	450	20	.96	.04	.75	.25
(7) 490	465	25	.95	.05	.75	.25
(8) 510	480	30	.94	.06	.75	.25
(9) 530	495	35	.93	.07	.75	.25
(10) 550	510	40	.93	.07	.75	.25

*The Greek letter Δ, delta, means "a change in."

9-1 and is plotted in Figure 9-2a (Key Graph). This consumption schedule reflects the consumption–disposable income relationship suggested by the empirical data of Figure 9-1, and is consistent with many empirical family budget studies. The relationship is direct—as common sense would suggest—and we note that households will spend a *larger proportion* of a small disposable income than of a large disposable income.

The Saving Schedule

It is simple to derive a **saving schedule.** Because disposable income equals consumption plus saving (DI = C + S), we need only subtract consumption (Table 9-1, column 2) from disposable income (column 1) to find the amount saved (column 3) at each level of DI. That is, DI − C = S. Thus, columns 1 and 3 of Table 9-1 constitute the saving schedule, plotted in Figure 9-2b. Note there is a direct relationship between saving and DI but that saving is a smaller proportion (fraction) of a small DI than of a large DI. If households consume a smaller and smaller proportion of DI as DI goes up (column 4), they must save a larger and larger proportion (column 5).

Remembering that at each point on the 45-degree line DI equals consumption, we see that dissaving would occur at the relatively low DI of, say, $370 billion (column 1, row 1), where consumption is actually $375 billion. Households will consume more than their current incomes by liquidating (selling for cash)

accumulated wealth or by borrowing. Graphically, the vertical distance of the consumption schedule *above* the 45-degree line is equal to the vertical distance of the saving schedule *below* the horizontal axis at the $370 billion level of output and income (see Figure 9-2a and b). In this instance, each of these two vertical distances measures the $5 billion of *dissaving* occurring at the $370 billion income level.

The **break-even income** is at the $390 billion income level (row 2). This is the level where households consume their entire incomes. Graphically, the consumption schedule cuts the 45-degree line, and the saving schedule cuts the horizontal axis (saving is zero) at the break-even income level.

At all higher incomes, households will plan to save part of their income. The vertical distance of the consumption schedule *below* the 45-degree line measures this saving, as does the vertical distance of the saving schedule *above* the horizontal axis. For example, at the $410 billion level of income (row 3), both these distances indicate $5 billion worth of saving (see Figure 9-2a and b).

Average and Marginal Propensities

Columns 4 to 7 of Table 9-1 show additional characteristics of the consumption and saving schedules.

APC and APS   That fraction, or percentage, of any total income which is consumed is called the **average propensity to consume** (APC). That fraction of any

KEY GRAPH

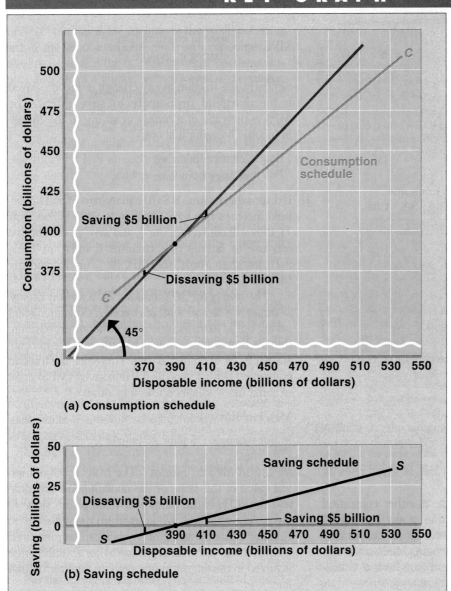

(a) Consumption schedule

(b) Saving schedule

FIGURE 9-2 Consumption (a) and saving (b) schedules The two parts of this figure show the income-consumption and income-saving relationships graphically. Each point on the 45-degree line in (a) indicates a point where DI equals consumption. Therefore, because saving equals DI minus consumption, the saving schedule in (b) is found by subtracting the consumption schedule vertically from the 45-degree guideline. Consumption equals DI (and saving therefore equals zero) at $390 billion for these hypothetical data.

total income which is saved is the **average propensity to save** (APS). That is,

$$APC = \frac{consumption}{income}$$

and

$$APS = \frac{saving}{income}$$

For example, at the $470 billion level of income (row 6) in Table 9-1, the APC is $\frac{450}{470} = \frac{45}{47}$, or about 96 percent, while the APS is $\frac{20}{470} = \frac{2}{47}$, or about 4 percent. By calculating the APC and APS at each of the ten levels of DI shown in Table 9-1, we find that the APC falls and the APS rises as DI increases. This quantifies a point just made: The fraction of total DI which is consumed declines as DI

25 percent of their current incomes are committed to installment payments on previous purchases, consumers may well retrench on current consumption to reduce indebtedness. Conversely, if consumer indebtedness is relatively low, households may consume at an unusually high rate by increasing this indebtedness.

4 Taxation In Chapter 10, we will find that changes in taxes will shift the consumption and saving schedules. Taxes are paid partly at the expense of consumption *and* partly at the expense of saving. Therefore, an *increase* in taxes will shift *both* the consumption and saving schedules *downward*. Conversely, a tax reduction will be partly consumed and partly saved by households. A tax *decrease* will shift *both* the consumption and saving schedules *upward*.

Shifts and Stability

Three final, related points are relevant to our discussion of the consumption and saving schedules.

1 Terminology The movement from one point to another on a stable consumption schedule (for example, a to b on C_0 in Figure 9-4a) is called a *change in the amount consumed*. The sole cause of this change in consumption is a change in disposable income. On the other hand, a *change in the consumption schedule* refers to an upward or downward shift of the entire schedule—for example, a shift from C_0 to C_1 or to C_2 in Figure 9-4a. A relocation of the consumption schedule is caused by changes in any one or more of the four nonincome determinants just discussed.

A similar distinction in terminology applies to the saving schedule in Figure 9-4b.

2 Schedule Shifts The first three nonincome determinants of consumption will shift the consumption and saving schedules in opposite directions. If households decide to consume *more* at each possible level of disposable income, they want to save *less,* and vice versa. Graphically, if the consumption schedule shifts upward from C_0 to C_1 in Figure 9-4, the saving schedule will shift downward from S_0 to S_1. Similarly, a downshift in the consumption schedule from C_0 to C_2 means an upshift in the saving schedule from S_0 to S_2. The exception to this is the fourth nonincome determinant—taxation. Households will consume less *and* save less to pay higher taxes. Thus, a tax increase

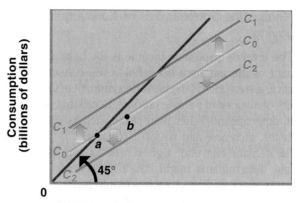

Disposable income (billions of dollars)

(a) Consumption schedule

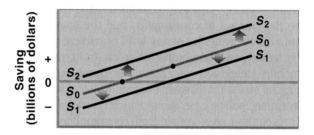

Disposable income (billions of dollars)

(b) Saving schedule

FIGURE 9-4 Shifts in the consumption (a) and saving (b) schedules
A change in any one or more of the nonincome determinants will cause the consumption and saving schedules to shift. If households consume more at each level of DI, they are necessarily saving less. Graphically this means that an upshift in the consumption schedule (C_0 to C_1) entails a downshift in the saving schedule (S_0 to S_1). If households consume less at each level of DI, they are saving more. A downshift in the consumption schedule (C_0 to C_2) is reflected in an upshift of the saving schedule (S_0 to S_2).

will lower *both* consumption and saving schedules, while a tax cut will shift *both* schedules upward.

3 Stability Economists generally agree that, aside from deliberate governmental actions designed to shift them, the consumption and saving schedules are generally stable. This may be because consumption-saving decisions are strongly influenced by habit or because the nonincome determinants are diverse and changes in them frequently work in opposite directions and therefore may be self-canceling.

INVESTMENT

We now turn to investment, the second component of private spending. Recall that investment consists of expenditures on new plants, capital equipment, machinery, and so on. The investment decision is a marginal benefit–marginal cost decision (Chapters 1 and 2). The marginal benefit from investment is the expected rate of net profits businesses hope to realize. The marginal cost is the interest rate—the cost of borrowing. We will see that businesses will invest in all projects for which expected net profits exceed the interest rate. Expected net profits and the interest rate therefore are the two basic determinants of investment spending.

Expected Rate of Net Profit, r

Investment spending is guided by the profit motive; businesses buy capital goods only when they expect such purchases to be profitable. Suppose the owner of a small cabinetmaking shop is considering investing in a new sanding machine costing $1000 and having a useful life of only one year. The new machine will presumably increase the firm's output and sales revenue. Suppose the *net* expected revenue (that is, net of such operating costs as power, lumber, labor, certain taxes, and so forth) from the machine is $1100.

In other words, after operating costs have been accounted for, the remaining expected net revenue is sufficient to cover the $1000 cost of the machine and leave a profit of $100. Comparing this $100 profit with the $1000 cost of the machine, we find that the expected *rate* of net profit, r, on the machine is 10 percent (= $100/$1000). Businesses sometimes refer to the "return" on an investment, meaning the profits that resulted from the investment. Thus, our use of r for this "return" or "profit."

The Real Interest Rate, i

One important cost associated with investing which our example has ignored is the interest rate—the financial cost the firm must pay to borrow the *money* capital required to purchase the *real* capital (the sanding machine).

We can consider the interest rate in the context of an investment and its expected return with the following generalization: If the expected rate of net profits (10 percent) exceeds the interest rate (say, 7 percent), it will be profitable to invest. But if the interest rate (say, 12 percent) exceeds the expected rate of net profits (10 percent), it will be unprofitable to invest.

But what if the firm does *not* borrow, instead financing the investment internally out of funds saved from past profits? The role of the interest rate as a cost in investing in real capital doesn't change. By using money from savings to invest in the sander, the firm incurs an opportunity cost (Chapter 2) because it forgoes the interest income it could have realized by lending the funds to someone else.

The *real* rate of interest, rather than the nominal rate, is crucial in making investment decisions. Recall from Chapter 8 that the nominal interest rate is expressed in dollars of current value, while the real interest rate is stated in dollars of constant or inflation-adjusted value. The real interest rate is the nominal rate less the rate of inflation. In our sanding machine illustration we implicitly assumed a constant price level so that all our data, including the interest rate, were in real terms.

But what if inflation is occurring? Suppose a $1000 investment is estimated to yield a real (inflation-adjusted) expected rate of net profits of 10 percent and the nominal interest rate is 15 percent. At first, we would say the investment will be unprofitable. But assume there is ongoing inflation of 10 percent per year. This means the investor will pay back dollars vate sector of the economy, the aggregate expenditures schedule shows the combined amount of consumption and planned gross investment spending $(C + I_g)$ forthcoming at each output-income level. Aggregate expenditures are the sum of columns 3 and 5 at each level of GDP.

We'll start by focusing on *planned* or intended investment in column 5 of Table 9-4. Later we'll see that imbalances in aggregate expenditures and real output will result in unplanned or unintended investment in the form of inventory changes (column 7).

Equilibrium GDP Of the ten possible levels of GDP in Table 9-4, which will be the equilibrium level? Which level of total output will the economy be capable of sustaining?

The equilibrium level of output is that output whose production will create total spending just sufficient to purchase that output. The equilibrium level of GDP is where the total quantity of goods produced (GDP) equals the total quantity of goods purchased $(C + I_g)$. Look at the domestic output schedule of column 2 and the aggregate expenditures schedule of column 6 and you see that this equality exists only at $470 billion of GDP (row 6). This is the only output at which the economy is willing to spend precisely the amount necessary to take that output off the market. Here the annual rates of production and spending are in balance. There is no overproduction, which would result in a piling up of unsold goods and therefore cutbacks in the production rate. Nor is there an excess of total spending, which would draw down inventories and prompt increases in the rate of production. In short, there is no reason for businesses to alter this rate of production; $470 billion is therefore the **equilibrium GDP.**

Disequilibrium To understand better the meaning of the equilibrium level of GDP, let's examine other levels of GDP to see why they cannot be sustained.

At the $410 billion level of GDP (row 3), businesses would find that if they produced this output, the income created would produce $405 billion in consumer spending. Supplemented by $20 billion of planned investment, total expenditures $(C + I_g)$ would be $425 billion, as shown in column 6. The economy provides an annual rate of spending more than sufficient to purchase the current $410 billion rate of production. Because businesses are producing at a lower rate than buyers are taking goods off the shelves, an unintended decline in business inventories of $15 billion would occur (column 7) if this situation were sus-

tained. But businesses will adjust to this imbalance between aggregate expenditures and real output by stepping up production. A higher rate of output will mean more jobs and a higher level of total income. In brief, if aggregate expenditures exceed the domestic output, those expenditures will drive domestic output upward.

By making the same comparisons of GDP (column 2) and $C + I_g$ (column 6) at all other levels of GDP below the $470 billion equilibrium level, we find that the economy wants to spend in excess of the level at which businesses are willing to produce. The excess of total spending at all these levels of GDP will drive GDP upward to the $470 billion level.

The reverse is true at all levels of GDP above the $470 billion equilibrium level. Businesses will find that the production of these total outputs fails to generate the levels of spending needed to take them off the market. Being unable to recover their costs, businesses will cut back on production.

To illustrate: At the $510 billion level of output (row 8), business managers will find there is insufficient spending to permit the sale of that output. Of the $510 billion of income which this output creates, $480 billion is received back by businesses as consumption spending. Though supplemented by $20 billion of planned investment spending, total expenditures ($500 billion) fall $10 billion short of the $510 billion quantity produced. If this imbalance persisted, $10 billion of inventories would pile up (column 7). But businesses will react to this unintended accumulation of unsold goods by cutting back on the rate of production. This decline in GDP will mean fewer jobs and a decline in total income. You should verify that deficiencies of total spending exist at all other levels of GDP above the $470 billion level.

The equilibrium level of GDP occurs where the total output, measured by GDP, and aggregate expenditures, $C + I_g$, are equal. Any excess of total spending over total output will drive GDP upward. Any deficiency of total spending will pull GDP downward.

Graphical Analysis

The same analysis can be shown in a graph. In Figure 9-8 (Key Graph) the **45-degree line** now takes on increased significance. Recall that the special property of this line is that at any point on it, the value of what is being measured on the horizontal axis (in this case GDP) is equal to the value of what is being measured on the vertical axis (here, aggregate expendi-

KEY GRAPH

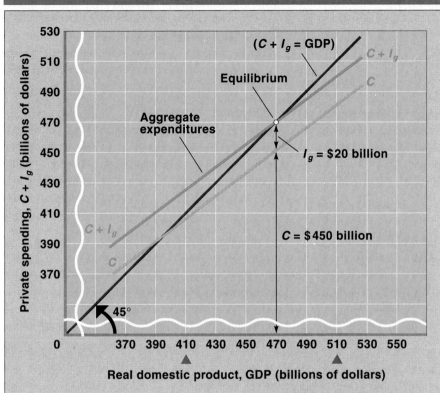

FIGURE 9-8 The aggregate expenditures–domestic output approach to the equilibrium GDP

The aggregate expenditures schedule, $C + I_g$, is determined by adding a fixed amount of investment to the upsloping consumption schedule. The equilibrium level of GDP is determined where the aggregate expenditures schedule intersects the 45-degree line, in this case at $470 billion.

---

tures or $C + I_g$). Having discovered in our tabular analysis that the equilibrium level of domestic output is determined where $C + I_g$ equals GDP, we can say that the 45-degree line in Figure 9-8 is a graphical statement of this equilibrium condition.

Next, we must add the aggregate expenditures schedule to Figure 9-8. To do this we graph the consumption schedule of Figure 9-2a and add to it *vertically* the constant $20 billion amount I_g from Figure 9-6, which, we assume, businesses plan to invest at each possible level of GDP. More directly, we can plot the $C + I_g$ data of column 6 in Table 9-4.

Observe that the aggregate expenditures line $C + I_g$ shows total spending rising with output and income, but not as much as income rises. This is because the marginal propensity to consume—the slope of line C—is less than 1. Because the aggregate expenditures line $C + I_g$ is parallel to the consumption line, the slope of the aggregate expenditures line equals the MPC and is also less than 1. A part of any increase in disposable income will *not* be spent; it will

be saved. For our particular data, aggregate expenditures rise by $15 billion for every $20 billion increase in real output and income because $5 billion of each $20 billion income increment is saved.

The equilibrium level of GDP is that GDP level corresponding to the intersection of the aggregate expenditures schedule and the 45-degree line. This intersection locates the only point at which aggregate expenditures (on the vertical axis) are equal to GDP (on the horizontal axis). Because our aggregate expenditures schedule is based on the data of Table 9-4, we once again find that equilibrium output is $470 billion. Observe that consumption at this output is $450 billion and investment is $20 billion.

It is evident from Figure 9-8 that no levels of GDP above the equilibrium level are sustainable, because $C + I_g$ falls short of GDP. Graphically, the aggregate expenditures schedule lies *below* the 45-degree line. At the $510 billion GDP level, $C + I_g$ is only $500 billion. Inventories of unsold goods rise to undesired levels, prompting businesses to readjust production sights downward in the direction of the $470 billion output level.

Conversely, at all possible levels of GDP less than $470 billion, the economy wants to spend in excess of what businesses are producing. $C + I_g$ exceeds the value of the corresponding output. Graphically, the aggregate expenditures schedule lies *above* the 45-degree line. At the $410 billion GDP, for example, $C + I_g$ totals $425 billion. Inventories decline as the rate of spending exceeds the rate of production, prompting businesses to raise production toward the $470 billion GDP. Unless there is some change in the location of the aggregate expenditures line, the $470 billion level of GDP will be sustained indefinitely.

EQUILIBRIUM GDP: LEAKAGES-INJECTIONS APPROACH

The expenditures-output approach to determining GDP spotlights total spending as the immediate determinant of the levels of output, employment, and income. Though the **leakages-injections** ($S = I_g$) **approach** is less direct, it does have the advantage of underscoring the reason $C + I_g$ and GDP are unequal at all levels of output except the equilibrium level.

The idea of the leakages-injections approach is this: Under our simplifying assumptions we know that the production of any level of real output will generate an identical amount of disposable income. But we also know a part of that income may be saved—*not* consumed—by households. Saving therefore represents a *leakage* or withdrawal of spending from the income-expenditures stream. Saving is what keeps consumption short of total output or GDP; thus, by itself consumption is insufficient to take the domestic output off the market, setting the stage, it would seem, for a decline in total output.

However, the business sector does not intend to sell its entire output to consumers; some domestic output will consist of capital or investment goods sold within the business sector. Investment can therefore be thought of as an *injection* of spending into the income-expenditures stream which supplements consumption. Investment is a potential offset to, or replacement for, the leakage of saving.

If the leakage of saving exceeds the injection of investment, then $C + I_g$ will fall short of GDP and this level of GDP will be too high to be sustained. Any GDP where saving exceeds investment will be an above-equilibrium GDP. Conversely, if the injection of investment exceeds the leakage of saving, then $C + I_g$ will be greater than GDP and GDP will be driven upward. Any GDP where investment exceeds saving will be a below-equilibrium GDP.

Only where $S = I_g$—where the leakage of saving is exactly offset by the injection of investment—will aggregate expenditures equal real output. And we know this equality defines the equilibrium GDP.

In the closed private economy assumed here, there are only one leakage (saving) and one injection (investment). In general terms, a *leakage* is any use of income other than its expenditure on domestically produced output. In the more realistic models which follow (in Chapter 10), we will need to incorporate the additional leakages of imports and taxes into our analysis.

Similarly, an *injection* is any supplement to consumer spending on domestic production. Again, in later models we must add injections of exports and government purchases to our discussion. But for now we need only compare the single leakage of saving with the sole injection of investment to assess the impact on GDP.

Tabular Analysis

Our $C + I_g$ = GDP approach has led us to conclude that all levels of GDP less than $470 billion are unstable because the corresponding $C + I_g$ exceeds these GDPs, driving GDP upward. Now let's look at the saving schedule (columns 2 and 4) and the investment schedule (columns 2 and 5) of Table 9-4. Comparing the amounts households and businesses want to save and invest at each of the below-equilibrium GDP levels explains the excesses of total spending. At each of these lower GDP levels, businesses plan to invest more than households want to save.

For example, at the $410 billion level of GDP (row 3), households will save only $5 billion, spending $405 of their $410 billion incomes. Supplemented by $20 billion of business investment, aggregate expenditures ($C + I_g$) are $425 billion. Aggregate expenditures exceed GDP by $15 billion (= $425 − $410) *because* the amount businesses plan to invest at this level of GDP exceeds the amounts households save by $15 billion. The fact is that a very small leakage of saving at this relatively low income level will be more than compensated for by the relatively large injection of investment spending which causes $C + I_g$ to exceed GDP and induce GDP upward.

Similarly, all levels of GDP above the $470 billion level are also unstable, because they exceed $C + I_g$. The reason for this insufficiency of aggregate expenditures is that at all GDP levels above $470 billion, households will want to save more than businesses plan to invest. The saving leakage is not compensated for by the injection of investment.

For example, households will choose to save at the high rate of $30 billion at the $510 billion GDP (row 8). Businesses, however, will plan to invest only $20 billion. This $10 billion excess of saving over planned investment will reduce total spending to $10 billion below the value of total output. Specifically, aggregate expenditures are $500 billion and real GDP is $510 billion. This spending deficiency will reduce GDP.

Again we verify that the equilibrium GDP is $470 billion. Only at this level are the saving desires of households and the investment plans of businesses equal. Only when businesses and households attempt to invest and save at the same rate—where the leakages and injections are equal—will $C + I_g = $ GDP. Only here will the annual rates of production and spending be in balance; only here will there be no unplanned changes in inventories.

Think of it this way: If saving were zero, consumer spending would always be sufficient to clear the market of any GDP; consumption would equal GDP. But saving can and does occur, causing consumption to fall short of GDP. Only when businesses are willing to invest at the same rate at which households save

will the amount by which consumption falls short of GDP be precisely counterbalanced.

Graphical Analysis

The leakages-injections approach to determining the equilibrium GDP can be demonstrated graphically, as in Figure 9-9. Here we have combined the saving schedule of Figure 9-2b and the investment schedule of Figure 9-6. The numerical data for these schedules are in columns 2, 4, and 5 of Table 9-4. We see the equilibrium level of GDP is at $470 billion, where the saving and investment schedules intersect. Only here do businesses and households invest and save at the same rates; therefore, only here will GDP and $C + I_g$ be equal.

At all higher levels of GDP, households will save at a higher rate than businesses plan to invest. The saving leakage exceeds the investment injection which causes $C + I_g$ to fall short of GDP, driving GDP downward. At the $510 billion GDP, for example, saving of $30 billion will exceed investment of $20 billion by $10 billion, with the result that $C + I_g$ is $500 billion, $10 billion short of GDP.

At all levels of GDP below the $470 billion equilibrium level, businesses will plan to invest more than households save. Here the injection of investment exceeds the leakage of saving so that $C + I_g$ exceeds GDP, driving GDP upward. To illustrate: At the $410 billion level of GDP the $5 billion leakage of saving is more than compensated for by the $20 billion that

FIGURE 9-9   The leakages-injections approach to the equilibrium GDP
A second approach is to view the equilibrium GDP as determined by the intersection of the saving (S) and the planned investment (I_g) schedules. Only at the point of equilibrium will households plan to save the amount businesses want to invest. It is the consistency of these plans which equates GDP and $C + I_g$.

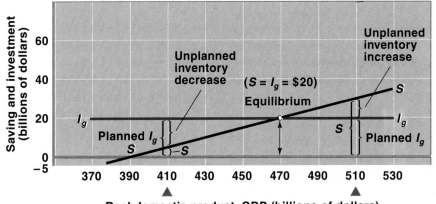

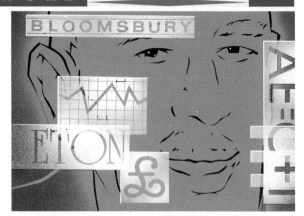
businesses plan to invest. The result is that $C + I_g$ exceeds GDP by $15 billion, inducing businesses to produce a larger GDP. *(Key Question 10)*

PLANNED VERSUS ACTUAL INVESTMENT

We have emphasized that discrepancies in saving and investment can occur and bring about changes in the equilibrium GDP. Now we must recognize that, in another sense, saving and investment must always be equal! This apparent contradiction concerning the equality of saving and investment is resolved when we distinguish between **planned investment** and saving (which need not be equal) and **actual investment** and saving (which by definition must be equal). The catch is that *actual investment consists of both planned and unplanned investment (unplanned changes in inventory investment), and unplanned investment acts as a balancing item which always equates the actual amounts saved and invested in any period of time.*

Disequilibrium and Inventories

Consider, for example, the $490 billion above-equilibrium GDP (row 7 of Table 9-4). What would happen if businesses produced this output, thinking they could sell it? At this level, households save $25 billion of their $490 billion DI, so consumption is only $465 billion. *Planned* investment (column 5) is $20 billion; businesses plan or desire to buy $20 billion worth of capital goods. This means aggregate expenditures $(C + I_g)$ are $485 billion, and sales therefore fall short of production by $5 billion. This extra $5 billion of goods is retained by businesses as an *unintended* or *unplanned* increase in inventories (column 7). It is unintended because it results from the failure of total spending to take total output off the market. Remembering that, by definition, changes in inventories are a part of investment, we note that *actual* investment of $25 billion ($20 planned *plus* $5 unintended or unplanned) equals saving of $25 billion, even though saving exceeds *planned* investment by $5 billion. Businesses, being unwilling to accumulate un-

Music and the Arts, bursar of King's College, Cambridge, editor of the *Economic Journal,* chairman of the *Nation* and later the *New Statesman* magazines, and chairman of the National Mutual Life Assurance Society. He also ran an investment company, organized the Camargo Ballet (his wife, Lydia Lopokova, was a renowned star of the Russian Imperial Ballet), and built (profitably) the Arts Theatre at Cambridge.*

In addition, Keynes found time to amass a $2 million personal fortune by speculating in stocks, international currencies, and commodities. He was also a leading figure in the "Bloomsbury group," an *avant-garde* group of intellectual luminaries who greatly influenced the artistic and literary standards of England.

Most importantly, Keynes was a prolific scholar.

*E. Ray Canterbery, *The Making of Economics,* 3d ed. (Belmont, Calif.: Wadsworth Publishing Company, 1987), p. 126.

His books encompassed such widely ranging topics as probability theory, monetary economics, and the economic consequences of the World War I peace treaty. His *magnum opus,* however, was the *General Theory,* which has been described by John Kenneth Galbraith as "a work of profound obscurity, badly written and prematurely published." Yet the *General Theory* attacked the classical economists' contention that recession will automatically cure itself. Keynes' analysis suggested that recession could easily spiral downward into a depression. Keynes claimed that modern capitalism contained no automatic mechanism which would propel the economy back toward full employment. The economy might languish for many years in depression. Indeed, the massive unemployment of the worldwide depression of the 1930s seemed to provide sufficient evidence that Keynes was right. His basic policy recommendation—a startling one in view of the balanced-budget sentiment at the time—was for government in these circumstances to increase its spending to induce more production and put the unemployed back to work.

wanted inventories at this annual rate, will cut back production.

Now look at the below-equilibrium $450 billion output (row 5 of Table 9-4). Because households save only $15 billion of their $450 billion DI, consumption is $435 billion. Planned investment by businesses is $20 billion, so aggregate expenditures are $455 billion. Sales exceed production by $5 billion. This is so because an unplanned decline in business inventories has occurred. Businesses have unintentionally *disinvested* $5 billion in inventories (column 7). Note once again that *actual* investment is $15 billion ($20 planned *minus* $5 unintended or unplanned) and equal to saving of $15 billion, even though *planned* investment exceeds saving by $5 billion. This unplanned decline in investment in inventories due to the excess of sales over production will induce businesses to increase the GDP by expanding production.

To summarize:

At all *above-equilibrium* levels of GDP (where saving exceeds planned investment), actual investment and saving are equal because of unintended increases in inventories which are a part of actual investment. Graphically (Figure 9-9), the unintended inventory increase is measured by the vertical distance by which the saving schedule lies above the (planned) investment schedule.

At all *below-equilibrium* levels of GDP (where planned investment exceeds saving), actual investment will be equal to saving because of unintended decreases in inventories which must be subtracted from planned investment to determine actual investment. These unintended inventory declines are shown graphically as the vertical distance by which the (planned) investment schedule lies above the saving schedule.

Achieving Equilibrium

These distinctions are important because they mean that *it is the equality of planned investment and saving which determines the equilibrium level of GDP.* We can think of the process by which equilibrium is achieved as follows:

1 A difference between saving and planned investment causes a difference between the production and spending plans of the economy as a whole.

2 This difference between aggregate production and spending plans results in unintended investment or disinvestment in inventories.

3 As long as unintended investment in inventories persists, businesses will revise their production plans downward and reduce GDP. Conversely, as long as unintended disinvestment in inventories exists, firms will revise their production plans upward and increase GDP. Both movements in GDP are toward equilibrium because they bring about the equality of planned investment and saving.

4 Only where planned investment and saving are equal will the level of GDP be in equilibrium. Only where planned investment equals saving will there be no unintended investment or disinvestment in inven-

tories to drive the GDP downward or upward. Note in column 7 of Table 9-4 that only at the $470 billion equilibrium GDP is there no unintended investment or disinvestment in inventories. *(Key Question 11)*

QUICK REVIEW 9-4

■ In a private closed economy, equilibrium GDP occurs where aggregate expenditures equal real domestic output $(C + I_g = GDP)$.

■ Alternatively, equilibrium GDP is established where saving equals planned investment $(S = I_g)$.

■ Actual investment consists of planned investment plus unplanned changes in inventories and is always equal to saving.

■ At equilibrium GDP, changes in inventories are zero; no unintended investment or disinvestment occurs.

CHAPTER SUMMARY

1 Classical economists argued that because supply creates its own demand (Say's law), general underspending was improbable. Thus the economy would provide virtually continuous full employment. Even if temporary declines in total spending occurred, these declines would be compensated for by downward price-wage adjustments which would boost spending and employment, restoring the economy to its full-employment level of output.

2 The Great Depression and Keynes's *General Theory* undermined classical macroeconomics. The Great Depression challenged the classical precept that full employment was the norm in a capitalist economy. Keynes's aggregate expenditures analysis showed how periods of underspending or overspending could occur.

3 The basic tools of the aggregate expenditures model are the consumption, saving, and investment schedules, which show the various amounts households intend to consume and save and businesses plan to invest at the various income-output levels, assuming a fixed price level.

4 The *average* propensities to consume and save show the fraction of any level of *total* income consumed and saved. The *marginal* propensities to consume and save show the fraction of any *change* in total income consumed or saved.

5 The locations of the consumption and saving schedules are determined by **a** the amount of wealth owned by households; **b** expectations of future income, future prices, and product availability; **c** the relative size of consumer indebtedness; and **d** taxation. The consumption

and saving schedules are relatively stable.

6 The immediate determinants of investment are **a** the expected rate of net profit and **b** the real rate of interest. The economy's investment-demand curve can be determined by cumulating investment projects and arraying them in descending order according to their expected net profitability and applying the rule that investment will be profitable up to the point at which the real interest rate, *i*, equals the expected rate of net profit, *r*. The investment-demand curve reveals an inverse relationship between the interest rate and the level of aggregate investment.

7 Shifts in the investment-demand curve can occur as the result of changes in **a** the acquisition, maintenance, and operating costs of capital goods; **b** business taxes; **c** technology; **d** the stocks of capital goods on hand; and **e** expectations.

8 For simplicity we assume the level of investment determined by the current interest rate and the investment-demand curve does not vary with the level of real GDP.

9 The durability of capital goods, the irregular occurrence of major innovations, profit volatility, and the variability of expectations all contribute to the instability of investment spending.

10 For a private closed economy the equilibrium level of GDP is where aggregate expenditures and real output are equal or, graphically, where the $C + I_g$ line intersects the 45-degree line. At any GDP greater than equilibrium GDP, real output will exceed aggregate spending, resulting in unintended investment in inventories, depressed profits, and eventual declines in output, employment, and income. At any below-equilibrium GDP, aggregate expenditures will exceed real output, resulting in unintended disinvestment in inventories, substantial profits, and eventual increases in GDP.

11 The leakages-injections approach determines equilibrium GDP at the point where the amount households save and the amount businesses plan to invest are equal. This is at the point where the saving and planned investment schedules intersect. Any excess of saving over planned investment will cause a shortage of total spending, forcing GDP

to fall. Any excess of planned investment over saving will cause an excess of total spending, inducing GDP to rise. These changes in GDP will in both cases correct the indicated discrepancies in saving and planned investment.

12 Actual investment consists of planned investment and unplanned changes in inventories. When planned investment diverges from planned saving, unintended investment or disinvestment in inventories occur which equate actual investment and saving. At equilibrium GDP, planned investment equals saving; inventory levels are constant (there is no unplanned investment or disinvestment).

TERMS AND CONCEPTS

Say's law	average propensities to	investment schedule	45-degree line
Keynesian economics	consume and save	aggregate	leakages-injections
consumption and	marginal propensities	expenditures–	approach
saving schedules	to consume and save	domestic output	planned versus actual
break-even income	investment-demand	approach	investment
	curve	equilibrium GDP	

QUESTIONS AND STUDY SUGGESTIONS

1 Relate Say's law to the perspective held by classical economists that the economy generally will operate at a position *on* its production possibilities curve (Chapter 2). Use production possibilities analysis to demonstrate the Keynesian perspective on this matter.

2 Explain what relationships are shown by **a** the consumption schedule, **b** the saving schedule, **c** the investment-demand curve, and **d** the investment schedule.

3 Precisely how are the APC and the MPC different? Why must the sum of the MPC and the MPS equal 1? What are the basic determinants of the consumption and saving schedules? Of your own level of consumption?

4 Explain how each of the following will affect the consumption and saving schedules or the investment schedule:

    a A decline in the amount of government bonds which consumers are holding

    b The threat of limited, nonnuclear war, leading the public to expect future shortages of consumer durables

    c A decline in the real interest rate

    d A sharp decline in stock prices

    e An increase in the rate of population growth

    f The development of a cheaper method of manufacturing pig iron from ore

    g The announcement that the social security program is to be restricted in size of benefits

    h The expectation that mild inflation will persist in the next decade

    i An increase in the Federal personal income tax

5 Explain why an upshift in the consumption schedule typically involves an equal downshift in the saving schedule. What is the exception?

6 *Key Question* *Complete the accompanying table.*

Level of output and income (GDP = DI)	Consumption	Saving	APC	APS	MPC	MPS
$240	$_____	$−4	__	__		
260	_____	0	__	__	__	__
280	_____	4	__	__	__	__
300	_____	8	__	__	__	__
320	_____	12	__	__	__	__
340	_____	16	__	__	__	__
360	_____	20	__	__	__	__
380	_____	24	__	__	__	__
400	_____	28	__	__	__	__

    a *Show the consumption and saving schedules graphically.*

    b *Locate the break-even level of income. How is it possible for households to dissave at very low income levels?*

    c *If the proportion of total income consumed decreases and the proportion saved increases as income rises, explain both verbally and graphically how the MPC and MPS can be constant at various levels of income.*

7 What are the basic determinants of investment? Explain the relationship between the real interest rate and the level of investment. Why is the investment schedule less stable than the consumption and saving schedules?

8 *Key Question* *Assume there are no investment projects in the economy which yield an expected rate of net profit of 25 percent or more. But suppose there are $10 billion of investment projects yielding expected net profit of between 20 and 25 percent; another $10 billion yielding between 15 and 20 percent; another $10 billion between 10 and 15 percent; and so forth. Cumulate these data and present them graphically, putting the expected rate of net profit on the vertical axis and the amount of investment on the horizontal axis. What will be the equilibrium level of aggregate investment if the real interest rate is* **a** *15 percent,* **b** *10 percent, and* **c** *5 percent? Explain why this curve is the investment-demand curve.*

9 Explain graphically the determination of the equilibrium GDP by **a** the aggregate expenditures–domestic output approach and **b** the leakages-injections approach for a private closed economy. Why must these two approaches always yield the same equilibrium GDP? Explain why the intersection of the aggregate expenditures schedule and the 45-degree line determines the equilibrium GDP.

10 *Key Question* *Assuming the level of investment is $16 billion and independent of the level of total output, complete the following table and determine the equilibrium levels of output and employment which this private closed economy would provide. What are the sizes of the MPC and MPS?*

Possible levels of employment, millions	Real domestic output (GDP = DI), billions	Consumption, billions	Saving, billions
40	$240	$244	$____
45	260	260	____
50	280	276	____
55	300	292	____
60	320	308	____
65	340	324	____
70	360	340	____
75	380	356	____
80	400	372	____

11 *Key Question* *Using the consumption and saving data given in question 10 and assuming the level of investment is $16 billion, what are the levels of saving and planned investment at the $380 billion level of domestic output? What are the levels of saving and actual investment? What are saving and planned investment at the $300 billion level of domestic output? What are the levels of saving and actual investment? Use the concept of unintended investment to explain adjustments toward equilibrium from both the $380 and $300 billion levels of domestic output.*

12 "Planned investment is equal to saving at all levels of GDP; actual investment equals saving only at the equilibrium GDP." Do you agree? Explain. Critically evaluate: "The fact that households may save more than businesses want to invest is of no consequence, because events will in time force households and businesses to save and invest at the same rates."

13 **Advanced analysis:** Linear equations (see appendix to Chapter 1) for the consumption and saving schedules take the general form $C = a + bY$ and $S = -a + (1 - b)Y$, where C, S, and Y are consumption, saving, and national income, respectively. The constant a represents the vertical intercept, and b is the slope of the consumption schedule.

    a Use the following data to substitute specific numerical values into the consumption and saving equations.

National income (Y)	Consumption (C)
$ 0	$ 80
100	140
200	200
300	260
400	320

    b What is the economic meaning of b? Of $(1 - b)$?

    c Suppose the amount of saving which occurs at each level of national income falls by $20, but that the values for b and $(1 - b)$ remain unchanged. Restate the saving and consumption equations for the new numerical values and cite a factor which might have caused the change.

14 **Advanced analysis:** Suppose that the linear equation for consumption in a hypothetical economy is $C = 40 + .8Y$. Also suppose that income (Y) is $400. Determine **a** the marginal propensity to consume, **b** the marginal propensity to save, **c** the level of consumption, **d** the average propensity to consume, **e** the level of saving, and **f** the average propensity to save.

15 **Advanced analysis:** Assume that the linear equation for consumption in a hypothetical private closed economy is $C = 10 + .9Y$, where Y is total real income (output). Also suppose that the equation for investment is $I_g = I_{g0} = 40$, meaning that I_g is 40 at all levels of real income (output). Using the equation $Y = C + I_g$, determine the equilibrium level of Y. What are the total amounts of consumption, saving, and investment at equilibrium Y?

16 (Last Word) What is the significance of John Maynard Keynes's book, *The General Theory,* published in 1936?

AGGREGATE EXPENDITURES: THE MULTIPLIER, NET EXPORTS, AND GOVERNMENT

We have seen why a particular level of real GDP exists, specifically in a private closed economy. Now we want to see why and how that level might change, as it often does in the real economy. Also, we gain realism by adding the foreign sector and government to our aggregate expenditures model.

First, we analyze changes in investment spending and how they affect real GDP, income, and employment, finding that a change in investment creates a multiple change in output and incomes. Then we "open" our simplified "closed" economy to show how exports and imports affect it. Government—with its expenditures and taxes—is next brought into the model; the "private" economy becomes the "mixed" economy. Finally, we apply our model to two historical periods and consider some of its deficiencies. We continue to assume the price level remains constant unless stated otherwise. Our focus therefore remains on real GDP.

CHANGES IN EQUILIBRIUM GDP AND THE MULTIPLIER

Thus far, we have been concerned with using the aggregate expenditures model to explain the equilibrium levels of total output and income. But we saw in Chapter 8 that the GDP of American capitalism is seldom stable; rather, it is characterized by long-run growth and punctuated by cyclical fluctuations. Let's see *why* and *how* the equilibrium level of real GDP fluctuates.

The equilibrium level of GDP will change in response to changes in the investment schedule or the saving-consumption schedules. Because investment spending generally is less stable than the consump-

tion-saving schedules, we will assume the investment schedule changes.

The impact of changes in investment can be seen through Figure 10-1a and b. Suppose the expected rate of net profit on investment rises (shifting the investment-demand curve of Figure 9-5 to the right) *or* the interest rate falls (the investment-demand curve in Fig. 9-5 doesn't shift; we move down the stable curve). As a result, investment spending increases by, say, $5 billion. This is indicated in Figure 10-1a by an upward shift in the aggregate expenditures schedule from $(C + I_g)_0$ to $(C + I_g)_1$, and in Figure 10-1b by an upward shift in the investment schedule from I_{g0} to I_{g1}. In each graph the consequence is a rise in the equilibrium GDP from $470 to $490 billion.

TABLE 10-1   The multiplier: a tabular illustration *(in billions)*

	(1) Change in income	(2) Change in consumption (MPC = .75)	(3) Change in saving (MPS = .25)
Assumed increase in investment	$ 5.00	$ 3.75	$1.25
Second round	3.75	2.81	0.94
Third round	2.81	2.11	0.70
Fourth round	2.11	1.58	0.53
Fifth round	1.58	1.19	0.39
All other rounds	4.75	3.56	1.19
Totals	$20.00	$15.00	$5.00

sumed flows to still other households as income (third round). This process continues.

Figure 10-2, derived from Table 10-1, shows the cumulative effects of the rounds of the multiplier process. Each round *adds* the orange blocks to national income and GDP. The cumulation of the additional income in each round—the sum of the orange blocks—is the total change in income or GDP. Though the spending and respending effects of the

FIGURE 10-2   The multiplier process (MPC = .75)
An initial change in investment spending of $5 billion creates an equal $5 billion of new income in round 1. Households spend $3.75 (= .75 × $5) billion of this new income, creating $3.75 of added income in round 2. Of this $3.75 of new income, households spend $2.81 (= .75 × $3.75) billion and income rises by that amount in round 3. The cumulation of such income increments over the entire process eventually results in a total change of income and GDP of $20 billion. The multiplier therefore is 4 (= $20 billion ÷ $5 billion).

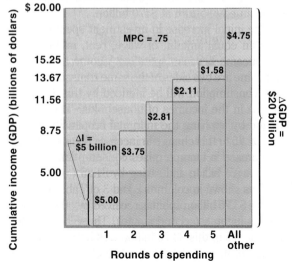

increase in investment diminish with each successive round of spending, the cumulative increase in the output-income level will be $20 billion if the process is carried through to the last dollar. The $5 billion increase in investment will therefore increase the equilibrium GDP by $20 billion, from $470 to $490 billion. Thus, the multiplier is 4 (= $20 billion ÷ $5 billion).

It is no coincidence that the multiplier effect ends at the point where exactly enough saving has been generated to offset the initial $5 billion increase in investment spending. Only then will the disequilibrium created by the investment increase be corrected. GDP and total incomes must rise by $20 billion to create $5 billion in additional saving to match the $5 billion increase in investment spending. Income must increase by four times the initial excess of investment over saving, because households save one-fourth of any increase in their incomes (that is, the MPS is .25). In this example the multiplier—the number of times the ultimate increase in income exceeds the initial increase in investment spending—is 4.

The Multiplier and the Marginal Propensities
You may have sensed from Table 10-1 a relationship between the MPS and the size of the multiplier. The fraction of an increase in income saved—the MPS—determines the cumulative respending effects of any initial change in I_g, G, X_n or C, and therefore the multiplier. *The size of the MPS and the size of the multiplier are inversely related.* The smaller the fraction of any change in income saved, the greater the respending at each round and, therefore, the greater the multiplier. If the MPS is .25, as in our example, the multiplier is 4. If the MPS were .33, the multiplier would be 3. If the MPS were .2, the multiplier would be 5.

Look again at Table 9-4 and Figure 10-1b. Initially the economy is in equilibrium at the $470 billion level of GDP. Now businesses increase investment by $5 billion so that planned investment of $25 billion exceeds saving of $20 billion at the $470 billion level. This means $470 billion is no longer the equilibrium GDP. By how much must GDP or national income rise to restore equilibrium? By enough to generate $5 billion of additional saving to offset the $5 billion increase in investment. Because households save $1 out of every $4 of additional income they receive (MPS = .25), GDP must rise by $20 billion—four times the increase in investment—to create the $5 billion of extra saving necessary to restore equilibrium. Thus, the multiplier is 4.

If the MPS were .33, GDP would only have to rise by $15 billion (three times the increase in investment) to generate $5 billion of additional saving and restore equilibrium, and the multiplier therefore would be 3. But if the MPS were .20, GDP would have to rise by $25 billion for people to save an extra $5 billion and equilibrium to be restored, yielding a multiplier of 5.

Also, recall the MPS measures the slope of the saving schedule. In the leakages-injections ($S = I_g$) approach, this means that if the MPS is relatively large (say, .5) and the slope of the saving schedule is therefore relatively steep (.5), any upward shift in investment spending will be subject to a relatively small multiplier. A $5 billion increase in investment will entail a new point of intersection of the S and I_g schedules only $10 billion to the right of the original equilibrium GDP. The multiplier is only 2.

But if the MPS is relatively small (say, .10), the slope of the saving schedule will be relatively gentle. Therefore, the same $5 billion upward shift in the investment schedule will provide a new intersection point $50 billion to the right of the original equilibrium GDP. The multiplier is 10 in this case. You should verify these two examples by drawing appropriate saving and investment diagrams.

We can summarize by saying *the multiplier is equal to the reciprocal of the MPS*. The reciprocal of any number is the quotient you obtain by dividing 1 by that number:

$$\text{The multiplier} = \frac{1}{\text{MPS}}$$

This formula is a shorthand way to determine the multiplier. All you need to know is the MPS to calculate the size of the multiplier.

Recall, too, from Chapter 9 that since MPC + MPS = 1, it follows that MPS = 1 − MPC. Therefore, we can also write our multiplier formula as

$$\text{The multiplier} = \frac{1}{1 - \text{MPC}}$$

Significance of the Multiplier   The significance of the multiplier is that a small change in the investment plans of businesses or the consumption-saving plans of households can trigger a larger change in the equilibrium level of GDP. The multiplier magnifies the fluctuations in business activity initiated by changes in spending.

As illustrated in Figure 10-3, the larger the MPC (the smaller the MPS), the greater will be the multiplier. If the MPC is .75, the multiplier is 4, a $10 billion decline in planned investment will reduce the equilibrium GDP by $40 billion. But if the MPC is only .67, the multiplier is 3, the same $10 billion drop in investment will reduce the equilibrium GDP by only $30 billion. This makes sense intuitively: A large MPC means the chain of induced consumption shown in Figure 10-2 dampens down slowly and thereby cumulates to a large change in income. Conversely, a small MPC (a large MPS) causes induced consumption to decline quickly so the cumulative change in income is small.

Generalizing the Multiplier   The multiplier we have presented here is called the *simple multiplier* because it is based on a simple model of the economy. In terms of $\frac{1}{\text{MPS}}$, the simple multiplier reflects only

FIGURE 10-3   The MPC and the multiplier
The larger the MPC (the smaller the MPS), the greater is the size of the multiplier.

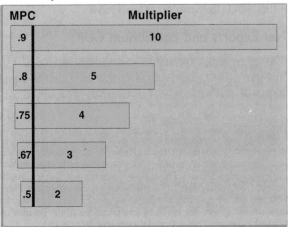

for by adding $5 billion to the $C + I_g$ schedule in Figure 10-4a. Aggregate expenditures at each level of GDP are $5 billion higher than represented by the $C + I_g$ schedule alone. The aggregate expenditures schedule for the open economy thus becomes $C + I_g + X_{n1}$. International trade has increased equilibrium GDP from $470 billion in the private closed economy to $490 billion in the more realistic private open economy.

You should verify that the new equilibrium GDP is $490 billion by adding $5 billion to each level of aggregate expenditures in Table 9-4 and then determining where $C + I_g + X_n$ equals GDP.

Generalization: *Positive net exports increase aggregate expenditures beyond what they would be in a closed economy and thus have an expansionary effect on domestic GDP.* Adding net exports of $5 billion has increased GDP by $20 billion, in this case implying a multiplier of 4.

Negative Net Exports An extension of our reasoning enables us to determine the impact of negative net exports on equilibrium GDP. If net exports are X_{n2} as shown in Figure 10-4b, $5 billion of net export spending by the rest of the world must be subtracted from the aggregate expenditure schedule $C + I_g$ to establish aggregate expenditures for the private open economy. The $5 billion of negative net exports mean that our hypothetical economy is importing $5 billion more of goods than it is selling abroad. The aggregate expenditures schedule shown as $C + I_g$ in Figure 10-4a therefore has overstated the expenditures on *domestic* output at each level of GDP. We must reduce the sum of consumption and investment expenditures by the $5 billion net amount expended on imported goods. If imports are $15 billion and exports are $10 billion, we must subtract the $5 billion of *net* imports (= − $5 billion of net exports) from the combined domestic consumption and investment expenditures.

After we subtract $5 billion from the $C + I_g$ schedule in Figure 10-4a, the relevant aggregate expenditures schedule becomes $C + I_g + X_{n2}$ and equilibrium GDP falls from $470 to $450. Again, a change in net exports of $5 billion has resulted in a fourfold change in GDP, reminding us that the multiplier is 4. Confirmation of the new equilibrium GDP can be obtained by subtracting $5 billion from aggregate expenditures at each level of GDP in Table 9-4 and ascertaining the new equilibrium GDP.

A corollary to our first generalization emerges: *Negative net exports reduce aggregate expenditures relative to what they would be in the closed economy and therefore have a contractionary effect on domestic GDP.* Imports add to the stock of goods available in the economy, but they diminish real GDP by reducing expenditures on domestically produced products.

Our generalizations concerning positive and negative net exports and equilibrium GDP mean that a decline in net exports—a decrease in exports or an increase in imports—decreases aggregate expenditures and contracts domestic GDP. Conversely, an increase in net exports—the result of either an increase in exports or a decrease in imports—increases aggregate expenditures and expands domestic GDP.

Net exports vary greatly among the major industrial nations, as shown in Global Perspective 10-1. *(Key Question 5)*

International Economic Linkages

Our analysis of net exports and real GDP reveals how circumstances or policies abroad can affect our GDP.

Prosperity Abroad A rising level of national income among our trading partners permits us to sell more goods abroad, thus raising our net exports and increasing our real GDP. We should be interested in the prosperity of our trading partners because their good fortune enables them to buy more of our exports and transfer some of their prosperity to us.

Tariffs Suppose our trading partners impose high tariffs on American goods to reduce their imports and stimulate production in their economies. But their imports are our exports. When they restrict their imports to stimulate *their* economies, they are reducing our exports and depressing *our* economy. We may retaliate by imposing trade barriers on their products. If so, their exports will decline and their net exports may be unchanged or even fall. In the Great Depression of the 1930s various nations, including the United States, imposed trade barriers as a way to reduce domestic unemployment. But rounds of retaliation simply throttled world trade, worsened the depression, and increased unemployment.

Exchange Rates Depreciation of the dollar relative to other currencies (Chapter 6) will permit people abroad to obtain more dollars per unit of their currencies. The price of American goods in terms of these currencies will fall, stimulating purchases of our exports. Also, American consumers will find they need more dollars to buy foreign goods and consequently will reduce their sending on imports. Higher American exports and lower imports will result, increasing our net exports and expanding our GDP.

Whether depreciation of the dollar raises real GDP or produces inflation depends on the initial position of the economy relative to its full-employment level of output. If the economy is operating below its production capacity, the depreciation of the dollar and the resulting rise in net exports will increase real GDP. But if the economy is fully employed, the depreciation of the dollar and higher level of net exports will cause domestic inflation.

Finally, while this last example has been cast in terms of a depreciation of the dollar, you should think through the impact that an *appreciation* of the dollar will have on net exports and equilibrium GDP.

QUICK REVIEW 10-1

■ The multiplier is the principle that initial changes in spending can cause magnified changes in national income and GDP.

■ The higher the marginal propensity to consume (the lower the marginal propensity to save), the larger is the simple multiplier.

■ Positive net exports increase aggregate expenditures on domestic output and increase equilibrium GDP; negative net exports decrease aggregate expenditures on domestic output and reduce equilibrium GDP.

ADDING THE PUBLIC SECTOR

Our final step in constructing the aggregate expenditures model is to move the analysis from that of a private (no government) open economy to a mixed economy having a public sector. Unlike private expenditures, government expenditures and taxes are subject to direct public control. Government can manipulate them to counter private underspending or overspending, thereby promote economic stability.

Simplifying Assumptions

For clarity, the following simplifying assumptions are made.

GLOBAL PERSPECTIVE 10-1

Merchandise net exports, selected nations

Some nations, such as Japan and Germany, have positive net exports; other countries, such as the United States and the United Kingdom, have negative net exports.

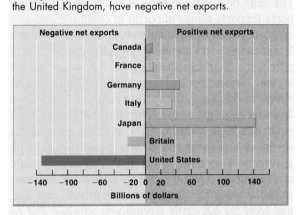

Source: *Organization for Economic Cooperation and Development. Data are for 1993.*

1 We continue to use the simplified investment and net export schedules, where levels of investment and net exports are independent of the level of GDP.
2 We suppose government purchases neither depress nor stimulate private spending. They do not cause any upward or downward shifts in consumption and investment schedules.
3 We assume government's net tax revenues—total tax revenues less "negative taxes" in the form of transfer payments—are derived entirely from personal taxes. Although DI will fall short of PI by the amount of government's tax revenues, GDP, NI, and PI will remain equal.
4 We assume that a fixed amount of taxes is collected regardless of the level of GDP.
5 We continue to suppose that, unless otherwise indicated, the price level is constant.

These assumptions will give us a simple and uncluttered view of how government spending and taxes fit within the aggregate expenditures model. Most of these assumptions will be dropped in Chapter 12 when we discuss how government uses changes in its expenditures and taxes to alter equilibrium GDP and the rate of inflation.

TABLE 10-4 Determination of the equilibrium levels of employment, output, and income: private and public sectors

(1) Real domestic output and income (GDP = NI = PI), billions	(2) Taxes, T, billions	(3) Disposable income, DI, billions, or (1) − (2)	(4) Con-sump-tion, C_a, billions	(5) Saving, S_a, billions, or (3) − (4)	(6) Invest-ment, I_g, billions	(7) Net exports, X_n, billions Exports, X	Imports, M	(8) Govern-ment purchases, G, billions	(9) Aggregate expenditures $(C_a + I_g + X_n + G)$, billions, or (4) + (6) + (7) + (8)
(1) $370	$20	$350	$360	$−10	$20	$10	$10	$20	$400
(2) 390	20	370	375	−5	20	10	10	20	415
(3) 410	20	390	390	0	20	10	10	20	430
(4) 430	20	410	405	5	20	10	10	20	445
(5) 450	20	430	420	10	20	10	10	20	460
(6) 470	20	450	435	15	20	10	10	20	475
(7) 490	20	470	450	20	20	10	10	20	490
(8) 510	20	490	465	25	20	10	10	20	505
(9) 530	20	510	480	30	20	10	10	20	520
(10) 550	20	530	495	35	20	10	10	20	535

Tabular Example In Table 10-4 we find taxes in column 2 and we see in column 3 that disposable (after-tax) income is reduced by $20 billion—the amount of the taxes—at each level of GDP. Because DI consists of consumer spending and saving, a decline in DI will lower both consumption and saving. But by how much will each decline as a result of taxes? The MPC and MPS hold the answer: The MPC tells us what fraction of a decline in DI will be at the expense of consumption, and the MPS indicates what fraction of a drop in DI will be at the expense of saving. Since the MPC equals .75 (= 15/20) and the MPS equals .25 (= 5/20), if government collects $20 billion in taxes at each possible level of GDP, the amount of consumption at each level of GDP will drop by $15 billion (.75 × $20 billion), and the amount of saving at each level of GDP will fall by $5 billion (.25 × $20 billion).

In columns 4 and 5 of Table 10-4 the amounts of consumption and saving *at each level of GDP* are $15 and $5 billion smaller, respectively, than in Table 10-3. For example, before taxes, where GDP equaled DI, consumption was $420 billion and saving $10 billion at the $430 billion level of GDP (row 4 of Table 10-3). After taxes are imposed, DI is $410 billion, $20 billion short of the $430 billion GDP, with the result that consumption is only $405 billion and saving is $5 billion (columns 4 and 5 of Table 10-4).

Taxes cause DI to fall short of GDP by the amount of the taxes. This decline in DI reduces both consumption and saving at each level of GDP. The sizes of the declines in C and S are determined by MPC and MPS.

What is the effect of taxes on equilibrium GDP? We calculate aggregate expenditures again as shown in column 9 of Table 10-4. Note that aggregate spending is $15 billion less at each level of real output than it was in Table 10-3. The reason is that after-tax consumption, designated by C_a, is $15 billion less at each level of GDP. Comparing real output and aggregate expenditures in columns 1 and 9, we see the aggregate amounts produced and purchased are equal only at $490 billion of GDP (row 7). The $20 billion lump-sum tax has caused equilibrium GDP to fall by $60 billion from $550 billion (row 10 in Table 10-3) to $490 billion (row 7 in Table 10-4).

Our alternative leakages-injections approach confirms this result. Taxes, like saving and imports, are a leakage from the domestic income-expenditures stream. Saving, importing, and paying taxes are all uses of income which do not involve domestic consumption. Consumption will now fall short of domestic output—creating a potential spending gap—in the amount of after-tax saving and imports *plus* taxes. This gap may be filled by planned investment, exports, and government purchases. Thus, our new equilibrium condition for the leakages-injections approach is: After-tax saving, S_a, plus imports plus taxes equals planned investment plus exports plus government purchases. Symbolically, $S_a + M + T = I_g + X + G$. You should verify in Table 10-4 that this equality of leakages and injections is fulfilled *only* at the $490 billion GDP (row 7).

Graphical Analysis In Figure 10-6a the $20 billion *increase* in taxes shows up as a $15 (*not* $20) billion *decline* in the aggregate expenditures $(C_a + I_g + X_n + G)$ schedule. Under our continuing assumption

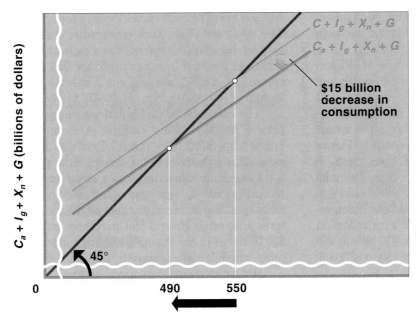

(a) Aggregate expenditures-domestic output approach

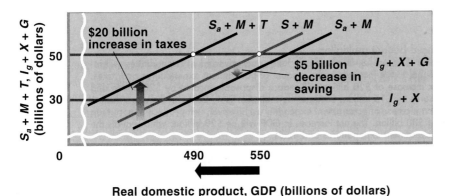

(b) Leakages-injections approach

FIGURE 10-6 Taxes and the equilibrium GDP

(a) *The aggregate expenditures–domestic output approach.* If the MPC is .75, the imposition of $20 billion of taxes will lower the consumption schedule by $15 billion and cause a decline in the equilibrium GDP. (b) *The leakages-injections approach.* Here taxes have a twofold effect. First, with an MPS of .25, the imposition of taxes of $20 billion will reduce disposable income by $20 billion and saving by $5 billion at each level of GDP. This is shown by the shift from S (saving before taxes) + M to S_a (saving after taxes) + M. Second, the $20 billion of taxes is an additional $20 billion leakage at each GDP level, giving us S_a + M + T. By adding government, the equilibrium condition changes from $S + M = I_g + X$ to $S_a + M + T = I_g + X + G$.

that all taxes are personal income taxes, this decline in aggregate expenditures solely results from a decline in the consumption component of the aggregate expenditures schedule. The equilibrium GDP shifts from $550 billion to $490 billion because of this tax-caused drop in consumption. *Increases in taxes will lower the aggregate expenditures schedule relative to the 45-degree line and reduce the equilibrium GDP.*

Consider now the leakages-injections approach: The analysis here is slightly more complex because the $20 billion in taxes has a twofold effect in Figure 10-6b.

1 The taxes reduce DI by $20 billion and, with the MPS at .25, cause saving to fall by $5 billion at each level of GDP. In Figure 10-6b this is shown as a shift from $S + M$ (saving before taxes plus imports) to $S_a + M$ (saving after taxes plus imports).

2 The $20 billion in taxes is a $20 billion leakage at each GDP level which must be added to $S_a + M$ (not $S + M$), giving us $S_a + M + T$.

Equilibrium now exists at the $490 billion GDP, where the total amount which households save plus imports plus the amount of taxes government intends to collect are equal to the total amount businesses plan picted in Figure 10-8a is failing to employ 5 million of its 75 million full-employment labor force and, as a result, is sacrificing $20 billion of output.

The amount by which aggregate expenditures fall short of those required to achieve the full-employment level of GDP is called the **recessionary gap,** since this deficiency of spending has a contractionary or depressing impact on the economy. In Table 10-4, assuming the full-employment GDP is $510 billion (column 1), the corresponding level of total expenditures is only $505 billion (column 9). The recessionary gap is $5 billion, the amount by which the aggregate expenditures schedule would have to shift upward to realize the full-employment GDP. Graphically, the recessionary gap is the *vertical* distance by which the aggregate expenditures schedule $(C_a + I_g + X_n + G)_1$ lies below the full-employment point on the 45-degree line. Because the multiplier is 4, we observe a $20 billion differential (the recessionary gap, $5 billion, *times* the multiplier of 4) between the equilibrium GDP and the full-employment GDP. This $20 billion gap is the GDP gap which we encountered in Figure 8-5.

Inflationary Gap

If aggregate expenditures are at $(C_a + I_g + X_n + G)_2$ in Figure 10-8b, a demand-pull inflationary gap will exist. The amount by which aggregate spending exceeds that necessary to achieve the full-employment level of GDP is called an **inflationary gap.** In this case, there is a $5 billion inflationary gap, shown by the *vertical* distance between $(C_a + I_g + X_n + G)_2$ and the full-employment point on the 45-degree line. The inflationary gap is the amount by which the aggregate expenditures schedule would have to shift downward to realize the full-employment noninflationary GDP.

The effect of this inflationary gap—this excess demand—will be to pull up the prices of the economy's output. In this model, businesses as a whole cannot respond to the $5 billion in excess demand by expanding their real outputs, so pure *demand-pull inflation* will occur. Nominal GDP will rise, but real GDP will not. *(Key Question 10)*

HISTORICAL APPLICATIONS

Let's see how these concepts of recessionary and inflationary gaps apply to two economic events.

Great Depression

In October 1929 the stock market collapsed. At the same time the most severe and prolonged depression of modern times began. In the United States real GDP (1987 dollars) plummeted from $822 billion in 1929 to a low of $587 billion in 1933. The unemployment rate rose from 3.2 percent in 1929 to 24.9 percent in the same period. As late as 1939, real GDP was only slightly above its level of ten years earlier and the unemployment rate still was 17.2 percent! (As shown in Global Perspective 10-2, the Great Depression was worldwide.)

A sagging level of investment spending was the major weight that pulled American capitalism into the economic chaos of the 1930s. In real terms, gross investment spending shrunk from $153 billion in 1929 to $27 billion in 1933—an 82 percent decline. In Figure 10-8, we would depict this decline in investment as a large downward shift in the nation's aggregate expenditure schedule. The outcome in the 1930s was a severe recessionary (depressionary) gap and an historic decline in real GDP.

What factors caused this steep decline in investment?

1 Overcapacity and Business Indebtedness Flush with the prosperity of the 1920s, businesses overexpanded their production capacity. In particular, the tremendous expansion of the automobile industry—and the related petroleum, rubber, steel, glass, and textile industries—ended as the market for new autos became saturated. Business indebtedness also increased rapidly during the 1920s. Furthermore, by the late 1920s much of the income of businesses was committed for the payment of interest and principal on past purchases, and thus was not available for current expenditures on new capital.

2 Decline in Residential Construction The 1920s experienced a boom in residential construction in response to population growth and housing demand deferred because of World War I. This investment spending began to level off as early as 1926, and by the late 1920s the construction industry had virtually collapsed.

3 Stock Market Crash The most striking aspect of the Great Depression was the stock market crash of October 1929. The optimism of the prosperous

1920s had elevated stock market speculation to something of a national pastime. This speculation had bid up stock prices to the point where they did not reflect financial reality—stock prices were far beyond the profit-making potentials of the firms they represented. A downward adjustment was necessary and it came suddenly and quickly in 1929.

The stock market crash had significant secondary effects. Most important were the psychological repercussions. The buoyant optimism of the 1920s gave way to a wave of crippling pessimism, and the crashing of stock prices created highly unfavorable conditions for acquiring additional money for investment.

4 Shrinking Money Supply The nation's money supply plummeted in the early years of the Great Depression, from $27 billion in 1929 down to $20 billion by 1933 (Last Word, Chapter 14). This shrinkage resulted from forces operating both abroad and at home, including inappropriate policies of the Federal Reserve Banks (Chapters 14–16). It was this drastic reduction of the money supply that contributed to the sharp decline in the volume of aggregate expenditures which characterized the early 1930s.

Vietnam War Inflation

The 1960s was a period of prolonged economic expansion, fueled by increases in consumption spending and investment. Perhaps the major factor in this long expansion was the revolution in economic policy which occurred under the Kennedy–Johnson administrations. This policy called for government to manipulate its tax collections and expenditures in such a way to increase aggregate demand, increasing employment and real GDP. For example, in 1962 legislation was enacted which provided for a 7 percent tax credit on investment in new machinery and equipment, thus strengthening the incentives of businesses to invest. In 1964 the government cut personal and corporate income taxes, boosting consumption spending and further increasing investment spending. The unemployment rate fell from 5.2 percent in 1964 to 4.5 percent in 1965.

At this time another expansionary force came into play. The escalation of the war in Vietnam resulted in a 40 percent increase in government spending on national defense between 1965 and 1967. Another 15 percent increase in war-related spending occurred in

GLOBAL PERSPECTIVE 10-2

Changes in industrial production, selected countries, 1929–1930 and 1937–1938

The Great Depression of the 1930s was global, with large declines in industrial output occurring in most countries. The Depression began in 1929–1930 for many countries. Precipitous declines in industrial output again occurred in some nations in 1937–1938.

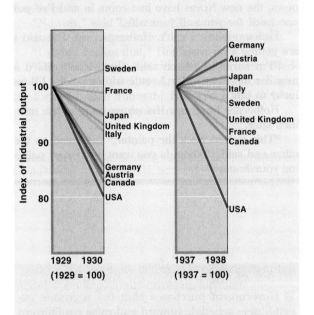

Source: *League of Nations, World Economic Survey, 1938–1939,* p. 107.

1968. Simultaneously, the draft claimed more and more young people from the ranks of the unemployed.

Remarkably, the unemployment rate fell below 4 percent during the entire 1966–1969 period. But the increased government expenditures, imposed on an already booming economy, also brought about the worse inflation in two decades. Inflation jumped from 1.6 percent in 1965 to 5.7 percent by 1970. In terms of Figure 10-8, the booming investment expenditures and the added government expenditures shifted the aggregate expenditures schedule sharply upward, creating a sizable inflationary gap.

CHAPTER SUMMARY

1 Shifts in the saving-consumption schedules or in the investment schedule will change the equilibrium output–income level by several times the amount of the initial change in spending. This multiplier effect accompanies both increases and decreases in aggregate expenditures.

2 The multiplier is equal to the reciprocal of the marginal propensity to save: The higher the marginal propensity to save, the smaller the size of the multiplier; the higher the marginal propensity to consume, the greater the multiplier.

3 The net export schedule relates net exports (exports minus imports) to levels of real GDP. We have assumed in our model that the level of net exports is the same at all levels of real GDP.

4 Positive net exports increase aggregate expenditures above their level in a private closed economy, raising American real GDP by a multiple amount; negative net exports decrease aggregate expenditures below their level in a private closed economy, decreasing American real GDP by a multiple amount. Increases in exports or decreases in imports have an expansionary effect on real GDP, while decreases in exports or increases in imports have a contractionary effect.

5 Government purchases shift the aggregate expenditures schedule upward and raise equilibrium GDP.

6 Taxation reduces disposable income, lowers both consumption spending and saving, shifts the aggregate expenditures schedule downward, and reduces equilibrium GDP.

7 The balanced-budget multiplier is 1, meaning that equal increases in government spending and taxation will increase the equilibrium real GDP by the amount of the increases in government expenditures and taxes.

8 The equilibrium level of real GDP and the full-employment GDP need not coincide. The amount by which aggregate expenditures fall short of the aggregate expenditures consistent with the full-employment GDP is called the recessionary gap; this gap prompts a multiple decline in real GDP. The amount by which aggregate expenditures exceed the aggregate expenditures consistent with the full-employment GDP is the inflationary gap; it causes demand-pull inflation.

9 The Great Depression of the 1930s resulted from a precipitous decline in aggregate expenditures which produced a severe and long-lasting recessionary (depressionary) gap. The Vietnam war period provides a good example of an inflationary gap. An abrupt increase in aggregate demand caused by war spending led to a sizable inflationary gap, with its accompanying demand-pull inflation.

10 The aggregate expenditures model provides many insights about the macroeconomy, but does not **a** show price level changes, **b** account for premature demand-pull inflation, **c** allow for real GDP to temporarily expand beyond the full-employment level of output, or **d** account for cost-push inflation.

TERMS AND CONCEPTS

multiplier effect	balanced-budget	recessionary gap
net exports	multiplier	inflationary gap
lump-sum tax		

QUESTIONS AND STUDY SUGGESTIONS

1 What effect will each of the changes designated in question 4 at the end of Chapter 9 have on the equilibrium level of GDP? Explain your answers.

📖 2 *Key Question   What is the multiplier effect? What relationship does the MPC bear to the size of the multiplier? The MPS? What will the multiplier be when the MPS is 0, .4, .6, and 1? When the MPC is 1, .90, .67, .50, and 0? How much of a change in GDP will result if businesses increase their level of investment by $8 billion and the MPC in the economy is .80? If the MPC is .67? Explain the difference between the simple and the complex multiplier.*

3 Graphically depict the aggregate expenditures model for a private closed economy. Next, show a decrease in the aggregate expenditures schedule and explain why the decrease in real GDP in your diagram is greater than the initial decline in aggregate expenditures. What would be the ratio of a decline in real GDP to the initial drop in aggregate expenditures if the slope of your aggregate expenditures schedule were .8?

4 Speculate on why a planned increase in saving by households, unaccompanied by an increase in investment spending by businesses, might result in a decline in real GDP and *no* increase in actual saving. Demonstrate this point graphically, using the leakages-injections approach to equilibrium real GDP. Now assume in your diagram that investment instead increases to match the initial increase in desired saving. Using your knowledge from Chapter 2, explain why these joint increases in saving and investment might be desirable for a society.

AGGREGATE EXPENDITURES: THE MULTIPLIER, NET EXPORTS, AND GOVERNMENT

5 Key Question *The data in columns 1 and 2 of the table below are for a private closed economy.*

(1) Real domestic output (GDP = DI), billions	(2) Aggregate expenditures, private closed economy, billions	(3) Exports, billions	(4) Imports, billions	(5) Net exports, billions	(6) Aggregate expenditures, private open economy, billions
$200	$240	$20	$30	$_____	$_____
250	280	20	30	_____	_____
300	320	20	30	_____	_____
350	360	20	30	_____	_____
400	400	20	30	_____	_____
450	440	20	30	_____	_____
500	480	20	30	_____	_____
550	520	20	30	_____	_____

a *Use columns 1 and 2 to determine the equilibrium GDP for this hypothetical economy.*

b *Now open this economy for international trade by including the export and import figures of columns 3 and 4. Calculate net exports and determine the equilibrium GDP for the open economy. Explain why equilibrium GDP differs from the closed economy.*

c *Given the original $20 billion level of exports, what would be the equilibrium GDP if imports were $10 billion larger at each level of GDP? Or $10 billion smaller at each level of GDP? What generalization concerning the level of imports and the equilibrium GDP is illustrated by these examples?*

d *What is the size of the multiplier in these examples?*

6 Assume that, without taxes, the consumption schedule of an economy is as shown below:

GDP, billions	Consumption, billions
$100	$120
200	200
300	280
400	360
500	440
600	520
700	600

a Graph this consumption schedule and note the size of the MPC.

b Assume now a lump-sum tax system is imposed such that the government collects $10 billion in taxes at all levels of GDP. Graph the resulting consumption schedule and compare the MPC and the multiplier with that of the pretax consumption schedule.

7 Explain graphically the determination of equilibrium GDP through both the aggregate expenditures–domestic output approach and the leakages-injections approach for the private sector. Now add government spending and taxation, showing the impact of each on the equilibrium GDP.

8 Key Question *Refer to columns 1 and 6 of the tabular data for question 5. Incorporate government into the table by assuming that it plans to tax and spend $20 billion at each possible level of GDP. Also assume that all taxes are personal taxes and that government spending does not induce a shift in the private aggregate expenditures schedule. Explain the changes in the equilibrium GDP which the addition of government entails.*

9 What is the balanced-budget multiplier? Demonstrate the balanced-budget multiplier in terms of your answer to question 8. Explain: "Equal increases in government spending and tax revenues of *n* dollars will increase the equilibrium GDP by *n* dollars." Does this hold true regardless of the size of the MPS?

10 Key Question *Refer to the accompanying table in answering the questions which follow.*

(1) Possible levels of employment, millions	(2) Real domestic output, billions	(3) Aggregate expenditures, $C_a + I_g + X_n + G$, billions
90	$500	$520
100	550	560
110	600	600
120	650	640
130	700	680

a *If full employment in this economy is 130 million, will there be an inflationary or a recessionary gap? What will be the consequence of this gap? By how much would aggregate expenditures in column 3 have to change at each level of GDP to eliminate the inflationary or recessionary gap? Explain.*

b *Will there be an inflationary or recessionary gap if the full-employment level of output is $500 billion? Explain the consequences. By how much would aggregate expenditures in column 3 have to change at each level of GDP to eliminate the inflationary or recessionary gap? Explain.*

NATIONAL INCOME, EMPLOYMENT, AND FISCAL POLICY

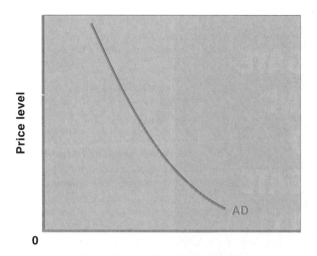

FIGURE 11-1 **The aggregate demand curve**
The downsloping aggregate demand curve indicates an inverse relationship between the price level and the amount of real domestic output purchased.

Why? The rationale is *not* the same as it is for the demand for a single product. That explanation centered on income and substitution effects. When the price of an individual product falls, the consumer's (constant) nominal income will enable him or her to purchase more of the product (the income effect). And, as price falls, the consumer wants to buy more of the product because it becomes relatively less expensive than other goods (the substitution effect).

But these explanations do not work for aggregates. In Figure 11-1 prices in general are falling as we move down the aggregate demand curve so the rationale for the substitution effect (a product becoming cheaper relative to all other products) is not applicable. Similarly, while an individual's demand curve for a specific product assumes the consumer's nominal income is fixed, the aggregate demand curve implies differing levels of aggregate incomes. As we move up the aggregate demand curve we move to higher price levels. But, recalling our circular flow model, higher prices paid for goods and services will flow to resources suppliers as expanded wage, rent, interest, and profit incomes. As a result, an increase in the price level does *not* necessarily mean a decline in the nominal income of the economy as a whole.

If substitution and income effects do not explain the downsloping aggregate demand curve, what does? The rationale rests on the following three factors.

1 Wealth Effect The first reason why the aggregate demand curve is downsloping involves the **wealth** or **real balances effect.** A higher price level reduces the real value or purchasing power of the public's accumulated financial assets. In particular, the real value of assets with fixed money values such as savings accounts or bonds diminish. Because of the erosion of purchasing power of such assets, the public is poorer in real terms and will retrench on its spending. A household might buy a new car or a sailboat if the purchasing power of its financial asset balances is, say, $50,000. But if inflation erodes the purchasing power of these asset balances to $30,000, the family may defer its purchase.

Conversely, a decline in the price level will increase the real value or purchasing power of a person's wealth and increase spending.

2 Interest-Rate Effect The **interest-rate effect** suggests that the rationale for the downsloping aggregate demand curve lies in the impact of the changing price level on interest rates and in turn on consumption and investment spending. As the price level rises so do interest rates, and rising interest rates reduce certain kinds of consumption and investment spending.

Elaboration: *The aggregate demand curve assumes the supply of money in the economy is fixed.* When the price level increases, consumers need more money for purchases and businesses similarly require more money to meet their payrolls and to buy other needed inputs. In short, a higher price level increases the demand for money.

With a fixed supply of money, this increase in demand for money drives up the price paid for its use. That price is the interest rate. Higher interest rates curtail interest-sensitive expenditures by businesses and households. A firm expecting a 10 percent return on a potential purchase of capital will find that purchase profitable when the interest rate is, say, only 7 percent. But the purchase is unprofitable and will not be made when the interest rate has risen to, say, 12 percent. Similarly, some consumers will decide *not* to purchase houses or automobiles because of the rise in the interest rate.

Conclusion: A higher price level—by increasing the demand for money and the interest rate—reduces the amount of real output demanded.

3 Foreign Purchases Effect We found in Chapter 7's discussion of national income accounting that im-

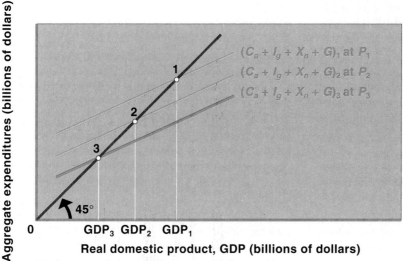

(a) Aggregate expenditures model

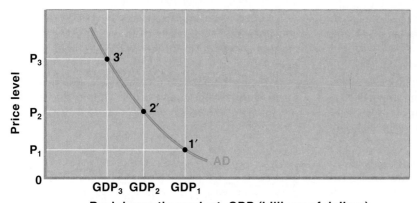

(b) Aggregate demand–aggregate supply model

FIGURE 11-2 Deriving the aggregate demand curve from the expenditures-output model

Through the wealth, interest-rate, and foreign purchases effects, the consumption, investment, and net exports schedules and therefore the aggregate expenditures schedule will rise when the price level declines and fall when the price level increases. If the aggregate expenditure schedule is at $(C_a + I_g + X_n + G)_2$ when the price level is P_2, we can combine that price level and the equilibrium output, GDP_2, to determine one point ($2'$) on the aggregate demand curve. A lower price level such as P_1 increases aggregate expenditures to $(C_a + I_g + X_n + G)_1$, providing point I' on the aggregate demand curve. Similarly, a higher price level at P_3 shifts aggregate expenditures down to $(C_a + I_g + X_n + G)_3$ so P_3 and GDP_3 yield another point on the aggregate demand curve at $3'$.

ports and exports are components of total spending. The volumes of our imports and exports depend on, among other things, relative price levels here and abroad. If the price level rises in the United States relative to foreign countries, American buyers will purchase more imports and fewer American goods. Similarly, the rest of the world will buy fewer American goods, reducing American exports. In brief, a rise in our price level will increase our imports and reduce our exports, reducing the amount of net export (export minus import) spending on American-produced products.

Conclusion: The **foreign purchases effect** of a price-level increase results in a decline in the aggregate amount of American output demanded. Conversely, a relative decline in our price level reduces our imports and increases our exports, increasing the

net exports component of American aggregate demand.

Deriving the Aggregate Demand Curve from the Aggregate Expenditures Model[1]

We can directly derive the downsloping aggregate demand curve shown in Figure 11-1 from the aggregate expenditures model developed in Chapters 9 and 10. The aggregate demand curve in Figure 11-1 merely relates the various possible price levels to corresponding GDPs. Note in Figure 11-2 that we can stack the aggregate expenditures model of Figure 11-2a and

---

[1]This section presumes knowledge of the aggregate expenditures model discussed in Chapters 9 and 10 and can be skipped by readers who are not assigned those chapters.

the aggregate demand curve of Figure 11-2b vertically because real output is measured on the horizontal axis of both models. Now we can start at the top with the aggregate expenditures schedule $(C_a + I_g + X_n + G)_2$. The price level relevant to this schedule is P_2, as shown in the graph to remind us of that fact. From this information we can plot the equilibrium real output, GDP$_2$, and the corresponding price level P_2. This gives us one point—namely 2′—on Figure 11-2b's aggregate demand curve.

Let's now assume the price level is P_1. Other things equal, this lower price level will: (1) increase the value of wealth, boosting consumption expenditures; (2) reduce the interest rate, promoting investment expenditures; and (3) reduce imports and increase exports, increasing net export expenditures. The aggregate expenditures schedule will rise from $(C_a + I_g + X_n + G)_2$ to, say, $(C_a + I_g + X_n + G)_1$, giving us equilibrium at GDP$_1$. In Figure 11-2b we locate this new price level–real output combination, P_1 and GDP$_1$, at point 1′.

Now suppose the price level increases from the original P_2 level to P_3. The real value of wealth falls, the interest rate rises, exports fall, and imports rise. Consequently, the consumption, investment, and net export schedules fall, shifting the aggregate expenditures schedule downward from $(C_a + I_g + X_n + G)_2$ to $(C_a + I_g + X_n + G)_3$ where real output is GDP$_3$. This lets us locate a third point on Figure 11-2b's aggregate demand curve, namely point 3′ where the price level is P_3 and real output is GDP$_3$.

In summary, a decrease in the price level shifts the aggregate expenditures schedule upward and increases real GDP. An increase in the price level shifts the aggregate expenditures schedule downward, reducing real GDP. The resulting price level–real GDP combinations yield various points such as 1′, 2′, and 3′, which locate a specific downsloping aggregate demand curve.

Determinants of Aggregate Demand

Thus far we have found that changes in the price level change the level of spending by domestic consumers, businesses, government, and foreign buyers such that we can predict changes in the amount of real GDP. That is, an increase in the price level, *other things equal,* will decrease the quantity of real GDP demanded; a decrease in the price level will increase the amount of real GDP desired. This relationship is represented graphically as movements along a stable ag-

gregate demand curve. However, if one or more of those "other things" change, the entire aggregate demand curve shifts. We refer to those "other things" as **determinants of aggregate demand;** they "determine" the location of the aggregate demand curve.

To understand what causes changes in real output, you must distinguish between *changes in the quantity of real output demanded* caused by changes in the price level and *changes in aggregate demand* caused by changes in one or more of the determinants of aggregate demand. We made a similar distinction when discussing single-product demand curves in Chapter 3.

As shown in Figure 11-3, an increase in aggregate demand is depicted by the rightward movement of the curve from AD$_1$ to AD$_2$. This shift indicates that, at each price level, the desired amount of real goods and services is larger than before.

A decrease in aggregate demand is shown as the leftward shift of the curve from AD$_1$ to AD$_3$, indicating that people desire to buy less real output at each price level.

To reemphasize: The changes in aggregate demand shown in the graph occur when changes happen in one or more of the factors previously assumed

FIGURE 11-3   Changes in aggregate demand
A change in one or more of the determinants of aggregate demand listed in Table 11-1 will change aggregate demand. An increase in aggregate demand is shown as the rightward shift of the AD curve from AD$_1$ to AD$_2$; a decrease in aggregate demand, as a leftward shift from AD$_1$ to AD$_3$.

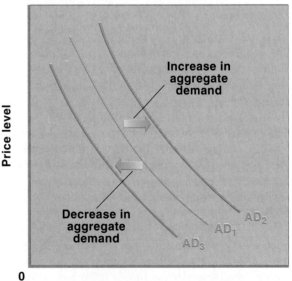

Real domestic output, GDP

TABLE 11-1 Determinants of aggregate demand: factors that shift the aggregate demand curve

1 **Change in consumer spending**
   a **Consumer wealth**
   b **Consumer expectations**
   c **Consumer indebtedness**
   d **Taxes**
2 **Change in investment spending**
   a **Interest rates**
   b **Profit expectations on investment projects**
   c **Business taxes**
   d **Technology**
   e **Degree of excess capacity**
3 **Change in government spending**
4 **Change in net export spending**
   a **National income abroad**
   b **Exchange rates**

to be constant. These determinants of aggregate demand, or *aggregate demand shifters,* are listed in Table 11-1. Let's examine each element of the table.

Consumer Spending   Independently of changes in the price level, domestic consumers collectively may alter their purchases of American-produced real output. When this happens the entire aggregate demand curve shifts. It shifts leftward as from AD_1 to AD_3 in Figure 11-3 when consumers buy less output than before at each possible price level; it moves rightward as from AD_1 to AD_2 when they buy more at each possible price level.

Changes in one or more of several non-price-level factors may change consumer spending, shifting the aggregate demand curve. As indicated in Table 11-1, these factors are real consumer wealth, consumer expectations, consumer indebtedness, and taxes.

Consumer Wealth   Consumer wealth comprises all consumer assets, including financial assets such as stocks and bonds and physical assets such as houses and land. A sharp decline in the real value of consumer assets encourages people to save more (buy fewer products) to restore their wealth. The resulting decline in consumer spending will decrease aggregate demand—shift the aggregate demand curve leftward. An increase in the real value of consumer wealth will increase consumption spending at each price level; the aggregate demand curve will shift rightward.

Warning: We are *not* referring here to the previously discussed "wealth effect" or "real balances effect." It assumes a fixed aggregate demand curve and

results from a change in the price level. In contrast, the change in real wealth addressed here is independent of a change in the price level; it is a *non-price-level factor* which shifts the entire aggregate demand curve. An example would be a rocketing boost in stock prices which increases consumer wealth, even though the price level has not changed. Similarly, a sharp decline in the real value of houses and land reduces consumer wealth, independent of changes in the general price level.

Consumer Expectations   Changes in expectations about the future may alter consumer spending. When people expect their future real income to rise, they spend more of their current income. Present consumption spending increases (present saving falls), and the aggregate demand curve shifts rightward. An expectation that real income will decline in the future reduces present consumption spending and therefore reduces aggregate demand.

Similarly, a widely held expectation of surging future inflation increases aggregate demand today, because consumers buy products before prices escalate. Just the opposite, expectations of lower price levels in the near future may reduce present consumption since people may postpone some of their present consumption to take advantage of the future lower prices.

Consumer Indebtedness   Consumers with high levels of indebtedness from past buying financed by installment loans may be forced to cut present spending to pay off their existing debt. The result is a decline in consumption spending and a leftward shift of the aggregate demand curve. When consumers' indebtedness is low, their present consumption spending increases. This produces an increase in aggregate demand.

Taxes   A reduction in personal income tax rates raises take-home income and increases consumer purchases at each possible price level. Tax cuts shift the aggregate demand curve rightward. Tax increases reduce consumption spending and shift the aggregate demand curve to the left.

Investment Spending   Investment spending—the purchase of capital goods—is a second determinant of aggregate demand. A decline in the amount of new capital goods desired by businesses at each price level will shift the aggregate demand curve leftward. An increase in the desired amount of investment goods will increase aggregate demand. Let's consider the factors which can alter the level of investment spending as listed in Table 11-1.

Interest Rates All else equal, an increase in the interest rate caused by a factor other than a change in the price level will lower investment spending and reduce aggregate demand. We are *not* referring here to the so-called "interest-rate effect" due to a change in the price level. Instead, we are identifying a change in the interest rate resulting from, say, a change in the nation's money supply. An increase in the money supply reduces the interest rate, increasing investment. A decrease in the supply of money increases the interest rate and reduces investment.

Profit Expectations on Investment Projects Improved profit expectations on investment projects will increase the demand for capital goods and shift the aggregate demand curve rightward. For example, an anticipated rise in spending by consumers may improve the profit expectations of possible investment projects. Alternatively, if the profit outlook on possible investment projects dims because of an expected decline in consumer spending, investment spending will decline. Consequently, aggregate demand will also decline.

Business Taxes An increase in business taxes reduces after-tax profits from corporate investment and reduces investment spending and aggregate demand. Conversely, tax reductions increase after-tax profits from corporate investment, boost investment spending, and push the aggregate demand curve rightward.

Technology New and improved technologies stimulate investment spending and increase aggregate demand. Example: Recent advances in microbiology and electronics have spawned new labs and production facilities to exploit the new technologies.

Degree of Excess Capacity A rise in excess capacity—unused existing capital—will retard the demand for new capital goods and reduce aggregate demand. Firms operating factories at well below capacity have little incentive to build new factories. But when firms collectively discover their excess capacity is dwindling, they build new factories and buy more equipment. Thus, investment spending rises and the aggregate demand curve shifts to the right.

Government Spending Government's desire to buy goods and services is a third determinant of aggregate demand. An increase in government purchases of real output at each price level will increase aggregate demand so long as tax collections and interest rates do not change as a result. An example would be a decision by government to expand the interstate highway system. A reduction in government spending, such as a cutback in orders for military hardware, will reduce aggregate demand.

Net Export Spending The final determinant of aggregate demand is net export spending. When foreign consumers change their purchases of U.S. goods independently of changes in our price level, the American aggregate demand curve shifts. We again specify "independent of changes in our price level" to distinguish clearly from changes in spending arising from the foreign purchases effect. That effect helps explain why a change in the American price level moves the economy *along* its existing AD curve.

In discussing aggregate demand shifters we instead address changes in net exports caused by factors other than changes in the price level. Increases in net exports (exports minus imports) caused by these other factors push our aggregate demand curve rightward. The logic is as follows. First, a higher level of American exports constitutes an increased *foreign demand* for American goods. Second, a reduction of our imports implies an increased *domestic demand* for American-produced products.

The non-price-level factors which alter net exports are primarily national income abroad and exchange rates.

National Income Abroad Rising national income in a foreign nation increases the foreign demand for United States goods, increasing aggregate demand in America. As income levels rise in a foreign nation, its citizens can afford to buy both more products made at home *and* made in the United States. Our exports therefore rise in step with increases in the national income levels of our trading partners. Declines in national income abroad have the opposite effect: Our net exports decline, shifting the aggregate demand curve leftward.

Exchange Rates A change in the exchange rate (Chapter 6) between the dollar and other currencies also affects net exports and hence aggregate demand. Suppose the dollar price of yen rises, meaning the *dol-*

lar depreciates in terms of the yen. This is the same as saying the yen price of dollars falls—the *yen appreciates.* The new relative values of dollars and yen means consumers in Japan can obtain *more* dollars with any particular number of yen and that consumers in the United States will obtain *fewer* yen for each dollar. Japanese consumers will therefore discover that American goods are cheaper in terms of yen. American consumers will find that fewer Japanese products can be purchased with a set number of dollars.

With respect to our *exports,* a $30 pair of American-made blue jeans now might be bought for 2880 yen compared to 3600 yen. And in terms of our *imports,* a Japanese watch might now cost $225 rather than $180. In these circumstances our exports will rise and imports will fall. This increase in net exports translates into an increase in American aggregate demand.

You are urged to think through the opposite scenario in which the dollar appreciates (yen depreciates).

Aggregate Demand Shifts and the Aggregate Expenditures Model[2]

The determinants of aggregate demand in Table 11-1 are the components of Chapter 10's aggregate expenditures model. When one of these determinants changes, so does the location of the aggregate expenditures schedule. We can easily link shifts in the

---

[2]This section presumes knowledge of the aggregate expenditures model (Chapters 9 and 10). It may be skipped by instructors who wish to rely exclusively on the aggregate demand–aggregate supply framework.

aggregate expenditures schedule to shifts in the aggregate demand curve.

Let's suppose that the price level is constant. In Figure 11-4 we begin with the aggregate expenditures schedule at $(C_a + I_g + X_n + G)_1$ in the top diagram, yielding real output of GDP_1. Assume now that more optimistic business expectations increase investment so the aggregate expenditures schedule rises from $(C_a + I_g + X_n + G)_1$ to $(C_a + I_g + X_n + G)_2$. (The P_1 labels remind us that the price level is assumed to be constant.) The result will be a multiplied increase in real output from GDP_1 to GDP_2.

FIGURE 11-4   Shifts in the aggregate expenditures schedule and in the aggregate demand curve
In (a) we assume that some determinant of consumption, investment, or net exports other than the price level shifts the aggregate expenditures schedule from $(C_a + I_g + X_n + G)_1$ to $(C_a + I_g + X_n + G)_2$, increasing real GDP from GDP_1 to GDP_2. In (b) we find that the aggregate demand counterpart of this is a rightward shift of the aggregate demand curve from AD_1 to AD_2 which is just sufficient to show the same increase in real output as in the expenditures-output model. The "aggregate demand shifters" are summarized in Table 11-1.

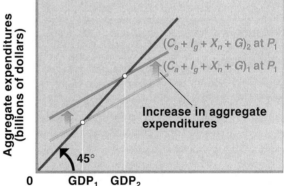

(a) Aggregate expenditures model

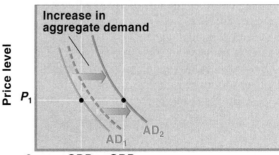

(b) Aggregate demand-aggregate supply model

In the lower graph the initial increase in investment spending is reflected in the horizontal distance between AD_1 and the broken line to its right. The immediate effect of the increase in investment is to increase aggregate demand by the amount of this new spending. The multiplier process then magnifies the initial change in investment into successive rounds of consumption spending and an ultimate increase in aggregate demand from AD_1 to AD_2. Equilibrium real output rises from GDP_1 to GDP_2, the same multiplied increase in real GDP as in the top graph. *The initial increase in investment in the top graph has shifted the AD curve in the lower graph by a horizontal distance equal to the change in investment times the multiplier.* In this case, the change in real GDP is associated with the constant price level P_1. To generalize,

$$\text{Shift in AD curve} = \text{initial change in spending} \times \text{multiplier}$$

AGGREGATE SUPPLY

Aggregate supply *is a schedule, graphically represented by a curve, showing the level of real domestic output which will be produced at each price level.* Higher price levels create an incentive for enterprises to produce and sell additional output, while lower price levels reduce output. As a result, the relationship between the price level and the amount of real output businesses offer for sale is direct or positive.

Aggregate Supply Curve

For now let's think of the aggregate supply curve as comprising three distinct segments or ranges. Also assume the aggregate supply curve itself does not shift when the price level changes.

The three segments of the aggregate supply curve are identified as (1) the horizontal, (2) the intermediate (upsloping), and (3) the vertical range. Let's examine these three ranges and explain what each represents. You are already familiar with our explanations from our discussion of Figure 8-7. The shape of the aggregate supply curve reflects what happens to per unit production costs as GDP expands or contracts. We know from Chapter 8 that per unit production cost is found by dividing the total cost of the inputs (resources) used by the quantity of output. That is, the per unit production cost of a particular level of output is the average cost of that output.

Horizontal Range   In Figure 11-5 Q_f designates the full-employment or potential level of real output. Recall from Chapter 8 that the natural rate of unemployment occurs at this output. Observe that the **horizontal range** (*ab*) of aggregate supply comprises real levels of output substantially less than the full-employment output Q_f. Thus, the horizontal range implies the economy is in a severe recession or depression and that large amounts of unused machinery and equipment and unemployed workers are available for production. These idle resources—both human and property—can be put back to work with little or no upward pressure on the price level. As output expands over this *ab* range, no shortages or production bottlenecks will be incurred to raise prices. Workers unemployed for two or three months will hardly expect a wage increase when recalled to their jobs. Because producers can acquire labor and other inputs at stable prices, production costs will not rise as output is expanded and so there is no reason to raise product prices.

This horizontal range also implies that, if real output falls, product and resource prices will be downwardly inflexible. That means real output and employment will fall, but product prices and wages will remain rigid. Indeed, real output and employment will decline in this range *because* prices and wages are inflexible.

Vertical Range   At the other extreme, we find that the economy reaches its absolute full-capacity level of real output at Q_c. Any increase in the price level in this **vertical range** (*cd*) will fail to elicit additional real output because the economy is operating at full capacity. Individual firms may try to expand production by bidding resources away from other firms. But the resources and additional production one firm gains will be lost by some other firm. This will raise resource prices (costs) and ultimately product prices, but real output will remain unchanged.

Intermediate (Upsloping) Range   Finally, in the *bc* **intermediate range** between Q_u and Q_c, an expansion of real output is accompanied by a rising price level. The aggregate economy is comprised of innumerable product and resource markets, and full employment is not reached evenly or simultaneously in various sectors or industries. As the economy expands in the $Q_u Q_f$ real output range, the high-tech computer industry may encounter shortages of skilled workers while the automobile or steel indus-

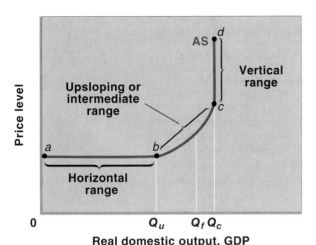

FIGURE 11-5   The aggregate supply curve
The aggregate supply curve shows the level of real domestic output which will be produced at various price levels. It comprises three ranges: (a) a horizontal range where the price level remains constant as domestic output varies; (b) a vertical range where real domestic output is constant at the absolute full-capacity level and only the price level can vary; and (c) an intermediate range where both real output and the price level are variable.

Determinants of Aggregate Supply

Our discussion of the shape of the aggregate supply curve revealed that real output increases as the economy moves from left to right through the horizontal and intermediate ranges of aggregate supply. These changes in output result from *movements along* the aggregate supply curve and must be distinguished from *shifts* in the curve itself. An existing aggregate supply curve identifies the relationship between the price level and real output, *other things being equal.* But when one or more of these "other things" change, the curve itself shifts.

The shift of the curve from AS_1 to AS_2 in Figure 11-6 shows an *increase* in aggregate supply. Over the intermediate and vertical ranges this shift is rightward, indicating that businesses collectively will produce more output at each price level. Over the horizontal range of the aggregate supply curve, an increase in aggregate supply can be thought of as a decline in the price level at each level of output (a downward shift of aggregate supply). We will refer to an increase in aggregate supply as a "rightward" shift of the curve. Also, the shift of the curve from AS_1 to AS_3 is a "leftward" shift, depicting a *decrease* in ag-

tries still face substantial unemployment. Similarly, in certain industries raw-material shortages or other production bottlenecks may begin to appear. Expansion also means some firms will be forced to use older and less efficient machinery as they approach capacity production. Additional employees will create congestion in workplaces and productivity will decline, increasing per unit costs and product prices. Also, less capable workers may be hired as output expands.

Once the full-employment level of GDP is reached at Q_f, for a time further price level increases may bring forth added real output. We know from Chapter 8 that employment and real GDP can expand beyond the full-employment level of output until the economy reaches its absolute maximum capacity. Recall from Figure 8-5 that periodically actual GDP exceeds full-employment or potential GDP. In a prosperous economy the size of the labor force, daily working hours, and the workweek can be extended. Workers can also "moonlight"—hold more than one job. But once the economy's absolute full capacity is reached at Q_c, the aggregate supply curve becomes vertical.

In the intermediate range of aggregate supply, per unit production costs rise and firms must receive higher product prices for their output to be profitable. In this range a rising real output is accompanied by a higher price level.

FIGURE 11-6   Changes in aggregate supply
A change in one or more of the determinants of aggregate supply listed in Table 11-2 will cause a change in aggregate supply. An increase in aggregate supply is shown as a rightward shift of the AS curve from AS_1 to AS_2; a decrease in aggregate supply, as a leftward shift from AS_1 to AS_3.

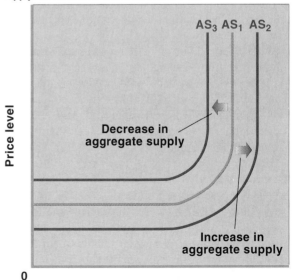

gregate supply. That means businesses now will produce less output at each price level than before (or charge higher prices at each level of output).

Table 11-2 lists the "other things" which shift the aggregate supply curve when they change. Called the **determinants of aggregate supply,** they collectively "determine" or establish the location of the aggregate supply curve. These determinants have one thing in common: When they change, per unit production costs also change. We saw earlier that supply decisions of businesses are based on production costs and revenues. Businesses are profit seekers and profits arise from the difference between product prices and per unit production costs. Producers respond to higher prices for their products—to higher price levels—by increasing their real output. And, production bottlenecks mean that per unit production costs rise as output expands toward—and beyond—full employment. For this reason the aggregate supply curve slopes upward in its intermediate range.

But there are factors *other than changes in real output* which alter per unit production costs (see Table 11-2). When one or more change, per unit production costs change *at each price level* and the aggregate supply curve shifts. Decreases in per unit production costs of this type shift the aggregate supply curve rightward; increases in per unit production costs shift it leftward. *When per unit production costs change for reasons other than a change in real output, firms collectively alter the amount of output they produce at each price level.*

Let's examine how changes in the aggregate supply shifters listed in Table 11-2 affect per unit production costs and shift the aggregate supply curve.

Input Prices   Input or resource prices—to be distinguished from the output prices comprising the price level—are a major determinant of aggregate supply. All else equal, higher input prices increase per unit production costs and reduce aggregate supply. Lower input prices do just the opposite. A number of factors influence input prices.

Domestic Resource Availability   We noted in Chapter 2 that a society's production possibilities curve shifts outward when the resources available to it increase. Rightward shifts in the production possibilities curve translate to rightward shifts of our aggregate supply curve. Increases in the supply of domestic resources lower input prices and decrease per unit production costs. At any specific price level, firms col-

TABLE 11-2   Determinants of aggregate supply: factors that shift the aggregate supply curve
1 Change in input prices
a Domestic resource availability
a_1 **Land**
a_2 **Labor**
a_3 **Capital**
a_4 **Entrepreneurial ability**
b Prices of imported resources
c Market power
2 Change in productivity
3 Change in legal-institutional environment
a Business taxes and subsidies
b Government regulation

lectively will produce and offer for sale more real output than before. Declines in resource supplies increase input prices and shift the aggregate supply curve to the left.

How might changes in the availability of land, labor, capital, and entrepreneurial resources work to shift the aggregate supply curve? Let's look at several examples.

Land   Land resources might expand through discoveries of mineral deposits, irrigation of land, or technical innovations, permitting us to transform what were previously "nonresources" into valuable factors of production. An increase in the supply of land resources lowers the price of land inputs, lowering per unit production costs. For example, the recent discovery that widely available materials at low temperatures can act as superconductors of electricity is expected eventually to reduce per unit production costs by reducing electricity loss during transmission. This lower price of electricity will increase aggregate supply.

Two examples of reductions in land resources availability may also be cited: (1) the widespread depletion of the nation's underground water through irrigation, and (2) the nation's loss of topsoil through intensive farming. Eventually, these problems may increase input prices and shift the aggregate supply curve leftward.

Labor   About 75 percent of all business costs are wages or salaries. All else being equal, changes in wages have a significant impact on per unit production costs and on the location of the aggregate supply curve. An increase in the availability of labor resources reduces the price of labor; a decrease raises labor's price. Examples: The influx of women into the labor force during the past two decades placed a downward pressure on wages and expanded American aggregate supply. Emigration of employable workers from abroad also has historically increased the availability of labor in the United States.

The great loss of life during World War II greatly diminished the postwar availability of labor in the United States, raising per unit production costs. Currently, the AIDS epidemic threatens to reduce the supply of labor and thus diminish the nation's aggregate supply of real output.

Capital   Aggregate supply usually increases when society adds to its stock of capital. Such an addition would happen if society saved more of its income and directed the savings toward purchase of capital goods. In much the same way, an improvement in the quality of capital reduces production costs and increases aggregate supply. For example, businesses over the years have replaced poor quality equipment with new, superior equipment.

On the other hand, aggregate supply declines when the quantity and quality of the nation's stock of capital diminishes. Example: In the depths of the Great Depression of the 1930s, our capital stock deteriorated because new purchases of capital were insufficient to offset the normal wearing out and obsolescence of plant and equipment.

Entrepreneurial Ability   Finally, the amount of entrepreneurial ability available to the economy can occasionally change and shift the aggregate supply curve. Recent media focus on individuals such as Ted Turner and Bill Gates who have amassed fortunes through entrepreneurial efforts might conceivably increase the number of people who have entrepreneurial aspirations. If so, the aggregate supply curve might shift rightward.

Prices of Imported Resources   Just as foreign demand for American goods contributes to our aggregate demand, resources imported from abroad add to our aggregate supply. Resources, whether domestic or imported, boost our production capacity. Imported resources reduce input prices and decrease the per unit cost of producing American real output. Generally, a decrease in the prices of imported resources expands our aggregate supply; an increase in the prices of these resources reduces our aggregate supply.

Exchange rate fluctuations alter the price of imported resources. Suppose the dollar price of foreign currency falls—the dollar appreciates—enabling American firms to obtain more foreign currency with each American dollar. This means that American producers face a lower dollar price of imported resources. Under these conditions, American firms would expand their imports of foreign resources and realize reductions in per unit production costs at each level of output. Falling per unit production costs of this type shift the American aggregate supply curve to the right.

Also, an increase in the dollar price of foreign currency—dollar depreciation—raises the prices of imported resources. Our imports of these resources fall, our per unit production costs jump upward, and our aggregate supply curve moves leftward.

Market Power   A change in the degree of market power or monopoly power held by sellers of resources can also affect input prices and aggregate supply. *Market power* is the ability to set a price above the price that would occur in a competitive situation. The rise and fall of market power held by the Organization of Petroleum Exporting Countries (OPEC) during the past three decades is a good illustration. The tenfold increase in the price of oil OPEC achieved during the 1970s permeated our economy, drove up per unit production costs, and jolted the American aggregate supply curve leftward. But then a steep reduction in OPEC's market power during the mid-1980s reduced the cost of manufacturing and transporting products, and as a direct result, increased American aggregate supply.

A change in labor union market power also can affect the location of the aggregate supply curve. Some observers believe that unions experienced growing market power in the 1970s, resulting in union wage increases which widened the gap between union and nonunion workers. This higher pay may have increased per unit production costs and produced leftward shifts of aggregate supply. But union market power greatly waned during the 1980s. The price of union labor fell in many industries, resulting in lower per unit production costs. The outcome was an increase in aggregate supply.

Productivity   Productivity relates a nation's level of real output to the quantity of input used to produce that output. In other words, **productivity** is a measure of average output, or of real output per unit of input:

$$\text{Productivity} = \frac{\text{real output}}{\text{input}}$$

An increase in productivity means the economy can obtain more real output from its resources—or inputs.

How does an increase in productivity affect the aggregate supply curve? We first need to see how a change in productivity alters per unit production costs. Suppose real output is 10 units, the input quantity needed to produce that quantity is 5, and the price of each input unit is $2. Productivity—output per input—is 2 (= 10/5). The per unit cost of output would be found as follows:

$$\text{Per unit production cost} = \frac{\text{total input cost}}{\text{units of output}}$$

Per unit cost is $1, found by dividing $10 of input cost (= $2 × 5 units of input) by 10 units of output.

Now suppose real output doubles to 20 units, while the input price and quantity remain constant at $2 and 5 units. That means productivity rises from 2 (= 10/5) to 4 (= 20/5). Because the total cost of the inputs stays at $10 (= $2 × 5 units of input), the per unit cost of the output falls from $1 to $.50 (= $10 of input cost/20 units of output).

By reducing per unit production costs, an increase in productivity shifts the aggregate supply curve rightward; a decline in productivity increases per unit production costs and shifts the aggregate supply curve leftward.

We will see in Chapter 19 that productivity growth is a major factor explaining the long-term expansion of aggregate supply in the United States and the corresponding growth of real GDP. More machinery and equipment per worker, improved production technology, a better-educated and trained labor force, and improved forms of business enterprises have raised productivity and increased aggregate supply.

Legal-Institutional Environment   Changes in the legal-institutional setting in which businesses collectively operate may alter per unit costs of output and shift the aggregate supply curve. Two changes of this type are (1) changes in taxes and subsidies, and (2) changes in the extent of regulation.

Business Taxes and Subsidies   Higher business taxes, such as sales, excise, and payroll taxes, increase per unit costs and reduce aggregate supply in much the same way as a wage increase. Example: An increase in payroll taxes paid by businesses will increase production costs and reduce aggregate supply.

Similarly, a business subsidy—a payment or tax break by government to firms—reduces production costs and increases aggregate supply. Example: During the 1970s, the government subsidized producers of energy from alternative sources such as wind, oil shale, and solar power. The purpose was to reduce production costs and encourage development of energy sources which might substitute for oil and natural gas. To the extent that these subsidies were successful, the aggregate supply curve moved rightward.

Government Regulation   It is usually costly for businesses to comply with government regulations. Thus, regulation increases per unit production costs and shifts the aggregate supply curve leftward. "Supply-side" proponents of deregulation of the economy have argued forcefully that, by increasing efficiency and reducing paperwork associated with complex regulations, deregulation will reduce per unit costs. In this way, the aggregate supply curve purportedly will shift rightward. Conversely, increases in regulation raise production costs and reduce aggregate supply. *(Key Question 5)*

QUICK REVIEW 11-2

■ The aggregate supply curve has three distinct ranges: the horizontal range, the upsloping intermediate range, and the vertical range.

■ In the intermediate range, per unit production costs and therefore the price level rise as output expands toward—and beyond—its full-employment level.

■ By altering per unit production cost independent of changes in the level of output, changes in one or more of the determinants of aggregate supply (Table 11-2) shift the location of the aggregate supply curve.

■ An increase in aggregate supply is shown as a rightward shift of the aggregate supply curve, a decrease by a leftward shift of the curve.

KEY GRAPH

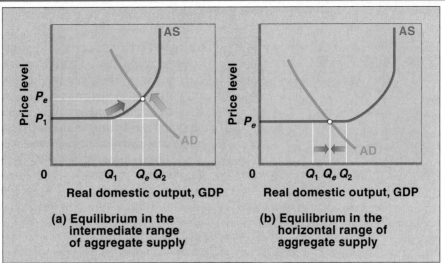

FIGURE 11-7   The equilibrium price level and equilibrium real GDP
The intersection of the aggregate demand and supply curves determines the equilibrium price level
and equilibrium real output. In (a) where aggregate demand intersects aggregate supply in its intermediate range, the price level will change to eliminate underproduction or overproduction of
output; in (b) where the aggregate demand curve intersects the aggregate supply curve in its horizontal range, no change in the price level accompanies the move toward equilibrium real output.

EQUILIBRIUM: REAL OUTPUT AND THE PRICE LEVEL

We found in Chapter 3 that the intersection of the demand for and supply of a particular product will determine its equilibrium price and output. Similarly, as
we see in Figure 11-7a and b (Key Graph), the intersection of the aggregate demand and aggregate supply curves determines the **equilibrium price level**
and **equilibrium real domestic output.**

In Figure 11-7a, where aggregate demand
crosses aggregate supply in its intermediate range,
the equilibrium price level and level of real output are
P_e and Q_e, respectively. To illustrate why P_e is the equilibrium price and Q_e is the equilibrium level of output,
suppose the price level were P_1 rather than P_e. We observe from the aggregate supply curve that price level
P_1 would entice businesses to produce (at most) real
output level Q_1. How much real output would domestic consumers, businesses, government, and foreign buyers want to purchase at P_1? The aggregate

demand curve tells us the answer is Q_2. Competition
among buyers to purchase the available real output of
Q_1 will drive up the price level to P_e.

As arrows in Figure 11-7a indicate, the rise in the
price level from P_1 to P_e encourages *producers* to increase their real output from Q_1 to Q_e and simultaneously causes *buyers* to scale back their purchases from
Q_2 to Q_e. When equality occurs between the amount
of real output produced and the amount purchased,
as it does at P_e, the economy has achieved equilibrium.

In Figure 11-7b aggregate demand intersects aggregate supply in the range where aggregate supply
is perfectly horizontal. Here, the price level does *not*
play a role in bringing about the equilibrium level
of real output. To understand why, first observe that
the equilibrium price and real output levels in Figure
11-7b are P_e and Q_e. If the business sector had produced a larger output, such as Q_2, it could not dispose
of it. Aggregate demand would be insufficient to take
the output off the market. Faced with unwanted in-

ventories of goods, businesses would reduce their production to Q_e—shown by the leftward pointing arrow—and the market would clear.

If firms had only produced output of Q_1, businesses would find their inventories of goods would quickly diminish because sales would exceed production. Businesses would react by increasing production, and output would rise to its equilibrium as shown by the rightward pointing arrow. *(Key Questions 4 and 7)*

CHANGES IN EQUILIBRIUM

Let's shift the aggregate demand and aggregate supply curves and see the effects on equilibrium real output and the price level.

Shifting Aggregate Demand

Suppose households, businesses, and government decide to increase their spending, shifting the aggregate demand curve to the right. Our list of determinants of aggregate demand (Table 11-1) provides several reasons why this could occur. Perhaps consumers become more optimistic about future economic conditions. These favorable expectations might stem from new American technological advances which promise to increase the competitiveness of our products in

both domestic and world markets and therefore to increase future real income. As a result, consumers would consume more (save less) of their current incomes. Similarly, firms anticipate that future business conditions will enhance profits from current investments in new capital. They increase their investment spending to enlarge their production capacities.

As shown in Figure 11-8, the precise effects of an *increase* in aggregate demand depend on whether the economy is currently in the horizontal, intermediate, or vertical range of the aggregate supply curve.

In the horizontal range of Figure 11-8a, where there is high unemployment and much unused production capacity, the increase in aggregate demand (AD_1 to AD_2) creates a large increase in real output (Q_1 to Q_2) and employment with no increase in the price level (P_1).

In the vertical range of Figure 11-8b, where labor and capital are at their absolute full capacities, an increase in aggregate demand (AD_5 to AD_6) will affect the price level only, increasing it from P_5 to P_6. Real output will remain at Q_c.

In the intermediate range of Figure 11-8c an increase in aggregate demand (AD_3 to AD_4) will raise both real output (Q_3 to Q_4) *and* the price level (P_3 to P_4).

The price level increases associated with aggregate demand increases in both the vertical and intermediate ranges of the aggregate supply curve con-

FIGURE 11-8   The effects of increases in aggregate demand
The effects of an increase in aggregate demand depend on the range of the aggregate supply curve in which it occurs. (a) An increase in aggregate demand in the horizontal range will increase real output, but leave the price level unaffected. (b) In the vertical range, an increase in aggregate demand will increase the price level, but real output cannot increase beyond the absolute full-capacity level. (c) An increase in demand in the intermediate range will increase both real output and the level of prices. The increases in aggregate demand shown in (b) and (c) depict demand-pull inflation.

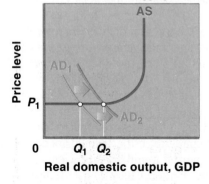

(a) Increasing demand in the horizontal range

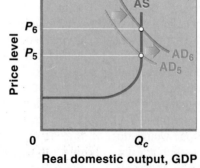

(b) Increasing demand in the vertical range

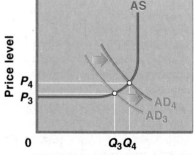

(c) Increasing demand in the intermediate range

stitute **demand-pull inflation** because shifts in aggregate demand are pulling up the price level.

Multiplier with Price Level Changes[3]

Close inspection reveals that real GDP does not increase as much in Figure 11-8c as it does in Figure 11-8a, even though the shifts in aggregate demand are of equal magnitudes. In Figure 11-9, which combines Figures 11-8a and 11-8b, we see the shift in aggregate demand from AD_1 to AD_2 occurs in the horizontal range of aggregate supply. In other words, the economy is in recession with excess production capacity and a high unemployment rate. Businesses are willing to produce more output *at existing prices.* Any initial change in spending and resulting multiple change in aggregate demand over this range is translated fully into a change in real GDP and employment while the price level remains constant. In the horizontal range of aggregate supply a "full-strength" multiplier is at work.

If the economy is in either the intermediate or vertical range of the aggregate supply curve, part or all of any initial increase in aggregate demand will be dissipated in inflation and therefore *not* reflected in increased real output and employment. In Figure 11-9 the shift of aggregate demand from AD_2 to AD_3 is of the same magnitude as the AD_1 to AD_2 shift, but look what happens. Because we are now in the intermediate range of the aggregate supply curve, a portion of the increase in aggregate demand is absorbed as inflation as the price level rises from P_1 to P_2. Real GDP rises to only GDP'. If the aggregate supply curve had been horizontal, then the AD_2 to AD_3 shift would have increased real output to GDP_3. But inflation has reduced the multiplier so that the actual increase is to GDP' which is only about half as much.

Our conclusion is that, *for any initial increase in aggregate demand, the resulting increase in real GDP will be smaller the larger the increase in the price level.* Price level increases weaken the multiplier.

You should sketch an increase in demand equal to the AD_2 to AD_3 shift in the vertical range to confirm that this increase in spending would be entirely absorbed as inflation. The multiplier would be zero because real GDP would be unchanged.

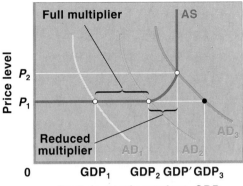

FIGURE 11-9   Inflation and the multiplier
The aggregate demand–aggregate supply model shows how inflation reduces the size of the multiplier. For the AD_1 to AD_2 increase in aggregate demand the price level is constant and the multiplier is at full strength. Although the increase in aggregate demand from AD_2 to AD_3 is of equal magnitude, it is partly dissipated in inflation (P_1 to P_2) and real output only increases from GDP_2 to GDP'.

A Ratchet Effect?

What of *decreases* in aggregate demand? Our model predicts that in the horizontal range of aggregate supply real GDP will fall and the price level will remain unchanged. In the vertical range prices fall and real output remains at the absolute full-capacity level. In the intermediate range the model suggests that both real output and the price level will diminish.

But a complicating factor raises doubts about the predicted effects of declines in aggregate demand in the vertical and intermediate ranges. The reverse movements of aggregate demand—from AD_6 to AD_5 in Figure 11-8b and from AD_4 to AD_3 in Figure 11-8c —may *not* restore the initial equilibrium positions, at least in the short term. The complication is that many prices—both of products and resources—are "sticky" or inflexible in a downward direction. Some economists envision a **ratchet effect** at work (a ratchet is a mechanism which cranks a wheel forward but not backward).

Graphical Depiction   The workings of the ratchet effect are shown in Figure 11-10. If aggregate demand increases from AD_1 to AD_2, the economy moves from the P_1Q_1 equilibrium at *a* in the horizontal range to the P_2Q_c equilibrium at *b* in the vertical range. But while prices readily move up, they do not easily come down, at least not in the short term. If aggregate demand should reverse itself and decrease from AD_2 to

---

[3]Instructors who do not assign Chapters 9 and 10 may want to use this section as a springboard for introducing the MPC, MPS, and multiplier concepts.

QUICK REVIEW 11-3

■ The equilibrium price level and amount of real output are determined at the intersection of the aggregate demand and aggregate supply curves.

■ Increases in aggregate demand in the upsloping and vertical ranges of aggregate supply cause demand-pull inflation.

■ The price level is "sticky" or inflexible in a downward direction in the short run.

■ Decreases in aggregate supply cause cost-push inflation.

■ Increases in aggregate supply expand real output; they result in economic growth.

CHAPTER SUMMARY

1 For purposes of analysis we consolidate—or aggregate—the outcomes from the enormous number of individual product markets into a composite market in which there are two variables—the price level and the level of real output. This is accomplished through an aggregate demand–aggregate supply model.

2 The aggregate demand curve shows the level of real output which the economy will purchase at each price level.

3 The rationale for the downsloping aggregate demand curve is based on the wealth or real balances effect, the interest-rate effect, and the foreign purchases effect. The wealth or real balances effect indicates that inflation will reduce the real value or purchasing power of fixed-value financial assets held by households, causing them to retrench on their consumer spending. The interest-rate effect means that, with a specific supply of money, a higher price level will increase the demand for money, raising the interest rate and reducing consumption and investment purchases. The foreign purchases effect suggests that an increase in the United States' price level relative to other countries will reduce the net exports component of American aggregate demand.

*4 A change in the price level alters the location of the aggregate expenditures schedule through the wealth, interest rate, and foreign purchases effects. The aggregate demand curve is derived from the aggregate expenditures model by allowing the price level to change and observing the effect on the aggregate expenditures schedule and thus on equilibrium GDP.

5 The determinants of aggregate demand are spending by domestic consumers, businesses, government, and foreign buyers. Changes in the factors listed in Table 11-1 cause changes in spending by these groups and shift the aggregate demand curve.

*6 Holding the price level constant, increases in consumption, investment, and net export expenditures shift the aggregate expenditures schedule upward and the aggregate demand curve to the right. Decreases in these spending components produce the opposite effects.

7 The aggregate supply curve shows the levels of real output which businesses will produce at various possible price levels.

8 The shape of the aggregate supply curve depends on what happens to per unit production costs—and therefore to the prices which businesses must receive to cover costs and make a profit—as real output expands. In the horizontal range of aggregate supply, there is substantial unemployment and thus production can be increased without raising per unit cost or prices. In the intermediate range, per unit costs increase as production bottlenecks appear and less efficient equipment and workers are employed. Prices must therefore rise as real output is expanded. The vertical range coincides with absolute full capacity; real output is at a maximum and cannot be increased, but the price level will rise in response to an increase in aggregate demand.

9 As indicated in Table 11-2, the determinants of aggregate supply are input prices, productivity, and the legal-institutional environment. A change in one of these factors will change per unit production costs at each level of output and therefore alter the location of the aggregate supply curve.

10 The intersection of the aggregate demand and aggregate supply curves determines the equilibrium price level and real GDP.

11 Increases in aggregate demand will a increase real output and employment but not alter the price level in the horizontal range of aggregate supply; b increase both real output and the price level in the intermediate range; and c increase the price level but not change real output in the vertical range.

12 In the intermediate and vertical ranges of the aggregate supply curve, the aggregate demand–aggregate supply model shows that the multiplier will be weakened because a portion of any increase in aggregate demand will be dissipated in inflation.

13 The ratchet effect is at work when prices are flexible upward, but inflexible downward. An increase in aggregate demand will raise the price level, but in the short term, the price level cannot be expected to fall when aggregate demand decreases.

14 Leftward shifts of the aggregate supply curve reflect

---

*This summary point presumes knowledge of the aggregate expenditures model presented in Chapters 9 and 10.

LAST WORD

WHY IS UNEMPLOYMENT IN EUROPE SO HIGH?

Are the high unemployment rates in Europe the result of structural problems or deficient aggregate demand?

Several European economies have had high rates of unemployment in the past several years. For example, in 1994 France had an unemployment rate of 12.4 percent; Great Britain, 9.5 percent; Italy, 11.6 percent; and all of Germany, 10.2 percent.

There is little dispute that recessions in Europe in the early 1990s contributed to these high rates. Declines in aggregate demand reduced real GDP and increased unemployment. Nevertheless, a mystery remains: Why were unemployment rates in many European nations so high even *before* their recessions? In 1990 the unemployment rate in France was 9.1 percent; in Great Britain, 6.9 percent; and in Italy, 7.0 percent (compared to only 5.5 percent in the United States). And why have European unemployment rates remained far higher than in the United States during economic recovery? There are two views on these questions:

1 High Natural Rates of Unemployment Many economists believe the high unemployment rates in Europe largely reflect high natural rates of unemployment. They envision a situation as in Figure 11-7a, where aggregate demand and aggregate supply have produced the full-employment level of real output Q_e. But high levels of frictional and structural unemployment accompany this level of output. In this view, the recent extensive unemployment in Europe has resulted from a high natural rate of unemployment, not from deficient aggregate demand. An increase in aggregate demand would push these economies beyond their full-employment levels of output, causing demand-pull inflation.

The alleged sources of the high natural rates of unemployment are government policies and union contracts which have increased the costs of hiring workers and reduced the cost of being unemployed. Examples: High minimum wages have discouraged employers from hiring low-skilled workers; generous welfare benefits have weakened incentives for people to take available jobs; restrictions against firings have discouraged firms from employing workers; thirty to forty days per year of paid vacations and holidays have boosted the cost of hiring workers; high worker absenteeism has reduced productivity; and high employer costs of health, pension, disability, and other benefits have discouraged hiring.

2 Deficient Aggregate Demand Not all economists agree that government and union policies have ratcheted up Europe's natural rate of unemployment. Instead, they point to insufficient aggregate demand as the culprit. They see the European economies in terms of Figure 11-7b, where the Q_e real output is less than it would be if aggregate demand were stronger. The argument is that the European governments have been so fearful of inflation that they have not undertaken appropriate fiscal and monetary policies (Chapters 12 and 15) to increase aggregate demand. In this view, increases in aggregate demand would not be inflationary, since these economies have considerable excess capacity. If they are operating in the horizontal range of their aggregate supply curves, a rightward shift in aggregate demand curves would expand output and employment, without increasing inflation.

Conclusion: The debate over high unemployment in Europe reflects disagreement on where European aggregate demand curves lie relative to full-employment levels of output. If these curves are *at* the full-employment real GDP, as in Figure 11-7a, then the high levels of unemployment are "natural." Public policies should focus on lowering minimum wages, reducing vacation time, reducing welfare benefits, easing restrictions on layoffs, and so on. But if the aggregate demand curves in the European nations lie to the left of their full-employment levels of output, as in Figure 11-7b, then expansionary government policies such as reduced interest rates or tax cuts may be in order.

Increased Taxes Just as government can use tax cuts to increase consumption spending, it can use tax increases to reduce it. If the economy in Figure 12-2 has an MPC of .75, government must raise taxes by $6.67 billion to reduce consumption by $5. The $6.67 tax will reduce saving by $1.67 (= the MPS of .25 × $6.67 billion) and this $1.67 billion reduction in saving, by definition, is not a spending reduction. But the $6.67 billion tax increase *will* reduce consumption spending by $5 billion (= the MPC of .75 × $6.67), as shown by the distance between AD$_4$ and the dashed line to its left. After the multiplier process, aggregate demand will shift leftward by $20 billion at each price level (= multiplier of 4 × $5 billion) and the price level will fall from P$_4$ to P$_3$. Demand-pull inflation will have been controlled.

Combined Government Spending Decreases and Tax Increases Government can combine spending decreases and tax increases to reduce aggregate demand and check inflation. To test your understanding you should determine why a $2 billion decline in government spending *paired* with a $4 billion increase in taxes would shift the aggregate demand curve from AD$_4$ to AD$_3$.

Also, if you were assigned Chapters 9 and 10, you should be able to explain the three fiscal policy options for fighting inflation in terms of the inflationary gap concept developed in the aggregate expenditures model (Figure 10-8). Recall from Chapter 11 that leftward shifts in the aggregate demand curve are associated with downshifts in the aggregate expenditures schedule. *(Key Question 3)*

Financing Deficits and Disposing of Surpluses

The expansionary effect of a specific budget deficit on the economy will depend on the method used to finance it. Similarly, the deflationary impact of a particular budget surplus will depend on what is done with it.

Borrowing versus New Money There are two ways the Federal government can finance a deficit: borrowing from (selling interest-bearing bonds to) the public, or issuing new money to its creditors. The impact on aggregate demand will be different in each case.

1 **Borrowing** If the government enters the money market and borrows, it will be competing with private

business borrowers for funds. This added demand for funds may drive up the equilibrium interest rate. Investment spending is inversely related to the interest rate. Government borrowing therefore may increase the interest rate and "crowd out" some private investment spending and interest-sensitive consumer spending.

2 **Money Creation** If deficit spending is financed by issuing new money, crowding out of private expenditures can be avoided. Federal spending can increase without any adverse effect on investment or consumption. *The creation of new money is a more expansionary way of financing deficit spending than is borrowing.*

Debt Retirement versus Idle Surplus Demand-pull inflation calls for fiscal action which will result in a budget surplus. But the anti-inflationary effect of this surplus depends on what government does with it.

1 **Debt Reduction** Since the Federal government has an outstanding debt of $4.6 trillion, it is logical that government should use a surplus to retire outstanding debt. The anti-inflationary impact of a surplus, however, may be reduced by paying off debt. In retiring debt held by the general public, the government transfers its surplus tax revenues back into the money market. This causes the interest rate to fall, stimulating investment and consumption.

2 **Impounding** On the other hand, government can realize a greater anti-inflationary impact from its budgetary surplus by impounding the surplus funds, meaning to allow them to stand idle. An impounded surplus means that the government is extracting and withholding purchasing power from the economy. If surplus tax revenues are not reinjected into the economy, there is no possibility of some portion of that surplus being spent. There is no chance that the funds will create inflationary pressure to offset the deflationary impact of the surplus itself. We conclude that *the impounding of a budgetary surplus is more contractionary than the use of the surplus to retire public debt.*

Policy Options: *G* or *T*?

Is it preferable to use government spending or taxes to eliminate recession and inflation? The answer depends largely on one's view as to whether the public sector is too large or too small.

"Liberal" economists, who think the public sector needs to be enlarged to meet various failures of the market system (Chapter 5), can recommend that aggregate demand be expanded during recessions by increasing government purchases *and* that aggregate demand should be constrained during inflationary periods by increasing taxes. Both actions either expand or preserve the absolute size of government.

"Conservative" economists, who think the public sector is too large and inefficient, can advocate that aggregate demand be increased during recessions by cutting taxes *and* that aggregate demand be reduced during inflation by cutting government spending.

An active fiscal policy designed to stabilize the economy can be associated with either an expanding or a contracting public sector.

QUICK REVIEW 12-1

■ The Employment Act of 1946 commits the Federal government to promote "maximum employment, production, and purchasing power."

■ Fiscal policy is the purposeful manipulation of government expenditures and tax collections by Congress to promote full employment, price stability, and economic growth.

■ Government uses expansionary fiscal policy—shown as a rightward shift of the aggregate demand curve—to stimulate spending and expand real output. It involves increases in government spending, reductions in taxes, or some combination of the two.

■ Contractionary fiscal policy—shown as a leftward shift of the aggregate demand curve—is aimed at demand-pull inflation. It entails reductions in government expenditures, tax increases, or some combination of each.

■ The expansionary effect of fiscal policy depends on how the budget deficit is financed; the contractionary effect of fiscal policy depends on the disposition of the budget surplus.

NONDISCRETIONARY FISCAL POLICY: BUILT-IN STABILIZERS

To some degree appropriate changes in the levels of government expenditures and taxes occur automatically. This automatic or *built-in stability* is not included in our discussion of discretionary fiscal policy because we implicitly assumed a simple lump-sum tax where the same amount of tax revenue was collected at each level of GDP. Built-in stability arises because in reality our net tax system (net taxes equal taxes minus transfers and subsidies) is such that *net tax revenues*[1] *vary directly with GDP.*

Virtually all taxes will yield more tax revenues as GDP rises. In particular, personal income taxes have progressive rates and result in more than proportionate increases in tax collections as GDP expands. Furthermore, as GDP increases and more goods and services are purchased, revenues from corporate income taxes and sales and excise taxes will increase. And, similarly, payroll tax payments increase as economic expansion creates more jobs. Conversely, when GDP declines, tax receipts from all these sources will decline.

Transfer payments (or "negative taxes") behave in the opposite way as tax collections. Unemployment compensation payments, welfare payments, and subsidies to farmers all *decrease* during economic expansion and *increase* during a contraction.

Automatic or Built-In Stabilizers

Figure 12-3 helps us understand how the tax system creates built-in stability. Government expenditures G are fixed and assumed to be independent of the level of GDP; expenditures are decided on at some specific level by Congress. But Congress does *not* determine the *level* of tax revenues; rather, it establishes tax *rates*. Tax revenues then vary directly with the level of GDP which the economy actually realizes. The direct relationship between tax revenues and GDP is shown in the upsloping T line.

Economic Importance   The economic importance of this direct relationship between tax receipts and GDP comes into focus when we consider two things.
1 Taxes reduce spending and aggregate demand.
2 It is desirable from the standpoint of stability to reduce spending when the economy is moving toward inflation and to increase spending when the economy is slumping.

In other words, the tax system portrayed in Figure 12-3 builds some stability into the economy. It automatically brings about changes in tax revenues and

---

[1]From now on, we will use the term "taxes" in referring to net taxes.

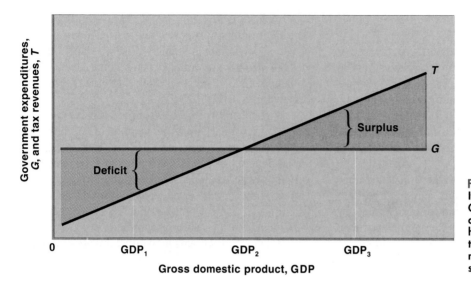

FIGURE 12-3 **Built-in stability** If tax revenues vary directly with GDP the deficits which will occur automatically during recession will help alleviate that recession. Also, the surpluses which occur automatically during expansion will assist in offsetting possible inflation.

therefore in the public budget which counter both inflation and unemployment. A **built-in stabilizer** is *anything which increases the government's deficit (or reduces its surplus) during a recession and increases its surplus (or reduces its deficit) during inflation without requiring explicit action by policy makers.* As Figure 12-3 reveals, this is precisely what our tax system does.

As GDP rises during prosperity, tax revenues *automatically* increase and, because they reduce spending, they restrain the economic expansion. In other words, as the economy moves toward a higher GDP, tax revenues automatically rise and move the budget from a deficit toward a surplus.

Conversely, as GDP falls during recession, tax revenues *automatically* decline, increasing spending and cushioning the economic contraction. With a falling GDP, tax receipts decline and move the public budget from a surplus toward a deficit. In Figure 12-3, the low level of income GDP_1 will automatically yield an expansionary budget deficit; the high and perhaps inflationary income level GDP_3 will automatically generate a contractionary budget surplus.

Tax Progressivity It is clear from Figure 12-3 that the size of the automatic budget deficits or surpluses and therefore built-in stability depends on the responsiveness of changes in taxes to changes in GDP. If tax revenues change sharply as GDP changes, the slope of line T in the figure will be steep and the vertical distances between T and G—the deficits or surpluses—will be large. If tax revenues change very

little when GDP changes, the slope will be gentle and built-in stability will be low.

The steepness of T in Figure 12-3 depends on the tax system in place. If it is **progressive,** meaning the average tax rate (= tax revenue/GDP) rises with GDP, the T line will be steeper than if the tax system is **proportional** or **regressive.** In a proportional tax system the average tax rate remains constant as GDP rises; in a regressive tax system the average tax rate falls as GDP rises. Tax revenues will rise with GDP under progressive and proportional tax systems and may either rise, fall, or remain the same when GDP increases under a regressive system. But what you should realize is this: *The more progressive the tax system, the greater is the economy's built-in stability.*

Changes in public policies or laws which alter the progressivity of the net tax system (taxes minus transfers and subsidies) affect the degree of built-in stability. For example, in 1993 the Clinton administration increased the highest marginal tax rate on personal income from 31 percent to 39.6 percent and boosted the corporate income tax one percentage point to 35 percent. These rises in tax rates increase the overall progressivity of the tax system, slightly bolstering the economy's built-in stability.

The built-in stability provided by our tax system has reduced the severity of business fluctuations. But built-in stabilizers can only diminish, *not* correct, major changes in equilibrium GDP. Discretionary fiscal policy—changes in tax rates and expenditures—may be needed to correct inflation or recession of any appreciable magnitude.

Full-Employment Budget

Built-in stability—the fact that tax revenues vary directly with GDP—means the **actual budget** surplus or deficit in any specific year is not a good measure of the status of fiscal policy. Here's why: Suppose the economy is at full employment at GDP_f in Figure 12-4 and the government has an actual budget deficit shown by the vertical distance *ab*. Now, assume investment spending plummets, causing a recession to GDP_r. The government, let's assume, takes no discretionary fiscal action. Therefore, the *G* and *T* lines remain in the positions shown in the diagram. As the economy moves to GDP_r, tax revenues fall, and with government expenditures unaltered, the deficit rises to *ec,* expanding from *ab* (= *ed*) by the amount *dc*. This **cyclical deficit** of *dc*—so named because it relates to the business cycle—is not the result of positive countercyclical fiscal actions by government; rather it is the by-product of fiscal inaction as the economy slides into recession.

We cannot gain a meaningful picture of the government's fiscal posture—whether Congress was manipulating taxes and expenditures—by looking at the historical record of budget deficits or surpluses. The actual budget deficit or surplus reflects not only possible discretionary fiscal decisions about spending and taxes (as shown by the locations of the *G* and *T* lines in Figure 12-4), but also the level of GDP (where the economy is operating on the horizontal axis of Figure 12-4). Because tax revenues vary with GDP, the problem of comparing deficits or surpluses in any two years is that the level of GDP may be different in each year. In Figure 12-4, the actual budget deficit in year 2 (GDP_r) differs from that in year 1 (GDP_f) only because GDP is lower in year 2 than in year 1.

Resolving the Problem Economists have resolved the problem of comparing budget deficits for different years in the business cycle by using the full-employment budget. The **full-employment budget,** also called the *structural budget, measures what the Federal budget deficit or surplus would be with existing tax and government spending structures, if the economy were at full employment throughout the year.* In Figure 12-4 the full-employment deficit or **structural deficit** is the same in year 1 and year 2 (*ab* = *ed*). This is the budget deficit that would have existed in year 2 even if there were no recession. It is called "structural" because it reflects the configuration of *G* and *T,* independent of the state of the economy.

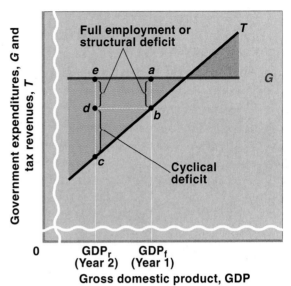

FIGURE 12-4 Full-employment (structural) deficits and cyclical deficits
The actual budget deficit for any specific year consists of the full-employment deficit (or structural deficit) and the cyclical deficit. The *full-employment* or *structural deficit* is the difference between government expenditures and tax collections which would occur if there were full-employment output (GDP_f). Here, this deficit is positive, since government spending exceeds tax collections at GDP_f. The *cyclical deficit* results from a below full-employment output (GDP_r). At GDP_f the structural deficit is *ab*, while the cyclical budget is zero. The structural deficit at GDP_r is *ed*(= *ab*); the cyclical deficit, *dc*.

In year 2 the actual budget deficit exceeds the full-employment or structural budget by *dc*. This is the amount of the cyclical budget deficit. To eliminate the *dc* cyclical deficit, government must move the economy back to full-employment output at GDP_f. Ironically, this may require a temporary increase in the full-employment deficit, or structural deficit, via expansionary discretionary fiscal policy. That is, government must cut taxes (shift *T* downward) or increase government spending (shift *G* upward) to move the economy from GDP_r to GDP_f. Once prosperity is restored, government can, if it wishes, eliminate the structural deficit by increasing tax rates (shift the *T* line upward) or by reducing government spending (shift the *G* line downward).

To emphasize: Discretionary fiscal policy is reflected in deliberate *changes* in the full-employment or structural deficit, not in changes in the cyclical deficit. Since the actual budget deficit comprises both the structural and cyclical deficits, the actual budget deficit is an unreliable measure of the government's fiscal policy stance.

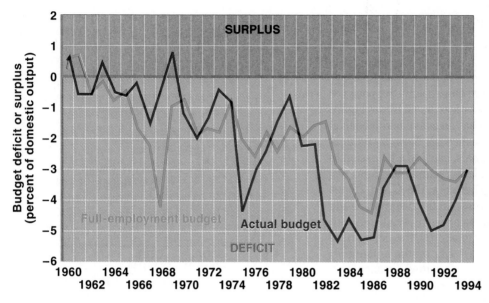

FIGURE 12-5 The full-employment budget and the actual budget Full-employment (or structural) budget deficits and surpluses often are different in size from actual budget deficits and surpluses. The full-employment budget surplus or deficit is a better indicator of the government's fiscal posture than is the actual surplus or deficit.

Historical Comparison Figure 12-5 compares the full-employment budget and the actual budget as percentages of GDP since 1959. In many years the sizes of the actual budget deficits or surpluses differ from the sizes of the deficits or surpluses of the full-employment budget. The key to assessing discretionary fiscal policy is to disregard the actual budget and instead observe the change in the *full-employment budget* in a particular year or period. For example, fiscal policy was very expansionary between 1965 and 1968 and between 1981 and 1986, reflected in the rapid increase in the full-employment deficit. Fiscal policy was contractionary in 1959, 1969, 1973, and 1987.

Also observe in Figure 12-5 that full-employment or structural deficits have been particularly large since 1981. A large part of the actual deficits during the 1980s and early 1990s were not cyclical deficits resulting from automatic deficiencies in tax revenues brought forth from below-full-employment GDP. Rather, much of the actual deficits reflected structural imbalances between government spending and tax collections caused by large cuts in tax rates in the 1980s, together with increases in government spending. The year 1989 is an example. Although the economy had achieved full employment, a sizable full-employment or structural deficit remained.

Large full-employment budget deficits have persisted into the 1990s. During the 1990s the American government has largely abandoned countercyclical

fiscal policy in its attempt to reduce the large structural deficits. These deficits were so massive that financing them increased real interest rates and may have crowded out much private investment, a scenario we will discuss shortly. Thus, in the 1990s the role of stabilizing the economy has fallen nearly exclusively to the nation's central bank, the Federal Reserve. This institution and its policies are the subject of Chapters 13 to 15, while budget deficits and the public debt are the subject of Chapter 18. *(Key Question 7)*

Global Perspective 12-1 shows that budget deficits are not confined to the United States.

QUICK REVIEW 12-2

■ Tax revenues automatically increase in economic expansions and decrease in recessions; transfers automatically decrease in expansions and increase in recessions.

■ Automatic changes in taxes and transfers add a degree of built-in stability to the economy.

■ The full-employment budget compares government spending to the tax revenues that would accrue if there were full employment; it is more useful than the actual budget in revealing the status of fiscal policy.

■ Full-employment budget deficits are also called structural deficits, as distinct from cyclical deficits.

GLOBAL PERSPECTIVE 12-1

Budget deficits as a percentage of GDP, selected nations

In 1993 all the major industrial nations had budget deficits, but these deficits varied greatly as a percentage of GDP. In some cases the deficits were largely cyclical; in other instances they were mainly full-employment or structural deficits.

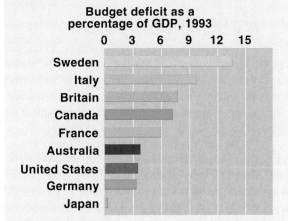

Budget deficit as a percentage of GDP, 1993

Sweden
Italy
Britain
Canada
France
Australia
United States
Germany
Japan

Source: *Organization for Economic Cooperation and Development.*

PROBLEMS, CRITICISMS, AND COMPLICATIONS

Unfortunately, there is much difference between fiscal policy on paper and fiscal policy in practice. Let's examine specific problems government may encounter in enacting and applying fiscal policy.

Problems of Timing

Several problems of timing may arise in connection with fiscal policy.

1 Recognition Lag The recognition lag refers to the time between the beginning of a recession or inflation and the certain awareness that it is actually happening. It is difficult to predict accurately the future course of economic activity. Although forecasting tools such as the index of leading indicators (see this chapter's Last Word) provide clues to the direction of

the economy, the economy may be four or six months into a recession or inflation before that fact appears in relevant statistics and is acknowledged.

2 Administrative Lag The wheels of democratic government turn slowly. There will typically be a significant lag between the time the need for fiscal action is recognized and the time action is actually taken. Congress has on occasion taken so much time in adjusting fiscal policy that the economic situation has turned around in the interim, rendering the policy action inappropriate.

3 Operational Lag There will also be a lag between the time that fiscal action is taken by Congress and the time that action affects output, employment, or the price level. Although changes in tax rates can be put into effect quickly, government spending on public works—the construction of dams, interstate highways, and so on—requires long planning periods and even longer periods of construction. Such spending is of questionable usefulness in offsetting short— for example, six- to eighteen-month—periods of recession. Because of these problems, discretionary fiscal policy has increasingly relied on tax changes.

Political Problems

Fiscal policy is created in the political arena and this greatly complicates its use in stabilizing the economy.

1 Other Goals Economic stability is *not* the sole objective of government spending and taxing policies. Government is also concerned with providing public goods and services and redistributing income (Chapter 5). A classic example occurred during World War II when massive government spending for military goods caused strong and persistent inflationary pressures in the early 1940s. The defeat of Nazi Germany and Japan was simply a higher priority goal than achieving price level stability.

2 State and Local Finance Fiscal policies of state and local governments are frequently procyclical— they do not counter recession or inflation. Unlike the Federal government, most state and local governments face constitutional or other legal requirements to balance their budgets. Like households and private businesses, state and local governments increase expenditures during prosperity and cut them during recession. During the Great Depression of the 1930s, most of the increase in Federal spending was offset by decreases in state and local spending. During the recession of 1990–1991, many state and local governments had to increase tax rates, impose new taxes, and reduce spending to offset falling tax revenues resulting from the reduced personal income and spending of their citizens.

3 Expansionary Bias? Rhetoric to the contrary, deficits may be politically attractive and surpluses politically painful. There may well be a political bias in favor of deficits; fiscal policy may have an expansionary-inflationary bias. Tax reductions are politically popular, and so are increases in government spending, provided the constituents of the politicians promoting them share in the benefits. But higher taxes upset voters and reducing government expenditures can be politically precarious. For example, it might be political suicide for a farm-state senator to vote for tax increases and against agricultural subsidies.

4 A Political Business Cycle? Some economists contend the goal of politicians is not to act in the interests of the national economy, but rather to get reelected. A few economists have suggested the notion of a **political business cycle.** They argue that politicians might manipulate fiscal policy to maximize voter support, even though their fiscal decisions *destabilize* the economy. In this view, fiscal policy, as we have described it, may be corrupted for political purposes and cause economic fluctuations.

The populace, it is assumed, takes economic conditions into account in voting. Incumbents are penalized at the polls if economic conditions are depressed; they are rewarded if the economy is prosperous. As an election approaches, the incumbent administration (aided by an election-minded Congress) will cut taxes and increase government spending. Not only will these actions be popular, the resulting stimulus to the economy will push all the critical economic indicators in proper directions. Output and real incomes will rise; unemployment will fall; and the price level will be relatively stable. As a result, incumbents will enjoy a very cordial economic environment for reelection.

But after the election, continued expansion of the economy is reflected increasingly in a rising price level and less in growing real incomes. Growing public concern over inflation will prompt politicians to invoke a contractionary fiscal policy. Crudely put, a "made-in-Washington" recession will be engineered by trimming government spending and increasing taxes to restrain inflation. This recession will not hurt incumbents because the next election is still two or three years away and the critical consideration for most voters is the performance of the economy in the year or so before the election. Indeed, the recession provides a new starting point from which fiscal policy can again be used to generate another expansion in time for the next election campaign.

This possible perversion of fiscal policy is disturbing but difficult to document. Although empirical evidence is inconclusive, there is some evidence to support this political theory of the business cycle.

Crowding-Out Effect

We now move from practical problems in the application of fiscal policy to a basic criticism of fiscal policy. The essence of the **crowding-out effect** is that an expansionary (deficit) fiscal policy will increase the interest rate and reduce investment spending, weakening or canceling the stimulus of the fiscal policy.

Suppose the economy is in recession and government invokes discretionary fiscal policy in the form of an increase in government spending. To do so government enters the money market to finance the deficit. The resulting increase in the demand for money raises the interest rate, the price paid for borrowing money. Because investment spending varies inversely with the interest rate, some investment will be choked off or crowded out.[2]

While few would question this logic, there is disagreement as to the size of the crowding-out effect. Some economists argue that there will be little crowding-out when there is considerable unemployment. Their rationale is that, given a recession, the stimulus provided by an increase in government spending will likely improve business profit expectations which are an important determinant of investment. Thus, investment spending need not fall—it may even increase—even though interest rates are higher.

Another consideration concerns monetary policy, which we will discuss in detail in later chapters. The monetary authorities may increase the supply of money by just enough to offset the deficit-caused increase in the demand for money. In this case the equilibrium interest rate would not change and the crowding-out effect would be zero. In the 1980s the monetary authorities restrained the growth of the

---

[2]Some interest sensitive consumption spending—for example, automobile purchases—may also be crowded out.

money supply and, consequently, the crowding-out effect of the large deficits of the 1980s may have been quite large. In comparison, in the 1960s the monetary authorities were strongly disposed to stabilize interest rates. They consequently would increase the money supply in response to higher interest rates caused by government borrowing. As a result, crowding-out was less significant.

Offsetting Saving

A few economists theorize that deficit spending is offset by an equal increase in private saving. Supposedly, people recognize that today's deficit spending will eventually require higher taxes for themselves or their heirs. People therefore increase their present saving (reduce their current consumption) in anticipation of these higher taxes. A budget deficit—*public dissaving*—produces an increase in *private saving.* This concept is termed the **Ricardian equivalence theorem,** named after British economist David Ricardo who first suggested it in the early 1800s. More formally, the theorem states that financing a deficit by borrowing has the same limited effect on GDP as financing it through a present tax increase.

In Figure 12-1, the increase in spending from the rise in government spending or decline in taxes is partially or fully offset by a decline in consumption caused

by the increase in saving. Aggregate demand and real GDP therefore do not expand as predicted. Fiscal policy is either rendered totally ineffective or is severely weakened.

Although research continues on this theory, mainstream economists reject it as unrealistic and contrary to historical evidence. They point out that the large budget deficits of the 1980s were accompanied by *declines*—not increases—in the national saving rate.

Aggregate Supply and Inflation

Our discussion of complications and criticisms of fiscal policy has thus far been entirely demand-oriented. We now consider a supply-side complication. With an upsloping aggregate supply curve, some portion of the potential effect of an expansionary fiscal policy on real output and employment may be dissipated in the form of inflation. We stressed this idea in Figure 11-9.

Graphical Portrayal: Crowding Out and Inflation

Let's look at the impact of crowding out and inflation on fiscal policy through Figure 12-6. Suppose there

FIGURE 12-6   Fiscal policy: the effects of crowding-out, the net export effect, and inflation
With a simplified aggregate supply curve, we observe in (a) that fiscal policy is uncomplicated and works at full strength. In (b) it is assumed that some amount of private investment is crowded out by the expansionary fiscal policy so that fiscal policy is weakened. In (c) a more realistic aggregate supply curve reminds us that, when the economy is in the intermediate range of the aggregate supply curve, part of the impact of an expansionary fiscal policy will be reflected in inflation rather than in increases in real output and employment. In (d)—the same graph as (b)—we assume that fiscal policy increases the interest rate, which attracts foreign financial capital to the United States. The dollar therefore appreciates and our net exports fall, weakening the expansionary fiscal policy.

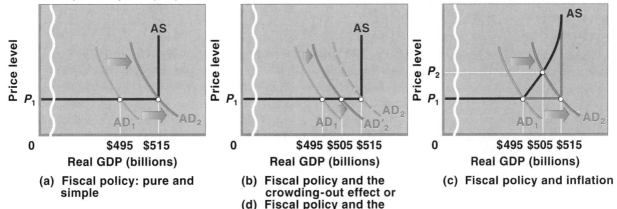

(a) **Fiscal policy: pure and simple**

(b) **Fiscal policy and the crowding-out effect or**
(d) **Fiscal policy and the net export effect**

(c) **Fiscal policy and inflation**

is a noninflationary absolute full-capacity level of real GDP at $515 billion, as shown in Figure 12-6a. For simplicity our aggregate supply curve here has no real-world intermediate range. Up to full capacity, the price level is constant. After the economy achieves full capacity the vertical range of AS prevails so that any further increase in aggregate demand would be purely inflationary.

We begin with aggregate demand at AD_1 which gives us a real output equilibrium at $495 billion. Assume now that government undertakes an expansionary fiscal policy which shifts the aggregate demand curve rightward by $20 billion to AD_2. The economy thus achieves absolute full-capacity output without inflation at $515 of GDP. We know from our previous discussion of discretionary fiscal policy (Figure 12-1) that an increase in government spending of $5 billion or a decrease in taxes of $6.67 billion would create this expansionary effect, assuming the economy's multiplier is 4. With no offsetting or complicating factors, this "pure and simple" expansionary fiscal policy moves the economy from recession to full-capacity output, greatly increasing employment.

In Figure 12-6b we complicate matters by adding the crowding-out effect. While fiscal policy is expansionary and designed to shift aggregate demand from AD_1 to AD_2, some investment may be crowded out so that aggregate demand ends up at AD_2'. Equilibrium GDP increases to only $505 billion rather than the desired $515 billion. *The crowding-out effect may weaken fiscal policy.*

In Figure 12-6c we switch to a more realistic aggregate supply curve which includes an intermediate range. We ignore the crowding-out effect so that the expansionary fiscal policy is successful in shifting aggregate demand from AD_1 to AD_2. If the aggregate supply curve was shaped as in Figure 12-6a and b, full employment would now be realized at $515 billion and the price level would remain at P_1. But we find that the upsloping intermediate range on the aggregate supply curve causes a part of the increase in aggregate demand to be dissipated in higher prices. The increase in real GDP is diminished. Specifically, the price level rises from P_1 to P_2 and real output increases to only $505 billion.

That is, the aggregate demand curve in Figure 12-6c shifts from AD_1 to AD_2, but the upsloping AS segment means we move upward along AD_2 from price level P_1 to P_2. In the real world, demand-side fiscal policy designed to achieve full employment does

not escape the realities imposed by the upsloping portion of the aggregate supply curve. *(Key Question 9)*

Fiscal Policy in the Open Economy

Additional complications arise when we recognize that our economy is a component of the world economy.

Shocks Originating from Abroad   Events and policies abroad that affect our net exports have an impact on our economy. Economies are susceptible to unforeseen international *aggregate demand shocks* which can alter domestic GDP and render domestic fiscal actions inappropriate.

Suppose we are incurring recession and have changed government expenditures and taxes to bolster aggregate demand and GDP without igniting inflation (as from AD_1 to AD_2 in Figure 12-6a). Now suppose the economies of our major trading partners unexpectedly and abruptly expand rapidly. Greater employment and rising incomes in those nations translate into more purchases of American goods. Our net exports rise, aggregate demand increases too rapidly, and we experience demand-pull inflation. Had we known in advance that our net exports would rise significantly, we would have enacted a less expansionary fiscal policy. The point is that our growing participation in the world economy brings with it the *complications* of mutual interdependence along with the *gains* from specialization and trade.

Net Export Effect   The **net export effect** may also work through international trade to reduce the effectiveness of fiscal policy. We concluded in our discussion of the crowding-out effect that an expansionary fiscal policy might boost interest rates, reducing *investment* and weakening fiscal policy. Now we want to know what effect an interest rate increase might have on our *net exports* (exports minus imports).

Suppose we undertake an expansionary fiscal policy which causes a higher interest rate. The higher interest rate will attract financial capital from abroad where interest rates are unchanged. But foreign financial investors must acquire U.S. dollars to invest in American securities. We know that an increase in the demand for a commodity—in this case dollars—will raise its price. So the price of dollars will rise in terms of foreign currencies; that is, the dollar will appreciate.

TABLE 12-1 Fiscal policy and the net export effect

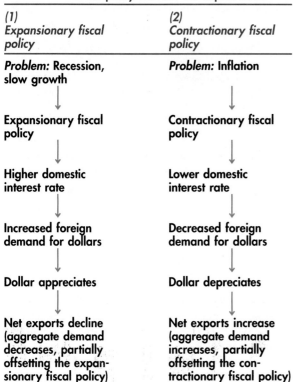

(1) Expansionary fiscal policy	(2) Contractionary fiscal policy
Problem: Recession, slow growth	**Problem:** Inflation
↓	↓
Expansionary fiscal policy	Contractionary fiscal policy
↓	↓
Higher domestic interest rate	Lower domestic interest rate
↓	↓
Increased foreign demand for dollars	Decreased foreign demand for dollars
↓	↓
Dollar appreciates	Dollar depreciates
↓	↓
Net exports decline (aggregate demand decreases, partially offsetting the expansionary fiscal policy)	Net exports increase (aggregate demand increases, partially offsetting the contractionary fiscal policy)

What will be the impact of this dollar appreciation on our net exports? Because more units of foreign currencies are needed to buy our goods, the rest of the world will see our exports as being more expensive. Hence, our exports will decline. Conversely, Americans, who can now exchange their dollars for more units of foreign currencies, will buy more imports. Consequently, with American exports falling and imports rising, net export expenditures in the United States will diminish and our expansionary fiscal policy will be partially negated.[3]

A return to our aggregate demand and supply analysis in Figure 12-6b, now labeled d, will clarify this point. An expansionary fiscal policy aimed at increasing aggregate demand from AD_1 to AD_2 may hike the domestic interest rate and ultimately reduce our net exports through the process just described.

The decline in the net export component of aggregate demand will partially offset the expansionary fiscal policy. The aggregate demand curve will shift rightward from AD_1 to AD'_2, *not* to AD_2, and equilibrium GDP will increase from $495 to $505, *not* to $515. Thus, the net export effect of fiscal policy joins the problems of timing, politics, crowding out, Ricardian effects, and inflation in complicating the "management" of aggregate demand.

Table 12-1 summarizes the net export effect resulting from fiscal policy. Column 1 reviews the analysis just discussed (Figure 12-6d). But note the net export effect works in both directions. By reducing the domestic interest rate, a *contractionary* fiscal policy *increases* net exports. In this regard, you should follow through the analysis in column 2 of Table 12-1 and relate it to the aggregate demand–aggregate supply model.

QUICK REVIEW 12-3

■ Time lags and political problems complicate fiscal policy.

■ The crowding-out effect indicates that an expansionary fiscal policy may increase the interest rate and reduce investment spending.

■ A few economists believe in the Ricardian equivalence theorem which says deficit spending creates expectations of future tax increases and therefore people privately save a dollar for each dollar of taxes they anticipate.

■ The upsloping range of the aggregate supply curve means that part of an expansionary fiscal policy may be dissipated in inflation.

■ Fiscal policy may be weakened by a net export effect which works through changes in *a* the interest rate, *b* the international value of the dollar, and *c* exports and imports.

Supply-Side Fiscal Policy

We have seen how movements along the aggregate supply curve can complicate the operation of fiscal policy. Let's now turn to the possibility of a more direct link between fiscal policy and aggregate supply. Economists recognize that fiscal policy—especially tax changes—*may* alter aggregate supply and affect the price level–real output outcomes of a change in fiscal policy.

[3]The appreciation of the dollar will also reduce the dollar price of foreign resources such as oil imported to the United States. As a result, aggregate supply will increase and part of the contractionary net export effect described here may be offset.

LAST WORD

THE LEADING INDICATORS

One tool policy makers use to forecast the future direction of real GDP is a monthly index of a group of variables which in the past has provided advance notice of changes in GDP.

"Index of Leading Indicators Falls for Third Month—Recession Feared"; "Index of Leading Indicators Surges Again"; "Decline in Stock Market Drags Down Index of Leading Indicators." Headlines such as these appear regularly in newspapers. The focus of these articles is the Commerce Department's weighted average—or composite index—of eleven economic variables which has historically reached its peak or trough in advance of the corresponding turns in the business cycle. Changes in the index of leading indicators thus provide a clue to the future direction of the economy and may therefore shorten the length of the "recognition lag" associated with the implementation of macroeconomic policy.

Let's examine the eleven components of the index of leading indicators in terms of a predicted *decline* in GDP, keeping in mind that the opposite changes forecast a *rise* in GDP.

1 Average Workweek Decreases in the length of the average workweek of production workers in manufacturing foretell declines in future manufacturing output and GDP.

2 Initial Claims for Unemployment Insurance Higher first-time claims for unemployment insurance are as-

sociated with falling employment and subsequently sagging production.

3 New Orders for Consumer Goods A slump in the number of orders received by manufacturers for consumer goods portends reduced future production—a decline in GDP.

4 Stock Market Prices Declines in stock prices often are reflections of expected declines in corporate sales and profits. Furthermore, lower stock prices diminish consumer wealth, leading consumers to cut back on their spending. Lower stock market values also make it less attractive for firms to issue new shares of stock as a way to raise funds for investment. Hence, declines in stock prices can bring forth declines in aggregate demand and GDP.

Suppose in Figure 12-7 that aggregate demand and aggregate supply are AD_1 and AS_1 so that the equilibrium level of real GDP is Q_1 and the price level is P_1. Assume further that government concludes the level of unemployment associated with Q_1 is too high and thus invokes an expansionary fiscal policy in the form of a tax cut. The demand-side effect is to increase aggregate demand from AD_1 to, say, AD_2. This shift increases real GDP to Q_2, but also boosts the price level to P_2.

How might tax cuts affect aggregate supply? Some economists—labeled "supply-side" economists—feel that tax reductions will shift the aggregate supply curve to the right.

1 Saving and Investment Lower taxes will increase disposable incomes, increasing household saving. Similarly, tax reductions on businesses will increase the profitability of investment. In brief, lower taxes will increase saving and investment, increasing the rate of capital accumulation. The size of our "national factory"—our productive capacity—will grow more rapidly.

2 Work Incentives Lower personal income tax rates also increase after-tax wages—the price paid for work—and stimulate work incentives. Many people not already in the labor force will offer their services because after-tax wages are higher. Those already in

5 Contracts and Orders for New Plant and Equipment
A drop in orders for capital equipment and other investment goods implies reduced future aggregate demand and domestic output.

6 Building Permits for Houses Decreases in the number of building permits taken out for new homes augur future declines in investment and therefore the distinct possibility that GDP will fall.

7 Vendor Performance Somewhat ironically, better performance by sellers of inputs in supplying buyers in a timely fashion indicates slackening business demand and potentially falling GDP.

8 Change in Unfilled Orders of Durable Goods Decreases in the dollar amounts of unfilled orders of durable manufactured goods imply falling aggregate demand and therefore ensuing declines in GDP.

9 Change in Sensitive Raw Material Prices Declines in certain sensitive raw material prices often precede declines in domestic output.

10 The Money Supply Decreases in the money supply are associated with falling GDP. (The components of the money supply and its role in the macro economy are the subjects of Chapters 13 through 16.)

11 Index of Consumer Expectations Declines in consumer confidence indicated by this index compiled by the University of Michigan's Survey Research Center foreshadow curtailed consumption expenditures and eventual declines in domestic output.

None of these factors *alone* consistently predicts the future course of the economy. It is not unusual in any month, for example, for one or two of the indicators to be decreasing while the other indicators are increasing. Rather, changes in the *weighted average*—or composite index—of the eleven components are what in the past have provided advance notice of a change in the direction of GDP. The rule of thumb is that three successive monthly declines or increases in the index indicate the economy will soon turn in that same direction.

Although the composite index has correctly signaled business fluctuations on numerous occasions, it has not been infallible. At times the index has provided false warnings of recessions which never happened. In other instances, recessions have so closely followed the downturn in the index that policy makers have not had sufficient time to make use of the "early" warning. Moreover, changing structural features of the economy on occasion have rendered the existing index obsolete and have necessitated its revision.

Given these caveats, the index of leading indicators can best be thought of as a useful but not totally reliable signaling device which authorities must employ with considerable caution in formulating macroeconomic policy.

---

the labor force will want to work more hours and take fewer vacations.

3 Risk Taking Lower tax rates prod risk takers. Individuals and businesses will be more willing to risk their energies and financial capital on new production

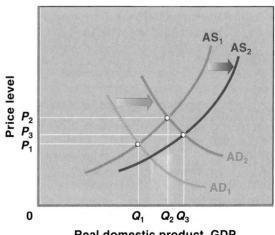

FIGURE 12-7 Supply-side effects of fiscal policy
The traditional view is that tax cuts will increase aggregate demand as from AD_1 to AD_2, increasing both real domestic output (Q_1 to Q_2) and the price level (P_1 to P_2). If the tax reductions induce favorable supply-side effects, aggregate supply will shift rightward as from AS_1 to AS_2. This allows the economy to realize an even larger output (Q_3 compared to Q_2) and a smaller price level increase (P_3 compared to P_2).

methods and new products when lower tax rates promise a larger potential after-tax reward.

Through all these avenues, lower taxes will shift aggregate supply to the right as from AS_1 to AS_2 in Figure 12-7, reducing inflation and further increasing real GDP.

Supply-siders also contend that lower tax *rates* need not result in lower tax *revenues*. In fact, lower tax rates that cause a substantial expansion of output and income may generate increases in tax revenues. This enlarged tax base may enhance total tax revenues even though tax rates are lower. While the mainstream view is that a reduction in tax rates will reduce tax revenues and increase budget deficits, the supply-side view is that tax rate reductions can be structured to increase tax revenues and reduce deficits.

Mainstream Skepticism Most economists are skeptical concerning the supply-side effects of tax cuts, particularly in view of the evidence from the supply-side tax cuts of the 1980s. First, these critics feel the hoped-for positive effects of a tax reduction on incentives to work, save and invest, and bear risks are not nearly as strong as supply-siders believe. Second, any rightward shifts of the aggregate supply curve will occur over an extended period of time, while the demand-side impact will be more immediate.

CHAPTER SUMMARY

1 Government responsibility for achieving and maintaining full employment is specified in the Employment Act of 1946. The Council of Economic Advisers (CEA) was established to advise the President on policies to fulfill the goals of the act.

2 Increases in government spending expand, and decreases contract, aggregate demand and equilibrium GDP. Increases in taxes reduce, and decreases expand, aggregate demand and equilibrium GDP. Fiscal policy therefore calls for increases in government spending and decreases in taxes—a budget deficit—to correct for recession. Decreases in government spending and increases in taxes— a budget surplus—are appropriate fiscal policy for correcting demand-pull inflation.

3 Built-in stability refers to net tax revenues that vary directly with the level of GDP. During a recession, the public budget automatically moves toward a stabilizing deficit; during expansion, the budget automatically moves toward an anti-inflationary surplus. Built-in stability lessens, but does not correct, undesired changes in the GDP.

4 The full-employment budget or structural budget measures what the Federal budgetary surplus or deficit would be *if* the economy operated at full employment throughout the year. The full-employment budget is a meaningful indicator of the government's fiscal posture, while its actual budgetary surplus or deficit is not.

5 The enactment and application of appropriate fiscal policy are subject to certain problems and questions. The important ones are: **a** Can the enactment and application of fiscal policy be better timed to maximize its effectiveness in heading off economic fluctuations? **b** Can the economy rely on Congress to enact appropriate fiscal policy? **c** An expansionary fiscal policy may be weakened if it crowds out some private investment spending. **d** Do people increase their saving in anticipation of the future higher taxes they think deficit spending will entail? **e** Some of the effect of an expansionary fiscal policy may be dissipated in inflation. **f** Fiscal policy may be rendered ineffective or inappropriate by unforeseen events occurring within the world economy. Also, fiscal policy may precipitate changes in exchange rates which weaken its effects. **g** Supply-side economists contend that traditional fiscal policy fails to consider the effects of tax changes on aggregate supply.

TERMS AND CONCEPTS

Employment Act of
  1946
Council of Economic
  Advisers
discretionary fiscal
  policy
expansionary fiscal
  policy

budget deficit
contractionary fiscal
  policy
progressive,
  proportional, and
  regressive tax
  systems

budget surplus
built-in stabilizer
actual budget
cyclical deficit
full-employment
  budget
structural deficit

political business cycle
crowding-out effect
Ricardian equivalence
  theorem
net export effect

QUESTIONS AND STUDY SUGGESTIONS

1 What is the central thrust of the Employment Act of 1946? What is the role of the Council of Economic Advisers (CEA) in responding to this law? Class assignment: Determine the names and educational backgrounds of the present members of the CEA.

2 *Key Question* Assume that a hypothetical economy with an MPC of .8 is experiencing severe recession. By how much would government spending have to increase to shift the aggregate demand curve rightward by $25 billion? How large a tax cut would be needed to achieve this same increase in aggregate demand? Why the difference? Determine one possible combination of government spending increases and tax decreases which would accomplish this same goal.

3 *Key Question* What are government's fiscal policy options for ending severe demand-pull inflation? Use the aggregate demand–aggregate supply model to show the impact of these policies on the price level. Which of these fiscal policy options do you think a "conservative" economist might favor? A "liberal" economist?

4 (For students assigned Chapters 9 and 10) Use the aggregate expenditures model to show how government fiscal policy could eliminate either a recessionary gap or an inflationary gap (Figure 10-8). Use the concept of the balanced budget multiplier to explain how equal increases in *G* and *T* could eliminate a recessionary gap and how equal decreases in *G* and *T* could eliminate an inflationary gap.

5 Designate each statement *true* or *false* and justify your answer.

   a Expansionary fiscal policy during a depression will have a greater positive effect on real GDP if government borrows the money to finance the budget deficit than if it creates new money to finance the deficit.

   b Contractionary fiscal policy during severe demand-pull inflation will be more effective if government impounds the budget surplus rather than using the surplus to pay off some of its past debt.

6 Explain how built-in (or automatic) stabilizers work. What are the differences between a proportional, progressive, and regressive tax system as they relate to an economy's built-in stability?

7 *Key Question* Define the "full-employment budget" and explain its significance. How does it differ from the "actual budget"? What is the difference between a structural deficit and a cyclical deficit? Suppose the economy depicted in Figure 12-4 is operating at its full-employment, noninflationary level of real output, GDP$_f$. What is the size of its structural deficit? Its cyclical deficit? Should government raise taxes or reduce government spending to eliminate this structural deficit? What are the risks of so doing?

8 The actual budget deficit increased significantly in 1990 and 1991, but the full-employment budget deficit remained relatively constant. Can you think of a logical explanation?

9 *Key Question* Briefly state and evaluate the problem of time lags in enacting and applying fiscal policy. Explain the notion of a political business cycle. What is the crowding-out effect and why is it relevant to fiscal policy? In what respect is the net export effect similar to the crowding-out effect? Do you think people increase their saving in anticipation of the future higher taxes they believe will follow government's use of expansionary fiscal policy?

10 In view of your answers to question 9, explain the following statement: "While fiscal policy clearly is useful in combating the extremes of severe recession and demand-pull inflation, it is impossible to use fiscal policy to 'fine-tune' the economy to the full-employment, noninflationary level of real GDP and keep the economy there indefinitely."

11 Discuss: "Mainstream economists tend to focus on the aggregate demand effects of tax-rate reductions; supply-side economists emphasize the aggregate supply effects." What are the routes through which a tax cut might increase aggregate supply? If tax cuts are so good for the economy, why don't we cut taxes to zero?

12 Using Figure 12-3 as a basis for your response, explain the stabilizing or destabilizing impacts of fiscal policy if a constitutional amendment requiring an annually balanced budget were passed.

13 Use Figure 12-4 to explain why a deliberate increase in the full-employment or structural deficit which causes the economy to expand from GDP$_r$ to GDP$_f$ might reduce the size of the actual deficit. In requesting a tax cut in the early 1960s, President Kennedy said, "It is a paradoxical truth that tax rates are too high today and tax revenues are too low and the soundest way to raise tax revenues in the long run is to cut tax rates now." Relate this quotation to your previous answer.

14 **Advanced analysis:** (For students assigned Chapters 9 and 10) Assume that, without taxes, the consumption schedule for an economy is as shown below:

GDP, billions	Consumption, billions
$100	$120
200	200
300	280
400	360
500	440
600	520
700	600

holds and businesses and use these financial resources to make available a wide variety of loans. Commercial bank loans provide short-term working capital to businesses and farmers, finance consumer purchases of automobiles and other durable goods, and so on.

2 Thrift Institutions The commercial banks are supplemented by other financial institutions—savings and loan associations (S&Ls), mutual savings banks, and credit unions—collectively designated as **thrift** or **savings institutions** or simply, "thrifts." **Savings and loan associations** and **mutual savings banks** marshal the savings of households and businesses which are then used, among other things, to finance housing mortgages. **Credit unions** accept the deposits of "members"—usually a group of individuals who work for the same company—and lend these funds to finance installment purchases.

The checkable deposits of banks and thrifts are known by various names—demand deposits, NOW (negotiable order of withdrawal) accounts, ATS (automatic transfer service) accounts, and share draft accounts. Nevertheless, they are all similar in that depositors can write checks on them whenever, and in whatever amount, they choose.

Qualification We must qualify our definition of money: Currency and checkable deposits owned by government (the Treasury) and by the Federal Reserve Banks, commercial banks, or other financial institutions are excluded from $M1$ and other money measures.

A paper dollar in the hands of Sally Sorenson obviously constitutes just $1 of the money supply. But, if we counted dollars held by banks as part of the money supply, the same $1 would count for $2 when deposited in a bank. It would count for a $1 demand deposit owned by Sorenson and also for $1 of currency resting in the bank's vault. This problem of double counting is avoided by excluding currency resting in banks (and currency redeposited in the Federal Reserve Banks or other commercial banks) in determining the total money supply.

Excluding currency held by, and demand deposits owned by, government is somewhat more arbitrary. This exclusion permits us better to gauge the money supply and rate of spending in the private sector of the economy apart from spending initiated by government policy.

Near-Monies: M2 and M3

Near-monies are certain highly liquid financial assets such as noncheckable savings accounts, time deposits, and short-term government securities. Although they do not directly function as a medium of exchange, they can be readily and without risk of financial loss converted into currency or checkable deposits. Thus, on demand you may withdraw currency from a **noncheckable savings account** at a commercial bank or thrift institution. Or, you may request that funds be transferred from a noncheckable savings account to a checkable account.

You can withdraw funds quickly from a **money market deposit account (MMDA).** These are interest-bearing accounts offered by banks and thrifts, which pool individual deposits to buy a variety of short-term securities. MMDAs have minimum balance requirements and limit how often money can be withdrawn.

As the term implies, **time deposits** only become available to a depositor at maturity. For example, a 90-day or 6-month time deposit is only available without penalty when the designated period expires. Although time deposits are somewhat less liquid than noncheckable savings accounts, they can be taken as currency or shifted into checkable accounts when they mature.

Or, through a telephone call, you can redeem shares in a **money market mutual fund (MMMF)** offered through a financial investment company. These companies use the combined funds of individual shareholders to buy short-term credit instruments such as certificates of deposit and U.S. government securities.

Money Definition M2 Thus our monetary authorities offer a second and broader definition of money:

$$\text{Money, } M2 = \begin{array}{l} M1 + \text{noncheckable savings} \\ \text{deposits} + \text{MMDAs} + \text{small} \\ \text{(less than \$100,000) time deposits} \\ + \text{MMMFs} \end{array}$$

In other words, **M2** includes (1) the medium of exchange items (currency and checkable deposits) comprising $M1$ *plus* (2) other items such as noncheckable savings deposits, money market deposit accounts, small time deposits, and individual money market mutual fund balances. These other items can be quickly and without loss converted into currency and checkable deposits. Table 13-1 shows that the addition of noncheckable savings deposits, MMDAs, small time deposits, and MMMFs yields an $M2$ money supply of $3595 billion compared to the narrower $M1$ money supply of $1152 billion.

Money Definition M3   A third "official" definition, **M3,** recognizes that large ($100,000 or more) time deposits—usually owned by businesses as certificates of deposit—are also easily convertible into checkable deposits. There is a market for these certificates and they can be sold (liquidated) at any time, although perhaps at the risk of a loss. Adding these large time deposits to $M2$ yields a still broader definition of money:

$$\text{Money, } M3 = \frac{M2 + \text{large (\$100,000 or}}{\text{more) time deposits}}$$

Consulting Table 13-1 again, we find the $M3$ money supply is $4247 billion.

There are still other slightly less liquid assets such as certain government securities (for example, Treasury bills and U.S. savings bonds) which can be easily converted into $M1$ money. A whole spectrum of assets exists which vary slightly from one another in terms of their liquidity or "moneyness."

Which definition of money shall we use? The simple $M1$ definition includes only items *directly* and *immediately* usable as a medium of exchange. For this reason it is an often-cited statistic in discussions of the money supply. However, for some purposes economists prefer the broader $M2$ definition. For example, $M2$ is used as one of the eleven trend variables in the index of leading indicators (Last Word, Chapter 12). And what of $M3$ and still broader definitions of money? These definitions are so inclusive that many economists question their usefulness.

We will use the narrow $M1$ definition of money in our discussion and analysis, unless stated otherwise. The important principles applying to $M1$ are also applicable to $M2$ and $M3$ because $M1$ is a base component in these broader measures.

Near Monies: Implications

Near-monies are important for several related reasons.

1   Spending Habits   These highly liquid assets affect people's consuming-saving habits. Usually, the

greater the amount of financial wealth people hold as near-monies, the greater is their willingness to spend out of their money incomes.

2   Stability   Conversion of near-monies into money or vice versa can affect the economy's stability. For example, during the prosperity-inflationary phase of the business cycle, converting noncheckable deposits into checkable deposits or currency adds to the money supply which could increase inflation. Such conversions can complicate the task of the monetary authorities in controlling the money supply and the level of economic activity.

3   Policy   The specific definition of money used is important for monetary policy. For example, the money supply as measured by $M1$ might be constant, while money defined as $M2$ might be increasing. If the monetary authorities feel it is appropriate to have an expanding supply of money, the narrow $M1$ definition would call for specific actions to increase currency and checkable deposits. But the broader $M2$ definition would suggest that the desired expansion of the money supply is already taking place and that no specific policy action is required. *(Key Question 5)*

Credit Cards

You may wonder why we have ignored credit cards —Visa, MasterCard, American Express, Discover, and so forth—in our discussion of how money is defined. After all, credit cards are a convenient means of making purchases. The answer is that credit cards are *not* really money, but rather a means of obtaining a short-term loan from the commercial bank or other financial institution which has issued the card.

When you purchase a sweatshirt with a credit card, the issuing bank will reimburse the store. Later, you reimburse the bank. You pay an annual fee for the services provided and, if you repay the bank in installments, you pay a sizable interest charge. Credit cards are merely a means of deferring or postponing payment for a short period. Your purchase of the sweatshirt is not complete until you have paid your credit-card bill.

However, credit cards—and all other forms of credit—allow individuals and businesses to "economize" in the use of money. Credit cards permit you to have less currency and checkable deposits on hand for transactions. Credit cards help you synchronize your expenditures and your receipt of income, reducing the cash and checkable deposits you must hold.

WHAT "BACKS" THE MONEY SUPPLY?

This is a slippery question. Any complete answer is likely to be at odds with preconceptions about money.

Money as Debt

The major components of the money supply—paper money and checkable deposits—are debts, or promises to pay. *Paper money is the circulating debt of the Federal Reserve Banks. Checkable deposits are the debts of commercial banks and thrift institutions.*

Paper currency and checkable deposits have no intrinsic value. A $5 bill is just a piece of paper. A checkable deposit is merely a bookkeeping entry. And coins, we know, have less intrinsic value than their face value. Nor will government redeem the paper money you hold for anything tangible, such as gold. In effect, we have chosen to "manage" our money supply. The monetary authorities attempt to provide the amount of money needed for that particular volume of business activity which will foster full employment, price level stability, and a healthy rate of economic growth.

Most economists feel that managing the money supply is more sensible than linking it to gold or any other commodity whose supply might arbitrarily and capriciously change. A large increase in the nation's gold stock as the result of new gold discovery might increase the money supply far beyond the amount needed to transact a full-employment level of business activity. Therefore rapid inflation might occur. Or, the historical decline in domestic gold production could reduce the domestic money supply to the point where economic activity was choked off and unemployment and a retarded growth rate resulted.

The point is that paper money cannot be converted into a fixed amount of gold or some other precious metal but is exchangeable only for other pieces of paper money. The government will swap one paper $5 bill for another bearing a different serial number. That is all you can get if you ask the government to redeem some of your paper money. Similarly, check money cannot be exchanged for gold but only for paper money, which, as we have just seen, will not be redeemed by the government for anything tangible.

Value of Money

If currency and checkable deposits have no intrinsic characteristics giving them value *and* if they are not backed by gold or other precious metals, then why are they money? What gives a $20 bill or a $100 checking account entry its value? A reasonably complete answer to these questions involves three points.

1   Acceptability   Currency and checkable deposits are money because they are accepted as money. By virtue of long-standing business practice, currency and checkable deposits perform the basic function of money; they are acceptable as a medium of exchange. Suppose you swap a $20 bill for a shirt or blouse at a clothing store. Why does the merchant accept this piece of paper in exchange for that product? The merchant accepts paper money because he or she is confident that others will also accept it in exchange for goods and services. The merchant knows that paper money can purchase the services of clerks, acquire products from wholesalers, and pay the rent on the store. We accept paper money in exchange because we are confident it will be exchangeable for real goods and services when we spend it.

2   Legal Tender   Our confidence in the acceptability of paper money is partly a matter of law; currency has been designated as **legal tender** by government. This means paper currency must be accepted in the payment of a debt or the creditor forfeits both the privilege of charging interest and the right to sue the debtor for nonpayment. Put bluntly, paper dollars are accepted as money because government says they are money. The paper money in our economy is **fiat money;** it is money because the government says it is, not because it can be redeemed for precious metal. The general acceptability of currency is also enhanced by the willingness of government to accept it in the payment of taxes and other obligations due the government.

Don't be overimpressed by the power of government. Paper currency's general acceptance in exchange is more important than government's legal tender decree in making these pieces of paper work as money. The government has *not* decreed checks to be legal tender, but they successfully perform the vast bulk of the economy's exchanges of goods, services, and resources. It's true, though, that a governmental agency—the Federal Deposit Insurance Corporation (FDIC)—insures the deposits of commercial banks and S&Ls, undoubtedly contributing to the willingness of individuals and businesses to use checkable deposits as a medium of exchange.

3   Relative Scarcity   The value of money, like the economic value of anything else, is a supply and demand phenomenon. Money derives its value from its scarcity relative to its utility (want-satisfying power). The utility of money lies in its unique capacity to be exchanged for goods and services, now or in the future. The economy's demand for money thus depends on its total dollar volume of transactions in any period plus the amount of money individuals and businesses want to hold for possible future transactions. With a reasonable constant demand for money, the supply of money will determine the value or "purchasing power" of the monetary unit.

Money and Prices

The real value or purchasing power of money is the amount of goods and services a unit of money will buy. When money rapidly loses its purchasing power, it rapidly loses its role as money.

Value of the Dollar   The amount a dollar will buy varies inversely with the price level; *a reciprocal relationship exists between the general price level and the value of the dollar.* Figure 13-1 shows this inverse relationship. When the consumer price index or "cost-of-living" index goes up, the purchasing power of the dollar goes down, and vice versa. Higher prices lower the value of the dollar because more dollars will be needed to buy a particular amount of goods and services.

133-35

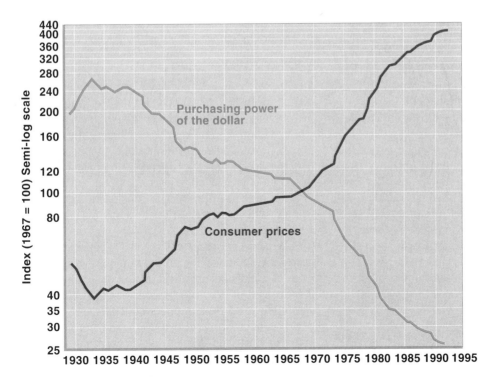

FIGURE 13-1   The price level and the value of money
A reciprocal or inverse relationship exists between the general price level and the purchasing power of the dollar. (This figure is called a "ratio" or "semilog chart" because equal vertical distances measure equal percentage changes rather than equal absolute changes.)

Lower prices increase the purchasing power of the dollar because you will need fewer dollars to obtain a specific quantity of goods and services. If the price level doubles, the value of the dollar will decline by one-half, or 50 percent. If the price level falls by one-half, or 50 percent, the purchasing power of the dollar will double.

If we let P equal the price level expressed as an index number (in hundredths) and D equal the value of the dollar, then the reciprocal relationship between them is

$$D = \frac{1}{P}$$

If the price level P equals 1.00, then the value of the dollar D is 1.00. But, if P rises from 1.00 to 1.20, D will be 0.833, meaning a 20 percent increase in the price level will reduce the value of the dollar by 16.67 percent. Check your understanding of this reciprocal relationship by determining the value of D and its percentage rise when P falls by 20 percent to 0.80. *(Key Question 7)*

Inflation and Acceptability   We saw in Chapter 8 situations in which a nation's currency became worthless and unacceptable in exchange. These were circumstances where government issued so many pieces of paper currency that the value of each of these units of money was almost totally undermined. The infamous post-World War I inflation in Germany is an example. In December of 1919 there were about 50 billion marks in circulation. Four years later this figure had expanded to 496,585,345,900 billion marks! The result? The German mark in 1923 was worth an infinitesimal fraction of its 1919 value.[3]

How might inflation and the accompanying decreases in the value of a nation's currency affect the acceptability of paper currency as money? Households and businesses will accept paper currency as a medium of exchange so long as they know they can spend it without any noticeable loss in its purchasing power. But, with spiraling inflation, this is not the case. Runaway inflation, such as in Germany in the early 1920s and in several Latin-American nations in the 1980s, may significantly depreciate the value of money between the time of its receipt and its expenditure. Money will be "hot" money. It is as if the government

were constantly taxing away the purchasing power of its currency. Rapid depreciation of the value of a currency may cause it to cease functioning as a medium of exchange. Businesses and households may refuse to accept paper money in exchange because they do not want to bear the loss in its value which will occur while it is in their possession. (All this despite the fact that government says the paper currency is legal tender!) Without an acceptable domestically provided medium of exchange, the economy may try to substitute a more stable currency from another nation. Example: Many transactions in Russia and South America now occur in dollars rather than highly unstable rubles or pesos (see Last Word). At the extreme, the economy may simply revert to inefficient barter.

Similarly, people will use money as a store of value so long as there is no sizable deterioration in the value of those stored dollars because of inflation. And the economy can effectively employ the monetary unit as a measure of value only when its purchasing power is relatively stable. A yardstick of value subject to drastic shrinkage no longer permits buyers and sellers to establish the terms of trade clearly. When the value of the dollar is declining rapidly, sellers will not know what to charge and buyers will not know what to pay for goods and services.

Maintaining Money's Value

What "backs" paper money is the government's ability to keep the value of money reasonably stable. Stability entails (1) appropriate fiscal policy, as explained in Chapter 12 and (2) intelligent management or regulation of the money supply, as just explained. Businesses and households accept paper money in exchange for goods and services so long as they expect it to command a roughly equivalent amount of goods and services when they spend it. In our economy a blending of legislation, government policy, and social practice inhibit imprudent expansion of the money supply which might seriously jeopardize money's value in exchange.

What we have said with respect to paper currency also applies to checking account money—the debt of commercial banks and thrift institutions. Your checking account of $200 means your bank or thrift is indebted to you for that number of dollars. You can collect this debt in one of two ways. You can go to the bank or thrift and demand paper currency for your checkable deposit; this amounts to changing the debts

---

[3]Frank G. Graham, *Exchange, Prices and Production in Hyperinflation Germany, 1920–1923* (Princeton, N.J.: Princeton University Press, 1930), p. 13.

you hold from the debts of a bank or thrift to government-issued debts. Or, and this is more likely, you can "collect" the debt which the bank or savings institution owes you by transferring this claim by check to someone else.

For example, if you buy a $200 coat from a store, you can pay for it by writing a check, which transfers your bank's indebtedness from you to the store. Your bank now owes the store the $200 it previously owed to you. The store accepts this transfer of indebtedness (the check) as a medium of exchange because it can convert it into currency on demand or can transfer the debt to others in making purchases of its choice. Thus, checks, as means of transferring the debts of banks and thrifts, are acceptable as money because we know banks and thrifts will honor these claims.

The ability of banks and thrifts to honor claims against them depends on their not creating too many of these claims. We will see that a decentralized system of private, profit-seeking banks does not contain sufficient safeguards against the creation of too much check money. Thus, the American banking and financial system has substantial centralization and governmental control to guard against the imprudent creation of checkable deposits.

Caution: This does not mean that in practice the monetary authorities have always judiciously controlled the supplies of currency and checkable-deposit money to achieve economic stability. Indeed, many economists allege that most of the inflationary woes we have encountered historically are the consequence of imprudent increases in the money supply.

QUICK REVIEW 13-2

■ In the United States and other advanced economies, all money is essentially the debts of government, commercial banks, and thrift institutions.

■ These debts efficiently perform the functions of money so long as their value, or purchasing power, is relatively stable.

■ The value of money is not rooted in carefully defined quantities of precious metals (as in the past), but rather, in the amount of goods and services money will purchase in the marketplace.

■ Government's responsibility in stabilizing the value of the monetary unit involves (1) the application of appropriate fiscal policies, and (2) effective control over the supply of money.

THE DEMAND FOR MONEY

Now that we know what constitutes the supply of money and how the money supply is "backed," let's turn to the demand for money. There are two reasons why the public wants to hold money.

Transactions Demand, D_t

People want money as a medium of exchange to conveniently negotiate the purchase of goods and services. Households must have enough money on hand to buy groceries and pay mortgage and utility bills until the next paycheck. Businesses need money to pay for labor, materials, power, and so on. Money demanded for all such purposes is called the **transactions demand** for money.

The basic determinant of the amount of money demanded for transaction purposes is the level of nominal GDP. The larger the total money value of all goods and services exchanged in the economy, the larger will be the amount of money needed to negotiate these transactions. *The transactions demand for money varies directly with nominal GDP.* We specify *nominal* GDP because households and firms will want more money for transactions purposes if *either* prices rise *or* real output increases. In both instances there will be a larger dollar volume of transactions to accomplish.

In Figure 13-2a (Key Graph) we show the relationship between the transactions demand for money, D_t, and the interest rate. Because the transactions demand for money depends on the level of nominal GDP and is independent of the interest rate, we draw the transactions demand as a vertical line. For simplicity we assume the amount of money demanded for transactions is unrelated to changes in the interest rate. That is, higher interest rates will not reduce the amount of money demanded for transactions.[4]

The transactions demand is at $100 billion arbitrarily, but a rationale can be provided. For example, if each dollar held for transactions purposes is spent on the average three times per year *and* nominal GDP is assumed to be $300 billion, then the public would need $100 billion of money to purchase that GDP.

---

[4]This is a simplification. We would also expect the amount of money held by businesses and households to negotiate transactions to vary inversely with the interest rate. When interest rates are high, consumers and businesses will try to reduce the amount of money held for transactions purposes to have more funds to put into interest-earning assets.

KEY GRAPH

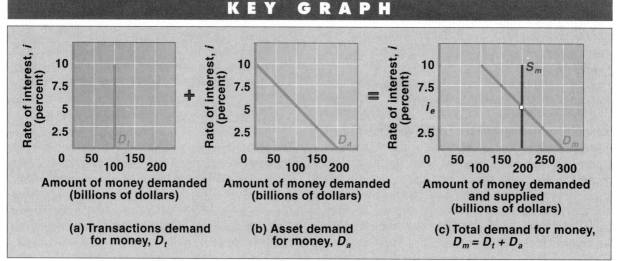

(a) Transactions demand for money, D_t

(b) Asset demand for money, D_a

(c) Total demand for money, $D_m = D_t + D_a$

FIGURE 13-2 The demand for money and the money market
The total demand for money, D_m, is determined by horizontally adding the asset demand for money, D_a, to the transactions demand, D_t. The transactions demand is vertical because it is assumed to depend on nominal GDP rather than the interest rate. The asset demand varies inversely with the interest rate because of the opportunity cost involved in holding currency and checkable deposits which do not pay interest. Combining the money supply (stock), S_m, with total money demand, D_m, portrays the money market and determines the equilibrium interest rate, i_e.

Asset Demand, D_a

The second reason for holding money is rooted in money's function as a store of value. People may hold their financial assets in many forms—as corporate stocks, private or government bonds, or as $M1$ money. Thus, there is an **asset demand** for money.

What determines the asset demand for money? First, we must recognize that each of the various forms of holding our financial assets has advantages and disadvantages. To simplify, let's compare holding bonds with holding money as an asset. The advantages of holding money are its liquidity and lack of risk. Money is the most liquid of all assets; it is immediately usable in making purchases. Money is an attractive asset to be holding when the prices of goods, services, and other financial assets are expected to decline. When the price of a bond falls, the bondholder will suffer a loss if the bond must be sold before maturity. There is no such risk with holding money.

The disadvantage of holding money as an asset is that, compared to holding bonds, it does *not* earn interest income or, in the case of an interest-bearing

checking account, earn as much interest income as on bonds or noncheckable deposits. And idle currency earns no interest at all. Some banks and thrifts require minimum-sized checkable deposits for the depositor to be paid interest; hence, many depositors do not achieve these minimum deposit balances and therefore earn no interest. The interest paid on checkable deposits which exceed the required minimums is less than that paid on bonds and the various noncheckable deposits.

Knowing this, the problem is deciding how much of your financial assets to hold as, say, bonds and how much as money. The solution depends primarily on the rate of interest. A household or business incurs an opportunity cost when holding money (Chapter 2); interest income is forgone or sacrificed. If a bond pays 10 percent interest, then it costs $10 per year of forgone income to hold $100 as cash or in a noninterest checkable account.

It is no surprise that *the asset demand for money varies inversely with the rate of interest.* When the interest rate or opportunity cost of holding money as an asset is low, the public will choose to hold a large amount of money as assets. When the interest rate is high, it is costly to "be liquid" and the amount of assets held in the form of money will be small. When it is expensive to hold money as an asset, people will hold less of it; when money can be held cheaply, people will hold more of it. This inverse relationship between the interest rate and the amount of money people will want to hold as an asset is shown by D_a in Figure 13-2b.

Total Money Demand, D_m

As shown in Figure 13-2c, the **total demand** for money, D_m, is found by adding the asset demand horizontally to the transactions demand. (The vertical line in Figure 13-2a represents the transactions demand to which Figure 13-2b's asset demand has been added.) The resulting downsloping line in Figure 13-2c represents the total amount of money the public will want to hold for transactions and as an asset at each possible interest rate.

Also note that a change in the nominal GDP— working through the transactions demand for money —will shift the total money demand curve. Specifically, an increase in nominal GDP will mean that the public will want to hold a larger amount of money for transactions purposes and this will shift the total money demand curve to the right. For example, if nominal GDP increases from $300 to $450 billion and we continue to suppose that the average dollar held for transactions is spent three times per year, then the transactions demand line will shift from $100 to $150 billion. Thus the total money demand curve will lie $50 billion further to the right at each possible interest rate. A decline in nominal GDP will shift the total money demand curve to the left.

THE MONEY MARKET

We can combine the demand for money with the supply of money to portray the **money market** and determine the equilibrium rate of interest. In Figure 13-2c we have drawn a vertical line, S_m, to represent the money supply. The money supply is shown as a vertical line because we assume our monetary authorities and financial institutions have provided the economy with some particular *stock* of money, such as the $M1$ total shown in Table 13-1. Just as in a product or resource market (Chapter 3), the intersection of money demand and money supply determines equilibrium price. The "price" in this case is the equilib-

rium interest rate, that is, the price paid for the use of money.

If disequilibrium existed in the money market, how would the money market achieve equilibrium? Consider Figure 13-3, which replicates Figure 13-2c and adds two alternative supply-of-money curves.

1   Shortage   Suppose the supply of money is reduced from $200 billion, S_m, to $150 billion, S_{m1}. Note the quantity of money demanded exceeds the quantity supplied by $50 billion at the previous equilibrium interest rate of 5 percent. People will attempt to make up for this shortage of money by selling some of the financial assets they own (we assume for simplicity that these assets are bonds). But one person's receipt of money through the sale of a bond is another person's loss of money through the purchase of that bond. Overall, there is only $150 billion of money available. The collective attempt to get more money by selling bonds will increase the supply of bonds relative to demand in the bond market and drive down bond prices.

FIGURE 13-3   Restoring equilibrium in the money market
A decrease in the supply of money creates a temporary shortage of money in the money market. People and institutions attempt to gain more money by selling bonds. The supply of bonds therefore increases, which reduces bond prices and raises interest rates. At higher interest rates, people reduce the amount of money they wish to hold. Thus, the amount of money supplied and demanded once again is equal at the higher interest rate. An increase in the supply of money creates a temporary surplus of money, resulting in an increase in the demand for bonds and higher bond prices. Interest rates fall and equilibrium is reestablished in the money market.

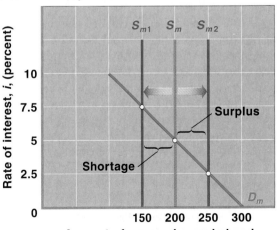

Generalization: *Lower bond prices are associated with higher interest rates* (Last Word, Chapter 5). To clarify this, suppose a bond with no expiration date pays a fixed $50 annual interest and is selling for its face value of $1000. The interest yield on this bond is 5 percent.

$$\frac{\$50}{\$1000} = 5\%$$

Now suppose the price of this bond falls to $667 because of the increased supply of bonds. The $50 fixed annual interest payment will now yield $7\frac{1}{2}$ percent to whomever buys the bond:

$$\frac{\$50}{\$667} = 7\frac{1}{2}\%$$

Because all borrowers must compete by offering to pay lenders interest yields similar to those available on bonds, a higher general interest rate emerges. In Figure 13-3 the interest rate rises from 5 percent at the money supply of $200 billion to $7\frac{1}{2}$ percent when the money supply is $150 billion. This higher interest rate raises the opportunity cost of holding money and reduces the amount of money firms and households want to hold. Specifically, the amount of money demanded declines from $200 billion at the 5 percent interest rate to $150 billion at the $7\frac{1}{2}$ percent interest rate. The money market is back into equilibrium: The quantity of money demanded and supplied are each $150 billion at the $7\frac{1}{2}$ percent interest rate.

2 Surplus An increase in the supply of money from $200 billion, S_m, to $250 billion, S_{m2}, will result in a surplus of $50 billion at the initial 5 percent interest rate. People will try to rid themselves of money by purchasing more bonds. But one person's expenditure of money is another person's receipt of money. The collective attempt to buy more bonds will increase the demand for bonds and pull bond prices upward.

Corollary: *Higher bond prices are associated with lower interest rates.* In terms of our example, the $50 interest payment on a bond now priced at, say, $2000, will yield a bond buyer only $2\frac{1}{2}$ percent:

$$\frac{\$50}{\$2000} = 2\frac{1}{2}\%$$

The point is that interest rates in general will fall as people unsuccessfully attempt to reduce their money holdings below $250 billion by buying bonds. In this case, the interest rate will fall to a new equilibrium at $2\frac{1}{2}$ percent. Because the opportunity cost of holding money now is lower—being liquid is less expensive—consumers and businesses will increase the amount of currency and checkable deposits they are willing to hold from $200 billion to $250 billion. Once again equilibrium in the money market is restored: The quantities of money demanded and supplied are each $250 billion at an interest rate of $2\frac{1}{2}$ percent.

In Chapter 15 we will discover how monetary policy attempts to change the money supply to alter the equilibrium real interest rate. A higher interest rate will reduce investment and consumption spending, decreasing aggregate demand. A lower rate will increase investment and consumption spending, increasing aggregate demand. Either situation ultimately affects the levels of real output, employment, and prices. *(Key Question 8)*

QUICK REVIEW 13-3

■ People hold money for transaction and asset purposes.

■ The total demand for money is the sum of the transaction and asset demands; it graphs as an inverse relationship between the interest rate and the quantity of money demanded.

■ The equilibrium interest rate is determined by money demand and supply; it occurs where people are willing to hold the exact amount of money being supplied by the monetary authorities.

■ Bond prices and interest rates are inversely related.

THE UNITED STATES FINANCIAL SYSTEM

In the past twenty-five years the American financial system has undergone sweeping changes and today the system remains in a state of flux. Early regulatory legislation rigidly defined the kind of business various financial institutions could conduct. For example, commercial banks provided checking accounts and made business and consumer loans. Savings and loan associations accepted savings deposits and provided these savings for mortgage lending. But a combination of competitive pressures, innovation, and deregulation in the recent past has expanded the functions of the various financial institutions and blurred the traditional distinctions between them.

The **Depository Institutions Deregulation and Monetary Control Act** (DIDMCA) of 1980 reduced or eliminated many of the historical distinctions between commercial banks and various thrift institutions. DIDMCA permitted all depository institutions to offer checkable deposits. But in extending the privilege of offering checkable deposits to the thrifts, DIDMCA requires in turn that the thrifts be subject to the same limitations on the creation of checkable deposits that apply to commercial banks. With these observations as an introduction, let's examine the framework of our financial system.

Centralization and Regulation

Although the trend has been toward deregulation of the financial system, considerable centralization and governmental control remain. This centralization and regulation has historical roots. It became painfully apparent rather early in American history that, like it or not, centralization and public control were essential for an efficient banking system.

Congress became increasingly aware of this about the turn of the twentieth century. Decentralized banking fostered the inconvenience and confusion of a heterogeneous currency, monetary mismanagement, and a money supply inappropriate to the needs of the economy. "Too much" money can precipitate dangerous inflationary problems; "too little" money can stunt the economy's growth by hindering the production and exchange of goods and services.

The United States and many foreign countries have learned through bitter experience that a decentralized, unregulated banking system is not likely to provide that particular money supply which is most conducive to the welfare of the economy as a whole.

An unusually acute money panic in 1907 was the straw that broke Congress's back. A National Monetary Commission was established to study the monetary and banking problems of the economy and to outline a course of action for Congress. The result was the Federal Reserve Act of 1913.

The Federal Reserve System

The monetary control system which has developed under the frequently amended Federal Reserve Act and DIDMCA is sketched in Figure 13-4. We must understand the nature and roles of the various segments which compose the banking system and the relationships the parts bear to one another.

Board of Governors   The kingpin of our money and banking system is the **Board of Governors** of the Federal Reserve System ("the Fed"). The seven members of this Board are appointed by the President with the confirmation of the Senate. Terms are long—fourteen years—and staggered so one member is replaced every two years. The intention is to provide the Board with continuity, experienced membership, and autonomy or independence. The Board is staffed by long-term appointment rather than elections as a way to divorce monetary policy from partisan politics.

The Board of Governors supervises and controls the operation of the money and banking system of the nation. The Board chairman is the most powerful central banker in the world. The Board's actions, which are to be in the public interest and designed to promote the general economic welfare, are made effective through certain monetary control techniques which alter the money supply.

Assistance and Advice   Several entities assist the Board of Governors in determining banking and monetary policy. The first is clearly the most important.
1   The **Federal Open Market Committee (FOMC),** made up of the Board plus five of the presidents of the Federal Reserve Banks, sets the System's policy on the purchase and sale of government securities (bills, notes, and bonds) in the open market. The open-market operations are the most significant technique available to the monetary authorities for affecting the money supply (Chapter 15).
2   Three **Advisory Councils** composed of private citizens meet periodically with the Board of Governors to voice their views on banking and monetary policy. The Federal Advisory Council comprises twelve commercial bankers, one selected annually by each of the twelve Federal Reserve Banks. The Thrift Institutions Advisory Council consists of representatives from S&Ls, savings banks, and credit unions. The third advisory group is the thirty-member Consumer Advisory Council, which includes representatives of consumers of financial services and academic and legal specialists in consumer matters. But, as their names indicate, the Councils are purely advisory. They have no policy-making powers and the Board has no obligation to heed their advice.

The Twelve Federal Reserve Banks   The twelve **Federal Reserve Banks** are (1) central banks, (2) quasi-public banks, and (3) bankers' banks.

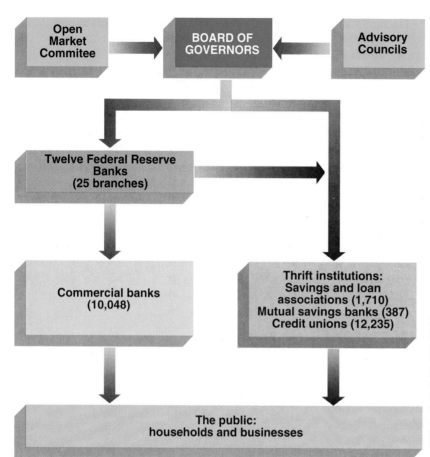

FIGURE 13-4 Framework of the Federal Reserve System and its relationship to the public
With the advice and counsel of the Open Market Committee and three Advisory Councils, the Board of Governors makes the basic policy decisions providing monetary control of our money and banking systems. These decisions are made effective through the twelve Federal Reserve Banks.

1 Central Banks Most nations have one central bank, for example, Britain's Bank of England or Germany's Bundesbank. The United States has twelve separate "central" banks, although their policies are coordinated by the Board of Governors. The twelve Federal Reserve Banks partly reflect our geographic size and economic diversity and the fact that we have a large number of commercial banks. They also are the result of a political compromise between proponents of centralization and advocates of decentralization.

Figure 13-5 locates the twelve Federal Reserve Banks and indicates the district each serves. Through these central banks the basic policy directives of the Board of Governors are made effective. The Federal Reserve Bank of New York City is the most important of these central banks; it's where Open Market Operations are centered (Chapter 15). The development of modern communication and transportation facilities has undoubtedly lessened the geographic need for a system of regional banks.

2 Quasi-Public Banks The twelve Federal Reserve Banks are quasi-governmental banks. They reflect a blend of private ownership and public control. The Federal Reserve Banks are owned by the member banks in their districts. Upon joining the Federal Reserve System, commercial banks are required to purchase shares of stock in the Federal Reserve Bank in their district. But the basic policies which the Federal Reserve Banks pursue are set by a governmental body—the Board of Governors. The central banks of American capitalism are privately owned but governmentally controlled. And the owners control neither the officials of the central banks nor their policies.

To understand Federal Reserve Banks you need to realize they are essentially public institutions. In particular, the Federal Reserve Banks are *not* motivated by profits, as are private enterprises. The policies followed by the central banks are perceived by the Board of Governors to promote the well-being of the economy as a whole. Thus, the activities of the

FIGURE 13-5 The twelve Federal Reserve Districts
The Federal Reserve System divides the United States into twelve districts, each of which has one central bank and in some instances one or more branches of the central bank. Hawaii and Alaska are included in the twelfth district. *(Federal Reserve Bulletin.)*

Federal Reserve Banks will frequently be at odds with the profit motive.[5] Also, the Federal Reserve Banks do not compete with commercial banks. With rare exceptions, the Federal Reserve Banks do not deal with the public, but rather, with the government and the commercial banks.

3 Bankers' Banks The Federal Reserve Banks are "bankers' banks." They perform essentially the same functions for depository institutions as depository institutions perform for the public. Just as banks and thrifts accept the deposits of and make loans to the public, so the central banks accept the deposits of and make loans to banks and thrifts. But the Federal Reserve Banks have a third function which banks and thrifts do not perform—they issue currency. Congress has authorized the Federal Reserve Banks to put into circulation Federal Reserve Notes, which constitute the economy's paper money supply.

Commercial Banks The workhorses of the American financial system are its 10,048 **commercial banks.** Roughly two-thirds of these are **state banks,** private banks operating under state charters. One-third received their charters from the Federal gov-

ernment; they are **national banks.** Only two of these national banks rank among the world's largest (see Global Perspective 13-1).

Thrift Institutions Thrift institutions are regulated by agencies which are separate and apart from the Board of Governors and the Federal Reserve Banks. For example, the operation of savings and loan associations is regulated and monitored by the Treasury Department's Office of Thrift Supervision. But, as we have noted, the Depository Institutions Deregulation and Monetary Control Act (DIDMCA) expanded the lending authority of all thrifts, so that S&Ls and mutual saving banks can now make consumer and business loans.

DIDMCA also has subjected S&Ls and other depository institutions to monetary control by the Federal Reserve System. In particular, thrifts now must meet the same reserve requirements as commercial banks, *and* they now can borrow from the Fed. We will find in Chapter 15 that the changing of reserve requirements and the terms under which depository institutions can borrow from the Federal Reserve Banks are two basic ways the Fed's Board of Governors controls the supply of money. In Figure 13-4 we have noted with arrows that the thrift institutions are partially subject to the control of the Board of Governors and the central banks. Decisions concerning monetary policy affect the thrifts along with the commercial banks.

---

[5]Though it is not their basic goal, the Federal Reserve Banks have actually operated profitably, largely as the result of Treasury debts held by them. Part of the profits has been used to pay dividends to member banks on their holdings of stock; the bulk of the remaining profits has been turned over to the United States Treasury.

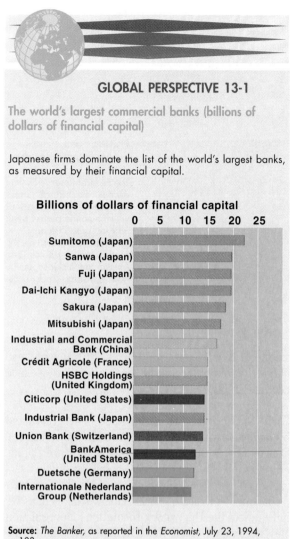

Source: *The Banker*, as reported in the *Economist*, July 23, 1994, p. 103.

Fed Functions and the Money Supply

The Fed performs a number of functions.[6]

1   Reserves   The Federal Reserve Banks hold deposits, called *reserves,* which are made by banks and thrifts. We will find in Chapter 15 that these deposits are of strategic importance in managing the economy's money supply.

2   Check Collection   Another important function of the Fed is to provide the mechanism for the collection of checks. If Sarah writes a check on her Salem bank or thrift to Sam who deposits it in his San Diego bank or thrift, how does the San Diego bank collect the check against the Salem bank? Answer: The Fed handles it in two or three days by adjusting the aforementioned reserves of the two banks.

3   Fiscal Agents   The Federal Reserve Banks act as fiscal agents for the Federal government. The government collects huge sums through taxation, spends equally astronomical amounts, and sells and redeems bonds. The government avails itself of the Fed's facilities in carrying out these activities.

4   Supervision   The Fed supervises the operations of member banks. Periodic bank examinations assess member bank profitability; ascertain that banks perform in accordance with the myriad regulations to which they are subject; and uncover questionable practices or fraud.[7]

5   Control of Money Supply   Finally—and most important of all—the Federal Reserve System has ultimate responsibility for regulating the supply of money. *The major task of the Federal Reserve authorities is to manage the money supply in accordance with the needs of the economy as a whole.* This involves making that amount of money available which is consistent with high and rising levels of output and employment and a relatively constant price level. While all the other functions are of a more-or-less routine or service nature, the goal of correctly managing the money supply entails making basic but unique policy decisions. Chapter 15 discusses Federal Reserve monetary policy and its effectiveness. But before we turn to that subject we must explore how banks create money (Chapter 14).

Federal Reserve Independence

The Fed is essentially an independent institution. It cannot be abolished or rendered ineffective by presi-

---

[6]For a detailed look at the service functions of the Federal Reserve Banks, see Board of Governors of the Federal Reserve System, *The Federal Reserve System: Purposes and Functions.* 7th ed. (1984), chaps. 1, 2, 7.

[7]The Federal Reserve is not alone in the task of supervision. The individual states supervise all banks which they charter. The Comptroller of the Currency supervises all national banks and the Office of Thrift Supervision oversees all thrifts. Finally, the Federal Deposit Insurance Corporation has the power to supervise all banks and thrifts whose deposits it insures.

dential whim, nor can its role and functions be altered by Congress except by specific legislative action. As noted, the long terms of the Board's members are designed to provide them with security and isolate them from political pressures.

The independence of the Fed has been a matter of ongoing controversy.

Opponents of an independent Fed argue it is undemocratic to have a powerful agency whose members are not directly subject to the will of the people. Also, because the legislative and executive branches of government bear ultimate responsibility for the economic well-being of the nation, they should be able to manipulate *all* the policy tools essential to the economy's health. Why should Congress and the administration be responsible for the consequences of policies they do not fully control? Critics cite instances of the Fed using monetary policy to counter the effects of fiscal policy.

Proponents of independence contend that the Fed must be protected from political pressures so that it can effectively control the money supply and maintain price stability (Global Perspective 13-2). They argue it is politically expedient for Congress and the executive branch to invoke expansionary fiscal policies —tax cuts and special-interest spending win votes— and there is thus a need for an independent monetary authority to guard against consequent inflation. Without an acceptable domestically provided medium of exchange, the economy may try to substitute a more stable currency from another nation. Example: Many transactions in Russia and South America now occur in dollars rather than highly unstable rubles or pesos (Last Word). At the extreme, the economy may simply revert to inefficient barter. You will be able to clarify your own position on Federal Reserve independence after we have analyzed the working of monetary policy in Chapter 15.

BANK AND THRIFT FAILURES

Financial innovation and deregulation have enhanced competition among financial institutions and undoubtedly increased economic efficiency. Deregulation and competition, however, have also produced an unpleasant and costly side effect: a rising tide of bank and thrift failures. As we see in Table 13-2, more than 2000 banks and thrifts have failed since 1980. Saving and loan associations (S&Ls) accounted for most of

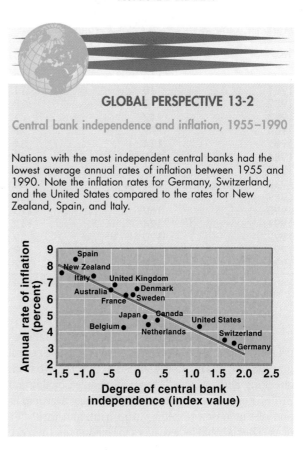

GLOBAL PERSPECTIVE 13-2

Central bank independence and inflation, 1955–1990

Nations with the most independent central banks had the lowest average annual rates of inflation between 1955 and 1990. Note the inflation rates for Germany, Switzerland, and the United States compared to the rates for New Zealand, Spain, and Italy.

the approximately 1000 insolvent thrifts.

We know business failures occur everyday in competitive market economies; they are a means of eliminating persistent and significant economic inefficiencies. Many observers believe there are too many banks and thrifts and that a major consolidation of the financial industry is required. So why are bank and thrift failures of special concern? There are two reasons.

1 Crucial Institutions Banks and thrifts are collectively and in some cases individually instrumental to the monetary system underlying the financial health of the entire economy. These financial institutions hold the money deposits of businesses and households, and as we will discover in Chapter 14, create the major portion of the nation's money supply by making loans to the public. Several of the banks and thrifts which failed in the late 1980s and early 1990s were large financial institutions. Without timely governmental action their collapse might have threatened the regional or even the national economy.

MONEY, BANKING, AND MONETARY POLICY

TABLE 13-2 Bank and thrift failures, 1980–1994

Year	Banks	Thrifts
1980	10	3
1981	10	11
1982	10	28
1983	42	71
1984	79	27
1985	124	34
1986	145	49
1987	206	48
1988	221	220
1989	207	327
1990	169	215
1991	124	142
1992	120	59
1993	42	9
1994	13	2

Source: Federal Deposit Insurance Corporation and Resolution Trust Corporation.

2   Bailouts by Taxpayers   Bank and thrift failures present a special problem for taxpayers. The Federal government has in effect pledged its full credit to back checking and savings deposits in insured banks and thrifts. For this reason it has agreed to pay a large portion of the losses resulting from bank and thrift failures. The final bill to taxpayers for bailing out the S&L industry may approach $250 billion!

Commercial Bank Difficulties

Although a handful of large commercial banks failed in the early 1980s, bank failures throughout the rest of the 1980s consisted mainly of small institutions operating in agricultural and energy-producing regions. Poor crop prices and declines in oil and natural gas prices resulted in loan defaults and consequent bank failures in regions where the economy depends on these products. Regional recessions and falling local real estate prices in the late 1980s added to the problems facing banks and forced several to close.

The 1990–1991 recession struck a more general blow, producing significant losses in some major banks and causing several financially troubled banks to fail. One was the relatively large Bank of New England. In 1991 the Federal government moved to shore up the bank deposit insurance fund by granting the Federal Deposit Insurance Corporation (FDIC) authority to borrow from the government. Nevertheless, the banking industry remains generally sound, and

most large banks have again prospered in recent years.

Savings and Loan Collapse

Of greater concern and magnitude, however, is the collapse of the savings and loan industry. More than one-third of 3000 S&Ls existing in 1987 are no longer in business! The reasons for S&L failures are somewhat complex.

Deregulation and Competition   Deregulation of the banking and thrift industry in the early 1980s contributed to the S&L crisis by removing the S&Ls' previously protected role. Before the 1980s, banking laws had carved out a near monopoly for the S&Ls on home mortgage loans. When the government lifted interest-rate ceilings on deposits in banks and thrifts, competition drove up the interest on deposits. Many S&Ls were caught holding fixed-rate, long-term mortgages issued at interest rates far below rates needed to maintain and attract deposits. S&Ls responded to the resulting losses by using the provisions of new thrift legislation to shift their lending toward riskier commercial, consumer, and real estate loans which earned higher interest rates.

Deposit Insurance   Banks and thrifts pay premiums to the FDIC to insure the deposits they hold. In 1980 the Federal government increased deposit insurance from $40,000 to $100,000 per account. The main purpose of deposit insurance is to prevent "bank panics" —sudden and massive deposit withdrawals by worried customers. Such bank panics destabilized the economy in the early 1930s and contributed to the Great Depression (Last Word, Chapter 14).

Somewhat ironically, deposit insurance—designed to *add* stability to the financial system—inadvertently contributed to the S&L problem. As with all insurance, deposit insurance creates a **moral hazard problem.** *This problem is that insuring an individual against risk of loss reduces the insured's incentive to prevent the loss from occurring.* In last-chance attempts to salvage their enterprises, financially troubled S&Ls offered extraordinarily high interest rates to attract deposits away from competing institutions. Knowing that accounts of $100,000 or less were fully insured, savers directed their funds to these financially shaky S&Ls. These S&Ls began making risky high-interest loans to attempt to earn interest returns above returns being paid on their expensive, newly acquired funds.

In brief, deposit insurance enabled shaky S&Ls to attract funds by removing the incentive for depositors to direct funds toward healthy financial institutions. It also encouraged S&Ls to gamble with insured deposits, or to incur more risk than otherwise was prudent for their stockholders. If the risky ventures paid off, shareholders would win. If the loans defaulted and caused the S&Ls to collapse, the government insurance fund, not S&L shareholders, would pay for depositors' losses.

Loan Defaults and Fraud   Major defaults on many of these risky loans forced several large S&Ls into bankruptcy. Particularly hard hit were savings and loans in Texas and other "oil patch" states. Loan defaults in these areas increased rapidly as oil prices fell and economic conditions worsened. Speculative loans on office buildings and other real estate went into default. Furthermore, the looser banking regulations provided a convenient opportunity for some S&L officers to defraud their failing institutions. As indicated in Table 13-2, more than 1000 S&Ls failed in the late 1980s and early 1990s. Federal investigators have now detected criminal conduct in 40 percent of these failed S&Ls.

The Thrift Bailout

The losses at S&Ls eventually plunged the S&L deposit insurance fund severely into the red, forcing government to face the crisis. In August 1989 the Financial Institutions Reform, Recovery, and Enforcement Act (FIRREA) became law. The new law established the **Resolution Trust Corporation** and directed it to oversee the closing or sale of all failed S&Ls. The total cost to date has been about $200 billion, most of it paid by taxpayers.

The FIRREA also placed deposit insurance for the thrifts and banks under FDIC control. It increased premiums paid by banks and thrifts for deposit insurance and raised the thrift's capital requirements—the percentage of their assets financed by owners—to match requirements of banks. The law also for the first time permitted S&Ls to accept deposits from commercial businesses. Finally, FIRREA directs the Federal Reserve to allow bank holding companies to acquire healthy S&Ls.

Recent Developments and Reform

Sweeping changes continue to transform the financial services industry.

Declining Shares   Although banks and thrifts remain the main institutions offering checkable deposits, their share of total financial assets (things of monetary value owned) has significantly fallen. In the 1980s commercial banks saw their market share fall from 37 percent to 27 percent, while the thrifts experienced a decline from 23 percent to 16 percent. Meanwhile, the market share of financial assets held by insurance companies, pension and trust funds, investment companies (mutual funds), and finance companies jumped from 39 to 57 percent. Clearly, American households and businesses are channeling more of their saving and borrowing away from banks and thrifts and toward these other financial institutions.

Globalization   The world's financial markets have become increasingly integrated. Major American financial institutions have off-shore operations and foreign financial institutions have operations in the United States. Moreover, investment companies now offer a variety of international stock and bond funds. Financial capital increasingly flows globally in search of the highest risk-adjusted returns.

We must take care not to overstate this extent of international financial integration, however. Studies show that the bulk of investment in the major nations still is financed via domestic saving in those countries. But there is no doubt that money and banking has increasingly become a global activity.

Reform   The fast and vast changes in the financial services industry aroused calls for regulatory reform. Legislation has been introduced to strengthen banks and thrifts, promote further competition among financial institutions, and hasten a perceived need for consolidation. Several proposed reforms would remove regulatory restrictions on banks and thrifts, increasing their competitiveness with other financial institutions. For example, in 1994 Congress enacted legislation removing Federal restrictions on interstate banking. Other proposed legislation would allow

LAST WORD

THE GLOBAL GREENBACK

Two-thirds of the $350 billion of American currency is circulating abroad.

Russians use them. So do Argentineans, Brazilians, Poles, Vietnamese, Chinese, and even Cubans. They are American dollars. Like blue jeans, computer software, and movie videos, the dollar has become a major American "export." About $235 billion of American currency is circulating overseas. Russians hold more than $20 billion in American cash, while another $5 billion to $7 billion is circulating freely in Argentina. The Polish government estimates that $5 billion of American dollars is circulating in Poland.

American currency leaves the United States when Americans buy imports, travel in other countries, or send dollars to relatives living abroad. The United States profits when American dollars stay in other countries. It costs the government about 4 cents to print a dollar. For someone abroad to obtain this new dollar, $1 worth of resources, goods, or services must be sold to Americans. These items are Ameri-

can gains. The dollar goes abroad, and assuming it stays there, it presents no claim on American resources or goods or services. Americans in effect make 96 cents on the dollar (= $1 gain in resources, goods, or services *minus* the 4-cent printing cost). It's like American Express selling travelers checks which never get cashed.

---

banks to own brokerage houses and insurance companies (and vice versa).

There is also a current move to streamline the regulation of banking. In 1994 the Clinton administration proposed creating a single new Federal Banking Commission to assume the regulatory duties currently exercised by the Federal Deposit Insurance Corporation, the Comptroller of the Currency, and the Office of Thrift Supervision.

Apparently the revolution in banking begun a decade or two ago has yet to run its full course. (In Chapter 15 we will examine the implications of these changes for monetary policy.)

QUICK REVIEW 13-4

■ The Federal Reserve System consists of the Board of Governors, twelve Federal Reserve Banks, commercial banks, and thrift institutions.

■ The Federal Reserve's major role is to regulate the supply of money in the economy.

■ The 1980s and early 1990s witnessed a sharp rise in the number of bank and thrift failures.

■ The government has bailed out failed savings and loan associations using taxpayer dollars.

■ The American financial industry remains in a state of flux.

CHAPTER SUMMARY

1   Anything that functions as   a a medium of exchange, b a measure of value, and   c a store of value is money.

2   The Federal Reserve System recognizes three "official" definitions of the money supply. *M*1 is currency and checkable deposits; *M*2 is *M*1 plus noncheckable savings

deposits, money market deposit accounts, small (less than $100,000) time deposits, and money market mutual fund balances; and *M*3 is *M*2 plus large ($100,000 or more) time deposits. In our analysis we concentrate on *M*1 since its components are immediately spendable.

Black markets and other illegal activity undoubtedly fuel some of the demand for American cash abroad. The dollar is king in covert trading in diamonds, weapons, and pirated software. Billions of cash dollars are involved in the narcotics trade. But the illegal use of dollars is only a small part of the story. The massive volume of dollars in other nations reflects a global search for monetary stability. Based on past experience, foreign citizens are confident the dollar's purchasing power will remain relatively steady.

Argentina has pegged its peso directly to the dollar, with the central bank issuing new pesos only when it has more dollars, gold, or other convertible reserves on hand. The result has been a remarkable decline in inflation. In Russia and the newly independent countries of eastern Europe, the dollar has retained its buying power while that of domestic currencies has plummeted. As a result, many Russian workers demand to be paid at least partially in dollars. In Brazil, where the inflation rate is more than 1000 percent annually, people have long sought the stability of dollars. In the shopping districts of Beijing and Shanghai, Chinese consumers trade their domestic renminda for dollars. In Bolivia half of all bank accounts are denominated in dollars. There is a thriving "dollar economy" in Vietnam, and even Cuba has partially legalized the use of the American currency. The dollar is the official currency in Panama and Liberia.

There is little risk to the United States in satisfying the world's demand for dollars. If all the dollars came rushing back to the United States at once, the nation's money supply would surge, possibly causing demand-pull inflation. But there is not much chance of that happening. Overall, the global greenback is a positive economic force. It is a reliable medium of exchange, measure of value, and store of value facilitating transactions which might not otherwise occur. Dollar holdings have helped buyers and sellers abroad overcome special monetary problems. The result has been increased output in those countries and thus greater output and income globally.

Source: Based partly on "The Global Greenback," *Business Week,* August 9, 1993, pp. 40–44; and "Dollar Drain: Most U.S. Greenbacks Are Overseas," *Lincoln-Star,* March 15, 1994, p. 3.

3 Money—the debts of government and depository institutions (commercial banks and thrift institutions)—has value because of the goods and services it will command in the market. Maintaining the purchasing power of money depends largely on the government's effectiveness in managing the money supply.

4 The total demand for money consists of the transactions and asset demands for money. The transactions demand varies directly with nominal GDP; the asset demand varies inversely with the interest rate. The money market combines the total demand for money with the money supply to determine the equilibrium interest rate.

5 Disequilibria in the money market are corrected through changes in bond prices. As bond prices change, interest rates move in the opposite direction. At the equilibrium interest rate, bond prices are stable and the amounts of money demanded and supplied are equal.

6 The American banking system is composed of a the Board of Governors of the Federal Reserve System, b the twelve Federal Reserve Banks, and c some 10,048 commercial banks and 14,332 thrift institutions. The Board of Governors is the basic policy-making body for the entire banking system. The directives of the Board are made effective through the twelve Federal Reserve Banks, which are simultaneously a central banks, b quasi-public banks, and c bankers' banks.

7 The major functions of the Federal Reserve System are a to hold the deposits or reserves of commercial banks and other depository institutions, b to provide facilities for the rapid collection of checks, c to act as fiscal agent for the Federal government, d to supervise the operations of member banks, and e to regulate the supply of money in terms of the best interests of the economy as a whole.

8 There were a rising number of bank and thrift failures in the 1980s and early 1990s. The collapse of major S&Ls resulted from deregulation and competition, the moral hazard problem associated with deposit insurance, loan defaults by borrowers, and criminal conduct. Thus far, the government bailout of the failed S&Ls has cost taxpayers about $200 billion.

9 Banks and thrifts recently have lost considerable market share to insurance companies, pension and trust funds, investment companies (mutual funds), and finance companies. Financial markets have increasingly become globalized. Major reform legislation has been proposed and passed relating to banks and thrifts.

TERMS AND CONCEPTS

medium of exchange	savings and loan	legal tender	Federal Open Market
measure of value	associations	fiat money	Committee
store of value	credit unions	transactions, asset,	Advisory Councils
M1, M2, M3	near-monies	and total demand for	Federal Reserve
token money	noncheckable savings	money	Banks
intrinsic value	accounts	money market	commercial banks
Federal Reserve Notes	MMDA (money market	Depository Institutions	state banks
checkable deposits	deposit account)	Deregulation and	national banks
thrift or savings	time deposits	Monetary Control	moral hazard problem
institutions	MMMF (money market	Act	Resolution Trust
mutual savings banks	mutual fund)	Board of Governors	Corporation

QUESTIONS AND STUDY SUGGESTIONS

1 Describe how rapid inflation can undermine money's ability to perform its three basic functions.

2 What are the disadvantages of commodity money? What are the advantages of **a** paper money and **b** check money compared with commodity money?

3 "Money is only a bit of paper or a bit of metal that gives its owner a lawful claim to so much bread or beer or diamonds or motorcars or what not. We cannot eat money, nor drink money, nor wear money. It is the goods that money can buy that are being divided up when money is divided up."[8] Evaluate and explain.

4 Fully evaluate and explain the following statements:

a "The invention of money is one of the great achievements of the human race, for without it the enrichment that comes from broadening trade would have been impossible."

b "Money is whatever society says it is."

c "When prices of everything are going up, it is not because everything is worth more, but because the dollar is worth less."

d "The difficult questions concerning paper [money] are . . . not about its economy, convenience or ready circulation but about the amount of the paper which can be wisely issued or created, and the possibilities of violent convulsions when it gets beyond bounds."[9]

e "In most modern industrial economies of the world the debts of government and of commercial banks are used as money."

---

[8]George Bernard Shaw, *The Intelligent Woman's Guide to Socialism and Capitalism* (New York: Brentano's, Inc., 1982), p. 9. Used by permission of the Public Trustee and the Society of Authors.

[9]F. W. Taussig, *Principles of Economics,* 4th ed. (New York: The Macmillan Company, 1946), pp. 247–248.

5 *Key Question What items constitute the M1 money supply? What is the most important component of the M1 money supply? Why is the face value of a coin greater than its intrinsic value? Distinguish between M2 and M3. What are near-monies? Of what significance are they? What arguments can you make for including savings deposits in a definition of money?*

6 What "backs" the money supply in the United States? What determines the value of money? Who is responsible for maintaining the value of money? Why is it important to be able to alter the money supply? What is meant by **a** "sound money" and **b** a "52-cent dollar"?

7 *Key Question Suppose the price level and value of the dollar in year 1 are 1.0 and $1.00, respectively. If the price level rises to 1.25 in year 2, what is the new value of the dollar? If instead the price level had fallen to .50, what would have been the value of the dollar? What generalization can you draw from your answers.*

8 *Key Question What is the basic determinant of **a** the transactions demand and **b** the asset demand for money? Explain how these two demands might be combined graphically to determine total money demand. How is the equilibrium interest rate determined in the money market? How might **a** the expanded use of credit cards, **b** a shortening of worker pay periods, and **c** an increase in nominal GDP affect the transactions demand for money and the equilibrium interest rate?*

9 Suppose that a bond having no expiration date has a face value of $10,000 and annually pays a fixed amount of interest of $800. Compute and enter in the space provided either the interest rate which a bond buyer could secure at each of the bond prices listed or the bond price at each of the interest rates shown. What generalization can be drawn from the completed table?

Bond price	Interest rate %
$ 8,000	
	8.9
$10,000	
$11,000	
	6.2

10 Assume the money market is initially in equilibrium and that the money supply is now increased. Explain the adjustments toward a new equilibrium interest rate. Will bond prices be higher at the new equilibrium rate of interest? What effects would you expect that interest-rate change to have on the levels of output, employment, and prices? Answer the same questions for a decrease in the money supply.

11 How did the Depository Institutions Deregulation and Monetary Control Act of 1980 change the American banking system?

12 What is the major responsibility of the Board of Governors? Discuss the major characteristics of the Federal Reserve Banks. Of what significance is the fact that the Federal Reserve Banks are quasi-public? Do you think the Fed should be an independent institution?

13 What are the two basic functions of commercial banks and thrift institutions? State and briefly discuss the major functions of the Federal Reserve System.

14 Explain the "moral hazard problem" associated with insurance and relate this problem to the collapse of major savings and loan associations during the late 1980s and early 1990s.

15 (Last Word) Over the years the Federal Reserve Banks have printed about $235 billion more in currency than American households, businesses, and financial institutions now hold. Where is this "missing" money? Why is it there?

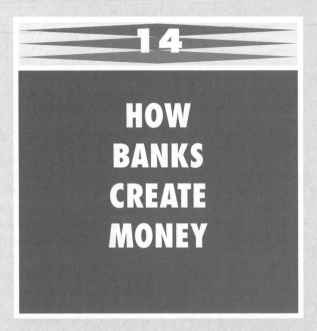

14

HOW BANKS CREATE MONEY

If you visit Washington, D.C., you might enjoy touring the United States Bureau of Engraving and Printing. There, each day more than $25 million of Federal Reserve Notes roll off the printing presses in large sheets. After machines cut the sheets into individual bills, employees ship them to twelve Federal Reserve Banks for distribution.

We are all fascinated by large amounts of money. Nevertheless, we use checkable deposits of commercial banks and thrift institutions, not currency, for most of our transactions. The amount of these deposits far exceeds the amount of currency banks hold. Who creates these checkable deposits? Loan officers at commercial banks. Their tools? Computers and computer printers. Sounds like something *60 Minutes* and a congressional committee should investigate. But in truth, banking authorities are well aware banks and thrifts create checking deposit money. In fact, the Federal Reserve *relies* on these institutions to create a large part of the nation's money supply.

Because the bulk of all checkable deposits are the demand deposits of commercial banks, this chapter will explain how they can *create* demand-deposit money. Specifically, we explain and compare how money can be created by (1) a *single* commercial bank which is part of a multibank system, and by (2) the commercial bank *system* as a whole. Keep in mind throughout our discussion that thrift institutions also provide checkable deposits. Therefore, when we say "commercial bank" we also mean "depository institution." And "checkable deposit" can be substituted for "demand deposit."

THE BALANCE SHEET OF A COMMERCIAL BANK

An understanding of the basic items on a bank's balance sheet, and how various transactions change these items, will give us the tools for analyzing the workings of our monetary and banking systems.

A **balance sheet** is a statement of assets and claims summarizing the financial position of a firm—in this case a commercial bank—at some point in time. Every balance sheet must balance, because each and every known *asset,* being something of economic value, will be claimed by someone. Can you think of an asset—something of monetary value—which no one claims? A balance sheet balances because the value of assets equals the amount of claims against those assets. The claims shown on a balance sheet are divided into two groups: the claims of the owners of a firm against the firm's assets, called _net worth,_ and the claims of nonowners, called _liabilities._ Thus, a balance sheet balances because

Assets = liabilities + net worth

A balance-sheet approach to our study of the money-creating ability of commercial banks is valuable in two respects.
1 A bank's balance sheet provides a convenient point of reference from which we can introduce new terms and concepts in an orderly manner.
2 The use of balance sheets allows us to quantify certain concepts and relationships which would defy comprehension if discussed in verbal terms alone.

PROLOGUE: THE GOLDSMITHS

Using balance sheets, let's see how a **fractional reserve system of banking** operates. The characteristics and working of such a system can be better understood by considering a bit of economic history.

When the ancients began to use gold in making transactions, it became apparent that it was both unsafe and inconvenient for consumers and merchants to carry gold and have it weighed and assessed for purity every time a transaction was negotiated. It therefore became commonplace to deposit one's gold with goldsmiths whose vaults or strongrooms could be used for a fee. Upon receiving a gold deposit, the goldsmith issued a receipt to the depositor. Soon goods were traded for the goldsmiths' receipts and the receipts became the first kind of paper money.

At this point the goldsmiths—embryonic bankers—used a 100 percent reserve system; their circulating paper money receipts were fully backed by gold. But, given the public's acceptance of the goldsmiths' receipts as paper money, the goldsmiths became aware that the gold they stored was rarely redeemed. In fact, they found themselves in charge of "going concerns" where the amount of gold deposited with them in any week or month was likely to exceed the amount withdrawn.

Then some adroit goldsmith hit on the idea that paper money could be issued _in excess of_ the amount of gold held. Goldsmiths would put these additional

"receipts" redeemable in gold—paper money—into circulation by making interest-earning loans to merchants, producers, and consumers. Borrowers were willing to accept loans in the form of gold receipts because they were accepted as a medium of exchange.

This was the beginning of the _fractional reserve system_ of banking. If, for example, our ingenious goldsmith made loans equal to the amount of gold stored, then the total value of paper money in circulation would be twice the value of the gold. Reserves would be 50 percent of outstanding paper money.

Fractional reserve banking—the system we have today—has two significant characteristics.

1 Money Creation and Reserves Banks in such a system can _create money._ When our goldsmith made loans by giving borrowers paper money which was not fully backed by gold reserves, money was being created. The quantity of such money the goldsmith could create would depend on the amount of reserves deemed prudent to keep on hand. The smaller the amount of reserves deemed necessary, the larger the amount of paper money the goldsmith could create. Although gold is no longer used to "back" our money supply (Chapter 13), bank lending (money creation) today is constrained by the amount of reserves banks feel obligated, or are required, to keep.

2 Bank Panics and Regulation Banks which operate on the basis of fractional reserves are vulnerable to bank "panics" or "runs." Our goldsmith who issued paper money equal to twice the value of gold reserves could not convert all that paper money into gold in the event all holders of that paper money appeared simultaneously demanding gold. In fact, many Europeans and American banks were once ruined by this unfortunate circumstance. However, a bank panic is highly unlikely _if_ the banker's reserve and lending policies are prudent. Indeed, a basic reason why banking systems are highly regulated industries is to prevent bank runs. This is also the reason why the United States has in place a system of deposit insurance (Chapter 13).

A SINGLE COMMERCIAL BANK

We now will explore how money can be created by a single bank which is part of a multibank banking system. What accounts make up a commercial bank's balance sheet? How does a single commercial bank create money? If it can create money, can it destroy it? What factors govern how a bank creates money?

Formation of a Commercial Bank

To answer these questions we must understand what's on a commercial bank's balance sheet and how certain transactions affect it. We start with the organization of a local commercial bank.

Transaction 1: The Birth of a Bank Suppose farsighted citizens of the metropolis of Wahoo, Nebraska (yes, there is such a place), decide their town needs a new commercial bank to provide banking services for that growing community. Assuming these enterprising individuals can secure a state or national charter for their bank, they then turn to the task of selling, say, $250,000 worth of capital stock (equity shares) to buyers, both in and out of the community. These financing efforts meet with success and the Merchants and Farmers Bank of Wahoo now exists —at least on paper. How does the Wahoo bank's balance statement appear at its birth?

The new owners of the bank have sold $250,000 worth of shares of stock in the bank—some to themselves, some to other people. As a result, the bank now has $250,000 in cash on hand and $250,000 worth of capital stock outstanding. The cash is an asset to the bank. Cash held by a bank is sometimes called **vault cash** or *till money*. The outstanding shares of stock constitute an equal amount of claims which the owners have against the bank's assets. The shares of stock are the net worth of the bank, though they are assets from the viewpoint of those who possess these shares. The bank's balance sheet reads:

BIRTH OF A BANK		
BALANCE SHEET 1: WAHOO BANK		
Assets	Liabilities and net worth	
Cash $250,000	Capital stock $250,000	

Transaction 2: Becoming a Going Concern The board of directors must now get their newborn bank off the drawing board and make it a reality. First, property and equipment must be acquired. Suppose the directors, confident of the success of their venture, purchase a building for $220,000 and $20,000 worth of office equipment. This simple transaction changes

the composition of the bank's assets. The bank now has $240,000 less in cash and $240,000 of new property assets. Using blue to denote those accounts affected by each transaction, we find that the bank's balance sheet at the end of transaction 2 appears as follows:

ACQUIRING PROPERTY AND EQUIPMENT		
BALANCE SHEET 2: WAHOO BANK		
Assets	Liabilities and net worth	
Cash $ 10,000	Capital stock $250,000	
Property 240,000		

Note the balance sheet still balances, as it must.

Transaction 3: Accepting Deposits Commercial banks have two basic functions: to accept deposits of money and to make loans. Now that our bank is operating, suppose that the citizens and businesses of Wahoo decide to deposit $100,000 in the Merchants and Farmers Bank. What happens to the bank's balance sheet?

The bank receives cash, which we know is an asset to the bank. Suppose this money is placed in the bank as demand deposits (checking accounts), rather than time deposits or savings accounts. These newly created demand deposits constitute claims which depositors have against the assets of the Wahoo bank. Thus the depositing of money in the bank creates a new liability account—demand deposits. The bank's balance sheet now looks like this:

ACCEPTING DEPOSITS		
BALANCE SHEET 3: WAHOO BANK		
Assets	Liabilities and net worth	
Cash $110,000	Demand deposits $100,000	
Property 240,000	Capital stock 250,000	

Although there is no direct change in the total supply of money, a change in the composition of the economy's money supply has occurred as a result of transaction 3. Bank money, or demand deposits, have *increased* by $100,000 and currency held by the nonbank public has *decreased* by $100,000. Currency held by a bank, you will recall, is *not* part of the economy's money supply.

It is apparent that a withdrawal of cash will reduce the bank's demand-deposit liabilities and its holdings of cash by the amount of the withdrawal. This, too, changes the composition, but not the total supply, of money.

Transaction 4: Depositing Reserves in a Federal Reserve Bank

All commercial banks and thrift institutions which provide checkable deposits must keep a **legal reserve** or, **required reserve**. This legal or required reserve is *an amount of funds equal to a specified percentage of its own deposit liabilities which a member bank must keep on deposit with the Federal Reserve Bank in its district or as vault cash.* To simplify we suppose our bank keeps its legal reserve *entirely* as deposits in the Federal Reserve Bank of its district. But remember that vault cash is counted as reserves and real-world banks keep a significant portion of their reserves in their vaults.

The "specified percentage" of its deposit liabilities which the commercial bank must keep as reserves is known as the **reserve ratio**—a ratio between the size of the required reserves the commercial bank must keep and the commercial bank's own outstanding deposit liabilities.

$$\text{Reserve ratio} = \frac{\text{commercial bank's required reserves}}{\text{commercial bank's demand-deposit liabilities}}$$

If the reserve ratio were $\frac{1}{10}$, or 10 percent, our bank, having accepted $100,000 in deposits from the public, would have to keep $10,000 as reserves. If the ratio were $\frac{1}{5}$, or 20 percent, $20,000 of reserves would be required. If $\frac{1}{2}$, or 50 percent, $50,000 would be required.

The Board of Governors has the authority to establish and vary the reserve ratio within limits legislated by Congress. The reserve ratio limits which now prevail are shown in Table 14-1. A 3 percent reserve is required on the first $54.0 million of demand or other checkable deposits held by an institution. The reserve requirement on an institution's checkable deposits over $54.0 million is currently 10 percent, although the Board of Governors can vary this between 8 and 14 percent. Currently, no reserves are required against noncheckable nonpersonal (business) savings and time deposits. This ratio can be varied between 0 and 9 percent. Also, after consultation with appropriate congressional committees, the Federal Reserve may impose reserve requirements for 180 days in excess of those specified in Table 14-1.

TABLE 14-1 Reserve requirements of depository institutions

Type of deposit	Current requirement	Statutory limits
Checkable deposits		
$0–54.0 million	3%	3%
Over $54.0 million	10	8–14
Noncheckable nonpersonal savings and time deposits	0	0–9

Source: Federal Reserve. Data are for 1995.

To simplify our discussion suppose the reserve ratio for commercial banks is $\frac{1}{5}$, or 20 percent, and that this requirement applies only to demand deposits. Although it's really too high, 20 percent is convenient to use in computations. And, because we are concerned with checkable (spendable) demand deposits, we ignore reserves on noncheckable savings and time deposits. The point is that reserve requirements are *fractional,* meaning they are less than 100 percent. This consideration is vital in our analysis of the lending ability of the banking system.

The Wahoo bank will just be meeting the required 20 percent ratio between its deposit in the Federal Reserve Bank and its own deposit liabilities by depositing $20,000 in the Federal Reserve Bank. We will use *reserves* in referring to those funds commercial banks deposit in the Federal Reserve Banks to distinguish them from the public's *deposits* in commercial banks.

But suppose the Wahoo bank anticipates that its holdings of the public's demand deposits will grow in the future. Thus, instead of sending just the minimum amount, $20,000, they send an extra $90,000, for a total of $110,000. In so doing, the bank will avoid the inconvenience of sending additional reserves to the Federal Reserve Bank each time its own demand-deposit liabilities increase. And, as we will see, it is on the basis of extra reserves that banks can lend and thereby earn interest income.

Actually, the bank would not deposit *all* its cash in the Federal Reserve Bank. However, because (1) banks as a rule hold vault cash only in the amount of $1\frac{1}{2}$ or 2 percent of their total assets, and (2) vault cash can be counted as reserves, we assume all the bank's cash is deposited in the Federal Reserve Bank and therefore constitutes the commercial bank's total reserves. We don't need to bother adding two assets— "cash" and "deposits in the Federal Reserve Bank"— to determine "reserves."

After depositing $110,000 of reserves at the Fed, the balance sheet of Merchants and Farmers Bank becomes:

DEPOSITS AT THE FED			
BALANCE SHEET 4: WAHOO BANK			
Assets		**Liabilities and net worth**	
Cash	$ 0	Demand	
Reserves	110,000	deposits	$100,000
Property	240,000	Capital stock	250,000

There are three things about this latest transaction you must understand.

1 Excess Reserves Some terminology: The amount by which the bank's **actual reserves** exceed its **required reserves** is the bank's **excess reserves.**

$$\frac{\text{Actual}}{\text{reserves}} - \frac{\text{required}}{\text{reserves}} = \frac{\text{excess}}{\text{reserves}}$$

In this case,

Actual reserves	$110,000
Required reserves	−20,000
Excess reserves	$90,000

The only reliable way of computing excess reserves is to multiply the bank's demand-deposit liabilities by the reserve ratio to obtain required reserves ($100,000 times 20 percent equals $20,000), then to subtract required reserves from the actual reserves listed on the asset side of the bank's balance sheet.

To understand this, you should compute excess reserves for the bank's balance sheet as it stands at the end of transaction 4, assuming that the reserve ratio is (1) 10 percent, (2) $33\frac{1}{3}$ percent, and (3) 50 percent.

Because the ability of a commercial bank to make loans depends on the existence of excess reserves, this concept is crucial in seeing how money is created by the banking system.

2 Control What is the rationale underlying the requirement that member banks deposit a reserve in the Federal Reserve Bank of their district? You might think the basic purpose of reserves is to enhance the liquidity of a bank and protect commercial bank depositors from losses. Reserves would constitute a ready source of funds from which commercial banks can meet large and unexpected cash withdrawals by depositors.

But this reasoning breaks down under scrutiny. Although historically reserves were seen as a source of liquidity and therefore protection for depositors, a bank's *legal,* or required, reserves are not great enough to meet sudden, massive cash withdrawals. If the banker's nightmare should materialize—everyone with demand deposits appearing at once to demand these deposits in cash—the legal reserves held as vault cash or at the Federal Reserve bank would be insufficient. The banker simply could not meet this "bank panic." Because reserves are fractional, demand deposits may be ten to twenty times greater than a bank's required reserves.

Commercial bank deposits must be protected by other means. We saw in Chapter 13 that periodic bank examinations are one way for promoting prudent commercial banking practices. And banking laws restrict banks as to the kinds of assets they may acquire; for example, banks are generally prohibited from buying common stocks. Furthermore, insurance funds administered by the Federal Deposit Insurance Corporation (FDIC) exist to insure individual deposits in banks and thrifts up to $100,000.

If the purpose of reserves is not to provide for commercial bank liquidity, what is their function? *Control* is the basic answer. Legal reserves permit the Board of Governors to influence the lending ability of commercial banks. Chapter 15 will examine how the Board of Governors can invoke certain policies which either increase or decrease commercial bank reserves and affect the ability of banks to grant credit. The objective is to prevent banks from *over*extending or *under*extending bank credit. To the degree that these policies are successful in influencing the volume of commercial bank credit, the Board of Governors can help the economy avoid the business fluctuations which lead to bank runs, bank failures, and collapse of the monetary system. In this indirect way—controlling commercial bank credit and thereby stabilizing the economy—reserves function to protect depositors, not as a source of liquidity. Another function of reserves is to facilitate the collection or "clearing" of checks. *(Key Question 2)*

3 Asset and Liability Note there is an apparent accounting matter which transaction 4 entails. Specifically, *the reserve created in transaction 4 is an asset to the depositing commercial bank but a liability to the Federal Reserve Bank receiving it.* To the Wahoo bank

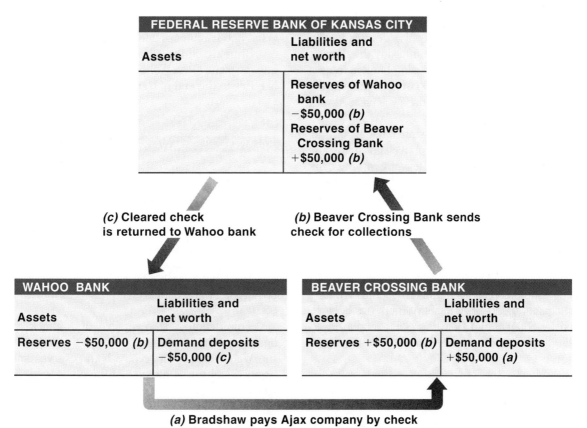

FIGURE 14-1   The collection of a check through a Federal Reserve Bank
The bank against which a check is drawn and cleared loses both reserves and deposits; the bank in which the check is deposited acquires reserves and deposits.

the reserve is an asset; it is a claim this bank has against assets of another institution—the Federal Reserve Bank. To the Federal Reserve Bank this reserve is a liability, a claim which another institution—the Wahoo bank—has against it. Just as the demand deposit you get by depositing money in a commercial bank is an asset to you and a liability to that bank, so the deposit or reserve which a commercial bank establishes by depositing money in a bankers' bank is an asset to that bank and a liability to the Federal Reserve Bank. Understand this clearly before proceeding to transaction 5.

Transaction 5: A Check is Drawn Against the Bank
Suppose Clem Bradshaw, a Wahoo farmer who deposited a substantial portion of the $100,000 in demand deposits which the Wahoo bank received in transaction 3, buys $50,000 worth of farm machinery from the Ajax Farm Implement Company of Beaver

Crossing, Nebraska. Bradshaw pays for this machinery by writing a $50,000 check, against his deposit in the Wahoo bank, to the Ajax company. We need to know (1) how this check is collected or cleared, and (2) the effect the collection of the check has on the balance sheets of the banks involved in the transaction.

To learn this, we must consider the Wahoo bank (Bradshaw's bank), the Beaver Crossing bank (the Ajax Company's bank), and the Federal Reserve Bank of Kansas City.[1] For simplicity, we deal only with changes which occur in those specific accounts affected by this transaction.

We trace this transaction in three steps, keying the steps by letters to Figure 14-1.

---

[1]Actually, the Omaha branch of the Federal Reserve Bank of Kansas City would handle the process of collecting this check.

a Bradshaw gives his $50,000 check, drawn against the Wahoo bank, to the Ajax company. Ajax deposits the check in its account with the Beaver Crossing bank. The Beaver Crossing bank increases Ajax's demand deposit by $50,000 when it deposits the check. Ajax is now paid off. Bradshaw is pleased with his new machinery.

b Now the Beaver Crossing bank has Bradshaw's check. This check is simply a claim against the assets of the Wahoo bank. The Beaver Crossing bank will collect this claim by sending this check (along with checks drawn on other banks) to the Federal Reserve Bank of Kansas City. Here a clerk will clear, or collect, this check for the Beaver Crossing bank by *increasing* Beaver's reserve in the Federal Reserve Bank by $50,000 and by *decreasing* Wahoo's reserve by a like amount. The check is collected merely by making bookkeeping notations that the Wahoo's claim against the Federal Reserve Bank has been reduced by $50,000 and Beaver's claim increased accordingly. Note these changes on the balance sheets in Figure 14-1.

c Finally, the Federal Reserve Bank sends the cleared check back to the Wahoo bank, and for the first time the Wahoo bank discovers that one of its depositors has drawn a check for $50,000 against his demand deposit. Accordingly, the Wahoo bank reduces Bradshaw's demand deposit by $50,000 and recognizes that the collection of this check has entailed a $50,000 decline in its reserves at the Federal Reserve Bank. Note that the balance statements of all three banks will balance. The Wahoo bank will have reduced both its assets and liabilities by $50,000. The Beaver Crossing bank will have $50,000 more in reserves and in demand deposits. Ownership of reserves at the Federal Reserve Bank will have changed—Wahoo owning $50,000 less, Beaver owning $50,000 more—but total reserves will stay the same.

Whenever a check is drawn against a bank and deposited in another bank, collection of that check will reduce both reserves and demand (checkable) deposits of the bank on which the check is drawn. Conversely, if a bank receives a check drawn on another bank, the bank receiving the check will, in the process of collecting it, have its reserves and deposits *increased* by the amount of the check. In our example, the Wahoo bank loses $50,000 in both reserves and deposits to the Beaver Crossing bank. But there is no loss of re-

serves or deposits for the banking system as a whole. What one bank loses another bank gains.

Bringing all the other assets and liabilities back into the picture, the Wahoo bank's balance sheet looks like this at the end of transaction 5:

CLEARING A CHECK

BALANCE SHEET 5: WAHOO BANK

Assets		Liabilities and net worth	
Reserves	$ 60,000	Demand deposits	$ 50,000
Property	240,000	Capital stock	250,000

You should verify that with a 20 percent reserve requirement, the bank's *excess* reserves now stand at $50,000.

Transaction 5 is reversible. If a check drawn against another bank is deposited in the Wahoo bank, the Wahoo bank will receive both reserves and deposits equal to the amount of the check as it is collected.

QUICK REVIEW 14-1

■ When a bank accepts deposits of cash, the composition of the money supply is changed, but the total supply of money is not directly altered.

■ Commercial banks and other depository institutions are required to keep legal reserve deposits, or required reserves, equal to a specified percentage of their own deposit liabilities as cash or on deposit with the Federal Reserve Bank of their district.

■ The amount by which a bank's actual reserves exceed its required reserves is called "excess reserves."

■ A bank which has a check drawn and collected against it will lose to the recipient bank both reserves and deposits equal to the value of the check.

Money-Creating Transactions of a Commercial Bank

The next three transactions are crucial because they explain (1) how a commercial bank can literally create money by making loans, (2) how money is destroyed when loans are repaid, and (3) how banks create money by purchasing government bonds from the public.

Transaction 6: Granting a Loan

In addition to accepting deposits, commercial banks grant loans to borrowers. What effect does lending by a commercial bank have on its balance sheet?

Suppose Grisley Meat Packing Company of Wahoo decides it's time to expand its facilities. Suppose, too, the company needs exactly $50,000—which just happens to be equal to the Wahoo bank's excess reserves—to finance this project.

Grisley approaches the Wahoo bank and requests a loan for this amount. The Wahoo bank knows the Grisley company's fine reputation and financial soundness and is convinced of its ability to repay the loan. So the loan is granted. The president of Grisley hands a promissory note—a high-class IOU—to the Wahoo bank. Grisley wants the convenience and safety of paying its obligations by checks. So, instead of receiving a bushelbasket full of currency from the bank, Grisley will get a $50,000 increase in its demand deposit in the Wahoo bank. From the Wahoo bank's standpoint it has acquired an interest-earning asset (the promissory note) and has created demand deposits (a liability) to "pay" for this asset.

Grisley has swapped an IOU for the right to draw an additional $50,000 worth of checks against its demand deposit in the Wahoo bank. Both parties are pleased. The Wahoo bank now possesses a new asset—an interest-bearing promissory note which it files under the general heading of "Loans." Grisley, sporting a fattened demand deposit, can now expand operations.

At the moment the loan is negotiated, the Wahoo bank's position is shown by balance sheet 6a.

WHEN A LOAN IS NEGOTIATED			
BALANCE SHEET 6a: WAHOO BANK			
Assets		**Liabilities and net worth**	
Reserves	$ 60,000	Demand	
Loans	50,000	deposits	$100,000
Property	240,000	Capital stock	250,000

All this looks simple enough. But a close examination of the Wahoo bank's balance statement will reveal a startling fact: *When a bank makes loans, it cre-*

ates money. The president of the Grisley company went to the bank with something which is *not* money—her IOU—and walked out with something that *is* money—a demand deposit.

Contrast transaction 6a with transaction 3 where demand deposits were created, but only by currency going out of circulation. There was a change in the *composition* of the money supply in that situation but no change in the total *supply* of money. But when banks lend, they create demand (checkable) deposits which *are* money. By extending credit the Wahoo bank has "monetized" an IOU. Grisley and the Wahoo bank have created and then swapped claims. The claim created by Grisley and given to the bank is not money; an individual's IOU is not generally acceptable as a medium of exchange. But the claim created by the bank and given to Grisley is money; checks drawn against a demand deposit are acceptable as a medium of exchange.

The bulk of the money we use in our economy is created through the extension of credit by commercial banks. This checking account money may be thought of as "debts" of commercial banks and thrift institutions. Checks are bank "debts" in the sense that they are claims banks and thrifts promise to pay "on demand."

But there are forces limiting the ability of a commercial bank to create demand deposits—"bank money"—by lending. The Wahoo bank can expect the newly created demand deposit of $50,000 to be a very active account. Grisley would not borrow $50,000 at, say, 7, 10, or 12 percent interest for the sheer joy of knowing funds were available if needed.

Assume that Grisley awards a $50,000 contract to the Quickbuck Construction Company of Omaha. Quickbuck, true to its name, completes the expansion job and is paid with a check for $50,000 drawn by Grisley against its demand deposit in the Wahoo bank. Quickbuck, with headquarters in Omaha, does *not* deposit this check in the Wahoo bank but instead deposits it in the Fourth National Bank of Omaha. Fourth National now has a $50,000 claim against the Wahoo bank. This check is collected in the manner described in transaction 5. As a result, the Wahoo bank *loses* both reserves and deposits equal to the amount of the check; Fourth National *acquires* $50,000 of reserves and deposits.

In summary, assuming a check is drawn by the borrower for the entire amount of the loan ($50,000) and given to a firm which deposits it in another bank, the Wahoo bank's balance sheet will read as follows *after the check has been cleared against it.*

AFTER A CHECK IS DRAWN ON THE LOAN

BALANCE SHEET 6b: WAHOO BANK

Assets		Liabilities and net worth	
Reserves	$ 10,000	Demand	
Loans	50,000	deposits	$ 50,000
Property	240,000	Capital stock	250,000

After the check has been collected, the Wahoo bank barely meets the legal reserve ratio of 20 percent (= $50,000 ÷ $10,000). The bank has *no excess reserves.* This poses a question: Could the Wahoo bank have lent more than $50,000—an amount greater than its excess reserves—and still have met the 20 percent reserve requirement if a check for the full amount of the loan were cleared against it? The answer is "No."

Here's why. Suppose the Wahoo bank had loaned $55,000 to the Grisley company. Collection of the check against the Wahoo bank would have lowered its reserves to $5,000 (= $60,000 − $55,000) and deposits would once again stand at $50,000 (= $105,000 − $55,000). The ratio of actual reserves to deposits would now be $5,000/$50,000, or only 10 percent. The Wahoo bank could thus *not* have lent $55,000.

By experimenting with other amounts over $50,000, you will find that the maximum amount the Wahoo bank could lend at the outset of transaction 6 is $50,000. This amount is identical with the amount of excess reserves the bank had available when the loan was negotiated. *A single commercial bank in a multibank banking system can lend only an amount equal to its initial preloan excess reserves.* When it lends, it faces the likelihood that checks for the entire amount of the loan will be drawn and cleared against the lending bank. A lending bank can anticipate the loss of reserves to other banks equal to the amount it lends.[2]

Transaction 7: Repaying a Loan If commercial banks create demand deposits—money—when they

make loans, is money destroyed when loans are repaid? Yes. Using balance sheets 6b and 7, we see what happens when Grisley repays the $50,000 it borrowed.

To simplify, we (1) suppose the loan is repaid not in installments but in one lump sum two years after the date of negotiation, and (2) ignore interest charges on the loan. Grisley will write a check for $50,000 against its demand deposit, which we assume was $50,000 before the Grisley loan was negotiated. As a result, the Wahoo bank's demand-deposit liabilities decline by $50,000; Grisley has given up $50,000 worth of its claim against the bank's assets. In turn, the bank will surrender Grisley's IOU which it has been holding these many months. The bank and the company have reswapped claims. But the claim given up by Grisley is money; the claim it is repurchasing —its IOU—is not. The supply of money has therefore been reduced by $50,000; that amount of demand deposits has been destroyed, unaccompanied by an increase in the money supply elsewhere in the economy.

The Grisley company's IOU has been "demonetized" as shown in balance sheet 7. The Wahoo bank's demand deposits and loans have each returned to zero. The decline in demand deposits increases the bank's holdings of excess reserves (= $10,000); this provides the basis for new loans to be made. *(Key Questions 4 and 8)*

REPAYING A LOAN

BALANCE SHEET 7: WAHOO BANK

Assets		Liabilities and net worth	
Reserves	$ 10,000	Demand	
Loans	0	deposits	$ 0
Property	240,000	Capital stock	250,000

In the unlikely event Grisley repays the loan with cash, the money supply will still decline by $50,000. In this case, Grisley would repurchase its IOU by handing over $50,000 in cash to the bank. Loan balances decline in the asset column by $50,000 and cash increases by $50,000. Remember, we exclude currency held by banks from the money supply because to include such cash would be double counting; it is apparent that this constitutes a $50,000 reduction in the supply of money.

Transaction 8: Buying Government Securities When a commercial bank buys government bonds

---

[2]Qualification: If some of the checks written on a loan are redeposited back in the lending bank by their recipients, then that bank will be able to lend an amount somewhat greater than its initial excess reserves.

from the public, the effect is substantially the same as lending. New money is created.

Assume that the Wahoo bank's balance sheet initially stands as it did at the end of transaction 5. Now suppose that, instead of making a $50,000 loan, the bank buys $50,000 of government securities from a securities dealer. The bank receives the interest-bearing bonds which appear on its balance statement as the asset "Securities" and gives the dealer an increase in its demand-deposit account. The Wahoo bank's balance sheet would appear as follows:

BUYING GOVERNMENT SECURITIES			
BALANCE SHEET 8: WAHOO BANK			
Assets		Liabilities and net worth	
Reserves	$ 60,000	Demand	
Securities	50,000	deposits	$100,000
Property	240,000	Capital stock	250,000

Demand deposits, that is, the supply of money, have been increased by $50,000, as in transaction 6. *Commercial bank bond purchases from the public increase the supply of money in the same way as does lending to the public.* The bank accepts government bonds (which are not money) and gives the securities dealer an increase in its demand deposits (which is money).

Of course, when the securities dealer draws and clears a check for $50,000 against the Wahoo bank, the bank will lose both reserves and deposits in that amount and therefore will just be meeting the legal reserve requirement. Its balance sheet will now read precisely as in 6b except that "Securities" is substituted for "Loans" on the asset side.

Finally, the selling of government bonds to the public by a commercial bank—like the repayment of a loan—will reduce the supply of money. The securities buyer will pay by check and both "Securities" and "Demand deposits" (the latter being money) will decline by the amount of the sale.

Profits, Liquidity, and the Federal Funds Market

The asset items on a commercial bank's balance sheet reflect the banker's pursuit of two conflicting goals.

1 Profits One goal is profits. Commercial banks, like any other business, seek profits. This is why the bank makes loans and buys securities—the two major earning assets of commercial banks.

2 Liquidity The other goal is safety. For a bank, safety lies in liquidity—specifically such liquid assets as cash and excess reserves. Banks must be on guard for depositors' transforming their demand deposits into cash. Similarly, more checks may be cleared against a bank than are cleared in its favor, causing a net outflow of reserves. Bankers thus seek a balance between prudence and profits. The compromise is between earning assets and highly liquid assets.

An interesting way banks can partly reconcile the goals of profits and liquidity is to lend temporary excess reserves held at the Federal Reserve banks to other commercial banks. Normal day-to-day flows of funds to banks rarely leave all banks with their exact levels of legally required reserves. Furthermore, funds held at the Federal Reserve banks are highly liquid, but they do not draw interest. Banks therefore lend these excess reserves to other banks on an overnight basis as a way to earn additional interest without sacrificing long-term liquidity. Banks which borrow in this *Federal funds market*—the market for immediately available reserve balances at the Federal Reserve—do so because they are temporarily short of required reserves. The interest rate paid on these overnight loans is called the **Federal funds rate.**

In Figure 14-1, we would show an overnight loan of reserves from the Beaver Crossing bank to the Wahoo bank as a decrease in reserves at the Beaver Crossing bank and an increase in reserves at the Wahoo bank. Ownership of reserves at the Federal Reserve Bank of Kansas City will have changed, but total reserves there are not affected.

QUICK REVIEW 14-2

■ Banks create money when they make loans; money vanishes when bank loans are repaid.

■ New money is created when banks buy government bonds from the public; money disappears when banks sell government bonds to the public.

■ Banks balance profitability and safety in determining their mix of earning assets and highly liquid assets.

■ Banks borrow and lend temporary excess reserves on an overnight basis in the Federal funds market; the interest rate on these loans is the Federal funds rate.

1 It affects the size of excess reserves.

2 It changes the size of the monetary multiplier.

For example, in raising the legal reserve ratio from 10 to 20 percent, excess reserves are reduced from $3000 to $1000 and the demand-deposit multiplier is reduced from 10 to 5. The money-creating potential of the banking system declines from $30,000 (= $3000 × 10) to $5000 (= $1000 × 5).

Changing the reserve ratio is a powerful technique of monetary control, but it is used infrequently. Nevertheless, in 1992 the Federal Reserve reduced the reserve ratio from 12 to 10 percent.

The Discount Rate

One of the functions of a central bank is to be a "lender of last resort." Central banks lend to commercial banks which are financially sound but have unexpected and immediate needs for additional funds. Thus, each Federal Reserve Bank will make short-term loans to commercial banks in its district.

When a commercial bank borrows, it gives the Federal Reserve Bank a promissory note or IOU drawn against itself and secured by acceptable collateral—typically United States government securities. Just as commercial banks charge interest on their loans, so do Federal Reserve Banks charge interest on loans they grant to commercial banks. This interest rate is called the **discount rate.**

As a claim against the commercial bank, the borrowing bank's promissory note (IOU) is an asset to the lending Federal Reserve Bank and appears on its balance sheet as "Loans to commercial banks." To the commercial bank the IOU is a liability, appearing as "Loans from the Federal Reserve Banks" on the commercial bank's balance sheet.

In providing the loan the Federal Reserve Bank will *increase* the reserves of the borrowing commercial bank. Since no required reserves need be kept against loans from Federal Reserve Banks, *all* new reserves acquired by borrowing from Federal Reserve Banks would be excess reserves. These changes are reflected in the balance sheets as shown in the right column.

Note that this transaction is analogous to a private person's borrowing from a commercial bank (see Chapter 14, transaction 6).

The point is that *commercial bank borrowing from the Federal Reserve Banks increases the reserves of commercial banks, enhancing their ability to extend credit.*

COMMERCIAL BANK BORROWING FROM THE FED

FEDERAL RESERVE BANKS

Assets	Liabilities and net worth
+ Loans to commercial banks	+ Reserves of commercial banks
↑	
IOUs	+ Reserves
	↓

COMMERCIAL BANKS

Assets	Liabilities and net worth
+ Reserves	+ Loans from the Federal Reserve Banks

The Fed's Board of Governors has the power to establish and manipulate the discount rate at which commercial banks can borrow from Federal Reserve Banks. From the commercial banks' point of view, the discount rate is a cost entailed in acquiring reserves. When the discount rate is decreased, commercial banks are encouraged to obtain additional reserves by borrowing from Federal Reserve Banks. Commercial bank lending based on these new reserves will constitute an increase in the money supply.

An increase in the discount rate discourages commercial banks from obtaining additional reserves through borrowing from the central banks. An increase in the discount rate therefore is consistent with the monetary authorities' desire to restrict the supply of money. *(Key Question 2)*

Easy Money and Tight Money

Suppose the economy is faced with recession and unemployment. The monetary authorities decide an increase in the supply of money is needed to stimulate aggregate demand to help absorb idle resources. To increase the supply of money, the Board of Governors must expand the excess reserves of commercial banks. What policies will bring this about?

1 **Buy Securities** The Board of Governors should order Federal Reserve Banks to buy securities in the open market. These bond purchases will be paid for by increases in commercial bank reserves.

2   Reduce Reserve Ratio The reserve ratio should be reduced, automatically changing required reserves into excess reserves and increasing the size of the monetary multiplier.

3   Lower Discount Rate The discount rate should be lowered to induce commercial banks to add to their reserves by borrowing from Federal Reserve Banks.

This set of policy decisions is called an **easy money policy.** Its purpose is to make credit cheaply and easily available, to increase aggregate demand and employment.

Suppose, on the other hand, excessive spending is pushing the economy into an inflationary spiral. The Board of Governors should attempt to reduce aggregate demand by limiting or contracting the supply of money. The key to this goal lies in reducing the reserves of commercial banks. How is this done?

1   Sell Securities Federal Reserve Banks should sell government bonds in the open market to tear down commercial bank reserves.

2   Increase Reserve Ratio Increasing the reserve ratio will automatically strip commercial banks of excess reserves and decrease the monetary multiplier.

3   Raise Discount Rate A boost in the discount rate will discourage commercial banks from building up their reserves by borrowing at Federal Reserve Banks.

This group of directives is labeled a **tight money policy.** The objective is to tighten the supply of money to reduce spending and control inflation.

Relative Importance

Of the three monetary controls, open-market operations clearly are the most important control mechanism.

The discount rate is less important for two interrelated reasons.

1 The amount of commercial bank reserves obtained by borrowing from the central banks is typically very small. On the average only 2 or 3 percent of bank reserves are acquired in this way. Indeed, open-market operations often induce commercial banks to borrow from Federal Reserve Banks. That

is, to the extent that central bank bond sales leave commercial banks temporarily short of reserves, commercial banks will be prompted to borrow from Federal Reserve Banks. Rather than being a primary tool of monetary policy, commercial bank borrowing from the Fed occurs largely in response to monetary policy as carried out by open-market operations.

2 While the manipulation of commercial bank reserves through open-market operations and the changing of reserve requirements are initiated by the Federal Reserve System, the discount rate depends on the initiative of commercial banks to be effective. For example, if the discount rate is lowered at a time when very few banks are inclined to borrow from Federal Reserve Banks, the lower rate will have little or no impact on bank reserves or the money supply.

Nevertheless, a change in the discount rate may have an "announcement effect"; it may be a clear and explicit way of communicating to the financial community and the economy as a whole the intended direction of monetary policy. Other economists doubt this, arguing that changes in the discount rate are often "passive"; it is changed to keep it in line with other short-term interest rates, rather than to invoke a policy change.

What about changes in reserve requirements? The Fed has used this instrument of monetary control only sparingly. Normally, it can accomplish its monetary goals through open-market operations, without resorting to changes in reserve requirements. The limited use of changes in the reserve ratio undoubtedly is related to the fact that reserve balances earn no interest. Higher or lower reserve requirements can have substantial effects on bank profits.

But there are more positive reasons why open-market operations have evolved as the primary technique of monetary policy. This mechanism of monetary control has the advantage of flexibility—government securities can be purchased or sold in large or small amounts—and the impact on bank reserves is prompt. Yet, compared with reserve-requirement changes, open-market operations work subtly and less directly. Furthermore, quantitatively there is no question about the potential of the Federal Reserve Banks to affect commercial bank reserves through bond sales and purchases. A glance at the consolidated balance sheet for the Federal Reserve Banks (Table 15-1) reveals very large holdings of government bonds ($355 billion), the sales of which could theoretically reduce commercial bank reserves from $30 billion to zero.

MONETARY POLICY, REAL GDP, AND THE PRICE LEVEL

Although there is no disagreement as to the tools available to the Federal Reserve to change the money supply, there is some disagreement on how changes in the money supply affect the economy. We will look at the conventional view here, waiting until Chapter 16 to present an alternative perspective.

Cause-Effect Chain

We can explain how monetary policy works toward the goal of full employment and price stability by using the three diagrams comprising Figure 15-2 (Key Graph).

Money Market Figure 15-2a shows the money market, where the demand for money curve and the supply of money curve are brought together. Recall from Chapter 13 that the total demand for money comprises the transactions and asset demands. The transactions demand is directly related to the level of economic transactions as reflected in the size of the nominal GDP. The asset demand is inversely related to the in-

terest rate. The interest rate is the opportunity cost of holding money as an asset; the higher the cost, the smaller the amount of money the public wants to hold. In Figure 15-2a the total demand for money is inversely related to the interest rate. Also, recall that an increase in nominal GDP would shift D_m to the right and a decline in nominal GDP would shift D_m to the left.

We complete our graphical portrayal of the money market by showing three potential money supply curves, S_{m1}, S_{m2}, and S_{m3}. In each case the money supply is shown as a vertical line representing some fixed amount of money determined by the Fed's Board of Governors. While monetary policy (the supply of money) helps determine the interest rate, the interest rate does not determine the location of the money supply curve.

Figure 15-2a shows the equilibrium interest rate —the interest rate equating the amount of money demanded and supplied. With money demand of D_m, if the supply of money is $125 billion ($S_{m1}$), the equilibrium interest rate will be 10 percent. At a money supply of $150 billion ($S_{m2}$), the interest rate will be 8 percent; at $175 billion ($S_{m3}$), 6 percent.

We know from Chapter 10 that the real, not the nominal, rate of interest is critical for investment decisions. So here we assume Figure 15-2a portrays real interest rates.

Investment These 10, 8, and 6 percent interest rates are carried rightward to the investment demand curve of Figure 15-2b. This curve shows the inverse relationship between the interest rate—the cost of borrowing to invest—and amount of the nation's investment spending. At the 10 percent interest rate it will be profitable for businesses to invest $15 billion; at 8 percent, $20 billion; and at 6 percent, $25 billion.

The investment component of total spending is more likely to be affected by changes in the interest rate than is consumer spending. Of course, consumer purchases of automobiles—which depend heavily on installment credit—are sensitive to interest rates. But overall the interest rate is *not* a very crucial factor in determining how households divide their disposable income between consumption and saving.

The impact of changing interest rates on investment spending is great because of the large cost and long-term nature of such purchases. Capital equipment, factory buildings, and warehouses are tremendously expensive. In absolute terms, interest charges on funds borrowed for these purchases are considerable.

KEY GRAPH

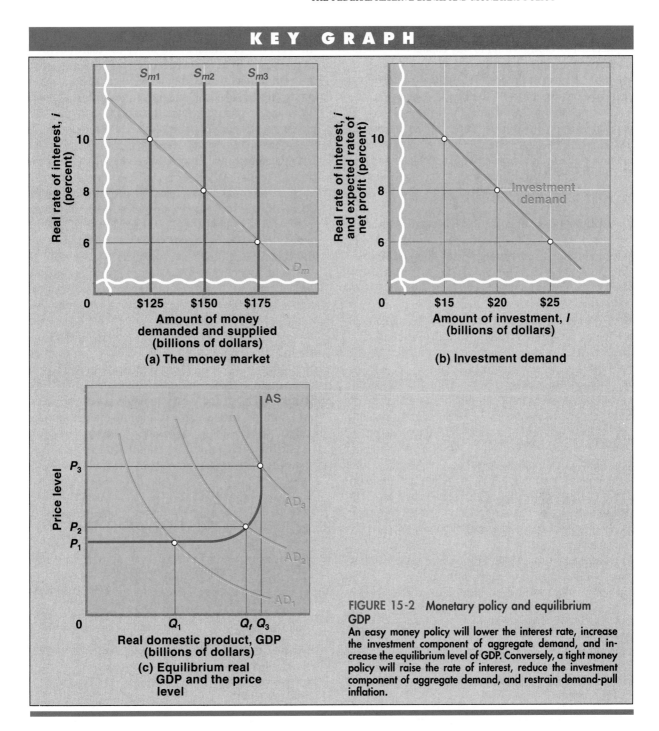

(a) The money market

(b) Investment demand

(c) Equilibrium real GDP and the price level

FIGURE 15-2 Monetary policy and equilibrium GDP
An easy money policy will lower the interest rate, increase the investment component of aggregate demand, and increase the equilibrium level of GDP. Conversely, a tight money policy will raise the rate of interest, reduce the investment component of aggregate demand, and restrain demand-pull inflation.

Similarly, the interest cost on a house purchased on a long-term contract will be very large: A one-half percentage point change in the interest rate could amount to thousands of dollars on the total cost of a home.

Also, changes in the interest rate may affect investment spending by changing the attractiveness of capital equipment purchases versus bond purchases. If the interest rate rises on bonds, then, given the profit expectations on capital goods purchases, businesses will be more inclined to use business savings to purchase securities than to buy capital equipment. Conversely, given profit expectations on investment spending, a fall in the interest rate makes capital goods purchases more attractive than bond ownership.

In brief, the impact of changing interest rates will be primarily on investment spending and, through this channel, on aggregate demand, output, employment, and the level of prices. More specifically, as Figure 15-2b indicates, investment spending varies inversely with the interest rate.

Equilibrium GDP   Figure 15-2c shows the impact of our three interest rates and corresponding levels of investment spending on aggregate demand. Aggregate demand curve AD_1 is associated with the $15 billion level of investment, AD_2 with investment of $20 billion, and AD_3 with investment of $25 billion. That is, investment spending is one of the determinants of aggregate demand (Chapter 11). All else equal, the greater this investment spending, the further to the right lies the aggregate demand curve.

Suppose the money supply in Figure 15-2a is $125 billion ($Sm_1$), producing an equilibrium interest rate of 10 percent. In Figure 15-2b we see this 10 percent interest rate will bring forth $15 billion of investment spending. This $15 billion of investment spending joins with consumption spending, net exports, and government spending to yield aggregate demand curve AD_1 in Figure 15-2c. The equilibrium levels of real output and prices are Q_1 and P_1, as determined by the intersection of AD_1 and the aggregate supply curve AS.

To test your understanding of these relationships, you should explain why each of the other two levels of money supply shown in Figure 15-2a results in a different interest rate, level of investment, aggregate demand curve, and real output-price level combination.

Effects of an Easy Money Policy

We have assumed the money supply is $125 billion ($Sm_1$) in Figure 15-2a. Because the resulting real output Q_1 in Figure 15-2c is far below the full employment output, Q_f, the economy must be experiencing substantial unemployment. The Federal Reserve therefore should institute an *easy money policy.*

To increase the money supply the Federal Reserve Banks will take some combination of the following actions: (1) buy government securities from banks and the public in the open market, (2) lower the legal reserve ratio, or (3) lower the discount rate. The result will be an increase in excess reserves in the commercial banking system. Because excess reserves are the basis on which commercial banks and thrifts can expand the money supply by lending, the nation's money supply likely will rise. An increase in the money supply will lower the interest rate, increasing investment, aggregate demand, and equilibrium GDP.

For example, an increase in the money supply from $125 to $150 billion will reduce the interest rate from 10 to 8 percent, as indicated in Figure 15-2a, and increase investment from $15 billion to $20 billion, as shown in Figure 15-2b. This $5 billion increase in investment spending will shift the aggregate demand curve rightward by more than the increase in investment because of the multiplier effect. Assuming the economy's MPC is .75, the multiplier will be 4, meaning that the $5 billion increase in investment will shift the AD curve rightward by $20 billion (= $4 \times$5) at each price level. Specifically, aggregate demand will shift from AD_1 to AD_2, as shown in Figure 15-2c. This rightward shift in aggregate demand moves the economy from Q_1 to the desired full-employment output at Q_f.

Column 1 in Table 15-3 summarizes the chain of events associated with an easy money policy.

TABLE 15-3 Monetary policy: Mainstream interpretation

(1) *Easy money policy*	(2) *Tight money policy*
Problem: unemployment and recession	**Problem:** inflation
Federal Reserve buys bonds, lowers reserve ratio, or lowers the discount rate ↓	**Federal Reserve sells bonds, increases reserve ratio, or increases the discount rate** ↓
Money supply rises ↓	**Money supply falls** ↓
Interest rate falls ↓	**Interest rate rises** ↓
Investment spending increases ↓	**Investment spending decreases** ↓
Aggregate demand increases ↓	**Aggregate demand decreases** ↓
Real GDP rises by a multiple of the increase in investment	**Inflation declines**

Effects of a Tight Money Policy

Now let's assume the money supply and interest rate are $175 billion ($S_{m3}$) in Figure 15-2a. This results in an interest rate of 6 percent, investment spending of $25 billion, and aggregate demand of AD_3. As observed in Figure 15-2c, we have depicted severe demand-pull inflation. Aggregate demand AD_3 is excessive relative to the economy's full-employment level of real output Q_f. To reign in spending, the Fed will institute a *tight money policy* (column 2 of Table 15-3).

The Federal Reserve Board will direct Federal Reserve Banks to undertake some combination of the following actions: (1) sell government securities to depository institutions and to the public in the open market, (2) increase the legal reserve ratio, or (3) increase the discount rate. Banks then will discover their reserves are too low to meet the legal reserve ratio. They therefore will need to reduce their demand deposits by refraining from issuing new loans as old loans are paid back. This will shrink the money supply and increase the interest rate. The higher interest rate will reduce investment, decreasing aggregate demand and restraining demand-pull inflation.

If the Fed reduces the money supply from $175 billion ($S_{m3}$) to $150 billion ($S_{m2}$), as shown in Figure 15-2a, the interest rate will increase from 6 to 8 percent and reduce investment from $25 to $20 billion (Figure 15-2b). The consequent $5 billion decrease in investment, bolstered by the multiplier process, will shift the aggregate demand curve leftward from AD_3 to AD_2. For example, if the MPC is .75, the multiplier will be 4 and the aggregate demand curve will shift leftward by $20 billion ($= 4 \times$ $5 billion of investment) at each price level. This leftward shift of the aggregate demand curve will eliminate the excessive spending and thus the demand-pull inflation. In the real world, of course, the goal will be to stop inflation—halt further increases in the price level—rather than actually driving down the price level.

Column 2 of Table 15-3 summarizes the cause-effect chain of tight money policy on demand-pull inflation. *(Key Question 3)*

Refinements and Feedbacks

The components of Figure 15-2 allow us to (1) appreciate some of the factors determining the effectiveness of monetary policy and (2) note the existence of a "feedback" or "circularity" problem complicating monetary policy.

Policy Effectiveness   Figure 15-2 reveals the magnitudes by which an easy or tight money policy will change the interest rate, investment, and aggregate demand. These magnitudes are determined by the particular shapes of the demand for money and investment-demand curves. Pencil in other curves to see that *the steeper the D_m curve, the larger will be the effect of any given change in the money supply on the equilibrium rate of interest. Furthermore, any given change in the interest rate will have a larger impact on investment—and hence on aggregate demand and GDP—the flatter the investment-demand curve.* A specific change in quantity of money will be most effective when the demand for money curve is relatively steep and the investment-demand curve is relatively flat.

A particular change in the quantity of money will be relatively ineffective when the money-demand curve is flat and the investment-demand curve is steep. As we will find in Chapter 16, there is controversy as to the precise shapes of these curves and therefore the effectiveness of monetary policy.

Feedback Effects   You may have sensed in Figure 15-2 a feedback or circularity problem which complicates monetary policy. The problem is this: By reading from Figure 15-2a to 15-2c we discover that the interest rate, working through the investment-demand curve, is a determinant of the equilibrium GDP. Now we must recognize that causation also runs the other way. The level of GDP is a determinant of the equilibrium interest rate. This link comes about because the transactions component of the money-demand curve depends directly on the level of nominal GDP.

How does this feedback from Figure 15-2c to 15-2a affect monetary policy? It means that the increase in the GDP which an easy money policy brings about will *increase* the demand for money, partially offsetting the interest-reducing effect of the easy money policy. A tight money policy will reduce the nominal GDP. But this will *decrease* the demand for money and dampen the initial interest-increasing effect of the tight money policy. This feedback is also at the core of a policy dilemma, as we will see later. *(Key Question 4)*

Monetary Policy and Aggregate Supply

As with fiscal policy (Chapter 12), monetary policy is subject to the constraints implicit in the aggregate

KEY GRAPH

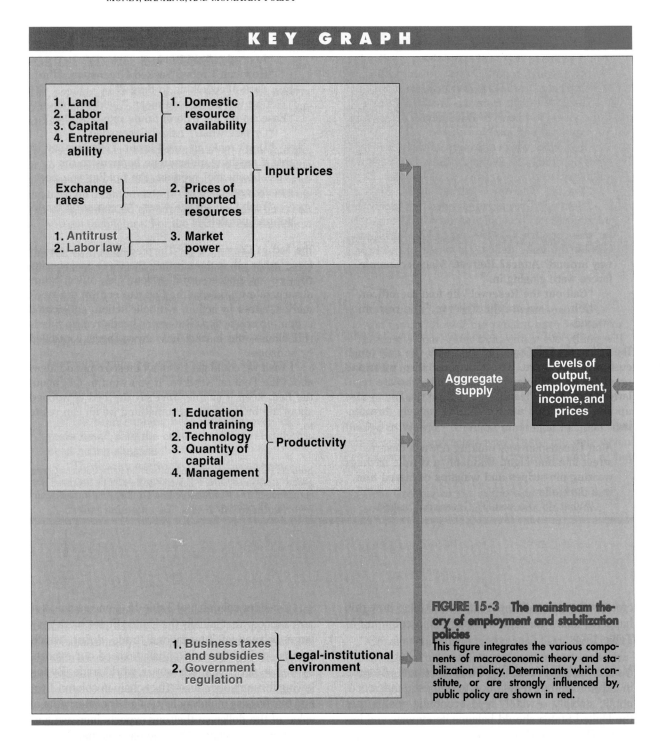

FIGURE 15-3 The mainstream theory of employment and stabilization policies
This figure integrates the various components of macroeconomic theory and stabilization policy. Determinants which constitute, or are strongly influenced by, public policy are shown in red.

gish growth is compatible with the goal of correcting a balance of trade deficit. If initially our exports were greatly in *excess* of our imports—that is, the United States had a large balance of trade *surplus*—an easy money policy would aggravate the surplus.

Now consider column 2 of Table 15-4 and assume again that at the outset the United States has a large balance of trade deficit. In invoking a tight money policy to restrain inflation we would find that net exports would decrease—our exports would fall and imports

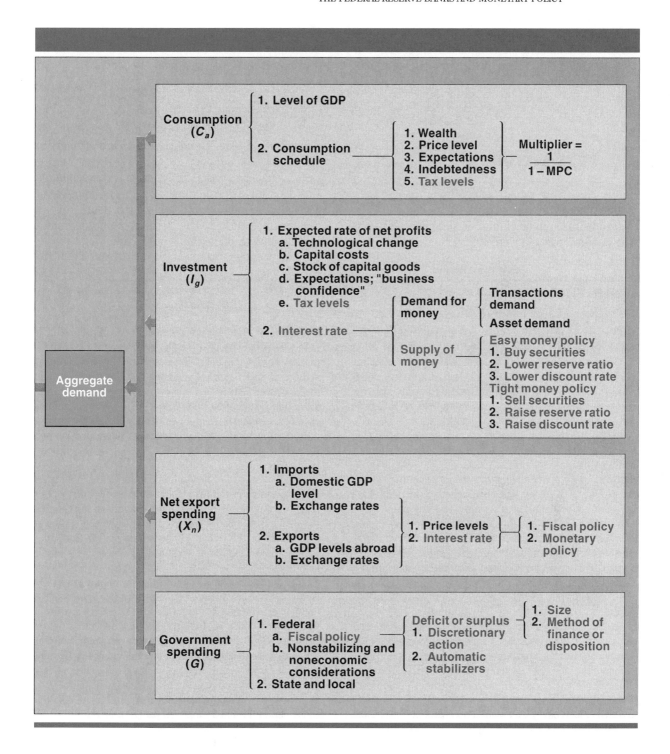

would rise. This means the trade deficit would be enlarged.

Conclusion: *A tight money policy invoked to alleviate inflation conflicts with the goal of correcting a balance of trade deficit.* If our initial problem was a trade surplus, a tight money policy would tend to resolve that surplus.

Overall we find that an easy money policy alleviates a trade deficit and aggravates a trade surplus. Similarly, a tight money policy alleviates a trade surplus and aggravates a trade deficit. The point is that certain combinations of circumstances create conflicts or tradeoffs between the use of monetary policy to achieve domestic stability and the realization of balance in the nation's international trade. *(Key Question 8)*

THE "BIG PICTURE"

Figure 15-3 (Key Graph) brings together the many analytical and policy aspects of macroeconomics discussed in this and the eight preceding chapters. This "big picture" shows how the many concepts and principles discussed relate to one another and how they constitute a coherent theory of what determines the level of resource use in a market economy.

Study this diagram and you will see that the levels of output, employment, income, and prices all result from the interaction of aggregate supply and aggregate demand. In particular, note those items—shown in red—which constitute, or are strongly influenced by, public policy.

Self-test: Suppose the economy represented by this diagram was experiencing a severe, long-lasting recession. What specific stabilization policies would you recommend? Use the linkages in this diagram to explain how your policies would work.

CHAPTER SUMMARY

1 Like fiscal policy, the goal of monetary policy is to assist the economy in achieving a full-employment, noninflationary level of total output.

2 For a consideration of monetary policy, the most important assets of the Federal Reserve Banks are securities and loans to commercial banks. The basic liabilities are the reserves of member banks, Treasury deposits, and Federal Reserve Notes.

3 The three instruments of monetary policy are **a** open-market operations, **b** changing the reserve ratio, and **c** changing the discount rate.

4 Monetary policy operates through a complex cause-effect chain: **a** Policy decisions affect commercial bank reserves; **b** changes in reserves affect the money supply; **c** changes in the money supply alter the interest rate; and **d** changes in the interest rate affect investment; **e** changes in investment affect aggregate demand; **f** changes in aggregate demand affect the equilibrium real GDP and the price level. Table 15-3 draws together all the basic notions relevant to applying easy and tight money policies.

5 The advantages of monetary policy include its flexibility and political acceptability. In the past fifteen years monetary policy has been used successfully both to reduce rapid inflation and push the economy from recession. Today, almost all economists view monetary policy as a significant stabilization tool.

6 Monetary policy has some limitations and problems. **a** Financial innovations and global considerations have made this policy more difficult to administer and its impact less certain. **b** Policy-instigated changes in the supply of money may be partially offset by changes in the velocity of money. **c** The impact of monetary policy will be lessened if the money-demand curve is flat and the investment-demand curve is steep. The investment-demand curve may also shift, negating monetary policy. **d** Changes in interest rates resulting from monetary policy change the amount of interest income received by lenders, altering some people's spending in a way counter to the intent of the monetary policy.

7 Monetary authorities face a policy dilemma in that they can stabilize interest rates *or* the money supply, but not both. Recent monetary policy has been pragmatic, focusing on the health of the economy and not on stabilizing either interest rates or the money supply exclusively. In particular, the Fed has recently focused on the Federal funds rate in setting its policy.

8 The impact of an easy money policy on domestic GDP is strengthened by an accompanying increase in net exports precipitated by a lower domestic interest rate. Likewise, a tight money policy is strengthened by a decline in net exports. In some situations, there may be a tradeoff between the use of monetary policy to affect the international value of the dollar and thus to correct a trade imbalance and the use of monetary policy to achieve domestic stability.

9 Figure 15-3 summarizes mainstream macroeconomic theory and policy and deserves your careful study.

TERMS AND CONCEPTS

monetary policy	discount rate	velocity of money	prime interest rate
open-market operations	easy and tight money	target dilemma	net export effect
reserve ratio	policies	Federal funds rate	

QUESTIONS AND STUDY SUGGESTIONS

1 Use commercial bank and Federal Reserve Bank balance sheets to demonstrate the impact of each of the following transactions on commercial bank reserves:

    a Federal Reserve Banks purchase securities from private businesses and consumers.

    b Commercial banks borrow from Federal Reserve Banks.

    c The Board of Governors reduces the reserve ratio.

2 *Key Question* *In the table below you will find simplified consolidated balance sheets for the commercial banking system and the twelve Federal Reserve Banks. In columns 1 through 3, indicate how the balance sheets would read after each of the three ensuing transactions is completed. Do not cumulate your answers; that is, analyze each transaction separately, starting in each case from the given figures. All accounts are in billions of dollars.*

ties from commercial banks. Show the new balance-sheet figures in column 3.

    d *Now review each of the above three transactions, asking yourself these three questions: (1) What change, if any, took place in the money supply as a direct and immediate result of each transaction? (2) What increase or decrease in commercial banks' reserves took place in each transaction? (3) Assuming a reserve ratio of 20 percent, what change in the money-creating potential of the commercial banking system occurred as a result of each transaction?*

3 *Key Question* *Suppose you are a member of the Board of Governors of the Federal Reserve System. The economy is experiencing a sharp and prolonged inflationary trend. What changes in* **a** *the reserve ratio,* **b** *the discount rate, and* **c** *open-market operations would you recommend? Explain in*

Consolidated balance sheet: all commercial banks

		(1)	(2)	(3)
Assets:				
Reserves	$ 33	____	____	____
Securities	60	____	____	____
Loans	60	____	____	____
Liabilities and net worth:				
Demand deposits	$150	____	____	____
Loans from the Federal Reserve Banks	3	____	____	____

Consolidated balance sheet: twelve Federal Reserve Banks

		(1)	(2)	(3)
Assets:				
Securities	$60	____	____	____
Loans to commercial banks	3	____	____	____
Liabilities and net worth:				
Reserves of commercial banks	$33	____	____	____
Treasury deposits	3	____	____	____
Federal Reserve Notes	27	____	____	____

    a *Suppose a decline in the discount rate prompts commercial banks to borrow an additional $1 billion from the Federal Reserve Banks. Show the new balance-sheet figures in column 1.*

    b *The Federal Reserve Banks sell $3 billion in securities to the public, who pay for the bonds with checks. Show the new balance-sheet figures in column 2.*

    c *The Federal Reserve Banks buy $2 billion of securi-*

each case how the change you advocate would affect commercial bank reserves, the money supply, interest rates, and aggregate demand.

4 *Key Question* *What is the basic objective of monetary policy? Describe the cause-effect chain through which monetary policy is made effective. Using Figure 15-2 as a point of reference, discuss how* **a** *the shapes of the demand for money and investment-demand curves and* **b** *the size of the MPC* *influence the effectiveness of monetary policy. How do feedback effects influence the effectiveness of monetary policy?*

5 Evaluate the overall effectiveness of monetary policy. Why have open-market operations evolved as the primary means of controlling commercial bank reserves? Discuss the specific limitations of monetary policy.

6 Explain the observation that the Fed cannot simultaneously stabilize interest rates and the money supply. Explain why the target of a stable interest rate might contribute to ongoing inflation.

7 *Key Question Distinguish between the Federal funds rate and the prime interest rate. In what way is the Federal funds rate a measure of the tightness or looseness of monetary policy? In 1994 the Fed used open-market operations to increase the Federal funds rate. What was the logic? What was the effect on the prime interest rate?*

8 *Key Question Suppose the Federal Reserve decides to engage in a tight money policy as a way to reduce demand-pull inflation. Use the aggregate demand–aggregate supply model to show the intent of this policy for a closed economy. Next, introduce the open economy and explain how changes in the international value of the dollar might affect the location of your aggregate demand curve.*

9 Design an antirecession stabilization policy, involving both fiscal and monetary policies, which is consistent with **a** a relative decline in the public sector, **b** greater income equality, and **c** a high rate of economic growth. Explain: "Truly effective stabilization policy presumes the coordination of fiscal and monetary policy."

10 (Last Word) How do each of the following metaphors apply to the Federal Reserve's role in the economy: Fed as a mechanic; Fed as a warrior; Fed as a fall guy?

Problems and Controversies in Macro-economics

—classical and Keynesian—can be restated and compared in their simple forms through aggregate demand and aggregate supply curves.

Classical View

The classical view is that the aggregate supply curve is vertical and exclusively determines the level of real output. The downsloping aggregate demand curve is stable and solely establishes the price level.

Vertical Aggregate Supply Curve In the classical perspective, the aggregate supply curve is a vertical line as shown in Figure 16-1a. This line is located at the full-employment level of real output, which in this particular designation is also the absolute full-capacity level of real output. According to the classical economists, the economy will operate at its full-employment level of output, Q_f, because of (1) Say's law (Chapter 9) and (2) responsive, flexible prices and wages.

We stress that classical economists believed that Q_f does *not* change in response to changes in the price level. Observe that as the price level falls from P_1 to P_2 in Figure 16-1a, real output remains anchored at Q_f.

But this stability of output might seem at odds with Chapter 3's upsloping supply curves for individual products. There we found that lower prices would make production less profitable and cause producers to offer *less* output and employ *fewer* workers. The classical response to this view is that input costs would fall along with product prices to leave *real* profits and output unchanged.

Consider a one-firm economy in which the firm's owner must receive a *real* profit of $20 to produce the full-employment output of 100 units. Recall from Chapter 8 that what ultimately counts is the *real* reward one receives and not the level of prices. Assume the owner's only input (aside from personal entrepreneurial talent) is 10 units of labor hired at $8 per worker for a total wage cost of $80 (= $10 \times 8). Also suppose the 100 units of output sell for $1 per unit so that total revenue is $100 (= $100 \times 1). This firm's *nominal* profit is $20 (= $100 - 80) and, using the $1 price to designate the base price index of 100 percent, its *real* profit is also $20 (= $20 \div 1.00$). Well and good; full employment is achieved. But suppose the price level declines by one-half. Would our producer still earn the $20 of real profits needed to induce production of a 100-unit full-employment output?

The classical answer is "Yes." Now that product price is only $.50, total revenue will only be $50 (= $100 \times $.50$). But the cost of 10 units of labor will be reduced to $40 (= $10 \times 4) because the wage rate will be halved. Although *nominal* profits fall to $10 (= $50 - 40), *real* profits remain at $20. By dividing money profits of $10 by the new price index (expressed as a decimal) we obtain *real* profits of $20 (= $10 \div .50$).

With perfectly flexible wages there would be no change in the real rewards and therefore the production behavior of businesses. With perfect wage flexibility, a change in the price level will not cause the economy to stray from full employment.

Stable Aggregate Demand The classical economists theorized that money underlies aggregate demand. The amount of real output which can be purchased depends on (1) the quantity of money households and businesses possess and (2) the purchasing power or real value of that money as determined by the price level. The purchasing power of the dollar refers to the real quantity of goods and services a dollar will buy. Thus, as we move down the vertical axis of Figure 16-1a, the price level is falling. This means the purchasing power of each dollar increases and therefore the specific quantity of money can buy a larger quantity of real output. If the price level declined by one-half, a particular quantity of money would now purchase a real output twice as large. With a fixed money supply, the price level and real output are inversely related.

And what of the *location* of the aggregate demand curve? According to the classical economists, aggregate demand will be stable if the nation's monetary authorities maintain a constant supply of money. With a fixed aggregate supply, increases in the supply of money will shift the aggregate demand curve rightward and spark demand-pull inflation. Reductions in the supply of money will shift the curve leftward and trigger deflation. The key to price-level stability, then, said the classical economists, is to control the nation's money supply to prevent unwarranted shifts in aggregate demand.

A final observation: Even if there are declines in the money supply and therefore in aggregate demand, the economy depicted in Figure 16-1a will *not* experience unemployment. Admittedly, the immediate effect of a decline in aggregate demand from AD_1 to AD_2 is an excess supply of output since the aggregate output of goods and services exceeds aggregate

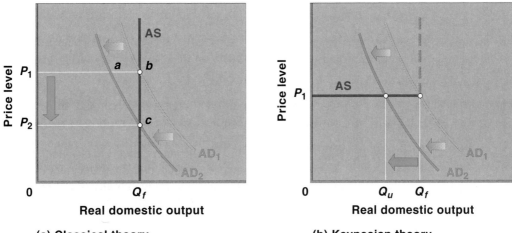

(a) Classical theory **(b) Keynesian theory**

FIGURE 16-1 Classical and Keynesian views of the macroeconomy
According to classical theory (a), aggregate supply will determine the full-employment level of real domestic output while aggregate demand will establish the price level. Aggregate demand normally is stable, but if it should decline, say, as shown from AD_1 to AD_2, the price level will quickly fall from P_1 to P_2 to eliminate the temporary excess supply of ab and to restore full employment at c. The Keynesian view (b) is that aggregate demand is unstable and that price and wages are downwardly inflexible. An AD_1 to AD_2 decline in aggregate demand has no effect on the price level. Rather, real output falls from Q_f to Q_u and can remain at this equilibrium indefinitely.

spending by the amount ab. But, with the presumed downward flexibility of product and resource prices, this excess supply will reduce product prices along with workers' wages and the prices of other inputs. As a result, the price level will quickly decline from P_1 to P_2 until the amounts of output demanded and supplied are brought once again into equilibrium, this time at c. While the price level has fallen from P_1 to P_2, real output remains at the full-employment level.

Keynesian View

The core of crude, or extreme, **Keynesianism** is that product prices and wages are downwardly inflexible, resulting in what is graphically represented as a horizontal aggregate supply curve. Also, aggregate demand is subject to periodic changes caused by changes in the determinants of aggregate demand (Table 11-1).

Horizontal Aggregate Supply Curve (to Full-Employment Output) The downward inflexibility of prices and wages discussed in Chapter 11 translates to a horizontal aggregate supply curve as shown in Figure 16-1b. Here, a decline in real output from Q_f to Q_u will have no impact on the price level. Con-

versely, an increase in real output from Q_u to Q_f will also leave the price level unchanged. The aggregate supply curve therefore extends from zero real output rightward to the full-employment output Q_f. Once full employment is reached, the aggregate supply curve becomes vertical in this simplified view. This is shown by the vertical (dashed) line extending upward from the horizontal aggregate supply curve at Q_f.

Unstable Aggregate Demand Keynesian economists view aggregate demand as unstable from one period to the next, even without changes in the money supply. In particular, the investment component of aggregate demand fluctuates, altering the location of the aggregate demand curve. Suppose aggregate demand in Figure 11-1b declines from AD_1 to AD_2. The sole impact of this decline in aggregate demand will be on output and employment because real output falls from Q_f to Q_u while the price level remains constant at P_1. Moreover, Keynesians believe that unless there is a fortuitous offsetting increase in aggregate demand, real output may remain at Q_u, which is below the full-employment level Q_f. Active macroeconomic policies of aggregate demand management by government are essential to avoid the wastes of recession and depression. *(Key Question 1)*

KEYNESIANS AND MONETARISM

Classical economics has emerged in modern forms. One is **monetarism,** which holds that markets are highly competitive and that a competitive market system gives the economy a high degree of macroeconomic stability. Like classical economics, monetarism argues that the price and wage flexibility provided by competitive markets would cause fluctuations in aggregate demand to alter product and resource prices rather than output and employment. Thus the market system would provide substantial macroeconomic stability *were it not for governmental interference in the economy.*

The problem, as the monetarists see it, is that government has fostered and promoted downward wage-price inflexibility through the minimum-wage law, pro-union legislation, farm price supports, pro-business monopoly legislation, and so forth. The free-market system could provide macroeconomic stability, but, despite good intentions, government interference has undermined this capability. Furthermore, monetarists argue that government has contributed to the instability of the system—to the business cycle—through its clumsy and mistaken attempts to achieve greater stability through *discretionary* fiscal and monetary policies.

In view of the preceding comments, it is no surprise that monetarists have a strong *laissez faire* or free-market orientation. Governmental decision making is held to be bureaucratic, inefficient, harmful to individual incentives, and frequently characterized by policy mistakes which destabilize the economy. Furthermore, as emphasized by Friedman, centralized decision making by government inevitably erodes in-

dividual freedoms.[1] The public sector should be kept to the smallest possible size.

Keynesians and monetarists therefore are opposed in their conceptions of the private and public sectors.

To the Keynesian, the instability of private investment causes the economy to be unstable. Government plays a positive role by applying appropriate stabilization medicine.

To the monetarist, government has harmful effects on the economy. Government creates rigidities which weaken the capacity of the market system to provide stability. It also embarks on monetary and fiscal measures which, although well intentioned, aggravate the instability they are designed to cure.

The Basic Equations

Keynesian economics and monetarism each build their analysis on specific equations.

Aggregate Expenditures Equation As indicated in Chapters 9 and 10, Keynesian economics focuses on aggregate spending and its components. The basic Keynesian equation is:

$$C_a + I_g + X_n + G = \text{GDP} \qquad (1)$$

This theory says that the aggregate amount of after-tax consumption, gross investment, net exports, and government spending determines the total value of the goods and services sold. In equilibrium, $C_a + I_g + X_n + G$ (aggregate expenditures) is equal to GDP (real output).

Equation of Exchange Monetarism focuses on money. The fundamental equation of monetarism is the **equation of exchange:**

$$MV = PQ \qquad (2)$$

where M is the supply of money; V is the **velocity of money,** that is, *the number of times per year the average dollar is spent on final goods and services;* P is the price level or, more specifically, *the average price at which each unit of physical output is sold;* and Q is the physical volume of all goods and services produced.

The label "equation of exchange" is easily understood. The left side, MV, represents the total

[1] Friedman's philosophy is effectively expounded in two of his books: *Capitalism and Freedom* (Chicago: The University of Chicago Press, 1962); and, with Rose Friedman, *Free to Choose* (New York: Harcourt Brace Jovanovich, 1980).

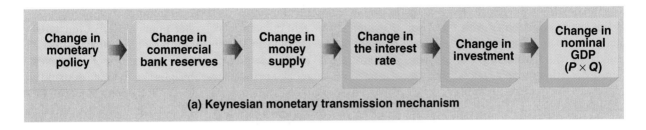

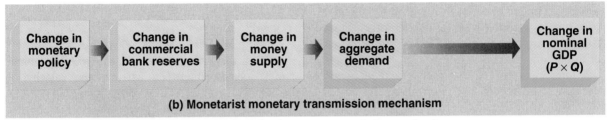

FIGURE 16-2 Alternative views of the monetary transmission mechanism
Keynesians (a) emphasize the roles of interest rates and investment spending in explaining how changes in the money supply affect nominal GDP. On the other hand, monetarists (b) contend that changes in the money supply cause direct changes in aggregate demand and thereby changes in nominal GDP.

amount *spent* by purchasers of output, while the right side, *PQ*, represents the total amount *received* by sellers of that output.

> The difference between the two approaches can be compared with two ways of looking at the flow of water through a sewer pipe—say, at the rate of 6000 gallons per hour. A neo-Keynesian investigator might say that the flow of 6000 gallons an hour consisted of 3000 gallons an hour from a paper mill, 2000 gallons an hour from an auto plant, and 1000 gallons an hour from a shopping center. A monetarist investigator might say that the sewer flow of 6000 gallons an hour consisted of an average of 200 gallons in the sewer at any one time with a complete turnover of the water 30 times every hour.[2]

Both the Keynesian and monetarist approaches are helpful in understanding macroeconomics. In fact, the Keynesian equation can be readily "translated" into monetarist terms. In the monetarist approach, total spending is the supply of money multiplied by its velocity. In short, MV is the monetarist counterpart of equilibrium $C_a + I_g + X_n + G$. Because MV is the total amount spent on final goods in one year, it is equal to nominal GDP. Furthermore, nominal GDP is the sum of the physical outputs of various goods and services (Q) multiplied by their respective prices (P).

That is, GDP = *PQ*. We can therefore restate the Keynesian $C_a + I_g + X_n + G$ = GDP equation in nominal terms as the monetarist equation of exchange, $MV = PQ$.[3]

The two approaches are two ways of looking at much the same thing. But the critical question remains: Which theory more accurately portrays macroeconomics and therefore is the better basis for economic policy?

Spotlight on Money The Keynesian equation puts money in a secondary role. Indeed, the Keynesian conception of monetary policy (Chapter 15) entails a rather lengthy transmission mechanism, as shown in Figure 16-2a. A change in monetary policy alters the nation's supply of money. The change in the money supply affects the interest rate, which changes the level of investment. When the economy is operating at less than capacity, changes in investment affect nominal GDP (= *PQ*) by changing real output (*Q*) through the income multiplier effect. Alternatively, when the economy is achieving full employment, changes in investment affect nominal GDP by altering the price level (*P*).

---

[2]Werner Sichel and Peter Eckstein, *Basic Economic Concepts* (Chicago: Rand McNally College Publishing Company, 1974), p. 344.

[3]Technical footnote: There is an important conceptual difference between the Keynesian $C_a + I_g + X_n + G$ and the MV component of the equation of exchange. The former indicates planned or *intended* expenditures, which equal actual expenditures only in equilibrium, while MV reflects *actual* spending.

Keynesians contend there are many loose links in this cause-effect chain with the result that monetary policy is an uncertain and weak stabilization tool compared with fiscal policy. For example, recall from Figure 15-2 that monetary policy will be relatively ineffective if the demand for money curve is flat and the investment-demand curve is steep. Also, the investment-demand curve may shift adversely so that the impact of a change in the interest rate on investment spending is muted or offset. Nor will an easy money policy be very effective if banks and other depository institutions are not anxious to lend or the public eager to borrow.

Monetarists believe that money and monetary policy are more important in determining the level of economic activity than do the Keynesians. *Monetarists hold that changes in the money supply are the single most important factor in determining the levels of output, employment, and prices.* They see a different cause-effect chain between the supply of money and the level of economic activity than the Keynesian model suggests. Rather than limiting the effect of an increase in money to bond purchases and consequent declines in the interest rate, monetarists theorize that an increase in the money supply drives up the demand for all assets—real or financial—as well as for current output. Under conditions of full employment, the prices of all these items will rise. Monetarists also say the velocity of money is stable—meaning it does not fluctuate wildly and does not change in response to a change in the money supply itself. Thus, changes in the money supply will have a predictable effect on the level of nominal GDP ($= PQ$). More precisely, an increase in M will increase P or Q, or some combination of both P and Q; a decrease in M will do the opposite.

Monetarists believe that, although a change in M may cause short-run changes in real output and employment as market adjustments occur, the long-run impact of a change in M will be on the price level. Monetarists think the private economy is inherently stable and usually operates at the full-employment level of output. The exact level of that full-employment output depends on such "real" factors as the quantity and quality of labor, capital, and land and upon technology (Chapter 19). The point is that, if Q is constant at the economy's capacity output, then changes in M will lead to changes in P.

Monetarism implies a more direct transmission mechanism than does the Keynesian model. Observe in Figure 16-2b that monetarists view changes in the money supply as producing direct changes in aggregate demand which alter nominal GDP. Monetarists contend that changes in the money supply affect all components of aggregate demand, not just investment. Furthermore, changes in aggregate demand allegedly affect nominal GDP in the long run primarily through changes in the price level, not through changes in real output.

Velocity: Stable or Unstable?

A critical theoretical issue in the Keynesian–monetarist debate centers on whether the velocity of money, V, is stable. As used here, "stable" is *not* synonymous with "constant." Monetarists are aware that velocity is higher today than in 1945. Shorter pay periods, greater use of credit cards, and faster means of making payments have increased velocity since 1945. These factors have enabled people to reduce their cash and checkbook holdings relative to the size of the nominal GDP.

What monetarists mean when they say velocity is stable is that the factors altering velocity change gradually and predictably. Changes in velocity from one year to the next can be easily anticipated. Moreover, velocity does *not* change in response to changes in the supply of money itself.

If velocity is stable, the equation of exchange tells us that monetarists are correct in claiming that a direct, predictable relationship exists between the money supply and nominal GDP ($= PQ$).

Suppose M is 100, V is 1, and nominal GDP is 100. Also assume velocity increases annually at a stable rate of 2 percent. Using the equation of exchange, we can predict that a 5 percent annual growth rate of the money supply will result in about a 7 percent increase in nominal GDP. M will increase from 100 to 105, V will rise from 1 to 1.02, and nominal GDP will increase from 100 to about 107 ($= 105 \times 1.02$).

But if V is not stable, then the Keynesian contention that money plays a secondary role in macroeconomics is quite plausible. If V is variable and unpredictable from one period to another, the link between M and PQ will be loose and uncertain. A steady growth of M will not necessarily translate into a steady growth of nominal GDP.

Monetarists: V Is Stable What rationale do monetarists offer for their contention that V is stable? They argue that people have a stable desire to hold money relative to holding other financial and real assets and buying current output. The factors determining the amount of money people and businesses wish to hold at any specific time are independent of the supply of money. Most importantly, the amount of money the public will want to hold will depend on the level of nominal GDP.

Example: Suppose that, when the level of nominal GDP is $400 billion, the amount of money the public wants or *desires* to hold to buy this output is $100 billion ($V$ is 4). If we further assume that the *actual* supply of money is $100 billion, we can say that the economy is in equilibrium with respect to money; the *actual* amount of money supplied equals the amount the public *desires* to hold.

In the monetarist view an increase in the money supply of, say, $10 billion will upset this equilibrium since the public will find itself holding more money or liquidity than it wants; the actual amount of money held exceeds the amount of holdings desired. The reaction of the public (households and businesses) is to restore its desired balance of money relative to other items such as stocks and bonds, factories and equipment, houses and automobiles, and clothing and toys. The public has more money than it wants; the way to get rid of it is to buy things. But one person's spending of money leaves more cash in someone else's checkable deposit or billfold. That person, too, tries to "spend down" excess cash balances.

The collective attempt to reduce cash balances will increase aggregate demand, boosting the nominal GDP. Because velocity is 4—the typical dollar is spent four times per year—nominal GDP must rise by $40 billion. When nominal GDP reaches $440 billion, the *actual* money supply of $110 billion again will be the amount which the public *desires* to hold, and equilibrium will be reestablished. Spending on goods and services will increase until nominal GDP has increased enough to restore the original equilibrium relationship between nominal GDP and the money supply.

The relationship GDP/M defines V. A stable relationship between GDP and M means a stable V.

Keynesians: V Is Unstable In the Keynesian view the velocity of money is variable and unpredictable. This position can be understood through the Keynesian conception of the demand for money (Chapter 13). Money is demanded, not only to use in negotiating transactions, but also to hold as an asset. Money demanded for *transactions* purposes will be "active"

money—money changing hands and circulating through the income-expenditures stream. Transactions dollars have some positive velocity; the average transactions dollar may be spent, say, six times per year and buy $6 of output. In this case V is 6 for each transactions dollar.

But money demanded and held as an *asset* is "idle" money. These dollars do *not* flow through the income-expenditures stream, so their velocity is zero. Therefore, the overall velocity of the entire money supply will depend on how it is divided between transactions and asset balances. The greater the relative importance of "active" transactions balances, the larger will be V. The greater the relative significance of "idle" asset balances, the smaller will be V.

Using this framework, Keynesians discredit the monetarist transmission mechanism—the allegedly dependable relationship between changes in M and changes in GDP—arguing that a significant portion of any increase in the money supply may go into asset balances, *causing V to fall.* In the extreme, assume *all* the increase in the money supply is held by the public as additional asset balances. The public simply hoards the additional money and uses none of it for transactions. The money supply will have increased, but velocity will decline by an offsetting amount so that there will be no effect on the amount of aggregate demand and the size of nominal GDP.

We can consider the Keynesian position on a more advanced level by referring to Figure 13-2. There, the relative importance of the asset demand for money varies inversely with the rate of interest. An *increase* in the money supply will *lower* the interest rate. That will make it less expensive to hold money as an asset, so the public will hold larger zero-velocity asset balances. Therefore, the overall velocity of the money supply will fall. A *reduction* in the money supply will *raise* the interest rate, increasing the cost of holding money as an asset. The resulting decline in asset balances will increase the overall velocity of money.

In the Keynesian view velocity varies (1) directly with the rate of interest and (2) inversely with the supply of money. If this is correct, the stable relationship between M and nominal GDP in the monetarist's transmission mechanism does *not* exist because V will vary whenever M changes.

We can now better appreciate a point made at the end of Chapter 15 in discussing possible shortcomings of monetary policy. We indicated that V tends to change in the opposite direction from M. Our present

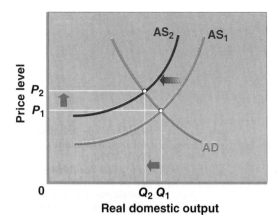

FIGURE 17-4 Adverse aggregate supply shocks and stagflation

In the mainstream interpretation, in 1973–1975 a series of supply shocks, including sharply increased energy costs, higher agricultural commodity prices, higher import prices, diminishing productivity growth, and inflationary expectations, shifted the aggregate supply curve leftward. The result was stagflation—a higher price level accompanied by a decline in real output. A similar scenario occurred in 1978–1980.

shift) of *aggregate supply* causes the unemployment rate and the price level to vary *directly*. Both increase to cause stagflation. This, say mainstream economists, is what happened in 1973–1975 and again in 1978–1980.

Let's consider the series of more-or-less random adverse shocks which raised unit production costs and shifted the aggregate supply curve leftward, as from AS$_1$ to AS$_2$ in Figure 17-4, to generate the Great Stagflation of 1973–1975. More technically, we want to examine how changes in several of the determinants of aggregate supply (Chapter 11) contributed to stagflation.

1 OPEC and Energy Prices First and foremost, the Organization of Petroleum Exporting Countries (OPEC) oil cartel quadrupled oil prices. The cost of producing and distributing virtually every product and service rose sharply.

2 Agricultural Shortfalls Severe global agricultural shortfalls occurred in 1972 and 1973, particularly in Asia and the Soviet Union. In response, American agricultural exports expanded sharply, reducing domestic supplies of agricultural commodities. The resulting higher prices for raw agricultural products in the United States meant higher costs to industries producing food and fiber products. These higher costs were passed on to consumers as higher prices.

3 Depreciated Dollar In 1971–1973, the dollar was reduced in value to achieve greater balance between national exports and imports. Depreciation of the dollar meant that it took more dollars to buy a unit of foreign money, which increased prices of all American imports. Because many American imports are production inputs, unit production costs increased and the aggregate supply curve shifted leftward.

4 Demise of Wage-Price Controls In 1971–1974 the Nixon administration imposed wage and price controls which suppressed inflationary pressures. When these were abandoned in 1974, both businesses and input suppliers pushed up their prices rapidly to recoup the price increases they had to forgo during the control period. This upsurge increased unit costs and product prices.

5 Productivity Decline The stagflation episodes of the 1970s and early 1980s were not due solely to the four supply shocks just discussed. More subtle considerations involving productivity and expectations were also at work. The rate of growth of labor productivity—the efficiency of labor—began to decline in the mid-1960s and continued to fall throughout the 1970s (Chapter 19). This decline in the growth rate of output per worker-hour increased unit production costs. An increase in unit labor costs (that is, labor cost per unit of output) approximates the difference between the increase in nominal-wage rates and the increase in labor productivity. More precisely:

$$\begin{array}{ccccc} \text{Percentage} & & \text{percentage} & & \text{percentage} \\ \text{change in} & & \text{change in} & & \text{change in} \\ \text{unit labor} & \approx & \text{nominal-wage} & - & \text{labor} \\ \text{costs} & & \text{rates} & & \text{productivity} \end{array} \quad (1)$$

If hourly nominal wages are currently \$5.00 and a worker produces 10 units per hour, unit labor costs will be \$.50.

If nominal wages increase by 10 percent to \$5.50 per hour and productivity also increases by 10 percent to 11 units per hour, then unit labor costs will be unchanged. That is, \$5.00/10 = \$5.50/11 = \$.50. In equation (1), 10 percent (change in nominal wages) *minus* 10 percent (change in productivity) *equals* no increase in unit labor costs.

Similarly, if nominal wages were to rise by 10 percent and labor productivity does not increase at all, unit labor costs would go up by 10 percent. If the wage rate was \$5.00 initially and output per hour was 10 units, labor costs would be \$.50. But with wages \$5.50

and output still at 10 units per hour, unit labor costs would be $.55, a 10 percent increase. In equation (1), 10 percent *minus* zero percent *equals* a 10 percent increase in unit labor costs. Since labor costs are 70 to 80 percent of production costs, product prices rise roughly with increases in unit labor costs.

What should we conclude from our simple equation when we think about stagflation? Answer: For any specific size of nominal wage increase, a decline in productivity will boost unit production costs and shift the aggregate supply curve leftward.

6 Inflationary Expectations and Wages The inflation of the 1970s had its genesis in the inflation of the late 1960s which was caused by expanded military spending on the Vietnam war. By the early 1970s workers had been exposed to a period of accelerating inflation. As a result, nominal-wage demands of labor began to include the expectation of an increasing rate of inflation. Most employers, expecting to pass on higher wage costs in this context of mounting inflation, did not resist labor's demands for larger and larger increases in nominal wages. These nominal-wage increases raised unit production costs and reduced aggregate supply, as from AS_1 to AS_2 in Figure 17-4.

We can incorporate both **inflationary expectations** *and* declining labor productivity in equation (1) as causes of stagflation. If nominal wage increases are accelerating and the growth rate of labor productivity is falling, there will be a double impetus for unit labor costs—and ultimately product prices—to rise.

Synopsis All these factors combined in the 1970s to adversely shift the aggregate supply curve to yield the worst possible macroeconomic world—falling output and rising unemployment combined with a rising price level (Figure 17-4). The unemployment rate shot up from 4.8 percent in 1973 to 8.3 percent in 1975, contributing to a $47 billion *decline* in real GDP. In the same period the price level increased by 21 percent.

Like a bad dream, the 1973–1975 stagflation scenario recurred in 1978–1980. In this instance OPEC imposed an enormous $21 per barrel increase in oil prices. Coupled with rising prices of agricultural commodities, the price level rose by 26 percent over the 1978–1980 period, while unemployment jumped from 6.0 to 7.5 percent. Real GDP grew by a very modest 2 percent annual rate over the three-year period.

Regardless of the causes of stagflation, it was clear in the 1970s that the Phillips Curve did not rep-resent a stable relationship. Adverse (leftward) shifts in aggregate supply were at work, which explained those unhappy occasions when the inflation rate and the unemployment rate increased simultaneously. To many economists the experience in the 1970s and early 1980s suggested the Phillips Curve was shifting to the right and confronting the economy with higher rates of inflation *and* unemployment. *(Key Question 1)*

Stagflation's Demise: 1982–1989

A return look at Figure 17-3 reveals a clear inward movement of the inflation-unemployment points between 1982 and 1989. By 1989 the stagflation of the 1970s and early 1980s had subsided. One precursor to this favorable trend was the deep recession of 1981–1982, largely caused by a purposely tight money policy. The recession propelled the unemployment rate to 9.5 percent in 1982. With so many workers unemployed, those who were working accepted smaller increases in their nominal wages—or in some cases wage reductions—to preserve their jobs. Firms, in turn, had to restrain price hikes to maintain their relative shares of a greatly diminished market.

Other factors were at work. Foreign competition throughout 1982–1989 suppressed wage and price hikes in several basic industries such as automobiles and steel. Deregulation of the airline and trucking industries also resulted in wage reductions or so-called "wage-givebacks." A decline in OPEC's monopoly power produced a stunning fall in the price of oil and its derivative products.

All these factors combined to reduce unit production costs and to shift the aggregate supply curve rightward (as from AS_2 to AS_1 in Figure 17-4). Meanwhile, a record-long peacetime economic expansion created 17 million new jobs between 1982 and 1989. The previously high unemployment rate fell from 9.5 percent in 1983 to 6.1 percent in 1987 and to 5.2 percent in 1989. Figure 17-3 reveals that the inflation unemployment points for 1987–1989 are closer to the points associated with the Phillips Curve for the 1960s than to the points in the late 1970s and early 1980s.

During the Great Stagflation of the mid-1970s, inflation and unemployment simultaneously *increased;* during some of the years of the economic expansion of 1983–1989 inflation and unemployment simultaneously *declined*. Global Perspective 17-1 is relevant to this latter period.

GLOBAL PERSPECTIVE 17-1

The misery index, selected nations, 1984–1994

The so-called "misery index" adds together a nation's unemployment rate and its inflation rate to get a measure of national economic discomfort. For example, a nation with a 5 percent rate of unemployment and 5 percent inflation rate would have a misery index number of 10, as would a nation with an 8 percent unemployment rate and 2 percent inflation.

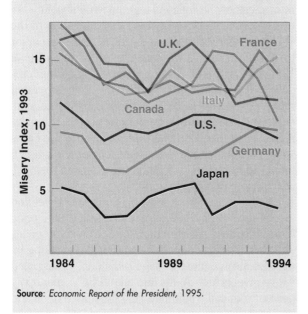

Source: *Economic Report of the President, 1995.*

NATURAL RATE HYPOTHESIS

The standard explanation for the scattering of inflation rate–unemployment points to the right of the 1960s Phillips Curve is that a series of supply shocks shifted the aggregate supply curve *leftward,* moving the Phillips Curve rightward and upward as in Figure 17-3. The inward collapse of inflation rate–unemployment points in the 1980s occurred because of *rightward* shifts of the aggregate supply curve. This Keynesian-based view holds that a tradeoff between the inflation rate and the unemployment rate still exists, but that changes in aggregate supply may alter the menu of inflation and unemployment choices—shift the Phillips Curve itself—during abnormal periods.

A second explanation of simultaneously higher rates of unemployment and inflation, the **natural rate**

hypothesis, is associated with new classical thinking. It questions the existence of the downsloping Phillips Curve as in Figure 17-2. This view says the economy is stable in the long run at the natural rate of unemployment. We know from Chapter 8 that the natural rate of unemployment is the rate of unemployment existing when cyclical unemployment is zero; it is the full-employment rate of unemployment.

According to the natural rate hypothesis, misguided full-employment policies, based on the incorrect assumption of a stable Phillips Curve, will result in an increasing rate of inflation. The natural rate hypothesis has its empirical roots in Figure 17-3, where you can argue that a vertical line located at a presumed 6 percent natural rate of unemployment represents the inflation-unemployment "relationship" better than the traditional downsloping Phillips Curve. In the natural rate hypothesis, any rate of inflation is compatible with the economy's natural rate of unemployment.

There are two variants of the natural rate interpretation of the inflation-unemployment data points shown in Figure 17-3: the adaptive expectations and rational expectations theories.

Adaptive Expectations Theory

The **theory of adaptive expectations** assumes people form their expectations of future inflation on the basis of previous and present rates of inflation and only gradually change their expectations as experience unfolds. The adaptive expectations theory was popularized by Milton Friedman and is consistent with both the traditional monetarist and new classical perspectives.

Adaptive expectations suggest there may be a tradeoff between inflation and unemployment in the short run, but not in the long run. Any attempt to reduce the unemployment rate below the natural rate sets in motion forces which destabilize the Phillips Curve and shift it rightward. Thus, the adaptive expectations view distinguishes between a "short-run" and "long-run" Phillips Curve.

Short-Run Phillips Curve   Consider Phillips Curve PC_1 in Figure 17-5. Suppose the economy initially is experiencing a 3 percent rate of inflation and a 6 percent natural rate of unemployment. In the adaptive expectations theory, such short-run curves as PC_1 (drawn as straight lines for simplicity) exist because

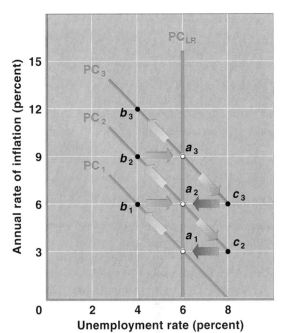

FIGURE 17-5   The adaptive expectations theory
The expansion of aggregate demand may temporarily increase profits and therefore output and employment (a_1 to b_1). But nominal wages will soon rise, reducing profits and thereby negating the short-run stimulus to production and employment (b_1 to a_2). Consequently, in the long run there is no tradeoff between the rates of inflation and unemployment; the long-run Phillips Curve is vertical. This suggests expansionary policies will generate increasing inflation rather than a lower rate of unemployment. On a more positive note, it also implies restrictive stabilization policies can reduce inflation without creating long-lived increases in unemployment.

the actual rate of inflation is not always the same as the expected rate.

Establishing an additional point on Phillips Curve PC_1 will clarify this. We begin at a_1, where we assume nominal wages are set on the expectation that the 3 percent rate of inflation will continue. But now suppose that government mistakenly judges the full-employment unemployment rate to be 4 percent instead of 6 percent. This misjudgment might occur because the economy temporarily achieved a 4 percent rate of unemployment in an earlier period. To achieve the targeted 4 percent rate of unemployment, suppose government invokes expansionary fiscal and monetary policy.

The resulting increase in aggregate demand boosts the rate of inflation to 6 percent. With a specific level of nominal wages, *set on the expectation that the rate of inflation would continue to be 3 percent,* the higher product prices raise business profits. Firms re-

spond to expanded profits by increasing output and therefore hiring more workers. In the short run, the economy moves to b_1, which, in contrast with a_1, entails a lower rate of unemployment (4 percent) and a higher rate of inflation (6 percent). This movement from a_1 to b_1 is consistent with our earlier interpretation of the Phillips Curve. Presumably, the economy has accepted some inflation as the "cost" of achieving a reduced level of unemployment. But the natural rate theorists interpret the movement from a_1 to b_1 differently. They see it as only a manifestation of the following principle: *When the actual rate of inflation is higher than expected, profits temporarily rise and the unemployment rate temporarily falls.*

Long-Run Vertical Phillips Curve   Point b_1 is *not* a stable equilibrium position in this theory. Workers will recognize their nominal wages have not been rising as fast as inflation and will therefore obtain nominal wage increases to restore their lost purchasing power. But, as nominal wages rise to restore the previous level of real wages existing at a_1, business profits fall to their earlier level. This profit reduction means that the original motivation of businesses to increase output and employ more workers disappears.

Unemployment then returns to its natural level at point a_2. Note, however, that the economy now faces a higher actual *and* expected rate of inflation—6 percent rather than 3 percent. Because the higher level of aggregate demand which originally moved the economy from a_1 to b_1 still exists, the inflation it engendered persists.

In view of the higher 6 percent expected rate of inflation, the short-run Phillips Curve shifts upward from PC_1 to PC_2. An "along-the-Phillips Curve" kind of movement from a_1 to b_1 on PC_1 is merely a short-run or transient phenomenon. In the long run—after nominal wages catch up with price level increases—unemployment will return to the natural rate at a_2 and a new short-run Phillips Curve PC_2 exists at the higher expected rate of inflation.

This process may now be repeated. Government may reason that certain extraneous, chance events have frustrated its expansionist policies, and will try again. Policy measures are used to increase aggregate demand and the scenario repeats. Prices rise momentarily ahead of nominal wages, profits expand, and output and employment increase (a_2 to b_2). But, in time, workers press for, and are granted, higher nominal wages to restore their level of real wages. Profits thus fall to their original level, pushing employment back to the normal rate at a_3. Government's "reward" for forcing the actual rate of unemployment below the natural rate is the perverse one of a still higher (9 percent) rate of inflation.

If we conceive of a_1b_1, a_2b_2, and a_3b_3 as a series of short-run Phillips Curves, the adaptive expectations theory says that governmental attempts through policy to move along the short-run Phillips Curve (a_1 to b_1 on PC_1) *cause* the curve to shift to a *less* favorable position (PC_2, then PC_3, and so on). A stable Phillips Curve with the dependable series of unemployment rate–inflation rate tradeoffs does not exist.

There is, in fact, no higher rate of inflation (such as 6 percent at b_1) which can be accepted as the "cost" of reduced unemployment in the *long run*. The *long-run relationship* between unemployment and inflation is shown by the vertical line through a_1, a_2, and a_3. Any rate of inflation is consistent with the 6 percent natural rate of unemployment. The Phillips Curve tradeoff portrayed earlier in Figure 17-2 does not exist.

Disinflation   We can also employ the adaptive expectations theory to explain **disinflation**—reductions in the rate of inflation. Suppose in Figure 17-5 the economy is at a_3 where the inflation rate is 9 percent and the unemployment rate is 6 percent. A significant decline in aggregate demand such as that occurring in the 1981–1982 recession will reduce inflation below the 9 percent expected rate, say, to 6 percent. Business profits will fall because product prices are rising less rapidly than wages. The nominal wage increases, remember, were set on the assumption that the 9 percent rate of inflation would continue. In response to the profit decline, firms will reduce their employment and consequently the unemployment rate will rise. The economy will temporarily slide downward from point a_3 to c_3 along the short-run Phillips Curve PC_3. In the natural rate theory, *when the actual rate of inflation is lower than the expected rate, profits temporarily fall and the unemployment rate temporarily rises.*

Firms and workers will eventually adjust their expectations to the new 6 percent rate of inflation and thus newly negotiated wage increases will decline. Profits will be restored, employment will rise, and the unemployment rate will return to its natural rate of 6 percent at point a_2. Because the expected rate of inflation is now 6 percent, the short-run Phillips Curve PC_3 will shift leftward to PC_2.

If aggregate demand falls further, the scenario will continue. Inflation will decline from 6 percent to,

say, 3 percent, moving the economy from a_2 to c_2 along PC_2. The lower-than-expected rate of inflation (lower prices) has squeezed profits and reduced employment. But, in the long run, firms will respond to the lower profits by reducing their nominal wage increases. Profits will be restored and unemployment will return to its natural rate at a_1 as the short-run Phillips Curve moves from PC_2 to PC_1. Once again, the long-run Phillips Curve is vertical at the natural rate of unemployment. *(Key Question 2)*

Rational Expectations Theory

The adaptive expectations theory assumes increases in nominal wages lag behind increases in the price level. This lag gives rise to *temporary* increases in profits which *temporarily* stimulate employment.

The **rational expectations theory** (Chapter 16) is the second variant of the natural rate hypothesis. This theory contends that businesses, consumers, and workers understand how the economy functions and they use available information to protect or further their own self-interests. In particular, people understand how government policies will affect the economy and anticipate these impacts in their own decision making.

Suppose that, when government invokes expansionary policies, workers anticipate inflation and a subsequent decline in real wages. They therefore immediately incorporate this expected inflation into their nominal wage demands. If workers correctly and fully anticipate the amount of price inflation and adjust their current nominal wage demands accordingly to maintain their real wages, then even the temporary increases in profits, output, and employment will *not* occur. Instead of the temporary increase in employment from a_1 to b_1 in Figure 17-5, the movement will be directly from a_1 to a_2. Fully anticipated inflation by labor means there will be no short-run decline in unemployment. Price inflation, fully anticipated in the nominal-wage demands of workers, will generate a vertical line through a_1, a_2 and a_3.

The policy implication is this: Fiscal and monetary policy designed to achieve a misspecified full-employment rate of unemployment will increase inflation, not lower unemployment. Note that the adaptive and rational expectations theories are consistent with the conservative philosophy that government's attempts to do good deeds typically fail and at considerable cost to society. In this instance the "cost" is accelerating inflation.

Changing Interpretations

Interpretations of the Phillips Curve have changed dramatically over the past three decades. The original idea of a stable tradeoff between unemployment and inflation gave way to the adaptive expectations view that, while a short-run tradeoff existed, no such tradeoff occurred in the long run. The more controversial rational expectations theory stresses that macroeconomic policy is completely ineffective because it is anticipated by workers. Not even a short-run tradeoff between unemployment and inflation exists. Taken together, the natural rate hypotheses (adaptive and rational expectations theories) conclude that demand-management policies cannot influence real output and employment in the long run, but only the price level. This conclusion is clearly contrary to predictions of the original Phillips Curve (Figure 17-2b).

Which perspective is correct? Does an inverse relationship exist between the unemployment rate and the inflation rate as the original Phillips Curve implied? Or is there no long-run tradeoff as the natural rate theory contends? Perhaps the safest answer is that most economists accept the notion of a short-run tradeoff while recognizing that in the long run such a tradeoff is much less likely. They also believe aggregate supply shocks can cause stagflation. The episodes of rising unemployment and inflation during the 1970s and early 1980s were *not* exclusively the results of misguided stabilization policies.

QUICK REVIEW 17-1

■ The original Phillips Curve showed an apparently stable, inverse relationship between annual unemployment rates and inflation rates over a period of years.

■ Stagflation occurred in 1973–1975 and 1978–1980 and produced Phillips Curve data points above and to the right of the Phillips Curve for the 1960s.

■ The following aggregate supply shocks caused stagflation during the 1970s and early 1980s: *a* OPEC oil price hikes, *b* poor agricultural harvests, *c* rapid dollar depreciation, *d* the demise of wage-price controls, *e* a productivity decline, and *f* inflationary expectations.

■ According to the natural rate hypothesis, the economy automatically gravitates to its natural rate of unemployment; therefore the Phillips Curve is vertical in the long run.

AGGREGATE SUPPLY REVISITED

The distinction between short-run Phillips Curves and the long-run vertical Phillips Curve has stimulated new thinking about aggregate supply.

In Figures 17-1 and 17-2a we derived the Phillips Curve by shifting aggregate demand rightward along a *stable* aggregate supply curve. Firms responded to the increasing price level by producing more output and increasing their employment. Thus, the unemployment rate fell as the price level rose.

The natural rate theory suggests, however, that the aggregate supply curve in Figure 17-1 is stable only so long as nominal wages do not increase in response to the rise in the price level. Once workers fully recognize the price level has risen, they will demand and receive higher nominal wages to restore their real wages. An increase in nominal wages, other things equal, will shift the aggregate supply curve leftward. That is, a change in nominal wages is one of the determinants of aggregate supply (Table 11-2).

The simplified aggregate supply curve—with its horizontal, intermediate, and vertical ranges—therefore needs to be refined to account for changes in nominal wages *induced* by changes in the price level. That means we must distinguish between short-run and long-run aggregate supply.

Definitions: Short Run and Long Run

Here *the short run is a period in which input prices—particularly nominal wages—remain fixed as the price level changes.* There are two reasons why input prices may remain constant for a time even though the price level has changed.

1 Workers may not immediately be aware of the existence of a higher or lower price level. If so, they will not know their real wages have changed and will not adjust their wage demands accordingly.

2 Many employees are hired under fixed-wage contracts. Unionized employees, for example, receive nominal wages based on their collective bargaining agreements. Also, most managers and many professionals receive set salaries established in annual contracts.

The upshot of both—the lack of information about the price level and the existence of labor contracts—is that changes in the price level do not immediately change nominal wages.

The long run is a period in which input prices (wages) are fully responsive to changes in the price level.

and price controls of 1971–1974 not only failed to achieve their purposes, but worsened stagflation by causing inefficiencies in the allocation of resources. The Carter administration guideposts of 1979 also failed dismally.

In view of this historical record, there remains little support for incomes policies among American macroeconomists. Nevertheless, wage and price controls are still occasionally tried in other nations, particularly those facing hyperinflation. Normally, these controls are a part of a larger set of policies—including a tight money policy—designed to break the price-wage inflationary spiral. *(Key Question 8)*

SUPPLY-SIDE ECONOMICS

In the past two decades, some economists have stressed low growth of productivity and real output as causes of stagflation and the relatively weak performance of our economy. These **supply-side economists** assert that mainstream economics does not come to grips with stagflation because its focal point is aggregate demand.

Supply-side economists contend that changes in aggregate supply—shifts in the short-run and long-run aggregate supply curve—must be recognized as an "active" force in determining both the levels of inflation *and* unemployment. Economic disturbances can be generated on the supply side, as well as on the demand side. By emphasizing the demand side, mainstream economists have neglected certain supply-side policies which might alleviate stagflation.

Tax-Transfer Disincentives

Supply-side economists argue that the spectacular growth of our tax-transfer system has negatively affected incentives to work, invest, innovate, and assume entrepreneurial risks. The tax-transfer system allegedly has eroded the economy's productivity and this decline in efficiency has meant higher production costs and stagflation. The argument is that higher taxes reduce the after-tax rewards of workers and producers, making work, innovations, investing, and risk bearing less financially attractive. According to supply-side economists, *marginal tax rates* are most relevant to decisions to undertake *additional* work and *additional* saving and investing.

Incentives to Work
Supply-siders believe that how long and how hard individuals work depends on how much additional *after-tax* earnings they derive from this extra work. To induce more work—to increase aggregate inputs of labor—marginal tax rates on earned incomes should be reduced. Lower marginal tax rates increase the attractiveness of work and increase the opportunity cost of leisure. Thus, individuals will choose to substitute work for leisure. This increase in productive effort can occur in many ways: by increasing the number of hours worked per day or week; by encouraging workers to postpone retirement; by inducing more people to enter the labor force; by making people willing to work harder; and by discouraging long periods of unemployment.

Transfer Disincentives
Supply-side economists also believe the existence of a wide variety of public transfer programs has eroded incentives to work. Unemployment compensation and welfare programs have made the job loss less of an economic crisis for some people. The fear of being unemployed and therefore the need to be a disciplined, productive worker is simply less acute than previously. Most transfer programs are structured to discourage work! Our social security and aid to families with dependent children programs are such that transfers are reduced sharply if recipients earn income. These programs encourage recipients *not* to be productive by imposing a "tax" in the form of a loss of transfer benefits on those who work.

Incentives to Save and Invest
The rewards to saving and investing have also been reduced by high marginal tax rates. Assume you save $1000 at 10 percent, so that you earn $100 interest per year. If your marginal tax rate is 40 percent, your after-tax interest earnings will be $60 and the after-tax interest rate you receive is only 6 percent. While you might be willing to save (forgo current consumption) for a 10 percent return on your saving, you might prefer to consume when the return is only 6 percent.

Saving, remember, is the prerequisite of investment. Thus supply-side economists recommend lower marginal tax rates on saving. They also call for lower taxes on investment income to ensure there are ready investment outlets for the economy's enhanced pool of saving. One of the determinants of investment spending is the *after-tax* net profitability of that spending.

To summarize: Lower marginal tax rates encourage saving and investing. Workers will therefore find themselves equipped with more and technologically superior machinery and equipment. Labor productivity will rise, and this will hold down increases in unit labor costs and the price level.

Laffer Curve

In the supply-side view, reductions of marginal tax rates will shift Figure 17-4's aggregate supply curve from AS_2 toward AS_1, alleviating inflation, increasing real output, and reducing the unemployment rate. Moreover, according to supply-side economist Arthur Laffer, lower tax *rates* are compatible with constant or even enlarged tax *revenues*. Supply-side tax cuts need not cause Federal budget deficits.

This idea is based on the **Laffer Curve.** As shown in Figure 17-8, this curve depicts the relationship between tax rates and tax revenues. As tax rates increase from zero to 100 percent, tax revenues increase from zero to some maximum level (at m) and then decline to zero. Tax revenues decline beyond some point because higher tax rates discourage economic activity, diminishing the tax base (domestic output and national income). This is easiest to see at the extreme where tax rates are 100 percent. Tax revenues here are reduced to zero because the 100 percent confiscatory tax rate has halted production. A 100 percent tax rate applied to a tax base of zero yields no revenue.

In the early 1980s Laffer suggested we were at some point such as n where tax rates were so high that production had been discouraged to the extent that tax revenues were below the maximum at m. If the economy is at n, then lower tax *rates* are quite compatible with constant total tax *revenues*. In Figure 17-8 we simply lower tax rates, moving from point n to point l, and government will collect the same amount of tax revenue. Laffer's reasoning is that lower tax rates will stimulate incentives to work, save and invest, innovate, and accept business risks, thus triggering an expansion of domestic output and national income. This enlarged tax base will sustain tax revenues even though tax rates are lower. Indeed, between n and m lower tax rates will result in increased tax revenues.

Supply-side economists think tax rates can be lowered without incurring budget deficits for two additional reasons.

1   Less Tax Evasion Tax avoidance and evasion will decline. High marginal tax rates prompt taxpayers to avoid taxes through various tax shelters (for example, buying municipal bonds on which interest earned is tax free) or to conceal income from the In-

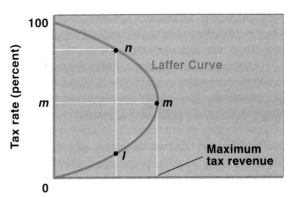

FIGURE 17-8 The Laffer Curve
The Laffer Curve suggests that up to point m higher tax rates will result in larger tax revenues. But still higher rates will adversely affect incentives to produce, reducing the size of the national income tax base to the extent that tax revenues decline. It follows that, if tax rates are above $0m$, tax reductions will produce increases in tax revenues. The controversial empirical question is to determine at what actual tax rates will tax revenues begin to fall.

ternal Revenue Service. Lower tax rates reduce the inclination to engage in such activities.

2   Reduced Transfers The stimulus to production and employment which a tax cut provides reduces government transfer payments. For example, more job opportunities reduce unemployment compensation payments and decrease a budget deficit.

Criticisms of the Laffer Curve

The Laffer Curve and its supply-side policy implications have been subject to severe criticism.

1   Taxes: Incentives and Time A fundamental criticism has to do with the sensitivity of economic incentives to changes in tax rates. Skeptics say there is ample empirical evidence that the impact of a tax reduction on incentives is small, of uncertain direction, and relatively slow to emerge. For example, with respect to work incentives, studies indicate that decreases in tax rates lead some people to work more, but others to work less. Those who work more are enticed by the higher after-tax pay; they substitute work for leisure because the opportunity cost of leisure has increased. Those who work less do so because the higher after-tax pay increases their ability to "buy leisure." They can meet their after-tax income goals while working fewer hours.

PROBLEMS AND CONTROVERSIES IN MACROECONOMICS

TABLE 17-1   Alternative macroeconomic theories and policies

Issue	Keynesianism	Natural rate hypothesis		Supply-side economics
		Monetarism	Rational expectations	
View of the private economy	Inherently unstable	Stable in long run at natural rate of unemployment	Stable in long run at natural rate of unemployment	May stagnate without proper work, saving, and investment incentives
Cause of the observed instability of the private economy	Investment plans unequal to saving plans (changes in AD); AS shocks	Inappropriate monetary policy	Unanticipated AD and AS shocks in the short run	Changes in AS
Appropriate macro policies	Active fiscal and monetary policy; occasional use of incomes policies	Monetary rule	Monetary rule	Policies to increase AS
How changes in the money supply affect the economy	By changing the interest rate, which changes investment, and real GDP	By directly changing AD which changes GDP.	No effect on output because price-level changes are anticipated	By influencing investment and thus AS
View of the velocity of money	Unstable	Stable	No consensus	No consensus
How fiscal policy affects the economy	Changes AD and GDP via the multiplier process	No effect unless money supply changes	No effect on output because price-level changes are anticipated	Affects GDP and price level via changes in AS
View of cost-push inflation	Possible (wage-push, AS shock)	Impossible in the long run in the absence of excessive money supply growth	Impossible in the long run in the absence of excessive money supply growth	Possible (productivity decline, higher costs due to regulation, etc.)

vice versa. This inverse relationship is known as the Phillips Curve and empirical data for the 1960s were generally consistent with it. Labor market imbalances explain the Phillips Curve tradeoff.

2   In the 1970s the Phillips Curve apparently shifted rightward, reflecting stagflation. A series of supply shocks in the form of higher energy and food prices, a depreciated dollar, and the demise of the Nixon wage-price freeze were involved in the 1973–1975 stagflation. More subtle factors such as inflationary expectations and a decline in productivity growth also contributed to stagflationary tendencies. Following the recession of 1981–1982, the Phillips Curve shifted inward toward its original position. By 1989 stagflation had subsided.

3   The adaptive expectations variant of the natural rate hypothesis argues that in the long run the traditional Phillips Curve tradeoff does not exist. Expansionary demand-management policies will shift the short-run Phillips Curve upward, resulting in increasing inflation with no permanent decline in unemployment.

4   The rational expectations variant of the natural rate hypothesis contends that the inflationary effects of expansionary policies will be anticipated and reflected in nominal wage demands. As a result, there will be no short-run increase in employment and thus no short-run Phillips Curve.

5   In the short run—where nominal wages are fixed—an increase in the price level increases profits and real output. Conversely, a decrease in the price level reduces profits and real output. Thus, the short-run aggregate supply curve is upward-sloping. In the long run—where nominal wages are variable—price level increases raise nominal wages and shift the short-run aggregate supply curve leftward. Conversely, price level declines shift the short-run aggregate supply curve rightward. The long-run aggregate supply curve therefore is vertical at the full-employment level of output.

6   In the short run, demand-pull inflation increases the price level *and* real output. Once nominal wages have increased, the temporary increase in real output dissipates.

7   In the short run, cost-push inflation increases the price level and reduces real output. Unless government expands aggregate demand, nominal wages eventually will decline

LAST WORD

PROFIT SHARING: MAKING WAGES FLEXIBLE

One of the problems of reducing inflation is that unemployment may result. Can greater downward wage flexibility be achieved to soften the impact of a decline in aggregate demand on employment?

Our comparisons of Keynesian and new classical views of the macroeconomy suggest that if wages are stable, employment will decline when aggregate demand falls. Most economists recognize that labor contracts, among other considerations, make wages downwardly inflexible, at least in the short run. The declines in labor demand accompanying recessions therefore primarily affect employment. This problem has led some economists to propose profit sharing as a way to increase the downward flexibility of wage rates. The idea is to make labor markets operate more like the new classical model, with its vertical aggregate supply curve, by creating greater employment stability.*

The essence of these profit-sharing proposals is to tie some portion of wages directly to the firm's profitability, making profit-sharing payments a part of workers' pay. Instead of paying workers a guaranteed wage rate of, say, $10 per hour, workers might be guaranteed $5 per hour (the base wage) and additional compensation equal to some predetermined percentage of the firm's profits (the profit-share wage). Total compensation (base wage + profit-share wage) may exceed or fall short of $10 per hour, depending on the firm's economic fortunes.

How would such a plan affect employment? Initially assume workers are receiving $10 per hour—$5 as a guaranteed wage and another $5 as profit-sharing compensation. Now suppose a recession occurs and the employer's sales and profits plummet. The $5 of profit-sharing income will fall and might decline to zero so that the actual wages paid by the firm fall from $10 to $5 an hour. With the new depressed demand for labor, the firm would clearly

*This idea is developed in detail in Martin L. Weitzman, *The Share Economy* (Cambridge, Mass.: Harvard University Press, 1984).

choose to employ more workers under this wage system than the standard system. Hourly wages will have automatically fallen from $10 to $5.

There are a number of criticisms of these profit-sharing wage plans. The plans might jeopardize the wage uniformity and wage gains achieved by organized labor. A further criticism is that employers might respond to the low base wage by adopting production techniques which use relatively more labor and less capital. Because the amount of capital equipment per worker is critical to productivity and economic growth, this pay scheme might impair the long-run expansion of real GDP. At the pragmatic level, critics point out that wage plans linked to profits eliminate the present certainty which workers have as to whether their employers have properly fulfilled the labor contract. With profit sharing, employers might use accounting and other techniques to hide profits and therefore evade paying share wages.

Finally, there is the fundamental question as to whether workers will accept more jobs and greater employment stability in exchange for a reduced hourly wage guarantee and higher variability of earnings. But it should be noted that in the past decade a growing number of union and nonunion contracts have contained profit-sharing arrangements. Although a full-blown profit-sharing economy seems improbable, limited profit-sharing appears to be spreading.

---

under conditions of recession and the short-run aggregate supply curve will shift back to its initial location. Prices and real output will eventually return to their original levels.

8 Employment and training policies, wage-price (incomes) policies, and supply-side policies have been used as antistagflation measures.

9 Employment and training programs are designed to reduce labor market imbalances; they include vocational training, job information, and nondiscrimination programs.

10 Incomes policies comprise wage-price guideposts or controls. Economists debate the desirability of these policies in terms of their workability and their impact on re-

balance its budget—not annually, but over a period of years.

The problem with this budget philosophy is that the upswings and downswings of the business cycle may not be of equal magnitude and duration. The goal of stabilization may therefore conflict with balancing the budget over the cycle. A long and severe slump, followed by a modest and short period of prosperity, would mean a large deficit during the slump, little or no surplus during prosperity, and a cyclical deficit in the budget.

Functional Finance

With **functional finance,** a balanced budget—annually or cyclically—is secondary. The primary purpose of Federal finance is to provide for noninflationary full employment—to balance the economy, not the budget. If this objective causes either persistent surpluses or a large and growing public debt, so be it. In this philosophy, the problems of government deficits or surpluses are minor compared with the undesirable alternatives of prolonged recession or persistent inflation. The Federal budget is first and foremost an instrument for achieving and maintaining macroeconomic stability. How best to finance government spending—through taxation or borrowing—depends on existing economic conditions. Government should not hesitate to incur any deficits and surpluses required to achieve macroeconomic stability and growth.

To those who express concern about the large Federal debt which the pursuit of functional finance might entail, proponents of this budget philosophy offer three arguments.

1 Our tax system is such that tax revenues automatically increase as the economy expands. Assuming constant government expenditures, a deficit successful in stimulating equilibrium GDP will be partially self-liquidating (Figure 12-3).

2 Because of its taxing powers and the ability to create money, the government's capacity to finance deficits is virtually unlimited.

3 Those who support functional finance contend that a large Federal debt is less burdensome than most people think. *(Key Question 1)*

TABLE 18-1 Quantitative significance of the public debt: the public debt and interest payments in relation to GDP, selected years, 1929–1994*

(1) Year	(2) Public debt, billions	(3) Gross domestic product, billions	(4) Interest payments, billions	(5) Public debt as percentage of GDP, (2) ÷ (3)	(6) Interest payments as percentage of GDP, (4) ÷ (3)	(7) Per capita public debt
1929	$ 16.9	$ 103.2	$ 0.7	16%	0.7%	$ 134
1940	50.7	100.1	1.1	51	1.1	384
1946	271.0	211.6	4.2	128	2.0	1917
1950	256.9	286.7	4.5	90	1.6	1667
1955	274.4	403.3	5.1	68	1.3	1654
1960	290.5	513.4	6.8	57	1.3	1610
1965	322.3	702.7	8.4	46	1.2	1659
1970	380.9	1010.7	14.1	38	1.4	1858
1975	541.9	1585.9	23.0	34	1.5	2507
1980	909.1	2708.0	52.7	34	1.9	3992
1982	1137.3	3149.6	84.4	36	2.7	4898
1984	1564.7	3777.2	113.1	41	3.0	6620
1986	2120.6	4268.6	131.0	50	3.1	8812
1988	2601.3	4900.4	146.0	53	3.0	10,616
1990	3206.6	5546.1	176.5	58	3.2	12,831
1992	4002.1	6020.2	186.8	66	3.1	15,670
1994	4643.7	6736.9	191.6	69	2.8	17,816

*In current dollars.

Source: Economic Report of the President, 1994; U.S. Department of Commerce.

THE PUBLIC DEBT: FACTS AND FIGURES

Because modern fiscal policy endorses unbalanced budgets to stabilize the economy, its application may lead to a growing public debt. Let's consider the public debt—its causes, characteristics, and size; and its burdens and benefits.

The public debt, as column 2 of Table 18-1 shows, has grown considerably since 1929. As noted, the public debt is the accumulation of all past deficits, minus surpluses, of the Federal budget.

Causes

Why has our public debt increased historically? What has caused us to incur these large and persistent deficits? The answer is fourfold: wars, recessions, tax cuts, and lack of political will.

Wars   Some of the public debt has resulted from the deficit financing of wars. The public debt increased substantially during World War I and grew more than fivefold during World War II.

Consider World War II and the options it posed. The task was to reallocate a substantial portion of the economy's resources from civilian to war goods production. Government expenditures for armaments and military personnel soared. There were three financing options: increase taxes, print the needed money, or use deficit financing. Government feared that tax financing would require tax rates so high they would diminish incentives to work. The national interest required attracting more people into the labor force and encouraging those already participating to work longer hours. Very high tax rates were felt to interfere with these goals. Printing and spending additional money would be inflationary. Thus, much of World War II was financed by selling bonds to the public, thereby draining off spendable income and freeing resources from civilian production so they would be available for defense industries.

Recessions   Another cause of the public debt is recessions and, more specifically, the built-in stability characterizing our fiscal system. In periods when the national income declines, tax collections automatically fall and deficits arise. Thus the public debt rose during the Great Depression of the 1930s and, more recently, during the recessions of 1974–1975, 1980–1982, and 1990–1991.

Tax Cuts   A third consideration has accounted for much of the large deficits since 1981. The Economic Recovery Tax Act of 1981 provided for substantial cuts in both individual and corporate income taxes. The Reagan administration and Congress did *not* make offsetting reductions in government outlays, thereby building a *structural deficit* into the Federal budget in the sense that the budget would not balance even if the economy were operating at full-employment. Unfortunately, the economy was not at full employment during most of the early 1980s. The 1981 tax cuts combined with the severe 1980–1982 recessions to generate rapidly rising annual deficits which were $128 billion in 1982, accelerating to $221 billion by 1986. Although annual budget deficits declined between 1986 and 1989, they remained historically high even though the economy reached full employment. Due partly to the earlier tax rate cuts, tax revenues were not high enough to cover rising Federal spending. Annual deficits, and thus the public debt, rose again in 1991–1993 as the economy experienced recession and the Federal government incurred massive expenses in bailing out failed savings and loan associations.

Lack of Political Will   Without being too cynical we might also assert that deficits and a growing public debt are the result of lack of political will and determination. Spending often gains votes; tax increases precipitate political disfavor. While opposition to deficits is expressed by politicians and their constituencies, *specific* proposals to cut spending programs or raise taxes typically encounter more opposition than support.

Particularly difficult to cut are **entitlement programs,** the subject of this chapter's Last Word. These programs, such as social security, Medicaid (health care for the poor), Medicare (health care for those on social security), and veterans' benefits, "entitle" or guarantee particular levels of transfer payments (Chapter 5) to all who fit the programs' criteria. Total spending on these programs automatically rises along with the number of qualifying individuals and has rocketed in recent years, contributing to budget deficits and the rising public debt. Cutting these benefits produces severe political opposition. For example, older Americans may favor smaller budget deficits so long as funds for social security and Medicare are not reduced.

Similarly, new taxes or tax increases to reduce budget deficits may be acceptable in the abstract, but far less popular when specific tax changes are pro-

PROBLEMS AND CONTROVERSIES IN MACROECONOMICS

posed. The popular view of taxation seems to be "Don't tax me, don't tax thee, tax the person behind the tree." But there are not enough taxpayers "behind the tree" to raise the amounts of new revenue needed to close the budget deficit.

The Clinton administration's struggle to pass a deficit-reduction package in 1993 is an example of the political difficulties of reducing spending and increasing taxes. The specific package of spending cuts and tax increases passed the Senate by only a single vote, even though nearly all senators agreed that deficit reduction was a worthy goal.

Quantitative Aspects

In 1994 the public debt reached $4600 billion—that's $4.6 trillion. That's more than twice what it was a mere eight years ago. If every sesame seed on every Big Mac ever sold was worth one dollar, the total wouldn't be sufficient to pay off the public debt. As of 1993, McDonald's had used 2.49 trillion seeds (178 on each of 14 billion Big Macs) in 25 years, compared to the $4.6 trillion debt.[3]

But we must not fear large, seemingly incomprehensible numbers. You will see why when we put the size of the public debt into better perspective.

Debt and GDP A bald statement of the absolute size of the debt ignores that the wealth and productive ability of our economy have also increased tremendously. A wealthy nation can more easily incur and carry a large public debt than a poor nation. That's why it is more meaningful to measure changes in the public debt *in relation to* changes in the economy's GDP, as shown in column 5 in Table 18-1. Instead of the seventeenfold increase in the debt between 1950 and 1994 shown in column 2, we find that the relative size of the debt was less in 1994 than in 1950. However, our data show that the relative size of the debt has doubled since the early 1980s. Also, column 7 indicates that on a per capita basis the nominal debt has increased more or less steadily through time.

International Comparisons As shown in Global Perspective 18-1, other industrial nations have public debts similar to, or greater than, those in the United States. As a percentage of GDP, public debt in 1994 was larger in Belgium, Italy, Canada, the Netherlands,

[3]Sam Ward, "How Big Is Our Debt?" *USA Today,* May 6, 1993, p. 1.

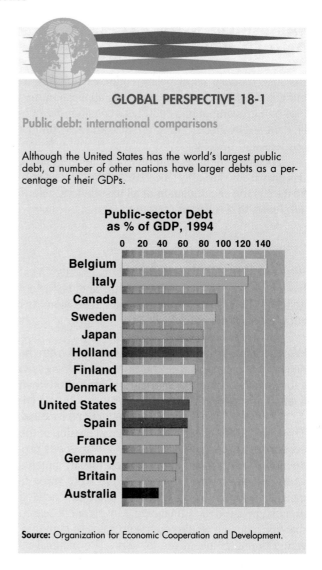

GLOBAL PERSPECTIVE 18-1

Public debt: international comparisons

Although the United States has the world's largest public debt, a number of other nations have larger debts as a percentage of their GDPs.

Public-sector Debt as % of GDP, 1994

	0 20 40 60 80 100 120 140
Belgium	
Italy	
Canada	
Sweden	
Japan	
Holland	
Finland	
Denmark	
United States	
Spain	
France	
Germany	
Britain	
Australia	

Source: Organization for Economic Cooperation and Development.

Sweden, Japan, and Denmark than in the United States.

Interest Charges Many economists think the primary burden of the debt is the annual interest charge accruing as a result. The absolute size of these interest payments is shown in column 4 of Table 18-1. Interest payments have increased sharply beginning in the 1970s. This reflects not only increases in the debt, but also periods of very high interest rates. Interest on the debt is now the fourth largest item of expenditures in the Federal budget (Figure 5-7). Interest charges as a percentage of the GDP are shown in column 6 of Table 18-1. Interest payments as a proportion of GDP have increased significantly in recent years. This ratio reflects the level of taxation (the average tax rate) required to service the public debt. In 1994 government had to collect taxes equal to 2.8 percent of GDP to pay interest on its debt.

Ownership Figure 18-1 indicates that about two-thirds of the total public debt is held outside the Federal government by state and local governments, banks and other financial institutions, and private parties. The remaining one-third is held by Federal agencies and the Federal Reserve. Foreign individuals and institutions hold only about 14 percent of the total debt, a percentage which has not changed much in the past few years. This statistic is significant because, as we will see shortly, the implications of internally and externally held debt are different.

Accounting and Inflation The data on budget deficits and public debt may not be as straightforward as they appear. Governmental accounting procedures may not reflect government's actual financial position. Private firms have a separate capital budget because, in contrast to current expenses on labor and raw materials, expenditures for capital equipment represent tangible money-making assets. The Federal government treats expenditures for highways, harbors, and

public buildings the same as it does welfare payments, while in fact the former outlays are investments in physical assets. Federal budget deficits in the 1980s and 1990s would have been smaller had the Federal government employed a capital budget which included depreciation costs.

Also, inflation works to benefit debtors. A rising price level reduces the real value or purchasing power of the dollars paid back by borrowers. Taking this "inflationary tax" into account further reduces the sizes of budget deficits and public debt.

All of this is quite controversial. But the point is there are different ways of measuring the public debt and government's overall financial position. Some of these alternative measures differ greatly from the data presented in Table 18-1.

QUICK REVIEW 18-1

■ A budget deficit is an excess of government expenditures above tax revenues in a particular year; the public debt is the total accumulation of budget deficits and surpluses through time.

■ The three major budget philosophies are *a* an annually balanced budget; *b* a budget balanced over the business cycle; and *c* functional finance.

■ The $4.6 trillion public debt has resulted mainly from wartime financing, recessions, tax cuts, and lack of political will.

■ United States public debt as a percentage of GDP is less than it was in 1950 and is in the midrange of such debt among major industrial nations.

ECONOMIC IMPLICATIONS: FALSE ISSUES

How does the public debt and its growth affect the economy? Can a mounting public debt bankrupt the nation? Does the debt place a burden on our children and grandchildren?

These are false or bogus issues. The debt is not about to bankrupt the government or the nation. Nor, except under certain specific circumstances, does the debt place a burden on future generations.

Going Bankrupt?

Can a large public debt bankrupt the government, making it unable to meet its financial obligations? No, for the following three reasons.

FIGURE 18-1 Ownership of the public debt
Two-thirds of the public debt is held outside the Federal government; one-third is held internally by Federal agencies and the Federal Reserve. Only 14 percent of the public debit is foreign owned.

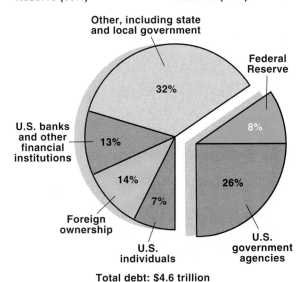

Debt held outside the Federal government and Federal Reserve (66%)

Debt held by the Federal government and Federal Reserve (34%)

Other, including state and local government

Federal Reserve

32%

8%

U.S. banks and other financial institutions

13%

14%

7%

26%

Foreign ownership

U.S. individuals

U.S. government agencies

Total debt: $4.6 trillion

1 Refinancing There is no reason why the public debt need be reduced, much less eliminated. As portions of the debt fall due each month, government does not cut expenditures or raise taxes to provide funds to *retire* the maturing bonds. (We know that with depressed economic conditions, this would be unwise fiscal policy.) Rather, the government *refinances* the debt; it sells new bonds and uses the proceeds to pay off holders of the maturing bonds.

2 Taxation Government has the constitutional authority to levy and collect taxes. A tax increase is a government option for gaining sufficient revenue to pay interest and principal on the public debt. Financially distressed private households and corporations *cannot* raise revenue via taxes; government *can*. Private households and corporations *can* go bankrupt; the Federal government *cannot*.

3 Creating Money Bankruptcy is also difficult to imagine because the Federal government can print money to pay both principal and interest on the debt. A government bond obligates the government to redeem that bond for some specific amount of money on its maturity date. Government can use the proceeds from the sale of other bonds *or* it can create the needed money to retire the maturing bonds. The creation of new money to pay interest on debt or to retire debt *may* be inflationary. But it is difficult to conceive of governmental bankruptcy when government has the power to create new money by running the printing presses.

Shifting Burdens

Does the public debt impose a burden on future generations? Recall that per capita debt in 1994 was $17,816. Does each newborn child in 1994 enter the world to be handed a $17,816 bill from Uncle Sam? Not really!

We first must ask to whom we owe the public debt. The answer is that, for the most part, we owe it to ourselves. About 86 percent of our government bonds are owned and held by citizens and institutions —banks, businesses, insurance companies, governmental agencies, and trust funds—within the United States. Thus *the public debt is also a public credit.* While the public debt is a liability to the American people (as taxpayers), most of the same debt is simultaneously an asset to the American people (as holders of

Treasury bills, Treasury notes, Treasury bonds, and U.S. Saving Bonds).

To retire the public debt would call for a gigantic transfer payment where Americans would pay higher taxes and government would pay out most of those tax revenues to those same taxpaying individuals and institutions in the aggregate in redeeming the U.S. securities they hold. Although a redistribution of income would result from this huge financial transfer, it need not entail any immediate decline in the economy's aggregate wealth or standard of living. Repayment of an internally held public debt entails no leakage of purchasing power from the economy as a whole. New babies who on the average inherit the $17,816 per person public debt obligation will also be bequeathed that same amount of government securities.

We noted earlier that the public debt increased sharply during World War II. Was some of the economic burden of World War II shifted to future generations by the decision to finance military purchases through the sale of government bonds? No. Recalling the production possibilities curve, we realize that the economic cost of World War II was the civilian goods society had to forgo in shifting scarce resources to war goods production. Regardless of whether society financed this reallocation through higher taxes or borrowing, the real economic burden of the war would have been the same. The burden of the war was borne almost entirely by those who lived during the war; they were the ones who did without a multitude of consumer goods to permit the United States to arm itself and its allies.

Also, wartime production may slow the growth of a nation's stock of capital as resources are shifted from production of capital goods to production of war goods. As a result, future generations inherit a smaller stock of capital goods. This occurred in the United States during World War II. But, again, this shifting of costs is independent of how a war is financed.

QUICK REVIEW 18-2

■ There is no danger of the Federal government going bankrupt because it need only refinance (not retire) the public debt and can raise revenues, if needed, through higher taxes or printing money.

■ Usually, the public debt is not a means of shifting economic burdens to future generations.

IMPLICATIONS AND ISSUES

We must be careful not to leave the impression that the public debt is of no concern among economists. The large debt *does* pose some real potential problems, although economists attach varying importance to them.

Income Distribution

The distribution of government security ownership is uneven. Some people own much more than their $17,816 per capita share; others less or none at all. Although our knowledge of the ownership of the public debt by income class is limited, we presume that ownership is concentrated among wealthier groups. Because the tax system is mildly progressive, payment of interest on the public debt probably increases income inequality. If greater income equality is one of our social goals, then this redistributive effect is clearly undesirable.

Incentives

Table 18-1 indicates that the present public debt necessitates annual interest payments of $192 billion. With no increase in the size of the debt, this annual interest charge must be paid out of tax revenues. These added taxes may dampen incentives to bear risk, to innovate, to invest, and to work. In this indirect way, a large public debt can impair economic growth. As noted earlier, the ratio of interest payments to GDP indicates the level of taxation needed to pay interest on the debt. Thus, many economists are concerned that this ratio is roughly twice as high as it was two decades earlier (column 6 of Table 18-1).

External Debt

External debt—U.S. debt held by citizens and institutions of foreign countries—*is* a burden. This part of the public debt is *not* "owed to ourselves," and in real terms the payment of interest and principal requires transferring some of our real output to other nations. Foreign ownership of the public debt is higher today than in earlier periods. In 1960 only 5 percent of the debt was foreign-owned; today foreign ownership is 14 percent. The assertion that "we owe the debt to ourselves" and the implication that the debt should thus be of little concern is less accurate

than it was four decades ago. But, we must also note that an increased foreign share of the public debt is not a continuing trend; it has remained relatively constant since 1988. *(Key Question 3)*

Curb on Fiscal Policy

A large and growing public debt makes it politically difficult to use fiscal policy during a recession. For example, in 1991 and 1992 the Fed substantially reduced interest rates to stimulate a sluggish economy. But this easy money policy was slow to expand output and reduce unemployment. Had the public debt not been at an historic high and increasing due to the aforementioned structural deficit, it would have been politically feasible to reduce taxes or increase government spending to generate the stimulus of a deficit. But the growing "debt problem" ruled out this stimulus on political grounds. In general, a large and growing public debt creates political impediments to the use of antirecessionary fiscal policy.

Crowding Out and the Stock of Capital

There is a potentially more serious problem. One way the public debt can transfer a real economic burden to future generations is by causing future generations to inherit a smaller stock of capital goods—a smaller "national factory." This possibility involves Chapter 12's **crowding-out effect,** the notion that deficit financing will increase interest rates and reduce private investment spending. If this happens, future generations would inherit an economy with a smaller production capacity and, other things equal, the standard of living would be lower than otherwise.

Suppose the economy is operating at its full-employment level of output and the Federal budget is initially in balance. Now for some reason government increases its level of spending. The impact of this increase in government spending will fall on those living when it occurs. Think of Chapter 2's production possibilities curve with "government goods" on one axis and "private goods" on the other. In a full-employment economy an increase in government spending will move the economy *along* the curve toward the government-goods axis, meaning fewer private goods.

But private goods may be consumer or investment goods. If the increased government goods are provided at the expense of *consumer goods,* then the present generation bears the entire burden as a lower current standard of living. The current investment level is *not* affected and therefore neither is the size of the national factory inherited by future generations. But if the increase in government goods means a reduction in production of *capital goods,* then the present generation's level of consumption (standard of living) will be unimpaired. But in the future our children and grandchildren will inherit a smaller stock of capital goods and will have lower income levels.

Two Scenarios Let's sketch the two scenarios yielding these different results.

First Scenario Suppose the presumed increase in government spending is financed by an increase in taxation, say, personal income taxes. We know most income is consumed. Therefore, consumer spending will fall by almost as much as the increase in taxes. Here, the burden of the increase in government spending falls primarily on today's generation; it has fewer consumer goods.

Second Scenario Assume the increase in government spending is financed by increasing the public debt, meaning government enters the money market and competes with private borrowers for funds. With the supply of money fixed, this increase in money demand will increase the interest rate—the "price" paid for the use of money.

In Figure 18-2 the curve I_{d1} reproduces the investment-demand curve of Figure 9-5. (Ignore curve I_{d2} for now.) The investment-demand curve is downsloping, indicating investment spending varies inversely with the interest rate. Here, government deficit financing drives up the interest rate, reducing private investment. If government borrowing increases the interest rate from 6 to 10 percent, investment spending would fall from $25 to $15 billion. That is, $10 billion of private investment would be crowded out.

Conclusion: An assumed increase in public goods production is more likely to come at the expense of private investment goods when financed by deficits. In comparison with tax financing, the future generation inherits a smaller national factory and therefore has a lower standard of living with deficit financing.

Two Qualifications But there are two loose ends to our discussion which might mitigate or even elimi-

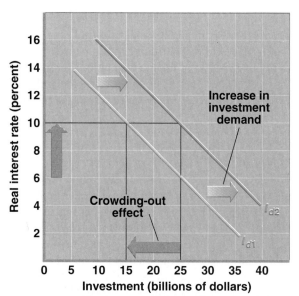

FIGURE 18-2 **The investment-demand curve and the crowding-out effect**
The crowding-outing effect suggests that, with a fixed investment-demand curve (I_{d1}), an increase in the interest rate caused by a government deficit will reduce private investment spending and decrease the size of the "national factory" inherited by future generations. In this case an increase in the interest rate from 6 to 10 percent crowds out $10 billion of private investment. However, if the economy is initially in a recession, the government deficit may improve profit expectations of businesses and shift the investment-demand curve rightward as from I_{d1} to I_{d2}. This shift may offset the crowding-out effect wholly or in part.

nate the size of the economic burden shifted to future generations.

1 Public Investment Our discussion has neglected the character of the increase in government spending. Just as private goods may involve consumption or investment, so it is with public goods. If the increase in government spending consists of consumption-type outlays—subsidies for school lunches or provision of limousines for government officials—then our second scenario's conclusion that the debt increase has shifted a burden to future generations is correct. But what if the government spending is investment-type outlays, for example, for construction of highways, harbors, and flood-control projects? Similarly, what if they are "human capital" investments in education, job training, and health?

Like private expenditures on machinery and equipment, **public investments** increase the economy's future production capacity. The capital stock of future generations need not be diminished, but rather its composition is changed so there is more public capital and less private capital.

2   Unemployment   The other qualification relates to our assumption that the initial increase in government expenditures occurs when the economy is at full employment. Again the production possibilities curve reminds us that, *if* the economy is at less than full employment or, graphically, at a point inside the production possibilities curve, then an increase in government expenditures can move the economy *to* the curve without any sacrifice of either current consumption or private capital accumulation. If unemployment exists initially, deficit spending by government need *not* mean a burden for future generations in the form of a smaller national factory.

Look at Figure 18-2 again. If deficit financing increases the interest rate from 6 to 10 percent, a crowding-out effect of $10 billion will occur. But the increase in government spending will stimulate a recession economy via the multiplier effect, improving profit expectations and shifting private investment demand rightward to I_{d2}. In the case shown, investment spending remains at $25 billion despite the higher 10 percent interest rate. Of course, the increase in investment demand might be smaller or larger than that in Figure 18-2. In the former case the crowding-out effect would not be fully offset; in the latter, it would be more than offset. The point? An increase in investment demand counters the crowding-out effect. *(Key Question 7)*

RECENT FEDERAL DEFICITS

Federal deficits and the growing public debt have been in the economic spotlight in the last decade.

Enormous Size

As Figure 18-3 makes clear, the absolute size of annual Federal deficits increased enormously in the 1980s and 1990s. The average annual deficit for the 1970s was approximately $35 billion. In the 1980s annual deficits averaged five times that amount. Consequently, the public debt tripled during the same time (Table 18-1).

The Federal deficit jumped to $269 billion in 1991 and $290 billion in 1992, mainly because of the 1990–1991 recession and a weak recovery, which slowed the inflow of tax revenues. Government's expensive bailout of the savings and loan associations also contributed to the huge deficits in these years. The deficits then began to fall in 1993 and 1994 as the economy's expansion quickened and the Clinton administration's efforts to reduce the deficit took hold.

Understatement?   The most recent annual budget deficits shown in Figure 18-3 may be understated. Over the past few years government has raised more money from social security taxes than it has paid out as benefits to current retirees. The purpose of this surplus is to prepare for the future time when "baby boomers" retire. Some economists argue that these revenues should be excluded when calculating present deficits because they represent future government obligations on a dollar-for-dollar basis. In this view the social security surplus should not be considered as an offset to *current* government spending. When we exclude the social security surplus from the deficit figures, budget deficits rise by as much as $60 billion annually.

Rising Interest Costs   Column 4 of Table 18-1 indicates that interest payments on the public debt have increased more than thirteenfold since 1970. Interest payments were $192 billion in 1994, an amount greater than the entire deficit in many previous years! Because interest payments are part of government expenditures, the debt feeds on itself through interest charges. Interest payments on the debt are the only component of government spending which Congress cannot cut. The spiraling of such payments therefore complicates the problem of controlling government spending and the size of future deficits.

Inappropriate Policy   Some of our large annual deficits have occurred in an economy operating at or close to full employment. Historically, deficits—particularly sizable ones—have been associated with wartime finance and recessions. While the 1980–1982 and 1990–1991 recessions contributed to huge deficits, it is clear that the large continuing deficits reflects the 1981 tax cuts and rising government spending. In terms of Figure 12-3, the 1981 tax cuts shifted the tax line downward. Meanwhile, mainly due to increased entitlement spending, the government spending line shifted upward. Thus, even at a full-employment level of output (GDP$_2$) sizable structural deficits remained.

products cheaper and American auto and steel industries and find themselves with excess production capacity and redundant labor.

The foregoing comments reiterate our earlier analysis (Chapter 12) that an expansionary fiscal policy may be less stimulating to the economy than simple analysis suggests. The expansionary impact of a deficit might be weakened by both the resulting *crowding-out effect* (box 3) and the negative *net export effect* (box 9).

Related Effects

There are three complications here.

1 The inflow of foreign funds does augment domestic funds and helps keep American real interest rates lower than otherwise. The inflow of foreign funds to the United States diminishes the size of the crowding-out effect. From the standpoint of foreign nations transferring funds to the United States, their domestic investment and long-term economic growth will be smaller.

2 Deficit-caused high real interest rates in America impose an increased burden on heavily indebted developing countries such as Mexico and Brazil. Their dollar-denominated debts to American banks and the banks of other industrial nations become more costly to service when our real interest rates rise.

Our large budget deficits—particularly through the upward pressure they exert on domestic real interest rates—pose something of a threat to the international credit system and to American banks.

3 A trade deficit means we are not exporting enough to pay for our imports. The difference can be paid for in two ways. One, we can borrow from people and institutions in foreign lands. In the late 1980s when the American trade deficit was severe, the United States became the world's leading debtor nation. Two, U.S. assets such as factories, shopping centers, and farms can be sold to foreign investors. This, too, happened in the late 1980s and early 1990s. To pay our debts and repurchase these assets, we must in the future export more than we import. In the future we will need to consume and invest less than we produce.

Contrary View: Ricardian Equivalence Theorem

A few economists disagree with the analysis just outlined. They adhere to the **Ricardian equivalence**

theorem (Chapter 12) which says financing a deficit by borrowing has the same effect on GDP as financing it through a present tax increase. People are supposedly aware that deficits today will require higher future taxes to pay the added interest expense resulting from the increase in the public debt. Households therefore spend less today—saving more—in anticipation of having less future after-tax income available for consumption. Because the increase in private saving perfectly offsets the increase in government borrowing, the real interest rate does not change. Thus neither a crowding-out effect nor a trade deficit necessarily emerges from a budget deficit. In Figure 18-4 the Ricardian equivalence theorem breaks the chain between box 1 and box 2, negating all the effects purportedly following (boxes 3 through 9).

But most economists reject this unusual perspective. They claim instead that the 1980s and early 1990s provide ample evidence of negative foreign-sector effects of large budget deficits. A glance at line 4 on the inside back cover of this text shows that high trade deficits (negative net exports) accompanied the large budget deficits of the late 1980s and early 1990s (Figure 18-3). *(Key Question 8)*

QUICK REVIEW 18-3

■ The borrowing and interest payments associated with the public debt may *a* increase income inequality, *b* require higher taxes which dampen incentives, *c* curb the use of antirecessionary fiscal policy, and *d* impede the growth of the nation's capital stock *if* public borrowing significantly crowds out private investment.

■ Recent Federal deficits are of concern because of *a* their enormous size, *b* the possibility they may be understated, *c* rising total interest costs, and *d* their inappropriateness when the economy is near, or at, full-employment output.

■ Budget deficits can be linked to trade deficits as follows: Budget deficits increase domestic real interest rates; the dollar appreciates; American exports fall, and American imports rise.

Policy Responses

Concern with large budget deficits and an expanding public debt has spawned several policy responses.

Budget Legislation of 1990 In November 1990 Congress attacked the deficit problem by passing the **Budget Reconciliation Act of 1990,** a package of tax increases and spending cuts designed to reduce budget deficits by $500 billion between 1991 and 1996.

This act sought to enhance tax revenue through (1) an increase in the marginal tax rate for wealthy Americans from 28 to 31 percent; (2) lower allowable deductions and personal exemptions for wealthy individuals; (3) higher payroll taxes for medical care; (4) increased excise taxes on gasoline, tobacco, alcoholic beverages, and airline tickets; and (5) a new luxury tax on expensive jewelry, furs, cars, boats, and personal aircraft. This law also set a goal of lopping $260 billion from government spending between 1991 and 1996, the brunt of cuts being borne by national defense, farm programs, and Federal pensions.

Tax increases and expenditure cuts in the midst of recession are counter to conventional fiscal policy. But Congress and the Bush administration reasoned that deficit reduction was essential to lower real interest rates and increase investment—to achieve a reverse crowding-out effect. They also recognized that without these actions deficits would climb to unprecedented, politically costly heights.

The **Budget Enforcement Act of 1990** accompanied the Budget Reconciliation Act and established a "pay-as-you-go" test for new spending or tax decreases. Between 1991 and 1996 new legislation that increased government spending had to be offset by a corresponding decrease in existing spending or an increase in taxes. Likewise, new tax reductions had to be accompanied by offsetting tax increases or spending cuts. Also, this law placed legally binding caps (with exceptions for emergencies) on Federal spending for each of these five years.

Deficit Reduction Act of 1993

By 1992 it became clear that the budget legislation of 1990—although helpful in slowing government spending—would still leave budget deficits of $175 to $225 billion annually. Spurred by the Clinton administration, Congress passed the **Deficit Reduction Act of 1993.** This law is designed to increase tax revenues by $250 billion over five years and to reduce Federal spending by a similar amount.

The tax increases fall mainly, but not exclusively, on high-income households. The three major tax hikes are: (1) an increase in the top marginal tax rate of the personal income tax from 31 percent to 39.6 percent; (2) an increase in the corporate income tax rate from 34 percent to 35 percent; (3) and a boost in the Federal excise tax on gasoline from 14.1 cents per gallon to 18.4 cents per gallon.

The largest spending "cut" will result from holding all discretionary spending—spending not mandated by law—to 1993 nominal levels. Normally, this spending would rise at least as fast as inflation. Also, the law achieves major spending cuts via reductions in government health care payments to doctors and hospitals, delays in the cost-of-living adjustment for government retirees, and reform of the student-loan program.

The budget legislation of 1990 and the Deficit Reduction Act of 1993 will clearly reduce Federal deficits, barring a new recession. But economists agree that these laws will not soon reduce budget deficits to zero.

Other Proposals Concern with balancing the budget has prompted a variety of other deficit-reduction proposals. One calls for a constitutional amendment requiring a balanced budget. Another calls for reform enabling the President to veto spending measures on a line-item basis.

Constitutional Amendment The most extreme proposal is that a constitutional amendment should be passed which mandates that Congress balance the budget each year. This proposed **balanced budget amendment** assumes Congress will continue to act "irresponsibly" because government spending enhances and tax increases diminish a politician's popular support. Political rhetoric notwithstanding, Federal deficits allegedly will continue until a constitutional amendment forces a balanced budget. Critics of this proposal remind us that an annually balanced budget has a procyclical or destabilizing effect on the economy.

Line-Item Veto The **line-item veto** would permit the President to veto individual spending items in appropriation bills. A typical appropriations bill merges hundreds of programs and projects into a single piece of legislation. Governors in the majority of states currently possess line-item veto authority for their state budgets, but the President does not have this veto power for the Federal budget. Proponents of this reform argue it would allow the President to cull from appropriation bills "pork-barrel" projects for which local or regional benefits are less than the costs to the nation's taxpayers. The line-item veto might reduce government spending and help the Federal government balance its budget. Opponents argue that the line-item veto would give far too much power to the

LAST WORD

CUT ENTITLEMENTS TO REDUCE THE DEFICIT?

Spending on programs which "entitle" people to specified transfer payments is rising rapidly, contributing to budget deficits.

The accompanying figure divides Federal spending into three components and shows spending trends as a percentage of GDP.

1 *Interest spending* consists of Federal interest payments on the public debt. Since 1980 interest payments have increased from 1.2 percent to 2.8 percent of GDP, mainly because of the quadrupling of the public debt.

2 *Discretionary spending* involves programs controlled by annual appropriation bills. Congress can decide how much it wants to spend on these programs each year; it has full "discretion" over the amounts spent. This component of Federal expenditures includes spending on defense, transportation, law enforcement, and government operations. Observe that discretionary spending shrunk from 13.5 percent of GDP in 1962 to about 8 percent in 1994.

3 *Mandatory spending*—or "entitlement spending"—comprises benefits paid out in programs such as social security, Medicare, Medicaid, veterans' compensation and pensions, agricultural subsidies, aid to families with dependent children, Supplementary Security Income, and food stamps. This

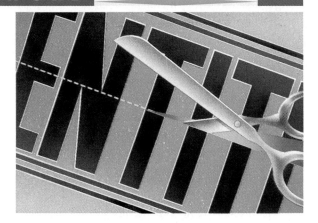

spending is mandated by past legislation which directs Congress to pay out specified benefits to all eligible recipients. Entitlement spending grows when Congress adds new transfer programs or raises benefit levels in existing programs. It also expands when more people become eligible for the benefits. Entitlement spending doubled between 1962 and 1994, rising from 6 percent to 12 percent of GDP.

It is clear from the diagram that rapidly rising Federal entitlements and interest payments are squeezing discretionary spending. Entitlements and

President—power, they say, which might easily be abused for political purposes.

Positive Role of Debt

Having completed this survey of imagined and real problems of deficits and the public debt, we conclude our discussion on a more positive note. Debt—both public and private—plays a positive role in a prosperous and growing economy. As income expands, so does saving. Macroeconomic theory and fiscal policy tell us that if aggregate demand is to be sustained at the full-employment level, this expanding volume of

saving or its equivalent must be obtained and spent by consumers, businesses, or government. The process by which saving is transferred to spenders is *debt creation.* Consumers and businesses *do* borrow and spend a great amount of saving. The total private debt in the United States is about $9 trillion.

But if households and businesses are not willing to borrow and thereby increase private debt sufficiently fast to absorb the growing volume of saving, an increase in public debt must absorb the remainder. If this doesn't happen the economy will falter from full employment and not realize its growth potential.

CHAPTER SUMMARY

1 A budget deficit is the excess of government expenditures over its receipts; the public debt is the total accumulation of its deficits and surpluses over time.

2 Budget philosophies include the annually balanced budget, the cyclically balanced budget, and functional finance. The basic problem with an annually balanced bud-

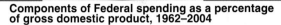

Components of Federal spending as a percentage of gross domestic product, 1962–2004

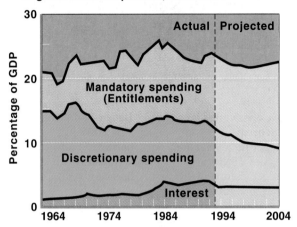

4 Denying wealthier citizens social security and Medicare benefits

5 Reducing health care benefits under Medicare

6 Fully taxing entitlement benefits as if they were ordinary income

None of these possibilities is politically popular. *About half of all American families receive benefits from one or more of the eleven largest entitlement programs.* A recent poll found that 61 percent of the public favored cutting government entitlement programs to curb the deficit. But when asked if they favored cuts in programs such as social security, Medicare, and farm subsidies, 66 percent said "no."

Social security and Medicare are the largest Federal entitlement programs. Social security is currently sound, collecting more revenues from 110 million workers than it pays to 41 million beneficiaries. But this self-financing will end in 2029 because of growing social security payments to the massive baby-boom generation. Spending for Medicare—the fastest growing entitlement program—will rise even more when the baby boomers retire.

Led by the Bipartisan Congressional Commission on Entitlements and Tax Reform, policy makers have begun to confront this issue. There is little doubt the question of what to do about entitlements will be the subject of intense discussion for some time to come.

Source: The Bipartisan Commission on Entitlements and Tax Reform, the Congressional Budget Office, and news sources.

interest are projected to consume *all* Federal tax revenues by 2015, leaving the Federal government with no money for education, children's programs, highways, national defense, or anything else.

Solutions proposed to avoid this startling scenario include:

1 Tax rate increases

2 Eliminating some entitlement programs

3 Reducing benefit levels in some or all entitlement programs

---

get is that it is procyclical rather than countercyclical. Similarly, it may be difficult to balance the budget over the course of the business cycle if upswings and downswings are not of roughly comparable magnitude. Functional finance is the view that the primary purpose of Federal finance is to stabilize the economy, and problems associated with consequent deficits or surpluses are of secondary importance.

3 Historically, growth of the public debt has been caused by the deficit financing of wars and by recessions. The large structural deficits in recent years are primarily the result of earlier tax reductions, accompanied by increases in entitlement spending.

4 The public debt was $4.6 trillion in 1994, two-thirds of which was held by the public and one-third by government agencies and the Federal Reserve. Since the 1970s the debt and associated interest charges have increased as a percentage of the GDP. The debt has also been rising on a per capita basis.

5 The argument that a large public debt may bankrupt the government is false because **a** the debt need only be

refinanced rather than refunded and **b** the Federal government has the power to levy taxes and create money.

6 The crowding-out effect aside, the public debt is not a vehicle for shifting economic burdens to future generations.

7 More substantive problems associated with public debt include the following: **a** Payment of interest on the debt probably increases income inequality. **b** Interest payments on the debt require higher taxes which may impair incentives. **c** A large and growing public debt creates political impediments to the use of antirecessionary fiscal policy. **d** Paying interest or principal on the portion of the debt held by foreigners entails a transfer of real output abroad. **e** Government borrowing to refinance or pay interest on the debt may increase interest rates and crowd out private investment spending.

8 Federal budget deficits have been much larger in the 1980s and 1990s than earlier. Many economists think these large deficits have increased real interest rates in the United States which have then **a** crowded out private investment and **b** increased foreign demand for American securities. Increased demand for American securities has increased

the international value of the dollar, causing American exports to fall and American imports to rise. The resulting trade deficits exert a contractionary effect on our domestic economy.

9 Proposed or enacted remedies for large deficits and public debt include **a** budget legislation of 1990 which raised taxes, cut expenditures, and forced Congress to offset new spending or tax cuts with either reductions in existing spending or tax increases; **b** the Deficit Reduction Act of 1993 which cut expenditures and raised personal income tax rates, the corporate income tax rate, and the Federal tax on gasoline; **c** a proposed constitutional amendment mandating an annually balanced budget; and **d** giving the President line-item veto authority.

TERMS AND CONCEPTS

budget deficit
public debt
annually balanced
  budget
cyclically balanced
  budget

functional finance
entitlement programs
external debt
crowding-out effect
public investments

Ricardian equivalence
  theorem
Budget Reconciliation
  Act of 1990
Budget Enforcement
  Act of 1990

Deficit Reduction Act
  of 1993
balanced budget
  amendment
line-item veto

QUESTIONS AND STUDY SUGGESTIONS

1 *Key Question* *Assess the potential for using fiscal policy as a stabilization tool under* **a** *an annually balanced budget,* **b** *a cyclically balanced budget, and* **c** *functional finance.*

2 What have been the major sources of the public debt historically? Why were deficits so large in the 1980s? Why did the deficit rise in 1991 and 1992?

3 *Key Question* *Discuss the two ways of measuring the size of the public debt. How does an internally held public debt differ from an externally held public debt? What would be the effects of retiring an internally held public debt? An externally held public debt? Distinguish between refinancing and retiring the debt.*

4 Explain or evaluate each of the following statements:
a "A national debt is like a debt of the left hand to the right hand."
b "The least likely problem arising from a large public debt is that the Federal government will go bankrupt."
c "The basic cause of our growing public debt is a lack of political courage."
d "The social security reserves are not being reserved. They are being spent, masking the real deficit."

5 Is the crowding-out effect likely to be larger during recession or when the economy is near full employment? Explain.

6 Some economists argue that the quantitative importance of the public debt can best be measured by interest payments on the debt as a percentage of the GDP. Can you explain why?

7 *Key Question* *Is our $4.6 trillion public debt a burden to future generations? If so, in what sense? Why might deficit financing be more likely to reduce the future size of our "national factory" than tax financing of government expenditures?*

8 *Key Question* *Trace the cause-and-effect chain through which large deficits might affect domestic real interest rates, domestic investment, the international value of the dollar, and our international trade. Comment: "There is too little recognition that the deterioration of America's position in world trade is more the result of our own policies than the harm wrought by foreigners." Provide a critique of this position, using the idea of Ricardian equivalence.*

9 Explain how a significant decline in the nation's budget deficit would be expected to affect **a** the size of our trade deficit, **b** the total debt Americans owe to foreigners, and **c** foreign purchases of U.S. assets such as factories and farms.

10 What was the essence of the 1990 Budget Reconciliation and Budget Enforcement Acts? What taxes were raised in the Deficit Reduction Act of 1993? Explain: "The success of the Deficit Reduction Act of 1993 in reducing the budget deficit is predicated on the expectation that there won't be a recession between 1993 and 1998."

11 Would you favor a constitutional amendment requiring the Federal budget to be balanced annually? Why or why not? Do you favor giving the president the authority to veto line-items of appropriation bills? Why or why not?

12 (Last Word) What is meant by the term "entitlement programs"? Cite several examples of these programs. Why have entitlement programs grown so rapidly? What are the implications for future generations if this growth continues?

19

ECONOMIC GROWTH

Despite periods of cyclical instability, economic growth in the United States has been impressive during this century. Real output has increased fifteenfold while population has only tripled, making five times more goods and services available to the average American than in 1900—and the quality of today's output is far superior. Economic growth has created material abundance, lifted the standard of living, and eased the unlimited wants–scarce resource dilemma.

But the American growth story is not all upbeat. Since 1970 economic growth in America has slowed considerably relative to earlier periods. Of twenty-four advanced industrial nations, only three grew more slowly than the United States over the past three decades.

We begin by defining economic growth. Next, we develop an analytical perspective on economic growth. How can we depict growth within our graphical models? Then, the long-term growth record of the United States and the various factors contributing to it are explored. This enables us to examine the causes of the slowdown in American productivity which began in the 1970s. So-called "doomsday" models of economic collapse are presented and critiqued. Finally, government policies designed to boost the rate of growth are briefly considered.

GROWTH ECONOMICS

Growth economics examines why production capacity increases over time. It also deals with the policy question of how to increase the economy's full employment level of real GDP.

Two Definitions

Economic growth can be defined and measured in two ways:
1 An increase in real GDP occurring over a period of time.

2 An increase in real GDP *per capita* occurring over time

In measuring military potential or political preeminence, the first definition is more relevant. But per capita output is superior for comparing living standards. While India's GDP is $215 billion compared to Denmark's $124 billion, per capita GDP is $26,000 in Denmark and only $310 in India.

Economic growth by either definition is usually calculated as annual percentage *rates* of growth. If real GDP was $200 billion last year and $210 billion this year, we can calculate the rate of growth by subtracting last year's real GDP from this year's real GDP and

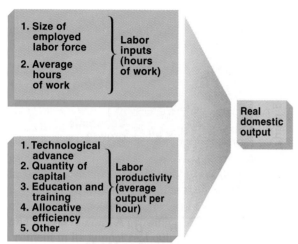

FIGURE 19-2   **The determinants of real output**
Real GDP can be usefully viewed as the product of the quantity of labor inputs multiplied by labor productivity.

real output per worker-hour—is $5, then total output or real GDP will be $100,000 (= 20,000 × $5).

What determines the number of hours worked each year? And what determines labor productivity? Figure 19-2 provides some answers. The hours of labor input depend on the size of the employed labor force and the length of the average workweek. Labor force size depends on the size of the working age population and the **labor force participation rate**—*the percentage of the working age population actually in the labor force.* The average workweek is governed by legal and institutional considerations and by collective bargaining.

Productivity is determined by technological progress, the quantity of capital goods available to workers, the quality of labor itself, and the efficiency with which inputs are allocated, combined, and managed. Productivity increases when the health, training, education, and motivation of workers are improved; when workers have more and better machinery and natural resources with which to work; when production is better organized and managed; and when labor is reallocated from less efficient industries to more efficient industries.

AD–AS Framework

We can also view economic growth through the long-run aggregate supply and aggregate demand analysis developed in Figures 17-6 and 17-7. Suppose aggre-

gate demand is AD_1 and long-run and short-run aggregate supply curves are AS_1 and AS_1' as shown in Figure 19-3. The initial equilibrium price level is P_1 and the level of real output is Q_1.

Recall that the upward slope of short-run aggregate supply curve AS_1' shows that a change in the price level will alter the level of real output. In the long run, however, wages and other input prices will fully adjust to the new price level, making the aggregate supply curve vertical at the economy's full-employment or potential level of real output. As with the location of the production possibilities curve, real supply factors—the quantity and quality of resources and technology—determine the long-run level of full-employment real output. Price level changes do not alter the location of the production possibilities curve; neither do they change the location of the long-run aggregate supply curve.

Aggregate Supply Shifts   Now assume changes in the supply factors listed in Figure 19-2 shift the long-run aggregate supply curve rightward from AS_1 to AS_2. This means the production possibilities curve in Figure 19-1 has been pushed outward.

Aggregate Demand Shifts   If aggregate demand remains at AD_1, the increase in long-run aggregate supply from AS_1 to AS_2 eventually will overcome downward price and wage rigidity and reduce the price level. But in recent decades a rising, not a falling, price level has accompanied economic growth. This suggests that aggregate demand has increased more rapidly than long-run aggregate supply. We show this in Figure 19-3 by shifting aggregate demand from AD_1 to AD_2, which results from changes in one or more of the determinants of aggregate demand (Table 11-1).

The combined increases in aggregate supply and aggregate demand in Figure 19-3 have produced economic growth of Q_1Q_2 and a rise in the price level from P_1 to P_2. At price level P_2, the economy confronts a new short-run aggregate supply curve AS_2'. (If not clear why, review Figure 17-6.)

Also, nominal GDP (= $P \times Q$) has increased more rapidly than real GDP (= Q) because of inflation. This diagram describes the secular trend of nominal GDP, real GDP, and the price level in the United States, a fact you can confirm by examining rows 5, 18, and 21 on the inside covers of this book. *(Key Question 3)*

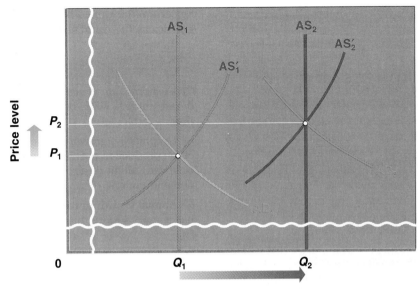

FIGURE 19-3 Economic growth and aggregate demand–aggregate supply analysis
Long-run and short-run aggregate supply curves have shifted rightward over time, as from AS₁ and
AS′₁ to AS₂ and AS′₂. Meanwhile, aggregate demand has shifted rightward even more rapidly. The outcome of these combined shifts has been economic growth, shown as the increase in real output from
Q_1 to Q_2, accompanied by inflation, shown as the rise in the price level from P_1 to P_2.

UNITED STATES GROWTH

Table 19-1 provides an overview of economic growth
in the United States over past decades as viewed
through our two definitions of growth. Column 2
shows the economy's growth as measured by increases in real GDP. Although not steady, the growth
of real GDP has been strong. *Real GDP has increased
nearly sixfold since 1940.* But our population has also
grown significantly. Using our second definition of
growth, we find in column 4 that *real per capita GDP
was almost three times larger in 1994 than in 1940.*

What about our *rate* of growth? Global Perspective 19-1 shows that the post-1948 growth rate of the
United States' real GDP has been 3.1 percent per year.
Not shown, real GDP per capita has grown at almost
2 percent per year.

These bare numbers must be modified.

1 Improved Products and Services The figures of Table 19-1 and Global Perspective 19-1 do *not*
fully take into account improvements in the quality of
products and services, and thus understate the
growth of economic well-being. Purely quantitative
data do not accurately compare an era of ice-boxes
and LPs and one of refrigerators and CDs.

2 Added Leisure The increases in real GDP and
per capita GDP shown in Table 19-1 were accomplished despite large increases in leisure. The standard workweek, once seventy hours, is now about

**TABLE 19-1 Real GDP and per capita GDP,
1929–1994**

(1) Year	(2) GDP, billions of 1987 dollars	(3) Population millions	(4) Per capita GDP, 1987 dollars (2) ÷ (3)
1929	$ 841	122	$ 6,893
1933	592	126	4,698
1940	919	132	6,962
1945	1615	140	11,536
1950	1428	152	9,395
1955	1773	166	10,681
1960	1973	181	10,902
1965	2474	194	12,753
1970	2876	205	14,029
1975	3222	214	15,056
1980	3776	228	16,561
1985	4280	239	17,908
1990	4897	250	19,588
1994	5342	261	20,467

Source: Economic Report of the President, 1995.

facilities, the municipal water systems, the airports —faces growing problems of deterioration, technological obsolescence, and insufficient capacity to serve future growth.

Also, public capital (infrastructure) and private capital are complementary. Investments in new highways promote private investment in new factories and retail establishments along their routes. Industrial parks which are developed by local governments in turn attract manufacturing firms. Some economists view the slowdown in the development of our infrastructure as a significant source of reduced private investment.

Education and Training

Ben Franklin once said: "He that hath a trade hath an estate." He meant that education and training improve a worker's productivity and result in higher earnings. Like investment in physical capital, investment in human capital is an important means of increasing labor productivity. Denison's estimates in Table 19-2 indicate that 14 percent of the growth in our real national income is attributable to such improvements in the quality of labor (item 5).

Perhaps the simplest measure of labor quality is the level of educational attainment. Figure 19-4 reflects educational gains in the past several decades. Currently 80 percent of the population, aged 25 or more, has at least a high school education. Twenty-two percent has acquired a college education or more.

It is clear from Figure 19-4 that education has become accessible to more and more people.

But there are concerns about the quality of American education. Scores on standardized college admissions tests have declined relative to scores of a few decades ago. Furthermore, American students in science and mathematics do not do as well as students in many other industrialized nations. Japanese children have a longer school day and attend school 240 days per year compared to 180 in the United States. Also, we have been producing fewer engineers and scientists, a problem which may trace back to inadequate training in math and science in elementary and high schools. And it is argued that on-the-job training (apprenticeship programs) in Japan and Germany— nations with fast rates of productivity growth—are more available and far superior to those in the United States.

Resource Allocation and Scale Economies

Table 19-2 also tells us that labor productivity has increased because of economies of scale (item 6) and improved resource allocation (item 7).

Improved Resource Allocation Improved resource allocation means that workers over time have reallocated themselves from low-productivity employment to high-productivity employment. Historically, much labor has shifted from agriculture, where labor productivity is low, to manufacturing, where it is quite high. More recently, labor has shifted away from some manufacturing industries to even higher-productivity industries such as legal, health, consulting, and financial services. As a result of such shifts, the average productivity of American workers in the aggregate has increased.

Also, labor market discrimination has historically denied women and minorities access to high-productivity jobs. The decline of such discrimination over time has shifted these groups from low-productivity jobs to higher-productivity jobs, increasing overall labor productivity and raising real GDP.

Tariffs, import quotas, and other barriers to international trade (Chapter 6) often keep resources in relatively unproductive employments. The long-run movement toward freer international trade has therefore improved the allocation of resources and expanded real output.

FIGURE 19-4   Changes in the educational attainment of the adult population
The percentage of the population, aged 25 or more, completing high school and college has been rising in recent decades. (*Statistical Abstract of the United States, 1994*, p. 157.)

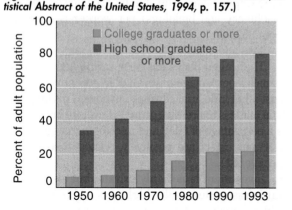

Economies of Scale Economies of scale are production advantages deriving from increased market
and firm size. A large corporation often can select
more efficient production techniques than can a small-
scale firm. A large manufacturer of autos can use elaborate assembly lines with computerization and robotics, while smaller producers must settle for less
advanced technologies. Markets have increased in
scope over time and firms have increased in size, allowing more efficient production methods to be used.
Accordingly, labor productivity has increased and economic growth has occurred.

Detriments to Growth

Some developments detract from the growth of real
output and income. The entry for the legal and human environment (item 8) in Table 19-2 aggregates
these detriments to productivity growth. Since 1929
there have been several changes in the regulation of
industry, environmental pollution, and worker health
and safety, which have negatively affected growth.
The expansion of government regulation in such areas as pollution control, worker health and safety, and
access for the disabled has diverted investment
spending away from growth-increasing capital goods
and toward expenditures for cleaner air and water,
greater worker protection, and improved access for
disabled workers and consumers. A firm required to
spend $1 million on a new scrubber to meet govern-
ment standards for air pollution or to make its stores
accessible to the disabled will not have that $1 million
to spend on machinery and equipment which would
expand real output. The diversion of resources to deal
with dishonesty and crime, the effects of work stoppages because of labor disputes, and the impact of bad
weather on agricultural output are also factors which
impede economic growth.

It should be noted that, while worker safety, clean
air and water, equal access for the disabled, and the
overall quality of life may come at the expense of economic growth, the reverse is also true. Economic
growth does not automatically enhance society's welfare. Growth of real output may involve opportunity
costs of other things (a clean environment, a fair society) we value more highly. Productivity measures
output per hour of work, *not* overall well-being per
hour of work. Increases in real GDP are not necessarily matched with equal increases in well-being.
Thus, society may rationally decide to "trade off"
some economic growth to achieve other desirable
ends. *(Key Question 5)*

Other Factors

There are other difficult-to-quantify considerations
which affect an economy's growth rate. For example,
America's generous and varied supplies of natural resources have been an important contributor to our
economic growth. We enjoy an abundance of fertile
soil, desirable climatic and weather conditions, large
quantities of most mineral resources, and generous
sources of power. With the possible exceptions of Russia and Canada, the United States has a larger variety
and greater quantity of natural resources than any
other nation.

While an abundant natural resource base is helpful to growth, a meager resource base does not doom
a nation to slow growth. Although Japan's natural resources are severely constrained, its post-World War
II growth has been remarkable (Global Perspective
19-1). In contrast, some of the impoverished countries
of Africa and South America have substantial amounts
of natural resources.

There are additional unmeasurable factors affecting a nation's growth rate. In particular, the overall social-cultural-political environment of the United
States generally has promoted economic growth. Several factors contribute to this favorable environment.
1 Unlike many other nations, there are virtually no
social or moral taboos on production and material
progress. American social philosophy has embraced
material advance as an attainable and desirable economic goal. The inventor, the innovator, and the business executive are accorded high degrees of prestige
and respect in American society.
2 Americans have traditionally possessed healthy
attitudes toward work and risk taking; our society has
benefited from a willing labor force and an ample supply of entrepreneurs.
3 Our market system has many personal and corporate incentives encouraging growth; our economy
rewards actions which increase output.
4 Our economy is founded on a stable political system characterized by democratic principles, internal
order, the right of property ownership, the legal status of enterprise, and the enforcement of contracts.
One recent study has shown that politically open societies grow much more rapidly on average than those
where freedom is limited.

tainment of the labor force has been slowing in recent years. The median number of years of school completed by the adult population was 12.1 in 1970 and increased to only 12.7 by 1993.

Technological Progress Technological advance—usually reflected in improvements in the quality of capital goods and the efficiency with which inputs are combined—may also have faltered. Technological progress is fueled by expenditures for formal research and development (R&D) programs. In the United States, R&D spending declined as a percentage of GDP from a peak of 3 percent in the mid-1960s to about 1 percent by the late 1970s, before rising again in the 1980s.

However, some economists discount the R&D decline in explaining the productivity slowdown. They say R&D *spending* alone tells us little about R&D *accomplishments*. There is clear evidence of continuing technological advance during the past two decades.

Investment A high positive correlation exists between the percentage of a nation's GDP devoted to investment goods and the productivity increases it achieves. A worker using a bulldozer can move more earth per hour than the same worker using a hand shovel. An engineer using a computer can complete a design task more rapidly than with pencil and paper.

The United States has been investing a smaller percentage of its GDP than in earlier periods. Several factors may have contributed to the weak growth of investment.

1 Low Saving Rate The United States has had a low saving rate which, coupled with strong private and public demands for credit, has resulted in high real interest rates relative to historical standards. High interest rates discourage investment spending.

2 Import Competition Growing import competition may have made some American producers reluctant to invest in new capital equipment. They may have shifted more investment overseas toward nations with low-wage workers.

3 Regulation The expansion of government regulations in the areas of pollution control, worker health and safety, and access for the disabled diverted some investment spending away from output-increasing capital goods. This investment spending may

have increased total utility to society, but did not directly increase output itself. The composition of investment may have shifted toward uses which do not increase productivity.

4 Reduced Infrastructure Spending Reduced spending on the economy's infrastructure may have slowed productivity growth. We have noted that these public capital goods are complementary to private capital goods. Data show that between 1950 and 1970 the public capital stock of infrastructure grew at a 4.1 percent annual rate, and labor productivity growth was 2.0 percent per year. During 1971–1985, however, the yearly increase in the infrastructure fell to 1.6 percent and the annual productivity increase dropped to 0.8 percent. A slowing of spending on public investment goods may have contributed to diminishing private investments and to declines in productivity growth.

Energy Prices Perhaps the prime suspect in the productivity slowdown was the large increases in oil prices occurring in 1973–1975 and in 1978–1980. Productivity growth diminished sharply after the quadrupling of oil prices in 1973–1975. Also, the impact of rocketing energy prices was worldwide, as was the productivity slowdown.

The direct impact of higher oil prices was to increase the cost of operating capital equipment, in effect raising the "price" of capital relative to labor. Producers were therefore more inclined to use less productive labor-intensive techniques.

The indirect macroeconomic effects of leaping energy prices may have had even more to do with reducing productivity growth. The two episodes of soaring energy prices produced stagflation—inflationary recessions. Government's restrictive macroeconomic policies to control inflation worsened and prolonged the periods of recession and slow economic growth. Recessions diminish productivity—output per worker—since output normally declines more rapidly than employment. The long periods of underuse of productive capacity in many industries probably contributed to the productivity slowdown.

Industrial Relations A different view of the productivity slowdown stresses institutional forces. The way work is organized, the attitudes and behavior of workers and managers, communication between labor and management, and the division of authority among managers and workers allegedly account for much of our poor productivity performance compared to Japan and western Europe. The argument is that American industrial relations reflect an adversarial relationship between managers and their employees. Feeling alienated from their employers, workers do not participate in the decisions governing their daily work lives; they do not identify with the objectives of their firms, and therefore are not motivated to work hard and productively. Managers are judged, rewarded, and motivated by short-term profits and thus, it is argued, give little attention to long-term plans and strategies critical to attaining high rates of productivity growth.

Japanese industries, in contrast, provide lifetime employment security for most of their work force, allow for worker participation in decision making, and use profit-sharing or bonuses to provide a direct link between the economic success of a firm and worker incomes. Furthermore, the direct interest workers have in the competitiveness and profitability of their enterprise reduces the need for supervisory personnel. The result is a commonality of interest and cooperation between management and labor, greater flexibility in job assignment, and more willingness of workers to accept technological change. Lifetime employment provides an incentive for heavy investment by employers in training and retraining their workers.

A Resurgence?

Since 1981 there has been a modest improvement in productivity growth. In Table 19-3 the 0.7 percent annual productivity growth for 1973–1981 improved to a 1.3 percent annual increase between 1981–1990. The recession of 1990–1991 halted this upward trend; productivity growth fell back to 0.7 percent in 1990 and was only 1.0 percent in 1991. But productivity surged to 3.0 percent in 1992 and averaged 2.0 percent over the 1990–1994 period.

Many of the factors depressing productivity growth have dissipated or been reversed. Energy prices are stable and the stagflation problem overcome. Since 1977 research and development spending has been increasing as a percentage of GDP. Innovations in computers, telecommunications, robotics, genetic engineering, and superconductors are providing a big stimulus to productivity. Although higher than a few years earlier, interest rates are still low, promoting purchases of new plant and equipment. Wages of college graduates have risen relative to wages of high school graduates and this wage premium should soon attract more students to universities.

The inexperienced baby-boomers who flooded labor markets in the 1960s and 1970s are now moving into the 25- to 54-year-old prime labor force as more mature, more productive workers. While American industrial relations remain distinctly different from the cooperative "shared vision" of Japanese managers and workers, the problems imposed by recession and increasing foreign competition are pushing American workers and managers in that direction. Worker involvement and profit-sharing plans are becoming more common in American industry.

Nevertheless, it is unclear at this point whether the recent revival of productivity is transitory or permanent. *(Key Question 8)*

DOOMSDAY MODELS

Annual 2 to 7 percent rates of economic growth in the industrial nations—compounded year after year—raise these questions: Can economic growth in industrially advanced nations continue over the next few decades? Can it continue over the next century?

Computer modelers[1] have developed complex simulation models called **doomsday models,** indicating that the world economy is using resources and dumping wastes at rates which the planet cannot sustain. Population and industrial production, it is argued, are expanding at exponential (2, 4, 16, 256, . . .) rates. Modern industrial production depends heavily on exhaustible natural resources which allegedly are fixed in supply. Industrial economies also employ the environment—which has a limited absorptive capacity—for waste disposal. In this view, we must ultimately run out of certain natural resources—oil, coal, copper, arable land—critical to the production process. Also, the increased waste inevitably resulting from economic growth will overwhelm the absorptive capacity of the world's ecological system. Air, water, and solid waste pollution will worsen.

The "Standard Run" Model

Figure 19-6 shows one computer simulation. This scenario assumes the world proceeds along its historical

[1]Donella H. Meadows, Dennis L. Meadows, and Jorgen Randers, *Beyond the Limits* (Post Mills, Vt.: Chelsea Green Publishers, 1992). Also see Dennis L. Meadows, et al., *The Limits to Growth* (Washington: Potomac Associates, 1972).

higher resource prices also spur resource producers to expand output by mining lower-grade ores or by recycling, both of which may have been economically unfeasible at lower prices. The point is the price mechanism automatically induces responses which alleviate resource shortages.

Recap

Whether you agree with the doomsday pessimists or with the critics of the doomsday models, certain messages and questions emerge from the limits-to-growth debate. For example, the fundamental question of scarcity has a time dimension. Absolutely exhaustible resources which are used today will not be available tomorrow. What is the optimal way to allocate such resources through time?

The debate also emphasizes that growth is not an unmitigated good. The impact of an ever-expanding output on the environment and on lifestyles must be taken into account in any evaluation of future growth.

Finally, the debate points out that factors which fall partially outside the realm of economics—in particular, population growth—have a critical bearing on our economic well-being. *(Key Question 12)*

QUICK REVIEW 19-3

■ Economists have cited the following reasons for America's slowdown in productivity in the past twenty-five years: *a* declines in labor quality, *b* a slowing of technological progress, *c* decreasing investment spending as a percentage of GDP, *d* higher energy prices, and *e* growth-impeding labor relations.

■ Computer modelers have developed simulation models indicating the world is using resources and dumping wastes at unsustainable rates.

■ To prevent complete economic collapse, "doomsday" modelers recommend slowing and eventually stopping the exponential growth of population and industrial output.

■ Critics of the "doomsday" models argue that *a* technological advance expands the supplies of existing resources and creates new resources, making it erroneous to assume that natural resource supplies are fixed; and *b* the price mechanism automatically reduces the use of increasingly scarce resources and encourages the development and use of new resources.

GROWTH POLICIES

If we accept the view that economic growth is desirable and sustainable, then the question arises as to what public policies might best stimulate growth. Several policies are either in use or have been suggested.

Demand-Side Policies

Low growth is often the consequence of inadequate aggregate demand and resulting GDP gaps. The purpose of demand-side policies is to eliminate or reduce the severity of recessions through active fiscal and monetary policy. The idea is to use government tools to increase aggregate demand at an appropriate, noninflationary pace. Adequate aggregate demand not only keeps present resources fully employed, it also creates an incentive for firms to expand their operations. In particular, low real interest rates (easy money policy) promote high levels of investment spending. This spending leads to capital accumulation, which expands the economy's capacity to produce.

Supply-Side Policies

These policies emphasize factors which will directly increase the potential or full-capacity output of the economy over time. The goal is to shift Figure 19-3's long-run and short-run aggregate supply curves rightward. Policies fitting this category include tax policies designed to stimulate saving, investment, and entrepreneurship. For example, by lowering or eliminating the tax on interest earned from savings accounts, the return on saving will increase and so will the amount of saving. Likewise, by lowering or eliminating the deduction of interest expenses on your personal income tax, consumption will be discouraged and saving encouraged. Some economists favor a national consumption tax as a full or partial replacement for the personal income tax. The idea is to penalize consumption and thereby encourage saving.

On the investment side, some economists propose eliminating the corporate income tax or allowing generous tax credits for business investment spending. If effective, this proposal would increase both aggregate demand and aggregate supply.

Industrial and Other Policies

There are other potential growth-stimulating policies which economists of various persuasions recommend. Some advocate an **industrial policy** whereby government would take a direct, active role in shaping the structure and composition of industry to promote growth. Thus government might take steps to hasten expansion of high-productivity industries and speed the movement of resources out of low-productivity industries. Government might also increase its expenditures on basic research and development to stimulate technological progress. Also, increased expenditures on basic education and apprenticeship skill training may help increase the quality and productivity of labor.

While the litany of potential growth-enhancing policies is long and involved, most economists agree it is not easy to increase a nation's growth rate.

CHAPTER SUMMARY

1 Economic growth may be defined either as **a** an expanding real output (income) or **b** an expanding per capita real output (income). Growth lessens the burden of scarcity and provides increases in real output which can be used to resolve domestic and international socioeconomic problems.

2 The supply factors in economic growth are **a** the quantity and quality of a nation's natural resources, **b** the quantity and quality of its human resources, **c** its stock of capital facilities, and **d** its technology. Two other factors —a sufficient level of aggregate demand and economic efficiency—are essential for the economy to realize its growth potential.

3 Economic growth can be shown graphically as an outward shift of a nation's production possibilities curve or as a rightward shift of its aggregate supply curve.

4 The post-World War II growth rate of real GDP for the United States has been more than 3 percent; real GDP per capita has grown at about 2 percent.

5 Real GDP in the United States has grown, partly because of increased inputs of labor, and primarily because of increases in the productivity of labor. Technological progress, increases in the quantity of capital per worker, improvements in the quality of labor, economies of scale, and improved allocation of labor are among the more important factors which increase labor productivity.

6 The rate of productivity growth declined sharply in the 1970s, causing a slowdown in the rise of our living standards and contributing to inflation. Although productivity growth has increased in the 1980s and early 1990s, it remains substantially below the rates attained in the two decades after World War II.

7 Suspected causes of the decline in productivity growth include decreases in labor quality, slowing of technological progress, declining investment spending as a percentage of GDP, higher energy prices, and adversarial labor relations.

8 Computer simulations called "doomsday models" indicate the world is using resources and dumping waste at rates which will result in the collapse of industrial output and food production somewhere near the year 2025. To stop this collapse, say the "doomsdayers," the world must quickly slow and eventually stop the exponential growth of population and industrial output.

9 Critics challenge the assumption of absolute limits on the supply of natural resources in the doomsday models, pointing out that technological advance expands the supplies of existing resources and creates new resources. Critics also argue these models overlook the role of the price mechanism in offsetting the predicted economic collapse. Declining resource supplies result in higher resource prices which automatically reduce the use of the higher-price inputs while expanding the development and use of new resources.

10 Growth-promoting policies include both demand-side and supply-side policies, along with efforts to shape the composition of industry.

TERMS AND CONCEPTS

supply, demand, and efficiency factors in growth	economic growth labor productivity	labor force participation rate infrastructure	doomsday models industrial policy

QUESTIONS AND STUDY SUGGESTIONS

1 Why is economic growth important? Explain why the difference between a 2.5 percent and a 3.0 percent annual growth rate might be of great significance.

2 *Key Question   What are the major causes of economic growth? "There are both a demand and a supply side to economic growth." Explain. Illustrate the operation of both sets*

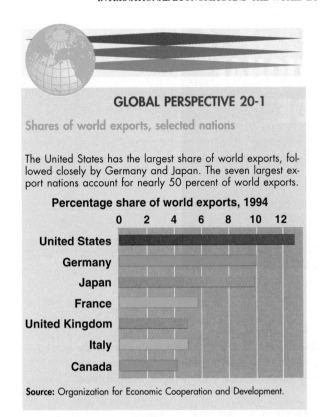

GLOBAL PERSPECTIVE 20-1

Shares of world exports, selected nations

The United States has the largest share of world exports, followed closely by Germany and Japan. The seven largest export nations account for nearly 50 percent of world exports.

Percentage share of world exports, 1994

Source: Organization for Economic Cooperation and Development.

5 America's principal commodity exports are chemicals, computers, consumer durables, and aircraft. Its main imports are automobiles, petroleum, computers, and clothing (Table 6-2).

6 Like other advanced industrial nations, America imports some of the same categories of goods that it exports. Examples: Autos, computers, chemicals, semiconductors, and telecommunications equipment (Table 6-2).

7 The bulk of United States export and import trade is with other industrially advanced nations, specifically Canada, nations of western Europe, and Japan (Table 6-3).

8 Improved transportation and communications technologies, declines in tariffs, and peaceful relations among major industrial nations have all helped expand world trade since World War II.

9 Although trade is still dominated by the United States, Japan, and western European nations, several new "players" have greatly increased their roles (Global Perspective 20-1). The four "Asian tigers"—Hong Kong, Singapore, South Korea, and Taiwan—have expanded their share of world trade from 3 percent in 1972 to nearly 10 percent today. China has

emerged as a new international trader and the collapse of communism has led eastern European nations and Russia to look globally for new trade partners.

10 International trade has recently been at the center of international policy. Examples: The North American Free Trade Agreement (NAFTA), the conclusion of negotiations on the General Agreement on Tariffs and Trade (GATT), and United States–Japan negotiations on reducing the American trade deficit with Japan.

Keeping these facts in mind, let's take a closer look at the economics of international trade.

THE ECONOMIC BASIS FOR TRADE

In Chapter 6 we found that international trade is a way nations can specialize, increase the productivity of their resources, and realize a larger total output. Sovereign nations, like individuals and regions of a nation, can gain by specializing in products they can produce with greatest relative efficiency and by trading for goods they cannot produce efficiently. This rationale for trade is correct, but a more detailed understanding is needed. The more complete answer to the question "Why do nations trade?" hinges on two points.

1 The distribution of economic resources—natural, human, and capital goods—among nations is uneven; nations are different in their endowments of economic resources.

2 Efficient production of various goods requires different technologies or combinations of resources.

The character and interaction of these two points can be readily illustrated. Japan, for example, has a large, well-educated labor force; skilled labor is abundant and therefore inexpensive. Japan can produce efficiently (at low cost) a variety of goods whose design and production require much skilled labor; cameras, transistor radios, and video recorders are examples of such **labor-intensive** commodities.

In contrast, Australia has vast amounts of land compared with its human and capital resources and can inexpensively produce such **land-intensive** commodities as wheat, wool, and meat. Brazil has the soil, tropical climate, rainfall, and lots of unskilled labor needed for efficient low-cost production of coffee.

Industrially advanced nations are in a position to produce inexpensively a variety of **capital-intensive** goods, for example, automobiles, agricultural equipment, machinery, and chemicals.

The economic efficiency with which nations produce various goods can change. Both the distribution of resources and technology can change, altering the relative efficiency with which goods can be produced by various countries. For example, in the past few decades South Korea has upgraded the quality of its labor force and has greatly expanded its stock of capital. Although South Korea was primarily an exporter of agricultural products and raw materials a half-century ago, it now exports large quantities of manufactured goods. Similarly, the new technologies which gave us synthetic fibers and synthetic rubber drastically altered the resource-mix needed to produce these goods and changed the relative efficiency of nations in manufacturing them.

As national economies evolve, the size and quality of their labor forces may change, the volume and composition of their capital stocks may shift, new technologies will develop, and even the quality of land and quantity of natural resources may be altered. As these changes occur, the efficiency with which a nation can produce goods will also change.

COMPARATIVE ADVANTAGE: GRAPHICAL ANALYSIS

Implicit in what we have just discussed is the principle of comparative advantage, described in Chapter 6. Let's again look at that idea, now using graphical analysis.

Two Isolated Nations

Suppose the world economy is composed of just two nations, the United States and Brazil. Each can produce both wheat and coffee, but at differing levels of economic efficiency. Suppose the United States' and Brazilian domestic production possibilities curves for coffee and wheat are as shown in Figure 20-1a and b. Let's look at two characteristics of these production possibilities curves.

1   Constant Costs   We have purposely drawn the "curves" as straight lines, in contrast to the concave-from-the-origin production possibilities boundaries introduced in Chapter 2. This means the law of increasing costs has been replaced with the assumption of constant costs. This simplification will make it easier for you to follow our discussion and will not impair the validity of our analysis and conclusions. We will consider later the effect of the more realistic increasing costs.

2   Different Costs   The production possibilities lines of the United States and Brazil are different, reflecting different resource mixes and differing levels of technological progress. Specifically, the opportunity costs of producing wheat and coffee differ between the two nations.

United States   In Figure 20-1a, with full employment, the United States can increase its output of wheat 30 tons by forgoing 30 tons of coffee output. That means the slope of the production possibilities curve is −1

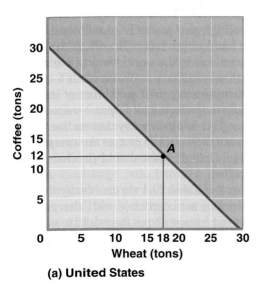

(a) United States

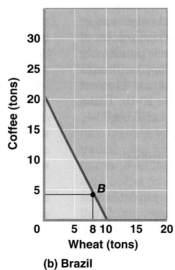

(b) Brazil

FIGURE 20-1   Production possibilities for the United States and Brazil The two production possibilities curves show the amounts of coffee and wheat the United States (a) and Brazil (b) can produce domestically. The production possibilities for both countries are straight lines because we are assuming constant costs. The different cost ratios—1*W* = 1*C* for the United States and 1*W* = 2*C* for Brazil—are reflected in the different slopes of the two lines.

and services were not sufficient to pay for our imports of goods and services. (We ignore transfer payments —item 8—in making this statement.) How did we finance the difference? The answer is that the United States must either borrow from abroad or give up ownership of some of its assets to foreigners as reflected in the capital account.

A simple analogy is useful here. Suppose in some year your expenditures exceed your earnings. How will you finance your "deficit"? You might sell some of your assets or borrow. You might sell some real assets (your car or stereo) or perhaps some financial assets (stocks or bonds) which you own. Or you might obtain a loan from your family or a bank.

Similarly, when a nation incurs a deficit in its current account, its expenditures for foreign goods and services (its imports) exceed the income received from the international sales of its own goods and services (its exports). It must finance that current account deficit by selling assets and by borrowing, that is, by going into debt. And that is what is reflected in the capital account surplus. Our capital account surplus of $33 billion (item 12) indicates that in 1993 the United States "sold off" real assets (buildings, farmland) and received loans from the rest of the world in that amount to help finance our current account deficit of $104 billion.

Recap: A nation's current account *deficit* will be financed essentially by a net capital *inflow* in its capital account. A nation's current account *surplus* would be accompanied by a net capital *outflow* in its capital account. The excess earnings from its current account surplus will be used to purchase real assets of, and make loans to, other nations.

Official Reserves

The central banks of nations hold quantities of foreign currencies called **official reserves** which are added to or drawn on to settle any *net* differences in current and capital account balances. In 1993 the surplus in our capital account was considerably less than the deficit in our current account so we had a $71 billion net deficit on the combined accounts (item 13). That is, the United States earned less foreign monies in all international trade and financial transactions than it used. This deficiency of earnings of foreign currencies was subtracted from the existing balances of foreign monies held by our central banks. The *plus* $71 billion of official reserves shown by item 14 represents this reduction of our stocks of foreign currencies. The plus sign indicates this is a credit or "export-type" transaction which represents a supply of foreign exchange.

Frequently the relationship between the current and capital account is just the opposite of that shown in Table 21-1. That is, the current account deficit is less than the capital account surplus. Hence, our central banks would experience an increase in their holdings of foreign currencies. This would show as a *minus* item in the balance of payments; it is a debit or "import-type" transaction because it represents a use of foreign exchange.

The point here is that *the three components of the balance of payments statement—the current account, the capital account, and the official reserves account—must sum to zero.* Every unit of foreign exchange used (as reflected in our "minus" outpayment or debit transactions) in our international transactions must have a source (our "plus" inpayment or credit transactions).

Payments Deficits and Surpluses

Although the balance of payments must always sum to zero, economists and political officials speak of **balance of payment deficits and surpluses.** In doing so they are referring to the "current and capital account balance" shown as item 13 in Table 21-1. If this is a negative item, there is a balance of payments deficit as was the case in 1993 when the United States earned less foreign monies from all its trade and financial transactions than it used. The United States did not "pay its way" in world trade and finance and therefore depleted its official reserves of foreign monies. If the current and capital account balance were positive, then the United States would face a balance of payments surplus. The United States would have earned sufficient foreign exchange from its export-type transactions to pay for its import-type transactions. As we have just seen, it would add to its stocks of foreign monies—that is, increase its official reserve holdings.

A decrease in official reserves (shown by a positive official reserves item in Table 21-1) measures a nation's balance of payments deficit; an increase in official reserves (shown by a negative official reserves item) measures its balance of payments surplus.

Deficits and Surpluses: Good, Bad, or Ugly?

Are deficits bad, as the term implies? Is a surplus desirable, as that word suggests? The answer to both is "not necessarily." A large merchandise trade deficit such as the United States has been incurring in recent years is regarded by many as "unfavorable" or "adverse," as it suggests American producers are losing their competitiveness in world markets. Our industries seem to be having trouble selling their goods abroad and are simultaneously facing strong competition from imported goods. On the other hand, a trade deficit is *favorable* from the vantage point of American consumers who are currently receiving more goods as imports than they are forgoing as exports.

Whether a balance of payments deficit or surplus is good or bad depends on (1) the events causing them and (2) their persistence through time. For example, the large payments deficits imposed on the United States and other oil-importing nations by OPEC's runup of oil prices in 1973–1974 and 1979–1980 were very disruptive, forcing the United States to invoke policies to curtail oil imports.

Also, any nation's official reserves are limited. Persistent or long-term payments deficits, which must be financed by drawing down those reserves, would ultimately deplete reserves. In this case that nation would have to undertake policies to correct its balance of payments. These policies might require painful macroeconomic adjustments, trade barriers and similar restrictions, or changing the international value of its currency. *(Key Question 3)*

QUICK REVIEW 21-1

■ American *exports* create a demand for dollars and a supply of foreign currencies; American *imports* create a demand for foreign currencies and a supply of American dollars.

■ The current account balance is a nation's exports of goods and services less its imports of goods and services plus its net investment income and net transfers.

■ The capital account balance is a nation's capital inflows less its capital outflows.

■ A balance of payments deficit occurs when the sum of the balances on current and capital accounts is negative; a balance of payments surplus arises when the sum of the balances on current and capital accounts is positive.

FREELY FLOATING EXCHANGE RATES

Both the size and persistence of a nation's balance of payments deficits and surpluses and the adjustments it must make to correct these imbalances depend on the system of exchange rates being used. There are two polar options: (1) a system of **flexible** or **floating exchange rates** where the rates at which national currencies exchange for one another are determined by demand and supply, and (2) a system of rigidly **fixed exchange rates** by which governmental intervention in foreign exchange markets or some other mechanism offsets the changes in exchange rates which fluctuations in demand and supply would otherwise cause.

Freely floating exchange rates are determined by the unimpeded forces of demand and supply. Let's examine the rate, or price, at which American dollars might be exchanged for, say, British pounds sterling. Figure 21-3 (Key Graph) shows the demand for pounds as downsloping; the supply of pounds as upsloping.

The downsloping *demand for pounds* shown by D indicates that, if pounds become less expensive to Americans, British goods will become cheaper to Americans. Americans will demand larger quantities of British goods and therefore larger amounts of pounds to buy those goods.

The *supply of pounds* S is upsloping because, as the dollar price of pounds *rises* (that is, the pound price of dollars *falls*), the British will purchase more American goods. At higher and higher dollar prices for pounds, the British can get more American dollars and therefore more American goods per pound. American goods become cheaper to the British, inducing them to buy more of these goods. When the British buy American goods, they supply pounds to the foreign exchange market because they must exchange pounds for dollars to purchase our goods.

The intersection of the supply and demand for pounds will determine the dollar price of pounds. Here, the equilibrium rate of exchange is $2 to £1.

Depreciation and Appreciation

An exchange rate determined by free-market forces can and does change frequently. When the dollar price of pounds increases, for example, from $2 for £1 to $3 for £1, the value of the dollar has **depreciated** relative to the pound. Currency depreciation means that

KEY GRAPH

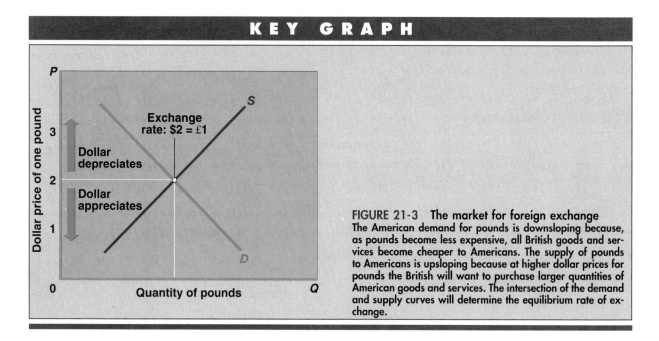

FIGURE 21-3   The market for foreign exchange
The American demand for pounds is downsloping because, as pounds become less expensive, all British goods and services become cheaper to Americans. The supply of pounds to Americans is upsloping because at higher dollar prices for pounds the British will want to purchase larger quantities of American goods and services. The intersection of the demand and supply curves will determine the equilibrium rate of exchange.

it take more units of a country's currency (dollars) to buy a single unit of some foreign currency (pounds).

When the dollar price of pounds decreases—from $2 for £1 to $1 for £1—the value of the dollar has **appreciated** relative to the pound. Currency appreciation means that it take fewer units of a country's currency (dollars) to buy a single unit of some foreign currency (pounds).

In our American-British illustrations, when the dollar depreciates the pound appreciates and vice versa. When the exchange rate between dollars and pounds changes from $2 = £1 to $3 = £1, it takes *more* dollars to buy £1 and the dollar has depreciated. But it takes *fewer* pounds to buy a dollar. At the initial rate it took £$\frac{1}{2}$ to buy $1; at the new rate it only takes £$\frac{1}{3}$ to buy $1. The pound has appreciated relative to the dollar. *If the dollar depreciates relative to the pound, the pound appreciates relative to the dollar. If the dollar appreciates vis-à-vis the pound, the pound depreciates vis-à-vis the dollar.* (You may want to review Figure 6-5.)

Determinants of Exchange Rates

Why are the demand for and the supply of pounds located as they are in Figure 21-3? What forces will cause the demand and supply curves for pounds to change, causing the dollar to appreciate or depreciate?

Changes in Tastes   Any change in consumer tastes or preferences for the products of a foreign country will alter the demand for, or supply of, that nation's currency and change its exchange rate. If American technological advances in computers make them more attractive to British consumers and businesses, then they will supply more pounds in exchange markets in purchasing more American computers and the dollar will appreciate. If British tweeds become more fashionable in the United States, our demand for pounds will increase and the dollar will depreciate.

Relative Income Changes   If the growth of a nation's relative income is more rapid than other countries', its currency is likely to depreciate. A country's imports vary directly with its level of income. As incomes rise in the United States, American consumers buy more domestically produced goods *and* more foreign goods. If the United States' economy is expanding rapidly and the British economy is stagnant, American imports of British goods—and therefore U.S. demand for pounds—will increase. The dollar price of pounds will rise, meaning the dollar has depreciated.

Relative Price Changes If the domestic price level rises rapidly in the United States and remains constant in Britain, American consumers will seek out low-priced British goods, increasing the demand for pounds. The British will purchase fewer American goods, reducing the supply of pounds. This combination of an increase in the demand for, and a reduction in the supply of, pounds will cause the dollar to depreciate.

Differences in price levels among nations—which reflect changes in price levels over time—help explain persistent differences in exchange rates. In 1995 an American dollar could buy .63 British pounds, 100 Japanese yen, or 40,887 Turkish lira. One reason for these differences is that the prices of British goods and services in pounds were far lower than the prices of Japanese goods and services in yen and the prices of Turkish goods and services in lira. For example, the same market basket of products costing $500 in the United States might cost 300 pounds in England, 50,000 yen in Japan, and 20 million lira in Turkey. *Generally, the higher the prices of a nation's goods and services in terms of its own currency, the greater the amount of that currency which can be obtained with an American dollar.*

Taken to extreme, this **purchasing power parity theory** holds that differences in exchange rates *equate* the purchasing power of various currencies. That is, the exchange rates among national currencies perfectly adjust to match the ratios of the nations' price levels. If a market basket of goods costs $100 in the United States and £50 in Great Britain, the exchange rate should be $2 = £1. Thus, a dollar spent on goods sold in Britain, Japan, Turkey, and other nations supposedly will have equal purchasing power. In practice, however, exchange rates depart significantly from purchasing power parity, even over long periods. Nevertheless, relative price levels are a determinant of exchange rates.

Relative Real Interest Rates What if the United States restricts the growth of its money supply (tight money policy), as it did in the late 1970s, early 1980s, and in 1994 to control inflation? As a result, *real* interest rates—nominal interest rates adjusted for the rate of inflation—rose in the United States compared to most other nations. Consequently, British individuals and firms found the United States an attractive place to make financial investments. This increase in the demand for American financial assets

TABLE 21-2 Determinants of exchange rates: factors which change demand or supply of a particular currency and thus alter the exchange rate

1 **Changes in tastes** Examples: Japanese autos decline in popularity in the United States (Japanese yen depreciates, American dollar appreciates); German tourists flock to the United States (American dollar appreciates, German mark depreciates)

2 **Changes in relative incomes** Example: England encounters a recession, reducing its imports, while American real output and real income surge, increasing American imports (British pound appreciates, American dollar depreciates)

3 **Changes in relative prices** Example: Germany experiences a 3 percent inflation rate compared to Canada's 10 percent rate (German mark appreciates, Canadian dollar depreciates)

4 **Changes in relative real interest rates** Example: The Federal Reserve drives up interest rates in the United States, while the Bank of England takes no such action (American dollar appreciates, British pound depreciates)

5 **Speculation** Examples: Currency traders believe France will have much more rapid inflation than Sweden (French franc depreciates; Swedish krona appreciates); currency traders think German interest rates will plummet relative to American rates (German mark depreciates, American dollar appreciates)

meant an increase in the supply of British pounds and the dollar therefore appreciated in value.

Speculation Suppose it is widely anticipated that the American economy will (1) grow faster than the British economy, (2) experience more rapid inflation than the British economy, and (3) have lower future real interest rates than Britain. All these expectations would lead us to believe that in the future the dollar will depreciate and the pound will appreciate. Holders of dollars will attempt to convert them into pounds, increasing the demand for pounds. This conversion causes the dollar to depreciate and the pound to appreciate. A self-fulfilling prophecy arises: The dollar depreciates and the pound appreciates because speculators act on the supposition that these changes in currency values will in fact happen. (Currency speculation is the subject of this chapter's Last Word.)

Table 21-2 provides additional illustrations to reinforce your understanding of the determinants of exchange rates.

Flexible Rates and the Balance of Payments

Proponents argue that flexible exchange rates have a compelling virtue: *They automatically adjust so as eventually to eliminate balance of payments deficits or surpluses.* We can explain this by looking at S and D in Figure 21-4 which restate the demand for, and supply of, pounds curves from Figure 21-3. The equilibrium exchange rate of $2 = £1 means there is no balance of payments deficit or surplus. At the $2 = £1 exchange rate the quantity of pounds demanded by Americans to import British goods, buy British transportation and insurance services, and pay interest and dividends on British investments in the United States equals the amount of pounds supplied by the British in buying American exports, purchasing services from Americans, and making interest and dividend payments on American investments in Britain. In brief, there would be no change in official reserves in Table 21-1.

Suppose tastes change and Americans buy more British automobiles. Or the American price level has increased relative to Britain, or interest rates have fallen in the United States compared to Britain. Any or all of these changes will cause the American demand for British pounds to increase from D to, say, D' in Figure 21-4.

We observe that *at the initial $2 = £1 exchange rate* an American balance of payments deficit has been created in the amount *ab*. That is, at the $2 = £1 rate there is a shortage of pounds in the amount of *ab* to Americans. American export-type transactions will earn *xa* pounds, but Americans will want *xb* pounds to finance import-type transactions. Because this is a free competitive market, the shortage will change the exchange rate (the dollar price of pounds) from $2 = £1 to, say, $3 = £1; that is, the dollar has *depreciated*.

At this point it must be emphasized that *the exchange rate is a special price which links all domestic (United States') prices with all foreign (British) prices.* The dollar price of a foreign good is found by multiplying the foreign product price by the exchange rate in dollars per unit of the foreign currency. At an exchange rate of $2 = £1, a British automobile priced at £9000 will cost an American $18,000 (= 9000 × $2).

A change in the exchange rate alters the prices of all British goods to Americans and all American goods to potential British buyers. The change in the exchange rate from $2 = £1 to $3 = £1 will alter the relative attractiveness of American imports and exports so as to restore equilibrium in the balance of

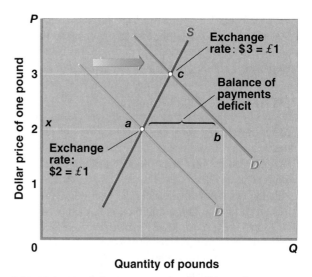

FIGURE 21-4 **Adjustments under flexible exchange rates, fixed exchange rates, and the gold standard** Under flexible rates an American trade deficit at the $2-for-£1 rate would be corrected by an increase in the rate to $3 for £1. Under fixed rates the *ab* shortage of pounds would be met out of international monetary reserves. Under the gold standard the deficit would cause changes in domestic price and income levels which would shift the demand for pounds (D') to the left and the supply (S) to the right, sustaining equilibrium at the $2-for-£1 rate.

payments of the United States. From the American point of view, as the dollar price of pounds changes from $2 to $3, the British auto priced at £9000, which formerly cost an American $18,000, now costs $27,000 (= 9000 × $3). Other British goods will also cost more to Americans, and American imports of British goods and services will decline. Graphically, this is shown as a move from point *b* toward point *c* in Figure 21-4.

From Britain's standpoint the exchange rate—the pound price of dollars—has fallen (from £$\frac{1}{2}$ to £$\frac{1}{3}$ for $1). The international value of the pound has *appreciated*. The British previously got only $2 for £1; now they get $3 for £1. American goods are therefore cheaper to the British, and American exports to Great Britain will rise. In Figure 21-4 this is shown by the move from point *a* toward point *c*.

The two adjustments described—a decrease in American imports from Great Britain and an increase in American exports to Great Britain—are precisely those needed to correct the American balance of payments deficit. (You should reason through the operation of freely fluctuating exchange rates in correcting an initial American balance of payments *surplus* in its trade with Great Britain.)

In summary, the free fluctuation of exchange rates in response to shifts in the supply of, and demand for, foreign monies automatically corrects balance of payments deficits and surpluses. *(Key Question 6)*

Disadvantages of Flexible Rates

Even though freely fluctuating exchange rates automatically work to eventually eliminate payments imbalances, they may cause several significant problems:

1 Uncertainty and Diminished Trade The risks and uncertainties associated with flexible exchange rates may discourage the flow of trade. Suppose an American automobile dealer contracts to purchase ten British cars for £90,000. At the current exchange rate of, say, $2 for £1, the American importer expects to pay $180,000 for these automobiles. But if in the three-month delivery period the rate of exchange shifts to $3 for £1, the £90,000 payment contracted by the American importer will now be $270,000.

This increase in dollar price of pounds may turn the potential American importer's anticipated profits into substantial losses. Aware of the possibility of an adverse change in the exchange rate, the American importer may not be willing to assume the risks involved. The American firm may confine its operations to domestic automobiles, with the result that international trade does not occur in this item.

The same rationale applies to investment. Assume that, when the exchange rate is $3 to £1, an American firm invests $30,000 (or £10,000) in a British enterprise. It estimates a return of 10 percent, that is, it anticipates earnings of $3000 or £1000. Suppose these expectations prove correct in that the British firm earns £1000 the first year on the £10,000 investment. But suppose that during the year, the value of the dollar *appreciates* to $2 = £1. The absolute return is now only $2000 (rather than $3000) and the rate of return falls from the anticipated 10 percent to only $6\frac{2}{3}$ percent (= $2000 ÷ $30,000). Investment is inherently risky. The added risk posed by adverse changes in exchange rates may persuade the potential American investor to avoid overseas ventures.[1]

---

[1]We will see in this chapter's Last Word, however, that a trader can circumvent part of the risk of unfavorable exchange rate fluctuations by "hedging" in the "futures market" for foreign exchange.

2 Terms of Trade A nation's terms of trade will be worsened by a decline in the international value of its currency. For example, an increase in the dollar price of pounds will mean that the United States must export more goods and services to finance a given level of imports from Britain.

3 Instability Freely fluctuating exchange rates may have destabilizing effects on the domestic economy as wide fluctuations stimulate and then depress industries producing internationally traded goods. If the American economy is operating at full employment and the international value of its currency depreciates as in our illustration, the results will be inflationary for two reasons. Foreign demand for American goods will increase—the net exports component of aggregate demand will increase and cause demand-pull inflation. Also, prices of all American imports will increase. Conversely, appreciation of the dollar would lower exports and increase imports, causing unemployment.

With regards to policy, floating exchange rates may complicate the use of domestic fiscal and monetary policies in seeking full employment and price stability. This is especially true for nations whose exports and imports are large relative to their GDPs (Table 6-1).

FIXED EXCHANGE RATES

At the other extreme nations have often fixed or "pegged" their exchange rates to circumvent the disadvantages associated with floating rates. To analyze the implications and problems associated with fixed rates, assume the United States and Britain agree to maintain a $2 = £1 exchange rate.

The problem is that a governmental proclamation that a dollar is worth so many pounds does *not* mandate stability of the demand for, and supply of, pounds. As demand and supply shift over time, government must intervene directly or indirectly in the foreign exchange market if the exchange rate is to be stabilized.

In Figure 21-4 suppose the American demand for pounds increases from D to D' and an American payments deficit of *ab* arises. This means the American government is committed to an exchange rate ($2 = £1) which is below the equilibrium rate ($3 = £1). How can the United States prevent the shortage of pounds—reflecting an American balance of payments deficit—from driving the exchange rate up to the equilibrium level? The answer is to alter market demand or supply or both so that they continue to intersect at the $2 = £1 rate of exchange. There are several ways to do this.

Use of Reserves

The most desirable means of pegging an exchange rate is to manipulate the market through the use of official reserves. International monetary *reserves* are stocks of foreign monies owned by a government. How do reserves originate? Let's assume that in the past the opposite market condition prevailed in which there was a surplus, rather than a shortage, of pounds, and the United States government had acquired that surplus. That is, at some earlier time the United States government spent dollars to buy surplus pounds which were threatening to reduce the $2 = £1 exchange rate to, say, $1 = £1. By selling part of its reserve of pounds, the United States government could shift the supply of pounds curve to the right so that it intersects D' at b in Figure 21-4, thereby maintaining the exchange rate at $2 = £1.

Historically nations have used gold as "international money" or as reserves. In our example the United States government might sell some of the gold it owns to Britain for pounds. The pounds acquired could be used to augment the supply of pounds earned through American trade and financial transactions to shift the supply of pounds to the right to maintain the $2 = £1 exchange rate.

It is critical that the amount of reserves be enough to accomplish the required increase in the supply of pounds. This is *not* a problem if deficits and surpluses occur more or less randomly and are about the same size. That is, last year's balance of payments surplus with Britain will increase the United States' reserve of pounds and this reserve can be used to "finance" this year's deficit. But if the United States encounters persistent and sizable deficits for an extended period, the reserves problem can become critical and force the abandonment of a system of fixed exchange rates. Or, at least, a nation whose reserves are inadequate must resort to less appealing options to maintain exchange rate stability. Let's consider these options.

Trade Policies

One set of policy options includes measures designed to control the flows of trade and finance directly. The United States might try to maintain the $2 = £1 exchange rate in the face of a shortage of pounds by discouraging imports (thereby reducing the demand for pounds) and by encouraging exports (thereby increasing the supply of pounds). Imports can be reduced by tariffs or import quotas. Special taxes may be levied on the interest and dividends Americans receive for foreign investments. Also, the United States government might subsidize certain American exports to increase the supply of pounds.

The fundamental problem with these policies is they reduce the volume of world trade and distort its composition or pattern away from that which is economically desirable. Tariffs, quotas, and the like can be imposed only at the sacrifice of some portion of the economic gains or benefits attainable from a free flow of world trade based on comparative advantage. These effects should not be underestimated; the imposition of trade barriers can elicit retaliatory responses from other nations which are adversely affected.

Exchange Controls: Rationing

Another option is exchange controls or rationing. Under exchange controls the United States government would handle the problem of a pound shortage by requiring all pounds obtained by American exporters be sold to it. Then the government allocates or rations this short supply of pounds (*xa* in Figure 21-4) among various American importers who demand the quantity *xb*. In this way the American government would restrict American imports to the amount of foreign exchange earned by American exports. American demand for British pounds in the amount of *ab* would be unfulfilled. Government eliminates a balance of payments deficit by restricting imports to the value of exports.

There are many objections to exchange controls.

1 Distorted Trade Like trade controls—tariffs, quotas, and export subsidies—exchange controls distort the pattern of international trade away from comparative advantage.

2 Discrimination The process of rationing scarce foreign exchange means discrimination among importers. Serious problems of equity and favoritism are implicit in the rationing process.

3 Restricted Choice Controls impinge on freedom of consumer choice. Americans who prefer Mazdas may be forced to buy Mercurys. The business opportunities of some American importers will be impaired because imports are constrained by government.

4 Black Markets There are likely to be enforcement problems. The market forces of demand and supply indicate there are American importers who want foreign exchange badly enough to pay *more* than the $2 = £1 official rate; this sets the stage or extralegal or "black market" foreign exchange dealings.

Domestic Macro Adjustments

A final means of maintaining a stable exchange rate is to use domestic fiscal and monetary policies to eliminate the shortage of pounds. Restrictive fiscal and monetary measures will reduce the United States' national income relative to Britain's. Because American imports vary directly with our national income, our demand for British goods, and therefore for pounds, will be restrained.

To the extent that these contractionary policies reduce our price level relative to Britain's, American buyers of consumption and investment goods will divert their demands from British to American goods, also restricting the demand for pounds.

Finally, a restrictive (tight) money policy will increase United States' interest rates compared to Britain and reduce American demand for pounds to make financial investments in Britain.

From Britain's standpoint lower prices on American goods and higher American interest rates will increase British imports of American goods and stimulate British financial investment in the United States. Both developments will increase the supply of pounds. The combination of a decrease in the demand for and an increase in the supply of pounds will eliminate the initial American payments deficit. In Figure 21-4 the new supply and demand curves will intersect at some new equilibrium point on the *ab* line where the exchange rates persists at $2 = £1.

This means of maintaining pegged exchange rates is hardly appealing. The "price" of exchange rate stability for the United States is falling output, employment, and price levels—in other words, a recession. Achieving a balance of payments equilibrium and realizing domestic stability are both important national economic objectives; but to sacrifice the latter for the former is to let the tail wag the dog.

QUICK REVIEW 21-2

◼ In a system where exchange rates are free to float, they are determined by the demand for, and supply of, individual national currencies.

◼ Determinants of freely floating exchange rates—factors which shift currency supply and demand curves—include changes in tastes, changes in relative national incomes, relative price level changes, relative real interest rate changes, and speculation.

◼ Under a system of fixed exchange rates, nations set their exchange rates and then maintain them by buying or selling reserves of foreign currencies, establishing trade barriers, employing exchange controls, or incurring inflation or recession

INTERNATIONAL EXCHANGE RATE SYSTEMS

There have been three different exchange rate systems which nations have employed in recent history.

The Gold Standard: Fixed Exchange Rates

Over the 1879–1934 period—except for the World War I years—an international monetary system known as the gold standard prevailed. The **gold standard** provided for fixed exchange rates. A look at its operation and ultimate downfall helps us see the functioning and some of the advantages and problems associated with fixed-rate systems. Currently a number of economists advocate fixed exchange rates and a few even call for a return to the international gold standard.

Conditions A nation is on the gold standard when it fulfills three conditions. It must:
1 Define its monetary unit in terms of a certain quantity of gold
2 Maintain a fixed relationship between its stock of gold and its domestic money supply
3 Allow gold to be freely exported and imported

If each nation defines its monetary unit in terms of gold, the various national currencies will have a fixed relationship to one another. Suppose the United

States defines a dollar as worth 25 grains of gold and Britain defines its pound sterling as worth 50 grains of gold. This means that a British pound is worth $\frac{50}{25}$ dollars or, £1 equals $2.

Gold Flows   Now, ignoring costs of packing, insuring, and shipping gold between countries, under the gold standard the rate of exchange would not vary from this $2-for-£1 rate. No one in the United States would pay more than $2 for £1, because you could always buy 50 grains of gold for $2 in the United States, ship it to Britain, and sell it for £1. Nor would the British pay more than £1 for $2. Why should they, when they could buy 50 grains of gold in Britain for £1, send it to the United States, and sell it for $2?

In practice the costs of packing, insuring, and shipping gold must be taken into account. But these costs would only amount to a few cents per 50 grains of gold. If these costs were 3 cents for 50 grains of gold, Americans wanting pounds would pay up to $2.03 for a pound rather than buy and export 50 grains of gold to get the pound. Why? Because it would cost them $2 for 50 grains of gold plus 3 cents to send it to Britain to be exchanged for £1. This $2.03 exchange rate, above which gold would begin to flow out of the United States, is called the **gold export point.**

The exchange rate would fall to $1.97 before gold would flow into the United States. The British, wanting dollars, would accept as little as $1.97 in exchange for £1, because from the $2 which they could get by buying 50 grains of gold in Britain and reselling it in the United States, 3 cents must be subtracted to pay shipping and related costs. This $1.97 exchange rate, below which gold would flow into the United States, is called the **gold import point.**

Under the gold standard the flow of gold between nations would result in exchange rates which for all practical purposes are fixed.

Domestic Macro Adjustments   Figure 21-4 helps explain the kinds of adjustments the gold standard would produce. Initially the demand for and the supply of pounds are D and S and their intersection point at *a* coincides with the fixed exchange rate of $2 = £1 which results from the "in gold" definitions of the pound and the dollar. Now suppose for some reason American preferences for British goods increase, shifting the demand for pounds curve to D'. In Figure 21-4 there is now a shortage of pounds equal to *ab,* implying an American balance of payments deficit.

What will happen? Remember that the rules of the gold standard prohibit the exchange rate from moving from the fixed $2 = £1 relationship; the rate can *not* move up to a new equilibrium of $3 = £1 at point *c* as it would under freely floating rates. Instead, the exchange rate would rise by a few cents to the American gold export point at which gold would flow from the United States to Britain.

Recall that the gold standard requires participants to maintain a fixed relationship between their domestic money supplies and their quantities of gold. The flow of gold from the United States to Britain would bring about a contraction of the money supply in America and an expansion of the money supply in Britain. Other things equal, this will reduce aggregate demand and, therefore, lower real domestic output, employment, and the price level in the United States. Also, the reduced money supply will boost American interest rates.

The opposite occurs in Britain. The inflow of gold boosts the money supply, increasing aggregate demand, national income, employment, and the price level. The increased money supply will also lower interest rates in Britain.

In Figure 21-4 declining American incomes and prices will reduce our demand for British goods and services and therefore reduce the American demand for pounds. Lower interest rates in Britain will make it less attractive for Americans to invest there, also lessening the demand for pounds. For all these reasons the D'curve will shift to the left.

Similarly, higher incomes and prices in Britain will increase British demand for American goods and services and higher American interest rates will encourage the British to invest more in the United States. These developments all increase the supply of pounds available to Americans, shifting the S curve of Figure 21-4 to the right.

In short, domestic macroeconomic adjustments in American and Britain, triggered by the international flow of gold, will produce new demand and supply for pound curves which intersect at some point on the horizontal line between points *a* and *b*.

Note the critical difference in the adjustment mechanisms associated with freely floating exchange rates and the fixed rates of the gold standard. With floating rates the burden of the adjustment is on the exchange rate itself. In contrast, the gold standard involves changes in the domestic money supplies of participating nations which precipitate changes in price levels, real output and employment, and interest rates.

Although the gold standard boasts the advantages of stable exchange rates and the automatic correction of balance of payments deficits and surpluses, its drawback is that nations must accept domestic adjustments in such distasteful forms as unemployment and falling incomes, on the one hand, or inflation, on the other. In using the gold standard nations must be willing to submit their domestic economies to painful macroeconomic adjustments. Under this system a nation's monetary policy would be determined largely by changes in the demand for and supply of foreign exchange. If the United States, for example, was already moving toward recession, the loss of gold under the gold standard would reduce its money supply and intensify the problem. Under the international gold standard nations forgo independent monetary policies.

Demise The worldwide Great Depression of the 1930s signaled the end of the gold standard. As domestic outputs and employment plummeted worldwide, the restoration of prosperity became the primary goal of afflicted nations. Protectionist measures such as the United States' Smoot-Hawley Tariff were enacted as nations sought to increase net exports and stimulate their domestic economies. And each nation was fearful that its economic recovery would be aborted by a balance of payments deficit which would lead to an outflow of gold and consequent contractionary effects. Indeed, nations attempted to devalue their currencies in terms of gold to make their exports more attractive and imports less attractive. These devaluations undermined a basic condition of the gold standard and the system broke down.

The Bretton Woods System

Not only did the Great Depression of the 1930s lead to the downfall of the gold standard, it also prompted erection of trade barriers which greatly impaired international trade. World War II was similarly disruptive to world trade and finance. Thus, as World War II drew to a close in the mid-1940s, the world trading and monetary systems were in shambles.

To lay the groundwork for a new international monetary system, an international conference of nations was held at Bretton Woods, New Hampshire, in 1944. This conference produced a commitment to an *adjustable-peg system* of exchange rates, called the **Bretton Woods system.** The new system sought to capture the advantages of the old gold standard (fixed exchange rates), while avoiding its disadvantages (painful domestic macroeconomic adjustments).

Furthermore, the conference created the **International Monetary Fund** (IMF) to make the new exchange rate system feasible and workable. This international monetary system, emphasizing relatively fixed exchange rates and managed through the IMF, prevailed with modifications until 1971. The IMF continues to play a basic role in international finance and in recent years has performed a major role in ameliorating debt problems of the less developed countries.

IMF and Pegged Exchange Rates Why did the Bretton Woods adjustable-peg system evolve? We have noted that during the depressed 1930s, various countries resorted to **devaluation**—devaluing[2] their currencies to try to stimulate domestic employment. For example, if the United States was faced with growing unemployment, it might devalue the dollar by *increasing* the dollar price of pounds from $2.50 for £1 to, say, $3 for £1. This action would make American goods cheaper to the British and British goods dearer to Americans, increasing American exports and reducing American imports. This increase in net exports, abetted by the multiplier effect, would stimulate output and employment in the United States.

But every nation can play the devaluation game, and most did. The resulting rounds of competitive devaluations benefited no one; on the contrary, they contributed to further demoralization of world trade. Nations at Bretton Woods therefore agreed that the postwar monetary system must provide for overall exchange rate stability whereby disruptive currency devaluations could be avoided.

What was the adjustable-peg system of exchange rates like? First, as with the gold standard, each IMF member was obligated to define its monetary unit in terms of gold (or dollars), thus establishing par rates of exchange between its currency and the currencies of all other members. Each nation was further obligated to keep its exchange rate stable with respect to any other currency.

---

[2]A note on terminology: We noted earlier in this chapter that the dollar has *appreciated (depreciated)* when its international value has increased (decreased) as the result of changes in the demand for, or supply of, dollars in foreign exchange markets. The terms *revalue* and *devalue* are used to describe an increase or decrease, respectively, in the international value of a currency which occurs as the result of governmental, rather than market, action.

But how was this obligation to be fulfilled? The answer, as we saw in our discussion of fixed exchange rates, is that governments must use international monetary reserves to intervene in foreign exchange markets. Assume that under the Bretton Woods system the dollar was "pegged" to the British pound at $2 = £1. Now suppose in Figure 21-4 the American demand for pounds temporarily increases from D to D' so that a shortage of pounds of ab arises at the pegged rate. How can the United States keep its pledge to maintain a $2 = £1 rate when the new market or equilibrium rate would be at $3 = £1? The United States could supply additional pounds in the exchange market, shifting the supply of pounds curve to the right so that it intersects D' at b and maintains the $2 = £1 rate of exchange.

Where would the United States obtain the needed pounds? Under the Bretton Woods system there were three main sources.

1   Reserves   The United States might currently possess pounds in a "stabilization fund" as the result of the opposite exchange market condition existing in the past. That is, at some earlier time the United States government may have spent dollars to purchase surplus pounds which were threatening to reduce the $2 = £1 exchange rate to, say, $1 = £1.

2   Gold Sales   The United States government might sell some of the gold it holds to Britain for pounds. The proceeds would then be offered in the exchange market to augment the supply of pounds.

3   IMF Borrowing   The needed pounds might be borrowed from the IMF. Nations participating in the Bretton Woods system were required to make contributions to the IMF on the basis of the size of their national income, population, and volume of trade. If necessary, the United States could borrow pounds on a short-term basis from the IMF by supplying its own currency as collateral.

Fundamental Imbalances: Adjusting the Peg   A fixed-rate system such as Bretton Woods functions well so long as a nation's payments deficits and surpluses occur more or less randomly and are approximately equal in size. If a nation's payments surplus last year allows it to add a sufficient amount to its international monetary reserves to finance this year's payments deficit, no problems will arise. But what if the United States encountered a "fundamental imbal-

ance" in its international trade and finance and was confronted with persistent and sizable payments deficits? In this case it is evident that the United States would eventually run out of reserves and be unable to maintain its fixed exchange rate.

Under the Bretton Woods system, a fundamental payments deficit was corrected by devaluation, that is, by an "orderly" reduction in the nation's pegged exchange rate. Also, the IMF allowed each member nation to alter the value of its currency by 10 percent without permission from the Fund to correct a "fundamental" balance of payments deficit. Larger exchange rate changes required the sanction of the Fund's board of directors. By requiring approval of significant rate changes, the Fund guarded against arbitrary and competitive currency devaluation prompted by nations seeking a temporary stimulus to their domestic economies. In our illustration, devaluing the dollar would increase American exports and lower American imports, correcting its persistent payments deficits.

The objective of the adjustable-peg system was a world monetary system which embraced the best features of both a fixed exchange rate system (such as the old international gold standard) and a system of freely fluctuating exchange rates. By reducing risk and uncertainty, short-term exchange rate stability— pegged exchange rates—would presumably stimulate trade and lead to the efficient use of world resources. Periodic exchange rate adjustments—adjustments of the pegs—made in an orderly fashion through the IMF, and on the basis of permanent or long-run changes in a country's payments position, provided a mechanism by which persistent international payments imbalances could be resolved by means other than painful changes in domestic levels of output and prices.

Demise of the Bretton Woods System   Under the Bretton Woods system gold and the dollar came to be accepted as international reserves. The acceptability of gold as an international medium of exchange was derived from its role under the international gold standard of an earlier era. The dollar became acceptable as international money for two reasons.
1   The United States emerged from World War II as the free world's strongest economy.
2   The United States had accumulated large quantities of gold and between 1934 and 1971 maintained a policy of buying gold from, and selling gold to, foreign monetary authorities at a fixed price of $35 per

ounce. The dollar was convertible into gold on demand; the dollar came to be regarded as a substitute for gold, or "as good as gold."

But the role of the dollar as a component of international monetary reserves contained the seeds of a dilemma. Consider the situation as it developed in the 1950s and 1960s. The problem with gold as international money was a quantitative one. The growth of the world's money stock depends on the amount of newly mined gold, less any amounts hoarded for speculative purposes or used for industrial and artistic purposes. Unfortunately, the growth of the gold stock lagged behind the rapidly expanding volume of international trade and finance. Thus the dollar came to occupy an increasingly important role as an international monetary reserve.

Economies of the world acquire dollars as reserves as the result of United States' balance of payments deficits. With the exception of some three or four years, the United States incurred persistent payments deficits throughout the 1950s and 1960s. These deficits were financed in part by drawing down American gold reserves. But mostly United States' deficits were financed by growing foreign holdings of American dollars which were "as good as gold" until 1971.

As the amount of dollars held by foreigners soared and as our gold reserves dwindled, other nations began to question whether the dollar was really "as good as gold." The ability of the United States to maintain the convertibility of the dollar into gold became increasingly doubtful, and so did the role of the dollar as generally accepted international monetary reserves. Thus, the dilemma was that to maintain the dollar as a reserve medium, the United States' payments deficit had to be eliminated. But elimination of the trade deficit would remove the source of additional dollar reserves for the system. The United States had to reduce or eliminate its payments deficits to preserve the dollar's status as an international medium of exchange. But success in this endeavor would limit the expansion of international reserves or liquidity and restrict the growth of international trade and finance.

This problem came to a head in the early 1970s. Faced with persistent and growing United States' payments deficits, President Nixon suspended the dollar's convertibility into gold on August 15, 1971. This suspension ended the thirty-seven-year-old policy to exchange gold for dollars at $35 per ounce. This new policy severed the link between gold and the international value of the dollar, thereby "floating" the dollar and allowing its value to be determined by market forces. The floating of the dollar withdrew American support from the old Bretton Woods system of fixed exchange rates and sounded its death knell.

The Managed Float

The present exchange rate system might best be labeled a system of **managed floating exchange rates** —floating exchange rates, accompanied by occasional currency interventions by central banks to stabilize or alter rates. It is recognized that changing economic conditions among nations require continuing changes in exchange rates to avoid persistent payment deficits or surpluses. Normally, the major trading nations allow their exchange rates to float to equilibrium levels based on supply and demand in the foreign exchange market. The result has been considerably more volatility in exchange rates than in the Bretton Woods era (see Global Perspective 21-2).

But nations also recognize that short-term changes in exchange rates—perhaps accentuated by purchases and sales by speculators—can disrupt and discourage the flow of trade and finance. Moreover, some longer-term moves in exchange rates may not be desirable. Thus, at times the central banks of the various nations intervene in the foreign exchange market by buying or selling large amounts of specific currencies. They "manage" or stabilize exchange rates by influencing currency demand and supply. Two examples:

1 *The 1987 G-7 Intervention* In 1987 the "Group of Seven" industrial nations (**G-7 nations**)— the United States, Germany, Japan, Britain, France, Italy, and Canada—agreed to stabilize the value of the dollar. In the previous two years the dollar had declined rapidly because of sizable American trade deficits. Although the United States' trade deficit remained large, these nations concluded that further dollar depreciation might disrupt economic growth in the G-7 economies. The G-7 nations therefore purchased large amounts of dollars to prop up the dollar's value. Since 1987 the G-7 has periodically intervened in foreign exchange markets to stabilize currency values.

2 *The 1994 Intervention* In 1994 the American dollar eroded in value relative to the Japanese yen and German mark. America's large, continuing trade deficit partly precipitated this depreciation. Another factor was that people from other countries began selling their holdings of American stocks and bonds, us-

GLOBAL PERSPECTIVE 21-2

Exchange rates in terms of dollars

The floating exchange rate system (managed float) introduced in 1971 has produced far more volatile exchange rates than in the earlier Bretton Woods era.

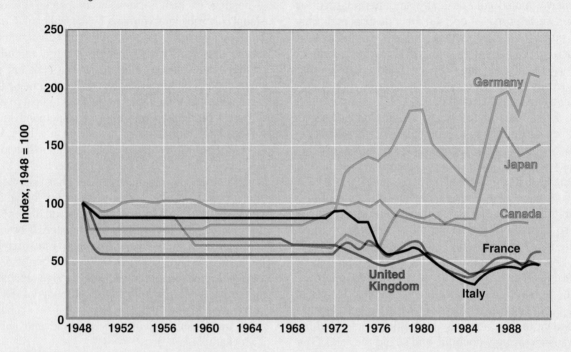

Source: *Economic Report of the President*, 1993, p. 287.

ing the dollar proceeds to buy other currencies to invest elsewhere.

Led by the United States, the central banks of sixteen nations countered this steep dollar depreciation by buying large amounts of dollars. These actions strengthened the demand for dollars and temporarily slowed the pace of the dollar's slide.

Actually, the current exchange rate system is more complicated than we just described. While the major currencies—German marks, American and Canadian dollars, Japanese yen, and the British pound—fluctuate in response to changing demand and supply conditions, some of the European Union nations attempt to peg their currencies to one another. Also, many less developed nations peg their currencies to the dollar and allow their currencies to fluctuate with it. And, finally, some nations peg the value of their currencies to a "basket" or group of other currencies.

How well has the managed floating system worked? It has both proponents and critics.

Pros Proponents argue that the system has functioned well—far better than anticipated.

1 Trade Growth In the first place, fluctuating exchange rates have not reduced world trade and finance as skeptics had predicted. In real terms world trade has grown at about the same rate under the managed float as during the decade of the 1960s under the fixed exchange rates of the Bretton Woods system.

2 Managing Turbulence Proponents argue the managed float has weathered severe economic turbulence which might have caused a fixed exchange regime to have broken down. Such events as worldwide agricultural shortfalls in 1972–1974, extraordinary oil-price increases in 1973–1974 and again in 1979–1980, worldwide stagflation in 1974–1976 and 1981–1983, and large U.S. budget deficits in the 1980s and 1990s all generated substantial international trade and financial imbalances. Flexible rates facilitated international adjustments to these developments, whereas the same events would have put unbearable pressures on a fixed-rate system.

Cons But there is still much sentiment in favor of greater exchange rate stability. Those favoring stable rates see problems with the current system.

1 Volatility and Adjustment Critics argue that exchange rates have been excessively volatile under the managed float (Global Perspective 21-2). This volatility, it is argued, has occurred even when underlying economic and financial conditions of particular nations have been stable. Perhaps more importantly, the managed float has not readily resolved balance of payments imbalances as flexible rates are supposed to do. Thus the United States has run persistent trade deficits in recent years, while Germany and Japan have had persistent surpluses. Changes in the international values of the dollar, mark, and yen have not yet corrected these imbalances.

2 A "Nonsystem"? Skeptics feel the managed float is basically a "nonsystem"; the rules and guidelines circumscribing the behavior of each nation as to its exchange rate are not sufficiently clear or constraining to make the system viable in the long run. Nations will inevitably be tempted to intervene in foreign exchange markets, not merely to smooth out short-term or speculative fluctuations in the value of their currencies, but to prop up their currency if it is chronically weak or to manipulate the value of their currency to achieve domestic stabilization goals. There is fear that in time there may be more "managing" and less "floating" of exchange rates, and this may be fatal to the present loosely defined system.

The jury is still out on floating exchange rates in general and the managed float in particular. Floating

exchange rates have neither worked perfectly nor failed miserably. But this can be said for them: They *have* survived—and no doubt eased—several shocks to the international trading system. Meanwhile, the "managed" part of the float has given nations some sense of control over their collective economic destiny.

QUICK REVIEW 21-3

■ Under the gold standard (1789–1934), nations fixed exchange rates by valuing their currencies in terms of gold, by tying their stocks of money to gold, and by allowing gold to flow between nations when balance of payment deficits and surpluses occurred.

■ The Bretton Woods, or adjustable-peg, system of exchange rates (1944–1971) fixed or pegged short-run exchange rates, but permitted orderly long-run adjustments of the pegs.

■ The managed floating system of exchange rates (1971–present) relies on foreign exchange markets to establish equilibrium exchange rates. But it also permits central banks to buy and sell foreign currencies to stabilize short-term speculative changes in exchange rates or to correct exchange rate imbalances negatively affecting the world economy.

RECENT UNITED STATES TRADE DEFICITS

As shown in Figure 21-5, American trade deficits have been large since the early 1980s. The merchandise trade deficit for 1994 was $166 billion. In 1994 the goods and services deficit was $108 billion and the current account deficit, $156 billion.

Causes of the Trade Deficits

Two central factors have contributed to the large trade deficits.

The Rise of the Dollar Figure 21-6 shows that the international value of the dollar rose significantly between 1980 and 1985. An appreciated dollar means foreign currencies are cheaper to Americans and dollars are more expensive to people abroad. Therefore, foreign goods are cheap to Americans and our imports rise. Conversely, American goods are expensive to the

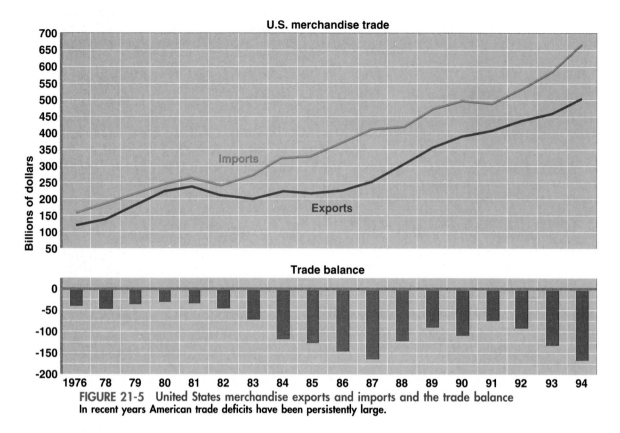

FIGURE 21-5 United States merchandise exports and imports and the trade balance
In recent years American trade deficits have been persistently large.

rest of the world and our exports decline. The pronounced appreciation of the dollar produced large American trade deficits.

Why did the value of the dollar surge between 1980 and 1985? The answer is that real interest rates —nominal interest rates less the rate of inflation— rose in the United States compared to other nations. These rises in real interest rates resulted from large Federal budgets deficits in the 1980s and a tight monetary policy early in that decade. Government borrowing to finance its deficits increased the domestic demand for money and boosted interest rates. The tight money policy directly increased interest rates by reducing the supply of money relative to its demand. Indirectly, the lower rate of inflation which resulted from the tight money policy kept the foreign demand for dollars high, because lower inflation meant higher real rates of return on investments in the United States.

By 1985 the dollar had reached record heights relative to other currencies. The major industrial nations then collectively pushed the dollar down by supplying dollars in the foreign exchange market. The purpose was to help correct the massive American trade deficits just discussed. Observe in Figure 21-6

that the dollar went into "free fall" during the next two years. This fall was aided by a sizable rise in the American demand for foreign currencies—an increase resulting from the expanded volume of United States imports.

Recall that in 1987 the G-7 nations halted the rapid decline in the value of the dollar. Meanwhile, as shown in Figure 21-5, American exports began to rise more rapidly than American imports, reducing somewhat the size of the trade deficit. The American recession of 1990–1991 contributed to a further decline in the American trade deficit. But what went up (the American trade deficit) when the dollar appreciated did not go down by the same amount when the dollar depreciated. We see from Figure 21-5 that large trade deficits remained.

One reason for the continuing overall trade deficit has been America's stubborn trade deficit with Japan (Global Perspective 21-1). Thus far this deficit has not declined as fast as the dollar has depreciated. Japanese firms have resisted increasing the dollar prices of their export goods by the same percentage as the decline in the value of the dollar. Instead, major Japanese exporters have accepted lower profit margins on goods sent to the United States.

Index, March 1973 = 1.0

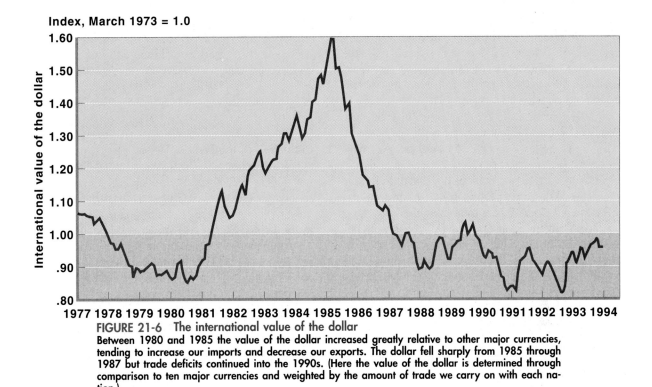

FIGURE 21-6   The international value of the dollar
Between 1980 and 1985 the value of the dollar increased greatly relative to other major currencies, tending to increase our imports and decrease our exports. The dollar fell sharply from 1985 through 1987 but trade deficits continued into the 1990s. (Here the value of the dollar is determined through comparison to ten major currencies and weighted by the amount of trade we carry on with each nation.)

American Growth   A second cause of the trade deficits is that the United States experienced a more rapid recovery from the 1980–1982 world recession than did its major trading partners. This is significant because, like domestic consumption, a nation's purchases of foreign goods (its imports) vary directly with its level of national income. Because our national income expanded more rapidly than the income of our major trading partners, our imports also increased more quickly.

Differences in growth rates also occurred in 1992–1994. Recession and slow growth in Japan and Europe meant that Japanese and European imports (our exports) grew only slowly. This disparity in economic growth kept the American trade deficit relatively high, even though the dollar had fallen in value relative to the yen and the mark.

Effects of American Trade Deficits

Are large trade deficits something that should concern us? There is disagreement on this issue, but most economists see both benefits and costs of trade deficits.

Increased Current Domestic Consumption   At the time a trade or current account deficit is occurring, American consumers benefit. A trade deficit means Americans are receiving more goods and services as imports from abroad than they are sending out as exports. Taken alone, a trade deficit allows us to operate outside our production possibilities curve, so it augments our domestic living standard. But there is a catch: The gain in present consumption will come at the expense of reduced future consumption.

Increased American Indebtedness   A trade deficit is considered "unfavorable" because it must be financed by borrowing from the rest of the world or selling off our assets. Our failure to "pay our way" in international trade has contributed to our net indebtedness to the rest of the world. Recall that current account deficits are financed primarily by net capital inflows to the United States. When our exports are insufficient to pay for our imports, we finance the difference by borrowing from foreign citizens—going into debt. The financing of our recent large trade deficits has enabled people abroad to accumulate a larger volume of claims against American assets than we have accumulated against foreign assets.

In 1985 the United States became a net debtor nation for the first time since 1914, and today it is the world's largest debtor nation. In 1994 foreign citizens abroad owned $600 billion more of American assets—corporations, land, stocks, and bonds—than Americans owned in foreign assets.

One implication: We can no longer look forward to our once-large net inflow of dividend and interest payments (see item 7 in Table 21-1's balance of payments) to help offset deficits in our goods and services trade. Another implication: If we want to regain ownership of these domestic assets, at some future time we will need to export more than we import. At that time domestic consumption will be lower, because we will need to send more of our domestic output abroad than we receive as imports. Therefore, the current consumption "gains" associated with trade deficits may mean consumption "losses" later.

There are other, more subtle "costs" of our large trade deficits. For example, these deficits have hurt industries which are most competitive with imports. Some of the problems faced by automobile manufacturers and steel producers in the 1980s, for example, were related to the strong dollar and the related trade deficits. These difficulties contributed to an upsurge in political pressure for protectionist policies. We know that such policies create efficiency losses for society. Moreover, our trade deficit with Japan and the bickering it has engendered have strained political relations between America and Japan. Finally, trade deficits have led to a series of aggressive Federal government policies to promote exports (Chapter 20), some of which perpetuate the myth that international trade is a battle against enemies rather than a source of mutual gain.

QUICK REVIEW 21-4

■ In the early and mid-1980s the United States experienced large and growing trade deficits, caused mainly by rapid appreciation of the dollar.

■ The dollar fell in value in 1986 and 1987 and the deficit declined somewhat. A recent cause of the continuing trade deficit is America's strong economic growth coupled with recession and sluggish growth in Europe and Japan.

■ American trade deficits benefit American consumers at the time of the deficits.

■ American trade deficits have increased American financial indebtedness to the rest of the world and will mean future "losses" to American consumers.

Reducing the Trade Deficit

Reducing the American trade deficit has been difficult. Nevertheless, economists suggest two ways for reducing future trade deficits: reduction of the Federal budget deficit and acceleration of economic growth abroad.

Reduction of the Budget Deficit Many economists agree that reductions in our large annual Federal budget deficits will lower the government's borrowing, reducing real interest rates in the United States. Lower real interest rates make financial investments in the United States less attractive to people abroad. The demand for dollars by foreign citizens declines and the dollar depreciates. With a depreciated dollar, our exports eventually increase and imports eventually fall, reducing our trade deficit.

Because of the Budget Deficit Reduction Act of 1993 and economic growth, American budget deficits have recently been declining. Along with this decline, the dollar has significantly fallen in value against the Japanese yen and the German mark. This slide was so steep that in 1994 the United States and other nations tried to halt further declines. There is general agreement that the dollar is now sufficiently low in value to begin having a *major* impact in reducing our trade deficit, particularly with Japan. A dollar that bought 262 yen in 1985 bought only 80 yen in April 1995. Japanese producers have no further profit margins to squeeze as a way to resist the dollar price increases necessitated by the depreciated dollar. Japanese firms need more dollars for their exports because each dollar now buys fewer yen—yen needed to pay workers and secure other resources in Japan.

Economic Growth Abroad Faster rates of growth among our major trading partners will also reduce the American trade deficit. Higher levels of foreign national income increase the demand for American exports. The G-7 group of industrial nations has recognized the importance of economic growth in nations with trade surpluses as a way to reduce these surpluses and lower the American trade deficit. Japan and Germany have established expansionary fiscal and monetary policies to bolster their national incomes. Faster economic growth in these nations should make a major impact on the stubborn American trade deficit.

Other "Remedies" There are other possible "remedies" to the persistent United States' trade deficits.

Easy Money Policy Under appropriate circumstances, an easy money policy lowers real interest rates and reduces a trade deficit. The process works as follows. The decline in interest rates reduces the international demand for dollars, which results in a depreciation of the dollar. Dollar depreciation raises our exports and lowers our imports.

Protective Tariffs Protective tariffs can be used to reduce imports, but this strategy results in the loss of the gains from specialization and international trade. Furthermore, it may not be successful: Tariffs which reduce our *imports* foster retaliatory tariffs abroad which reduce our *exports*. Trade deficits do not disappear; instead, all trading partners suffer declines in their living standards.

Recession Recessions in the United States reduce disposable income and spending on all goods, including imports. Because exports are largely unaffected, the decline in imports trims the trade deficit. This is what happened in the United States during the recession of 1990–1991. But recession is an undesirable way to reduce trade deficits; it imposes higher economic costs (lost output) on society than the costs associated with the trade deficit itself. Also, unless the fundamental causes of the deficits have in the meanwhile been remedied, imports and thus trade deficits again rise when the economy recovers from recession.

Increased American Competitiveness American trade deficits can be reduced by lowering the costs of, and improving the quality of, American goods and services relative to foreign goods. Cost-saving production technologies, development of improved products, and more efficient management techniques each can contribute to a decline in the trade deficit by lowering United States demand for imported goods and increasing foreign demand for American goods.

Direct Foreign Investment Ironically, our persistent trade deficit has set off a chain of events which has begun to feed back to reduce the trade deficit itself. The vast accumulation of American dollars in foreign hands has enabled foreign individuals and firms to buy American factories or to build new plants in the United States. Furthermore, the fall in the value of the dollar has provided an incentive for foreign firms to produce in the United States rather than in their own nations.

In short, the trade deficit has resulted in increased *direct foreign investment* in the form of plant and equipment. Foreign-owned factories are turning out increasing volumes of goods that otherwise would have been imported. Hondas and Mazdas, produced in American factories, have replaced Hondas and Mazdas formerly imported from Japan. Other examples abound. The upshot is that the American trade deficit may shrink as imports are replaced with goods produced in foreign-owned factories in the United States. *(Key Question 13)*

CHAPTER SUMMARY

1   American exports create a foreign demand for dollars and make a supply of foreign exchange available to Americans. Conversely, American imports simultaneously create a demand for foreign exchange and make a supply of dollars available to foreigners. Generally, a nation's exports earn the foreign currencies needed to pay for its imports.

2   The balance of payments records all international trade and financial transactions taking place between a given nation and the rest of the world. The trade balance compares merchandise exports and imports. The balance on goods and services compares exports and imports of both goods and services. The current account balance considers not only goods and services transactions, but also net investment income and net transfers.

3   A deficit on the current account will be largely offset by a surplus on the capital account. Conversely, a surplus on the current account will be largely offset by a deficit on the capital account. A balance of payments deficit occurs

when the sum of the current and capital accounts is in deficit. A payments deficit is financed by drawing down official reserves. A balance of payments surplus occurs when the sum of the current and capital accounts is in surplus. A payments surplus results in an increase in official reserves. The desirability of a balance of payments deficit or surplus depends on its causes and its persistence.

4   Flexible or floating exchange rates are determined by the demand for and supply of foreign currencies. Under floating rates a currency will depreciate or appreciate as a result of changes in tastes, relative income changes, relative price changes, relative changes in real interest rates, and speculation.

5   Maintenance of fixed exchange rates requires adequate reserves to accommodate periodic payments deficits. If reserves are inadequate, nations must invoke protectionist trade policies, engage in exchange controls, or endure undesirable domestic macroeconomic adjustments.

QUESTIONS AND STUDY SUGGESTIONS

1 Explain how an American automobile importer might finance a shipment of Toyotas from Japan. Demonstrate how an American export of machinery to Italy might be financed. Explain: "American exports earn supplies of foreign monies which Americans can use to finance imports."

2 *Key Question* *Indicate whether each of the following creates a demand for, or a supply of, French francs in foreign exchange markets:*

a *An American importer purchases a shipload of Bordeaux wine*

b *A French automobile firm decides to build an assembly plant in Los Angeles*

c *An American college student decides to spend a year studying at the Sorbonne*

d *A French manufacturer exports machinery to Morocco on an American freighter*

e *The United States incurs a balance of payments deficit in its transactions with France*

f *A United States government bond held by a French citizen matures*

g *It is widely believed that the international value of the franc will fall in the near future*

3 *Key Question* *Answer the following questions on the basis of Alpha's balance of payments for 1996 as shown below. All figures are in billions of dollars. What is the balance of trade? The balance on goods and services? The balance on current account? The balance on capital account? Does Alpha have a balance of payments deficit or surplus?*

Merchandise exports	+$40	Net transfers	+$10
Merchandise imports	− 30	Capital inflows	+ 10
Service exports	+ 15	Capital outflows	− 40
Service imports	− 10	Official reserves	+ 10
Net investment income	− 5		

4 "A rise in the dollar price of yen necessarily means a fall in the yen price of dollars." Do you agree? Illustrate and elaborate: "The critical thing about exchange rates is that they provide a direct link between the prices of goods and services produced in all trading nations of the world." Explain the purchasing power parity theory of exchange rates.

5 The Swedish auto company Saab imports car components from Germany and exports autos to the United States. In 1990 the dollar depreciated, and the German mark appreciated, relative to the Swedish krona. Speculate as to how this hurt Saab—twice.

6 *Key Question* *Explain why the American demand for Mexican pesos is downsloping and the supply of pesos to Americans is upsloping. Assuming a system of floating exchange rates between Mexico and the United States, indicate whether each of the following would cause the Mexican peso to appreciate or depreciate:*

a *The United States unilaterally reduces tariffs on Mexican products*

b *Mexico encounters severe inflation*

c *Deteriorating political relations reduce American tourism in Mexico*

d *The United States' economy moves into a severe recession*

e *The Federal Reserve embarks on a tight money policy*

f *Mexican products become more fashionable to Americans*

g *The Mexican government encourages American firms to invest in Mexican oil fields*

h *The rate of productivity growth in the United States diminishes sharply*

7 Explain whether or not you agree with the following statements:

a "A country which grows faster than its major trading partners can expect the international value of its currency to depreciate."

b "A nation whose interest rate is rising more rapidly than in other nations can expect the international value of its currency to appreciate."

c "A country's currency will appreciate if its inflation rate is less than that of the rest of the world."

8 "Exports pay for imports. Yet in 1994 the rest of the world exported about $108 billion more worth of goods and services to the United States than were imported from the United States." Resolve the apparent inconsistency of these two statements.

9 Explain in detail how a balance of payments deficit would be resolved under **a** the gold standard, **b** the Bretton Woods system, and **c** floating exchange rates. What are the advantages and shortcomings of each system?

10 Outline the major costs and benefits associated with a large trade or current account deficit. Explain: "A current account deficit means we are receiving more goods and services from abroad than we are sending abroad. How can that be called 'unfavorable'?"

11 Some people assert that the United States is facing a foreign trade crisis. What do you think they mean? What are the major causes of this "crisis"?

12 Cite and explain two reasons for the decline in the international value of the dollar between 1985 and 1987. Why did the United States trade deficit remain high, even though the dollar fell in value?

13 *Key Question* *Explain how a reduction in the Federal budget deficit could contribute to a decline in the United States trade deficit. Why do trade deficits fall during recessions? Is recession a desirable remedy to trade deficits?*

14 (Last Word) Suppose Winter Sports—a French retailer of snowboards—wants to order 5000 snowboards made in the United States. The price per board is $200, the present exchange rate is 6 francs = 1 dollar, and payment is due in dollars when the boards are delivered in three months. Use a numerical example to explain why exchange rate risk might make the French retailer hesitant to place the order. How might speculators absorb some of Winter Sports' risk?

22

GROWTH AND THE LESS DEVELOPED COUNTRIES

It is difficult for the typical American family, whose 1993 average income was $36,959, to grasp the fact that some two-thirds of the world's population lives at, or perilously close to, the subsistence level. Hunger, squalor, and disease are common in many nations of the world. The World Bank estimates that over 1 billion people—approximately 20 percent of the world's population—lives on less than $1 per day!

In this chapter we first identify the poor or less developed nations. Second, we seek to determine why they are poor. What are the obstacles to growth? Third, the potential role of government in economic development is considered. Fourth, international trade, private capital flows, and foreign aid are examined as vehicles of growth. Fifth, the external debt problems faced by many of the poor nations are analyzed. Finally, we present the demands of poor nations to establish a "new global contract" to improve their economies.

THE RICH AND THE POOR

Just as there is considerable income disparity among individual families within a nation, so there also is considerable economic inequality among the family of nations. Table 22-1 shows the remarkable degree of income disparity in the world. The richest one-fifth of the world's population receives almost 83 percent of world income; the poorest one-fifth obtains less than 1.5 percent. The poorest 60 percent of the world population gets less than 6 percent of the world's income.

Table 22-2 helps to sort out rich and poor by identifying the following groups of nations.

1 Industrially Advanced Countries The **industrially advanced countries (IACs)** include the United States, Canada, Australia, New Zealand, Japan, and most of the nations of western Europe. These nations have developed market economies based on large stocks of capital goods, advanced production technologies, and well-educated labor forces. As column 1 of Table 22-2 indicates, these twenty-three economies have a high per capita (per person) GNP.

2 Less Developed Countries Most of the remaining nations of the world—located in Africa, Asia, and Latin America—are underdeveloped or **less developed countries (LDCs).** These 109 nations are unindustrialized with their labor forces heavily committed to agriculture. Literacy rates are low, unemployment is high, population growth is rapid, and exports consist largely of agricultural commodities (cocoa, bananas, sugar, raw cotton) and raw materi-

TABLE 22-1   Global income disparity

World population	Percentage of world income
Richest 20%	82.7
Second 20%	11.7
Third 20%	2.3
Fourth 20%	1.9
Poorest 20%	1.4

Source: United Nations Development Program, *Human Development Report 1992* (New York: Oxford University Press, 1992), p. 36.

als (copper, iron ore, natural rubber). Capital equipment is scarce, production technologies are typically primitive, and labor force productivity is low. About three-fourths of the world's population lives in these nations, which share the characteristic of widespread poverty.

In Table 22-2 we have divided the poor nations into two groups. The first group comprises sixty-seven "middle-income" LDCs with an average annual per capita GNP of $2490. The range of per capita GNPs of this diverse group is from $670 to $7510. The other group is made up of forty-two "low-income" LDCs with per capita GNPs ranging from $60 to $670 and averaging only $390. This group is dominated by India, China, and the sub-Saharan nations of Africa.

Several comparisons may bring global income disparities into sharper focus.

1   The United States' 1992 GDP was approximately $5.9 trillion; the combined GDPs of the 109 LDCs in that year were only $5.7 trillion.

2   The United States with only about 5 percent of the world's population produces one-fourth of the world's output.

3   The annual sales of many large U.S. corporations exceed the GDPs of many of the LDCs. General Motors' annual revenues are greater than the GDPs of all but twenty or so nations.

4   Per capita GNP in the United States is 387 times greater than in Mozambique, the world's poorest nation.

Growth, Decline, and Income Gaps

We need to append two other points to our discussion of Table 22-2.

1   Miracles and Disasters   There have been considerable differences in the ability of the various LDCs to improve their circumstances over time. On the one hand, a group of so-called newly industrialized economies—Singapore, Hong Kong, Taiwan, and South Korea—have achieved very high annual growth rates of real GNP of 6 to 7 percent over the 1960–1989 period. As a consequence, real per capita GNPs rose fivefold in these nations. In vivid contrast, many of the highly indebted LDCs and the very poor sub-Saharan nations of Africa have had *declining* real per capita GNPs during the past decade.

2   Growing Absolute Gaps   The income gap between rich and poor nations has been widening. To demonstrate this point, let's assume the per capita GNPs of the advanced and less developed countries have both been growing at about 2 percent per year. Because the income base in the advanced countries is initially much higher, the income gap grows. If per capita income is $400 a year, a 2 percent growth rate means an $8 increase in income. Where per capita in-

TABLE 22-2   GNP per capita, population, and growth rates

	GNP per capita		Population	
	(1) Dollars, 1992	(2) Annual growth rate, 1980–1992	(3) Millions, mid-1992	(4) Annual growth rate, 1980–1992
Industrially advanced countries: IACs (23 nations)	$22,160	2.3%	828	0.7%
Less developed countries: LDCs (109 nations)				
Middle-income LDCs (67 nations)	2,490	−0.1	1,419	1.8
Low-income LDCs (42 nations)	390	3.9	3,191	2.0

Source: World Bank, *World Development Report, 1994* (New York: Oxford University Press), pp. 162–164, 210–211.

TABLE 22-3   Selected socioeconomic indicators of development

Country	(1) Per capita GNP, 1992	(2) Life expectancy at birth, 1992	(3) Infant mortality per 1000 live births, 1992	(4) Adult illiteracy rate, 1990	(5) Daily per capita calorie supply, 1990	(6) Per capita energy consumption, 1992*
Japan	$28,190	79 years	5	under 5	2,848	3,586
United States	23,240	77	9	under 5	3,666	7,662
Brazil	2,770	66	57	19	2,730	681
Mauritania	530	48	117	66	2,450	108
China	470	69	31	27	2,640	600
India	310	61	79	52	2,230	235
Bangladesh	220	55	91	65	2,040	59
Ethiopia	110	49	122	—	1,700	21
Mozambique	60	44	162	67	1,810	32

*Kilograms of oil equivalent.
Source: World Development Report, 1994.

come is $4000 per year, the same 2 percent growth rate translates into an $80 increase in income. Thus, the absolute income gap will have increased from $3600 (= $4000 − $400) to $3672 (= $4080 − $408). The LDCs must grow faster than the IACs to catch up.

In fact, the absolute income gap between rich and poor nations has widened significantly. The absolute difference in per capita income between the richest 20 percent and the poorest 20 percent of the world's population increased from $1854 in 1960 to $15,149 in 1989. *(Key Question 3)*

Implications

Mere statistics conceal the human implications of the extreme poverty characterizing so much of our planet:

> . . . let us examine a typical "extended" family in rural Asia. The Asian household is likely to comprise ten or more people, including parents, five to seven children, two grandparents, and some aunts and uncles. They have a combined annual income, both in money and in "kind" (i.e., they consume a share of the food they grow), of from $250 to $300. Together they live in a poorly constructed one-room house as tenant farmers on a large agricultural estate owned by an absentee landlord who lives in the nearby city. The father, mother, uncle, and the older children must work all day on the land. None of the adults can read or write; of the five school-age children, only one attends school regularly; and he cannot expect to proceed beyond three or four years of primary education. There is only one meal a day; it rarely changes and it is rarely sufficient to alleviate the childrens' constant hunger pains. The house has no electricity, sanitation, or fresh water supply. There is much sickness, but qualified doctors and medical practitioners are far away in the cities attending to the needs of wealthier families. The work is hard, the sun is hot and aspirations for a better life are constantly being snuffed out. In this part of the world the only relief from the daily struggle for physical survival lies in the spiritual traditions of the people.[1]

In Table 22-3 various socioeconomic indicators for selected LDCs are contrasted with those for the United States and Japan. These data confirm the major points stressed in the above quotation.

BREAKING THE POVERTY BARRIER

The avenues of economic growth are essentially the same for industrially advanced and less developed nations:

1 Greater Efficiency Existing supplies of resources must be used more efficiently in the future. This means not only eliminating unemployment but

---

[1]Michael P. Todaro, *Economic Development in the Third World*, 5th ed. (New York: Longman, 1994), p. 4.

also achieving greater efficiency in the utilization of resources.

2 Resource Enhancement   Supplies of productive resources must be altered—typically, increased. By expanding supplies of raw materials, capital equipment, effective labor, and technological knowledge, a nation can push its production possibilities curve to the right.

Why have some nations been successful in pursuing these avenues of growth while others lag far behind? The difference is in the physical, human, and sociocultural environments of the various nations.

Natural Resources

There is no simple generalization as to the role of natural resources in the economic development of LDCs. This is because the distribution of natural resources among these nations is very uneven. Some less developed nations have valuable deposits of bauxite, tin, copper, tungsten, nitrates, and petroleum. Some LDCs have been able to use their natural resource endowments to achieve rapid growth and a significant redistribution of income from the rich to the poor nations. The Organization of Petroleum Exporting Countries (OPEC) is a standard example. On the other hand, in many cases natural resources are owned or controlled by the multinational corporations of industrially advanced countries, with the economic benefits from these resources largely diverted abroad. Furthermore, world markets for many of the farm products and raw materials which the LDCs export are subject to great price fluctuations which contribute to instability in their economies.

Other LDCs lack mineral deposits, have little arable land, and have few sources of power. Also, most of the poor countries are in Central and South America, Africa, the Indian subcontinent, and Southeast Asia where tropical climates prevail. The hot, humid climate is not conducive to productive labor; human, crop, and livestock diseases are widespread; and weed and insect infestations plague agriculture.

A weak resource base can pose a serious obstacle to growth. Real capital can be accumulated and the quality of the labor force improved through education and training. But the natural resource base is largely unaugmentable. It may be unrealistic for many of the LDCs to envision an economic destiny comparable with that of, say, the United States and Canada. But we must be careful in generalizing: Switzerland and

Japan, for example, have achieved high levels of living *despite* restrictive natural resource bases.

Human Resources

Three statements describe many of the LDCs' circumstances with respect to human resources:
1   They are overpopulated.
2   Unemployment and underemployment are widespread.
3   Labor force productivity is low.

Overpopulation   As column 3 of Table 22-2 makes clear, many of the LDCs with the most meager natural and capital resources have the largest populations to support. Table 22-4 compares population densities and population growth rates of a few selected nations with those of the United States and the world as a whole.

Most important for the long run is the vivid contrast of population growth rates: The middle- and low-income LDCs of Table 22-2 are now experiencing approximately a 2 percent annual increase in population compared with a 0.7 percent annual rate for advanced countries. Recalling the "rule of 70," the current rate suggests that the total population of the LDCs will double in about 35 years.

These statistics indicate why the per capita income gap between the LDCs and the IACs has widened. In some of the less developed countries rapid population growth actually presses on the food supply to the extent that per capita food consumption is pulled down to the subsistence level or below. In

TABLE 22-4   Population statistics for selected countries

Country	Population per square mile, 1994	Annual rate of population increase, 1980–1992
United States	74	1.0%
Pakistan	429	3.1
Bangladesh	2,421	2.3
Venezuela	60	2.6
India	801	2.1
China	331	1.4
Kenya	128	3.6
Philippines	606	2.4
World	112	1.7

Source: Statistical Abstract of the United States, 1994.

GLOBAL PERSPECTIVE 22-1

Population growth in rich and poor countries

World population is expected to double over the next century, with the poorest nations accounting for most of the increase.

Projected population growth in rich and poor countries

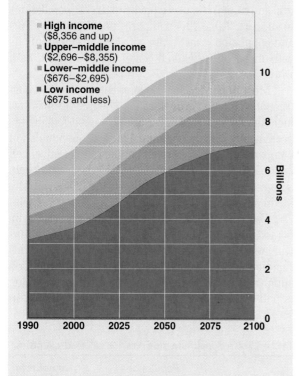

■ **High income**
($8,356 and up)
■ **Upper–middle income**
($2,696–$8,355)
■ **Lower–middle income**
($676–$2,695)
■ **Low income**
($675 and less)

1990 2000 2025 2050 2075 2100

Billions: 10, 8, 6, 4, 2, 0

Source: World Bank data.

the standard of living could be raised by boosting consumer goods—particularly food—production. But the problem is more complex than this, because any increase in consumer goods production which initially raises the standard of living is likely to induce a population increase. This increase, if sufficient in size, will dissipate the improvement in living standards, and subsistence living levels will again prevail.

But why does population growth in LDCs accompany increases in output? First, the nation's *death* or *mortality rate* will decline with initial increases in production. This decline is the result of (1) a higher level of per capita food consumption, and (2) the basic medical and sanitation programs which accompany the initial phases of economic development.

Second, the *birthrate* will remain high or may increase, particularly as medical and sanitation programs cut infant mortality. The cliché that "the rich get richer and the poor get children" is uncomfortably accurate for many LDCs. An increase in the per capita standard of living may lead to a population upsurge which will cease only when the standard of living has again been reduced to the level of bare subsistence.

In addition to the fact that rapid population growth can convert an expanding GDP into a stagnant or slow-growing GDP per capita, there are other reasons why population expansion is an obstacle to development.

1   *Saving and Investment*   Large families reduce the capacity of households to save, restricting the economy's ability to accumulate capital.

2   *Productivity*   As population grows, more investment is required to maintain the amount of real capital per person. If investment fails to keep pace, each worker will have fewer tools and equipment, reducing worker productivity (output per worker). Declining productivity implies stagnating or declining per capita incomes.

3   *Resource Exploitation*   Because most less developed countries are heavily dependent on agriculture, rapid population growth may result in overuse of limited natural resources such as land. The much-publicized African famines are partially the result of past overgrazing and overplanting of land caused by the pressing need to feed a growing population.

the worst instances, only malnutrition and disease and the high death rate they engender keep incomes near subsistence. This chapter's Last Word is relevant.

It would seem at first glance that, since

$$\text{Per capita standard of living} = \frac{\text{consumer goods (food) production}}{\text{population}}$$

4 Urban Problems Rapid population growth in the cities of the LDCs, accompanied by unprecedented flows of rural migrants, are generating massive urban problems. Substandard housing in impoverished slums, deteriorating public services, congestion, pollution, and crime are all problems worsened by rapid population growth. The resolution or lessening of these difficulties necessitates a diversion of resources from growth-oriented uses.

Most authorities advocate birth control as the most effective means for breaking out of this dilemma. And breakthroughs in contraceptive technology in recent decades have made this solution increasingly relevant. But obstacles to population control are great. Low literacy rates make it difficult to disseminate information on contraceptive devices. In peasant agriculture, large families are a major source of labor. Adults may regard having many children as a kind of informal social security system; the more children, the greater the probability of having a relative to care for you during old age. Finally, many nations which stand to gain the most through birth control are often the least willing, for religious and sociocultural reasons, to embrace contraception programs. Population growth in Latin America, for example, is among the most rapid in the world.

China—with about one-fifth of the world's population—adopted a harsh "one-child" program in 1980. The government advocated late marriages and one child per family. Couples having more than one child are fined or lose various social benefits. Even though the rate of population growth has diminished under this program, China's population continues to expand at about 100 million per decade. India, the world's second most populous nation, had a 103 million or 13 percent population increase in the 1986–1992 period. With a total population of 884 million, India has 16 percent of the world's population but less than 2.5 percent of its land mass.

Three Addenda But three additional points are worthy of note.

1 As with natural resources, the relationship between population and economic growth is less clear than one might expect. A high population density and rapid population growth do not necessarily mean poverty. China and India have immense populations and are poor; but Japan and Hong Kong are densely populated and relatively wealthy.

2 Population growth rates for the LDCs as a group have declined somewhat in recent decades. In the mid-1960s the annual population growth rate was about 2.35 percent. Currently it is about 2 percent and projections suggest further future declines.

3 The traditional view is that the reduction of population growth through the more widespread use of birth control techniques is the basic means for increasing per capita incomes in the LDCs. Reduce population growth in the denominator of our earlier equation and the standard of living will rise.

But there is a contrary view—known as the **demographic transition**—which reverses causation by arguing that rising incomes must first be achieved and only then will slower population growth follow. The demographic transition view observes that in low-income countries children are viewed as economic assets; they are a cheap source of labor and potentially provide financial support and security for their parents in their old age. Thus people in poor countries have high birthrates. But in wealthy IAC nations children are economic liabilities. Their care requires the sacrifice of high earnings or the need to purchase expensive child care. Also, children require extended and expensive education for the highly skilled jobs characteristic of IAC economies. Finally, the wealth of the IACs results in "social safety nets" which protect adults from the insecurity associated with old age and the inability to work. Thus people in the IACs recognize that high birthrates are neither necessary nor desirable, so they choose to have fewer children.

Note the differences in causation implied by the two views. The traditional view says reduced birthrates must come first and higher per capita incomes will follow; lower birthrates cause per capita income growth. The demographic transition view says higher incomes must first be achieved and lower rates of population growth will be the result; higher incomes are the cause of slower population growth. *(Key Question 6)*

Unemployment and Underemployment Reliable unemployment statistics for the LDCs are not readily available. But observation suggests that unemployment and underemployment are both quite high. **Unemployment** occurs when someone who is willing and able to work cannot find a job. **Underemployment** occurs when workers are employed fewer hours or days per week than they desire, work at jobs that do not fully use their skills, or spend much of the time on their job unproductively.

Many economists contend that unemployment is high—as much as 15 to 20 percent—in the rapidly growing urban areas of the LDCs. There has been substantial migration in most less developed countries from rural to urban areas, motivated by the *expectation* of finding jobs with higher wage rates than are available in agricultural and other rural employments. But this huge migration makes it unlikely that a migrant will in fact obtain a job. Migration to the cities has greatly exceeded the growth of urban job opportunities, resulting in very high urban unemployment rates. Thus, rapid rural-urban migration has given rise to urban unemployment rates which are two or three times as great as rural rates.

Underemployment is widespread and characteristic of most LDCs. In many LDCs rural agricultural labor may be so abundant relative to capital and natural resources that a significant percentage of this labor contributes little or nothing to agricultural output. Similarly, many LDC workers are self-employed as proprietors of small shops, in handicrafts, or as street vendors. A lack of demand means that small shop owners or vendors spend more time in idleness in the shop or on the street. While they are not without jobs, they are underemployed.

Low Labor Productivity Labor productivity tends to be very low in most LDCs. As we will see, the LDCs have found it difficult to invest in *physical capital*. As a result, their workers are underequipped with machinery and tools and are relatively unproductive. Keep in mind that rapid population growth tends to reduce the amount of physical capital available per worker which decreases labor productivity and real incomes.

In addition, most poor countries have not been able to invest sufficiently in their *human capital* (Table 22-3, columns 4 and 5); that is, expenditures on health and education have been meager. Low levels of literacy, malnutrition, absence of proper medical care, and insufficient educational facilities all contribute to populations ill equipped for economic development and industrialization. Attitudes may also play a role. In some countries hard work is associated with slavery, servitude, and inferiority. It is therefore to be avoided.

Particularly vital is the absence of a vigorous entrepreneurial class willing to bear risks, accumulate capital, and provide the organizational requisites essential to economic growth. Closely related is the dearth of labor prepared to handle the routine supervisory functions basic to any program of develop-

ment. Ironically, the higher education systems of many LDCs are oriented heavily toward the humanities and offer little work in business, engineering, and the sciences. Some LDCs are characterized by an authoritarian view of human relations—often fostered by repressive governments—which generates an environment hostile to independent thinking, taking initiatives, and assuming economic risks. Authoritarianism discourages experimentation and change—the essence of entrepreneurship.

An additional irony is that, while migration from the LDCs has modestly offset rapid population growth, it has also deprived some LDCs of highly productive workers. Often the best-trained and most highly motivated workers—physicians, engineers, teachers, and nurses—leave the LDCs to seek their fortunes in the IACs. This so-called **brain drain** contributes to the deterioration in the overall skill level and productivity of the labor force.

Capital Accumulation

An important focal point of economic development is the accumulation of capital goods. There are several reasons for this.

1 All LDCs suffer from shortages of capital goods—factories, machinery and equipment, public utilities, and so forth. Better-equipped labor forces would greatly enhance their productivity and help boost the per capita standard of living. There is a close relationship between output per worker (labor productivity) and real income per worker. A nation must produce more goods and services per worker to enjoy more goods and services per worker as income. One way of increasing labor productivity is to provide each worker with more tools and equipment. Indeed, empirical studies for the LDCs confirm a positive relationship between investment and the growth of GDP. On the average a 1 percentage point increase in the ratio of investment to GDP raises the overall growth rate by about one-tenth of 1 percentage point. Thus an increase in the investment-to-GDP ratio from 10 to 15 percent would increase the growth of real GDP by one-half of 1 percentage point.[2]

2 Increasing the stock of capital goods is crucial because of the very limited possibility of increasing the supply of arable land. If there is little likelihood of increasing agricultural output by increasing the supply

---

[2]International Monetary Fund, *World Economic Outlook* (Washington, 1988), p. 76.

of land, an alternative is to use more and better capital equipment with the available agricultural work force.

3 Once initiated, the process of capital accumulation *may* be cumulative. If capital accumulation can increase output faster than population grows, a margin of saving may arise which permits further capital formation. In a sense, capital accumulation can feed on itself.

Let's first consider the prospects for less developed nations to accumulate capital domestically. Then we will examine the possibility of foreign capital flowing into them.

Domestic Capital Formation   A less developed nation—or any nation—accumulates capital through saving and investing. A nation must save (refrain from consumption) to release resources from consumer goods production. Investment spending must then absorb these released resources in the production of capital goods. But impediments to saving and investing are much greater in a low-income nation than in an advanced economy.

Savings Potential   Consider first the savings side of the picture. The situation here is mixed and varies greatly between countries. Some of the very poor countries such as Ethiopia, Bangladesh, Uganda, Haiti, and Madagascar save only from 2 to 5 percent of their domestic outputs. They are too poor to save a significant portion of their incomes. Interestingly, however, other less developed countries save as large a percentage of their domestic outputs as do advanced industrial countries. In 1992 India and China saved 22 and 36 percent of their domestic outputs, respectively, compared to 34 percent for Japan, 28 percent for Germany, and 15 percent for the United States. The problem is that the domestic outputs of the LDCs are so low that even when saving rates are comparable to advanced nations, the total absolute volume of saving is not large. As we will see, foreign capital inflows and foreign aid are means of supplementing domestic saving.

Capital Flight   Many of the LDCs have suffered **capital flight.** Citizens of the LDCs have transferred their savings to, or invested their savings in, the IACs. Citizens of many LDCs regard the risks of investing at home to be high compared to the industrially advanced nations. These risks include loss of savings or real capital due to government expropriation, taxation,

higher rates of inflation, or changes in exchange rates. If an LDC's political climate is volatile, savers may shift their funds overseas to a "safe haven" in fear that a new government might confiscate their wealth. Likewise, rapid or galloping inflation in an LDC would have similar confiscatory effects. The transfer of savings overseas may also be a means of evading domestic taxes on interest income or capital gains. Finally, financial capital may flow to the IACs where there are higher interest rates or a greater variety of investment opportunities.

Whatever the motivation, studies suggest the amount of capital flight from the LDCs is significant. One estimate suggested that the five largest Latin American debtors had capital outflows of $101 billion of private assets between 1979 and 1984. At the end of 1987 Mexicans are estimated to have held some $84 billion in assets abroad. Foreign asset holdings for Venezuelans, Argentinians, and Brazilians were $58, $46, and $31 billion, respectively. It is estimated that $6 to $10 billion flees Brazil every year. Brazilians are sending more money abroad as interest on foreign debt and capital flight than they receive as foreign investment and foreign aid. The critical point is that a significant portion of capital lending by the IACs to the LDCs is offset by LDC capital flights to the IACs. The World Bank estimates that the inflows of foreign aid and loans to Latin America were essentially negated by their capital flight in the 1980s.

Investment Obstacles   The investment side of capital formation abounds with equally serious obstacles. These obstacles undermine the rate of capital formation even when a sufficient volume of saving is available to finance the needed investment. Obstacles to investment fall into two categories: lack of investors and lack of incentives to invest.

Oddly, in some less developed countries the major obstacle to investment is the lack of business executives willing to assume the risks associated with investment. This is a special case of qualitative deficiencies of the labor force previously discussed.

But even if substantial savings and a vigorous entrepeneurial class are present, an essential ingredient in capital formation—the incentive to invest—may be weak. A host of factors may combine in an LDC to cripple investment incentives. We have just mentioned such factors as political instability and higher rates of inflation in our discussion of capital flight. Similarly, very low incomes mean a limited domestic market—a lack of demand—for most nonagricultural goods.

This factor is crucial when we recognize that the chances of successfully competing with mature industries of advanced nations in international markets are meager. Then, too, lack of trained administrative and operating personnel may be a factor in retarding investment, Finally, many LDCs simply do not have an adequate **infrastructure,** that is, the public capital goods, which are prerequisite to private investment of a productive nature. Poor roads and bridges, inadequate railways, little gas and electricity production, antiquated communications, unsatisfactory housing, and meager educational and public health facilities scarcely provide an inviting environment for investment spending. It is significant that approximately four-fifths of the investment of multinational companies goes to IACs.

The absence of an adequate infrastructure presents more of a problem than you might first surmise. The dearth of public capital goods means that much investment spending which does not *directly* result in the production of goods and which may not be capable of bearing profits must take place before, and simultaneously with, productive investment in manufacturing machinery and equipment. Statistics for advanced nations indicate that about 60 percent of gross investment goes for housing, public works, and public utilities, leaving about 40 percent for directly productive investment in manufacturing, agriculture, and commerce. These figures probably understate the percentage of total investment which must be devoted to infrastructure in emerging nations. The volume of investment required to initiate economic development may be much greater than it first appears.

One bright spot is the possibility of accumulating capital through *in-kind* or **nonfinancial investment.** With leadership and willingness to cooperate, capital can be accumulated by transferring surplus agricultural labor to improvement of agricultural facilities or the infrastructure. If each agricultural village allocated its surplus labor to the construction of irrigation canals, wells, schools, sanitary facilities, and roads, significant amounts of capital might be accumulated at no significant sacrifice of consumer goods production. Nonfinancial investment simply bypasses the problems inherent in the financial aspects of the capital accumulation process. Such investment does not require consumers to save portions of their money income, nor does it presume the presence of an entrepreneurial class anxious to invest. When leadership and cooperative spirit are present, nonfinancial investment is a promising avenue for accumulation of basic capital goods. *(Key Question 8)*

Technological Advance

Technological advance and capital formation are frequently part of the same process. Yet, there are advantages in treating technological advance—the discovery and application of new methods of producing —and capital formation, or the accumulating of capital goods, as separate processes.

The rudimentary state of technology in the LDCs puts them far from the frontiers of technological advance. There already exists an enormous body of technological knowledge accumulated by advanced nations which less developed countries *might* adopt and apply without expensive research. Crop rotation and contour plowing require no additional capital equipment, and may contribute significantly to productivity. By raising grain storage bins a few inches above ground, a large amount of grain spoilage can be avoided. Such changes may sound trivial to people of advanced nations. However, resulting gains in productivity can mean the difference between subsistence and starvation in some poverty-ridden nations.

In most instances application of either existing or new technological knowledge involves new and different capital goods. But, within limits, this capital can be obtained without an increase in the rate of capital formation. If the annual flow of replacement investment is rechanneled from technologically inferior to technologically superior capital equipment, productivity can be increased out of a constant level of investment spending. Actually, some technological advances may be **capital-saving** rather than **capital-using.** A new fertilizer, better adapted to a nation's topography and climate, might be cheaper than one currently employed. A seemingly high-priced metal plow which will last ten years may be cheaper in the long run than an inexpensive but technologically inferior wooden plow which requires annual replacement.

To what extent have LDCs transferred and effectively used available IAC technological knowledge? The picture is mixed. There can be no doubt that such technological borrowing has been instrumental in the rapid growth of such Pacific Rim countries as Japan, South Korea, Taiwan, and Singapore. Similarly, the OPEC nations benefitted greatly from IAC knowledge of oil exploration, production, and refining. Recently the former Soviet Union and the nations of eastern Europe have been seeking western technology to hasten their conversions to viable market-based economies.

At the same time, we must be realistic about the transferability of advanced technologies to less developed countries. In industrially advanced nations technologies are usually predicated on relatively scarce, highly skilled labor and relatively abundant capital. Such technologies tend to be capital-using or, alternatively stated, labor-saving. In contrast, less developed economies require technologies appropriate to *their* resource endowments—abundant unskilled labor and very limited quantities of capital goods. Labor-using and capital-saving technologies are appropriate to LDCs. Much of the highly advanced technology of advanced nations is inappropriate in the less developed countries; they must develop their own technologies. Recall, too, that many less developed nations have "traditional economies" and are not highly receptive to change. This is particularly true in peasant agriculture which dominates the economies of most LDCs. A potential technological advance which fails can mean hunger and malnutrition; therefore, there is a strong propensity to retain traditional production techniques.

Sociocultural and Institutional Factors

Economic considerations alone do not explain why an economy does or does not grow. Substantial social and institutional readjustments are usually an integral part of the growth process. Economic development means not only changes in a nation's physical environment (new transportation and communications facilities, new schools, new housing, new plants and equipment), but also changes in the way people think, behave, and associate with one another. Emancipation from custom and tradition is frequently a prerequisite of economic development. A critical but intangible ingredient in economic development is **the will to develop.** Economic growth may hinge on "what individuals and social groups *want,* and *whether they want it badly enough to change their old ways of doing things and to work hard at installing the new.*"[3]

Sociocultural Obstacles Sociocultural impediments to growth are numerous and varied.

1 Some of the least developed countries have failed to achieve the preconditions for a national economic unit. Tribal and ethnic allegiances take precedence over national identity. Warring tribes confine all economic activity within the tribe, eliminating any possibility for production-increasing specialization and trade. The pathetic economic circumstances in Somalia, Sudan, Liberia, Zaire, and other sub-Saharan nations of Africa are due in no small measure to martial and political conflicts among rival clans.

2 The existence of a caste system—formal or informal—causes labor to be allocated to occupations on the basis of caste or tradition rather than on the basis of skill or merit. The result is a misallocation of human resources.

3 Religious beliefs and observances may seriously restrict the length of the workday and divert resources which might have been used for investment to ceremonial uses. In rural India total ceremonial expenditures are estimated at about 7 percent of per capita income.[4] Generally, religious and philosophical beliefs may be dominated by the fatalistic **capricious universe view,** that is, the notion that there is little or no correlation between an individual's activities and endeavors and the outcomes or experiences which that person encounters.

> If the universe is deemed capricious, the individual will learn to expect little or no correlation between actions and results. This will result in a fatalistic attitude. . . .
>
> These attitudes impinge on all activities including saving, investment, long-range perspective, supply of effort, and family planning. If a higher standard of living and amassing of wealth is treated as the result of providence rather than springing from hard work and saving, there is little rationale for saving, hard work, innovations, and enterprise.[5]

Other attitudes and cultural factors may impede economic activity and growth: emphasis on the per-

---

[3]Eugene Staley, *The Future of Underdeveloped Countries,* rev. ed. (New York: Frederick A. Praeger, 1961), p. 218.

[4]Inder P. Nijhawan, "Socio-Political Institutions, Cultural Values, and Attitudes: Their Impact on Indian Economic Development," in J. S. Uppal (ed.), *India's Economic Problems* (New Delhi: Tata McGraw-Hill Publishing Company, Ltd., 1975), p. 31.

[5]Ibid., p. 33.

formance of duties rather than the exertion of individual initiative; the focus on group rather than individual achievement; the notion of a preordained and unalterable universe; the belief in reincarnation which reduces the importance of one's present life.

Institutional Obstacles Political corruption and bribery are common in many LDCs. School systems and public service agencies are often ineptly administered and their functioning impaired by petty politics. Tax systems are frequently arbitrary, unjust, cumbersome, and detrimental to incentives to work and invest. Political decisions are often motivated by a desire to enhance the nation's international prestige, rather than to foster development.

Because of the predominance of farming in LDCs, the problem of achieving that institutional environment in agriculture most conducive to increasing production must be a vital consideration in any growth program. Specifically, the institutional problem of **land reform** demands attention in virtually all LDCs. But needed reform may vary tremendously between specific nations. In some LDCs the problem is excessive concentration of land ownership in the hands of a few wealthy families. This situation is demoralizing for tenants, weakening their incentive to produce, and is typically not conducive to capital improvements. At the other extreme is the absurd arrangement where each family owns and farms a minute fragment of land far too small for the application of modern agricultural technology. An important complication to the problem of land reform lies in the fact that political considerations sometimes push reform in that direction which is least defensible on economic grounds. For many nations, land reform may well be the most acute institutional problem to be resolved in initiating the process of economic development.

Examples: Land reform in South Korea undermined the political control of the landed aristocracy and made way for the development of strong commercial and industrial middle classes, all to the benefit of the country's economic development. In contrast, the prolonged dominance of the landed aristocracy in the Philippines has helped stifle the development of that economy.[6]

---

[6]Mrinal Datta-Chaudhuri, "Market Failure and Government Failure," *Journal of Economic Perspectives,* Summer 1990, p. 36.

QUICK REVIEW 22-1

■ About three-fourths of the world's population lives in the LDCs of Africa, Asia, and Latin America.

■ Natural resource scarcities and inhospitable climates restrict growth in many LDCs.

■ The LDCs are characterized by overpopulation, high unemployment rates, underemployment, and low labor productivity.

■ Low saving rates, capital flight, weak infrastructures, and lack of investors impair capital accumulation.

■ Sociocultural and institutional factors are often serious impediments to growth.

THE VICIOUS CIRCLE

Many of the characteristics of LDCs just described are simultaneously causes and consequences of their poverty. These countries are caught in a **vicious circle of poverty.** They *stay* poor because they *are* poor! Consider Figure 22-1. The fundamental feature of an LDC is low per capita income. Being poor, a family has little ability or incentive to save. Furthermore, low incomes mean low levels of demand. Thus, there are few available resources, on the one hand, and no strong incentives, on the other, for investment in physical or human capital. This means labor productivity is low. And, since output per person is real income per person, it follows that per capita income is low.

Many experts feel that the key to breaking out of this vicious circle is to increase the rate of capital accumulation, to achieve a level of investment of, say, 10 percent of the national income. But Figure 22-1 reminds us that the real villain for many LDCs—rapid population growth—may be waiting in the wings to undo the potentially beneficial effects of this higher rate of capital accumulation. Using hypothetical figures, suppose that initially an LDC is realizing no growth in its real GDP. But now it somehow manages to increase its saving and investment to 10 percent of its GDP. As a result, its real GDP begins to grow at, say, 2.5 percent per year. Given a stable population, real GDP per capita will also grow at 2.5 percent per year. If this persists, the standard of living will *double* in about 28 years. But what if population grows at the

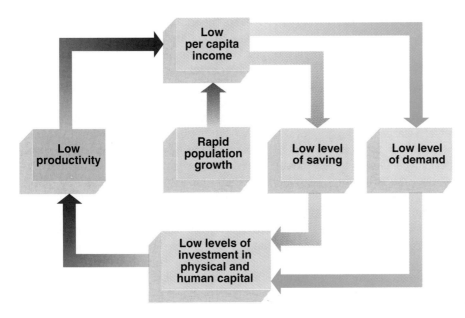

FIGURE 22-1   **The vicious circle of poverty**
Low per capita incomes make it extremely difficult for poor nations to save and invest, a condition that perpetuates low productivity and low incomes. Furthermore, rapid population growth may quickly absorb increases in per capita real income and thereby may negate the possibility of breaking out of the poverty circle.

Latin American rate of 2.5 percent per year? Then real income per person is unchanged and the vicious circle persists.

More optimistically, *if* population can be kept constant or constrained to some growth rate significantly below 2.5 percent, then real income per person will rise. This implies the possibility of still further enlargement in the flows of saving and investment, continued advances in productivity, and the continued growth of per capita real income. If a process of self-sustaining expansion of income, saving, investment, and productivity can be achieved, the self-perpetuating vicious circle of poverty can be transformed into a self-regenerating, beneficent circle of economic progress. The trick is to make effective those policies and strategies which will accomplish this transition. *(Key Question 14)*

ROLE OF GOVERNMENT

Economists do not agree on the appropriate role of government in seeking economic growth.

A Positive Role

One view is that, at least during initial stages of development, government should play a major role. The reasons for this stem from the character of the obstacles facing LDCs.

1   Law and Order   Some of the poorest countries are plagued by banditry and intertribal warfare which divert both attention and resources from the task of development. A strong and stable national government is needed to establish domestic law and order and to achieve peace and unity. Research demonstrates that political instability (as measured by the number of revolutions and coups per year) is associated with slow growth.

2   Lack of Entrepreneurship   The absence of a sizable and vigorous entrepreneurial class, ready and willing to accumulate capital and initiate production, indicates that in many cases private enterprise is intrinsically not capable of spearheading the growth process.

3   Infrastructure   Many obstacles to economic growth center on deficiencies of public goods and services—an inadequate infrastructure. Sanitation and basic medical programs, education, irrigation and soil conservation projects, and construction of highways and transportation-communication facilities are all essentially nonmarketable goods and services yielding widespread spillover benefits. Government is the sole institution in a position to provide these goods and services in required quantities.

4 Forced Saving and Investment Government action may also be required to break through the saving-investment dilemma which impedes capital formation in LDCs.

It may be that only governmental fiscal action can provide a solution by forcing the economy to accumulate capital. There are two alternatives. One is to force the economy to save by increasing taxes. These tax revenues can then be channeled into priority investment projects. The problems of honestly and efficiently administering the tax system and achieving a high degree of compliance with tax laws can be great.

The other alternative is to force the economy to save through inflation. Government can finance capital accumulation by creating and spending new money or by selling bonds to banks and spending the proceeds. The resulting inflation is the equivalent of an arbitrary tax on the economy.

There are serious arguments against the advisability of saving through inflation. In the first place, inflation often distorts the composition of investment away from productive facilities to such items as luxury housing, precious metals and jewels, or foreign securities, which provide a better hedge against rising prices. Furthermore, significant inflation may reduce voluntary private saving as potential savers become less willing to accumulate depreciating money or securities payable in money of declining value. Inflation also induces "capital flight." Internationally, inflation may boost the nation's imports and retard its flow of exports, creating balance of payments difficulties.

5 Social-Institutional Problems Government is in the key position to deal effectively with the social-institutional obstacles to growth. Controlling population growth and land reform are problems which call for the broad approach that only government can provide. And government is in a position to stimulate the will to develop, to change a philosophy of "Heaven and faith will determine the course of events" to one of "God helps those who help themselves."

Public Sector Problems

But serious problems and disadvantages may exist with a governmentally directed development pro-

gram. If entrepreneurial talent is lacking in the private sector, can we expect leaders of quality to be present in the ranks of government? Is there not a real danger that government bureaucracy will impede, not stimulate, much-needed social and economic change? And what of the tendency of some political leaders to favor spectacular "showpiece" projects at the expense of less showy but more productive programs? Might not political objectives take precedence over the economic goals of a governmentally directed development program?

Development experts are less enthusiastic about the role of government in the growth process than they were thirty years ago. Government maladministration and corruption are common in many LDCs. Government officials often line their own pockets with foreign aid funds. Similarly, political leaders frequently confer monopoly privileges on relatives, friends, and political supporters. A political leader may grant exclusive rights to relatives or friends to produce, import, or export certain products. These monopoly privileges lead to higher domestic prices for the relevant products and diminish the LDC's ability to compete in world markets. Similarly, managers of state-owned enterprises are often appointed on the basis of cronyism rather than competence. Many LDC governments, particularly in Africa, have created "marketing boards" as the sole purchaser of agricultural products from local farmers. The boards buy farm products at artificially low prices, sell the output at higher world prices, and the "profit" ends up in the pockets of government officials. In recent years the perception of government has shifted from that of catalyst and promoter of growth to that of a potential impediment to development.

A Mixed Bag

It is possible to muster casual evidence on both sides of this question. Positive government contributions to development are evident in the cases of Japan, South Korea, and Taiwan. In comparison, Mobutu's Zaire, Somoza's Nicaragua, Marcos' Philippines, and Haiti under the Duvaliers are recognized examples of corrupt and inept governments which functioned as impediments to economic progress. Certainly the revolutionary transformations of the former Soviet Union and other eastern European nations away from communism and toward market-oriented economies makes clear that central planning is no longer recognized as an effective mechanism for development.

Many LDCs are belatedly coming to recognize that competition and individual economic incentives are important ingredients in the development process, and that their citizens need to see direct personal gains from their efforts to motivate them to take actions which will expand production.

ROLE OF ADVANCED NATIONS

What are the ways by which industrially advanced nations can help less developed countries in their quest for growth? To what degree have these avenues of assistance been pursued?

Generally, less developed nations can benefit from (1) an expanding volume of trade with advanced nations; (2) foreign aid in the form of grants and loans from governments of advanced nations; and (3) flows of private capital from more affluent nations.

Expanding Trade

Some authorities maintain that the simplest and most effective way the United States and other industrially advanced nations can aid less developed nations is by lowering international trade barriers, enabling LDCs to expand their national incomes through increased trade.

Though there is some truth in this view, lowered trade barriers are not a panacea. It is true that some poor nations need only large foreign markets for their raw materials to achieve growth. But the problem for many is not obtaining markets for utilizing existing productive capacity or the sale of relatively abundant raw materials, but the more fundamental one of getting the capital and technical assistance needed to produce something for export.

Furthermore, close trade ties with advanced nations are not without disadvantages. The old quip, "When Uncle Sam gets his feet wet, the rest of the world gets pneumonia," contains considerable truth for many less developed nations. A recession among the IACs can have disastrous consequences for the prices of raw materials and the export earnings of the LDCs. For example, in mid-1974 copper was $1.52 per pound; by the end of 1975 it had fallen to $.53 per pound! Stability and growth in industrially advanced nations are important to progress in less developed countries.

Foreign Aid: Public Loans and Grants

Foreign capital—both public and private—can supplement an emerging country's saving and investment and play a crucial role in breaking the circle of poverty.

Most LDCs are sadly lacking in infrastructure—irrigation and public health programs and educational, transportation, and communications systems—prerequisites to attracting either domestic or foreign private capital. Foreign public aid is needed to tear down this roadblock to the flow of private capital to the LDCs.

Direct Aid   The United States and other IACs have assisted LDCs directly through a variety of programs and through participating in international institutions designed to stimulate economic development. Over the last decade American aid to the LDCs—including both loans and grants—averaged $10–$14 billion per year. The bulk of this aid is administered by our Agency for International Development (AID). Some, however, takes the form of grants of surplus food under the Food for Peace program. Other advanced nations have also embarked on substantial foreign aid programs. In recent years foreign aid from all industrially advanced nations has been about $60 billion per year.

The aid programs of the IACs merit several additional comments. First, aid is typically distributed on the basis of political and military, rather than economic, considerations. Israel, Turkey, Egypt, and Greece are major recipients of American aid at the expense of Asian, Latin American, and African nations with much lower standards of living. Second, aid from the IACs only amounts to about one-third of 1 percent of the IAC's collective GDPs (Global Perspective 22-2). Finally, LDCs are increasingly concerned that the shift of the former Soviet Union and eastern Europe toward more democratic, market-oriented systems will make these nations "new players" as foreign aid recipients. The LDCs worry that IAC aid which formerly flowed to Latin America, Asia, and Africa may be redirected to, say, Poland, Hungary, and Russia. Similarly, there is the prospect of a substantially larger aid flow to the Middle East if the PLO-Israeli peace accord is durable.

The World Bank Group   The United States is a participant in the **World Bank,** whose major objective is assisting LDCs in achieving growth. Supported by

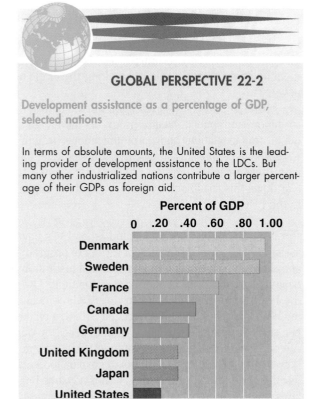

GLOBAL PERSPECTIVE 22-2

Development assistance as a percentage of GDP, selected nations

In terms of absolute amounts, the United States is the leading provider of development assistance to the LDCs. But many other industrialized nations contribute a larger percentage of their GDPs as foreign aid.

Percent of GDP

	0	.20	.40	.60	.80	1.00
Denmark						
Sweden						
France						
Canada						
Germany						
United Kingdom						
Japan						
United States						

Source: World Bank data.

nearly 180 member nations, the World Bank not only lends out of its capital funds, but also (1) sells bonds and lends the proceeds, and (2) guarantees and insures private loans.

Several characteristics of the World Bank are noteworthy.

1 The World Bank is a "last resort" lending agency; its loans are limited to productive projects for which private funds are not readily available.

2 Because many World Bank loans have been for basic development projects—dams, irrigation projects, health and sanitation programs, communications and transportation facilities—it has been hoped that the Bank's activities will provide the infrastructure needed to encourage flows of private capital.

3 The Bank has played a role in providing technical assistance to the LDCs by helping them discover what avenues of growth seem appropriate for their economic development.

Two World Bank affiliates function in areas where the World Bank has been weak. The *International Fi-*

nance Corporation (*IFC*) has the primary function of investing in *private* enterprises in the LDCs. The *International Development Association* (*IDA*) makes "soft loans"—loans which may not be self-liquidating—to the poorest of the LDCs on more liberal terms than does the World Bank.

Foreign Harm? But foreign aid to the LDCs has been subject to criticism.

1 *Dependency and Incentives* A basic criticism is that, like domestic welfare programs, foreign aid may generate dependency rather than self-sustaining growth. It is argued that transfers of wealth from the IACs allow the LDCs to avoid the painful economic decisions, the institutional and cultural changes, and the alterations in attitudes regarding thrift, industry, hard work, and self-reliance which are needed for growth. Critics say that, after some five decades of foreign aid, the LDCs' demand for foreign aid has increased; if aid programs had been successful in promoting sustainable growth, demand should have fallen.

2 *Bureaucracy and Centralized Government* IAC aid is given, not directly to the residents and businesses of the LDCs, but rather to their governments. The direct consequence is that aid typically generates massive, relatively unproductive government bureaucracies and centralizes government power over the economy. The recent stagnation and collapse of the centralized economies of the Soviet Union and eastern Europe provide evidence that market-oriented economies are much more conducive to growth and development. Furthermore, not only does the bureaucratization of the LDCs divert valuable human resources from the private to the public sector, but it shifts the nation's focus from the *production* of output and income to its *redistribution*.

3 *Corruption and Misuse* Critics also allege that foreign aid is ineffectively used. Corruption is rampant in many LDCs and some estimates suggest 10 to 20 percent of aid is diverted into the pockets of government officials. Some of the wealthiest individuals in the world—for example, Zaire's Mobutu, the Duvaliers in Haiti, the Philippines' Marcos—are (or were) rulers of LDCs. Foreign aid may create an ironic and perverse incentive for LDC leaders to keep their populations poor so they continue to qualify for aid.

Also, IAC-based aid consultants and multinational corporations are major beneficiaries of aid programs. Some economists contend that as much as one-fourth or more of each year's aid is spent on expert consultants. Furthermore, because IAC corporations carry out most aid projects, they are major beneficiaries of, and lobbyists for, foreign aid.

Private Capital Flows

The LDCs have also received substantial flows of private capital from the IACs. These private investors for the most part are large corporations and commercial banks. General Motors or Chrysler might finance construction of a plant in Mexico or Brazil to assemble autos or produce auto parts. Or Citicorp or Bank of America may make loans to the governments of Argentina or the Philippines.

Although these private capital flows were modest in the 1950s and 1960s—ranging from $2 to $4 billion per year—they grew in the 1970s. Specifically, average annual private flows of capital to the LDCs in the decade of the 1970s was $28 billion. Then in the early 1980s an LDC debt crisis developed which caused private capital flows to the poor nations to fall precipitously.

THE LDC DEBT CRISIS

What is the magnitude of LDC debt? What are its causes? And effects? What has been done to resolve the debt problem?

The Debt and Its Growth

The external debt (debts owed to foreign governments, businesses, individuals, and financial institutions) of the LDCs increased thirteenfold in the past two decades, from $100 billion in 1970 to about $1350 billion in 1990.

Causes of the Crisis

We have noted that private capital flows—particularly from large IAC commercial banks—increased greatly in the 1970s. But in the 1970s and early 1980s a series of converging world economic events had serious adverse effects on the LDCs and created a debt crisis.

1 Soaring Oil Prices The dramatic runup of oil prices by OPEC in 1973–1974 and again in 1979–1980 (raising the price of a barrel of oil from about $2.50 to $35) greatly increased the energy bills of the oil-importing LDCs. These nations were faced with growing current account deficits in their balance of payments which were financed largely by increased borrowing. Hence, the external debt of oil-importing LDCs grew from $130 billion in 1973 to $700 billion by 1982. Borrowed funds which could have been used for development were instead used to pay higher energy costs.

2 Tight Money Policy In the early 1980s the IACs —and the United States in particular—invoked strong anti-inflationary monetary policies. These tight money policies triggered two adverse effects for the LDCs. On the one hand, growth of IAC national incomes slowed; in 1980–1982 the United States suffered its most serious postwar recession. As a result, IAC demands for the raw material and farm product exports of LDCs declined. This meant sharp reductions in the export earnings which the LDCs needed to pay interest and principal on their debts. On the other hand, tight money policies in the IACs resulted in much higher interest rates. This greatly increased the cost to the LDCs in servicing their debts.

3 Appreciating Dollar The burden of LDC debt rose for another reason. Over the 1981–1984 period the international value of the dollar appreciated. This meant that LDCs had to pay more for their imports of American manufactured goods. And, because much LDC debt is denominated in dollars, it also meant that LDCs would have to export a larger amount of goods to acquire each dollar needed to pay interest and principal on their debts.

4 Unproductive Investments In a number of LDCs the improper use of borrowed funds contributed to the debt crisis. Because of political corruption and economic mismanagement, LDC investment of loan funds was frequently unproductive. Returns on such investments were not sufficient to cover interest and principal payments, thereby generating loan defaults.

5 Mexican Crisis In 1982 Mexico was on the verge of defaulting on its debt. Creditors were forced to reschedule that debt and make further loans to Mexico. This Mexican debt crisis precipitated an abrupt loss of confidence in the creditworthiness of many highly indebted LDCs. As a result, private voluntary lending to LDCs declined sharply. This was complicated by the fact that the United States was incurring very large Federal budget deficits during the 1980s. The sale of United States government bonds to finance these budget deficits absorbed a significant portion of the world's financial capital which might otherwise have been available to LDCs.

In short, higher prices on imported oil, declines in LDC export earnings, higher interest rates, appreciation of the dollar, unproductive investment by the LDCs, and declines in recent private lending to the LDCs all combined to create a debt crisis. By 1982 and 1983 many LDCs were unable to make scheduled payments on their external debts.

Economic Consequences

There has followed a period of "muddling through" during which creditor nations in cooperation with the International Monetary Fund attempted to deal with the LDC debt crisis on a nation-by-nation basis. The debts of many LDCs were rescheduled (stretched out over a longer period of time) to reduce the burden of annual interest and principal payments. In return for these concessions the LDCs had to agree to domestic austerity programs to improve their prospects for debt repayment. This meant that LDCs had to reduce their imports and increase their exports to realize more international trade earnings for debt repayment. But increased exports and reduced imports clearly imply a further impairment of living standards in the LDCs. Similarly, with net export earnings being used primarily for debt retirement little or nothing is left to invest in development projects. It is not by chance that, while the growth of real GDP for the LDCs as a group was 3.8 percent per year over the 1980–1989 period, the rate for highly indebted LDCs was only 1.9 percent.

The debt crisis has also had adverse repercussions in the IACs. IAC commercial banks have been forced to write off some LDC debt as uncollectible. In mid-1987 Citicorp increased its bad-debt reserves by $3 billion in recognition that as much as 25 percent of its loans to LDCs would not be repaid.

Reform and Revival

The 1980s was characterized by intensive negotiations between the IACs and the IMF, on the one hand, and the highly indebted LDCs, on the other, to resolve the debt crisis. The results included (1) restructuring of debt, that is, increasing the period of repayment and reducing interest rates; (2) writing-off or forgiving some of the debt; (3) making additional loans to the LDCs to help them make payments on existing debt; and (4) debt-equity swaps. **Debt-equity swaps** occur when LDC governments and businesses pay off debt by giving shares of stock (ownership claims to government-owned or private enterprises) to foreign creditors. The advantage of such swaps to LDCs is that no fixed interest or principal payments must be made to stockholders. The disadvantage to LDCs is that partial ownership of their businesses is transferred to foreigners. The advantage to lending IACs is that stock ownership is better than default.

Although private capital flows to the LDCs virtually ceased in the 1980s, there has been a modest revival in the 1990s. Two interrelated factors are involved.

LDC Economic Reforms As part of the debt negotiations, heavily indebted LDCs agreed to reform their economies so as to promote growth and avert future debt crises. At the macro level greater efforts are being made to reduce budget deficits and control chronically high levels of inflation. At the micro level many governments have privatized state-owned businesses and deregulated industry. Tariffs and other trade barriers, along with exchange rate controls, have been reduced. In general, the economic role of government has been lessened and that of free markets enhanced. These reforms have made the LDCs more attractive to foreign lenders.

Revived Investment The 1990s has witnessed a modest revival in private capital flows to the LDCs, particularly to those with reformed economies. However, the makeup of this revived investment flow is now different. First, private IAC firms and individuals, rather than commercial banks, are the primary lenders. Second, the loans are largely direct investment in LDC enterprises, rather than loans to LDC governments. The potential advantage of directly investing in LDC enterprises is that management skills and technological knowledge often accompany such capital flows.

Two words of caution. The revived flow of capital is highly selective. Most of the flow is directed toward the more affluent, reformed countries of Latin

America and not toward the extremely impoverished sub-Saharan nations of Africa. And it is premature to say that the LDC debt crisis has been resolved. Some LDC nations still face staggering debt burdens and there is no assurance that some combination of circumstances will not bring about future defaults. The debt crisis has been alleviated, not solved. Evidence: In early 1995 the United States, other G-7 Nations, and the IMF found it necessary to provide a $50 billion package of loan guarantees to offset the collapse of the Mexican peso. The immediate cause of the peso's dramatic fall was an expansion of Mexican debt in excess of its export earnings.

QUICK REVIEW 22-2

■ LDC governments may encourage growth by *a* providing law and order; *b* engaging in entrepreneurial activities; *c* improving the infrastructure; *d* forcing higher levels of saving and investing; and *e* resolving social-institutional problems.

■ The IACs can assist the LDCs through expanded trade, foreign aid, and private capital flows.

■ Many LDCs have huge external debts which have become an additional obstacle to growth.

TOWARD A NEW GLOBAL COMPACT[7]

As the income gap between the rich and the poor nations widens, spokespersons for the LDCs have put forth an agenda for reform which includes the following.

1 Sharing the Peace Dividend With the end of the Cold War, LDC leaders argue that IAC military spending can be reduced and the released resources shared with the poor nations. Specifically, all countries should reduce their military expenditures by at least 3 percent per year, making available a "peace dividend" of about $1.2 trillion in the IACs by the year 2000.

2 Reform of Foreign Aid The LDCs say foreign aid is (a) deficient quantitatively, (b) borne inequitably by donor nations, and (c) not allocated to the poorest nations.

---

[7]This section is based primarily on the United Nations Development Program, *Human Development Report 1992* (New York: Oxford University Press, 1992).

Quantity While the governments of IACs "recycle" from 15 to 25 percent of their GDPs to alleviate income inequality internally, they only provide 0.35 percent of their GDPs in foreign aid to impoverished peoples around the world. The LDCs advocate that this figure should by doubled to the 0.7 percent level recommended by the United Nations.

Equity The LDCs would like to see foreign aid restructured to resemble a progressive tax so that the percentage of aid donated by each nation would increase the larger its GDP. Currently we find that superrich United States and Japan donate only 0.20 and 0.32 percent of their GDPs, respectively, as aid while less-affluent Sweden and Denmark give 0.90 percent or more. If the United States and Japan were to pay recommended progressive rates of approximately 0.80 percent, most of the aid shortfall between the current 0.35 and the recommended 0.70 percent of GDP would disappear.

Allocation Foreign aid is strongly influenced by political and military—not economic—considerations. The consequence is that LDCs do *not* receive aid in accordance with their needs or degree of destitution. Only a quarter of foreign aid goes to those ten countries whose populations constitute 70 percent of the world's poorest people. The most affluent 40 percent of the LDC world population receives over twice as much aid as the poorest 40 percent.

3 Debt Relief The LDCs have also sought debt relief. They say their present debt is so large that it constitutes a severe obstacle to LDC growth. Arguing that the prosperity of the IACs depends on the prosperity of the LDCs, LDCs feel that forgiving some portion of the debt would be mutually beneficial. One proposal suggests that as much as two-thirds of all existing LDC external debt be canceled and the remainder be rescheduled for payment over a twenty-five-year period.

4 Improving Global Markets The LDCs complain that their export earnings have been impaired because of deteriorating terms of trade and trade barriers.

Terms of Trade The long-term price trend of LDC commodity exports (such as coffee, sugar, cocoa, bauxite, tin, and copper) has been downward. For example, in the 1980s the price index for a group of

FAMINE IN AFRICA

The roots of Africa's persistent famines include both natural and human causes.

The recent famine in Somolia—documented by shocking photos of fly-tormented, emaciated children with bloated bellies—is not uncommon in sub-Saharan Africa. Before U.S. armed forces and U.N. aid arrived in Somalia in late 1992, severe famine had caused an estimated 2000 deaths each day. One out of four Somali children under the age of 5—about 300,000—are believed to have died. Similarly, despite an outpouring of aid from the rich nations, the 1983–1984 Ethiopian famine caused 1 million deaths. A number of African nations—including Ethiopia, Sudan, Angola, Liberia, Zaire, Mozambique, and Malawi—are persistently threatened by famine. Estimates put from 5 to 20 million Africans at risk. This tragedy is ironic because most African countries were self-sufficient in food at the time they became independent nations; they are now heavily dependent on imported foodstuffs for survival.

The immediate cause of this catastrophe is drought. But the ultimate causes of Africa's declining ability to feed itself are more complex, an interplay of natural and human conditions. Lack of rainfall, chronic civil strife, rapid population growth, widespread soil erosion, and counterproductive public policies, all contribute to Africa's famines.

1   Civil Strife   Regional rebellions and prolonged civil wars have devastated some African nations. Both Ethiopia and Sudan, for example, have been plagued by decades of civil strife. Not only do these conflicts

divert precious resources from civilian uses, they also greatly complicate the ability of wealthy nations to provide famine and developmental aid. In the 1983–1984 famine the Ethiopian government denied food aid to areas occupied by rebel forces. Donated food is frequently diverted to the army and denied to starving civilians. During Ethiopia's 1973–1974 famine Haile Selassie sold much of the donated food on world markets to enrich his regime! In Somolia factional feuding has destroyed most institutions—schools, factories, and government ministries—and reduced the country to anarchy. Armed gangs steal water pumps, tractors, and livestock from farms and loot ports of donated foodstuffs.

2   Population Growth   In Africa population is growing more rapidly than is food production. Population is increasing about 3 percent per year while food output is growing only 2 percent per year. This grim arithmetic suggests declining living standards, hunger, and malnutrition. The World Bank reports

thirty-three primary commodities (excluding oil) fell by almost one-half. Part of this decline is explained by the slow growth of demand relative to supply. Ironically, many LDCs stepped up production of their commodity exports to increase their foreign exchange earnings to meet interest and principal payments on their external debts. But these attempts were largely frustrated by the price declines which resulted from the increased commodity supplies. Product substitution has also contributed to falling commodity prices. Synthetic fibers have been substituted for cotton and

jute; glass fibers have supplanted copper in communications; corn syrup and other sweeteners have tended to reduce the demand for sugar.

In contrast, the LDCs import manufactured goods produced by the corporate giants of the advanced nations which have the market power to charge high prices. The LDCs argue that the **terms of trade** have shifted against them; the prices of their exports tend to be depressed while the prices of their imports tend to rise. Hence, it takes more of the LDCs' exports to purchase a given quantity of imports.

that during the 1980s the per capita incomes of the sub-Saharan nations fell to about three-quarters of the level reached by the end of the 1970s.

3   Ecological Degradation   But apart from the simple numbers involved, population growth has contributed to the ecological degradation of Africa. With population pressures and the increasing need for food, marginal land has been deforested and put into crop production. In many cases trees which have served as a barrier to the encroachment of the desert have been cut for fuel, allowing the fragile topsoil to be blown away by desert winds. The scarcity of wood which has accompanied deforestation has forced the use of animal dung for fuel, thereby denying its traditional use as fertilizer. Furthermore, traditional fallow periods have been shortened, resulting in overplanting and overgrazing and a wearing out of the soil. Deforestation and land overuse have reduced the capacity of the land to absorb moisture, diminishing its productivity and its ability to resist drought. Some authorities feel that the diminished ability of the land to absorb water reduces the amount of moisture which evaporates into the clouds to return ultimately as rainfall. All of this is complicated by the fact that there are few facilities for crop storage. Even when crops are good, it is difficult to accumulate a surplus for future lean years. A large percentage of domestic farm output in some parts of Africa is lost to rats, insects, and spoilage.

4   Public Policies and Debt   Ill-advised public policies have contributed to Africa's famines. In the first place, African governments have generally neglected investment in agriculture in favor of industrial development and military strength. It is estimated that African governments on the average spend four times as much on armaments as they do on agriculture. Over 40 percent of Ethiopia's budget is for the support of an oppressive military. Second, many African governments have followed the policy of establishing the prices of agricultural commodities at low levels to provide cheap food for growing urban populations. This low-price policy has diminished the incentives of farmers to increase productivity. While foreign aid has helped to ease the effects of Africa's food-population problems, most experts reject aid as a long-term solution. Experience suggests that aid in the form of food can only provide temporary relief and may undermine the realization of long-run local self-sufficiency. Foreign food aid, it is contended, treats symptoms and not causes.

All of this is made more complex by the fact that the sub-Saharan nations are burdened with large and growing external debts. The IMF reports that the aggregate debt of these nations rose from $21 billion in 1976 to $127 billion in 1990. As a condition of further aid, these nations have had to invoke austerity programs which have contributed to declines in their per capita incomes. One tragic consequence is that many of these nations have cut back on social service programs for children.

To summarize: The famine confronting much of Africa is partly a phenomenon of nature and in part self-inflicted. Drought, civil strife, overpopulation, ecological deterioration, and errant public policies have all been contributing factors. This complex of causes implies that hunger and malnutrition in Africa may persist long after the rains return.

Trade Barriers   The LDCs lament that trade barriers are highest for the labor-intensive kinds of manufactured goods—textiles, clothing, footwear, and processed agricultural products—in which the LDCs have a comparative advantage. Some twenty of the twenty-four most industrialized nations are more protectionist than they were a decade ago. And, ironically, many tariffs increase with the degree of product processing—for example, tariffs on chocolate are higher than on cocoa—which effectively denies the LDCs the opportunity to develop processing industries. One estimate suggests that trade barriers reduce the gross domestic products of the LDCs by 3 percent, causing an annual loss of $75 billion in income.

5   Immigration   There are both quantitative and qualitative aspects to the LDCs' immigration complaints. Too few people are allowed to move from the LDCs to the IACs and IAC policies tend to favor movement of the most productive LDC workers.

LDC spokespersons believe that the IACs should liberalize their immigration laws to enlarge the flow of unemployed and underemployed workers from the LDCs. While some nations—the United States and Canada, for example—have abolished discrimination by country of origin, several European nations are moving toward more restrictive stances with respect to potential LDC immigrants. Some pressure is building to repatriate unemployed migrants. Not only is migration an outlet for surplus LDC labor, but also a source of income in the form of migrant remittances. Currently aggregate remittances from emigrants back to the LDCs is about $25 billion per year.

The United States, Canada, and other IACs have rewritten their immigration laws to favor workers with high skill levels such as researchers, physicians, engineers, and scientists. This, of course, encourages the "brain drain" where LDCs lose human capital in which they have made substantial investments. To illustrate: Estimates indicate that Africa as a whole lost some 60,000 middle-and high-level managers to migration in the 1985–1990 period.

6 Neocolonialism A more general grievance is that, despite the realization of political independence, many LDCs feel an economic-based **neocolonialism** persists. Over four-fifths of the world's direct investment by multinational companies is received by IACs and the remaining one-fifth goes largely to those LDCs which are already better off. And most of the contracts, leases, and concessions which multina-tional corporations of advanced countries have negotiated with the LDCs have benefitted the multinationals at the expense of the host countries. The poor countries argue that most benefits from the exploitation of their natural resources accrue to others. Furthermore, LDCs seek to achieve greater diversification and therefore greater stability in their economies. Foreign private capital, however, seeks out those industries which are currently the most profitable, that is, the ones now producing for the export market. In brief, while LDCs strive for less dependence on world markets, flows of foreign private capital enhance that dependence. Exxon, Alcoa, United Fruit, and the rest are after profits and allegedly have no particular interest in either the economic independence, diversification, or overall progress of the LDCs.

Whether the IACs will address these grievances, creating a "new global compact" with the LDCs is problematic. While the poor countries feel their proposals are egalitarian and just, many advanced nations see them as a demand for a massive redistribution of world income and wealth which is simply not in the cards. Many industrialized nations feel there is no "quick fix" for underdevelopment and that the LDCs must undergo the same process of patient hard work and gradual capital formation as did the advanced nations over the past two centuries.

CHAPTER SUMMARY

1 Most nations are less developed (low per capita income) nations. While some LDCs have been achieving quite rapid growth rates in recent years, others have realized little or no growth.

2 Initial scarcities of natural resources and the limited possibility of augmenting existing supplies may limit a nation's capacity to develop.

3 The large and rapidly growing populations in most LDCs contributes to low per capita incomes. Increases in per capita incomes frequently induce rapid population growth, again reducing per capita incomes to near subsistence levels. The "demographic transition" concept suggests that rising living standards must precede declining birthrates.

4 Most LDCs suffer from unemployment and underemployment. Labor productivity is low because of insufficient investment in physical and human capital.

5 In many LDCs both the saving and investment aspects of capital formation are impeded by formidable obstacles. In some of the poorest LDCs the savings potential is very low. Many LDC savers transfer their funds to the IACs rather than invest domestically. The absence of a vigorous entrepreneurial class and the weakness of investment incentives are also impediments to capital accumulation.

6 Appropriate social and institutional changes and, in particular, the presence of "the will to develop" are essential ingredients in economic development.

7 The vicious circle of poverty brings together many of the obstacles to growth, saying in effect that "poor countries stay poor because of their poverty." Low incomes inhibit saving and accumulation of physical and human capital, making it difficult to increase productivity and incomes. Rapid population growth can offset otherwise promising attempts to break the vicious circle.

8 The nature of the obstacles to growth—the absence of an entrepreneurial class, the dearth of infrastructure, the saving-investment dilemma, and the presence of social-institutional obstacles to growth—suggests the need for government action in initiating growth. However, the corruption and maladministration which are quite common to the public sectors of the LDCs suggest that government may be ineffective as an instigator of growth.

9 Advanced nations can assist in development by reducing trade barriers and by providing both public and private capital. Critics of foreign aid say it **a** creates LDC dependency; **b** contributes to the growth of bureaucracies and centralized economic control; and **c** is ineffective because of corruption and mismanagement.

10 Rising energy prices, declining export prices, depreci-

ation of the dollar, the unproductive use of borrowed funds, and concern about LDCs' creditworthiness combined to create an LDC debt crisis in the early 1980s. External debt problems of many LDCs remain serious and inhibit their growth.

11 The LDCs seek a "new global compact" with the IACs which entails **a** a larger and better allocated flow of aid; **b** debt relief; **c** greater LDC access to world markets; **d** liberalized immigration policies; and **e** an end to neocolonialism.

TERMS AND CONCEPTS

industrially advanced countries (IACs)
less developed countries (LDCs)
demographic transition
unemployment and underemployment

brain drain
capital flight
infrastructure
nonfinancial investment
the will to develop

capital-saving and capital-using technological advance
capricious universe view
land reform

vicious circle of poverty
World Bank
debt-equity swaps
new global compact
terms of trade
neocolonialism

QUESTIONS AND STUDY SUGGESTIONS

1 What are the characteristics of an LDC? List the avenues of economic development available to such a nation. State and explain obstacles which face LDCs in breaking the poverty barrier. Use the "vicious circle of poverty" to outline in detail steps an LDC might take to initiate economic development.

2 Explain how the absolute per capita income gap between rich and poor nations might increase, even though per capita GDP is growing faster in LDCs than it is in IACs.

3 *Key Question Assume an LDC and an IAC currently have real per capita outputs of $500 and $5000 respectively. If both nations realize a 3 percent increase in their real per capita outputs, by how much will the per capita output gap change?*

4 Discuss and evaluate:
   a "The path to economic development has been clearly blazed by American capitalism. It is only for the LDCs to follow this trail."
   b "Economic inequality is conducive to saving, and saving is the prerequisite of investment. Therefore, greater inequality in the income distribution of the LDCs would be a spur to capital accumulation and growth."
   c "The IACs fear the complications from oversaving; the LDCs bear the yoke of undersaving."
   d "The core of development involves changing human

beings more than it does altering a nation's physical environment."
   e "America's 'foreign aid' program is a sham. In reality it represents neocolonialism—a means by which the LDCs can be nominally free in a political sense but remain totally subservient in an economic sense."
   f "Poverty and freedom cannot persist side by side; one must triumph over the other."
   g "The biggest obstacle facing poor nations in their quest for development is the lack of capital goods."
   h "A high per capita GDP does not necessarily identify an industrially advanced nation."

5 Explain how population growth might be an impediment to economic growth. How would you define the optimal population of a country?

6 *Key Question Contrast the "demographic transition" view of population with the traditional view that slower population growth is a prerequisite for rising living standards in the LDCs.*

7 Much of the initial investment in an LDC must be devoted to infrastructure which does not directly or immediately lead to a greater production of goods and services. What bearing might this have on the degree of inflation which results as government finances capital accumulation through the creating and spending of new money?

8 *Key Question* *Since real capital is supposed to earn a higher return where it is scarce, how do you explain the fact that most international investment flows to the IACs (where capital is relatively abundant) rather than to the LDCs (where capital is very scarce)?*

9 "The nature of the problems faced by the LDCs creates a bias in favor of governmentally directed as opposed to a decentralized development process." Do you agree? Why or why not?

10 What is the LDC debt crisis? How did it come about? What solutions can you offer?

11 What types of products do the LDCs export? Use the law of comparative advantage to explain the character of these exports.

12 Outline the main components of the "new global compact" proposed by the LDCs. Which of these demands do you feel are justified?

13 What would be the implications of a worldwide policy of unrestricted immigration between nations for economic efficiency and the global distribution of income?

14 *Key Question* *Use Figure 22-1 (changing box labels as necessary) to explain rapid economic growth in a country such as Japan or South Korea. What factors other than those contained in the figure might contribute to growth?*

15 (Last Word) Explain how civil wars, population growth, and public policy decisions have contributed to periodic famines in Africa.

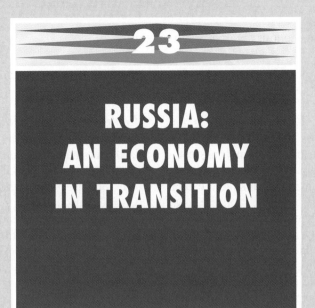

RUSSIA: AN ECONOMY IN TRANSITION

Arguably the most profound event of the past decade was the collapse of the Soviet Union in late 1991 and the decision by Russia and the other successor republics to transform themselves from centrally directed to market economies.

In this final chapter we examine the breakup of the Soviet Union and the problems the new republics now face. Specific questions are: What were the main characteristics and goals of the Soviet planned economy? Why did Soviet communism fail? What must be accomplished to achieve the transition to a market or capitalistic system? What role, if any, might the United States and other western nations play in this transition? What progress has been realized thus far? What problems remain?

The transition from central planning to markets has been widespread. Such eastern European nations as Poland, East Germany, Czechoslovakia, and Hungary, among others, preceded the former Soviet Union on this path. We focus on Russia because of its economic, political, and military importance. Russia encompasses about three-fourths of the territory of the former Soviet Union, and is two and one-half times larger than Canada, the world's second largest nation. Russia has about 150 million people, over half as many as were in the former Soviet Union. It also encompasses vast natural resources, including oil and gas, precious metals, diamonds, and timber.

IDEOLOGY AND INSTITUTIONS

To understand the planned economy of the former Soviet Union, we must look back at its ideology and institutions.

Marxian Ideology

The Communist Party was the dominant force in Soviet political and economic life. It viewed itself as a dictatorship of the proletariat or working class. Based on Marxism-Leninism, the Communists envisioned their system as the inevitable successor to capitalism, the latter being plagued by internal contradictions stemming from the exploitation, injustice, and insecurity which it was thought to generate. To communists, the market system was chaotic, unstable, and inequitable. Markets bred inflation, unemployment, and an unfair distribution of income. In contrast, central planning was viewed as a means for rationally organizing the economy's resources, achieving macroeconomic stability, and providing greater equality.

Especially important for our purposes is the Marxian concept of a **labor theory of value**—the idea that the economic or exchange value of any commodity is determined solely by the amount of labor time required for its production. Thanks to the capitalistic institution of private property, capitalists own the machinery and equipment necessary for production in an industrial society. The propertyless working class is therefore dependent on the capitalists for employment and for its livelihood. Because of the worker's inferior bargaining position and the capitalist's pursuit of profits, the capitalists will exploit labor by paying a daily wage far below the value of the worker's daily production. The capitalist can and will pay workers a subsistence wage and expropriate the remaining fruits of their labor as profits, or what Marx termed **surplus value.** In the Soviet system, surplus value was to be extracted by the state as an agency of the working class and distributed in large part through subsidies to what we would call public or quasi-public goods, for example, education, transportation, health care, and housing.

The function of communism was to overthrow capitalism and replace it with a classless society void of human exploitation. The Communist Party viewed itself as the vanguard of the working class, and its actions were held to be in keeping with the goals of the working class. In fact, it was a strong dictatorship. Many westerners characterized the Soviet government as a dictatorship *over* the proletariat, not *of* the proletariat.

Institutions

The two outstanding institutional characteristics of the Soviet economy were: (1) state ownership of property resources, and (2) authoritarian central economic planning.

State Ownership **State ownership** meant the Soviet state owned all land, natural resources, transportation and communication facilities, the banking system, and virtually all industry. Most retail and wholesale enterprises and most urban housing were governmentally owned. In agriculture many farms were state-owned; most, however, were government-organized collective farms—essentially cooperatives

to which the state assigned land "for free use for an unlimited time."

Central Economic Planning **Central economic planning** meant that the Soviet Union had a centralized "command" economy functioning in terms of a detailed economic plan. The Soviet economy was government-directed rather than market-directed. Choices made through the market in the United States' economy were made by bureaucratic decision in the Soviet Union. Through the plan "all the manifold activities of the Soviet economy [were] coordinated as if they were parts of one incredibly enormous enterprise directed from the central headquarters in Moscow."[1]

CENTRAL PLANNING AND ITS PROBLEMS

The Soviet system of central planning was put in place in the late 1920s and early 1930s. Despite occasional reforms, the system remained fundamentally unchanged for almost seven decades.

Ends and Means

The following generalizations describe how Soviet planning functioned historically.

1 Industrialization and Military Strength The economy of the former Soviet Union was a system of "totalitarianism harnessed to the task of rapid industrialization and economic growth." Planned goals stressed rapid industrialization and military strength. This was achieved through extensive investment in heavy industries—steel, chemicals, and machine tools—and the allocation of a large percentage of domestic output to the military. As a consequence, development of consumer goods industries, the distribution and service sectors, and the infrastructure were neglected.

2 Resource Overcommitment Production increases sought in the various plans were ambitious; they overcommitted the economy's available re-

---

[1]Harry Schwartz, *Russia's Soviet Economy,* 2d ed. (Englewood Cliffs, N.J.: Prentice-Hall, Inc., 1954), p. 146.

sources. As a result, not all planning targets could be achieved. And planning priorities were to achieve those goals associated with heavy industry and the military at the expense of consumption.

3 Resource Mobilization Industrialization and rapid economic growth were initially achieved through mobilization of labor, capital, and raw materials. In the early years of planning there was substantial surplus labor in agriculture which the plans reallocated to industrial production. Similarly, a larger proportion of the population was induced or coerced into the labor force. Early Soviet growth was achieved through more inputs rather than using fixed amounts of inputs more productivity. In the 1930s and again in the early post-World War II era, this strategy produced growth rates greater than the United States and other industrialized nations.

4 Allocation by Directives Soviet central planners directed the allocation of inputs among industries and firms, thereby determining the composition of output. Planning directives were substituted for the market or price system as an allocational mechanism.

5 Government Price Fixing Prices were set by government direction rather than by the forces of demand and supply. Consumer good prices were changed infrequently and, as a matter of social policy, the prices of "necessities"—for example, housing and basic foodstuffs—were established at low levels. Rents on Soviet housing averaged only about 3 percent of income and did not change between 1928 and 1992! Input prices and the price of an enterprise's output were also governmentally determined and were used primarily as accounting devices to gauge a firm's progress in meeting its production target.

6 Self-Sufficiency The Soviet Union viewed itself as a single socialist nation surrounded by hostile capitalistic countries. Therefore, the central plans stressed economic self-sufficiency. Trade with western nations was greatly restricted because the ruble was not convertible into other currencies. Soviet trade was largely with the other communist nations of eastern Europe.

7 Passive Macroeconomic Policies The Soviet economy was a quantity-directed system with money and prices playing only a limited role in resource allocation. Unlike most market economies, monetary and fiscal policies were passive rather than active in the Soviet Union. In the United States and other market systems, monetary and fiscal policies are used to manipulate the aggregate levels of output, employment, and prices. Historically, unemployment in the Soviet Union was very low, perhaps 1 or 2 percent of the labor force. This was partly the result of ambitious planning targets and various admonitions to work. Low unemployment was also due to overstaffing (managers could not fire redundant workers), a disinterest in cost-minimization (gross output was the overriding objective), and a population whose growth rate was steadily diminishing. Similarly, government price determination was the primary device used to control the price level.

The Coordination Problem

The market system is a powerful organizing force which coordinates millions of individual decisions by consumers, resource suppliers, and businesses, and fosters a reasonably efficient use of scarce resources. It is not easy to substitute central planning as a coordinating mechanism.

Example: Suppose an enterprise in Minsk is producing men's shoes. Planners must establish a realistic production target for that enterprise and then see that all the necessary inputs—labor, electric power, leather, rubber, thread, nails, appropriate machinery, transportation—for production and delivery of that product are made available. When we move from a simple product such as shoes to more complex products such as television sets and farm tractors, planners' allocational problems are greatly compounded.

Because the outputs of many industries are inputs to other industries, the failure of any single industry to fulfill its output target will cause a chain of adverse repercussions. If iron mines—for want of machinery or labor or transportation inputs—fail to supply the steel industry with the required inputs of iron ore, the steel industry will be unable to fulfill the input needs of the many industries dependent on steel. All these steel-using industries—automobiles, tractors, and transportation—will be unable to fulfill their planned production goals. And so the bottleneck chain reaction goes on to all firms using steel parts or components as inputs. Bottlenecks and production stoppages occurred with alarming regularity in the 1980s and early 1990s.

QUICK REVIEW 23-1

■ Marxian ideology is based on the labor theory of value and views capitalism as a system for expropriating profits or surplus value from workers.

■ The primary institutional features of the former Soviet economy were state ownership of property resources and central economic planning.

■ Soviet plans were characterized by *a* an emphasis on rapid industrialization and military power, *b* resource overcommitment; *c* growth through the use of more inputs rather than greater efficiency; *d* resource allocation by government directives rather than markets; *e* government price determination; *f* an emphasis on economic self-sufficiency; and *g* passive monetary and fiscal policies.

■ The basic planning problem is to direct needed resources to each enterprise so that production targets can be achieved and bottlenecks avoided.

COMMUNISM'S FAILURES

Diminishing economic growth, shoddy product quality, and the inability to meet consumer expectations all contributed to the Soviet system's collapse.

Declining Growth

Soviet economic growth in the 1950s and 1960s was impressive. In the 1950s Soviet real domestic output expanded at roughly 6 percent per year compared to about 3 percent for the United States. The Soviet economy continued to grow at about 5 percent per year in the 1960s. But growth fell to an annual rate of about $2\frac{1}{2}$ or 3 percent in the 1970s and further declined to 2 percent by the mid-1980s. In the last year or two before the system's breakdown, real output was falling sharply.

Poor Product Quality

Further evidence of economic failure was reflected in the quality of goods. In such vital manufacturing sectors as computers and machine tools, Soviet technology lagged some seven to twelve years behind the United States. Overall, the quality of most Soviet manufactured goods was far short of international standards. Consumer goods were of notoriously poor quality and product assortment was greatly limited. Durable goods—automobiles, refrigerators, and con-

sumer electronics products—were primitive by world standards. Furthermore, widespread shortages of basic goods, interminable shopper queues, black markets, and corruption in the distribution of products characterized the consumer sector.

Consumer Needs

The major contributing factor to the downfall of Soviet communism was its inability to efficiently supply the goods and services consumers wanted to buy. In the early decades of Soviet communism the government established a "social contract" with its citizenry to the effect that, by enduring the consumer sacrifices associated with the high rates of saving and investment necessary for rapid industrialization and growth, the population would be rewarded with consumer abundance in the future (Figure 2-5). The failure of the system to meet consumer expectations contributed to frustration and deteriorating morale among consumers and workers (Global Perspective 23-1).

Causes of the Collapse

Having chronicled the deteriorating performance of the economy of the former Soviet Union, we now consider causes of its collapse.

1 Military Burden Large Soviet military expenditures of 15 to 20 percent of domestic output—compared to 6 percent for the United States—absorbed great quantities of resources which would otherwise have been available for the development and production of consumer and investment goods. During the cold war era it was the government's policy to channel superior management and the best scientists and engineers to defense and space research, which adversely affected technological progress and the quality (productivity) of investment in the civilian sector.

2 Agricultural Drag By western standards agriculture in the former Soviet Union was something of a monument to inefficiency and a drag on economic growth, engulfing some 30 percent of the labor force and roughly one-fourth of annual investment. Furthermore, output per worker was only 10 to 25 percent of the United States' level. The low productivity of Soviet agriculture was attributable to many factors: relative scarcity of good land; vagaries in rainfall and length of growing season; serious errors in planning and administration; and, perhaps most important, the failure to construct an effective incentive system.

Once a major exporter of grain and other agricultural products, the Soviet Union became one of the world's largest importers of agricultural commodities. Agricultural imports were a serious drain on foreign currency reserves which its leadership wanted for financing imports of western capital goods and technology.

3 More Inputs versus Increased Efficiency

Much of the former Soviet Union's rapid growth in the early decades of central planning resulted from using more labor, capital, and land in the production process—taking up "slack" in the economy. But in time this means of increasing real output was exhausted. Soviet labor force participation rates were among the highest in the world so there was little or no opportunity to recruit more workers. Furthermore, population and labor force growth slowed significantly. While the annual average increase in the labor force was about 1.5 percent in the 1970s, it slowed to about 0.6 percent in the 1980s. Similarly, the percentage of domestic output devoted to investment was comparatively high and could only be increased by reducing output devoted to consumption. Because of the low standard of living in the former Soviet Union, it was unpopular and politically difficult to further increase the output of capital goods at the expense of consumption. Also, natural conditions limited the availability of additional farmland. Occasional attempts to bring more land of marginal quality into crop production were counterproductive in that yields were minimal and the land lost to grazing.

The alternative to growth through the use of more inputs is to increase the productivity or efficiency of available inputs. But this is a more complex and difficult way of achieving economic growth. Productivity growth requires modern capital equipment, innovation and technological progress, and strong material incentives for workers and managers—none of which characterized the traditional Soviet planning system. Indeed, labor productivity in the former Soviet Union was estimated to be only 35 to 40 percent that of American workers.

4 Planning Problems

The problem of centrally coordinating economic activity becomes much more difficult as an economy grows and develops. Early planning under Stalin in the 1930s and 1940s resembled the simple World War II planning of western cap-

GLOBAL PERSPECTIVE 23-1

Consumption and product availability: former Soviet Union and the United States, mid 1980s

Because the former Soviet Union allocated large quantities of resources to industrialization and the military, the availability of consumer goods was far below that found in the United States.

Product	United States	Soviet Union
Wheat (kilograms per capita)	329	322
Meat (kilograms per capita)	74	47
Automobiles (per 1000 persons)	555	42
Washing machines (% of households)	74	55
TVs (per 1000 persons)	815	396
Radios (per 1000 persons)	2123	306
Energy consumed (kilograms per capita)	9563	5549
Telephones (per 1000 persons)	501	120
Personal computers (per 1000 persons)	229	2

Source: *Statistical Abstract of the United States,* 1988.

italist nations. A few key production goals were established and resources were centrally directed toward fulfilling those goals regardless of costs or consumer welfare. But the past success of such "campaign planning" resulted in a more complex, industrially advanced economy. Products became more sophisticated and complex and there were more industries for which to plan. Planning techniques workable in the Stalinist era became inadequate and inefficient in the more advanced Soviet economy of the 1970s and 1980s. The Soviet economy outgrew its planning mechanisms.

5 Inadequate Success Indicators

Market economies have a single, comprehensive success indicator—profits. Each firm's success or failure is measured by its profits or losses. Profits depend on consumer demand, production efficiency, and product quality.

In contrast, the major success indicator of a Soviet enterprise was its fulfillment of a quantitative production target assigned by the central planners. This generated inefficient practices because production costs, product quality, and product-mix became secondary considerations at best. Achieving least-cost production is nearly impossible without a system of genuine market prices accurately reflecting the relative scarcity or economic value of various resources. Product quality was frequently sacrificed by managers and workers who were awarded bonuses for fulfilling quantitative, not qualitative, targets. If meeting production goals of a television or automobile manufacturing plan meant sloppy assembly work, so be it.

Finally, it is difficult for planners to assign quantitative production targets without unintentionally producing ridiculous distortions in output. If the production target for an enterprise manufacturing nails is specified in terms of weight (tons of nails), it will tend to produce all large nails. But if its target is a quantity (thousands of nails), it will be motivated to use available inputs to produce all small nails. The problem is that the economy needs *both* large and small nails.

6 Incentive Problems Perhaps the main deficiency of central planning was the lack of economic incentives. The market systems of western economies have built-in signals resulting in the efficient use of resources. Profits and losses generate incentives for firms and industries to increase or decrease production. If a product is in short supply, its price and profitability will increase and producers will be motivated to expand production. Conversely, surplus supply means falling prices and profits and a reduction in output. Successful innovations in the form of either product quality or production techniques are sought because of their profitability. Greater work effort by labor means higher money incomes which can be translated into a higher real standard of living.

These actions and adjustments do not occur under central planning. The output-mix of the former Soviet economy was determined by the central planners. If their judgments as to the quantities of automobiles, razor blades, underwear, and vodka wanted by the populace at governmentally determined prices were incorrect, there would be *persistent* shortages and surpluses of products. But the managers who oversaw the production of these goods were rewarded for fulfilling their assigned production goals; they had no incentive to adjust production in response to product shortages or surpluses. And they did not have changes in prices and profitability to signal that more or less of each product was desired. Thus in the for-

mer Soviet Union many products were unavailable or in short supply, while other unwanted goods languished in warehouses.

Incentives to innovate were almost entirely absent; indeed, innovation was often resisted. Soviet enterprises were essentially governmentally owned monopolies. As a result, there was no private gain to managers or workers for improving product quality or developing more efficient production techniques. Historically, government-imposed innovations were resisted by enterprise managers and workers. The reason was that new production processes were usually accompanied by higher and unrealistic production targets, underfulfillment, and loss of bonuses.

Innovation also lagged because there was no competition. New firms could not come into being to introduce better products, superior managerial techniques, or more efficient production methods. Similarly, the Soviet goal of economic self-sufficiency isolated its enterprises from the competitive pressures of international markets. In general, over an extended period Soviet enterprises produced the same products with the same techniques, with both goods and techniques becoming increasingly obsolete by world standards.

Nor were individual workers motivated to work hard, because of a lack of material incentives. Because of the low priority assigned to consumer goods in the plans, there was only a limited array of low-quality goods and services available to Soviet workers-consumers. (The price of an automobile was far beyond the means of average factory workers, and for those able to buy, the waiting period was one to five years.) While hard work might result in promotions and bonuses, the increase in *money* income did not translate into a proportionate increase in *real* income. Why work hard for additional income if there is nothing to buy with the money you earn? As a Soviet worker once lamented to a western journalist: "The government pretends to pay us and we pretend to work."

The Gorbachev Reforms

The deteriorating Soviet economy of the 1970s and early 1980s prompted then-President Mikhail Gorbachev to introduce in 1986 a reform program described as **perestroika,** a restructuring of the economy. This economic restructuring was accompanied by **glasnost,** a campaign for greater openness and democratization in both political and economic affairs. Under *glasnost,* workers, consumers, enterprise managers, political leaders, and others were provided greater opportunity to voice complaints and make suggestions for improving the economy.

The **Gorbachev reforms** involved six interrelated elements: (1) the modernization of industry; (2) greater decentralization of decision making; (3) provision for a limited private enterprise sector; (4) improved worker discipline and incentives; (5) a more rational price system; and (6) an enlarged role in the international economy.

While *perestroika* had some initial success, it did not comprehensively address the systemic economic problems facing the Soviet Union. In retrospect, *perestroika* was more in the nature of traditional Soviet "campaigns" to elicit better performance within the general framework of the planned economy. It was *not* an overall program of institutional change such as those adopted by Poland and Hungary. Thus, in the late 1980s the Soviet economy was stagnating; some estimates put its growth rate at only 2 percent per year, while others indicated it did not grow at all. In late 1991 Gorbachev's successor, Boris Yeltsin, outlined a program of radical or "shock therapy" reform to move the economy from planning to a market system.

QUICK REVIEW 23-2

■ The failure of central planning in the former Soviet Union was evidenced by diminished growth rates, low-quality goods, and the failure to provide a rising standard of living.

■ The collapse of the Soviet economy in the 1980s was attributable to *a* a large military burden; *b* chronic inefficiencies in agriculture; *c* the need to expand real output by increasing input productivity rather than increasing the quantity of inputs; *d* the inability of traditional planning techniques to deal with the growing complexity of the Soviet economy; *e* inadequate success indicators; and *f* ineffectual incentives to produce, innovate, and work.

■ The Gorbachev reforms of the late 1980s centered on *perestroika* ("restructuring") and *glasnost* ("openness") but failed to provide major systemic change.

TRANSITION TO A MARKET SYSTEM

The former Soviet republics—particularly Russia—have committed themselves to making the transition to a market economy. What are the components of such a dramatic reform program?

Privatization

If entrepreneurship is to come into existence, private property rights must be established and protected by law. This means that existing government property—farmland, housing, factories, machinery and equipment, stores—must be transferred to private owners. It also means that new private firms must be allowed to form and develop.

Promotion of Competition

The industrial sector of the former Soviet Union consisted of large state-owned enterprises in which average employment exceeded 800 workers. Thirty to 40 percent of total industrial production was produced by single-firm "industries." When several enterprises produced a product, their actions were coordinated by the planning process to create a cartel. In short, most production took place under monopoly or near-monopoly conditions.

Realization of an efficient market economy requires the dismantling of these public monopolies and the creation of antitrust laws to sustain competition. Privatization without "demonopolization" will be of limited benefit to the economy. Existing monopolies must be restructured or split apart as separate, competing firms. For example, a tractor manufacturing enterprise with four plants could be separated into four independent and competing firms. The establishment and guarantee of property rights are prerequisite to the creation and entry of new firms into previously monopolized industries. Joint ventures between Russia and foreign companies provide a further avenue for increasing competition, as does opening the economy to international trade. Recent legislation has opened the door for foreign firms to invest directly in Russia.

Limited and Reoriented Role for Government

The transition to a market economy will curtail government's economic role. The government must reduce its involvement to those tasks associated with a market economy: providing an appropriate legal framework; maintaining competition; reducing excessive inequality in the distribution of income and wealth; making market adjustments where spillover costs or benefits are large; providing public goods and services; and stabilizing the economy (Chapter 5).

Many of these functions will be new to the Russian government, at least in the environment of a market system. Unemployment and overt inflation were controlled by central planning. Historically, ambitious production plans and overstaffing of enterprises yielded low unemployment rates while government price-setting controlled the price level. The task will be to develop monetary and fiscal policies—and institutional arrangements appropriate to their implementation—to indirectly provide macroeconomic stability. Restructuring will likely result in substantial short-run unemployment as inefficient public enterprises are closed or fail to be viable under private ownership. Thus, a priority goal will be to establish a *social safety net* for Russian citizens. In particular, a program of unemployment insurance must be established, not only on equity grounds but also to reduce worker resistance to the transition. Similarly, antitrust legislation of some sort will be needed to maintain competitive markets.

Price Reform: Removing Controls

Unlike competitive market prices, the prices established by the Soviet government bore no relationship to the economic value of either products or resources. In an effectively functioning competitive market system the price of a product equates, at the margin, the value consumers place on that good ("benefits") and the value of the resources used in its production ("costs"). When free markets achieve this equality for all goods and services, the economy's scarce resources are being used efficiently to satisfy consumer wants.

But in the former Soviet Union both input and output prices were fixed by government and in many instances were not changed for long periods of time. Because input prices did not measure the relative scarcities of resources, it was impossible for a firm to minimize real production costs. With fixed prices it is impossible to produce a unit of X in such a way as to minimize the sacrifice of alternative goods.

Example: High energy prices have caused firms in market economies to curtail its use. But energy was underpriced in the former Soviet Union (the world's largest producer of energy) and its industries used two to three times as much energy per unit of output as leading industrial countries.

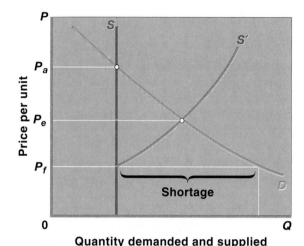

Quantity demanded and supplied

FIGURE 23-1   The effects of government price fixing
Central planners establish below-equilibrium prices such as P_f on many basic consumer goods to make them widely available to everyone. But in fact at such low prices quantity demanded exceeds quantity supplied and this shortage means that many consumers cannot obtain such goods. Assuming no privatization, abandonment of government price fixing would raise price from P_f to P_a. With privatization and an accompanying increase in output as price rises, price would increase from P_f to P_e. In either event, the decontrol of prices can be expected to be inflationary.

A difficult problem arises in making the transition from government- to market-determined prices because historically the prices of many basic consumer goods were fixed at low levels. The Soviet rationale for this was that low prices would ensure everyone access to such goods. As Figure 23-1 shows, this pricing policy helps explain the chronic product shortages and long lines which frustrated consumers in the former Soviet Union. The perfectly inelastic supply curve S reflects the fixed output of, say, shoes for which the plan provided. (Disregard supply curve S' for the moment.) The demand curve slopes downward as it would in a market economy. Given S, the equilibrium price would be P_a. But in an effort to make shoes accessible to those with lower incomes, the government fixed the price at P_f.

But not everyone who wanted shoes at price P_f could obtain them. At P_f quantity demanded was substantially greater than quantity supplied, so there was excess demand or, in other words, a shortage. This explains the long, impatient lines of consumers and the empty shelves we saw in television news clips of Soviet shoppers. Black markets—illegal markets where goods are sold at much higher prices than those fixed by the government—were widespread. *(Key Question 7)*

Joining the World Economy

The Soviet Union was largely isolated from the world economy for almost three-quarters of a century. A key aspect of transition is to open the economy to international trade and finance.

One basic task is to make the ruble a stable convertible currency, meaning that it is acceptable in exchange for other currencies. Convertibility and stability are necessary for Russia to achieve an enlarged role in international trade and finance. Firms cannot buy from or sell to Russia unless a realistic exchange rate is established for the ruble. Nor can western firms be expected to invest in the former Soviet Union unless they are certain that rubles can be exchanged for dollars and other "hard" currencies. American and other western firms want their profits in dollars, yen, pounds, and marks, not rubles.

Opening the Russian economy to world trade will be beneficial because world markets are sources of competition and a means of acquiring much-needed superior technologies from industrially advanced capitalist nations. Liberalized international trade will put pressure on privatized Russian firms to produce efficiently products which meet world quality standards. Also, free world trade will allow Russia to realize the benefits from production based on comparative advantage—income gains which its isolation has long denied it.

Macroeconomic Stability

The transition to free markets poses the possibility of high rates of inflation. Figure 23-1 is again relevant. As government price controls on shoes are eliminated, prices will rise from P_f to P_a. With privatization, this runup of prices will be dampened somewhat by the extra output induced by the rising prices. As shown by supply curve S' in Figure 23-1, private producers will respond to higher prices by increasing quantity supplied. Nevertheless, prices will rise substantially, as from P_f to P_e. Similarly, prices will also rise for butter, soap, meat, housing, vodka, and all other goods and services whose prices have been liberalized. An important need during the transition is to control inflationary pressures.

The worst scenario is hyperinflation, where there is a "flight from the currency" and the ruble ceases to function as an effective medium of exchange because businesses and consumers find it unacceptable. In these circumstances hoarding and speculation supplant production and the economy grinds to a halt. Rapidly and unevenly rising prices also create a hostile environment for microeconomic decision making. Achieving both least-cost production (productive efficiency) and production of the most desired output-mix (allocative efficiency) is predicated on a reasonable measure of price stability.

Finally, an environment of high and volatile inflation greatly complicates achieving other components of transition. The purchase of formerly public enterprises by private buyers, the establishing of a convertible ruble, and the encouragement of both domestic and foreign investment to modernize the economy are all more difficult with the uncertainties posed by a rapidly rising price level.

Public Support: Attitudes and Values

The reforms comprising the transition from planning to markets must have wide public support. Consider some of the difficulties.

1 Bureaucratic Resistance The reforms threaten the jobs and status of many former party members and bureaucrats. These individuals continue in many instances to have positions of power and prestige and want to maintain the status quo. Ironically, those most likely to have access to formerly state-owned enterprises and other assets are those very same bureaucrats who formerly administered the failed system of central planning.

2 Worker Incentives Under a system of capitalist incentives most workers and managers will be required to be more disciplined and to work harder and more productively. This may be difficult to accept in an economy which historically has served consumers-workers poorly. Money wage increases do not provide incentives without corresponding improvements in the quantity and quality of housing, food, and other consumer goods and services.

Some observers say that many citizens in the former Soviet Union and other communist nations have acquired work habits and personality traits which will only change slowly. These include working at a leisurely pace, avoiding responsibility, resistance to innovation and change, stressing output quantity over quality, and promotion based on connections and party affiliation rather than productive efficiency. It may be wishful thinking to assume that the populace possesses a strong work ethic and a latent entrepreneurial spirit, and that these attributes will emerge as the heavy hand of central planning is removed. The citizenry has been indoctrinated for some seventy years regarding the evils of private property, profits, and capitalist enterprise. The "mental residue" of communism may not be easily removed.

The Simultaneity Problem

A more subtle problem is that the reform components are interlinked. Not to move forward on all fronts may enhance the prospects for failure. Examples: Private ownership will do little to increase productive efficiency unless prices are reformed to accurately measure relative scarcities. Privatization—the selling off of state enterprises—may be helpful in reducing budget deficits. When market prices for inputs and output are unknown, it is difficult to determine the value of an enterprise when it is being privatized. The creation of a more competitive environment depends on the economy being opened to world trade and foreign investment. *(Key Question 8)*

ROLE OF ADVANCED NATIONS

The world's industrialized capitalistic nations can facilitate Russia's reforms in three ways: providing foreign aid; private investment in Russia by western firms; and helping to integrate Russia into the world economy.

Foreign Aid

Foreign aid can ease the painful transition process when planning is being abandoned and free enterprise has not yet been firmly established. In particular, foreign aid can help the Russian government avoid financing its deficits by money creation and thereby reduce the rate of inflation.

The United States and the other market democracies have a great economic stake in Russia's transition to democracy and capitalism. If the transition fails, the peace dividend associated with the end of the cold war may not be realized and the possibility of accelerated economic growth through expanded international trade with a free-market Russia will also be sacrificed. The political benefit is that a democratic Russia will isolate the last strongholds of communism—China, Cuba and North Korea—and perhaps force their leaders toward political and economic reform.

But there are serious reservations concerning aid to Russia. One is that aid is likely to be ineffectual and wasteful until the transition to market capitalism has been accomplished. Aside from humanitarian aid in the form of foodstuffs and medicine, economic aid is not likely to be of much help until capitalistic institutions are firmly in place.

A second contention is that Russia has not yet exploited the opportunity it now has to divert vast amounts of resources from the military to the civilian sector.

Finally, there is the hard political fact that foreign aid for a long-time cold war foe may not be popular among the voters of industrialized nations who see in their own countries unemployment, poor education, crime, poverty, and drug abuse.

The foreign aid issue involves a kind of chicken-or-egg problem. The west wants aid to be contingent upon a firm commitment to, or completion of, reforms; Russia contends that aid is necessary for reforms to be realized. Similarly, rapid inflation in Russia makes potential aid donors hesitant; but lack of aid forces Russia to finance its deficits with money creation, which fuels further inflation.

How much aid has been forthcoming? And in what forms? Table 23-1 shows that in 1992–1993 the west provided $23 billion in aid to Russia. International financial institutions made $3 billion available—$2.5 billion from the International Monetary Fund and $0.5 billion from the World Bank. The remaining $20 billion was bilateral or nation-to-nation aid. About $18 billion of this was in the form of export credits—government-subsidized credit—which allows Russia to buy a nation's exports via low-interest loans rather than paying cash. The remaining $2 billion is in the form of grants.

The United States' share in bilateral (nation-to-nation) aid is approximately $2 to $3 billion per year. In 1994 the United States pledged $2 billion in grants and almost $1 billion in credits.

Private Investment

As Russia moves toward a capitalistic system, will it be able to attract foreign investment to shore up its economy? In view of the vast potential market provided by some 150 million citizens, we would expect

TABLE 23-1   Foreign aid to Russia, 1992–1993

Type of aid		Amount (billions of dollars)
International financial institutions		$ 3
IMF	$2.5	
World Bank	0.5	
Bilateral aid		20
Export credits	$18	
Grants	2	
Total		$23

Source: International Monetary Fund.

the answer to be "Yes." These flows of private investment could be extremely helpful to the Russian economy, perhaps more so than public aid. In addition to providing real capital, profit-seeking private investors will bring in managerial skills, improved technologies, entrepreneurial behavior, and marketing connections.

But substantial obstacles face foreign firms doing business in Russia. One problem is determining who is in charge. Should you deal with the Trade Ministry in Moscow or regional officials or both? To whom does a foreign firm pay taxes, and with whom does one sign contracts? Who issues the necessary permits and licenses? Furthermore, the legislative underpinnings of commercial activities are often cumbersome, ambiguous, or simply nonexistent. In many cases reliable sources of inputs are not available. And the infrastructure—for example, communication and transportation systems—is primitive by western standards. Business taxes are among the world's highest. Racketeers regularly extort protection money from businesses and scam artists bilk investors. Bouts of hyperinflation create uncertainty and make private investors hesitant.

Membership in International Institutions

Historically the former Soviet Union distanced itself from the major international trade and financial institutions such as the International Monetary Fund (IMF), the World Bank, and the General Agreement on Tariffs and Trade (GATT). Membership in these institutions could benefit the Soviet Union. Russia was admitted to the IMF and World Bank in 1992 and, as we saw in Table 23-1, has received $3 billion in

aid from those institutions. Membership in GATT would result in lower tariff barriers for Russian exports.

A PROGRESS REPORT

What's the current status of Russia's reforms?

Accomplishments

On the positive side, several aspects of Russian economic reform have gone quite well.

1   Privatization   By late 1994 about 70 percent of the entire economy was privately held. About two-thirds of former state-owned enterprises have been privatized; 90 percent of small companies are privately owned; and 80 percent of service-sector companies are private.

The privatization process involved two phases. In the first phase the government gave vouchers, each with a designated monetary value, to 40 million Soviet citizens. Recipients could then pool these vouchers to purchase enterprises. The second phase, begun in 1994, allows state enterprises to be purchased for cash. This makes it possible for foreign investors to buy Russian enterprises and also provides much-needed capital to the enterprises.

Land reform, however, has progressed more slowly. Farmers fear the uncertainties and potential problems which might accompany privatization and free markets.

2   Price Reform   With some exceptions, government price fixing has been abandoned. In January 1992 the government decontrolled approximately 90 percent of all prices. The international value of the ruble was devalued to the current black market level and was allowed to float—that is, its value to be determined by demand and supply.

3   Low Unemployment   Despite vast structural changes and other dislocations associated with the transition to markets, massive unemployment has not yet occurred. In the spring of 1994 unemployment was slightly under 6 percent, close to full employment by international standards.

The downside of this is that many Russian workers have been forced to accept substantial wage cuts to save their jobs. The consequences have been sharply reduced living standards for such workers and growing wage inequality.

Problems

The problems Russia has encountered in its economic transition are substantial.

1 Inflation   As column 2 of Table 23-2 shows, inflation in Russia has been enormous. The sources of this inflation are several.

First, prices were decontrolled in January 1992 and, as expected, prices on many products tripled or quadrupled almost overnight (Figure 23-1).

Second, Russian households stored massive amounts of currency and deposits at savings banks during years of waiting for scarce consumer goods to become more abundant. This **ruble overhang** helped fuel inflation once prices were decontrolled.

The third and most important source of inflation has been large government deficits financed by increases in the money supply. The deficits in turn have many roots. First, privatization of state enterprises has caused the government to lose an important source of revenue—firm profits. Second, the uncertainties inherent in the transition have led to widespread tax avoidance. Many local governments have withheld tax payments to the central government. Large numbers of privatized businesses have avoided the new 28 percent value-added (sales) tax. And, ironically, the government's anti-alcohol campaign has led to a loss of vodka-tax revenues. Third, the government has extended massive subsidy credits to both industry and agriculture and has increased welfare benefits to ease transition problems.

One dramatic side effect of Russia's inflation has been the plunging international value of the ruble. When the ruble was floated in early 1992, the exchange rate was 90 rubles (R) for 1 dollar (R90 = $1). By January 1994 the ruble had fallen to R1607 = $1 and plunged to R3926 = $1 in the fall of 1994 before recovering somewhat as the result of Russian Central Bank intervention. Such drastic changes in the ruble's international value are obviously detrimental to Russia's world trade.

2 Falling Output and Living Standards   Real output began to fall in the 1980s, but its decline has accelerated during the reforms. Column 3 of Table

TABLE 23-2   Inflation and real GDP in Russia, 1991–1994

(1) Year	(2) Rate of inflation	(3) Growth of real GDP (percent)
1991	93	−13
1992	1353	−19
1993	896	−12
1994*	292	−12

*Estimate.

Source: International Monetary Fund and Russian authorities.

23-2 documents recent declines. Note that the fall in real GDP bottomed out in 1992 at 19 percent, and the government's program hopes to limit the drop to 12 percent in 1994.

Causes of these declines include: (1) rapid inflation, which created an uncertain environment for borrowing and investing; (2) the unraveling of Russia's international trade relationships with former communist-bloc nations of eastern Europe; (3) the bankruptcy and closing of many former state-owned enterprises which could not survive in a market environment; and (4) the massive reallocation of resources required by the reforms and the downgrading of the military.

We know that output is income. Declining real output has meant declines in Russian living standards. Farmers, government employees, and pensioners have been hard hit, and as we have noted, many workers have had to accept deep wage cuts to keep their jobs.

3 Inequality and Social Costs   Economic inequality has increased during the transition. As noted, many farmers, pensioners, and state employees have been impoverished. A small enriched elite—some associated with honest entrepreneurship and others with corruption, illegal activities, and speculation—is also emerging. Considerable friction between gainers and losers fuels public doubts as to the desirability of a market economy. Greater economic insecurity exists; medical and educational services have deteriorated, and school enrollments have declined. So has life expectancy. In 1988 the life expectancy of Russian men was 65 years. It is currently 59 years, thirteen less than American males.

QUICK REVIEW 23-3

■ Russia has made the commitment to become a capitalistic system. Ingredients in the transition from planning to markets include *a* creating private property and property rights; *b* promoting competition; *c* limiting and reformulating government's role; *d* removing domestic price controls; *e* opening the economy to international market forces; *f* establishing monetary and fiscal policies to stabilize the economy; and *g* sustaining public support for the reforms.

■ Russia's reform effort may be assisted by foreign aid, private investment by foreign firms, and membership in international trade and lending institutions.

■ Substantial progress has been made in privatization and price decontrol; unemployment has not yet been a serious problem. However, inflation has been severe; real output and living standards have fallen; and economic inequality has increased.

FUTURE PROSPECTS

There is widespread disagreement among experts as to the prospects for the success of Russia's transition to a market economy.

Destabilization and Collapse

The pessimistic view is that Russia is now plagued by highly volatile economic and political conditions which could undermine both economic reforms and democratization. In particular, the Russian government's persistent deficits, financed by money creation, pose the possibility of hyperinflation and collapse as inflation and government weaknesses feed upon one another. A weak and indecisive central government will find it difficult to impose and collect taxes. Businesses and political subdivisions will evade or withhold tax payments because the central government cannot effectively enforce collection. Widespread tax evasion means declining tax revenues, enlarged budget deficits, and therefore more inflation and financial instability. Declining tax revenues further weaken the government's ability to enforce tax laws, so a kind of vicious circle continues until political and economic collapse results. Declining revenues also cripple the central government's ability to perform other basic functions, such as maintaining law and order and providing a social safety net for its citizens. A longing may arise for the old political order and economic security of communism, leading to abandonment of economic reforms and democracy.

Muddling Through

A more optimistic view is that Russia's reform process is relatively new and that the most severe economic dislocations in the form of inflation and a declining real output may be behind it. As Table 23-2 suggests, while inflation and real GDP declines are still at serious levels, the rate of inflation is falling and production declines may be bottoming out.

More positively, the private sector is developing rapidly. Some 70,000 state enterprises have been at least partly privatized and about 18,000 new private firms have arisen. Financial and securities markets are beginning to emerge, and perhaps some of the estimated $40 billion which Russians hold abroad will return to fuel investment and growth. While Russia's central planning-to-markets transition might span another decade or so, with further hardships, collapse of its economic and political reforms and a return to socialism are unlikely.

CHAPTER SUMMARY

1 The labor theory of value is a central principle of Marxian ideology. Capitalists, as property owners, allegedly expropriate most of labor's value as profits or surplus value.

2 Virtually complete state ownership of property resources and central planning historically were the major institutional features of the Soviet economy.

3 Characteristics of Soviet planning included **a** emphasis on industrialization and military strength; **b** overcommitment of resources; **c** economic growth based on additional inputs rather than increased productivity; **d** allocation of resources by bureaucratic rather than market decisions; **e** economic self-sufficiency; and **f** passive macroeconomic policies.

4 The basic problem Soviet central planners faced was

LAST WORD

CHINA: EMERGING ECONOMIC SUPERPOWER?

The characteristics and consequences of China's reforms are quite different from those of Russia.

China has achieved a remarkable 8 to 9 percent growth of real output over the last decade. In 1992 its growth rate was a spectacular 12.8 percent! In terms of real GDP China has emerged as the world's third largest economy, behind only the United States and Japan. If the current 6 or $6\frac{1}{2}$ percentage point differential in the growth rates of China and America persist, China would become the world's largest economy shortly after 2010 (even though its per capita output will remain far below that of the major industrial nations because of its huge population).

The direction of reform in both China and Russia is the same—from central planning to markets. Why, then, has China done so well compared to Russia? While there is considerable disagreement among experts, the answer might lie in the different characteristics of China's reforms.

1 "Shock Therapy" versus Gradualism Russia pursued a rapid and radical "shock therapy" approach

to reform, seeking to institute privatization, price liberalization, competition, macroeconomic stability, and other elements of reform in a short time. China's reforms, begun in 1978, have been piecemeal and gradual.

2 Political and Economic Reform Russia believed its political apparatus—the Communist Party in particular—was an obstacle to economic reform. Political

achieving coordination or internal consistency in their plans to avoid bottlenecks and the chain reaction of production failures which they cause.

5 Diminishing growth rates, shoddy consumer goods, and the inability to provide a promised high standard of living were all outcomes of the failure of Soviet central planning.

6 Stagnation of the agricultural sector, a growing labor shortage, and the burden of a large military establishment contributed to the failure of the Soviet economy. However, the primary causes of failure were the inability of central planning to coordinate a more complex economy, the absence of rational success indicators, and the lack of adequate economic incentives.

7 The Gorbachev reforms attempted to restructure the economy and introduce greater political "openness," but did not address fundamental systemic deficiencies.

8 To change from central planning to a market economy, Russia must move from public to private ownership of property; establish a competitive environment for businesses; restructure government's role to activities appropriate to capitalism; abandon state-determined prices in favor of market-determined prices; integrate its system into the world economy; provide price level and employment stability; and sustain public support for the reforms.

9 Industrialized capitalist nations may assist Russia's transition by **a** providing foreign aid; **b** encouraging private firms to invest in Russia; and **c** facilitating Russian membership in international financial and tariff-determining institutions.

10 While progress has been made in privatization and price decontrol, Russia has experienced severe inflation and significant declines in real output and living standards.

TERMS AND CONCEPTS

labor theory of value	central economic	Gorbachev reforms	*glasnost*
surplus value	planning	*perestroika*	ruble overhang
state ownership			

reform or democratization preceded economic reform. China has sought economic reform under the strong guidance of its Communist Party. China's view is that the upsetting of the political system would generate endless debate, competition for power, and ultimate stagnation and failure of economic reforms. China feels communist dictatorship and markets are compatible; Russia does not.

3 Role of SOEs Russia focused most of its institutional reform on privatizing its state-owned enterprises (SOEs), which produce most of its GDP. China has protected the existence and development of its SOEs, while simultaneously encouraging the creation of competing private enterprises.

4 Ties to the World Economy Russia has sought to integrate itself into the world economy by floating the ruble, lowering international trade barriers, and seeking membership in international institutions such as the IMF. China established "special economic zones" along its coast which eliminated the government's monopoly on foreign trade and finance. The purpose was to attract foreign capital and foreign companies, along with their advanced technologies and business expertise. The result has been burgeoning growth in these zones, spearheaded by ethnic Chinese businesspersons in Hong Kong, Taiwan, and elsewhere in Asia.

Can China sustain its economic surge? Many experts are optimistic. The economy is highly competitive; saving rates are very high, encouraging the financing of industrial investment; rising agricultural productivity permits transfer of redundant farm labor to industry; the labor force has sufficient education and skills to support further industrialization; and its current low level of technology has the potential for substantial efficiency gains by adopting superior world technology.

Perhaps the main reason for pessimism is the widening gap between economic reform and political control. China remains a politically repressive society. As a rising standard of living permits its citizenry to make more economic choices, it may also decide it wants to choose the kind of government it wants and who will run that government. China's authoritarian capitalism may contain the seeds of upheaval, chaos, and even civil war, which bodes ill for continued economic progress.

QUESTIONS AND STUDY SUGGESTIONS

1 Compare the ideology and institutional framework of the former Soviet economy with that of American capitalism. Contrast the manner in which production was motivated in the Soviet Union compared to how it is motivated in the United States.

2 Discuss the problem of coordination which faced central planners in the former Soviet Union. Explain how a planning failure can cause a chain reaction of additional failures.

3 How was the number of automobiles to be produced determined in the former Soviet Union? In the United States? How are the decisions implemented in the two different types of economies?

4 What were the major characteristics and goals of Soviet central planning?

5 What was the evidence of the failure of Soviet planning? Explain why Soviet economic growth diminished after 1970.

6 Explain why the use of quantitative output targets as the major success indicator for Soviet enterprises contributed to economic inefficiency.

7 *Key Question Use a supply and demand diagram to explain why persistent shortages of many consumer goods occurred in the former Soviet Union. Why has the transformation to a market economy been accompanied by inflation? Why were black markets so common in the Soviet Union?*

8 *Key Question What specific changes must be made to transform the Soviet economy to a market system? Why is it important that these changes be introduced simultaneously?*

9 What progress has Russia achieved in its transition to a market economy? What problems has it encountered?

10 Briefly assess the quantity and types of foreign aid which have been made available to Russia.

11 (Last Word) In what specific respects have Chinese economic reforms differed from Russia's? Do you believe these differences account for China's superior growth?

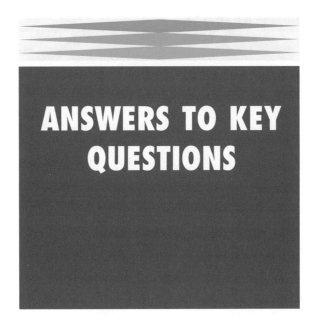

ANSWERS TO KEY QUESTIONS

Chapter 1

1-1 Effective policy must be based on sound theory—factually supported generalizations about behavior. Two methods are used to obtain sound economic theory: deduction and induction.

In *deduction,* the economist starts directly with an untested hypothesis. The hypothesis or theory is tested for accuracy by gathering and examining all relevant facts. If the facts support the hypothesis, the theory can be used for policy. The other approach is *induction,* in which the economist starts by gathering facts and then notes their relationship to each other. Eventually, the data may reveal a cause and effect pattern from which a theory results. From this theory, economic policy relevant to the real world can be formulated. Deduction and induction are complementary and often used simultaneously.

As for the quotation, the opposite is true; any theory not supported by facts is not a good theory. Good economics is empirically grounded; it is based on facts and highly practical.

1-5   (a), (d), and (f) are macro; (b), (c), and (e) are micro.

1-6   (a) and (c) are positive; (b) and (d) are normative.

1-9   (a) The fallacy of composition is the mistake of believing that something true for an individual part is necessarily true for the whole. Example: A single auto producer can increase its profits by lowering its price and taking business away from its competitors. But matched price cuts by all auto manufacturers will not necessarily yield higher industry profits.

(b) The "after this, therefore because of this" fallacy is incorrectly reasoning that when one event precedes another, the first event *necessarily* caused the second. Example: Interest rates rise, followed by an increase in the rate of inflation, leading to the erroneous conclusion the rise in interest rates caused the inflation. Higher interest rates slow inflation.

Cause and effect relationships are difficult to isolate because "other things" are continually changing.

1-13 This behavior can be explained in terms of marginal costs and marginal benefits. At a standard restaurant, items are priced individually—they have a positive marginal cost. If you order more, it will cost you more. You order until the marginal benefit from the extra food no longer exceeds the positive marginal cost. At a buffet you pay a flat fee no matter how much you eat. Once the fee is paid, additional food items have a zero marginal cost. You therefore continue to eat until your marginal benefit is also zero.

Appendix 1-2   (a) More tickets are bought at each price; the line plots to the right of the previous line. (b) and (c) Fewer tickets are bought at each price; the line plots to the left of the previous line.

Appendix 1-3   Income column: $0; $5,000; $10,000; $15,000; $20,000. Saving column: $-500; 0; $500; $1,000; $1,500. Slope = 0.1 (= $1,000 - $500)/($15,000 - $10,000). Vertical intercept = $-500. The slope shows how much saving will go up for every $1 increase in income; the intercept shows the amount of saving (dissaving) occurring when income is zero. Equation: $S = $-500 + 0.1Y$ (where S is saving and Y is income). Saving will be $750 at the $12,500 income level.

Appendix 1-6   Slopes: at $A = +4$; at $B = 0$; at $C = -4$.

Chapter 2

2-5   Economics deals with the "limited resources–unlimited wants" problem. Unemployment represents valuable resources which could have been used to produce more goods and services—to meet more wants and ease the economizing problem.

Allocative efficiency means that resources are being used to produce the goods and services most wanted by society. Society is located at the optimal point on its production possibilities curve where marginal benefit equals marginal cost for each good. *Productive efficiency* means the least costly production techniques are being used to produce wanted goods and services.

Example: manual typewriters produced using the least-cost techniques but for which there is no demand.

2-6 (a) See curve *EDCBA* in the accompanying figure. The assumptions are full employment and productive efficiency, fixed supplies of resources, and fixed technology.

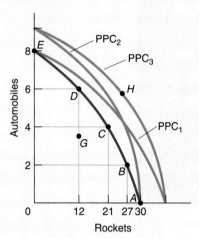

Rockets

(b) 4.5 rockets; .33 automobiles, as determined from the table. Increasing opportunity costs are reflected in the concave-from-the-origin shape of the curve. This means the economy must give up larger and larger amounts of rockets to get constant added amounts of automobiles—and vice versa.

(c) It must obtain full employment and productive efficiency.

2-9 The marginal benefit curve is downsloping; MB falls as more of a product is consumed. The first units of a good consumed yield greater additional satisfaction than subsequent units. The marginal cost curve is upsloping; MC increases as more of a product is produced. The opportunity cost of producing good A rises as resources increasingly better suited to other uses are used to produce A. The optimal amount of a particular product occurs where MB equals MC. If MC exceeds MB, fewer resources should be allocated to this use. The resources have more value in some alternative use (as reflected in MC) than in this use (as reflected in MB).

2-10 See the figure accompanying the answer to question 2-6. *G* indicates unemployment, productive inefficiency, or both. *H* is at present unattainable. Economic growth—through more inputs, better inputs, improved technology—must be achieved to attain *H*.

2-11 See question 2-6 figure. PPC₁ shows improved rocket technology. PPC₂ shows improved auto technology. PPC₃ shows improved technology in producing both products.

Chapter 3

3-2 Demand increases in (a), (c), (e), and (f); decreases in (b) and (d).

3-5 Supply increases in (a), (d), (e), and (g); decreases in (b), (c), and (f).

3-7 Data, from top to bottom: −13; −7; 0; +7; +14; and +21.
(a) $P_e = \$4.00$; $Q_e = 75,000$. Equilibrium occurs where there is neither a shortage nor surplus of wheat. At the im-

mediately lower price of $3.70, there is a shortage of 7000 bushels. At the immediately higher price of $4.30, there is a surplus of 7000 bushels.

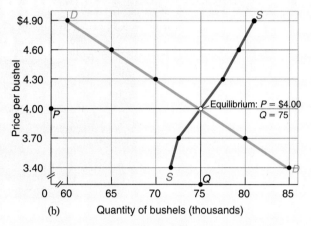

(b)   Quantity of bushels (thousands)

(c) Because at $3.40 there will be a 13,000 bushel shortage which will drive price up. Because at $4.90 there will be a 21,000 surplus which will drive the price down. Quotation is incorrect; just the opposite is true.

(d) A $3.70 ceiling causes a persistent shortage. Also, a black market (illegal sales above $3.70) might occur. Government might want to suppress inflation.

3-8 (a) Price up; quantity down; (b) Price down; quantity down; (c) Price down; quantity up; (d) Price indeterminate; quantity up; (e) Price up; quantity up; (f) Price down; quantity indeterminate; (g) Price up; quantity indeterminate; (h) Price indeterminate and quantity down.

Chapter 4

4-2 "Roundabout" production means using capital goods in the production process, enabling producers to obtain more output than through direct production. The direct way to produce a corn crop is to scatter seed about in an unplowed field. The roundabout way is to plow, fertilize, harrow, and till the field using machinery and then use a seed drill to sow the seeds in rows at the correct depth. The higher yield per acre will more than compensate the farmer for the cost of using the roundabout techniques.

To increase the capital stock at full employment, the current production of consumer goods must decrease. Moving along the production possibilities curve toward more capital goods comes at the expense of current consumption.

No, it can use its previously unemployed resources to produce more capital goods, without sacrificing consumption goods. It can move from a point inside to a point on the curve, thus obtaining more capital goods.

4-8 (a) Technique 2. Because it produces the output with least cost ($34 compared to $35 each for the other two). Economic profit will be $6 (= $40 − $34), which causes the industry to expand. Expansion continues until prices are competed down to where total revenue is $34 (equal to total cost).
(b) Adopt technique 4 because its cost is now lowest at $32.
(c) Adopt technique 1 because its cost is now lowest at $27.50.

(d) Increasing scarcity causes prices to rise. Firms ignoring higher prices will become high-cost producers and be competed out of business by firms switching to the less expensive inputs. The market system forces producers to conserve on the use of highly scarce resources. Question 8c confirms this because technique 1 was adopted because labor had become less expensive. The least-cost combination is *not* necessarily the one using the fewest inputs. The relative prices of inputs is important.

Chapter 5

5-2 The distribution of income is quite unequal. The highest 20 percent of the residents receive 10 times more income than the lowest 20 percent.

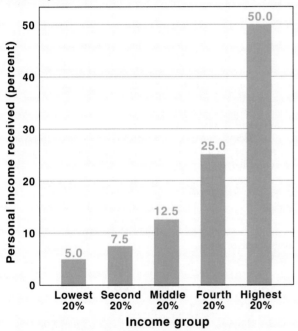

5-4 Sole proprietorship, partnership, and corporation.

Proprietorship advantages: easy to open and provides maximum freedom for the proprietor to do what she or he thinks best. Proprietorship disadvantages: limited financial resources; the owner must be a "Jack-or-Jill-of-all-trades"; and unlimited liability.

Partnership advantages: easy to organize; greater specialization of management; and greater financial resources. Disadvantages: financial resources are still limited; unlimited liability; possibility of disagreement among the partners; and precarious continuity.

Corporation advantages: can raise large amounts of money by issuing stocks and bonds; limited liability; and continuity.

Corporation disadvantages: red tape and expense in incorporating; potential for abuse of stockholder and bondholder funds; double taxation of profits; and separation of ownership and control.

The dominant role of corporations stems from the advantages cited, particularly unlimited liability and superior ability to raise money capital.

5-9 Public goods (a) are indivisible—they are produced in such large units that they cannot be sold to individuals and (b) the exclusion principle does not apply; once the goods are produced nobody—including free riders—can be excluded from the goods' benefits. The free-rider problem explains the significance of the exclusion principle. The government must provide public goods such as the judicial system, national defense, police protection, and weather warning systems since people can obtain the benefits without paying. Government must levy taxes to get revenues to pay for public goods.

5-10 If on the curve, the only way to obtain more public goods is to reduce the production of private goods (from C to B).

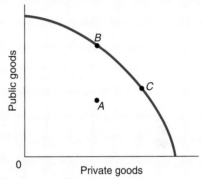

If operating inside the curve, it can expand the production of public goods without sacrificing private goods (from A to B).

5-15 Total tax = $13,000; marginal tax rate = 40%; average tax rate = 26%. This is a progressive tax; the average tax rate rises as income goes up.

Chapter 6

6-3 An export increases domestic output and revenues to domestic export firms. Because these firms would employ more resources, household income would rise. Households would then use part of their greater income to buy more imported goods.

United States exports in 1993 were $457 billion (flow 13) and imports were $590 billion (flow 16).

Flow 14 must equal flow 13. Flow 15 must equal flow 16.

6-4 (a) Yes, because the opportunity cost of radios is less (1R = 1C) in South Korea than in the United States (1R = 2C). South Korea should produce radios and the United States, chemicals.

(b) If they specialize, the United States can produce 20 tons of chemicals and South Korea can produce 30,000 radios. Before specialization South Korea produced alternative B and the United States alternative U for a total of 28,000 radios (24,000 + 4,000) and 18 tons of chemicals (6 tons + 12 tons). The gain is 2,000 radios and 2 tons of chemicals.

(c) The limits of the terms of trade are determined by the comparative cost conditions in each country before trade: 1R = 1C in South Korea and 1R = 2C in the United States. The terms of trade must be somewhere between these two ratios for trade to occur.

If the terms of trade are 1R = 1½C, South Korea would end up with 26,000 radios (= 30,000 − 4,000) and 6 tons of chemicals. The United States would have 4,000 radios and

14 tons of chemicals (= 20 − 6). South Korea has gained 2,000 radios. The United States has gained 2 tons of chemicals.

(d) Yes, the world is obtaining more output from its fixed resources.

6-6 The first part of this statement is incorrect. Our exports create a domestic *supply* of foreign currencies, not a domestic demand for them. The second part of the statement is accurate. The foreign demand for dollars (from our exports) generates a supply of foreign currencies to Americans.

A decline in American incomes or a weakening of American preferences for foreign goods would reduce our imports, reducing our demand for foreign currencies. These currencies would depreciate (the dollar would appreciate). Dollar appreciation means our exports will decline and our imports will rise.

6-10 GATT is the General Agreement on Tariffs and Trade. Its provisions apply to more than 120 nations, affecting people around the globe. The Uruguay Round of GATT negotiations produced an agreement which will reduce tariffs, liberalize trade in services, cut agricultural subsidies, protect intellectual property, reduce import quotas, and create the World Trade Organization.

The EU and NAFTA are free-trade blocs. GATT reduces tariffs and liberalizes trade for nearly *all* nations, not just countries in these blocs. The ascendancy of the EU and the passage of NAFTA encouraged nations to reach a new GATT agreement. No nation wanted to be disadvantaged by the formation of the trade blocs.

Chapter 7

7-2 Because the dollar value of final goods includes the dollar value of the intermediate goods. If intermediate goods were counted, then double (or triple or quadruple, etc.) counting would occur. The value of the steel used in autos is included in the price of the auto (the final product).

GNP is the dollar value of final goods and services produced by Americans within the United States and abroad. GDP is the value of final goods and services produced by Americans and others within the geographical borders of the United States.

NDP is GDP less depreciation—the physical capital used up in producing this year's output.

7-5 When gross investment exceeds depreciation, net investment is positive and the economy is said to be expanding; it ends the year with more physical capital. When gross investment equals depreciation, net investment is zero and the economy is said to be static; it ends the year with the same amount of physical capital. When depreciation is greater than gross investment, net investment is negative and the economy is said to be declining; it ends the year with less physical capital.

The first statement is wrong. Just because *net* investment was a minus $6 billion in 1933 doesn't mean the economy produced no new capital in that year. It simply means depreciation exceeded gross investment by $6 billion. Although gross investment was positive, the economy ended the year with $6 billion less capital.

The second statement is correct. If only one $20 spade is bought by a construction firm in the entire economy in a year and no other physical capital is bought, then gross investment is $20. This is true even though *net* investment will be highly negative, equaling the whole of depreciation less the $20 spade. If not even this $20 spade had been bought, then gross investment would have

been zero. But "gross investment can never be *less* than zero."

7-7 (a) GDP = $388; NDP = $361; (b) NI = $339; (c) PI = $291; (d) DI = $265.

7-10 In this hypothetical case, the GDP price index for 1974 was 0.65 (= $39/$60). Between 1974 and 1987, the price level rose by 53.85 percent [= (($60 − $39)/$39) × 100].

7-11 Values for real GDP, top to bottom of the column: $1930.5 (inflating); $2339.4 (inflating); $2687.4 (inflating); $3267.8 (inflating); $3702.7 (inflating); $4716.4 (deflating).

Chapter 8

8-1 The four phases of a typical business cycle, starting at the bottom, are: trough, recovery, peak, and recession. The length of a cycle varies from two to three years to as much as six or seven years or even longer.

Normally there will be a pre-Christmas spurt, followed by a slackening in January after post-Christmas sales. This normal seasonal variation must not be viewed as signaling a boom in the first case nor a recession in the second. From decade to decade the long-term, or secular, trend of the United States economy has been upward. If there is no growth of GDP over a period, this does not signal all is normal but rather the economy is functioning below its trend rate of output growth.

Because durable goods last, consumers can postpone buying replacements. This happens when people are worried about a recession and whether there will be a paycheck next month. And firms will soon quit producing what people are not buying. Durable goods industries therefore suffer large output declines during recessions.

In contrast, consumers cannot long postpone the buying of many nondurables such as food and therefore recessions only slightly reduce output.

8-3 GDP gap = 10 percent [= (9 − 5) × 2.5]; forgone output = $50 billion (= 10% of $500 billion).

8-5 Labor force = 230 [= 500 − (120 + 150)]; unemployment rate = 10% [= (23/230) × 100].

8-7 This year's rate of inflation = 10% [(121 − 110)/110] × 100.

Dividing 70 by the annual rate of increase of any variable (for instance, the rate of inflation or population growth) will give the approximate number of years for doubling of the variable.

(a) 35 years (= 70/2); (b) 14 years (= 70/5); (c) 7 years (= 70/10).

Chapter 9

9-6 Data for completing the table (top to bottom). Consumption: $244; $260; $276; $292; $308; $324; $340; $356; $372. APC: 1.02; 1.00; .99; .97; .96; .95; .94; .94; .93. APS: −.02; .00; .01; .03; .04; .05; .06; .06; .07. MPC: .80, throughout. MPS: .20, throughout.

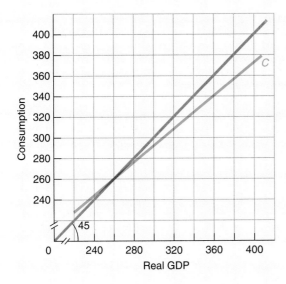

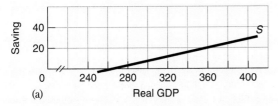

(a)

(b) Break-even income = $260. By borrowing or using past savings.

(c) Technically, the APC diminishes and the APS increases because these schedules have positive and negative vertical intercepts (Appendix to Chapter 1). MPC and MPS are measured by the *slopes* of the consumption and saving schedules; they relate to *changes* in consumption and saving as income changes. With straight-line consumption and saving schedules, these slopes do not change as the level of income changes; the slopes and thus the MPC and MPS are unrelated to the intercepts.

9-8 Aggregate investment: (a) $20 billion; (b) $30 billion; (c) $40 billion. This is the investment-demand curve because we have applied the rule of undertaking all investment up to the point where the expected rate of net profit, *r*, equals the interest rate, *i*.

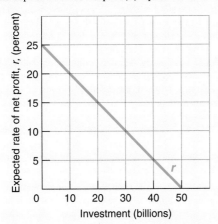

9-10 Saving data for completing the table (top to bottom): $−4; $0; $4; $8; $12; $16; $20; $24; $28.

Equilibrium GDP = $340 billion, determined where (1) aggregate expenditures equal GDP (*C* of $324 billion + *I* of $16 billion = GDP of $340 billion); or (2) where planned *I* = planned *S* (*I* of $16 billion = *S* of $16 billion). Equilibrium level of employment = 65 million; MPC = .8; MPS = .2.

9-11 At the $380 billion level of GDP, planned saving = $24 billion; planned investment = $16 billion (from the question). This deficiency of $8 billion of planned investment causes an unintended $8 billion *increase* in inventories—inventory investment. Actual investment is $24 billion (= $16 billion of planned investment *plus* $8 billion of unplanned inventory investment), matching the $24 billion of actual saving.

At the $300 billion level of GDP, planned saving = $8 billion; planned investment = $16 billion (from the question). This excess of $8 billion of planned investment causes an unintended $8 billion *decline* in inventories—inventory disinvestment. Actual investment is $8 billion (= $16 billion of planned investment *minus* $8 billion of an unplanned inventory disinvestment). Actual saving is also $8 billion.

When unintended investment in inventories occur, as at the $380 billion level of GDP, businesses revise their production plans downward and GDP falls. When unintended disinvestment in inventories occur, as at the $300 billion level of GDP, businesses revise their production plans upward and GDP rises. Equilibrium GDP—in this case, $340 billion—occurs were planned investment equals planned saving.

Chapter 10

10-2 The simple multiplier effect is the multiple by which the equilibrium GDP increases when any component of aggregate expenditures changes. The greater the MPC (the smaller the MPS), the greater the multiplier.

MPS = 0, multiplier = infinity; MPS = .4, multiplier = 2.5; MPS = .6, multiplier = 1.67; MPS = 1; multiplier = 1.

MPC = 1; multiplier = infinity; MPC = .9, multiplier = 10; MPC = .67; multiplier = 3; MPC = .5, multiplier = 2; MPC = 0, multiplier = 1.

Change in GDP = $40 billion (= $8 billion × multiplier of 5); change in GDP = $24 billion ($8 billion × multiplier of 3). The simple multiplier takes account of only the leakage of saving. The complex multiplier also takes account of leakages of taxes and imports, making the complex multiplier less than the simple multiplier.

10-5 (a) Equilibrium GDP for the closed economy = $400 billion.

(b) Net export data for column 5 (top to bottom): $−10 billion in each space. Aggregate expenditure data for column 6 (top to bottom): $230; $270; $310; $350; $390; $430; $470; $510. Equilibrium GDP for the open economy is $350 billion, $50 billion below the $400 billion equilibrium GDP for the closed economy. The $−10 billion of net exports reduces equilibrium GDP by $50 billion (= $400 billion − $350 billion) because the multiplier is 5. Since every rise of $50 billion of GDP increases aggregate expenditures by $40 billion, the MPC is .8, and the multiplier is 5.

(c) Net exports would fall by $10 billion and GDP would decline by $50 billion (= $10 billion × the multiplier of 5).

Net exports would increase by $10 billion and GDP would rise by $50 billion (= $10 billion × the multiplier of 5). Exports constant, increases in imports reduce GDP; decreases in imports, increase GDP.

(d) 5.

10-8 The addition of $20 billion of government expenditures and $20 billion of personal taxes increases the equilibrium GDP from $350 to $370 billion. The $20 billion increase in *G raises* equilibrium by $100 billion (= $20 billion × the multiplier of 5); the $20 billion increase in *T reduces* consumption by $16 billion (= $20 billion × the MPC of .8). This $16 billion decline in turn reduces equilibrium GDP by $80 billion (= $16 billion × multiplier of 5). The net change from adding government is $20 billion (= $100 billion − $80 billion.).

10-10 (a) Recessionary gap. Equilibrium GDP is $600 billion, while full employment GDP is $700 billion. Employment will be 20 million less than at full employment. Aggregate expenditures will have to increase by $20 billion at each level of GDP to eliminate the recessionary gap.

(b) Inflationary gap. Aggregate expenditures are excessive, causing demand-pull inflation. Aggregate expenditures will have to fall by $20 billion at each level of GDP to eliminate the inflationary gap.

(c) MPC = .8 (= $40 billion/$50 billion). MPS = .2 (= 1 − .8). Multiplier = 5 (= 1/.2).

Chapter 11

11-4 (a)

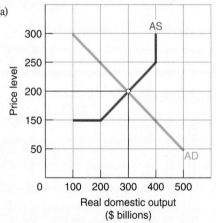

Equilibrium price level = 200. Equilibrium real output = $300 billion. No, the absolute full-capacity level of GDP is $400 billion, where the AS curve becomes vertical.

(b) At a price level of 150, real GDP supplied is a maximum of $200 billion, less than real GDP demanded of $400 billion. The shortage of real output will drive the price level up. At a price level of 250, real GDP supplied is $400 billion, which is more than real GDP demanded of $200 billion. The surplus of real output will drive down the price level. Equilibrium occurs at the price level where AS and AD intersect.

(c) Increases in consumer, investment, government, or net export spending shift the AD curve rightward. New equilibrium price level = 250. New equilibrium GDP = $400 billion. The intermediate range.

11-5 (a) Productivity level = 2.67; (b) Per unit cost of production = $.75; (c) New per unit production cost = $1.13. The AS curve would shift leftward. The price level would rise and real output would decrease; (d) New per unit cost of production = $0.375 [($2 × 150)/800]. AS curve shifts to the right; price level declines and real output increases.

11-7 (a) AD curve left; (b) AD curve right; (c) AS curve left; (d) AD curve right; (e) AD curve left; (f) AD curve right; (g) AS curve right; (h) AD curve right; (i) AS curve right; (j) AS curve left; (k) AD curve right; AS curve left; (l) AD curve left; (m) AS curve right.

11-9 (a) Price level rises and no change in real output; (b) price level drops and real output increases; (c) price level does not change, but real output rises; (d) price level does not change, but real output declines; (e) price level increases, but change in real output is indeterminate; (f) price level does not change, but real output declines.

Chapter 12

12-2 Increase in government spending = $5 billion. Decrease in taxes = $6.25 billion. (Initial new consumption spending would rise by $5 billion, because the MPC is .8.) Because part of the tax reduction ($1.25 billion) is saved, not spent. The multiplier applies only to that part of a tax cut which boosts consumption. Combination: a $1 billion increase in government spending and a $5 billion tax cut.

12-3 Reduce government spending, increase taxes, or some combination of both. See Figure 12-2 in the chapter. If the price level is flexible downward, it will fall. In the real world, the goal is to reduce *inflation*—to keep prices from rising so rapidly—not to reduce the *price level*. A "conservative" economist might favor cuts in government spending, since this would reduce the size of government. A "liberal" economist might favor a tax hike; it would preserve government spending programs.

12-7 The *full-employment budget* indicates what the Federal budgetary deficit or surplus would be if the economy were to achieve full employment throughout the year. This budget is a useful measure of fiscal policy. If the full-employment budget is moving toward deficit, fiscal policy is expansionary. If the full-employment budget is moving toward surplus, fiscal policy is contractionary. The *actual budget* simply compares *G* and *T* for the year and is an unreliable indicator of the government's fiscal policy. It does not account for shortfalls of tax revenues arising from less than full-employment output. A *structural deficit*—or a full-employment budget deficit—is the difference between *G* and *T* when the economy is at full employment. A *cyclical deficit* is the difference between *G* and *T* caused by tax revenues being below those accruing when the economy is at full employment.

At GDP$_f$, the structural deficit is *ab* and the cyclical deficit is zero. Government should raise *T* or reduce *G* to eliminate this deficit, but it may want to take this action over several years to avoid pushing the economy into recession.

12-9 It takes time to ascertain the direction the economy is moving (recognition lag), to get a fiscal policy enacted into law (administrative lag); and for the policy to have its full effect on the economy (operational lag). Meanwhile, other factors may change, rendering inappropriate a particular fiscal policy. Nevertheless, discretionary fiscal policy is a valuable tool in preventing severe recession or severe demand-pull inflation.

A political business cycle is the concept that politicians are more interested in reelection than in stabilizing the economy. Before the election, they enact tax cuts and spending increases even though this may fuel inflation. After the election, they apply the brakes to restrain inflation. The economy will slow and unemployment will rise. In this view the political process creates economic instability.

The crowding-out effect is the reduction in investment spending caused by the increase in interest rates arising from an increase in government spending, financed by borrowing. The increase in *G* was designed to increase AD but the resulting increase in interest rates may decrease *I,* thus reducing the impact of the expansionary fiscal policy.

The net export effect also derives from the higher interest rates accompanying fiscal policy. The higher interest rates make American bonds more attractive to foreign buyers. The inflow of foreign currency to buy dollars to purchase the bonds drives up the international value of the dollar, making imports less expensive for Americans and American exports more expensive for people abroad. American net exports decline, and like the crowding-out effect, diminish the expansionary fiscal policy.

It seems improbable to us that people respond to government budget deficits by reducing consumption and increasing saving in anticipation of a future tax increase tied to current budget deficits.

Chapter 13

13-5 *M*1 = currency (in circulation) + checkable deposits. The largest component of *M*1 is checkable deposits. If the face value of a coin were not greater than its intrinsic (metallic) value, people would remove them from circulation and sell them for their metallic content. *M*2 = *M*1 + noncheckable savings deposits + money market deposit accounts + small time deposits + money market mutual fund balances. *M*3 = *M*2 + large time deposits (those $100,000 or more). Near-monies include the components of *M*2 and *M*3 not included in *M*1 and, secondly, other less liquid assets such as Savings bonds and Treasury bills.

Near-monies represent wealth; the more wealth people have, the more they are likely to spend out of current income. Also, the fact that near-monies are liquid adds to potential economic instability. People may cash in their near-monies and spend the proceeds while the monetary authorities are trying to stem inflation by reducing the money supply. Finally, near-monies can complicate monetary policy because *M*1, *M*2, and *M*3 do not always change in the same direction.

The argument for including noncheckable savings deposits in a definition of money is that saving deposits can quickly be transferred to a checking account or withdrawn as cash and spent.

13-7 In the first case, the value of the dollar (year 2, relative to year 1) is $.80 (= 1/1.25); in the second case, $2 (= 1/.50). Generalization: The price level and the value of the dollar are inversely related.

13-8 (a) The level of nominal GDP. The higher this level, the greater the amount of money demanded for transactions. (b) The interest rate. The higher the interest rate, the smaller the amount of money demanded as an asset.

On a graph measuring the interest rate vertically and the amount of money demanded horizontally, the two demand for money curves can be summed horizontally to get the total demand for money. This total demand shows the total amount of money demanded at each interest rate. The equilibrium interest rate is determined at the intersection of the total demand for money curve and the supply of money curve.

(a) Expanded use of credit cards: transaction demand for money declines; total demand for money declines; interest rate falls. (b) Shortening of worker pay periods: transaction demand for money declines; total demand for money declines; interest rate falls. (c) Increase in nominal GDP: transaction demand for money increases; total demand for money increases; interest rate rises.

Chapter 14

14-2 Reserves provide the Fed a means of controlling the money supply. It is through increasing and decreasing excess reserves that the Fed is able to achieve a money supply of the size it thinks best for the economy.

Reserves are assets of commercial banks because these funds are cash belonging to them; they are a claim the commercial banks have against the Federal Reserve Bank. These reserves deposited at the Fed are a liability to the Fed because they are funds it owes; they are claims which commercial banks have against it.

Excess reserves = actual reserves − required reserves. Commercial banks can safely lend excess reserves, thereby increasing the money supply.

14-4 Banks create or add to checking account balances when they make loans; these checkable deposits are part of the money supply. People pay off loans by writing checks. Checkable deposits fall, meaning the money supply drops. Money is "destroyed."

14-8 Table data: Column (1) of Assets (top to bottom): $22,000; $38,000; $42,000. Column (2) of Assets (top to bottom): $20,000; $38,000; $42,000. Column (1) of Liabilities: $102,000. Column (2) of Liabilities: $100,000.

(a) $2000; (b) $2000; The bank has lent out its excess reserves, creating $2000 of new demand-deposit money. (c) See column (2) data; (d) Required reserves = $15,000 (= 15% of $100,000). Excess reserves = $7000 (= $22,000 − $15,000). When the bank lends out its excess reserves, the money supply increases by $7000.

14-13 (a) Required reserves = $50 billion (= 25% of $200 billion). Excess reserves = $2 billion (= $52 billion − $50 billion). Maximum amount banking system can loan = $8 billion (= 1/.25 × $2 billion). Column (1) of Assets data (top to bottom): $52 billion; $48 billion; $108 billion. Column (1) of Liabilities data: $208 billion. Monetary multiplier = 4 (1/.25).

(b) Required reserves = $40 billion (= 20% of $200 billion). Excess reserves = $12 billion (= $52 billion − $40 billion). Maximum amount banking system can lend = $60 billion (= 1/.20 × $12 billion). Column (1) data for assets after loans (top to bottom): $52 billion; $48 billion; $160 billion. Column (1) data for liabilities after loans (top to bottom): $260 billion. The decrease in the reserve ratio increases the banking systems' excess reserves from $2 billion to $12 billion and increases the size of the monetary multiplier from 4 to 5.

Chapter 15

15-2 (a) Column (1) data, top to bottom: (Commercial banks) $34; $60; $60; $150; $4; (Fed banks) $60; $4; $34; $3; $27.
(b) Column (2) data: (Commercial banks) $30; $60; $60; $147; $3; (Fed banks) $57; $3; $30; $3; $27.
(c) Column (3) data (top to bottom): $35; $58; $60; $150; $3; (Fed banks) $62; $3; $35; $3; $27.
(d1) Money supply (demand deposits) directly changes only in (b), where it decreases by $3 billion; (d2) See balance sheets; (d3) Money-creating potential of the banking system increases by $5 billion (a); decreases by $12 billion in (b) (not by $15 billion—the sale of $3 billion of bonds to the public reduced demand deposits by $3 billion, thus freeing $0.6 billion of reserves. Three billion dollars − $0.6 billion = $2.4 billion and this multiplied by the monetary multiplier of 5 = $12 billion); and increases by $10 billion in (c).

15-3 (a) Increase the reserve ratio. This would increase the size of required reserves. If the commercial banks were fully loaned up, they would have to call in loans. The money supply would decrease, interest rates would rise, and aggregate demand would decline.
(b) Increase the discount rate. This would decrease commercial bank borrowing from the Fed. Actual reserves of the commercial banks would fall, as would excess reserves and lending. The money supply would drop, interest rates would rise, and aggregate demand would decline.
(c) Sell government securities in the open market. Buyers of the bonds will write checks to the Fed on their demand deposits. When these checks clear, reserves will flow from the banking system to the Fed. The decline in reserves will reduce the money supply, which will increase interest rates and reduce aggregate demand.

15-4 The basic objective of monetary policy is to assist the economy in achieving a full-employment, noninflationary level of total output. Changes in the money supply affect interest rates, which affect investment spending and therefore aggregate demand.
(a) A steep demand for money curve makes monetary policy more effective since the steepness of the curve means that only a relatively small change in the money supply will be needed to produce large changes in interest rates. A relatively flat investment-demand curve means that only a small change in the interest rate will be sufficient to change investment sharply. (b) A high MPC (low MPS) yields a large income multiplier, meaning that a relatively small initial change in spending will multiply into a larger change in GDP.
The increase in GDP resulting from an easy money policy will increase the transactions demand for money, partially offsetting the reduction in the interest rate associated with the initial increase in the money supply. Investment spending, aggregate demand, and GDP will not rise by as much.

15-7 The Federal funds interest rate is the interest rate banks charge one another on overnight loans needed to meet the reserve requirement. The prime interest rate is the interest rate banks charge on loans to their most credit-worthy customers. The tighter the monetary policy, the fewer the excess reserves in the banking system and the higher the Federal funds rate.
The Fed wanted to reduce excess reserves, slowing the growth of the money supply. This would slow the expansion of AD and keep inflation from occurring. The prime interest rate went up.

15-8 The intent of a tight money policy would be shown as a leftward shift of the AD curve and a decline in the price level (or in the real world, a reduction in the rate of inflation). In an open economy, the interest rate hike resulting from the tight money policy would entice people abroad to buy American securities. Because they would need American dollars to buy these securities, the international demand for dollars would rise, causing the dollar to appreciate. Net exports would fall, pushing the AD curve farther leftward than in the closed economy.

Chapter 16

16-1 (a) Classical economists envision the AS curve as being perfectly vertical. When prices fall, real profits would not decrease because wage rates will fall in the same proportion. With constant real profits, firms would have no reason to change the quantities of output they supplied. Keynesians view the AS curve as being horizontal at outputs less than the full-employment output. Declines in aggregate demand in this range do not change the price level because wages and prices are assumed to be inflexible downward.
(b) Classical economists view AD as stable so long as the monetary authorities hold the money supply constant. Therefore inflation and deflation are unlikely. Keynesians view the AD curve as unstable—even if the money supply is constant—since investment spending is volatile. Decreases in AD can cause a recession; rapid increases in AD can cause demand-pull inflation.
Neither model—in these simple forms—is realistic. Wage rates and prices are not perfectly *flexible* downward as the classical vertical AS curve suggests; nor are they completely *inflexible* downward as implied by the Keynesian horizontal AS curve. A more realistic view of the economy would incorporate an AS curve having a horizontal, intermediate, and vertical range.
The Keynesian view of AD seems more realistic than the monetarist's view. Aggregate demand appears to be unstable, sometimes causing recession and other times causing demand-pull inflation.

16-5 (a) Keynesian mechanism: Change in monetary policy; change in commercial bank reserves; change in the money supply; change in the interest rate; change in investment; change in aggregate demand; change in nominal GDP (= PQ).
(b) Monetarists mechanism: Change in monetary policy; change in commercial bank reserves; change in the money supply; change in aggregate demand; change in nominal GDP (= PQ).
Because of the longer and more problematic chain in their transmission mechanism, Keynesians view monetary policy as less reliable than fiscal policy in achieving full-employment, noninflationary GDP. Monetarists believe there is a dependable link between the money supply and nominal GDP. The preferred monetary policy therefore is for the Fed to adhere to a monetary rule: increase the money supply at a constant 3 percent to 5 percent annual rate.

16-12 Refer to Figures 16-5a (Keynesian) and 16-5b (monetarism) and Figure 16-6 (rational expectations). Stabilization policy

—in this case, to increase AD—is highly effective in the Keynesian model; highly inflationary in the monetarist model; and totally ineffective in the rational expectations model.

In the RET model there is never any deviation from full-employment output—all changes in AD are fully anticipated. In the old classical model, there are temporary "lapses" from full employment until market adjustments are complete.

16-13 (b), (c), (d), and (e).

Chapter 17

17-1 To derive the Phillips Curve from the AD-AS model we accept that the AS curve has three ranges: horizontal (or near so), upsloping, and vertical. When the economy moves from its horizontal to upsloping range, there is a tradeoff between more output (or employment) and the price level. The economy can only have more output (and employment) if it is willing to accept a higher price level.

The 1970s saw a succession of supply shocks that destabilized the Phillips Curve and cast doubts on its existence. These included: the quadrupling of world oil prices; decreased agricultural production; depreciation of the dollar; the ending of wage-price controls; and a decline in productivity growth. All these factors shifted the AS curve to the left, causing stagflation—rising unemployment and inflation.

17-2 Check your answer against Figure 17-5 and its legend.

17-7 Check your answer against Figure 17-7a and b and its legend.

17-8 Guideposts are voluntary; controls have the force of law. Controls (1) cause product shortages, resulting in black markets; (2) lead to lowering of product quality to circumvent the controls; (3) result in an inefficient allocation of society's scarce resources.

The few economists who do favor controls see them as useful in ending the inflationary expectations which often propel rapid inflation. A highly credible wage-price control program can convince businesses and labor that large price and wage hikes are not warranted to keep up with inflation since "inflation is under control." Wage and price controls held down—or at least postponed—inflation during World War II. But guideposts and controls applied since then have been largely ineffective.

17-10 The major tenets of supply side economics are: (1) the tax-transfer system negatively affects incentives to work, invest, innovate, and assume entrepreneurial risks; (2) tax cuts can occur without loss of tax revenues; (3) business taxes such as payroll taxes cause higher business costs, reduced employment, and reduced GDP; (4) government regulation of business is excessive.

According to supply side economists, the basic cause of stagflation—leftward shifts of the AS curve—is rising costs and stagnating productivity. High taxes and excessive regulation reduce economic incentives and lower productivity. The AS curve shifts to the left, causing stagflation.

Refer to Figure 17-8. In the graph, the advocates of tax cuts contend the economy is somewhere above *m* (where tax revenues would be at their maximum). By lowering the tax rate from, say, *n* to *m,* the government would increase tax revenues. This increase would occur because the lower tax rate would increase incentives to produce output and earn income. Example: Suppose GDP in an economy is initially $100 billion. At an average tax rate of 30 percent, tax revenues will be $30 billion (= 30% of $30 billion). Now

suppose government drops the tax rate to 20 percent and, as a result, the economy expands to $200 billion. The new tax revenue rises to $40 billion (= 20% of $200 billion). Aggregate supply would rise, simultaneously decreasing unemployment and prices. In two words: remedy stagflation.

Chapter 18

18-1 (a) There is practically no potential for using fiscal policy as a stabilization tool under an annually balanced budget. In an economic downturn, tax revenues fall. To keep the budget in balance, fiscal policy would require the government to reduce its spending or increase its tax rates, adding to the deficiency in spending and accelerating the downturn. If the economy were booming and tax revenues were mounting, to keep the budget balanced fiscal policy would have to increase government spending or reduce taxes, thus adding to the already excessive demand and accelerating the inflationary pressures. An annually balanced budget would intensify cyclical ups and downs.

(b) A cyclically balanced budget would be countercyclical, as it should be, since it would bolster demand by lowering taxes and increasing government spending during a recession and restrain demand by raising taxes and reducing government spending during an inflationary boom. However, because boom and bust are not always of equal intensity and duration, budget surpluses during the upswing need not automatically match budget deficits during the downswing. Requiring the budget to be balanced over the cycle may necessitate inappropriate changes in tax rates or levels of government expenditures.

(c) Functional finance pays no attention to the balance of deficits and surpluses annually or over the cycle. What counts is the maintenance of a noninflationary full-employment level of spending. Balancing the economy is what counts, not the budget.

18-3 Two ways of measuring the public debt: (1) measure its absolute size; (2) measure its size as a percentage of GDP.

An internally held debt is one where the bondholders live in the nation having the debt; an externally held debt is one where the bondholders are citizens of other nations. Paying off an internally held debt would involve boosting taxes or reducing other government spending and using the proceeds to buy the government bonds. This would present a problem of income distribution, because holders of the government bonds generally have higher incomes than the average taxpayer. But paying off an internally held debt would not burden the economy as a whole—the money used to pay off the debt would stay within the domestic economy.

In paying off an externally held debt people abroad would use the proceeds of the bonds sales to buy goods from the country paying off its external debt. That nation would have to send some of its output abroad to be consumed by others (with no imported goods in exchange).

Refinancing the public debt simply means rolling over outstanding debt—selling "new" bonds to retire maturing bonds.

18-7 Economists do not view the large public debt as a burden for future generations. Future generations not only inherit the public debt, but they inherit the bonds which constitute the public debt. They also inherit public capital goods, some of which were financed by the debt.

Chapter 21

21-2 A demand for francs is created in (a), (c), and (f). A supply of francs is created in (b), (d), (e), and (g).

21-3 Balance of trade = $10 billion surplus (= merchandise exports of $40 billion minus merchandise imports of $30 billion). Balance of goods and services = $15 billion surplus (= $55 billion of exports of goods and services minus $40 billion of imports of goods and services). Balance on current account = $20 billion surplus (= credits of $65 billion minus debits of $45 billion). Balance on capital account = $30 billion deficit (= capital inflows of $10 billion minus capital outflows of $40 billion). Balance of payments deficit of $10 billion (= $10 billion decrease in official reserves).

21-6 The American demand for pesos is downsloping when the dollar price of pesos is used as the relevant exchange rate. As the peso depreciates relative to the dollar, Americans find that Mexican goods and services are less expensive in dollar terms and purchase more of them, demanding a greater quantity of pesos in the process. The supply of pesos to Americans is upsloping because as the peso appreciates relative to the dollar, American goods and services become cheaper to Mexicans in peso terms. Mexicans buy more dollars, supplying a larger quantity of pesos.

The peso appreciates in (a), (f), (g), and (h) and depreciates in (b), (c), (d), and (e).

21-13 A decline in the Federal budget deficit will cause real interest rates to fall (the crowding-out effect in reverse), decreasing foreign financial investment in the United States, and reducing the international value of the dollar. This depreciation eventually will increase American exports and reduce imports, diminishing the size of the merchandise trade deficit.

Trade deficits fall during recessions because national income declines and consumers buy fewer domestic and imported goods. Our exports do not decline; they depend on other nations' income, not our own. The result of the decline in imports is a lower trade deficit. Economists would not propose a recession as a remedy for trade deficits. This "cure" is worse than the "disease."

Chapter 22

22-3 Rise in per capita output gap = $135 (= 3% × $5000 − 3% × $500).

22-6 Demographic transition view: Expanded output and income in LDCs will result in lower birthrates and slower growth of population. As incomes of primary family members expand, they begin to see extra children as "liabilities," not "assets." The policy emphasis should therefore be on economic growth. Traditional view: Less developed nations should reduce population growth as a first priority. Slow population growth enables the growth of per capita income.

22-8 Capital earns a higher return where it is scarce, *other things equal*. But, when comparing investment opportunities between IACs and LDCs, other things aren't equal. Advanced factories filled with specialized equipment require a productive work force. IACs have an abundance of educated, experienced workers; these workers are scarce in LDCs. Also, IACs have extensive public infrastructures which increase the returns on private capital. Example: a network of highways makes it more profitable to produce goods which need to be widely transported. Finally, investment returns must be adjusted for risk. IACs have stable governments and "law and order," reducing the risk of capital being "nationalized" or pilfered by organized crime.

22-14 To describe countries such as Japan and South Korea, we would need to change labels on three boxes, leading to a change in the "results" boxes. "Rapid" population growth would change to "low" rate of population growth; "low" level of saving would change to "high" level of saving; "low" levels of investment in physical and human capital would change to "high" levels of investment in physical and human capital. These three changes would result in higher productivity and higher per capita income, which would produce a rising level of demand. Other factors: stable national government; homogeneous population; extensive investment in infrastructure; "will to develop"; strong private incentives.

Chapter 23

23-7 See Figure 23-1 in the text. Because prices were set by government and not allowed to change as supply or demand shifted, prices were below the market equilibrium for most goods and services. When the fixed price, *Pf,* is below the equilibrium price, *Pe,* there will be a shortage since the quantity demanded will exceed the quantity supplied. As fixed prices are abolished, they will rise to their significantly higher equilibrium levels, contributing to rapid inflation. Black markets are common where prices are fixed below equilibrium levels. People can buy goods at the fixed government prices (or pay off clerks to save such goods to sell to them), and because of the shortages at the low fixed price, resell these goods at a much higher price to those unable to find the goods in the government stores at controlled prices. Official attempts to interfere with the market mechanism often lead to an unofficial market system which is called the black market.

23-8 Privatization of state-owned property and enterprises; promotion of competition by "demonopolizing" the huge state-run enterprises; reduction of the government's role as owner, manager, price-setter, and production planner; removal of price controls; joining the global economy; achieving macroeconomic stability; and altering entrenched anticapitalist attitudes. Because these changes are interlinked, they need to be accomplished more or less simultaneously. Example: If price controls are lifted without competition or privatization, there is no incentive for producers to expand output. Rather there is incentive to behave like monopolists and take the higher price without expanding supply. Second example: Greater competition requires opening the economy to world trade and foreign investment.

GLOSSARY

A

Ability-to-pay principle The belief that those who have greater income (or wealth) should be taxed absolutely and relatively more than those who have less.

Abstraction Elimination of irrelevant and noneconomic facts to obtain an economic principle.

Actual budget The amount spent by the Federal government (to purchase goods and services and for transfer payments) less the amount of tax revenue collected by it in any (fiscal) year; and which can *not* reliably be used to determine whether it is pursuing an expansionary or contractionary fiscal policy. Compare (*see*) the Full-employment budget.

Actual deficit The size of the Federal government's Budget deficit (*see*) actually measured or recorded in any given year.

Actual investment The amount which business Firms do invest; equal to Planned investment plus Unplanned investment.

Actual reserves The funds which a Member bank has on deposit at the Federal Reserve Bank of its district (plus its Vault cash).

Adaptive expectations theory The idea that people determine their expectations about future events (for example, inflation) on the basis of past and present events (rates of inflation) and only change their expectations as events unfold.

Adjustable pegs The device used in the Bretton Woods system (*see*) to change Exchange rates in an orderly way to eliminate persistent payments deficits and surpluses: each nation defined its monetary unit in terms of (pegged it to) gold or the dollar, kept the Rate of exchange for its money stable in the short run, and changed (adjusted) it in the long run when faced with international disequilibrium.

Aggregate demand A schedule or curve which shows the total quantity of goods and services demanded (purchased) at different price levels.

Aggregate demand–aggregate supply model The macroeconomic model which uses Aggregate demand and Aggregate supply (*see* both) to determine and explain the Price level and the real Domestic output.

Aggregate expenditures The total amount spent for final goods and services in the economy.

Aggregate expenditures–domestic output approach Determination of the Equilibrium gross domestic product (*see*) by finding the real GDP at which aggregate expenditures are equal to the Domestic output.

Aggregate expenditures schedule A schedule or curve showing the total amount spent for final goods and services at different levels of GDP.

Aggregate supply A schedule or curve showing the total quantity of goods and services supplied (produced) at different Price levels.

Aggregation Combining individual units or data into one unit or number. For example, all prices of individual goods and services are combined into a Price level, or all units of output are aggregated into Real gross domestic product.

Annually balanced budget The equality of government expenditures and tax collections during a year.

Anticipated inflation Inflation (*see*) at a rate equal to the rate expected in that period of time.

Applied economics (*See* Policy economics.)

Appreciation of the dollar An increase in the value of the dollar relative to the currency of another nation; a dollar now buys a larger amount of the foreign currency. For example, if the dollar price of a British pound changes from $3 to $2, the dollar has appreciated.

"Asian tigers" The newly industrialized and rapidly growing nations of Hong Kong, Singapore, South Korea, and Taiwan.

Asset Anything of monetary value owned by a firm or individual.

Asset demand for money The amount of money people want to hold as a Store of value (the amount of their financial assets they wish to have in the form of Money); and which varies inversely with the Rate of interest.

Authoritarian capitalism An economic system in which property resources are privately owned and government extensively directs and controls the economy.

Average product The total output produced per unit of a resource employed (total product divided by the quantity of a resource employed).

Average propensity to consume Fraction of Disposable income which households spend for consumer goods and services; consumption divided by Disposable income.

Average propensity to save Fraction of Disposable income which households save; Saving divided by Disposable income.

Average tax rate Total tax paid divided by total (taxable) income; the tax rate on total (taxable) income.

B

Balanced-budget amendment Proposed constitutional amend-ment which would require Congress to balance the Federal budget annually.

Balanced budget multiplier The effect of equal increases (decreases) in government spending for goods and services and in taxes is to increase (decrease) the Equilibrium gross domestic product by the amount of the equal increases (decreases).

Balance of payments deficit The sum of the Balance on current account (*see*) and the Balance on the capital account (*see*) is negative.

Balance of payments surplus The sum of the Balance on current account (*see*) and the Balance on the capital account (*see*) is positive.

Balance on current account The exports of goods (merchandise) and services of a nation less its imports of goods (merchandise) and services plus its Net investment income and Net transfers.

Balance on goods and services The exports of goods (merchandise) and services of a nation less its imports of goods (merchandise) and services.

Balance on the capital account The Capital inflows (*see*) of a nation less its Capital outflows (*see*).

Balance sheet A statement of the Assets (*see*), Liabilities (*see*), and Net worth (*see*) of a firm or individual at some given time.

Bank deposits The deposits which banks have at the Federal Reserve Banks (*see*).

Bankers' bank A bank which accepts the deposits of and makes loans to Depository institutions; a Federal Reserve Bank.

Bank reserves Bank reserves held at the Federal Reserve Banks (*see*) plus bank Vault cash (*see*).

Barrier to entry Anything that artificially prevents the entry of Firms into an industry.

Barter The exchange of one good or service for another good or service.

Base year The year with which prices in other years are compared when a Price index (*see*) is constructed.

Benefit-cost analysis Deciding whether to employ resources and the quantity of resources to employ for a project or program (for the production of a good or service) by comparing the marginal benefits with the marginal costs.

Big business A business Firm which either produces a large percentage of the total output of an industry, is large (in terms of number of employees or stockholders, sales, assets, or profits) compared with other Firms in the economy, or both.

Board of Governors The seven-member group that supervises and controls the money and banking system of the United States; formally, the Board of Governors of the Federal Reserve System; the Federal Reserve Board.

Brain drain The emigration of highly educated, highly skilled workers from a country.

Break-even income The level of Disposable income at which Households plan to consume (spend) all of their income and to save none of it; also denotes that level of earned income at which subsidy payments become zero in an income maintenance program.

Bretton Woods system The international monetary system developed after World War II in which Adjustable pegs (*see*) were employed, the International Monetary Fund (*see*) helped to stabilize Foreign exchange rates, and gold and the dollar (*see*) were used as International monetary reserves (*see*).

Budget deficit The amount by which the expenditures of the Federal government exceed its revenues in any year.

Budget surplus The amount by which the revenues of the Federal government exceeds its expenditures in any year.

Built-in stability The effect of Nondiscretionary fiscal policy (*see*) on the economy; when Net taxes vary directly with the Gross domestic product, the fall (rise) in Net taxes during a recession (inflation) lessens unemployment (inflationary pressures).

Business cycle Recurrent ups and downs over a period of years in the level of economic activity.

C

Capital Human-made resources (machinery and equipment) used to produce goods and services; goods which do not directly satisfy human wants; capital goods.

Capital account The section in a nation's International balance of payments (*see*) in which are recorded the Capital inflows (*see*) and the Capital outflows (*see*) of that nation.

Capital account deficit A negative Balance on the capital account (*see*).

Capital account surplus A positive Balance on the capital account (*see*).

Capital flight The transfer of savings from less developed to industrially advanced countries to avoid government expropriation, taxation, and high rates of inflation or to realize better investment opportunities.

Capital gain The gain realized when securities or properties are sold for a price greater than the price paid for them.

Capital goods (*See* Capital.)

Capital inflow The expenditures made by the residents of foreign nations to purchase real and financial capital from the residents of a nation.

Capital-intensive commodity A product which requires a relatively large amount of Capital to produce.

Capital outflow The expenditures made by the residents of a nation to purchase real and financial capital from the residents of foreign nations.

Capital-saving technological advance An improvement in technology that permits a greater quantity of a product to be produced with a specific amount of Capital (or the same amount of the product to be produced with a smaller amount of Capital).

Capital-using technological advance An improvement in technology that requires the use of a greater amount of Capital to produce a specific quantity of a product.

Causation A cause-and-effect relationship; one or several events bring about or result in another event.

CEA (*See* Council of Economic Advisers.)

Central bank A bank whose chief function is the control of the nation's money supply.

Central economic planning Government determination of the objectives of the economy and the direction of its resources to the attainment of these objectives.

Ceteris paribus **assumption** (*See* "Other things equal" assumption.)

Change in amount consumed Increase or decrease in consumption spending that results from an increase or decrease in Disposable income, the Consumption schedule (curve) remaining unchanged; movement from one row (point) to another on the same Consumption schedule (curve).

Change in amount saved Increase or decrease in Saving that results from an increase or decrease in Disposable income, the Saving schedule (curve) remaining unchanged; movement from one row (point) to another on the same Saving schedule (curve).

Change in the consumption schedule An increase or decrease in consumption at each level of Disposable income caused by changes in the Nonincome determinants of consumption and saving (*see*); an upward or downward movement of the Consumption schedule.

Change in the saving schedule An increase or decrease in Saving at each level of Disposable income caused by changes in the Nonincome determinants of consumption and saving (*see*); an upward or downward movement of the Saving schedule.

Checkable deposit Any deposit in a commercial bank or Thrift institution against which a check may be written; includes Demand deposits and NOW, ATS, and share draft accounts.

Checking account A Checkable deposit (*see*) in a Commercial bank or Thrift institution.

Circular flow of income The flow of resources from Households to Firms and of products from Firms to Households accompanied in an economy using money by flows of money from Households to Firms and from Firms to Households.

Classical economics The Macroeconomic generalizations accepted by most economists before the 1930s which led to the conclusion that a capitalistic economy would employ its resources fully.

Closed economy An economy which neither exports nor imports goods and services.

Coincidence of wants The item (good or service) which one trader wishes to obtain is the same as another trader desires to give up and the item which the second trader wishes to acquire is the same as the first trader desires to surrender.

COLA (*See* Cost-of-living adjustment.)

Collection of checks The process by which funds are transferred from the checking accounts of the writers of checks to the checking accounts of the recipients of the checks; also called the "clearing" of checks.

Command economy An economic system (method of organization) in which property resources are publicly owned and Central economic planning (*see*) is used to direct and coordinate economic activities.

Commercial bank Firm which has a charter from either a state government or the Federal government to engage in the business of banking.

Commercial banking system All Commercial banks and Thrift institutions as a group.

Communism (*See* Command economy.)

Comparative advantage A lower relative or Comparative cost (*see*) than another producer.

Comparative cost The amount by which one product must be reduced to increase the production of another product; Opportunity cost (*see*).

Compensation to employees Wages and salaries paid by employers to workers plus Wage and salary supplements (*see*).

Competing goods (*See* Substitute goods.)

Competition The presence in a market of a large number of independent buyers and sellers and the freedom of buyers and sellers to enter and leave the market.

Complementary goods Goods and services for which there is an inverse relationship between the price of one and the demand for the other; when the price of one falls (rises) the demand for the other increases (decreases).

Complex multiplier The Multiplier (*see*) when changes in the Gross domestic product change Net taxes and Imports, as well as Saving.

Conglomerate combination A group of Plants (*see*) owned by a single Firm and engaged at one or more stages in the production of different products (of products which do not compete with each other).

Consumer goods Goods and services which satisfy human wants directly.

Consumer price index (CPI) An index which measures the prices of a fixed "market basket" of some 300 consumer goods bought by a "typical" consumer.

Consumer sovereignty Determination by consumers of the types and quantities of goods and services produced from the scarce resources of the economy.

Consumption of fixed capital Estimate of the amount of Capital worn out or used up (consumed) in producing the Gross domestic product; depreciation.

Consumption schedule A schedule showing the amounts Households plan to spend for Consumer goods at different levels of Disposable income.

Contractionary fiscal policy A decrease in Aggregate demand brought about by a decrease in Government expenditures for goods and services, an increase in Net taxes, or some combination of the two.

Corporate income tax A tax levied on the net income (profit) of Corporations.

Corporation A legal entity ("person") chartered by a state or the Federal government which is distinct and separate from the individuals who own it.

Correlation Systematic and dependable association between two sets of data (two kinds of events); does not necessarily indicate causation.

Cost-of-living adjustment An increase in the incomes (wages) of workers which is automatically received by them when there is inflation and guaranteed by a clause in their labor contracts with their employer.

Cost-push inflation Inflation resulting from a decrease in Aggregate supply (from higher wage rates and raw material prices) and accompanied by decrease in real output and employment (and by increases in the Unemployment rate).

Cost ratio The ratio of the decrease in the production of the product to the increase in the production of another product when resources are shifted from the production of the first to the second; the amount the production of one product decreases when the production of a second increases by one unit.

Council of Economic Advisers A group of three persons which advises and assists the President of the United States on economic matters (including the preparation of the economic report of the President to Congress).

Credit An accounting notation that the value of an asset (such as the foreign money owned by the residents of a nation) has increased.

Credit union An association of persons who have a common tie (such as being employees of the same Firm or members of the same Labor union) which sells shares to (accepts deposits from) its members and makes loans to them.

Crowding-out effect The rise in interest rates and the resulting decrease in planned investment spending in the economy caused by increased borrowing in the money market by the Federal government.

Currency Coins and Paper money.

Currency appreciation   (*See* Exchange rate appreciation.)

Currency depreciation   (*See* Exchange rate depreciation.)

Current account   The section in a nation's International balance of payments (*see*) which records its exports and imports of goods (merchandise) and services, its net investment income, and its net transfers.

Current account deficit   A negative Balance on current account (*see*).

Current account surplus   A positive Balance on current account (*see*).

Customary economy   (*See* Traditional economy.)

Cyclical deficit   A Federal Budget deficit which is caused by a recession and the consequent decline in tax revenues.

Cyclical unemployment   Unemployment caused by insufficient Aggregate expenditures (or by insufficient Aggregate demand).

Cyclically balanced budget   The equality of Government expenditures and Net tax collections over the course of a Business cycle; deficits incurred during periods of recession are offset by surpluses obtained during periods of prosperity (inflation).

D

Debit   An accounting notation that the value of an asset (such as the foreign money owned by the residents of a nation) has decreased.

Debt-equity swaps   The transfer of stock in private or government-owned enterprises of Less developed countries (*see*) to foreign creditors.

Declining economy   An economy in which Net private domestic investment (*see*) is less than zero (Gross private domestic investment is less than Depreciation).

Declining industry   An industry in which Economic profits are negative (losses are incurred) and which will, therefore, decrease its output as Firms leave the industry.

Decrease in demand   A decrease in the Quantity demanded of a good or service at every price; a shift of the Demand curve to the left.

Decrease in supply   A decrease in the quantity supplied of a good or service at every price; a shift of the Supply curve to the left.

Deduction   Reasoning from assumptions to conclusions; a method of reasoning that first develops a hypothesis (an assumption) and then compares the conclusions to which it leads with economic facts.

Deficit Reduction Act of 1993   Federal legislation intended to reduce the budget deficit by about $500 billion over five years by increasing taxes and cutting expenditures.

Deflating   Finding the Real gross domestic product (*see*) by decreasing the dollar value of the Gross domestic product produced in a year in which prices were higher than in the Base year (*see*).

Deflation   A fall in the general (average) level of prices in the economy.

Demand   A Demand schedule or a Demand curve (*see* both).

Demand curve   A curve showing the amounts of a good or service buyers wish to purchase at various prices during some period of time.

Demand deposit   A deposit in a Commercial bank or Thrift against which checks may be written; a Checking account or checking-account money.

Demand-deposit multiplier   (*See* Monetary multiplier.)

Demand factor   The increase in the level of Aggregate demand which brings about the Economic growth made possible by an increase in the productive potential of the economy.

Demand management   The use of Fiscal policy (*see*) and Monetary policy (*see*) to increase or decrease Aggregate demand.

Demand-pull inflation   Inflation resulting from an increase in Aggregate demand.

Demand schedule   A schedule showing the amounts of a good or service buyers will purchase at various prices during some period of time.

Dependent variable   A variable which changes as a consequence of a change in some other (independent) variable; the "effect" or outcome.

Depository institution   A Firm that accepts the deposits of Money of the public (businesses and persons); Commercial banks, Savings and loan associations, Mutual savings banks, and Credit unions.

Depository Institutions Deregulation and Monetary Control Act   Federal legislation of 1980 which, among other things, allowed Thrift institutions to accept Checkable deposits and to use the check-clearing facilities of the Federal Reserve and to borrow from the Federal Reserve Banks; subjected the Thrifts to the reserve requirements of the Fed; and provided for the gradual elimination of the maximum interest rates that could be paid by Depository institutions on Savings and Time deposits.

Depreciation   (*See* Consumption of fixed capital.)

Depreciation of the dollar A decrease in the value of the dollar relative to another currency; a dollar now buys a smaller amount of the foreign currency. For example, if the dollar price of a British pound changes from $2 to $3, the dollar has depreciated.

Derived demand The demand for a good or service which is dependent on or related to the demand for some other good or service; the demand for a resource which depends on the demand for the products it can be used to produce.

Descriptive economics The gathering or collection of relevant economic facts (data).

Determinants of aggregate demand Factors such as consumption, investment, government, and net export spending which, if they change, will shift the aggregate demand curve.

Determinants of aggregate supply Factors such as input prices, productivity, and the legal-institutional environment which, if they change, will shift the aggregate supply curve.

Determinants of demand Factors other than its price which determine the quantities demanded of a good or service.

Determinants of supply Factors other than its price which determine the quantities supplied of a good or service.

Devaluation A decrease in the governmentally defined value of a currency.

DI (*See* Disposable income.)

Diagnosis-related-group system (DRG) A program by which hospitals are paid a fixed amount for Medicare patients based on one of 468 diagnostic categories.

DIDMCA (*See* Depository Institutions Deregulation and Monetary Control Act.)

Directing function of prices (*See* Guiding function of prices.)

Directly related Two sets of economic data that change in the same direction; when one variable increases (decreases) the other increases (decreases).

Direct relationship The relationship between two variables which change in the same direction, for example, product price and quantity supplied.

Discount rate The interest rate which the Federal Reserve Banks charge on the loans they make to Depository institutions.

Discouraged workers Workers who have left the Labor force (*see*) because they have not been able to find employment.

Discretionary fiscal policy Deliberate changes in taxes (tax rates) and government spending (spending for goods and services and transfer payment programs) by Congress to achieve a full-employment noninflationary Gross domestic product and economic growth.

Disinflation A reduction in the rate of Inflation (*see*).

Disposable income Personal income (*see*) less personal taxes; income available for Personal consumption expenditures (*see*) and Personal saving (*see*).

Dissaving Spending for consumer goods and services in excess of Disposable income; the amount by which Personal consumption expenditures (*see*) exceed Disposable income.

Division of labor Dividing the work required to produce a product into a number of different tasks which are performed by different workers; Specialization (*see*) of workers.

Dollar votes The "votes" which consumers and entrepreneurs in effect cast for the production of the different kinds of consumer and capital goods, respectively, when they purchase them in the markets of the economy.

Domestic capital formation Adding to a nation's stock of Capital by saving and investing part of its own domestic output.

Domestic output Gross (or net) domestic product; the total output of final goods and services produced in the economy.

Domestic price The price of a good or service within a country, determined by domestic demand and supply.

Doomsday models Computer-based models which predict that continued growth of population and production will exhaust available resources and the environment, causing an economic collapse.

Double counting Including the value of Intermediate goods (*see*) in the Gross domestic product; counting the same good or service more than once.

Double taxation Taxation of both corporate net income (profits) and the dividends paid from this net income when they become the Personal income of households.

Dumping The sale of products below cost in a foreign country.

Durable good A consumer good with an expected life (use) of three years or more.

Dynamic progress The development over time of more efficient (less costly) techniques of producing existing products and of improved products; technological progress.

E

Earnings The money income received by a worker; equal to the Wage (rate) multiplied by the quantity of labor supplied (the amount of time worked) by the worker.

Easy money policy Expanding the Money supply.

EC European Economic Community. (*See* European Union.)

Economic analysis Deriving Economic principles (*see*) from relevant economic facts.

Economic cost A payment that must be made to obtain and retain the services of a resource; the income a Firm must provide to a resource supplier to attract the resource away from an alternative use; equal to the quantity of other products that cannot be produced when resources are employed to produce a particular product.

Economic efficiency The relationship between the input of scarce resources and the resulting output of a good or service; production of an output with a specific dollar-and-cents value with the smallest total expenditure for resources; obtaining the largest total production of a good or service with resources of a specific dollar-and-cents value.

Economic growth (1) An increase in the Production possibilities schedule or curve that results from an increase in resource supplies or an improvement in Technology; (2) an increase either in real output (Gross domestic product) or in real output per capita.

Economic integration Cooperation among and the complete or partial unification of the economies of different nations; the elimination of the barriers to trade among these nations; the bringing together of the markets in each of the separate economies to form one large (a common) market.

Economic law (*See* Economic principle.)

Economic model A simplified picture of reality; an abstract generalization.

Economic perspective A viewpoint which envisions individuals and institutions making rational or purposeful decisions based on a consideration of the marginal benefits and marginal costs associated with their actions.

Economic policy Course of action intended to correct or avoid a problem.

Economic principle Generalization of the economic behavior of individuals and institutions.

Economic profit The Total revenue of a firm less all its Economic costs; also called "pure profit" and "above normal profit."

Economic rent The price paid for the use of land and other natural resources, the supply of which is fixed (perfectly inelastic).

Economic resources Land, labor, capital, and entrepreneurial ability which are used in the production of goods and services.

Economics Social science concerned with using scarce resources to obtain the maximum satisfaction of the unlimited material wants of society.

Economic theory Deriving economic principles (*see*) from relevant economic facts; an Economic principle (*see*).

Economies of scale The forces which reduce the Average total cost of producing a product as the Firm expands the size of its Plant (its output) in the Long run (*see*); the economies of mass production.

Economizing problem Society's material wants are unlimited but the resources available to produce the goods and services that satisfy wants are limited (scarce); the inability to produce unlimited quantities of goods and services.

Efficiency factors in growth The capacity of an economy to combine resources effectively to achieve the growth of real output which the Supply factors (*see*) make possible.

Efficient allocation of resources That allocation of the resources of an economy among the production of different products which leads to the maximum satisfaction of the wants of consumers; producing the optimal mix of output.

Employment Act of 1946 Federal legislation which committed the Federal government to the maintenance of economic stability (a high level of employment, stable prices, and Economic growth); established the Council of Economic Advisors (*see*) and the Joint Economic Committee (*see*); and provided for the annual economic report of the President to Congress.

Employment and training policy Policies and programs involving vocational training, job information, and antidiscrimination which are designed to improve labor-market efficiency and lower unemployment at any level of aggregate demand.

Employment rate The percentage of the Labor force (*see*) employed at any time.

Entrepreneurial ability The human resource which combines the other resources to produce a product, makes nonroutine decisions, innovates, and bears risks.

Equation of exchange $MV = PQ$, in which M is the Money supply (*see*), V is the Velocity of money (*see*), P is the Price level, and Q is the physical volume of final goods and services produced.

Equilibrium gross domestic product   The Gross domestic product at which the total quantity of final goods and services produced (the Domestic output) is equal to the total quantity of final goods and services purchased (Aggregate expenditures); the real Domestic output at which the Aggregate demand curve intersects the Aggregate supply curve.

Equilibrium price   The price in a competitive market where the Quantity demanded (*see*) and the Quantity supplied (*see*) are equal; where there is neither a shortage nor a surplus; and where there is no tendency for price to rise or fall.

Equilibrium price level   The price level at which the Aggregate demand curve intersects the Aggregate supply curve.

Equilibrium quantity   The Quantity demanded (*see*) and Quantity supplied (*see*) at the Equilibrium price (*see*) in a competitive market.

European Common Market   (*See* European Union.)

European Union (EU)   The association of European nations initiated in 1958 to abolish gradually the Tariffs and Import quotas that exist among them, to establish common Tariffs for goods imported from outside the member nations, to allow the eventual free movement of labor and capital among them, and to create other common economic policies. (Earlier known as "European Economic Community" and the "Common Market.")

Excess reserves   The amount by which a bank or thrift's Actual reserves (*see*) exceed its Required reserves (*see*); Actual reserves minus Required reserves.

Exchange control   (*See* Foreign exchange control.)

Exchange rate   The Rate of exchange (*see*).

Exchange rate appreciation   An increase in the value of a nation's money in foreign exchange markets; an increase in the Rate of exchange for foreign monies.

Exchange rate depreciation   A decrease in the value of a nation's money in foreign exchange markets; a decrease in the Rate of exchange for foreign monies.

Exchange rate determinant   Any factor other than the Rate of exchange (*see*) that determines a currency's demand and supply in the Foreign exchange market (*see*).

Excise tax   A tax levied on the expenditure for a specific product or on the quantity of the product purchased.

Exclusion principle   The exclusion of those who do not pay for a product from the benefits of the product.

Exhaustive expenditure   An expenditure by government resulting directly in the employment of economic resources and in the absorption by government of the goods and services these resources produce; a Government purchase (*see*).

Expanding economy   An economy in which Net private domestic investment (*see*) is greater than zero (Gross private domestic investment is greater than Depreciation).

Expanding industry   An industry in which economic profits are obtained by the firms in the industry and which will, therefore, increase its output as new firms enter the industry.

Expansionary fiscal policy   An increase in Aggregate demand brought about by an increase in Government expenditures for goods and services, a decrease in Net taxes, or some combination of the two.

Expectations   What consumers, business Firms, and others believe will happen or what conditions will be in the future.

Expected rate of net profit   Annual profit a firm anticipates it will obtain by purchasing Capital (by investing) expressed as a percentage of the price (cost) of the Capital.

Expenditures approach   The method which adds all the expenditures made for Final goods and services to measure the Gross domestic product.

Expenditures-output approach   (*See* Aggregate expenditures–domestic output approach.)

Export controls   The limitation or prohibition of the export of certain high-technology products on the basis of foreign policy or national security objectives.

Export-Import Bank   A Federal institution which provides interest-rate subsidies to foreign borrowers who buy American exports on credit.

Exports   Goods and services produced in a nation and sold to customers in other nations.

Export subsidies   Government payments which reduce the price of a product to foreign buyers.

Export supply curve   An upsloping curve showing the amount of a product domestic firms will export at each World price (*see*) above the Domestic price (*see*).

Export transactions   A sale of a good or service which increases the amount of foreign money held by the citizens, firms, and governments of a nation.

External benefits   (*See* Spillover benefit.)

External cost   (*See* Spillover cost.)

External debt   Private or public debt (*see*) owed to foreign citizens, firms, and institutions.

Externality   (*See* Spillover.)

F

Face value   The dollar or cents value stamped on a coin.

Factors of production   Economic resources: Land, Capital, Labor, and Entrepreneurial ability.

Fallacy of composition   Incorrectly reasoning that what is true for the individual (or part) is therefore necessarily true for the group (or whole).

FDIC   (*See* Federal Deposit Insurance Corporation.)

Federal Advisory Committee   The group of twelve commercial bankers which advises the Board of Governors (*see*) on banking policy.

Federal Deposit Insurance Corporation (FDIC)   The Federally chartered corporation which insures the deposit liabilities of Commercial banks and Thrift institutions.

Federal funds rate   The interest rate banks and other depository institutions charge one another on overnight loans made out of their excess reserves.

Federal Open Market Committee   (*See* Open Market Committee.)

Federal Reserve Bank   Any one of the twelve banks chartered by the United States government to control the Money supply and perform other functions. (*See* Central bank, Quasi-public bank, *and* Banker's bank.)

Federal Reserve Note   Paper money issued by the Federal Reserve Banks.

Feedback effects   The effects which a change in the money supply will have (because it affects the interest rate, planned investment, and the equilibrium GDP) on the demand for money which is itself directly related to the GDP.

Fiat money   Anything that is Money because government has decreed it to be Money.

Final goods   Goods which have been purchased for final use and not for resale or further processing or manufacturing (during the year).

Financial capital   (*See* Money capital.)

Financing exports and imports   The use of Foreign exchange markets by exporters and importers to receive and make payments for goods and services they sell and buy in foreign nations.

Firm   An organization that employs resources to produce a good or service for profit and owns and operates one or more Plants (*see*).

Fiscal federalism   The system of transfers (grants) by which the Federal government shares its revenues with state and local governments.

Fiscal policy   Changes in government spending and tax collections designed to achieve a full-employment and noninflationary domestic output.

Five fundamental economic questions   The five questions which every economy must answer: what to produce, how to produce, how to divide the total output, how to maintain Full employment, and how to assure economic flexibility.

Fixed exchange rate   A Rate of exchange which is prevented from rising or falling.

Flexible exchange rate   A rate of exchange determined by the international demand for and supply of a nation's money; a rate free to rise or fall.

Floating exchange rate   (*See* Flexible exchange rate.)

Foreign exchange control   The control a government may exercise over the quantity of foreign money demanded by its citizens and business firms and over the Rates of exchange in order to limit its outpayments to its inpayments (to eliminate a Payments deficit, *see*).

Foreign exchange market   A market in which the money (currency) used by one nation is used to purchase (is exchanged for) the money used by another nation.

Foreign exchange rate   (*See* Rate of exchange.)

Foreign purchases effect   The inverse relationship between the Net exports (*see*) of an economy and its Price level (*see*) relative to foreign Price levels.

45-degree line   A line along which the value of the GDP (measured horizontally) is equal to the value of Aggregate expenditures (measured vertically).

Fractional reserve   A Reserve ratio (*see*) which is less than 100 percent of the deposit liabilities of a Commercial bank.

Freedom of choice   Freedom of owners of property resources and money to employ or dispose of these resources as they see fit, of workers to enter any line of work for which they are qualified, and of consumers to spend their incomes in a manner which they deem appropriate (best for them).

Freedom of enterprise   Freedom of business Firms to employ economic resources, to use these resources to produce products of the firm's own choosing, and to sell these products in markets of their choice.

Freely floating exchange rates   Rates of exchange (*see*) which are not controlled and which may, therefore, rise and fall; and which are determined by the demand for and the supply of foreign monies.

Free-rider problem   The inability of potential providers of an economically desirable but indivisible good or service to obtain payment from those who benefit, because the Exclusion principle (*see*) is not applicable.

Free Trade   The absence of artificial (government imposed) barriers to trade among individuals and firms in different nations.

Frictional unemployment. Unemployment caused by workers voluntarily changing jobs and by temporary lay-offs; unemployed workers between jobs.

Full employment (1) Using all available resources to produce goods and services; (2) when the Unemployment rate is equal to the Full-employment unemployment rate and there is Frictional and Structural but no Cyclical unemployment (and the Real output of the economy is equal to its Potential real output).

Full-employment budget What government expenditures and revenues and its surplus or deficit would be if the economy were to operate at Full employment throughout the year.

Full-employment unemployment rate The Unemployment rate (*see*) at which there is no Cyclical unemployment (*see*) of the labor force (*see*); and because some Frictional and Structural unemployment is unavoidable, equal to about 5.5 to 6 percent.

Full production The maximum amount of goods and services which can be produced from the employed resources of an economy; occurs when both Allocative efficiency and Productive efficiency are realized.

Functional distribution of income The manner in which national income is divided among those who perform different functions (provide the economy with different kinds of resources); the division of National income (*see*) into wages and salaries, proprietors' income, corporate profits, interest, and rent.

Functional finance Use of Fiscal policy to achieve a full-employment noninflationary Gross domestic product without regard to the effect on the Public debt (*see*).

G

G-7 Nations A group of seven major industrial powers (the United States, Japan, Germany, United Kingdom, France, Italy, and Canada) whose leaders meet regularly to discuss common economic problems and try to coordinate economic policies.

GATT (*See* General Agreement on Tariffs and Trade.)

GDP (*See* Gross domestic product.)

GDP deflator The Price index (*see*) for all final goods and services used to adjust the money (or nominal) GDP to measure the real GDP.

GDP gap Potential Real gross domestic product less actual Real gross domestic product.

General Agreement on Tariffs and Trade The international agreement reached in 1947 in which twenty-three nations agreed to give equal and nondiscriminatory treatment to the other nations, to reduce tariff rates by multi-national negotiations, and to eliminate Import quotas. Now includes 124 nations.

Generalization Statistical or probability statement; statement of the nature of the relation between two or more sets of facts.

Glasnost A Soviet campaign of the mid-1980s for greater "openness" and democratization in political and economic activities.

GNP (*See* Gross national product.)

Gold export point The rate of exchange for a foreign money above which—when nations participate in the International gold standard (*see*)—the foreign money will not be purchased and gold will be sent (exported) to the foreign country to make payments there.

Gold flow The movement of gold into or out of a nation.

Gold import point The Rate of exchange for a foreign money below which—when nations participate in the International gold standard (*see*)—a nation's own money will not be purchased and gold will be sent (imported) into that country by foreigners to make payments there.

Gorbachev's reforms A mid-1980s series of reforms designed to revitalize the Soviet economy. The reforms stressed the modernization of productive facilities, less centralized control, improved worker discipline and productivity, more emphasis on market prices, and an expansion of private economic activity.

Government purchases Disbursements of money by government for which government receives a currently produced good or service in return; the expenditures of all governments in the economy for Final goods (*see*) and services.

Government transfer payment The disbursement of money (or goods and services) by government for which government receives no currently produced good or service in return.

Gross domestic product (GDP) The total market value of all Final goods (*see*) and services produced annually within the boundaries of the United States, whether by American or foreign-supplied resources.

Gross national product (GNP) The total market value of all Final goods (*see*) and services produced annually by land, labor, and capital, and entrepreneurial talent supplied by American residents, whether these resources are located in the United States or abroad.

Gross private domestic investment Expenditures for newly produced Capital goods (*see*)—machinery, equipment, tools, and buildings—and for additions to inventories.

Guiding function of prices   The ability of price changes to bring about changes in the quantities of products and resources demanded and supplied. (*See* Incentive function of price.)

H

Horizontal axis   The "left-right" or "west-east" axis on a graph or grid.

Horizontal combination   A group of Plants (*see*) in the same stage of production which are owned by a single Firm (*see*).

Horizontal range   Horizontal segment of the Aggregate-supply curve along which the price level is constant as real domestic output changes.

Household   An economic unit (of one or more persons) which provides the economy with resources and uses the money paid to it for these resources to purchase goods and services which satisfy material wants.

Hyperinflation   A very rapid rise in the price level.

I

IMF   (*See* International Monetary Fund.)

Import competition   Competition which domestic firms encounter from the products and services of foreign suppliers.

Import demand curve   A downsloping curve showing the amount of a product which an economy will import at each World price (*see*) below the Domestic price (*see*).

Import quota   A limit imposed by a nation on the quantity of a good which may be imported during some period of time.

Imports   Spending by individuals, Firms, and governments for goods and services produced in foreign nations.

Import transaction   The purchase of a good or service which decreases the amount of foreign money held by citizens, firms, and governments of a nation.

Income approach   The method which adds all the incomes generated by the production of Final goods and services to measure the Gross domestic product.

Income effect   The effect of a change in price of a product on a consumer's Real income (purchasing power) and thus on the quantity of the product purchased, after the Substitution effect (*see*) has been determined and eliminated.

Income inequality   The unequal distribution of an economy's total income among persons or families.

Incomes policy   Government policy which affects the Nominal incomes of individuals (the wages workers receive) and the prices they pay for goods and services and alters their Real incomes. (*See* Wage-price policy.)

Income velocity of money   (*See* Velocity of money.)

Increase in demand   An increase in the Quantity demanded of a good or service at every price; a shift in the Demand curve to the right.

Increase in supply   An increase in the Quantity supplied of a good or service at every price; a shift in the Supply curve to the right.

Independent goods.   Goods or services for which there is no relationship between the price of one and the demand for the other; when the price of one rises or falls the demand for the other remains constant.

Independent variable   The variable causing a change in some other (dependent) variable.

Indirect business taxes   Such taxes as Sales, Excise, and business Property taxes (*see all*), license fees, and Tariffs (*see*) which Firms treat as costs of producing a product and pass on (in whole or in part) to buyers of the product by charging them higher prices.

Individual demand   The Demand schedule (*see*) or Demand curve (*see*) of a single buyer.

Individual supply   The Supply schedule (*see*) or Supply curve (*see*) of a single seller.

Induction   A method of reasoning which proceeds from facts to Generalization (*see*).

Industrially advanced countries (IACs)   Countries such as the United States, Canada, Japan, and the nations of western Europe which have developed Market economies based on large stocks of technologically advanced capital goods and skilled labor forces.

Industrial policy   Any policy in which government takes a direct and active role in promoting specific firms or industries to expand output and achieve economic growth.

Industry   A group of (one or more) Firms which produce identical or similar products.

Inferior good   A good or service of which consumers purchase less (more) at every price when their incomes increase (decrease).

Inflating   Finding the Real gross domestic product (*see*) by increasing the dollar value of the Gross domestic product produced in a year in which prices are lower than in the Base year (*see*).

Inflation   A rise in the general (average) level of prices in the economy.

Inflation premium   The component of the nominal interest rate which reflects anticipated inflation.

Long-run aggregate supply curve   The aggregate supply curve associated with a time period in which input prices (especially nominal wages) are fully responsive to changes in the price level.

Lotteries   Games of chance where people buy numbered tickets and winners are drawn by lot; a source of state and local government revenue.

Lump-sum tax   A tax which is a constant amount (the tax revenue of government is the same) at all levels of GDP.

M

M1   The narrowly defined Money supply; the Currency and Checkable deposits (*see*) not owned by the Federal government, Federal Reserve Banks, or Depository institutions.

M2   A more broadly defined Money supply; equal to *M*1 (*see*) plus Noncheckable savings deposits, Money market deposit accounts, small Time deposits (deposits of less than $100,000), and individual Money market mutual fund balances.

M3   Very broadly defined Money supply; equal to *M*2 (*see*) plus large Time deposits (deposits of $100,000 or more).

Macroeconomics   The part of economics concerned with the economy as a whole; with such major aggregates as the household, business, and governmental sectors and with totals for the economy.

Managed floating exchange rate   An Exchange rate allowed to change (float) to eliminate Payments deficits and surpluses and is controlled (managed) to reduce day-to-day fluctuations.

Marginal analysis   Decision making which involves a comparison or marginal ("extra" or "additional") benefits and marginal costs.

Marginal propensity to consume   Fraction of any change in Disposable income spent for Consumer goods; equal to the change in consumption divided by the change in Disposable income.

Marginal propensity to save   Fraction of any change in Disposable income which households save; equal to change in Saving (*see*) divided by the change in Disposable income.

Marginal tax rate   The fraction of additional (taxable) income which must be paid in taxes.

Market   Any institution or mechanism which brings together the buyers (demanders) and sellers (suppliers) of a particular good or service.

Market demand   (*See* Total demand.)

Market economy   An economy in which only the private decisions of consumers, resource suppliers, and business Firms determine how resources are allocated; the Market system.

Market failure   The failure of a market to bring about the allocation of resources which best satisfies the wants of society (that maximizes the satisfaction of wants). In particular, the over- or underallocation of resources to the production of a particular good or service (because of Spillovers or informational problems) and no allocation of resources to the production of Public goods (*see*).

Market policies   Government policies designed to reduce the market power of labor unions and large business firms and to reduce or eliminate imbalances and bottlenecks in labor markets.

Market socialism   An economic system (method of organization) in which property resources are publicly owned and markets and prices are used to direct and coordinate economic activities.

Market system   All the product and resource markets of the economy and the relationships among them; a method which allows the prices determined in these markets to allocate the economy's scarce resources and to communicate and coordinate the decisions made by consumers, business firms, and resource suppliers.

Medium of exchange   Money (*see*); a convenient means of exchanging goods and services without engaging in Barter (*see*); what sellers generally accept and buyers generally use to pay for a good or service.

Microeconomics   The part of economics concerned with such individual units within the economy as Industries, Firms, and Households; and with individual markets, particular prices, and specific goods and services.

Mixed capitalism   An economy in which both government and private decisions determine how resources are allocated.

Monetarism   An alternative to Keynesianism (*see*); the macroeconomic view that the main cause of changes in aggregate output and the price level are fluctuations in the money supply; advocates a Monetary rule (*see*).

Monetary multiplier   The multiple of its Excess reserves (*see*) by which the Commercial banking system (*see*) can expand the Money supply and Demand deposits by making new loans (or buying securities); and equal to one divided by the Required reserve ratio (*see*).

Monetary policy   Changing the Money supply (*see*) to assist the economy to achieve a full-employment, noninflationary level of total output.

Monetary rule   The rule suggested by Monetarism (*see*); the Money supply should be expanded each year at the same annual rate as the potential rate of growth of the Real gross domestic product; the supply of money should be increased steadily at from 3 to 5 percent per year.

Money Any item which is generally acceptable to sellers in exchange for goods and services.

Money capital Money available to purchase Capital goods (*see*).

Money income (*See* Nominal income.)

Money interest rate The Nominal interest rate (*see*).

Money market The market in which the demand for and the supply of money determine the Interest rate (or the level of interest rates) in the economy.

Money market deposit account (MMDA) Interest-earning accounts at banks and thrift institutions which pool the funds of depositors to buy various short-term securities.

Money market mutual funds (MMMF) Interest-bearing accounts offered by brokers which pool depositors' funds for the purchase of short-term securities; depositors may write checks in minimum amounts or more against their accounts.

Money supply Narrowly defined (*see*) $M1$, more broadly defined (*see*) $M2$ and $M3$.

Money wage The amount of money received by a worker per unit of time (hour, day, etc.); nominal wage.

Money wage rate (*See* Money wage.)

Monopoly A market in which the number of sellers is so small that each seller is able to influence the total supply and the price of the good or service. (Also *see* Pure monopoly.)

Most-favored-nation (MFN) clause A clause in a trade agreement between the United States and another nation which provides that the other nation's Imports into the United States will be subjected to the lowest tariff levied then or later on any other nation's Imports into the United States.

Multinational corporations A firm which owns production facilities in other countries and produces and sells its products abroad.

Multiplier The ratio of the change in the Equilibrium GDP to the change in Investment (*see*), or to the change in any other component of Aggregate expenditures or Aggregate demand; the number by which a change in any component of Aggregate expenditures or Aggregate demand must be multiplied to find the resulting change in the Equilibrium GDP.

Multiplier effect The effect on Equilibrium gross domestic product of a change in Aggregate expenditures or Aggregate demand (caused by a change in the Consumption schedule, Investment, Government expenditures, or Net exports).

Mutual savings bank A Firm without stockholders which accepts deposits primarily from small individual savers and which lends primarily to individuals to finance the purchases of residences.

Mutually exclusive goals Goals which conflict and cannot be achieved simultaneously.

N

National bank A Commercial bank (*see*) chartered by the United States government.

National income Total income earned by resource suppliers for their contributions to the production of the Gross domestic product (*see*); equal to the Gross domestic product minus the Nonincome charges (*see*) minus Net foreign factor income earned in the United States (*see*).

National income accounting The techniques employed to measure the overall production of the economy and other related totals for the nation as a whole.

Natural monopoly An industry in which Economies of scale (*see*) are so great the product can be produced by one Firm at a lower average total cost than if the product were produced by more than one Firm.

Natural rate hypothesis The idea that the economy is stable in the long run at the natural rate of unemployment; views the long-run Phillips Curve (*see*) as vertical at the natural rate of unemployment.

Natural rate of unemployment (*See* Full-employment unemployment rate.)

NDP (*See* Net domestic product.)

Near-money Financial assets, the most important of which are Noncheckable savings accounts, Time deposits, and U.S. short-term securities and savings bonds, which are not a medium of exchange but can be readily converted into Money.

Negative relationship (*See* Inverse relationship.)

Net capital movement The difference between the real and financial investments and loans made by individuals and Firms of one nation in the other nations of the world and the investments and loans made by individuals and Firms from other nations in a nation; Capital inflows less Capital outflows.

Net domestic product Gross domestic product (*see*) less that part of the output needed to replace the Capital goods worn out in producing the output (Consumption of fixed capital, *see*).

Net export effect The notion that the impact of a change in Monetary policy (Fiscal policy) will be strengthened

Positive economics The analysis of facts or data to establish scientific generalizations about economic behavior; compare Normative economics.

Positive relationship The relationship between two variables which change in the same direction, for example, product price and quantity supplied.

Post hoc, ergo propter hoc **fallacy** Incorrectly reasoning that when one event precedes another the first event is the cause of the second.

Potential output The real output (GDP) an economy is able to produce when it fully employs its available resources.

Premature inflation Inflation (*see*) which occurs before the economy has reached Full employment (*see*).

Price The quantity of money (or of other goods or services) paid and received for a unit of a good or service.

Price-decreasing effect The effect in a competitive market of a decrease in Demand or an increase in Supply upon the Equilibrium price (*see*).

Price guidepost A government exhortation that the price charged by an industry for its product should increase by no more than the increase in the Unit labor cost (*see*) of producing the product.

Price increasing effect The effect in a competitive market of an increase in Demand or a decrease in Supply on the equilibrium price.

Price index An index number which shows how the average price of a "market basket" of goods changes through time. A price index is used to change nominal output (income) into real output (income).

Price level The weighted average of the Prices paid for the final goods and services produced in the economy.

Price level surprises Unanticipated changes in the price level.

Price-wage flexibility Changes in the prices of products and in the Wages paid to workers; the ability of prices and Wages to rise or to fall.

Prime interest rate The interest rate banks charge their most credit-worthy borrowers, for example, large corporations with impeccable financing credentials.

Private good A good or service subject to the Exclusion principle (*see*) and which is provided by privately owned firms to those who are willing to pay for it.

Private property The right of private persons and Firms to obtain, own, control, employ, dispose of, and bequeath Land, Capital, and other Assets.

Private sector The Households and business firms of the economy.

Production possibilities curve (table) A curve (table) showing the different combinations of two goods or services that can be produced in a Full-employment (*see*), Full-production (*see*) economy where the available supplies of resources and technology are constant.

Productive efficiency The production of a good in the least costly way; occurs when production takes place at the output where Average total cost is at a minimum and where Marginal product per dollar's worth of each input is the same.

Productivity A measure of average output or real output per unit of input. For example, the productivity of labor may be determined by dividing hours of work into real output.

Productivity slowdown The recent decline in the rate at which Labor productivity (*see*) in the United States has increased.

Product market A market in which Households buy and Firms sell the products they have produced.

Profit (*see*) Economic profit and Normal profit; without an adjective preceding it, the income of those who supply the economy with Entrepreneurial ability (*see*) or Normal profit.

Progressive tax A tax such that the Average tax rate increases as the taxpayer's income increases and decreases as income decreases.

Property tax A tax on the value of property (Capital, Land, stocks and bonds, and other Assets) owned by Firms and Households.

Proprietors' income The net income of the owners of unincorporated Firms (proprietorships and partnerships).

Prosperous industry (*See* Expanding industry.)

Protective tariff A Tariff (*see*) designed to protect domestic producers of a good from the competition of foreign producers.

Public debt The total amount owed by the Federal government (to the owners of government securities) and equal to the sum of its past Budget deficits (less its budget surpluses).

Public finance The branch of economics which analyzes government revenues and expenditures.

Public good A good or service to which the Exclusion principle (*see*) is not applicable; and which is provided by government if it yields substantial benefits to society.

Public sector The part of the economy that contains all its governments; government.

Purchasing power parity The idea that exchange rates between nations equate the purchasing power of various currencies; exchange rates between any two nations adjust to reflect the price level differences between the countries.

Pure capitalism   An economic system in which property resources are privately owned and markets and prices are used to direct and coordinate economic activities.

Pure competition   (1) A market in which a very large number of Firms sells a Standardized product **(see)**, into which entry is very easy, in which the individual seller has no control over the price at which the product sells, and in which there is no Nonprice competition **(see)**; (2) a market in which there is a very large number of buyers.

Pure profit   (*See* Economic profit.)

Pure rate of interest   (*See The* rate of interest.)

Q

Quantity-decreasing effect   The effect in a competitive market of a decrease in Demand or a decrease in Supply on the Equilibrium quantity **(see)**.

Quantity demanded   The amount of a good or service buyers wish (or a buyer wishes) to purchase at a particular price during some period.

Quantity-increasing effect   The effect in a competitive market of an increase in Demand or an increase in Supply on the Equilibrium quantity **(see)**.

Quantity supplied   The amount of a good or service sellers offer (or a seller offers) to sell at a particular price during some period.

Quasi-public bank   A bank which is privately owned but governmentally (publicly) controlled; each of the Federal Reserve Banks.

Quasi-public good   A good or service to which the Exclusion principle **(see)** could be applied, but which has such a large Spillover benefit **(see)** that government sponsors its production to prevent an underallocation of resources.

R

R & D   Research and development; activities undertaken to bring about Technological progress.

Ratchet effect   The tendency for the Price level to rise when Aggregate demand increases, but not fall when Aggregate demand declines.

Rate of exchange   The price paid in one's own money to acquire one unit of a foreign money; the rate at which the money of one nation is exchanged for the money of another nation.

Rate of interest   Price paid for the use of Money or for the use of Capital; interest rate.

Rational   An adjective which describes the behavior of any individual who consistently does those things enabling him or her to achieve the declared objective of the individual; and which describes the behavior of a consumer who uses money income to buy the collection of goods and services yielding the maximum amount of Utility **(see)**.

Rational expectations theory   The hypothesis that business firms and households expect monetary and fiscal policies to have certain effects on the economy and take, in pursuit of their own self-interests, actions which make these policies ineffective.

Rationing function of price   The ability of a price in a competitive market to equalize Quantity demanded and Quantity supplied and to eliminate shortages and surpluses by rising or falling.

Reaganomics   The policies of the Reagan administration based on Supply-side economics **(see)** and intended to reduce inflation and the Unemployment rate (Stagflation).

Real-balances effect   The tendency for increases (decreases) in the price level to lower (raise) the real value (or purchasing power) of financial assets with fixed money values; and, as a result, to reduce (expand) total spending in the economy.

Real capital   (*See* Capital.)

Real gross domestic product   Gross domestic product **(see)** adjusted for changes in the price level; Gross domestic product in a year divided by the GDP deflator **(see)** for that year expressed as a decimal.

Real income   The amount of goods and services an individual or group can purchase with his, her, or its Nominal income during some period of time. Nominal income adjusted for changes in the Price level.

Real interest rate   The rate of interest expressed in dollars of constant value (adjusted for inflation); and equal to the Nominal interest rate **(see)** less the expected rate of inflation.

Real rate of interest   The Real interest rate **(see)**.

Real wage   The amount of goods and services a worker can purchase with his or her Nominal wage **(see)**; the purchasing power of the Nominal wage; the Nominal wage adjusted for changes in the Price level.

Real wage rate   (*See* Real wage.)

Recessionary gap   The amount by which the Aggregate expenditures schedule (curve) must increase (shift upward) to increase the real GDP to the full-employment noninflationary level.

Reciprocal Trade Agreements Act of 1934   The Federal act which gave the President the authority to negotiate agreements with foreign nations and lower American tariff rates by up to 50 percent if the foreign nations would reduce tariff rates on American goods and which incorporated Most-favored-nation clauses (*see*) in the agreements reached with these nations.

Refinancing the public debt Paying owners of maturing United States government securities with money obtained by selling new securities or with new securities.

Remittance A gift or grant; a payment for which no good or service is received in return; the funds sent by workers who have legally or illegally entered a foreign nation to their families in the nations from which they have migrated.

Rental income Income received by those who supply the economy with Land (*see*).

Required reserve ratio (*See* Reserve ratio.)

Required reserves (*See* Legal reserves.)

Reserve ratio The specified minimum percentage of its deposit liabilities which a Member bank (*see*) must keep on deposit at the Federal Reserve Bank in its district, or in Vault cash (*see*).

Resolution Trust Corporation (RTC) A Federal institution created in 1989 to oversee the closing and sale of failed Savings and loan institutions.

Resource market A market in which Households sell and Firms buy the services of resources.

Retiring the public debt Reducing the size of the Public debt by paying money to owners of maturing United States government securities.

Revaluation An increase in the governmentally defined value of a currency.

Revenue tariff A Tariff (*see*) designed to produce income for the (Federal) government.

Ricardian equivalence theorem The idea that an increase in the public debt will have little or no effect on real output and employment because taxpayers will save more in anticipation of future higher taxes to pay the higher interest expense on the debt.

Roundabout production The construction and use of Capital (*see*) to aide in the production of Consumer goods (*see*).

Ruble overhang The large amount of forced savings formerly held by Russian households due to the scarcity of consumer goods; these savings fueled inflation when Rus-sian prices were decontrolled.

Rule of 70 A method for determining the number of years it will take for the Price level to double; divide 70 by the annual rate of inflation.

S

Sales tax A tax levied on expenditures for a broad group of products.

Saving Disposable income not spent for Consumer goods (*see*); equal to Disposable income minus Personal consumption expenditures (*see*).

Savings account A deposit in a Depository institution (*see*) which is interest-earning and which can normally be withdrawn by the depositor at any time.

Savings and Loan association (S&L) A Firm which accepts deposits primarily from small individual savers, and lends primarily to individuals to finance purchases of residences.

Saving schedule Schedule which shows the amounts Households plan to save (plan not to spend for Consumer goods, *see*) at different levels of Disposable income.

Savings institution A Thrift institution (*see*).

Say's law The (discredited) macroeconomic generalization that the production of goods and services (supply) creates an equal Aggregate demand for these goods and services.

Scarce resources The fixed (limited) quantities of Land, Capital, Labor, and Entrepreneurial ability (*see all*) which are never sufficient to satisfy the virtually unlimited material wants of humans.

Seasonal variation An increase or decrease during a single year in the level of economic activity caused by a change in the season.

Secular trend The expansion or contraction in the level of economic activity over a long period of years.

Self-interest What each Firm, property owner, worker, and consumer believes is best for itself and seeks to obtain.

Separation of ownership and control Difference between the group that owns the Corporation (the stockholders) and the group that manages it (the directors and officers) and between the interests (goals) of the two groups.

Service That which is intangible (invisible) and for which a consumer, firm, or government is willing to exchange something of value.

Shortage The amount by which the Quantity demanded of a product exceeds the Quantity supplied at a particular (below-equilibrium) price.

Short-run aggregate supply curve The aggregate supply curve relevant to a time period in which input prices (particularly nominal wages) remain constant when the price level changes.

Simple multiplier The Multiplier (*see*) in an economy in which government collects no Net taxes (*see*), there are no Imports (*see*), and Investment (*see*) is independent of the level of income (Gross domestic product); equal to one divided by the Marginal propensity to save (*see*).

Slope of a line   The ratio of the vertical change (the rise or fall) to the horizontal change (the run) in moving between two points on a line. The slope of an upward sloping line is positive, reflecting a direct relationship between two variables; the slope of a downward sloping line is negative, reflecting an inverse relationship between two variables.

Smoot-Hawley Tariff Act   Passed in 1930, this legislation established some of the highest tariffs in United States history. Its objective was to reduce imports and stimulate the domestic economy.

Social accounting   (*See* National income accounting.)

Sole proprietorship   An unincorporated business firm owned and operated by a single person.

Specialization   The use of the resources of an individual, a Firm, a region, or a nation to produce one or a few goods and services for which there is a Comparative advantage.

Speculation   The activity of buying or selling with the motive of then reselling or rebuying to make a profit.

Spillover   A benefit or cost from production or consumption, accruing without compensation to nonbuyers and nonsellers of the product (*see* Spillover benefit and Spillover cost).

Spillover benefit   A benefit obtained without compensation by third parties from the production or consumption of other parties. Example: A bee keeper benefits when the neighboring farmer plants clover.

Spillover costs   A cost imposed without compensation on third parties by the production or consumption of other parties. Example: A manufacturer dumps toxic chemicals into a river, killing the fish sought by sport fishers.

Stabilization policy dilemma   The use of monetary and fiscal policy to decrease the Unemployment rate increases the rate of inflation, and the use of monetary and fiscal policy to decrease the rate of inflation increases the Unemployment rate.

Stagflation   Inflation accompanied by stagnation in the rate of growth of output and a high unemployment rate in the economy; simultaneous increases in both the Price level and the Unemployment rate.

State bank   A Commercial bank chartered to engage in the business of banking by a state government.

State ownership   The ownership of property (Land and Capital) by government (the state); in the former Soviet Union by the central government (the nation).

Static economy   (1) An economy in which Net private domestic investment (*see*) is zero—Gross private domestic investment (*see*) is equal to the Consumption of fixed capital (*see*); (2) an economy in which the supplies of resources, technology, and the tastes of consumers do not change and in which, therefore, the economic future is perfectly predictable and there is no uncertainty.

Store of value   Any asset (*see*) or wealth set aside for future use; a function of Money.

Strategic trade policy   The use of trade barriers to reduce the risk of product development by domestic firms, particularly products involving advanced technology.

Structural deficit   The difference between Federal tax revenues and expenditures when the economy is at full employment.

Structural unemployment   Unemployment caused by changes in the structure of demand for Consumer goods and in technology; workers who are unemployed because their skills are not demanded by employers, they lack sufficient skills to obtain employment, or they cannot easily move to locations where jobs are available.

Subsidy   A payment of funds (or goods and services) by a government, business firm, or household for which it receives no good or service in return. When made by a government, it is a Government transfer payment (*see*).

Substitute goods   Goods or services for which there is a direct relationship between the price of one and the Demand for the other; when the price of one falls (rises) the Demand for the other decreases (increases).

Substitution effect   (1) The effect which a change in the price of a Consumer good would have on the relative expensiveness of that good and the resulting effect on the quantity of the good a consumer would purchase if the consumer's Real income (*see*) remained constant; (2) the effect which a change in the price of a resource would have on the quantity of the resource employed by a firm if the firm did not change its output.

Superior good   (*See* Normal good.)

Supply   A Supply schedule or a Supply curve (*see both*).

Supply curve   A curve showing the amounts of a good or service sellers (a seller) will offer to sell at various prices during some period.

Supply factor   An increase in the availability of a resource, an improvement in its quality, or an expansion of technological knowledge which makes it possible for an economy to produce a greater output of goods and services.

Supply schedule   A schedule showing the amounts of a good or service sellers (or seller) will offer at various prices during some period.

Supply shock   One of several events of the 1970s and early 1980s which increased production costs, decreased Aggregate supply, and generated Stagflation in the United States.

Supply-side economics   A view of macroeconomics which emphasizes the role of costs and Aggregate supply in explaining Inflation, unemployed labor, and Economic growth.

Supply-side view   The view of fiscal policy held by the advocates of Supply-side economics which emphasizes increasing Aggregate supply (*see*) as a means of reducing the Unemployment rate and Inflation and encouraging Economic Growth.

Surplus   The amount by which the Quantity supplied of a product exceeds the Quantity demanded at a specific (above-equilibrium) price.

Surplus value   A Marxian term; the amount by which the value of a worker's daily output exceeds his daily wage; the output of workers appropriated by capitalists as profit.

T

Tangent   The point where a line touches, but does not intersect, a curve.

Target dilemma   A problem arising because monetary authorities cannot simultaneously stabilize both the money supply and the level of interest rates.

Tariff   A tax imposed by a nation on an imported good.

Tax   A nonvoluntary payment of money (or goods and services) to a government by a Household or Firm for which the Household or Firm receives no good or service directly in return.

Tax incidence   The income or purchasing power different persons and groups lose as a result of a tax after Tax shifting (*see*) has occurred.

Tax "wedge"   Such taxes as Indirect business taxes (*see*) and Payroll taxes (*see*) which are treated as a cost by business firms and reflected in the prices of their products; equal to the price of the product less the cost of the resources required to produce it.

Technology   The body of knowledge which can be used to produce goods and services from Economic resources.

Terms of trade   The rate at which units of one product can be exchanged for units of another product; the Price (*see*) of a good or service; the amount of one good or service given up to obtain one unit of another good or service.

The rate of interest   The Rate of interest (*see*) which is paid solely for the use of money over an extended period of time and which excludes the charges made for the riskiness of the loan and its administrative costs; and which is approximately equal to the rate of interest paid on the long-term and virtually riskless bonds of the United States government.

Thrift institution   A Savings and loan association, Mutual savings bank, or Credit union (*see all*).

Tight money policy   Contracting, or restricting the growth of, the nation's Money supply (*see*).

Till money   (*See* Vault cash.)

Time deposit   An interest-earning deposit in a Depository institution (*see*) which the depositor can withdraw without a loss of interest after the end of a specific period.

Token money   Coins having a Face value (*see*) greater than their Intrinsic value (*see*).

Total demand   The Demand schedule (*see*) or the Demand curve (*see*) of all buyers of a good or service.

Total demand for money   The sum of the Transactions demand for money (*see*) and Asset demand for money (*see*); the relationship between the total amount of money demanded, nominal GDP, and the Rate of Interest.

Total product   The total output of a particular good or service produced by a firm (a group of firms or the entire economy).

Total revenue   The total number of dollars received by a Firm (or Firms) from the sale of a product; equal to the total expenditures for the product produced by the Firm (or firms); equal to the quantity sold (demanded) multiplied by the price at which it is sold—by the Average revenue (*see*) from its sale.

Total spending   The total amount buyers of goods and services spend or plan to spend. Also called Aggregate expenditures.

Total supply   The Supply schedule (*see*) or the Supply curve (*see*) of all sellers of a good or service.

Trade balance   The export of merchandise (goods) of a nation less its imports of merchandise (goods).

Trade bloc   A group of nations which lower or abolish trade barriers among members. Examples include the European Union (*see*) and the North American Free Trade Agreement (*see*).

Trade controls   Tariffs (*see*), Export subsidies, Import quotas (*see*), and other means a nation may employ to reduce Imports (*see*) and expand Exports (*see*).

Trade deficit   The amount a nation's imports of merchandise (goods) exceed its exports of merchandise (goods).

Tradeoffs The notion that one economic goal or objective must be sacrificed to achieve some other goal.

Trade surplus The amount a nation's exports of merchandise (goods) exceed its imports of merchandise (goods).

Trading possibilities line A line which shows the different combinations of two products an economy is able to obtain (consume) when it specializes in the production of one product and trades (exports) this product to obtain the other product.

Traditional economy An economic system in which traditions and customs determine how the economy will use its scarce resources.

Transactions demand for money The amount of money people want to hold to use as a Medium of exchange (to make payments); and which varies directly with the nominal GDP.

Transfer payment A payment of money (or goods and services) by a government or a Firm to a Household or Firm for which the payer receives no good or service directly in return.

U

Unanticipated inflation Inflation (*see*) at a rate which was greater than the rate expected for that period of time.

Underemployment Failure to produce the maximum amount of goods and services that can be produced from the resources employed; failure to achieve Full production (*see*).

Undistributed corporate profits After-tax corporate profits not distributed as dividends to stockholders; corporate or business saving.

Unemployment Failure to use all available Economic resources to produce goods and services; failure of the economy to employ fully its Labor force (*see*).

Unemployment compensation (*See* Unemployment insurance).

Unemployment rate The percentage of the Labor force (*see*) unemployed at any time.

Unit labor cost Labor costs per unit of output; equal to the Nominal wage rate (*see*) divided by the Average product (*see*) of labor.

Unlimited liability Absence of any limit on the maximum amount which may be lost by an individual and which the individual may become legally required to pay; the amount which may be lost and which a sole proprietor or partner may be required to pay.

Unlimited wants The insatiable desire of consumers (people) for goods and services which will give them satisfaction or Utility.

Unplanned investment Actual investment less Planned investment; increases or decreases in the inventories of business firms resulting from production greater than sales.

Unprosperous industry (*See* Declining industry.)

Uruguay Round The eighth and most recent round of trade negotiations under GATT (*see*).

Utility The want-satisfying power of a good or service; the satisfaction or pleasure a consumer obtains from the consumption of a good or service (or from the consumption of a collection of goods and services).

V

Value added The value of the product sold by a Firm less the value of the goods (materials) purchased and used by the Firm to produce the product; and equal to the revenue which can be used for Wages, rent, interest, and profits.

Value judgment Opinion of what is desirable or undesirable; belief regarding what ought or ought not to be (regarding what is right or just and wrong or unjust).

Value of money The quantity of goods and services for which a unit of money (a dollar) can be exchanged; the purchasing power of a unit of money; the reciprocal of the Price level.

Vault cash The Currency (*see*) a bank has in its safe (vault) and cash drawers.

Velocity of money The number of times per year the average dollar in the Money supply (*see*) is spent for Final goods and services (*see*).

VERs (*See* Voluntary export restrictions.)

Vertical axis The "up-down" or "north-south" axis on a graph or grid.

Vertical combination A group of Plants (*see*) engaged in different stages of the production of a final product and owned by a single Firm (*see*).

Vertical intercept The point at which a line meets the vertical axis of a graph.

Vertical range Vertical segment of the Aggregate supply curve along which the economy is at full capacity.

Vicious circle of poverty A problem common to the less developed countries where their low per capita incomes are an obstacle to realizing the levels of saving and investment requisite to acceptable rates of economic growth.

Voluntary export restrictions The limitations by firms of their exports to particular foreign nations to avoid the erection of other trade barriers by the foreign nations.

W

Wage   The price paid for Labor (for the use or services of Labor, *see*) per unit of time (per hour, per day, etc.).

Wage and salary supplements   Payments made by employers of Labor into social insurance and private pension, health, and welfare funds for workers; and a part of the employer's cost of obtaining Labor.

Wage guidepost   A government exhortation that wages (*see*) in all industries in the economy should increase at an annual rate equal to the rate of increase in the Average product (*see*) of Labor in the economy.

Wage-price controls   A Wage-price policy (*see*) which legally fixes the maximum amounts Wages (*see*) and prices may be increased in any period.

Wage-price guideposts   A Wage-price policy (*see*) which depends on the voluntary cooperation of Labor unions and business firms.

Wage-price inflationary spiral   Increases in wage rates which bring about increases in prices and in turn result in further increases in wage rates and in prices.

Wage-price policy   Government policy that attempts to alter the behavior of Labor unions and business firms to make their Wage and price decisions more nearly compatible with the goals of Full employment and a stable Price level.

Wage rate   (*See* Wage.)

Wages   The income of those who supply the economy with Labor (*see*).

Wealth effect   (*See* Real balances effect.)

Welfare programs   (*See* Public assistance programs.)

(The) "will to develop"   Wanting economic growth strongly enough to change from old to new ways of doing things.

World Bank   A bank which lends (and guarantees loans) to less developed nations to assist them to grow; formally, the International Bank for Reconstruction and Development.

World price   The international price of a good or service, determined by world demand and supply.

World Trade Organization (WTO)   An organization established in 1994 by GATT (*see*) to oversee the provisions of the Uruguay Round (*see*) and resolve any disputes stemming therefrom.

INDEX

National income and related statistics for selected years, 1971–1994

National income statistics are in billions of current dollars. Details may not add to totals because of rounding.

			1971	1972	1973	1974	1975	1976	1977	1978	1979	1980
THE SUM OF	1	Personal consumption expenditures	700.3	767.8	848.1	927.7	1,024.9	1,143.1	1,271.5	1,421.2	1,583.7	1,748.1
	2	Gross private domestic investment	175.5	205.6	243.1	245.8	226.0	286.4	358.3	434.0	480.2	467.6
	3	Government purchases	224.3	241.5	257.7	288.3	321.4	341.3	368.0	403.6	448.5	507.1
	4	Net exports	–3.0	–8.0	0.6	–3.1	13.6	–2.3	–23.7	–26.1	–23.8	–14.7
EQUALS	5	Gross domestic product	1,097.2	1,207.0	1,349.6	1,458.6	1,585.9	1,768.4	1,974.1	2,232.7	2,488.6	2,708.0
LESS	6	Consumption of fixed capital	97.6	109.9	120.4	140.2	165.2	182.8	205.2	234.8	272.4	311.9
EQUALS	7	Net domestic product	996.6	1,097.1	1,229.2	1,318.4	1,420.7	1,585.6	1,768.9	1,997.9	2,216.2	2,396.1
LESS	8	Net foreign factor income earned in the U.S.	–7.7	–8.7	–12.7	–15.7	–13.3	–17.1	–20.5	–21.8	–32.2	–34.1
LESS	9	Indirect business taxes	107.8	112.9	122.4	135.3	148.7	167.2	180.3	189.9	209.5	232.0
EQUALS	10	National income	899.5	992.9	1,119.5	1,198.8	1,285.3	1,435.5	1,609.1	1,829.8	2,038.9	2,198.2
LESS	11	Social security contributions	68.9	79.0	97.6	110.5	118.5	134.5	149.8	171.7	197.8	216.5
	12	Corporate income taxes	37.7	41.9	49.3	51.8	50.9	64.2	73.0	83.5	88.0	84.8
	13	Undistributed corporate profits	28.8	35.6	39.0	22.3	40.8	47.3	61.9	70.4	62.1	33.9
PLUS	14	Transfer payments	129.4	144.1	165.1	191.5	232.2	256.8	276.9	303.7	342.1	402.4
EQUALS	15	Personal income	893.5	980.5	1,098.7	1,205.7	1,307.3	1,446.3	1,601.3	1,807.9	2,033.1	2,265.4
LESS	16	Personal taxes	108.7	132.0	140.6	159.1	156.4	182.3	210.0	240.1	280.2	312.4
EQUALS	17	Disposable income	784.9	848.5	958.1	1,046.5	1,150.9	1,264.0	1,391.3	1,567.8	1,753.0	1,952.9
	18	Real gross domestic product (in 1987 dollars)	2,955.9	3,071.1	3,268.6	3,248.1	3,221.7	3,380.8	3,533.2	3,703.5	3,796.8	3,776.3
	19	Percent change in real GDP	3.1	4.8	5.2	–0.6	–0.8	4.9	4.5	4.8	2.5	–0.5
	20	Real disposable income per capita (in 1987 dollars)	10,111.0	10,414.0	11,013.0	10,832.0	10,906.0	11,192.0	11,406.0	11,851.0	12,039.0	12,005.0

RELATED STATISTICS

		1971	1972	1973	1974	1975	1976	1977	1978	1979	1980
21	Consumer price index (1982–84 = 100)	40.5	41.8	44.4	49.3	53.8	56.9	60.6	65.2	72.6	82.4
22	Rate of inflation (%)	4.4	3.2	6.2	11.0	9.1	5.8	6.5	7.6	11.3	13.5
23	Index of industrial production (1987 = 100)	62.2	68.3	73.8	72.7	66.3	72.4	78.2	82.6	85.7	84.1
24	Supply of money, $M1$ (in billions of dollars)	228.4	249.3	262.9	274.4	287.6	306.4	331.3	358.4	382.8	408.8
25	Prime interest rate (%)	5.72	5.25	8.03	10.81	7.86	6.84	6.83	9.06	12.67	15.27
26	Population (in millions)	207.7	209.9	211.9	213.9	216.0	218.0	220.2	222.6	255.1	227.7
27	Civilian labor force (in millions)	84.4	87.0	89.4	91.9	93.8	96.2	99.0	102.3	105.0	106.9
28	Unemployment (in millions)	5.0	4.9	4.4	5.2	7.9	7.4	7.0	6.2	6.1	7.6
29	Unemployment rate as % of civilian labor force	5.9	5.6	4.9	5.6	8.5	7.7	7.1	6.1	5.8	7.1
30	Index of productivity (1982 = 100)	90.2	92.6	95.0	93.3	95.5	98.3	99.8	100.4	99.3	98.6
31	Annual change in productivity (%)	3.6	2.7	2.6	–1.8	2.3	3.0	1.6	0.6	–1.1	–0.7
32	Trade balance on current account (in billions of dollars)	–1.4	–5.8	7.1	2.0	18.1	4.3	–14.3	–15.1	–0.2	2.3
33	Public debt (in billions of dollars)	408.2	435.9	466.3	483.9	541.9	629.0	706.4	776.6	828.9	909.1

*Preliminary data

1981	1982	1983	1984	1985	1986	1987	1988	1989	1990	1991	1992	1993	1994*
1,926.2	2,059.2	2,257.5	2,460.3	2,667.4	2,850.6	3,052.2	3,296.1	3,523.1	3,761.2	3,902.4	4,136.9	4,378.2	4,627.0
558.0	503.4	546.7	718.9	714.5	717.6	749.3	793.6	832.3	808.9	744.8	788.3	882.0	1,037.5
561.1	607.6	652.3	700.8	772.3	833.0	881.5	918.7	975.2	1,047.4	1,097.4	1,125.3	1,148.4	1,174.5
−14.7	−20.6	−51.4	−102.7	−115.6	−132.5	−143.1	−108.0	−79.7	−71.4	−19.9	−30.3	−65.3	−102.1
3,030.6	3,149.6	3,405.0	3,777.2	4,038.7	4,268.6	4,539.9	4,900.4	5,250.8	5,546.1	5,724.8	6,020.2	6,343.3	6,736.9
362.4	399.1	418.4	432.2	454.5	478.6	502.2	534.0	580.4	602.7	626.5	658.5	691.1	715.5
2,668.2	2,750.5	2,986.6	3,345.0	3,584.2	3,790.0	4,037.7	4,366.4	4,670.4	4,943.4	5,098.3	5,361.7	5,652.2	6,021.4
−33.2	−30.2	−29.3	−24.3	−14.9	−9.1	−4.6	−7.9	−16.0	−21.7	−16.0	−5.6	−4.5	12.0
268.9	258.2	295.1	311.0	330.7	361.2	350.0	371.7	436.9	474.1	506.1	537.8	525.3	553.7
2,432.5	2,522.5	2,720.8	3,058.3	3,268.4	3,437.9	3,692.3	4,002.6	4,249.5	4,491.0	4,608.2	4,829.5	5,131.4	5,455.7
251.2	269.6	290.2	325.0	353.8	379.8	400.7	442.3	473.2	503.1	525.9	556.4	585.6	626.3
81.1	63.1	77.2	94.0	96.5	106.5	127.1	137.0	141.3	138.7	131.1	139.7	173.2	202.5
31.7	18.4	54.2	87.5	91.8	55.4	86.5	112.6	87.0	88.5	99.3	94.3	120.8	135.1
466.2	519.5	563.3	602.8	653.5	694.2	724.0	765.2	832.3	913.1	1,008.4	1,115.2	1,123.3	1,210.0
2,534.7	2,690.9	2,862.5	3,154.6	3,379.8	3,590.4	3,802.0	4,075.9	4,380.3	4,673.8	4,860.3	5,154.3	5,375.1	5,701.8
360.2	371.4	368.8	395.1	436.8	459.0	512.5	527.7	593.3	623.3	623.7	648.6	686.4	742.5
2,174.5	2,319.6	2,493.7	2,759.5	2,943.0	3,131.5	3,289.5	3,548.2	3,787.0	4,050.5	4,236.6	4,505.8	4,688.7	4,959.3
3,843.1	3,760.3	3906.6	4,148.5	4,279.8	4,404.5	4,540.0	4,718.6	4,838.0	4,897.3	4,867.6	4,979.3	5,134.5	5,342.3
1.8	−2.2	3.9	6.2	3.2	2.9	3.1	3.9	2.5	1.2	−0.6	2.3	3.1	4.0
12,156.0	12,146.0	12,349.0	13,029.0	13,258.0	13,552.0	13,545.0	13,890.0	14,005.0	14,101.0	14,003.0	14,279.0	14,341.0	14,696.0

1981	1982	1983	1984	1985	1986	1987	1988	1989	1990	1991	1992	1993	1994
90.9	96.5	99.6	103.9	107.6	109.6	113.6	118.3	124.0	130.7	136.2	140.3	144.5	148.2
10.3	6.2	3.2	4.3	3.6	1.9	3.6	4.1	4.8	5.4	4.2	3.0	3.0	2.6
85.7	81.9	84.9	92.8	94.4	95.3	100.0	104.4	106.0	106.0	104.3	107.6	112.0	118.1
436.4	474.4	521.2	552.2	619.9	724.3	750.1	787.4	794.7	826.4	897.7	1,024.8	1,128.4	1,147.6
18.87	14.86	10.79	12.04	9.93	8.33	8.21	9.32	10.87	10.01	8.46	6.25	6.00	7.15
230.0	232.3	234.3	236.4	238.5	240.7	242.9	245.1	247.3	250.0	252.7	255.4	258.1	260.7
108.7	110.2	111.6	113.5	115.5	117.8	119.9	121.7	123.9	124.8	125.3	127.0	128.0	131.1
8.3	10.7	10.7	8.5	8.3	8.2	7.4	6.7	6.5	6.9	8.4	9.4	8.8	8.0
7.6	9.7	9.6	7.5	7.2	7.0	6.2	5.5	5.3	5.5	6.7	7.4	6.8	6.1
99.9	100.0	102.3	104.8	106.3	108.5	109.6	110.7	109.9	110.7	112.1	115.5	117.2	119.9
1.3	0.1	2.3	2.4	1.4	2.1	1.0	1.0	−0.7	0.7	1.3	3.0	1.5	2.3
5.0	−11.4	−44.5	−99.8	−125.4	−151.2	−167.1	−128.2	−102.8	−91.7	−7.0	−67.9	−103.9	−155.7
994.8	1,137.3	1,371.2	1,564.7	1,817.5	2,120.6	2,346.1	2,601.3	2,868.0	3,206.6	3,598.5	4,002.1	4,351.4	4,643.7

Source: *Survey of Current Business, Federal Reserve Bulletin, Economic Report of the President, Economic Indicators.*